Going Forward by Looking Back

Catastrophes in Context

Catastrophes in Context aims to bring critical attention to the social, political, economic, and cultural structures that create disasters out of natural hazards or political events and that shape the responses. Combining long-term ethnographic fieldwork typical of anthropology and increasingly adopted in similar social science disciplines such as geography and sociology with a comparative frame that enlightens global structures and policy frameworks, *Catastrophes in Context* includes monographs and edited volumes that bring critical scrutiny to the multiple dimensions of specific disasters and important policy/practice questions for the field of disaster research and management. Theoretically innovative, our goal is to publish readable, lucid texts to be accessible to a wide range of audiences across academic disciplines and specifically practitioners and policymakers.

Volume 3
Going Forward by Looking Back: Archaeological Perspectives on Socio-ecological Crisis, Response, and Collapse
Edited by Felix Riede and Payson Sheets

Volume 2
Disaster upon Disaster: Exploring the Gap between Knowledge, Policy and Practice
Edited by Susanna M. Hoffman and Roberto E. Barrios

Volume 1
Contextualizing Disaster
Edited by Gregory V. Button and Mark Schuller

Going Forward by Looking Back

Archaeological Perspectives on Socio-ecological Crisis, Response, and Collapse

Edited by
Felix Riede and Payson Sheets

berghahn
NEW YORK • OXFORD
www.berghahnbooks.com

First published in 2020 by
Berghahn Books
www.berghahnbooks.com

First paperback edition published in 2023

Library of Congress Cataloging-in-Publication Data

Names: Riede, Felix, editor. | Sheets, Payson D., editor.
Title: Going Forward by Looking Back: Archaeological Perspectives on Socio-ecological Crisis, Response, and Collapse / edited by Felix Riede and Payson Sheets.
Other titles: Archaeological Perspectives on Socio-ecological Crisis, Response, and Collapse
Description: New York: Berghahn, 2020. | Series: Catastrophes in Context; volume 3 | Includes bibliographical references and index.
Identifiers: LCCN 2020018305 (print) | LCCN 2020018306 (ebook) | ISBN 9781789208641 (hardback) | ISBN 9781789208658 (ebook)
Subjects: LCSH: Archaeology and natural disasters--Case studies. | Disasters—Social aspects—Case studies. | Disaster relief—Social aspects—Case studies. | Emergency management—Social aspects—Case studies. | Environmental archaeology—Case studies. | Human ecology—History—Case studies. | Hazard mitigation—Social aspects—Case studies. | Climatic changes—Social aspects—Case studies.
Classification: LCC CC77.N36 G65 2020 (print) | LCC CC77.N36 (ebook) | D DC 363.34—dc23
LC record available at https://lccn.loc.gov/2020018305
LC ebook record available at https://lccn.loc.gov/2020018306

British Library Cataloguing in Publication Data

A catalogue record for this book is available from the British Library

ISBN 978-1-78920-864-1 hardback
ISBN 978-1-80073-928-4 paperback
ISBN 978-1-78920-865-8 ebook

https://doi.org/10.3167/9781789208641

Contents

Illustrations, Figures, and Tables

Illustrations

Figures

Tables

Introduction

Framing Catastrophes Archaeologically

FELIX RIEDE and PAYSON SHEETS

Summary for Stakeholders

Catastrophes are never natural; they occur when an extreme event—or a compound series of these—impacts an at-risk community. Communities are at risk when access to resources is limited or unevenly distributed or when political structures or cultural norms prevent effective and equitable responses. Such inequalities or inadequacies always have a history. They generate socially produced vulnerabilities. Hence, understanding vulnerability and its important counterpart resilience requires an attention to deep history. In many parts of the world, however, the actual written historical record is short and patchy and often only reflects the limited perspectives of literary and urban elites. In contrast, the archaeological record reflects the material conditions of past lives and livelihoods and can inform us about past vulnerability and resilience anywhere in the world. Many parts of the world are experiencing rising frequencies of disasters including extreme events of a nature or magnitude that have long recurrence intervals. In such cases, little or no local memories inform disaster responses. In other cases, traditional peoples maintained oral histories of disasters and salutary behavior to mitigate losses. Unfortunately, such oral history has often been lost when colonization occurred. This book catalogues a wide and diverse range of case studies of such disasters and human responses. This heritage of past disasters serves as inspiration for building culturally sensitive adaptations to present and future calamities to mitigate their impacts and facilitate recoveries.

Catastrophes Past, Present, Future

Catastrophes are on the rise, as is their toll in lives and livelihoods. Climate change is increasing the energy in hurricanes, typhoons, torrential rains, tornadoes, and other phenomena. The increase in world population is putting ever more people at risk, often in the most hazardous locations. Furthermore, the inequalities of wealth and power often place the disenfranchised in greatest vulnerability. Finally, those with greater resources often benefit from the inequality, as the extreme event intensifies preexisting disparities (Wisner et al. 2004; O'Keefe, Westgate, and Wisner 1976).

These trends lend a clear urgency to academic enquiry not only to attempt to better understand catastrophes per se, but also to reflect on how such understandings may inform contemporary practice. There is a substantial scholarship on the anthropology, history, and archaeology of catastrophes both in relation to specific hazards—there are major edited volumes on volcanic eruptions (Grattan and Torrence 2007; Riede 2015; Sheets and Grayson 1979; Boer and Sanders 2002; Oppenheimer 2011) and earthquakes (Ambraseys 2009; Boer and Sanders 2004), for instance—and more broadly in relation to extreme environmental events or catastrophes as an object of enquiry (Torrence and Grattan 2002; Hoffman and Oliver-Smith 1999; 2002; Cooper and Sheets 2012). In this tradition, the present volume presents a diversity of archaeological approaches to extreme events of various kinds and onset dynamics and their interactions with a wide variation of social constellations, as well as the immediate and long-term human/cultural responses. The volume also draws on the tradition of historical ecology (Crumley 1993), a school of thought and action that has been finding ways of making archaeological insights usable in the contemporary world (Stump 2013; Isendahl and Stump 2019; Armstrong et al. 2017).

Diversity is a deliberate element, and we feel a key strength, of the volume at hand. These chapters represent the full gamut of archaeological orientations—from the Paleolithic and paleoenvironmental to the contemporary and co-creative—and offer exciting and unexpected juxtapositions and pairings. We are pleased to present in this volume a range of phenomena spanning the breadth of scholarship from the natural sciences through the social sciences and including the humanities.[1]

The importance and urgency of better understanding disasters past, present, and future has not gone unnoticed in the social sciences and humanities. Scholars of literature, ethnographers, sociologists, and historians are grappling with the realization that extreme environmental events always were, are, and will be part of the fabric of human social lives (e.g.,

Dominey-Howes 2018; Rigby 2015; Barrios 2017; Bavel and Curtis 2016; Schenk 2015; Mauch and Pfister 2009); by the same token, it is becoming increasingly accepted among disaster risk reduction *practitioners* that *culture*—and with it prehistory, history, tangible and intangible heritage—needs to be taken seriously in reducing vulnerability (Mercer et al. 2012; K. Donovan 2010; A. R. Donovan 2017; Barclay et al. 2008; Migoń and Pijet-Migoń 2019). Sometimes a religious factor could predominate over an ecological one in people returning to their formerly devastated landscape. One could even picture the spirit of a deceased ancestor, buried prior to the disaster in the devastated zone, as a needed resource, as a resource for spiritual and emotional needs of the survivors. Therefore, access to the spirits of the deceased can function as an encouragement to reoccupy the abandoned area, perhaps even before environmental recovery is sufficiently complete for permanent reoccupation. The salient details of these entanglements among space, materials, and the environment vary from place to place, from time to time; the present volume offers an array of resources and templates for how they can be approached, understood, narrated, and made to work in the present and well into the future.

The great diversity of contributions collected together here also presents challenges. We have thought and communicated a great deal about defining some of the key concepts that pervade our thinking and writing. Considering the wide variety of already published definitions, one could and perhaps ought to define the concepts of "resilience" and "vulnerability." Attempts at providing exhaustive exegeses of these terms have been mounted (cf. Wolf et al. 2013; Alexander 2013; Lorenz 2013; Miller et al. 2010; J. Walker and Cooper 2011), but these inevitably proffer only disciplinarily narrow perspectives and often little practical outcome. Similarly, we feel that any attempts of this kind on our behalf would merely add to already long lists of bespoke definitions; in fact, using these seemingly innocuous vernaculars may create more confusion and frustration given the evident multiplicity of meanings that hide under the thin veneer of terminological identity. We did not want to prescribe specific theoretical or conceptual approaches to our contributors, so where they occur in the chapters that make up this book they are defined within and for those chapters' operationalizations.

That said, the traditional concept of resilience, it has been pointed out, focuses on a return to pre-existing conditions, inspired by systems-ecological thinking that operated with the notion of equilibrium. Yet, even for faunal and floral communities, such equilibrium states have been questioned (e.g., Svenning and Sandel 2013). With regard to human communities, post-disaster societal trajectories are rarely if ever identical to their pre-disaster counterparts. And in most cases, they should not be identical.

The efforts to rebuild the same community in place after a disaster, which so often occurs in the United States, may be satisfactory only until the next disaster strikes. Processes, changes, adjustments, and innovations by people, households, or societies under stress or released from societal strictures within the "eventful" fluidity of a catastrophe (Sewell 2005) deserve more attention than any preserved return to stability or even to prior conditions. In fact, the power of archaeological analysis of past disasters offers the possibility of explicating causal pathways from pre-existing conditions to whatever follows. Catastrophic events serve as analytical tools—as methodological and narrative caesura, just as in the original definition of the term in the context of stage play—rather than as sole drivers or dramatic distractions deployed to tell and sell our particular "stories." This acute attention to the structure and power of catastrophic narrative does not equate to doubting the relevance of the environment for human affairs, as it appears to have led some to do (e.g., Middleton 2017). We argue here that we need to seek a middle ground where narrative and evidence go hand in hand; where archaeology aligns itself with recent studies in the environmental humanities that accept the saliency, capriciousness, and relevance of the environment but also point at the cultural specificity of how these are perceived and handled (e.g., Rigby 2015; Bergthaller et al. 2014; Riede 2019). Hulme (2008, 5) reminds us:

> We are living in a climate of fear about our future climate. The language of the public discourse around global warming routinely uses a repertoire which includes words such as "catastrophe," "terror," "danger," "extinction," and "collapse." To help make sense of this phenomenon the story of the complex relationships between climates and cultures in different times and in different places is in urgent need of telling. If we can understand from the past something of this complex interweaving of our ideas of climate with their physical and cultural settings we may be better placed to prepare for different configurations of this relationship in the future.

Just as a disease can inform the doctor of the internal functioning of a body in stress, so can a disaster reveal much about a society during the impact, the initial devastation, the nature of recovery—none, partial, complete—and the knowledge gained and innovations emplaced to mitigate future impacts. Archaeology can tell these stories.

Resilience, Cyclicity, and History

Ever since Redman's (2005) important review, archaeological studies have been focusing increasingly on resilience (e.g., Gronenborn 2006; Bradtmöller, Grimm, and Riel-Salvatore 2017; Barton et al. 2018; Gerrard and Petley 2013). Most commonly, these approaches trace their roots to Holling's (1973) original view of resilience as a system successfully returning to its condition prior to a given perturbation—for instance, an extreme event. Cyclical models such as the traditional resilience model and its derivative tend to frame impact-and-recovery processes according to a uniform processual scheme. While this may serve as a useful first-pass heuristic, we see such models as fundamentally ahistorical and hence as detracting from the explanatory power inherent in the interpreted archaeological record. This power lies in charting how historically specific constellations structure eventual outcomes, in a path-dependent manner.

The insistence on empirical specificity should not, however, be understood as an argument in favor of particularism. There are similar and comparable processes and mechanisms at work; they just do not always lead to the same outcomes. Many of the chapters in this volume take their starting point in a particular case; others are inherently comparative. Collectively, however, this volume is, we believe, an important step toward a lateral and cross-temporal transfer of insights and inspirations—and analytical hinges—among and between case studies (Howe and Boyer 2015; Pedersen and Nielsen 2013; Nielsen, Sørensen, and Riede, 2020) and, eventually, perhaps even toward a formal comparison across cases (Diamond and Robinson 2010; Riede 2014). The temporal depth and spatial breadth of the global archaeological record presents us, in principle, with a substantial database of completed natural experiments. Indeed, some of these experiments are still running. If, for instance, prolonged mega-droughts characterized the latest subdivision of the Holocene, the so-called Meghalayan (M. J. C. Walker et al. 2012), perhaps they also characterize the onset of the Anthropocene. Quibbles about geological subdivisions aside, the widespread droughts of around 4200 BCE were likely associated with substantial societal change (e.g., Weiss and Bradley 2001), and perhaps we are witnessing—as documented by, for instance, Nick Shepherd in painful real time for the Cape Town water crisis in this volume—similar impacts and transitions in our time. While archaeological in its perspective, this volume takes us to the brink of the present, the brink of the societal collapse that may yet come to characterize our own near future.

The occurrence of major societal changes linked to and in part driven by environmental events is not cyclical in any meaningful sense then, but it is a recurring feature of the human career. The aim of our volume is to also speak also to practitioners and policy makers for whom a consideration of the anthropological perspective on resilience (e.g., Barrios 2017) should be instructive. As scholars, such as those in this volume, study societies in detail prior to, during, and after disasters, they often discover that novel understandings, practices, and religious elements were innovated by people under conditions of structural fluidity. This notion gels with conceptions of historical change promoted by Sewell (2005), who argues that "events" loosen otherwise rigid social structures and amplify agency to form new societal constellations. While there are usually winners and losers in any disaster (cf. Scanlon 1988), the resulting social change can be positive—opportunities for reform, for change, and for the creation of better societies do arise in these contexts (Birkmann et al. 2010; Solnit 2010). As hazard awareness increased, societies generally mitigated their risks from future extreme events and thus did not simply revert to prior conditions. Further, looking within societies, particularly nonegalitarian societies, there often were losers and winners, as the stress differentially impacted people. People with greater economic resources or political power often took advantage of those less fortunate, therefore intensifying pre-existing inequalities.

Many of the cases presented showed that the disaster stress served as an *intensifier* of pre-existing conditions of inequality or other factors, an insight that as such is hardly novel (Barrios 2017; García-Acosta 2002; Hoffman 1999). This intensification can be seen in many chapters, and they form a means of integration of the book, by creating linkages between chapters that go beyond a given primary disaster. The heterogeneity of responses to extreme events is reflected in the written chapters. The chapters have been divided into elemental categories of "fire" and "water" interactions and placed adjacent to each other so that salient linkages—often the hazard type—and obvious differences—the type of community under consideration, the theoretical or analytical angle—provide strong interpretative handles. This division by element is not perfect, but we wanted to break with traditional structures of chronology or geography. The comparative approach that binds the volume together follows a different logic, one that aims to uncover surprising and important patterns of socio-ecological vulnerability and resilience that are thickly contextualized that can also enter into dialogue across these contexts and suggest policy implications.

In some cases, elites benefit in the wake of a disaster, while others in the same society with meager resources suffer. In other cases, it is precisely the collapse of elite power—that is, collapse as traditionally understood—that ensues in the wake of a calamity. In fact, what seems important is to unpack notions of impact, response, and gains and losses according to meaningful social differentiators such as class, status, age, gender, and belief. In all societies, we claim, catastrophes and related processes of societal collapse are causally enmeshed in a political economy/ecology that *always* needs to include environmental and societal dimensions (Oliver-Smith 2004). Scale is important here, as large-scale comparative studies are unlikely to capture such heterogeneity. In contrast, small-scale particularist work does not allow generalizations and, hence, fails to produce anything other than cautionary and ultimately impotent tales from times gone by. The diversity of cases and the potential for meaningful and productive *dialogue* among them is important.

Can the Archaeology of Past Disasters Contribute to Risk Reduction?

All chapter authors were required to write a section of policy implications and/or practice suggestions to stakeholders, be they planners, first responders, politicians, other academics interested in impactful writing, or, as Holmberg reminds us in chapter 2, everyone. Our objective is to reach a reading audience beyond our discipline or subdiscipline. Putting it bluntly, authors were requested to do their best answering the question: So what? Authors were encouraged to think of knowledge gained, how ideas can be put into practice, and policy implications, either very specific or very general in nature. Occasionally, the archaeological record can recover sustainable practices of the past (Guttmann-Bond 2010; chapters in Isendahl and Stump 2019 and Cooper and Sheets 2012), but we remain cautious with regard to overly grandiose claims to useful knowledge.

The case studies collected together here can serve as effective modern-day parables, but what else can they do, given the radically different demographic and technological conditions of many cases to the present? One potential way to solve this apparent disjunction between the premodern and modern world is to think of social structures and interactions as not so much radically different, but as nested within each other, such as when considering neighborhoods or social networks within a complex society. The foundational disaster scholar Gilbert White (1974) suggested a long time ago that truly resilient communities would combine the best of traditional ways of handling calamities with technological acumen and infrastructure. White's distinction was insightful, simplistic, and evidence-free; he did not elaborate on his notion of preindustrial societies, nor did he follow up on this prescient suggestion. Perhaps we stand something to learn from how smaller-scale societies managed hazards for designing community resilience also within contemporary state societies. Perhaps we also stand something to gain by bringing relatively simple approaches to our cases such as, for instance, the schematic risk-management heuristic of Halstead and O'Shea (1989) that parcels response options out into five domains: physical storage, social networks, economic intensification and diversification, as well as mobility. These dimensions in fact articulate, albeit coarsely, with contemporary means of measuring socio-ecological vulnerability and may help in identifying patterns across case studies. Importantly, we may conclude in highlighting residential mobility—in other words, habitat tracking or disaster refugee behavior, depending on your preferred terminology—as a key response mechanism across many hazard types, communities, and periods. The net result of this mobility, migration, is then framed as an adaptive response, yet projected into the present, it carries with it numerous important and thorny corollaries (Black et al. 2011; Oliver-Smith 2009).

Archaeology is not ethnography, nor is it sociology. Our insights differ from those offered by these disciplines, and the pathways for our work to have impact on policies or on the livelihoods of at-risk communities are different. We have the advantage of a great sweep of time, especially before and after the perturbation. But we have trouble dealing with individuals or specific households in most cases. This volume attempts to emphasize the many strengths of the many archaeological perspectives on disaster. It is making a scholarly contribution, but the volume is also motivated by an anxiety that is as nagging as it is existential. The archaeological record offers arguably clear cases of impressively widespread climatic changes around the world and on a continental scale during, for instance, the late thirteenth-century drought and mid-sixth-century climatic disaster. Individuals, households, communities, and societies were affected. Networks were critical for robust responses but also conditioned the teleconnections that made some more vulnerable than others. There are powerful implications for our times of a rapidly warming planet. Indeed, if one can point at a single major conclusion of this volume, it is that social inequality is at the root of most if not all disasters. Egalitarian villagers, exemplified by the ancient Costa Ricans, showed both efficient disaster responses and no post-disaster increase in inequality, even after multiple disasters from Arenal Volcano's explosive eruptions (Sheets 1999, 2001). Perhaps future efforts of adaptation and mitigation should focus less on technological fixes and more on new forms of governance and of community life that attempt to integrate notions of equality *within* our so strongly stratified contemporary societies.

The looming catastrophe of our time is encapsulated in the notion of the Anthropocene. The Anthropocene narrative traces its roots into the deep past (Malm and Hornborg 2014) despite the fact that the most recent official suggestions of its starting age would let it coincide with the onset of modernity (Zalasiewicz et al. 2015, 2017) and overlap almost fully with a period of, at least in the West, unusually few major extreme events—what environmental historian Christian Pfister (2009, 239) has termed the "disaster gap." The coincidence of the rise of modern world systems and the relative quiescence vis-à-vis major disasters has blinded us, we feel, to the severity of the looming threat. Yet, ironically, this temporal separation of our present state from anything traditionally considered archaeological would boost the role of archaeology in contemporary discourse. This "mandate of the Anthropocene" makes it inevitable and unavoidable—even if uncomfortable—that our work is political (Riede, Andersen, and Price 2016). In this volume, we openly raise the question of the political involvement of an archaeology of catastrophe, climate change, and societal collapse. It is undeniable that our work relates to present quandaries—it draws its raison d'être, its fascination, and its finance from it, after all—but where do we draw the boundary between academia and activism? How are we to reconcile this evident bias with demands for scientific rigor and the validity of our conclusions as evidence-based? This volume makes one attempt to do so.

Acknowledgments

This work has been generously supported by grants awarded to Felix Riede by the Independent Research Fund Denmark *Sapere Aude* funding program (#11-106336/11-120673 and #6107-00059B), in the context of which the long-term collaboration between Payson Sheets and Felix Riede emerged. We also express our gratitude to Christian S. L. Jørgensen for expertly handling the index.

Felix Riede is German-born and British educated, with a PhD from Cambridge University. He is Professor of Archaeology at Aarhus University in Denmark. He heads the Laboratory for Past Disaster Science, and his research focuses on the Palaeolithic and Mesolithic of Europe.

Payson Sheets earned his PhD at the University of Pennsylvania. He is a professor in the Anthropology Department at the University of Colorado in Boulder. His lifelong research has focused on the interrelationships among human societies and volcanic activity in ancient Central America. His studies include the full range of social complexities, from small-scale egalitarian groups, through ranked societies, to complex civilizations. Societies reacted very differently to the massive sudden stresses of explosive volcanic eruptions in areas proximal to the eruption and in distal areas.

Note

1. The placement of archaeology into the natural sciences, social sciences, or humanities is highly arbitrary. While archaeology in the United States on the whole is seen as part of the anthropological projects and placed in the social sciences, its European counterpart can generally be found in humanities faculties. Elsewhere (i.e., in East Asia), archaeology departments can also be found in the natural sciences.

References

Alexander, David E. 2013. "Resilience and Disaster Risk Reduction: An Etymological Journey." *Natural Hazards and Earth System Sciences* 1 (2): 1257–84.

Ambraseys, Nicholas. 2009. *Earthquakes in the Mediterranean and Middle East: A Multidisciplinary Study of Seismicity up to 1900*. Cambridge: Cambridge University Press.

Armstrong, Chelsey Geralda, Anna C. Shoemaker, Iain McKechnie, Anneli Ekblom, Péter Szabó, Paul J. Lane, Alex C. McAlvay, et al. 2017. "Anthropological Contributions to Historical Ecology: 50 Questions, Infinite Prospects." *PLoS ONE* 12 (2): e0171883.

Barclay, Jenni, Katharine Haynes, Tom Mitchell, Carmen Solana, Richard Teeuw, Amii Darnell, H. Sian Crosweller, et al. 2008. "Framing Volcanic Risk Communication within Disaster Risk Reduction: Finding Ways for the Social and Physical Sciences to Work Together." *Geological Society, London, Special Publications* 305 (1): 163.

Barrios, Roberto E. 2017. "What Does Catastrophe Reveal for Whom? The Anthropology of Crises and Disasters at the Onset of the Anthropocene." *Annual Review of Anthropology* 46 (1): 151–66.

Barton, C. Michael, J. Emili Aura Tortosa, Oreto Garcia-Puchol, Julien G. Riel-Salvatore, Nicolas Gauthier, Margarita Vadillo Conesa, and Geneviève Pothier Bouchard. 2018. "Risk and Resilience in the Late Glacial: A Case Study from the Western Mediterranean." *Late Glacial to Early Holocene Socio-ecological Responses to Climatic Instability within the Mediterranean Basin* 184 (March): 68–84.

Bavel, Bas van, and Daniel R. Curtis. 2016. "Better Understanding Disasters by Better Using History: Systematically Using the Historical Record as One Way to Advance Research into Disasters." *International Journal of Mass Emergencies and Disasters* 34 (1): 143–69.

Bergthaller, Hannes, Rob Emmett, Adeline Johns-Putra, Agnes Kneitz, Susanna Lidström, Shane McCorristine, Isabel Pérez Ramos, et al. 2014. "Mapping Common Ground: Ecocriticism, Environmental History, and the Environmental Humanities." *Environmental Humanities* 5: 261–76.

Birkmann, Jörn, Philip Buckle, Jill Jaeger, Mark Pelling, Neysa J. Setiadi, Matthias Garschagen, Neil Fernando, and Jürgen Kropp. 2010. "Extreme Events and Disasters: A Window of Opportunity for Change? Analysis of Organizational, Institutional and Political Changes, Formal and Informal Responses after Mega-Disasters." *Natural Hazards* 55 (3): 637–55.

Black, Richard, Stephen R. G. Bennett, Sandy M. Thomas, and John R. Beddington. 2011. "Climate Change: Migration as Adaptation." *Nature* 478 (7370): 447–49.

Boer, Jelle Zeilinga de, and Donald Theodore Sanders. 2002. *Volcanoes in Human History: The Far-Reaching Effects of Major Eruptions*. Princeton, NJ: Princeton University Press.

———. 2004. *Earthquakes in Human History: The Far-Reaching Effects of Seismic Disruptions*. Princeton, NJ: Princeton University Press.

Bradtmöller, Marcel, Sonja Grimm, and Julien Riel-Salvatore. 2017. "Resilience Theory in Archaeological Practice—An Annotated Review." *Quaternary International* 446 (Supplement C): 3–16.

Cooper, Jago, and Payson Sheets. 2012. *Surviving Sudden Environmental Change*. Boulder: University Press of Colorado.

Crumley, Carole. 1993. *Historical Ecology: Cultural Knowledge and Changing Landscapes*. Santa Fe, NM: School of American Research Press.

Diamond, Jared M., and James A. Robinson. 2010. *Natural Experiments of History*. Cambridge, MA: Belknap Press.

Dominey-Howes, Dale. 2018. "Hazards and Disasters in the Anthropocene: Some Critical Reflections for the Future." *Geoscience Letters* 5 (1): 7.

Donovan, Amy R. 2017. "Geopower: Reflections on the Critical Geography of Disasters." *Progress in Human Geography* 41 (1): 44–67.

Donovan, Katherine. 2010. "Doing Social Volcanology: Exploring Volcanic Culture in Indonesia." *Area* 42 (1): 117–26.

García-Acosta, Virginia. 2002. "Historical Disaster Research." In *Catastrophe & Culture: The Anthropology of Disaster*, edited by Susanna M. Hoffman and Anthony Oliver-Smith, 49–66. School of American Research Advanced Seminar Series. Santa Fe, NM: School of American Research Press.

Gerrard, Christopher M., and David N. Petley. 2013. "A Risk Society? Environmental Hazards, Risk and Resilience in the Later Middle Ages in Europe." *Natural Hazards* 69 (1): 1051–79.

Grattan, John, and Robin Torrence, eds. 2007. *Living Under the Shadow: Cultural Impacts of Volcanic Eruptions*. One World Archaeology 53. Walnut Creek, CA: Left Coast Press.

Gronenborn, Detlef. 2006. "Climate Change and Socio-Political Crises: Some Cases from Neolithic Central Europe." *Journal of Conflict Archaeology* 2 (1): 13–32.

Guttmann-Bond, Erika. 2010. "Sustainability out of the Past: How Archaeology Can Save the Planet." *World Archaeology* 42 (3): 355–66.

Halstead, P., and J. O'Shea. 1989. "Introduction: Cultural Responses to Risk and Uncertainty." In *Bad Year Economics. Cultural Responses to Risk and Uncertainty*, edited by P. Halstead and J. O'Shea, 1–7. New Directions in Archaeology. Cambridge: Cambridge University Press.

Hoffman, Susanna M. 1999. "The Worst of Times, the Best of Times: Toward a Model of Cultural Response to Disaster." In *The Angry Earth: Disaster in Anthropological Perspective*, edited by Anthony Oliver-Smith and Susanna M. Hoffman, 134–55. London: Routledge.

Hoffman, Susanna M., and Anthony Oliver-Smith. 1999. *The Angry Earth: Disaster in Anthropological Perspective*. London: Routledge.

———. 2002. *Catastrophe & Culture: The Anthropology of Disaster*. School of American Research Advanced Seminar Series. Santa Fe, NM: School of American Research Press.

Holling, C. S. 1973. "Resilience and Stability of Ecological Systems." *Annual Review of Ecology and Systematics* 4: 1–23.

Howe, Cymene, and Dominic Boyer. 2015. "Portable analytics and lateral theory." In *Theory Can Be More than It Used to Be*, edited by Dominic Boyer, James Faubion, and George Marcus, 15–38. Ithaca, NY: Cornell University Press.

Hulme, Mike. 2008. "The Conquering of Climate: Discourses of Fear and Their Dissolution." *Geographical Journal* 174 (1): 5–16.

Isendahl, Christian, and Daryl Stump. 2019. *The Oxford Handbook of Historical Ecology and Applied Archaeology*. Oxford: Oxford University Press.

Lorenz, Daniel F. 2013. "The Diversity of Resilience: Contributions from a Social Science Perspective." *Natural Hazards* 67 (1): 7–24.

Malm, Andreas, and Alf Hornborg. 2014. "The Geology of Mankind? A Critique of the Anthropocene Narrative." *The Anthropocene Review* 1 (1): 62–69.

Mauch, Christof, and Christian Pfister. 2009. *Natural Disasters, Cultural Responses: Case Studies toward a Global Environmental History*. Lanham, MD: Lexington Books.

Mercer, Jessica, Jean-Christophe Gaillard, Katherine Crowley, Rachel Shannon, Bob Alexander, Simon Day, and Julia Becker. 2012. "Culture and Disaster Risk Reduction: Lessons and Opportunities." *Environmental Hazards* 11 (2): 74–95.

Middleton, Guy D. 2017. *Understanding Collapse: Ancient History and Modern Myths*. Cambridge: Cambridge University Press.

Migoń, Piotr, and Edyta Pijet-Migoń. 2019. "Natural Disasters, Geotourism, and Geo-Interpretation." *Geoheritage* 11 (2): 629–40.

Miller, Fiona, Henry Osbahr, Emily Boyd, Frank Thomalla, Sukaina Bharwani, Gina Ziervogel, Brian Walker, et al. 2010. "Resilience and Vulnerability: Complementary or Conflicting Concepts?" *Ecology and Society* 15 (3): 11.

Nielsen, Morten, Sørensen, Annette H., Riede, Felix, 2020. "Islands of Time: Unsettling Linearity Across Deep History." *Ethnos* 1–20.

O'Keefe, Phil, Ken Westgate, and Ben Wisner. 1976. "Taking the Naturalness out of Natural Disasters." *Nature* 260: 566–67.

Oliver-Smith, Anthony. 2004. "Theorizing Vulnerability in a Globalized World: A Political Ecological Perspective." In *Mapping Vulnerability: Disasters, Development, and People*, edited by Thea Hilhorst, Georg Frerks, and Greg Bankoff, 10–24. London: Earthscan Publications.

———. 2009. "Climate Change and Population Displacement: Disasters and Diasporas in the Twenty-First Century." In *Anthropology and Climate Change: From Encounters to Actions*, edited by Susan Alexandra Crate and Mark Nuttall, 116–36. Walnut Creek, CA: Left Coast Press.

Oppenheimer, Clive. 2011. *Eruptions That Shook the World*. Cambridge: Cambridge University Press.

Pedersen, Morten A., and Morten Nielsen, M. 2013. "Trans-temporal Hinges: Reflections on an Ethnographic Study of Chinese Infrastructural Projects in Mozambique and Mongolia." *Social Analysis* 57 (1): 122–42.

Pfister, Christian. 2009. "The 'Disaster Gap' of the 20th Century and the Loss of Traditional Disaster Memory." *GAIA—Ecological Perspectives for Science and Society* 18 (3): 239–46.

Redman, Charles L. 2005. "Resilience Theory in Archaeology." *American Anthropologist* 107 (1): 70–77.

Riede, Felix. 2014. "Towards a Science of Past Disasters." *Natural Hazards* 71 (1): 335–62.

———, ed. 2015. *Past Vulnerability. Volcanic Eruptions and Human Vulnerability in Traditional Societies Past and Present*. Aarhus: Aarhus University Press.

———. 2019. "Deep Pasts—Deep Futures: A Palaeoenvironmental Humanities Perspective from the Stone Age to the Human Age." *Current Swedish Archaeology* 26 (2018): 11–28.

Riede, Felix, Per Andersen, and Neil Price. 2016. "Does Environmental Archaeology Need an Ethical Promise?" *World Archaeology* 48 (4): 466–81.

Rigby, Kate. 2015. *Dancing with Disaster: Environmental Histories, Narratives, and Ethics for Perilous Times*. Under the Sign of Nature: Explorations in Ecocriticism. Charlottesville: University of Virginia Press.

Scanlon, Joseph. 1988. "Winners and Losers: Some Thoughts about the Political Economy of Disaster." *International Journal of Mass Emergencies and Disasters* 6 (1): 47–63.

Schenk, Gerrit Jasper. 2015. "'Learning from History'? Chances, Problems and Limits of Learning from Historical Natural Disasters." In *Cultures and Disasters: Understanding Cultural Framings in Disaster Risk Reduction*, edited by Fred Krüger, Greg Bankoff, Terry Cannon, Benedikt Orlowski, and Lisa E. Schipper, 72–87. London: Routledge.

Sewell, William H. 2005. *Logics of History: Social Theory and Social Transformation*. Chicago Studies in Practices of Meaning. Chicago: University of Chicago Press.

Sheets, Payson. 1999. "The Effects of Explosive Volcanism on Ancient Egalitarian, Ranked, and Stratified Societies in Middle America." In *The Angry Earth: Disaster in Anthropological Perspective*, edited by Anthony Oliver-Smith and Susanna M. Hoffman, 36–58. London: Routledge.

———. 2001. "The Effects of Explosive Volcanism on Simple to Complex Societies in Ancient Middle America." In *Interhemispheric Climate Linkages*, edited by Vera Markgraf, 73–86. London: Academic Press.

Sheets, Payson, and Donald K. Grayson. 1979. *Volcanic Activity and Human Ecology*. London: Academic Press.

Solnit, Rebecca. 2010. *A Paradise Built in Hell: The Extraordinary Communities That Arise in Disaster*. London: Penguin.

Stump, Daryl. 2013. "On Applied Archaeology, Indigenous Knowledge, and the Usable Past." *Current Anthropology* 54 (3): 268–98.

Svenning, Jens-Christian, and Brody S. Sandel. 2013. "Disequilibrium Vegetation Dynamics under Future Climate Change." *American Journal of Botany* 100 (7): 1266–86.

Torrence, Robin, and John Grattan, eds. 2002. *Natural Disasters and Cultural Change*. One World Archaeology. London: Routledge.

Walker, Jeremy, and Melinda Cooper. 2011. "Genealogies of Resilience: From Systems Ecology to the Political Economy of Crisis Adaptation." *Security Dialogue* 42 (2): 143–60.

Walker, Mike J. C., M. Berkelhammer, S. Björck, L. C. Cwynar, D. A. Fisher, Andrew J. Long, John J. Lowe, R. M. Newnham, Sune Olander Rasmussen, and Harvey Weiss. 2012. "Formal Subdivision of the Holocene Series/Epoch: A Discussion Paper by a Working Group of INTIMATE (Integration of Ice-Core, Marine and Terrestrial Records) and the Subcommission on Quaternary Stratigraphy (International Commission on Stratigraphy)." *Journal of Quaternary Science* 27 (7): 649–59.

Weiss, Harvey, and R. S. Bradley. 2001. "What Drives Societal Collapse?" *Science* 291 (5504): 609–10.

White, Gilbert F. 1974. "Natural Hazards Research: Concepts, Methods and Policy Implications." In *Natural Hazards: Local, National, Global*, edited by Gilbert F. White, 3–16. Oxford: Oxford University Press.

Wisner, Ben, Piers Blaikie, Terry Cannon, and Ian Davis. 2004. *At Risk: Natural Hazards, People's Vulnerability and Disasters*. 2nd ed. London: Routledge.

Wolf, Sarah, Jochen Hinkel, Mareen Hallier, Alexander Bisaro, Daniel Lincke, Cezar Ionescu, and Richard J. T. Klein. 2013. "Clarifying Vulnerability Definitions and Assessments Using Formalisation." *International Journal of Climate Change Strategies and Management* 5 (1): 54–70.

Zalasiewicz, Jan, Colin N. Waters, Colin P. Summerhayes, Alexander P. Wolfe, Anthony D. Barnosky, Alejandro Cearreta, Paul Crutzen, et al. 2017. "The Working Group on the Anthropocene: Summary of Evidence and Interim Recommendations." *Anthropocene* 19 (Supplement C): 55–60.

Zalasiewicz, Jan, Colin N. Waters, Mark Williams, Anthony D. Barnosky, Alejandro Cearreta, Paul Crutzen, Erle Ellis, et al. 2015. "When Did the Anthropocene Begin? A Mid-Twentieth Century Boundary Level Is Stratigraphically Optimal." *Quaternary International* 383: 196–203.

Section I

FIRE

The ancient Greeks, over two millennia ago, believed that everything in the world was composed of four basic elements: earth, water, fire, and air. Most of the research projects presented in this volume include many of these elements, in a variety of forms and contexts. In this first section of the book, these seven chapters focus on fire, in the form of volcanic eruptions. Each eruption impacts earth in the sense that lava or volcanic ash fell and to varying degrees destroyed, stressed, or preserved environments and evidence of human activities (e.g., Sheets 2015; Riede 2014). Lava did not travel through the air, but explosive eruptions emitted volcanic ash and gasses certainly did, occasionally so high that they circulated around the world and caused crises for many peoples. The research programs presented in this section were selected for variation in the magnitude and nature of the eruptions, the societies affected, how people reacted to eruptions and often innovated to decrease vulnerability to future eruptions, and environmental considerations (cf. Oppenheimer 2011; Grattan and Torrence 2007). Each chapter presents lessons from the past and suggestions for stakeholders today to improve their readiness for future extreme events.

The first chapter, by Felix Riede and Rowan Jackson, delves into the deep past of a great explosive eruption in what is now Germany and considers how that affected hunter-gatherer peoples about thirteen thousand years ago. It was continental Europe's last immense eruption, and it had intensive devastating impacts on nearby environments and human groups. At greater distances it had surprising effects. The authors graphically explain how much more devastating a similar eruption would be for present-day societies.

In chapter 2, by Karen Holmberg, we learn of the hazardous tradeoffs of the desire to decrease carbon dioxide emissions in Indonesian electrical production by constructing nuclear generators. She details the hazards of earthquakes and tsunamis to the nuclear plants, as well as volcanic eruptions, and the long-lived radioactive by-products. She delves deep into the humanities in seeking ways of depicting the fire and ice symbolism of these risks.

That is followed by Payson Sheets's chapter presenting how present-day cultures are handling ongoing or very recent disasters of fire and water. Unfortunately for the unfortunate citizens, they too often suffer greatly, while those with greater resources can profit handily from the extreme event. He does present a case, in detail, of egalitarian settled villages in ancient Costa Rica where repeated explosive eruptions did not enhance inequality.

In chapter 4, Peter Peregrine takes a quantitative approach to exploring the colossal volcanic impacts of droughts and chilling temperatures in 536 CE and following years. Most societies suffered greatly or even collapsed, yet a few survived well and even flourished. He reveals how the pre-stress social and structural nature of societies dramatically affect their resilience, along a spectrum of success to failure.

In chapter 5, Robin Torrence takes us to the tropics of Papua New Guinea to look closely at how traditional native communities can create oral history of past eruptions and their consequences, to enhance their handling of the next eruption. She deals with some forty thousand years of human occupation of that volcanically active area and the degrees of success people had in adapting to it.

A strikingly different environment is the subject of chapter 6, by Andrew Dugmore and colleagues. It is set in Iceland, an island totally built by the fire of volcanic activity, yet only occupied for some twelve centuries. They document the unfortunate and sustained erosion of the fragile soils and Icelanders' need for outside trade and assistance. The future does not look salutary for Icelanders and people in other areas of the world, with climate change and global warming.

The importance of social networks in assisting people under great stress in the Kuril Islands is convincingly presented by Erik Gjesfjeld and William A. Brown in chapter 7. The networks can provide early warnings, distribute needed resources, and offer loci for refuge. The advantages of social networks were delimited in other chapters of this volume, as well. Another advantage of the hunter-gatherer-fisher natives of the islands is their high degree of residential mobility. Gjesfjeld and Brown consider not only the hazardous relations of humans and volcanic fire but also those of humans and water; in so doing they build the bridge to the volume's second part, where watery hazards—too much water, too little water—move center stage.

References

Grattan, J., and R. Torrence. 2007. "Beyond Gloom and Doom: The Long-Term Consequences of Volcanic Disasters." In *Living Under the Shadow: Cultural Impacts of Volcanic Eruptions*, edited by J. Grattan and R. Torrence, 1–18. Walnut Creek, CA: Left Coast Press.

Oppenheimer, Clive. 2011. *Eruptions That Shook the World*. Cambridge: Cambridge University Press.

Riede, Felix. 2014. "Volcanic Activity." In *Encyclopedia of Global Archaeology*, edited by Claire Smith, 11:7657–66. New York: Springer.

Sheets, Payson. 2015. "Volcanoes, Ancient People, and Their Societies." In *The Encyclopedia of Volcanoes*, 2nd ed., 1313–19. Amsterdam: Academic Press.

CHAPTER 1

Do Deep-Time Disasters Hold Lessons for Contemporary Understandings of Resilience and Vulnerability?

The Case of the Laacher See Volcanic Eruption

FELIX RIEDE and ROWAN JACKSON

Summary for Stakeholders

Extreme events, including volcanic eruptions, have always affected human communities. Understanding the ways in which such events impact societies—past, present, and future—requires attention to both the physical parameters of the hazard in question and the societal nature of the affected communities. In many parts of the world, however, recent migration or the marked socioeconomic changes of recent centuries have resulted in a loss of collective memory relating to such events. Along with the memory of the events, any notion of how to respond to these events has also been lost. While the geosciences can reconstruct the magnitude and nature of such extreme events, archaeology can reconstruct past societal impacts and their responses. Such reconstructions that take account of both environmental and societal factors can inform scenarios of future impacts and facilitate holistic surge capacity tests. Furthermore, archaeology garners great public interest in many countries. When we accept that disaster risk reduction needs to include sociocultural aspects, archaeological data and heritage can be used much more effectively in (a) risk management, in (b) policy influencing, and in (c) boosting disaster literacy through museum engagement. In order to develop and implement such novel uses of our geo-cultural heritage, strategic alliances between academics, policy makers, planners, and public stakeholders are necessary.

Introduction

The fascination with past disasters in public and academic discourse can be traced back to the discovery of Pompeii and Herculaneum in the eighteenth century. This marked a significant step in the history of archaeology and is widely acknowledged in Romantic art and poetry of the nineteenth century. Yet, such fascination is rarely coupled with adequate explanations of how extreme events translate into disasters through their interaction with the contextual social, economic, and political structures of affected communities. At the same time, a growing literature on the cascading effects of volcanic eruptions on social and demographic networks over variable timescales has amassed, but this literature is rarely applied to future disasters.

Global climate change has been responsible for a higher frequency of extreme hydrometeorological events and associated social and economic losses since the 1980s (Schiermeier 2012; Smolka 2006). In contrast, geophysical events remain relatively stable, although even these may be responding to the radically altered conditions of a warming Earth: as mass is redistributed from land-based glaciers to the oceans, long quiescent tectonism and volcanism may be reactivated (McGuire 2013; Sigmundsson et al. 2010; Watt, Pyle, and Mather 2013). Volcanic eruptions again and again cause fatalities, and significantly, they also lead to migrations (Simkin, Siebert, and Blong 2001; Witham 2005). Explosive volcanism is a persistent hazard that, with eruptions at the high end of the magnitude scale, may have substantial impacts on future climates and one that presents a range of challenges for human communities (Bethke et al. 2017), especially in the rapidly warming world of the Anthropocene (Barrios 2017). By the same token, volcanic activity has had indirect but no less dramatic impacts on societies of the deep past (Riede 2014d; Sheets 2015) and recent past (e.g., Buntgen et al. 2016; Huhtamaa and Helama 2017; McCormick, Dutton, and Mayewski 2007; Toohey et al. 2016). Beyond simple devastation, a range of volcanic hazards, including ash falls, pyroclastic flows, lahars, flooding, environmental pollution, and lava flows, may impact communities nearby and at some distance, negatively as well as occasionally positively. Archaeologists and volcanologists have collaborated to reconstruct the long-term impacts of volcanic eruptions on human societies; arguably, understanding the spatial and temporal characteristics of risk for human societies in the *past* has the potential to inform disaster risk scenario planning in the *present* by providing an empirical basis for calculating *future* risks associated with volcanic hazards (Donovan and Oppenheimer 2018). Greater attention to the specific historical and societal contexts of at-risk communities can also assist in implementing improved risk-reduction measures (Barrios 2016; Mercer et al. 2012).

For some time now, archaeologists have been calling for a greater involvement of their discipline with the climate change debate and with disaster risk reduction (Djindjian 2011; Kaufman, Kelly, and Vachula 2018; Kintigh et al. 2014; Riede 2014a; Rockman 2012; Van de Noort 2013). Learning from past disasters is not straightforward, however (Pfister 2009a; Schenk 2015; Bavel and Curtis 2016), and we are fully cognizant that due caution is needed when attempting to offer *concrete* solutions to adaptive challenges (Cooper and Sheets 2012; Guttmann-Bond 2010) taken from disciplines such as history and archaeology (cf. Lane 2015). Similar to climate change adaptation research in general, the humanities and social sciences—and with them archaeology—remain peripheral to risk reduction policy making or intervention. This is in part due to a failing of the discipline to present results at large in those journals that feed into policy documents (Jackson, Dugmore, and Riede 2017, 2018). We nonetheless suggest that placing human-environment interactions in a deep historical perspective offers insights that can be translated into actionable knowledge and policy beyond the trope of "cautionary tales" (Kaufman, Kelly, and Vachula 2018, 5).

This chapter discusses how archaeology can contribute to environmental and disaster literacy by strengthening our understanding of the long-term vulnerability and resilience of communities to extreme environmental events. Drawing on the converging thinking of historians, disaster sociologists, and archaeologists, we develop the argument that the deep past is relevant in relation to contemporary and future calamities. We deploy one particular case study, the eruption of the Laacher See volcano—located in present-day western Germany—12,900 years ago and its impact on hunter-gatherer communities, to interrogate how our archaeological knowledge of such ancient calamities can be brought forward and made relevant in the context of contemporary and future vulnerability and resilience. We do so with reference to the Laacher See eruption exemplar and to a rapidly growing body of evidence for similar impacts of other volcanic events. Against this background, we outline three specific strategic positions for archaeologists interested in such engagement. First, we argue that such a view from the past can contribute in an evidence-based manner to drafting so-called realistic disaster scenarios, which are emergency planning tools regularly employed by policy makers and insurers. Second, we show through a systematic review of a key policy-influencing document—the Intergovernmental Panel on

Climate Change's extreme events (IPCC SREX) report (Field et al. 2012)—precisely what publication strategy archaeologists should follow if they want to increase the likelihood of their work making its way into future reports of this kind. Finally, we argue that in order to increase public awareness and risk literacy, extreme events such as volcanic eruptions and their societal impacts should play a greater role in the exhibitions of cultural history museums.

Mind the Disaster Gap

Vulnerability and resilience are widely adopted conceptual levers for studying disaster risk and the human dimensions of climate change (Adger 2006, 2000; Bankoff 2001, 2018; Birkmann 2006; Cutter et al. 2003; Smit and Wandel 2006; Pelling 2011; O'Brien et al. 2007; Tierney 2014; Wisner et al. 2004). Yet, there is a diverse array of terminologies and discourses largely contingent on the interests of the researcher and the availability of pertinent data. Generally, vulnerability indexes the potential for loss, while resilience captures the ability to respond to, rebuild, and rebound after a given calamity (Miller et al. 2010). Both vulnerability and resilience are socio-ecological in their composition. The latter term perhaps harbors a more positive attitude to how societies cope with calamities and has been widely discussed in archaeology (e.g., Bradtmöller, Grimm, and Riel-Salvatore 2017; Redman 2005), although anthropologists working with living communities take a more critical stance that often links resilience to conservative notions of political power (Barrios 2016, 2017). Whichever notion is favored, such crises should be viewed as opportunities for change and transformation (Birkmann et al. 2010; Pelling 2011; Nelson et al. 2007)—sometimes for the better (Solnit 2010). In this sense, social transformation is made possible by calamities that provide the stimulus for structural societal change. Therefore, rather than focus on vulnerability as a static phenomenon, we focus on vulnerability as revealed through an interplay of the social, economic, and environmental context and on societal changes following catastrophic events (Bankoff 2003, 2004, 2018; Costanza et al. 2007).

Where natural hazards occur frequently, effective response strategies often become incorporated into social and cultural practices, education, and policy, in what have become known as "cultures of coping" (Bankoff 2009, 265). Disasters that are experienced less frequently and at higher magnitudes, however, can be lost from the collective memory of a given community, leading to the emergence of a "disaster gap" (Pfister 2009b,

239). This refers to the false sense of security from extreme events in a given place. The eruption of Eyjafjallajökull (Iceland) in 2010 is a notable case of the cascading effects that such hazards can have on an entire region and economic sector that has a limited experience of volcanic disasters. By global volcanic standards the eruption was "ordinary" (Davies et al. 2010, 608), but social and economic impacts were catastrophic for many (Adey and Anderson 2011). Local farms in the volcano's immediate vicinity were negatively affected by tephra fall covering pastureland used for animal grazing, but the Eyjafjallajökull volcano also attracted tourists at a time of economic uncertainty in Iceland (Benediktsson, Lund, and Huijbens 2011). The regular experience of eruptions in Iceland has normalized risk management strategies so that communities and authorities rapidly assess and respond to volcanic hazards (cf. Gislason et al. 2011). This has increased the resilience of local communities and reduced their vulnerability to the impacts of eruption events.

At the regional scale, the dispersion of ash across Europe had economically disastrous consequences (Pedersen 2010). Airborne volcanic ash particles have the potential to cause jet engine failure, leading to the closure of large portions of European airspace 15–21 April 2010 (Langmann et al. 2012). This had a cascading effect on flight networks and global/regional airline hubs, logistical chains, and the organization of European airspace, with consequences for the wider global aviation industry across the North Atlantic and Eurasia especially (Adey and Anderson 2011). In all, more than one hundred thousand flights were canceled, and over ten million passengers were affected. The aviation industry alone suffered estimated losses of approximately $1.7 billion (Budd et al. 2011), but the criticality of airborne logistics amplified these economic losses: a report commissioned by Airbus estimated impacts on global gross domestic product in the first week at $4.7 billion (Oxford Economics 2010).

As the case illustrates, the remarkable effects of the Eyjafjallajökull eruption cannot be sought in its geophysical properties, but rather in the complex ways in which it interacted with the affected societies and their ways of socially, cognitively, legally, and technologically handling this event (Alexander 2013; Donovan and Oppenheimer 2012; Lund and Benediktsson 2011; Adey and Anderson 2011). Owing to its remote island location, the Eyjafjallajökull eruption offers a drastically simplified distinction between direct/short- and indirect/long-range impacts. The vulnerabilities it revealed relate to an interplay of contextual and impact-related factors that, in a highly networked and technologically interwoven society, can have cascading effects that are experienced across multiple spatial scales (Graham 2010; November 2008; Bennett 2005).

The Laacher See Eruption—Apocalypse Then?

Approximately 12,900 years ago, the Laacher See volcano located in the westernmost part of present-day Germany erupted violently. This highly explosive Plinian eruption scored a solid 6 on the volcanic explosivity index (VEI), making it "paroxysmal, colossal" (Newhall and Self 1982, 1232). The eruption itself has been studied in considerable detail (see table 1.1 for a summary and references); over several months—perhaps more than a year—eruptive activity waxed and waned (Schmincke 2006). Its ash column would have been seen, its explosions heard, its shockwaves and associated earthquakes felt across most of Europe (Riede 2017b). Furthermore, the nearby River Rhine was temporarily dammed by an accumulation of ejecta, forming a lake, as well as damming numerous upstream tributaries. Following dam collapse, one or several river flood waves traveled down the drained riverbed (Park and Schmincke 2009)—river-rafted debris from the eruption has been found far downstream (Janssens et al. 2012). Volcanic ash (= tephra) from the eruption's different phases was distributed by wind in a southwest-to-northeast swath that cuts Europe into two, from Italy in the south to Russia in the north, and from France in the west to Lithuania in the east. To the northeast of the eruptive center, areas as far away as 250 kilometers from the volcano still received several centimeters of ashfall (Riede et al. 2011).

Archaeological research highlights that contemporaneous highly mobile forager communities of Stone Age hunter-gatherers were affected by the eruption (Riede 2017b). The volcano's near field (within fifty kilometers) was devastated by massive ash deposition and appears to have been depopulated for decades (Baales and Jöris 2002). The eruption and its attendant tephra fallout also had societal effects in the far field beyond five hundred kilometers) that were at the same time subtler (no depopulation) and more pronounced (evident changes in the cultural repertoire) than those in the near field. The fallout likely affected ecosystem

Table 1.1. Summary of key characteristics of the Laacher See eruption.

Characteristic	Description	References
Best estimated dates based on various approaches	12,916 cal BP	Baales et al. (2002)
	12,900 ± 560 (Ar^{40}/Ar^{39}) BP	Bogaard (1995)
	12,880 varve years BP	Brauer, Endres, and Negendank (1999)
	12,980–12,890 cal BP	Bronk Ramsey et al. (2015)
	13,034 cal BP	Raden et al. (2013)

(continued)

Table 1.1. continued

Characteristic	Description	References
Correlated geophysical, cosmogenic, and climatic events	"Acid rain, increased rain fall, reduction of solar radiation and drop of temperature"	Schmincke (2006, 152); also Graf and Timmreck (2001) and Riede et al. (2019)
Fallout directions	NE > SSW	Bogaard and Schmincke (1984)
Maximum height of Plinian column	<40 km	Bogaard and Schmincke (1985)
Minimum height of Plinian column	>20 km	Schmincke, Park, and Harms (1999)
Volume of extruded magma	≥20 km^3 or 6.3 km^3 (dense rock equivalent [DRE])	Schmincke et al. (1999)
Estimated discharge rate	3–5 x 10^8 kg/s	Schmincke (2006)
Eruptive temperature	250°C (pressure blasts); 8800°C (magma)	Schmincke (2006)
Sulfur injected into the atmosphere	1.9–15 x 10^{12} g	Schmincke et al. (1999)
Area covered by pyroclastic currents	>1400 km^2	Bogaard and Schmincke (1984)
Area affected by ash fallout	>315,000 km^2 at a thickness of several m to mm	(Fisher and Schmincke, 1984; Riede et al., 2011)
High-latitude (> 60° N) amplifying factor for cooling	+4 (winter) / −4 (summer) °K	Graf and Timmreck (2001); see also Baldini, Brown, and Mawdsley (2018)
Human impacts	Affected part of the North European Plain abandoned	Riede (2008; 2016; 2017b)
VEI	6	Newhall and Self (1982)
Magnitude (M)	6.2	Calculated after Mason, Pyle, and Oppenheimer (2004)
Intensity (I)	11.5–11.7	Calculated after Pyle (2015)
Destructiveness (D)	≥3.1	Calculated after Pyle (2015)

functioning through negative impacts on animal and human respiratory health (Riede and Bazely 2009) and by increasing dental wear (Riede and Wheeler 2009). Ash storms fed by remobilized particles (cf. Wilson et al. 2011) may have plagued the areas affected by tephra fallout for decades following the eruption.

It is likely that these ash-induced effects interacted with the eruption's effects on weather and climate to also disrupt traditional travel routes, leading to a breakdown of the social networks that bound these communities together (Riede 2014b). Perhaps the entirely unexpected eruption event interacted with already ongoing climate change—the two hundred years prior to the eruption constitute the cold "Gerzensee oscillation" documented in paleoenvironmental archives across Europe (e.g., van Raden et al. 2013)—to form a so-called convergent catastrophe (Moseley 1999, 59) or compound event defined as "combinations of extreme events with underlying conditions that amplify the impact of the events" (Field et al. 2012, 118). In interaction with ecological and societal factors, the eruption led to the abandonment of affected regions in the middle distance (fifty to five hundred kilometers) toward the northeast of the volcano (Riede 2016). In turn, this resulted in the isolation of communities along the far-field margins of the tephra fallout in southern Scandinavia, which then led to culture change reflected in the stone tool repertoire of the period immediately following the eruption. Interestingly, these changes may indicate the loss of important technologies such as the bow and arrow (Riede 2009). At the same time, the eruption event perhaps also represented an opportunity to initiate social change. Living conditions in southern Scandinavia—a refuge area not directly impacted by the Laacher See ashfall—in the post-eruption period were favorable, and resources were fairly abundant. Perhaps some communities seized the opportunity to effect positive societal changes in a form of *splendid isolation* (Riede 2017b).

Volcanic Hazards of the Future

Broad comparative perspectives have already shown that volcanic events can have long-term social and political legacies (Cashman and Giordano 2008; J. Grattan and Torrence 2007; J. P. Grattan 2006; Riede 2015). Certainly, data resolution is sometimes coarse when investigating ancient calamities, but these limitations are arguably balanced out by access to unique long-term information on the affected societies and their material expressions of livelihood and a similarly long-term perspective on the critical magnitude/frequency relationship of the relevant natural hazards, by the ability to carefully select case studies, and by the sheer number of cases available once the chronological window is suitably enlarged.

The stakes are high in disaster risk reduction. Large volcanic eruptions are potentially destructive and disruptive, but they are also rare. The serious consideration of low-probability but high-impact occurrences—"possibilism" (Clarke 2008)—and the attendant tropes of destruction and apocalypse carry with them the danger of hysteria, but combined geological, archaeological, and historical data can be effectively used to modulate these by offering historically informed, evidence-based, and holistic information on both the environmental and sociocultural parameters of past disasters that, critically, retains a great deal of immediacy and intimacy. In recognizing the relevance of archaeological data for addressing the possible impacts of extreme events, it is necessary for archaeologists to develop strategies for engagement with disciplines that are currently debating such matters. Many archaeologists are already active in collaborations with volcanologists and other natural scientists but do not fully utilize the implications of their data vis-à-vis contemporary society. Here we outline a strategy for archaeologists studying extreme events to engage in impactful collaborations with contemporary disaster studies, contribute resourcefully to policy-relevant debates through targeted publication, and use museums creatively to engage with the public. In the following we outline three pathways for bringing these insights into play in the contemporary world.

An Extended Laacher See Scenario Storyline

The magma chamber that fueled the cataclysmic Laacher See eruption of 12,900 years ago remains active (Zhu et al. 2012), its lurking presence signaled by carbon dioxide continuously rising to the surface of the crater lake (e.g., Goepel et al. 2015); earthquake activity in the region is taken to signal chamber recharge (Hensch et al. 2019). The scale of impact that a Laacher See–type eruption would have on contemporary infrastructures, ecosystems, and human health is chilling. The Laacher See volcanic complex is located in the densely settled Rhineland-Palatinate region of Germany, close to multiple international borders and multiple critical infrastructure installations located within the immediate blast radius and the zone of potentially massive ashfall (figures 1.1a–c). The impacts of these volcanic hazards would likely have cascading effects on European transport, energy, and supply networks that are essential to human health, well-being, and the economy (Jenkins et al. 2015; Scandone, Bartolini, and Martí 2015; Newhall, Self, and Robock 2018).

a

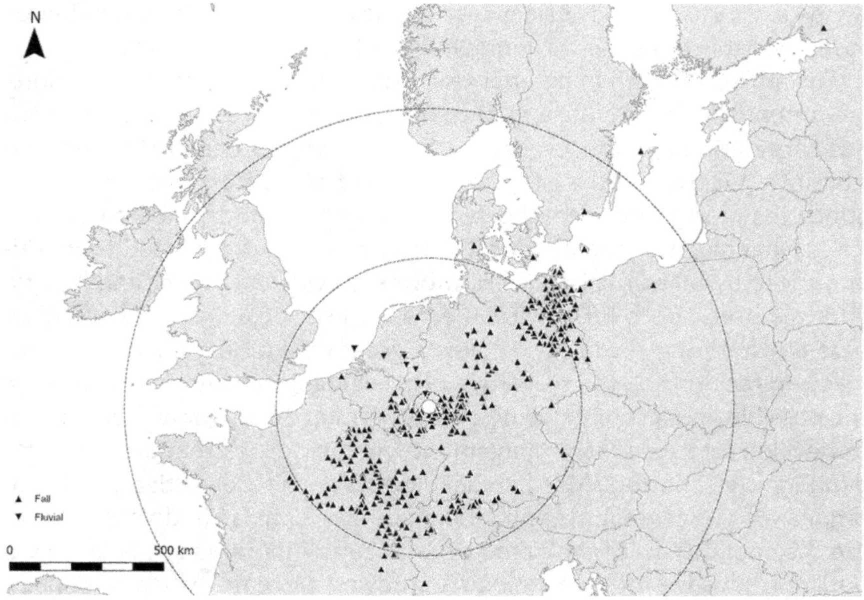

b

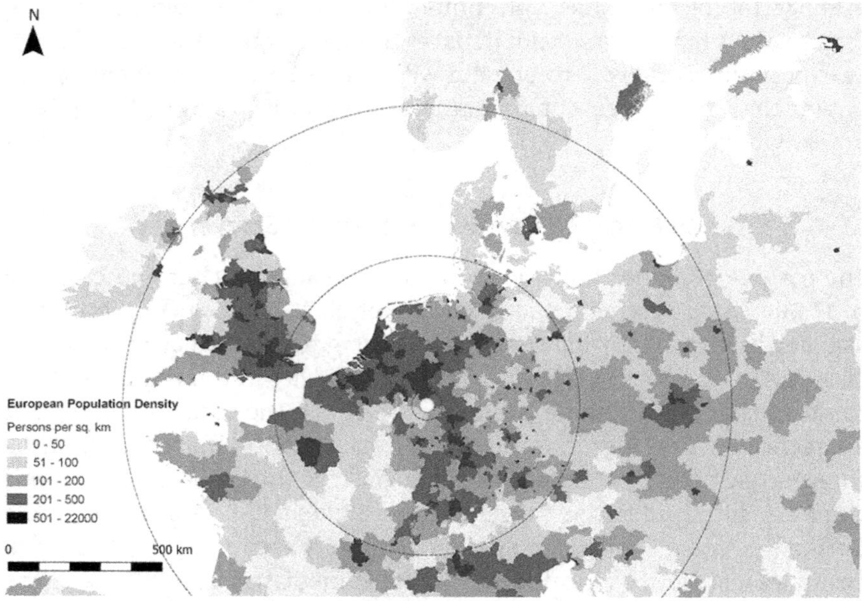

Figures 1.1a–c. The currently known distribution of Laacher See ash fallout of the ~13.000 BP eruption (a), contemporary population densities in Europe (b) (source: ESRI), the location of power plants in Europe (c). Stippled lines mark the proximal (<50 km), medial (50–500 km), distal (500–1000 km), and ultra-distal (>1000 km) hazard zones. Redrawn from http://maps.unomaha.edu/peterson. Figures originally published in Riede (2017a).

C

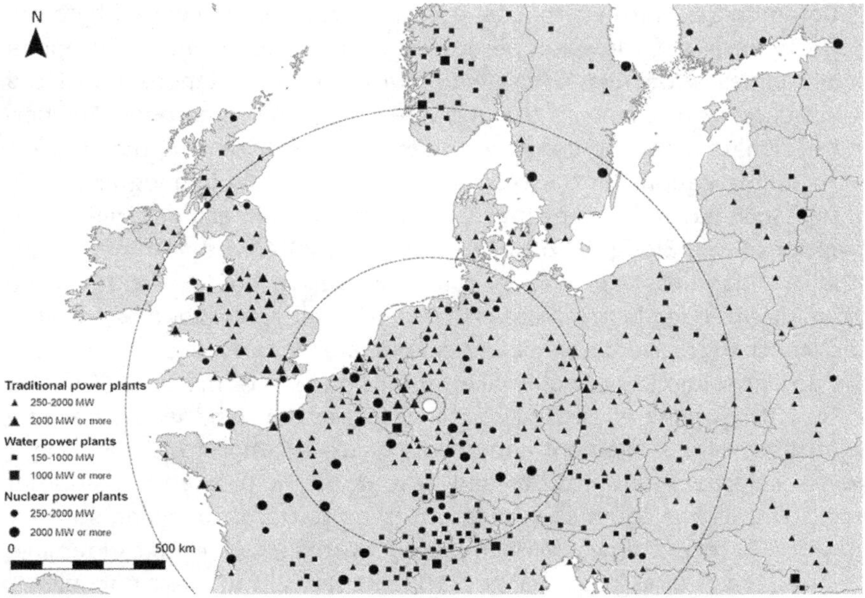

The longer-term cleanup and repair following tephra fall has been shown to require significant resources (Hayes, Wilson, and Magill 2015; Wilson, Jenkins, and Stewart 2015). A Laacher See eruption scenario would put the European economic and political systems under considerable strain, as emergency response systems would be ill-suited to respond to the scale, range, and complexity of impacts. With a focus on buildings, Leder and colleagues (2017) estimated the impacts of tephra fallout on Central Europe, including major cities such Cologne, Bonn, Koblenz, and Frankfurt. Estimates of building damage alone reach approximately $30 billion. The costs of clearing tephra fall from buildings and agricultural land, significant and prolonged disruption to European air traffic and various other supply chains, and responding to physical and mental health impacts (cf. Adams and Adams 1984; Hayes, Wilson, and Magill 2015) would also need to be considered. Tephra buildup on the River Rhine could block one of the most important economic highways in Europe, with direct impacts on major cities and industrial hubs (Uehlinger, Wantzen, and Leuven 2009). Frankfurt Airport is one of Europe's premier air traffic hubs, and its prolonged closure would have far-reaching consequences not only for personal travel but also for all the industries associated with its operation. Assuming ashfall comparable to that of thirteen thousand years ago, at least fourteen contemporary countries would be directly affected, raising the additional challenge of cross-border coordination and mitigation (Donovan and Oppenheimer 2012).

Communities thirteen thousand years ago were challenged by a period of consistently low temperatures prior to the eruption. European communities of the near future would face similar challenges associated with adapting to changing temperatures, albeit by rising ones. Furthermore, climate modeling not only indicates fairly substantial post-eruptive climatic fluctuations, but also directly attests to the dimming and darkness associated with the event (Riede et al. 2019). In analogy with other eruptions (e.g., Blong 1982; Horn 2014; Wood 2014) and anthropological studies of darkness (e.g., Galinier et al. 2010; Heijnen 2005), such sustained dimming often leads to increases in mental health issues and aggravated societal change. Scenario-building exercises have been used to consider the potential impacts of volcanic eruptions on long-term health (Schmidt et al. 2011; Sonnek et al. 2017). Significant areas of land would become unattractive for settlement and economic exploitation for some time—years or decades—potentially leading to domestic or even cross-border migration, as has commonly been observed to occur following volcanic eruption in recent times (Witham 2005). With such challenges looming, political, but also religious changes including radicalization are not unlikely (cf. Chester 2005)—effects of this kind must be taken seriously as potential outcomes of future eruptions.

In sum, a high-magnitude mid-continent eruption in Europe lasting several weeks or months would have substantial impacts on physical infrastructures, weather and climate, resource access and ecosystem structures, and human health and well-being both in the near and far field. The prolonged closure of European or even Eurasian airspace and at least a temporary collapse of air- and water-based supply chains that provide a high proportion of perishable goods, as well as the fragmentation of the highly interdependent European power supply system (Högselius et al. 2013), are among the most obvious consequences. Impacts on critical infrastructure (Wilson, Jenkins, and Stewart 2015) and agriculture (Arnalds 2013) could be significant, as the European resource system is highly interdependent across borders for matching energy surplus and the movement of short-term perishable goods. A breakdown of energy and food supply would present a significant challenge to national security and over prolonged periods could trigger large-scale population movement and geopolitical change.

Robust scenario-building excercises to assess the potential consequences of extreme events on societies of today require the holistic consideration of present conditions. Advances in science and technology since the Scientific and Industrial Revolutions of the eighteenth and nineteenth centuries transformed society's relationship with the natural environment (Golinski 1998; Latour 1987, 1994). The speed of technological advance in the nineteenth century ushered in a discourse of limitless growth and progress (Butzer 2012). Historians and sociologists of science have observed an ontological division of culture and nature, created by human rationalization and the perceived mastery over natural processes (Latour 1994). Bonneuil and Fressoz (2016) draw attention to Charles Lyell's (1835) *Principles of Geology*, which distinguished between the slow and regular geological processes from human timescales. As such, humans are seen to have become emancipated from natural determinants by their manipulation of nature as a source of energy that feeds into the ideas of "progress" and "mastery" by which modernity is defined (Urry 2015; cf. Latour 1994).

The great irony for so-called modern societies is that modernity is intrinsically dependent on a regular supply of energy to maintain material and economic growth, leading Latour (1994) to conclude that we have "never been modern" (Urry 2014). Dependence on natural resources to sustain human life is therefore a major concern for the future of humanity. Fear of the consequence of ecological destruction, catastrophic climate change, and resource crisis have become defining discourses for science, governance, and civil society (Hulme 2016, 2008), along with the expectation that modern ways of life are being protected through science-based risk management (Anderson 2010; Latour 2005).

Ulrich Beck (1987) and Anthony Giddens (1990) observed the emergence of "reflexive modernization" from problems created by eighteenth- to mid-twentieth-century modernization processes. Since the end of the twentieth century, societies have become increasingly oriented toward identifying and finding solutions to disease burdens, crime, and terror as well as natural hazards (Beck 2002). For Beck, the identification of otherwise invisible threats to society is the principal role of the sciences in a modern risk society (Demeritt 2006). According to Anderson (2010), multiple forms of anticipatory practices are used by liberal democracies to calculate, imagine, or perform possible futures. Calculation of futures often uses statistics and modeling based on historical information to enumerate threats. But when there is a limited understanding of the causal relationship within systems, quantification may not be possible, and (semi-)qualitative scenarios might be opted for to imagine or perform possible futures (Anderson 2010; Rounsevell and Metzger 2010).

Attempts to bridge the disaster gap between past, present, and future—scenario planning—has a long history but was systematized and became widespread in military strategy during the 1950s and in the economic strategies of major companies in the 1960s and 1970s (Bradfield et al. 2005; Urry 2015) for its ability to assess multiple plausible futures using extrapolations from the past (Son 2015). The combination of statistical modeling and qualitative scenario storylines have since become an important tool in climate change adaptation and disaster risk reduction research (Alexander 2000; Rounsevell and Metzger 2010). This information is used increasingly to inform policy and disaster management strategies for future risk. In volcanology, scenarios have been particularly important for developing evacuation procedures, improving infrastructure resilience, and co-producing community risk awareness (T. Davies et al. 2015). This involves imagining threats that translate from the physical properties of the eruption into the contextual vulnerabilities of societies. Good communication of the potential impacts and cascading effects associated with different eruption scenarios will be essential to designing adequate policy interventions (Donovan and Oppenheimer 2018, 2016).

Mazzorana, Hübl, and Fuchs (2009) proposed a time-incremented scenario method that integrates both natural and human information in a consistent framework. This realistic disaster scenario (RDS) framework can allow different eruption parameters to be conceptualized over space and time and integrated with vulnerabilities associated with the human domain. Such scenarios can be improved by feeding past societal data into these frameworks (figure 1.2). By increasing the number of eruption scenarios over space (the near and far areas) and time (the increase or decrease of vulnerability load) and by including salient sociocultural data on the affected communities, the analytical scope of such extended realistic disaster scenarios (eRDS) could reduce the risk of otherwise unforeseeable and catastrophic events—Taleb's (2010) infamous "black swans."

Such an extension of the realistic disaster scenario tool is timely, as deep-time natural hazards and disasters have not gone unnoticed in the social sciences and humanities. The nexus between society, technology, and environment has radically altered our susceptibility to persistent hazards, such as earthquakes and volcanic eruptions. Societies are now better equipped to anticipate, predict even, and respond to geo-hazards, but such is the rate of development in areas susceptible to long-term hazards that an asymmetry has grown between infrastructures and experience of risk. This becomes clear when statistics about the frequency and magnitude of volcanic eruptions and earthquakes are contrasted with the robustness of infrastructures, local knowledge of potential hazards, and emergency planning strategies. The Three Gorges Dam, for example, is located in an area of tectonic activity, and the pressure of the reservoir that it creates increases the risk of high-magnitude earthquakes (Huang et al. 2018). A historical case that illustrates this well is the experience of hurricanes in New Orleans since the city's foundation in 1718. As Rohland (2018) explains, the interrelationship among technology, politics, and scientific knowledge is an essential context for the population expansion and sustained use of inadequate storm surge defenses.

Increased global population, standards of well-being, access to and consumption of natural resources, vastly expanded scales of trade, and population movement, as well as flows of information and capital, characterize

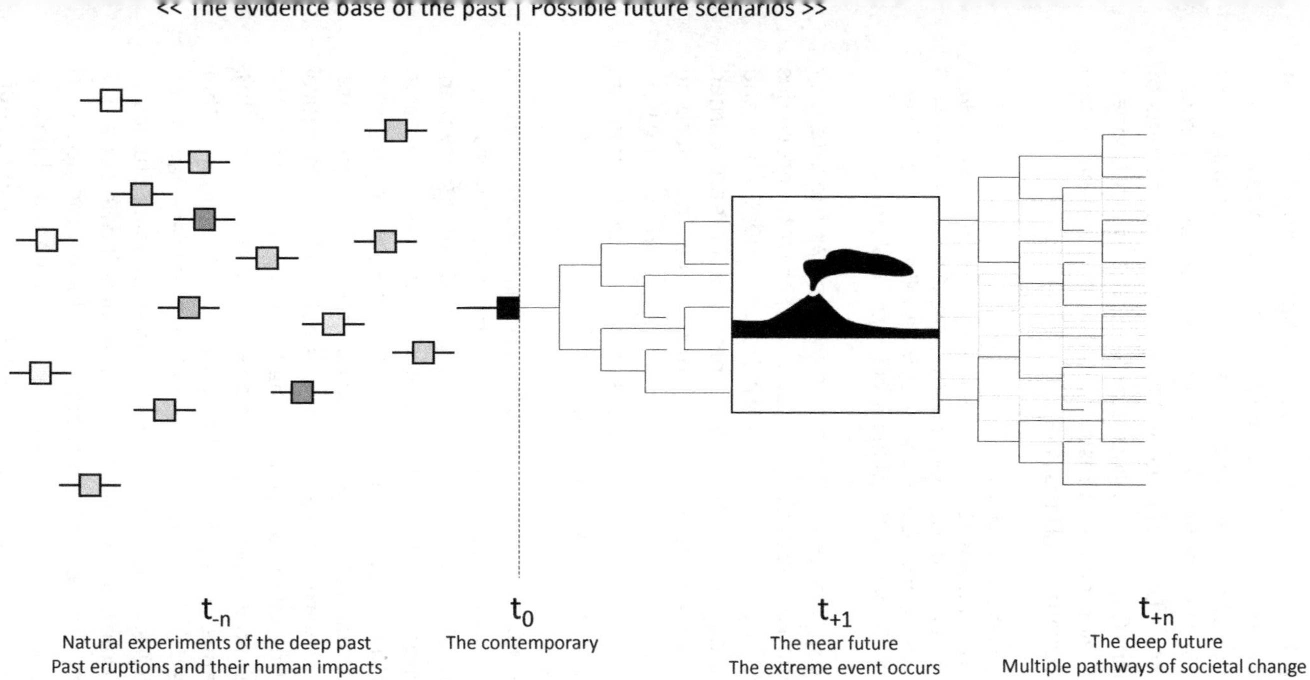

Figure 1.2. A conceptual schematic for extended realistic disaster scenarios (eRDS) as originally proposed by Mazzorana et al. (2009) and modified by Riede (2017a). The shaded squares represent archaeological/historical cases—completed natural experiments of history. The timeline passing through each case square indicates that the archaeological/historical record allows the investigation of the socio-ecological conditions both before and after a given event to be captured. Their variable placement in the left-hand part of the schematic reflects the variable chronological (t_{-n}) and cultural distance from the present (t_0); the variable shading indexes the evidential quality of each case. The stippled line at t_0 divides an evidentially constrained past from a future that can only be prognosticated. From the present, the pathways of societal development can be projected into the future where at t_{+1} an extreme event occurs and interacts with the different socio-ecological near futures. From this point, manifold but evidence-constrained deep futures (t_{+n}) unfold as a conjoined consequence of prior societal trajectories and the impacts of the extreme event in question. Figure originally published in Riede (2017a).

the contemporary world (Bonneuil and Fressoz 2016; Steffen et al. 2015). Although human settlements have always experienced environmental hazards and disasters, high-density urban agglomerations seriously aggravate vulnerability to volcanic disasters (Brown, Auker, and Sparks 2015; Chester et al. 2001). Nigel Clark (2011) has asked what contemporary societies can learn from the lived experience of natural catastrophes. In doing so, Clark draws attention to situating social thought and the analysis of natural hazards in deep time. Clark cites Mike Davis's (1998, 1990) ethnographic accounts of Los Angeles and Southern California to illustrate global asymmetry between the speed of human development—infrastructural and demographic—and the experience of geo-hazards. As Davis (1998: 35–36) writes:

> If there has been a single fatal flaw in the design of Southern California as a civilization, it has been the decision to base the safety of present and future generations almost entirely upon shortsighted extrapolations from the disaster record of the past half-century. . . . These spans are too short to serve as reliable proxies for ecological time or to sample the possibilities of future environmental stress.

The asymmetrical experience of hazardous events has the effect of "black boxing" disruption to the social (and technical) order that societies have come to expect (Adey and Anderson 2011; Graham 2010; Graham and Marvin 2001; Graham and Thrift 2007). Because infrastructures are learned and normalized by their users in conventions of practice, they become veiled physically and metaphorically (Kaika and Swyngedouw 2000). As Graham and Thrift (2007) have observed, our dependence on these infrastructures becomes visible only when they are disrupted by the breakdown of normal operation.

The dependence of modern life on so-called critical infrastructures is so important to the national security of nations that their "operational resilience" features dominantly in national strategy and emergency planning (Walker and Cooper 2011). The "catastrophic possibilities" reviewed by government departments span military and civil threats ranging from organized cyber threats and terrorist attacks to natural disasters and infrastructure failure. This elevates the future operational resilience of critical infrastructure supporting everyday life (ranging from health to economic transactions) as an essential oversight for national security (Graham 2010). Modern societies' relative inexperience of high-magnitude eruptions that would have impacts extending over multiple national borders have been cited across hazard literatures, and most vividly in expanding studies of existential risk (e.g., Martin Rees 2013). Future studies in the social sciences and humanities have expanded rapidly, exploring the potential consequences of advances in technology, climate change, and natural hazards on social and political organization (Bostrom and Cirkovic 2008; Oreskes and Conway 2014; Urry 2011, 2015). Yet, explicit considerations of effectively existential volcanic risk remain rare, with Denkenberger and Blair's (2018) detailed discussion of major threats to humanity on the whole being a recent exception. Such near-existential threats are difficult to imagine, let alone communicate (Turchin and Denkenberger 2018). Such imaginaries are necessarily speculative but could, precisely due to their inherent difficulty, be improved by a historical grounding in past disasters. This opens the possibility for collaboration among archaeologists, historians, volcanologists, natural and social sciences, and humanities to create scenarios that are grounded in the realism of past events but contextualized in the socio-technical complexities of contemporary societies.

The asymmetry among fading disaster memory, increasing vulnerability, and the steady, perhaps even increasing, rate of volcanic eruptions calls for greater attention to the implications of high-magnitude volcanic eruptions on human security in developed and developing nations alike. Consilience among volcanology, archaeology, and the social sciences has the potential to offer a deeper history of past human vulnerability and a structured understanding of the potential impacts of volcanic hazards on societies in the future. Natural and social sciences use a range of different methods to imagine possible futures, from hard statistical calculations of the probability that volcanic eruptions, earthquakes, and flooding of various magnitudes will occur in the twenty-first century (Newhall, Self, and Robock 2018; Self 2006) to scenarios and qualitative models of social and political organization following catastrophic events (Oreskes and Conway 2014; Urry 2011). Archaeologists studying past disasters have used data, method, and theory from natural and social sciences to interpret material culture and reconstruct the social consequences of risk to environmental hazards (e.g., Guedes et al. 2016). Scenario exercises in hazard management and adaptation planning, on the other hand, are reliant on historical information to construct storylines for the future (Rounsevell and Metzger 2010). This puts the historical sciences—archaeology in particular—in a position to explore future scenarios by expanding the chronological scope of disaster history (Costanza et al. 2007, 2012; Kaufman, Kelly, and Vachula 2018; Redman 2005).

Publication Strategy for Maximizing Policy Impacts

Archaeologists and historians have amassed a growing body of literature on the human impacts of past disasters. Many currently work in fruitful collaborations—both multidisciplinary and interdisciplinary—with the natural sciences and geosciences. But for this research to have an impact on academic debates that are pertinent to contemporary disaster studies and therein highlight policy relevance, research should aim to publish in journals that are read by authors beyond archaeology and history.

To provide a road map for publishing impactful historical studies of past disasters and hazard risk, we compiled a rank of research journals published in the IPCC SREX report and a refined literature search using the Scopus search engine. This builds upon previous research setting out a "New Social Contract" for archaeologists and historians who study climate change adaptation to publish in journal articles that are read by global change researchers (Jackson, Dugmore, and Riede 2017, 2018). Here, our results aim to highlight target journals for archaeologists (and historians) to synthesize their research for contribution to contemporary challenges of disaster risk reduction, climate change adaptation, and understanding human resilience/vulnerability.

We started our analysis by recording the citation frequency of journal articles within each chapter of the SREX report to provide a rank of journals. This was then combined with a rank collected using the Scopus search engine. Keyword and refinement criteria for the Scopus search results are given in figure 1.3. A mean rank was then calculated by combining the SREX and Scopus ranks (table 1.2). This provides a general representa-

	Inclusion	**Exclusion**
Document types	Article, review, book chapter, editorial, book, short survey, article in press	Publications not in English
Year range	1996–2017	
Search code	TITLE-ABS-KEY ("climat* change" AND "disaster*" OR "risk" OR "hazard*" OR "catastrop*")	

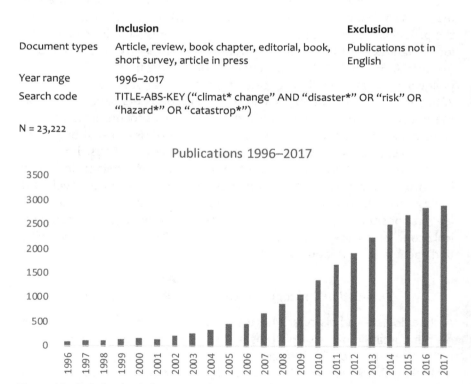

N = 23,222

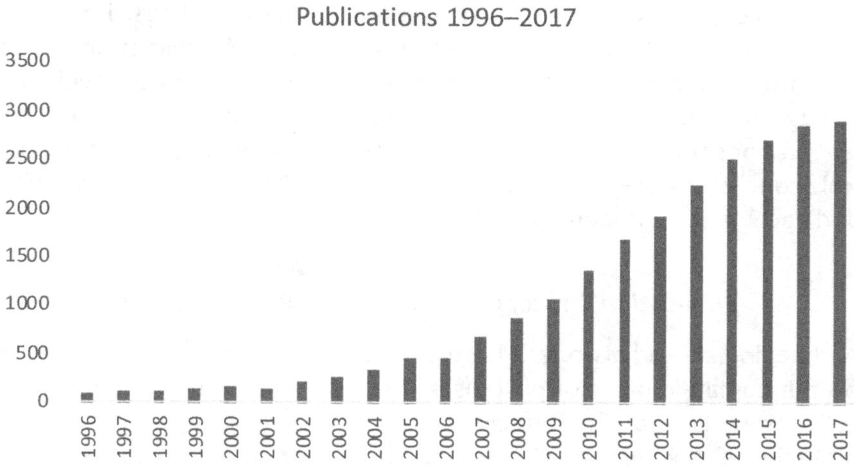

Figure 1.3. Search criteria for our semi-systematic literature search for impactful studies of past disasters.

Table 1.2. The ranked results of our semi-systematic review of the IPPC SREX report. This list offers signposts for impactful publication if the aim is to make archaeological studies of past human-environment interaction available to those drafting policy-making documents. It is worth noting that the articles in this table feature in the SREX report and Scopus keyword search for different reasons. The majority of the journals within the overall rank on the right-hand side of the table are interdisciplinary journals, but different journals place a greater or lesser emphasis on either the physical scientific basis for a given environmental hazard or human dimensions of the hazard (i.e., social, economic, health impacts, or political economic context of vulnerability and adaptive capacities). The *Journal of Climate* and *Geophysical Research Letters* for example, emphasizes research focusing on the physical scientific basis for a hazard, whereas *Global Environmental Change* and *Climate Policy* focuses on policy, human adaptation and resilience, and so on. Journals with an asterisk have the scope to include perspectives on cultural heritage and indigenous groups in disaster research.

IPCC SREX Report			Scopus Search				
Rank	**Journal Name**	**Citation Frequency**	**Rank**	**Journal Name**	**Publications**	**Journal**	**Overall Rank**
1	*Journal of Climate*	118	1	*Climatic Change*	551	*Climatic Change*	1
2	*Climatic Change*	105	2	PLoS ONE	329	*Global Environmental Change*	2
3	*Geophysical Research Letters*	98	3	*Science of the Total Environment*	249	*Science*	3
4	*Global Environmental Change*	86	4	*Natural Hazards*	244	*Natural Hazards*	4
5	*Science*	85	5	*Global Environmental Change*	222	*Nature*	5
6	*Disasters*	71	6	*Global Change Biology*	222	*PNAS*	6
7	*Nature*	69	7	*PNAS*	179	*Geophysical Research Letters*	7
8	*International Journal of Climatology*	58	8	*Regional Environmental Change*	172	**Mitigation and Adaptation Strategies for Global Change*	8

(continued)

Table 1.2. continued

IPCC SREX Report			Scopus Search				
Rank	**Journal Name**	**Citation Frequency**	**Rank**	**Journal Name**	**Publications**	**Journal**	**Overall Rank**
9	*Climate Dynamics*	53	9	*International Journal of Environmental Research and Public Health*	164	*International Journal of Climate*	9
10	*Journal of Geophysical Research*	42	10	*Science*	164	*Climate Research*	10
11	*Ecology and Society*	37	11	*Environmental Science and Policy*	156	*Journal of Climate*	10
12	*Natural Hazards*	34	12	*Environmental Research Letters*	148	*Ecology and Society*	12
13	*Climate Policy*	30	13	*Nature*	147	*Journal of Hydrology*	13
14	*Climate Research*	28	14	*Mitigation and Adaptation Strategies for Global Change*	140	*Risk Analysis*	14
15	*PNAS*	26	15	*Nature Climate Change*	135	**Environmental Science and Policy*	15
15	*Mitigation and Adaptation Strategies for Global Change*	26	16	*Environmental Health Perspectives*	122	*Climate Policy*	16

tion of journal impact/influence in hazards research. Each journal was then examined for evidence of published historical research or sufficient aims and scope to include multidisciplinary historical perspectives. This provided a criterion to determine the suitability for archaeologists to publish their deep-time perspectives in each journal. Journals highlighted in gray have sufficient scope to include such perspectives given sufficient attention to outlining the relevance of historical research—in order to boost the impact of archaeological/historical research on past extreme events, it is these journals that ought to be targeted.

Museums as Catalysts of Change

Museums of culture history have the potential to offer high-profile platforms for outreach, for education, and for debate around the role of climate and environmental change and extreme events in social change—past, present, and future. Recent research has drawn attention to the importance of museums as trusted educational spaces that can be used to increase public engagement with science (Cameron, Hodge, and Salazar 2013; Cameron and Deslandes 2011; Morien Rees 2017). We argue that disaster research from archaeology and history warrant greater attention in cultural history museums to disseminate knowledge and to engage with and educate the public. Much archaeological work already finds its way into museums of culture history. These museums are well visited in many countries—often with markedly higher visitor numbers than their natural history counterparts—and hence well positioned to frame debates on climate change and human impacts. The role of museums in addressing these issues and in providing democratic platforms for debate is increasingly recognized (e.g., Cameron and Neilson 2015), but the full potential of specifically culture history museums here remains as yet unrealized.

Archaeology cannot, except in very rare circumstances (e.g., Cooper and Sheets 2012; Guttmann-Bond 2010), provide concise blueprints for designing sustainable adaptations to volcanic hazards or other, climate-induced challenges. Rather, archaeology's strength is in its ability to provide evidence of the long-term relationship between human societies and the environments (Costanza et al. 2007). Intrinsic to this relationship is the ability of humans to adapt to changes resulting as a consequence of climate change, environmental degradation, or natural hazards. The archaeological process relies on the remains of deposited material culture to reconstruct cultural history. The resulting narratives have popular appeal across civil society as stories that are used to form identities and cultural sense of place. In addition, many themed cultural history exhibitions have captured significant attention in the media for the questions that they raise.

Material culture can be used as a tangible narrative of human history, recalling the impacts of volcanism and past disasters on human communities. The tangible nature of the archaeological record has made community archaeology a popular method for including and educating publics in the production of local history and challenges (Marshall 2002). This has also been applied in at-risk regions (Ryzewski and Cherry 2012) to contribute to environmental literacy and increased community resilience (Dix and Röhrs 2007; Van de Noort 2013). The Laacher See eruption and its impact on the culture history of Europe remains underutilized. Educational outreach about the eruption is currently largely limited to its geology and tourism (Bitschene and Schüller 2011; Erfurt-Cooper 2010), yet there is significant potential for museums to use this eruption and many others to communicate and raise awareness about extreme events.

Toward an Archaeology of Future Catastrophes

Self (2006) calculated the probability of a Mount St. Helens– or Krakatau-style VEI 5 eruption happening in the twenty-first century at 100 percent, whereas Oruanui- or Toba-style VEI 8 eruptions have a probability of less than 0.1 percent. The probability of a Laacher See–type VEI 6 eruption occurring in the near future lies somewhere in the middle. Rather than when, however, the decisive question is rather where such an eruption will occur. With the identification of a range of grand challenges for society and the environment in the twenty-first century, the possibility of such massive and potentially highly disruptive events has received increasing attention in academia, policy, and civil society. The current discourse about climate change and the impacts of extreme events is strongly catastrophic and apocalyptic in its rhetoric (see Dawdy 2009; Dörries 2010; Hulme 2008; Mauelshagen 2009; Nielsen 2013), and it is strongly focused on global "future narratives" rather than narratives that are centered on particular locales or regions and their deep histories. This global focus is reflected in the Intergovernmental Panel on Climate Change (IPCC) assessment reports and other international collaborations to address climate change, environmental degradation, and risk. Such reports often adopt a technocratic or natural science focus that can be distant, abstract, or outright alienating for many. As Van de Noort (2011) has noted, the IPCC reports—including in its special SREX report on extreme events (Field et al. 2012)—draw heavily on paleoclimatic data as a foundation for the prediction of future climate change, but they do not draw to any meaningful degree on corresponding "paleosocietal"—archaeological, historical—data when it comes to addressing future societal change (Riede 2014a).

Studies of past volcanism are plagued by a very similar dilemma: A suite of excellent databases of past volcanic activity as well as of other paleo-hazards (e.g., the NGDC/WDS Global Historical Tsunami Database, www.ngdc.noaa.gov/hazard/tsu_db.shtml) exist, some of which are expressly constructed to aid in risk reduction research (Bryson, Bryson, and Ruter 2006; Crosweller et al. 2012; Siebert, Simkin, and Kimberly 2010). Yet, none of these databases contain any or none other than trivial information on the societies actually affected by these eruptions. While we fully appreciate their utility in studies of past geological processes (e.g., Deligne, Coles, and Sparks 2010) and also fully appreciate the work that has gone into assembling these databases, they do not contribute to the investigation of past human vulnerability, resilience, or responses in a historically informed manner.

A better understanding of these past configurations could inform current debate. In the geosciences, there is increasing recognition that discussions of the threat posed by climate change and by extreme geophysical events are driven not by *information* but by *values*. The vulnerability of contemporary Europe, for instance, to extreme events such as a major volcanic eruption are therefore not merely "matters of fact" but "matters of concerns" (Stewart and Lewis 2017). What archaeology can add is immediacy and intimacy to specific volcanic hazard forecast scenarios by focusing on both the vulnerability and the resilience of past communities—a heritage that often generates a sense of place and the social capital for action. People relate readily to the past of the places they live and indeed draw much of their identity from historical and archaeological narratives (Sommer 2000). Adding this human dimension is hence likely to assist in framing such hazards not only in terms of facts but also in terms of concerns. Sustained archaeological investigations have advanced our understanding of the human ecology and human experience of volcanic eruptions through the comparison of different eruptions, different affected societies, and social-environmental impacts over different spatial and temporal ranges. So-called natural experiments of history (Diamond and Robinson 2010) have allowed the formal comparison of vulnerability before, during, and after eruption events comparatively between case studies (Riede 2014c).

Greater interdisciplinary and historical scope brought by collaboration between historical and contemporary disaster research would build a richer understanding of the "human ecology of extreme events" (Oppenheimer 2015, 245). Contributions come from multiple disciplines studying and bringing together human and environmental processes to understand the long-term impacts of environmental hazards using increasingly sophisticated techniques to resolve the past. But such approaches can be taken further. Orlove (2005) suggested that comparative approaches such as these could be adjoined with sociologies of the future. This closely resembles Clarke's (2007) "possibilistic thinking." The use of comparative history together with theory from the social sciences offers the potential for archaeologists to contribute to future studies and to what John Urry (2011) termed the "new catastrophism" discourse in academia.

We have here sought consilience among multiple disciplines occupied with prognosing and prognosticating socio-environmental futures. We propose connecting comparative studies of past disasters with social and natural sciences that study potential threats in the future. Large collaborative studies of existential risk are currently underway, such as the Centre for Existential Risk (University of Cambridge) and the Future of Humanity Institute (University of Oxford), but such projects rarely involve contributions from the deep history of archaeology as frames for the future of natural hazards. To understand the potential impacts of natural hazards, studies require collaborations that contextualize past disasters and consider the potential disruption of these events for modern networked societies. Efforts to exchange knowledge and data about the multiple environmental, social, and technological challenges in the twenty-first century can provide a platform for consilience in disaster research through global partnerships such as Knowledge Action Network on Emergent Risks and Extreme Events (https://www.risk-kan.org) under IRDR (http://www.irdrinternational.org) and Future Earth (http://www.futureearth.org). Participation in such initiatives could pave the way for improved knowledge of and action to address extreme events in the future.

Through its inherently interdisciplinary work, archaeology produces evidence-based narratives of past human-environment interactions that often generate a great deal of public interest. Narratives are powerful tools in translating environmental science into actionable ideas (Carter and van Eck 2014; Pancost 2017). We have therefore argued here that a fusion of environmental science and evidence-based narratives from the deep past can play a role in future-proofing society. Three avenues are particularly promising: (1) designing and using holistic extended realistic disaster scenarios (eRDS) for planning and policy making; (2) focusing publication strategies to target policy-influencing fora and documents such as the IPCC reports; and (3) taking the debate about climate change, extreme events, and human impacts into museum settings. Together, this practical three-pronged approach would allow for an engagement of archaeologists individually and collectively with environmental science, policy, and public debate in a way that makes the discipline's results more relevant without sacrificing intellectual rigor.

Acknowledgments

This work has been funded by the Independent Research Fund Denmark's *Sapere Aude* grant #6107-00059B *Apocalypse then? The Laacher See volcanic eruption (13,000 years before present), Deep Environmental History and Europe's geo-cultural heritage.*

Felix Riede is German-born and British educated, with a PhD from Cambridge University. He is Professor of Archaeology at Aarhus University in Denmark. He heads the Laboratory for Past Disaster Science, and his research focuses on the Palaeolithic and Mesolithic of Europe.

Rowan Jackson is university teacher in environmental sustainability and director of the MSc Environmental Sustainability programme at the University of Edinburgh. His most recent research explores human vulnerability, adaptation, and resilience in medieval Greenland and the application of archaeological data to contemporary human adaptation and vulnerability to climate change and natural hazards.

References

Adams, P. R., and G. R. Adams. 1984. "Mount Saint Helens's Ashfall: Evidence for a Disaster Stress Reaction." *American Pychologist* 39 (3): 252–60.

Adey, Peter, and Ben Anderson. 2011. "Anticipation, Materiality, Event: The Icelandic Ash Cloud Disruption and the Security of Mobility." *Mobilities* 6 (1): 11–20.

Adger, W. Neil. 2000. "Social and Ecological Resilience: Are They Related?" *Progress in Human Geography* 24 (3): 347–64.

———. 2006. "Vulnerability." *Global Environmental Change* 16 (3): 268–81.

Alexander, David E. 2000. *Confronting Catastrophe.* Oxford: Oxford University Press.

———. 2013. "Volcanic Ash in the Atmosphere and Risks for Civil Aviation: A Study in European Crisis Management." *International Journal of Disaster Risk Science* 4 (1): 9–19.

Anderson, Ben. 2010. "Preemption, Precaution, Preparedness: Anticipatory Action and Future Geographies." *Progress in Human Geography* 34 (6): 777–98.

Arnalds, Olafur. 2013. "The Influence of Volcanic Tephra (Ash) on Ecosystems." In *Advances in Agronomy*, edited by Donald Sparks, 121:331–80. Amsterdam: Academic Press.

Baales, Michael, and Olaf Jöris. 2002. "Between North and South—a Site with Backed Points from the Final Allerod: Bad Breisig, Kr. Ahrweiler (Central Rhineland, Germany)." *L'Anthropologie* 106 (2): 249–67.

Baales, Michael, Olaf Jöris, Martin Street, Felix Bittmann, Bernhard Weninger, and J. Wiethold. 2002. "Impact of the Late Glacial Eruption of the Laacher See Volcano, Central Rhineland, Germany." *Quaternary Research* 58 (3): 273–88.

Baldini, James U. L., Richard J. Brown, and Natasha Mawdsley. 2018. "Re-evaluating the Link between the Laacher See Volcanic Eruption and the Younger Dryas." *Climate of the Past* 14: 969–90.

Bankoff, Gregory. 2001. "Rendering the World Unsafe: 'Vulnerability' as Western Discourse." *Disasters* 25 (1): 19–35.

———. 2003. "Vulnerability as a Measure of Change in Society." *International Journal of Mass Emergencies and Disasters* 21 (2): 5–30.

———. 2004. "Time Is of the Essence: Disasters, Vulnerability and History." *International Journal of Mass Emergencies and Disasters* 22 (3): 23–42.

———. 2009. "Cultures of Disaster, Cultures of Coping: Hazard as a Frequent Life Experience in the Philippines, 1600–2000." In *Natural Disasters, Cultural Responses: Case Studies toward a Global Environmental History*, edited by Christof Mauch and Christian Pfister, 265–84. Lanham, MD: Lexington Books.

———. 2018. "Remaking the World in Our Own Image: Vulnerability, Resilience and Adaptation as Historical Discourses." *Disasters* 43 (2): 221–239.

Barrios, Roberto E. 2016. "Resilience: A Commentary from the Vantage Point of Anthropology." *Annals of Anthropological Practice* 40 (1): 28–38.

———. 2017. "What Does Catastrophe Reveal for Whom? The Anthropology of Crises and Disasters at the Onset of the Anthropocene." *Annual Review of Anthropology* 46 (1): 151–66.

Bavel, Bas van, and Daniel R. Curtis. 2016. "Better Understanding Disasters by Better Using History: Systematically Using the Historical Record as One Way to Advance Research into Disasters." *International Journal of Mass Emergencies and Disasters* 34 (1): 143–69.

Beck, Ulrich. 1987. *Risikogesellschaft: Auf dem Weg in eine andere Moderne*. 4. Druck. Frankfurt am Main: Suhrkamp.

———. 2002. "The Cosmopolitan Society and Its Enemies." *Theory, Culture & Society* 19 (1–2): 17–44.

Benediktsson, Karl, Katrin Anna Lund, and Edward Huijbens. 2011. "Inspired by Eruptions? Eyjafjallajökull and Icelandic Tourism." *Mobilities* 6 (1): 77–84.

Bennett, Jane. 2005. "The Agency of Assemblages and the North American Blackout." *Public Culture* 17 (3): 445–65.

Bethke, Ingo, Stephen Outten, Odd Helge Otterå, Ed Hawkins, Sebastian Wagner, Michael Sigl, and Peter Thorne. 2017. "Potential Volcanic Impacts on Future Climate Variability." *Nature Climate Change* 7 (11): 799.

Birkmann, Jörn. 2006. *Measuring Vulnerability to Natural Hazards: Towards Disaster Resilient Societies*. New York: United Nations University.

Birkmann, Jörn, Philip Buckle, Jill Jaeger, Mark Pelling, Neysa J. Setiadi, Matthias Garschagen, Neil Fernando, and Jürgen Kropp. 2010. "Extreme Events and Disasters: A Window of Opportunity for Change? Analysis of Organizational, Institutional and Political Changes, Formal and Informal Responses after Mega-Disasters." *Natural Hazards* 55 (3): 637–55.

Bitschene, Peter Rene, and Andreas Schüller. 2011. "Geo-education and Geopark Implementation in the Vulkaneifel European Geopark." *GSA Field Guide* 22: 29–34.

Blong, Russell J. 1982. *The Time of Darkness: Local Legends and Volcanic Reality in Papua New Guinea*. Seattle: University of Washington Press.

Bogaard, Paul van den. 1995. "$^{40}Ar/^{39}Ar$ Ages of Sanidine Phenocrysts from Laacher See Tephra (12,900 Yr BP): Chronostratigraphic and Petrological Significance." *Earth and Planetary Science Letters* 133 (1–2): 163–74.

Bogaard, Paul van den, and Hans-Ulrich Schmincke. 1984. "The Eruptive Center of the Late Quaternary Laacher See Tephra." *Geologische Rundschau* 73 (3): 933–80.

———. 1985. "Laacher See Tephra: A Widespread Isochronous Late Quaternary Tephra Layer in Central and Northern Europe." *Geological Society of America Bulletin* 96 (12): 1554–71.

Bonneuil, C., and J.-B. Fressoz. 2016. *The Shock of the Anthropocene*. London: Verso.

Bostrom, N., and M. M. Cirkovic. 2008. *Global Catastrophic Risks*. Oxford: Oxford University Press.

Bradfield, Ron, George Wright, George Burt, George Cairns, and Kees Van Der Heijden. 2005. "The Origins and Evolution of Scenario Techniques in Long Range Business Planning." *Futures* 37 (8): 795–812.

Bradtmöller, Marcel, Sonja Grimm, and Julien Riel-Salvatore. 2017. "Resilience Theory in Archaeological Practice—An Annotated Review." *Quaternary International* 446 (Supplement C): 3–16.

Brauer, A., C. Endres, and J. F. W. Negendank. 1999. "Lateglacial Calendar Year Chronology Based on Annually Laminated Sediments from Lake Meerfelder Maar, Germany." *Quaternary International* 61: 17–25.

Bronk Ramsey, Christopher, Paul G. Albert, Simon P. E. Blockley, Mark Hardiman, Rupert A. Housley, Christine S. Lane, Sharen Lee, Ian P. Matthews, Victoria C. Smith, and John J. Lowe. 2015. "Improved Age Estimates for Key Late Quaternary European Tephra Horizons in the RESET Lattice." *Quaternary Science Reviews* 118: 18–32.

Brown, Sarah K., M. R. Auker, and R. S. J. Sparks. 2015. "Populations around Holocene Volcanoes and Development of a Population Exposure Index." In *Global Volcanic Hazards and Risk*, edited by Charlotte Vye-Brown, Sarah K. Brown, Steve Sparks, Susan C. Loughlin, and Susanna F. Jenkins, 223–32. Cambridge: Cambridge University Press.

Bryson, Robert U., Reid A. Bryson, and Anthony Ruter. 2006. "A Calibrated Radiocarbon Database of Late Quaternary Volcanic Eruptions." *eEarth Discussions* 1: 123–34.

Budd, Lucy, Steven Griggs, David Howarth, and Stephen Ison. 2011. "A Fiasco of Volcanic Proportions? Eyjafjallajökull and the Closure of European Airspace." *Mobilities* 6 (1): 31–40.

Buntgen, Ulf, Vladimir S. Myglan, Fredrik Charpentier Ljungqvist, Michael McCormick, Nicola Di Cosmo, Michael Sigl, Johann Jungclaus, et al. 2016. "Cooling and Societal Change during the Late Antique Little Ice Age from 536 to around 660 AD." *Nature Geoscience* 9 (3): 231–36.

Butzer, Karl W. 2012. "Collapse, Environment, and Society." *Proceedings of the National Academy of Sciences* 109 (10): 3632–39.

Cameron, Fiona R., and Ann Deslandes. 2011. "Museums and Science Centres as Sites for Deliberative Democracy on Climate Change." *Museum and Society* 9 (2): 136–53.

Cameron, Fiona R., Bob Hodge, and Juan Francisco Salazar. 2013. "Representing Climate Change in Museum Space and Places." *Wiley Interdisciplinary Reviews: Climate Change* 4 (1): 9–21.

Cameron, Fiona R., and Brett Neilson, eds. 2015. *Climate Change and Museum Futures*. Routledge Research in Museum Studies. London: Routledge.

Carter, Adam, and Christel van Eck. 2014. *Science & Stories: Bringing the IPCC to Life.* Oxford: Climate Outreach & Information Network (COIN).

Cashman, Katharine V., and Giudo Giordano. 2008. "Volcanoes and Human History." *Journal of Volcanology and Geothermal Research* 176 (3): 325–29.

Chester, David K. 2005. "Theology and Disaster Studies: The Need for Dialogue." *Journal of Volcanology and Geothermal Research* 146 (4): 319–28.

Chester, David K., Martin Degg, Angus M. Duncan, and John E. Guest. 2001. "The Increasing Exposure of Cities to the Effects of Volcanic Eruptions: A Global Survey." *Environmental Hazards* 2 (3): 89–103.

Clark, Nigel. 2011. *Inhuman Nature.* London: Sage.

Clarke, Lee. 2007. "Thinking Possibilistically in a Probabilistic World." *Significance* 4 (4): 190–92.

———. 2008. "Possibilistic Thinking: A New Conceptual Tool for Thinking about Extreme Events." *Social Research* 75 (3): 669–90, 1033.

Cooper, Jago, and Payson D. Sheets. 2012. *Surviving Sudden Environmental Change.* Boulder: University of Colorado Press.

Costanza, Robert, L. Graumlich, Will Steffen, Carole Crumley, J. Dearing, K. Hibbard, R. Leemans, Charles L. Redman, and D. Schimel. 2007. "Sustainability or Collapse: What Can We Learn from Integrating the History of Humans and the Rest of Nature?" *Ambio* 36: 522–27.

Costanza, Robert, Sander van der Leeuw, Kathy Hibbard, Steve Aulenbach, Simon Brewer, Michael Burek, Sarah Cornell, et al. 2012. "Developing an Integrated History and Future of People on Earth (IHOPE)." *Open Issue* 4 (1): 106–14.

Crosweller, Helen Sian, Baneet Arora, Sarah Krystyna Brown, Elizabeth Cottrell, Natalia Irma Deligne, Natalie Ortiz Guerrero, Laura Hobbs, et al. 2012. "Global Database on Large Magnitude Explosive Volcanic Eruptions (LaMEVE)." *Journal of Applied Volcanology* 1 (1): 4.

Cutter, Susan L., Bryan J. Boruff, and W. Lynn Shirley. 2003. "Social Vulnerability to Environmental Hazards." *Social Science Quarterly* 84 (2): 242–61.

Davies, S. M., G. Larsen, S. Wastegård, C. S. M. Turney, V. A. Hall, L. Coyle, and T. Thordarson. 2010. "Widespread Dispersal of Icelandic Tephra: How Does the Eyjafjöll Eruption of 2010 Compare to Past Icelandic Events?" *Journal of Quaternary Science* 25 (5): 605–11.

Davies, Tim, Sarah Beaven, David Conradson, Alex Densmore, Jean-Christophe Gaillard, David Johnston, Dave Milledge, et al. 2015. "Towards Disaster Resilience: A Scenario-Based Approach to Co-Producing and Integrating Hazard and Risk Knowledge." *International Journal of Disaster Risk Reduction* 13: 242–47.

Davis, Mike. 1990. *City of Quartz: Excavating the Future in Los Angeles.* London: Verso.

———. 1998. *Ecologies of Fear: Los Angeles and the Imagination of Disaster.* New York: Picador.

Dawdy, Shannon Lee. 2009. "Millennial Archaeology: Locating the Discipline in the Age of Insecurity." *Archaeological Dialogues* 16 (02): 131–42.

Deligne, Natalia I., S. G. Coles, and Steve R. J. Sparks. 2010. "Recurrence Rates of Large Explosive Volcanic Eruptions." *Journal of Geophysical Research* 115 (B6): B06203.

Demeritt, David. 2006. "Science Studies, Climate Change and the Prospects for Constructivist Critique." *Economy and Society* 35 (3): 453–79.

Denkenberger, David C., and Robert W. Blair. 2018. "Interventions That May Prevent or Mollify Supervolcanic Eruptions." *Futures of Research in Catastrophic and Existential Risk* 102 (September): 51–62.

Diamond, Jared M., and James A. Robinson. 2010. *Natural Experiments of History*. Cambridge, MA: Belknap Press.

Dix, Andreas, and Matthias Röhrs. 2007. "Vergangenheit versus Gegenwart? Anmerkungen Zu Potentialen, Risiken Und Nebenwirkungen Einer Kombination Historischer Und Aktueller Ansätze Der Naturgefahrenforschung." *Historical Social Research* 32 (3): 215–34.

Djindjian, François. 2011. "The Role of the Archaeologist in Present-Day Society." *Diogenes* 58 (1–2): 53–63.

Donovan, Amy R., and Clive Oppenheimer. 2012. "Governing the Lithosphere: Insights from Eyjafjallajokull Concerning the Role of Scientists in Supporting Decision-Making on Active Volcanoes." *Journal of Geophysical Research: Solid Earth* 117 (3).

———. 2016. "Resilient Science: The Civic Epistemology of Disaster Risk Reduction." *Science and Public Policy* 43 (3): 363–74.

———. 2018. "Imagining the Unimaginable: Communicating Extreme Volcanic Risk." In *Observing the Volcano World: Volcano Crisis Communication*, edited by Carina J. Fearnley, Deanne K. Bird, Katharine Haynes, William J. McGuire, and Gill Jolly, 149–63. Cham: Springer International.

Dörries, Matthias. 2010. "Climate Catastrophes and Fear." *Wiley Interdisciplinary Reviews: Climate Change* 1 (6): 885–90.

Erfurt-Cooper, Patricia. 2010. "The Vulkaneifel in Germany. A Destination for Geotourism." In *Volcano and Geothermal Tourism: Sustainable Geo-Resources for Leisure and Recreation*, edited by Patricia Erfurt-Cooper and Malcolm Cooper, 281–85. London: Earthscan.

Field, Christopher B., Vicente Barros, Thomas F. Stocker, Dahe Qin, David Jon Dokken, Kirstie L. Ebi, Michael D. Mastrandrea, et al. 2012. *Managing the Risks of Extreme Events and Disasters to Advance Climate Change Adaptation*. Working Groups I and II of the Intergovernmental Panel on Climate Change, Special Report. Cambridge: Cambridge University Press.

Fisher, Richard V., and Hans-Ulrich Schmincke. 1984. *Pyroclastic Rocks*. Berlin: Springer.

Galinier, Jacques, Aurore Monod Becquelin, Guy Bordin, Laurent Fontaine, Francine Fourmaux, Juliette Roullet Ponce, Piero Salzarulo, Philippe Simonnot, Michèle Therrien, and Iole Zilli. 2010. "Anthropology of the Night: Cross-Disciplinary Investigations." *Current Anthropology* 51 (6): 819–47.

Giddens, Anthony. 1990. *The Consequences of Modernity*. Cambridge: Polity Press.

Gislason, Sigudur R., Tue Hassenkam, Sorin Nedel, Nicolas Emile Bovet, Eydís S. Eiriksdottir, Helgi Arnar Alfredsson, Caroline Piper Hem, et al. 2011. "Characterization of Eyjafjallajökull Volcanic Ash Particles and a Protocol for Rapid Risk Assessment." *Proceedings of the National Academy of Sciences* 108 (18): 7307–12.

Goepel, Andreas, Martin Lonschinski, Lothar Viereck, Georg Büchel, and Nina Kukowski. 2015. "Volcano-Tectonic Structures and CO2-Degassing Patterns in the Laacher See Basin, Germany." *International Journal of Earth Sciences* 104 (5): 1483–1495.

Golinski, J. 1998. *Making Natural Knowledge: Constructivism and the History of Science*. Cambridge: Cambridge University Press.

Graf, Hans-F., and Claudia Timmreck. 2001. "A General Climate Model Simulation of the Aerosol Radiative Effects of the Laacher See Eruption (10,900 B.C.)." *Journal of Geophysical Research* 106 (14): 14747–56.

Graham, Stephen. 2010. *Disrupted Cities: When Infrastructure Fails*. London: Routledge.

Graham, Stephen, and S. Marvin. 2001. *Splintering Urbanism: Networked Infrastructures, Technological Mobilities and the Urban Condition*. London: Routledge.

Graham, Stephen, and Nigel Thrift. 2007. "Out of Order: Understanding Repair and Maintenance." *Theory, Culture & Society* 24 (3): 1–25.

Grattan, John P. 2006. "Aspects of Armageddon: An Exploration of the Role of Volcanic Eruptions in Human History and Civilization." *Quaternary International* 151: 10–18.

Grattan, John, and Robin Torrence, eds. 2007. *Living Under the Shadow: Cultural Impacts of Volcanic Eruptions*. One World Archaeology 53. Walnut Creek, CA: Left Coast Press.

Guedes, Jade A. d'Alpoim, Stefani A. Crabtree, R. Kyle Bocinsky, and Timothy A. Kohler. 2016. "Twenty-First Century Approaches to Ancient Problems: Climate and Society." *Proceedings of the National Academy of Sciences* 113 (51): 14483.

Guttmann-Bond, Erika. 2010. "Sustainability Out of the Past: How Archaeology Can Save the Planet." *World Archaeology* 42 (3): 355–66.

Hayes, Josh L., Thomas M. Wilson, and Christina Magill. 2015. "Tephra Fall Clean-Up in Urban Environments." *Journal of Volcanology and Geothermal Research* 304 (Spring): 359–77.

Heijnen, Adrienne. 2005. "Dreams, Darkness and Hidden Spheres: Exploring the Anthropology of the Night in Icelandic Society." *Paideuma* 51: 193–207.

Hensch, Martin, Torsten Dahm, Joachim Ritter, Sebastian Heimann, Bernd Schmidt, Stefan Stange, and Klaus Lehmann. 2019. "Deep Low-Frequency Earthquakes Reveal Ongoing Magmatic Recharge beneath Laacher See Volcano (Eifel, Germany)." *Geophysical Journal International* 216 (3): 2025–36.

Högselius, Per, Anique Hommels, Arne Kajser, and Erik van der Vleuten, eds. 2013. *The Making of Europe's Critical Infrastructure: Common Connections and Shared Vulnerbilities*. Houndmills: Palgrave Macmillan.

Horn, Eva. 2014. *Zukunft Als Katastrophe*. Frankfurt am Main: S. Fischer.

Huang, Rong, Lupei Zhu, John Encarnacion, Yixian Xu, Chi-Chia Tang, Song Luo, and Xiaohuan Jiang. 2018. "Seismic and Geologic Evidence of Water-Induced Earthquakes in the Three Gorges Reservoir Region of China." *Geophysical Research Letters* 45 (12): 5929–36.

Huhtamaa, Heli, and Samuli Helama. 2017. "Distant Impact: Tropical Volcanic Eruptions and Climate-Driven Agricultural Crises in Seventeenth-Century Ostrobothnia, Finland." *Journal of Historical Geography* 57: 40–51.

Hulme, Mike. 2008. "The Conquering of Climate: Discourses of Fear and Their Dissolution." *Geographical Journal* 174 (1): 5–16.

———. 2016. *Weathered: Cultures of Climate*. London: Sage.

Jackson, Rowan C., Andrew J. Dugmore, and Felix Riede. 2017. "Towards a New Social Contract for Archaeology and Climate Change Adaptation." *Archaeological Review from Cambridge* 32 (2): 197–221.

———. 2018. "Rediscovering Lessons of Adaptation from the Past." *Global Environmental Change* 52: 58–65.

Janssens, M. M., C. Kasse, S. J. P. Bohncke, H. Greaves, K. M. Cohen, J. Wallinga, and W. Z. Hoek. 2012. "Climate-Driven Fluvial Development and Valley Abandonment at the Last Glacial-Interglacial Transition (Oude IJssel-Rhine, Germany)." *Netherlands Journal of Geosciences-Geologie En Mijnbouw* 91 (1–2): 37–62.

Jenkins, Susanna F., T. M. Wilson, C. Magill, V. Miller, C. Stewart, Russell J. Blong, W. Marzocchi, M. Boulton, Costanza Bonadonna, and A. Costa. 2015. "Volcanic Ash Fall Hazard and Risk." In *Global Volcanic Hazards and Risk*, edited by Charlotte Vye-Brown, Sarah K. Brown, Steve Sparks, Susan C. Loughlin, and Susanna F. Jenkins, 173–222. Cambridge: Cambridge University Press.

Kaika, Maria, and Erik Swyngedouw. 2000. "Fetishizing the Modern City: The Phantasmagoria of Urban Technological Networks." *International Journal of Urban and Regional Research* 24 (1): 120–38.

Kaufman, Brett, Christopher S. Kelly, and Richard S. Vachula. 2018. "Paleoenvironment and Archaeology Provide Cautionary Tales for Climate Policymakers." *Geographical Bulletin* 59 (1): 5–24.

Kintigh, Keith W., Jeffrey H. Altschul, Mary C. Beaudry, Robert D. Drennan, Ann P. Kinzig, Timothy A. Kohler, W. Fredrick Limp, et al. 2014. "Grand Challenges for Archaeology." *Proceedings of the National Academy of Sciences* 111 (3): 879–80.

Lane, Paul J. 2015. "Archaeology in the Age of the Anthropocene: A Critical Assessment of Its Scope and Societal Contributions." *Journal of Field Archaeology* 40 (5): 485–98.

Langmann, Baerbel, Arnau Folch, Martin Hensch, and Volker Matthias. 2012. "Volcanic Ash over Europe during the Eruption of Eyjafjallajökull on Iceland, April–May 2010." *Atmospheric Environment* 48: 1–8.

Latour, Bruno. 1987. *Science in Action*. Cambridge, MA: Harvard University Press.

———. 1994. *We Have Never Been Modern*. Cambridge, MA: Harvard University Press.

———. 2005. *Reassembling the Social: An Introduction to Actor-Network-Theory*. Oxford: Oxford University Press.

Leder, Jan, Friedemann Wenzel, James E. Daniell, and Ellen Gottschämmer. 2017. "Loss of Residential Buildings in the Event of a Re-Awakening of the Laacher See Volcano (Germany)." *Journal of Volcanology and Geothermal Research* 337 (Spring): 111–23.

Lund, Katrín Anna, and Karl Benediktsson. 2011. "Inhabiting a Risky Earth: The Eyjafjallajökull Eruption in 2010 and Its Impacts." *Anthropology Today* 27 (1): 6–9.

Lyell, Charles. 1835. *Principles of Geology*. London: John Murray.

Marshall, Yvonne. 2002. "What Is Community Archaeology?" *World Archaeology* 34 (2): 211–19.

Mason, Ben G., David M. Pyle, and Clive Oppenheimer. 2004. "The Size and Frequency of the Largest Explosive Eruptions on Earth." *Bulletin of Volcanology* 66 (8): 735–48.

Mauelshagen, Franz. 2009. "Die Klimakatastrophe. Szenen Und Szenarien." In *Katastrophen. Vom Untergang Pompejis Bis Zum Klimawandel*, edited by Gerrit Jasper Schenk, 205–23. Ostfildern: Jan Thorbecke Verlag.

Mazzorana, Bruno, Johannes Hübl, and Sven Fuchs. 2009. "Improving Risk Assessment by Defining Consistent and Reliable System Scenarios." *Natural Hazards and Earth System Sciences* 9 (1): 145–59.

McCormick, Michael, Paul Edward Dutton, and Paul A. Mayewski. 2007. "Volcanoes and the Climate Forcing of Carolingian Europe, A.D. 750–950." *Speculum* 82: 865–95.

McGuire, W. J. 2013. *Waking the Giant: How a Changing Climate Triggers Earthquakes, Tsunamis, and Volcanoes*. Oxford: Oxford University Press.

Mercer, Jessica, Jean-Christophe Gaillard, Katherine Crowley, Rachel Shannon, Bob Alexander, Simon Day, and Julia Becker. 2012. "Culture and Disaster Risk Reduction: Lessons and Opportunities." *Environmental Hazards* 11 (2): 74–95.

Miller, Fiona, Henry Osbahr, Emily Boyd, Frank Thomalla, Sukaina Bharwani, Gina Ziervogel, Brian Walker, et al. 2010. "Resilience and Vulnerability: Complementary or Conflicting Concepts?" *Ecology and Society* 15 (3): 11.

Moseley, Michael E. 1999. "Convergent Catastrophe: Past Patterns and Future Implications of Collateral Natural Disasters in the Andes." In *The Angry Earth: Disaster in Anthropological Perspective*, edited by Anthony Oliver-Smith and Susanna M. Hoffman, 59–71. London: Routledge.

Nelson, Donald R., W. Neil Adger, and Katrina Brown. 2007. "Adaptation to Environmental Change: Contributions of a Resilience Framework." *Annual Reviews of Environment and Resources* 32 (1): 395–419.

Newhall, Chris G., and Stephen Self. 1982. "The Volcanic Explosivity Index (VEI): An Estimate of Explosive Magnitude for Historical Volcanism." *Journal of Geophysical Research* 87: 1231–38.

Newhall, Chris G., Stephen Self, and Alan Robock. 2018. "Anticipating Future Volcanic Explosivity Index (VEI) 7 Eruptions and Their Chilling Impacts." *Geosphere* 14 (2): 1–32.

Nielsen, Esben Bjerggaard. 2013. "Klima, apokalypse og en topos om sted." *Rhetorica Scandinavica* 63 (4): 39–53.

November, Valerie. 2008. "Spatiality of Risk." *Environment and Planning A* 40 (7): 1523–27.

O'Brien, Karen, Siri Eriksen, Lynn P. Nygaard, and Ane Scholden. 2007. "Why Different Interpretations of Vulnerability Matter in Climate Change Discourses." *Climate Policy* 9 (1): 73–88.

Oppenheimer, Clive. 2015. "Eruption Politics." *Nature Geoscience* 8 (4): 244–45.

Oreskes, Naomi, and Erik M. Conway. 2014. *The Collapse of Western Civilization: A View from the Future*. New York: Columbia University Press.

Orlove, Ben. 2005. "Human Adaptation to Climate Change: A Review of Three Historical Cases and Some General Perspectives." *Environmental Science & Policy* 8 (6): 589–600.

Oxford Economics. 2010. *The Economic Impacts of Air Travel Restrictions Due to Volcanic Ash*. Oxford. Retrieved 13 May 2020 from https://www.oxfordeconomics.com/my-oxford/projects/129051.

Pancost, Richard D. 2017. "Climate Change Narratives." *Nature Geoscience* 10 (7): 466–68.

Park, Cornelia, and Hans-Ulrich Schmincke. 2009. "Apokalypse Im Rheintal." *Spektrum Der Wissenschaften* 2009 (2): 78–87.

Pedersen, Rikke. 2010. *Eyjafjallajökull. Vulkanen Der Lammede Europa*. København: Gyldendal.

Pelling, Mark. 2011. *Adaptation to Climate Change: From Resilience to Transformation*. London: Routledge.

Pfister, Christian. 2009a. "Learning from Nature-Induced Disasters: Theoretical Considerations and Case Studies from Western Europe." In *Natural Disasters, Cultural Responses: Case Studies toward a Global Environmental History*, edited by Christof Mauch and Cristian Pfister, 17–40. Lanham, MD: Lexington Books.

———. 2009b. "The 'Disaster Gap' of the 20th Century and the Loss of Traditional Disaster Memory." *GAIA—Ecological Perspectives for Science and Society* 18 (3): 239–46.

Pyle, David M. 2015. "Sizes of Volcanic Eruptions." In *The Encyclopedia of Volcanoes*, 2nd ed., edited by Haraldur Sigurdsson, 257–64. Amsterdam: Academic Press.

Raden, Ulrike J. van, Daniele Colombaroli, Adrian Gilli, Jakob Schwander, Stefano M. Bernasconi, Jacqueline van Leeuwen, Markus Leuenberger, and Ueli Eicher. 2013. "High-Resolution Late-Glacial Chronology for the Gerzensee Lake Record (Switzerland): $\delta^{18}O$ Correlation between a Gerzensee-Stack and NGRIP." *Palaeogeography, Palaeoclimatology, Palaeoecology* 391, part B: 13–24.

Redman, Charles L. 2005. "Resilience Theory in Archaeology." *American Anthropologist* 107 (1): 70–77.

Rees, Martin. 2013. "Denial of Catastrophic Risks." *Science* 339 (6124): 1123.

Rees, Morien. 2017. "Museums as Catalysts for Change." *Nature Climate Change* 7: 166.

Riede, Felix. 2008. "The Laacher See-Eruption (12,920 BP) and Material Culture Change at the End of the Allerød in Northern Europe." *Journal of Archaeological Science* 35 (3): 591–99.

———. 2009. "The Loss and Re-introduction of Bow-and-Arrow Technology: A Case Study from the Southern Scandinavian Late Palaeolithic." *Lithic Technology* 34 (1): 27–45.

———. 2014a. "Climate Models: Use Archaeology Record." *Nature* 513 (7518): 315.

———. 2014b. "Eruptions and Ruptures—a Social Network Perspective on Vulnerability and Impact of the Laacher See Eruption (c. 13,000 BP) on Late Glacial Hunter-Gatherers in Northern Europe." *Archaeological Review from Cambridge* 29 (1): 67–102.

———. 2014c. "Towards a Science of Past Disasters." *Natural Hazards* 71 (1): 335–62.

———. 2014d. "Volcanic Activity." In *Encyclopedia of Global Archaeology*, edited by Claire Smith, 11:7657–66. New York: Springer.

———, ed. 2015. *Past Vulnerability: Volcanic Eruptions and Human Vulnerability in Traditional Societies Past and Present*. Aarhus: Aarhus University Press.

———. 2016. "Changes in Mid- and Far-Field Human Landscape Use Following the Laacher See Eruption (c. 13,000 BP)." *Quaternary International* 394: 37–50.

———. 2017a. "Past-Forwarding Ancient Calamities: Pathways for Making Archaeology Relevant in Disaster Risk Reduction Research." *Humanities* 6 (4), 79: 1–25.

———. 2017b. *Splendid Isolation: The Eruption of the Laacher See Volcano and Southern Scandinavian Late Glacial Hunter-Gatherers*. Aarhus: Aarhus University Press.

Riede, Felix, and Oliver Bazely. 2009. "Testing the 'Laacher See Hypothesis': A Health Hazard Perspective." *Journal of Archaeological Science* 36 (3): 675–83.

Riede, Felix, Oliver Bazely, Anthony J. Newton, and Christine S. Lane. 2011. "A Laacher See-Eruption Supplement to Tephrabase: Investigating Distal Tephra Fallout Dynamics." *Quaternary International* 246 (1–2): 134–44.

Riede, Felix, Christian Tegner, Claudia Timmreck, Ulrike Niemeier, Anja Schmidt, Clive Oppenheimer, and Anke Zernack. 2019. "Laacher See-Vulkanudbruddet Og Effekten På Klimaet." *Kvant* 30 (1): 19–23.

Riede, Felix, and Jeffrey M. Wheeler. 2009. "Testing the 'Laacher See Hypothesis': Tephra as Dental Abrasive." *Journal of Archaeological Science* 36 (10): 2384–91.

Rockman, Marcy. 2012. "The Necessary Roles of Archaeology in Climate Change Mitigation and Adaptation." In *Archaeology in Society*, edited by Marcy Rockman and Joe Flatman, 193–215. New York: Springer.

Rohland, Eleonora J. 2018. "Adapting to Hurricanes: A Historical Perspective on New Orleans from Its Foundation to Hurricane Katrina, 1718–2005." *Wiley Interdisciplinary Reviews: Climate Change* 9 (1): e488.

Rounsevell, Mark D. A., and Marc J. Metzger. 2010. "Developing Qualitative Scenario Storylines for Environmental Change Assessment." *Wiley Interdisciplinary Reviews: Climate Change* 1 (4): 606–19.

Ryzewski, Krysta, and John F. Cherry. 2012. "Communities and Archaeology under the Soufrière Hills Volcano on Montserrat, West Indies." *Journal of Field Archaeology* 37 (4): 316–27.

Scandone, Roberto, Stefania Bartolini, and Joan Martí. 2015. "A Scale for Ranking Volcanoes by Risk." *Bulletin of Volcanology* 78 (1): 1–8.

Schenk, Gerrit Jasper. 2015. "'Learning from History'? Chances, Problems and Limits of Learning from Historical Natural Disasters." In *Cultures and Disasters: Understanding Cultural Framings in Disaster Risk Reduction*, edited by Fred Krüger, Gregory Bankoff, Terry Cannon, Benedikt Orlowski, and Lisa E. Schipper, 72–87. London: Routledge.

Schiermeier, Quirin. 2012. "Disaster Toll Tallied." *Nature* 481 (7380): 124–25.

Schmidt, Anja, Bart Ostro, Kenneth S. Carslaw, Marjorie Wilson, Thorvaldur Thordarson, Graham W. Mann, and Adrian J. Simmons. 2011. "Excess Mortality in Europe Following a Future Laki-Style Icelandic Eruption." *Proceedings of the National Academy of Sciences* 108 (38): 15710–15.

Schmincke, Hans-Ulrich. 2006. "Environmental Impacts of the Lateglacial Eruption of the Laacher See Volcano, 12.900 Cal BP." In *150 Years of Neanderthal Discoveries*, edited by W. von Koenigswald and T. Litt, 2:149–53. Bonn: Terra Nostra.

Schmincke, Hans-Ulrich, Cornelia Park, and Eduard Harms. 1999. "Evolution and Environmental Impacts of the Eruption of Laacher See Volcano (Germany) 12,900 a BP." *Quaternary International* 61: 61–72.

Self, Stephen. 2006. "The Effects and Consequences of Very Large Explosive Volcanic Eruptions." *Philosophical Transactions of the Royal Society A: Mathematical, Physical and Engineering Sciences* 364 (1845): 2073–97.

Sheets, Payson. 2015. "Volcanoes, Ancient People, and Their Societies." In *The Encyclopedia of Volcanoes*, 2nd ed., 1313–19. Amsterdam: Academic Press.

Siebert, Lee, Tom Simkin, and Paul Kimberly. 2010. *Volcanoes of the World*. 3rd ed. Washington, DC: Smithsonian Institution.

Sigmundsson, Freysteinn, Virginie Pinel, Björn Lund, Fabien Albino, Carolina Pagli, Halldór Geirsson, and Erik Sturkell. 2010. "Climate Effects on Volcanism: Influence on Magmatic Systems of Loading and Unloading from Ice Mass Variations, with Examples from Iceland." *Philosophical Transactions of the Royal Society A: Mathematical, Physical and Engineering Sciences* 368 (1919): 2519–34.

Simkin, Tom, Lee Siebert, and Russell J. Blong. 2001. "Volcano Fatalities—Lessons from the Historical Record." *Science* 291 (5502): 255.

Smit, Barry, and Johanna Wandel. 2006. "Adaptation, Adaptive Capacity and Vulnerability." *Global Environmental Change* 16 (3): 282–92.

Smolka, Anselm. 2006. "Natural Disasters and the Challenge of Extreme Events: Risk Management from an Insurance Perspective." *Philosophical Transactions of the Royal Society A: Mathematical, Physical and Engineering Sciences* 364 (1845): 2147–65.

Solnit, Rebecca. 2010. *A Paradise Built in Hell: The Extraordinary Communities That Arise in Disaster*. London: Penguin.

Sommer, Ulrike. 2000. "Archaeology and Regional Identity in Saxony." *Public Archaeology* 1 (2): 125–42.

Son, Hyeonju. 2015. "The History of Western Futures Studies: An Exploration of the Intellectual Traditions and Three-Phase Periodization." *Futures* 66: 120–37.

Sonnek, Karin Mossberg, Tomas Mårtensson, Ester Veibäck, Peter Tunved, Håkan Grahn, Pontus von Schoenberg, Niklas Brännström, and Anders Bucht. 2017. "The Impacts of a Laki-like Eruption on the Present Swedish Society." *Natural Hazards* 88 (3): 1565–90.

Steffen, Will, Wendy Broadgate, Lisa Deutsch, Owen Gaffney, and Cornelia Ludwig. 2015. "The Trajectory of the Anthropocene: The Great Acceleration." *Anthropocene Review* 2 (1): 81–98.

Stewart, Iain S., and Deirdre Lewis. 2017. "Communicating Contested Geoscience to the Public: Moving from 'Matters of Fact' to 'Matters of Concern.'" *Earth-Science Reviews* 174 (November): 122–33.

Taleb, Nassim. 2010. *The Black Swan: The Impact of the Highly Improbable*. 2nd ed. London: Penguin.

Tierney, Kathleen J. 2014. *The Social Roots of Risk*. Redwood City, CA: Stanford University Press.

Toohey, Matthew, Kirstin Krüger, Michael Sigl, Frode Stordal, and Henrik Svensen. 2016. "Climatic and Societal Impacts of a Volcanic Double Event at the Dawn of the Middle Ages." *Climatic Change* 136 (3): 401–12.

Turchin, Alexey, and David Denkenberger. 2018. "Global Catastrophic and Existential Risks Communication Scale." *Futures of Research in Catastrophic and Existential Risk* 102 (September): 27–38.

Uehlinger, Urs, Karl M. Wantzen, and Rob S. E. W. Leuven. 2009. "The Rhine River Basin." In *Rivers of Europe*, edited by Klement Trockner, Urs Uehlinger, and Christopher T. Robinson, 199–245. London: Academic Press.

Urry, John. 2011. *Climate Change and Society*. Oxford: Polity Press.

———. 2014. "The Problem of Energy." *Theory, Culture & Society* 31 (5): 3–20.

———. 2015. *What Is the Future?* Cambridge: Polity Press.

Van de Noort, Robert. 2011. "Conceptualising Climate Change Archaeology." *Antiquity* 85 (329): 1039–48.

———. 2013. *Climate Change Archaeology: Building Resilience from Research in the World's Coastal Wetlands*. Oxford: Oxford University Press.

Walker, Jeremy, and Melinda Cooper. 2011. "Genealogies of Resilience: From Systems Ecology to the Political Economy of Crisis Adaptation." *Security Dialogue* 42 (2): 143–60.

Watt, Sebastian F. L., David M. Pyle, and Tamsin A. Mather. 2013. "The Volcanic Response to Deglaciation: Evidence from Glaciated Arcs and a Reassessment of Global Eruption Records." *Earth-Science Reviews* 122: 77–102.

Wilson, Thomas M., James W. Cole, Carol Stewart, Shane J. Cronin, and David M. Johnston. 2011. "Ash Storms: Impacts of Wind-Remobilised Volcanic Ash on Rural Communities and Agriculture Following the 1991 Hudson Eruption, Southern Patagonia, Chile." *Bulletin of Volcanology* 73 (3): 223–239.

Wilson, Thomas M., Susanna Jenkins, and Carol Stewart. 2015. "Impacts from Volcanic Ash Fall." In *Volcanic Hazards, Risks and Disasters*, edited by Paolo Papale, 47–86. Boston: Elsevier.

Wisner, Ben, Piers Blaikie, Terry Cannon, and Ian Davis. 2004. *At Risk: Natural Hazards, People's Vulnerability and Disasters*. 2nd ed. London: Routledge.

Witham, Claire S. 2005. "Volcanic Disasters and Incidents: A New Database." *Journal of Volcanology and Geothermal Research* 148 (3–4): 191–233.

Wood, Gillen D'Arcy. 2014. *Tambora: The Eruption That Changed the World*. Princeton, NJ: Princeton University Press.

Zhu, Hejun, Ebru Bozdag, Daniel Peter, and Jeroen Tromp. 2012. "Structure of the European Upper Mantle Revealed by Adjoint Tomography." *Nature Geoscience* 5 (7): 493–98.

CHAPTER 2

Risky Business and the Future of the Past

Nuclear Power in the Ring of Fire

KAREN HOLMBERG

Summary for Stakeholders

Data and understanding of past disasters from both the social sciences and natural sciences can help inform policy makers of possible outcomes in order to improve policy decisions. Creative new approaches are requisite for the challenges we face, particularly given the fact that science and policy processes generally do not interface as productively as they should to mitigate environmental risks. Creativity can take many forms, including the use of jurisprudence and new ways of conceiving the intended audiences of academic work or cultural heritage.

In this chapter, I discuss the uncertainties of the energy transition from fossil fuels to other sources as required by pledges made by Indonesia for the Paris Agreement to lower carbon emissions. The Indonesian government has ambitious plans to build nuclear reactors to supply its citizens with energy, yet their location in the volcanically active Indonesian Ring of Fire means that these reactors and their spent nuclear waste face a hazardous future. The problems of nuclear risk and transitions to new ways of creating power are, of course, not limited to Indonesia. I write this in New York City, which is currently grappling with an aging energy grid, rising sea levels, and concerns regarding nuclear reactors and terrorism.

The most significant recent nuclear disaster, the Fukushima meltdown following a tsunami in 2011, led to the creation of a "knowledge portal" by the International Atomic Energy Agency (IAEA) with data to inform policy makers and all other global stakeholders. I hold that archaeologists should be thought of as significant stakeholders and contributors in discussions of nuclear facilities and their waste through our research and perspectives that allow consideration of material and immaterial remnants of the past over the long time spans that need to be considered in nuclear discussions. We are all, in fact, stakeholders in such vital questions.

Introduction

In "Bad Weather: On Planetary Crisis," Joseph Masco (2010, 9) aptly writes that "we live in an age of crisis—multiple overlapping crises" characterized by the unanticipated by-products of environmental disaster. Energy production and consumption is the thread that connects our crises. As is incontrovertible, fossil fuel energy is the historically specific, focal component of our political and economic systems and (Mitchell 2011; Huber 2009). What comes after fossil fuels, though? We do not know yet. This chapter spans different geographical locations and time frames, looking at the past in the present and future in Indonesia, Japan, and New York City to query environmental risk and energy production.

My central focus is on plans to build nuclear reactors in Indonesia, a region that is part of what is termed "the Ring of Fire" in reference to its high level of volcanic activity. The reactors will, ostensibly, reduce the risk caused by carbon dioxide emissions and their link to anthropogenic climate change, though of course they incur their own risks, particularly in the long time frames that nuclear waste remains radioactive. Safety is an illusion in the present and future and perhaps always has been. Nihilism is not useful, nor is belief that social, economic, and political structures are immovable. Archaeology is reliant upon material culture from the past. In this discussion, however, I highlight the importance of nonmaterial remnants of the past that are creatively reused as well as consideration of material futures of nuclear materials.

Our society-nature relations are under a newly emerging "internationalized state" and "imperial way of living" (Brand and Wissen 2018). Alternate understandings of ecology and economy and how they comprise the globalized "environment" are difficult and problematic for those disempowered by international regulations (Mickelson and Natarajan 2017). As a species, the percentage of the world's population that will be disempowered is currently likely to increase to include many of us who might have felt "safe" prior per the report issued on 8 October 2018 from the United Nations Intergovernmental Panel on Climate Change (IPCC 2018). Food shortages, droughts, wildfires, and a mass die-off of coral reefs are foretold as early as 2040 due to the amount of carbon we continue to release (Davenport 2018). Safety is an illusion for the majority of the world's population.

There is a need for collective imagination when one system is crumbling and another is yet to form. Scientists can and should play greater roles in international efforts to reduce the prevalence and impact of disasters (Waddington 2014). To do so, the meshing of social data and environmental data is requisite to examine what gets awkwardly termed "coupled natural and human systems" (Crain, Cooper, and Dickinson 2014). Productive engagement between scientists and policy makers is generally hindered by poor communication when considering and modeling risk (Donovan and Oppenheimer 2015). I propose that archaeology is important to discussions of how different timescales and human life intersect and that archaeologists do have insights to communicate in ways that usefully inform policy. Rather than offer predictive or prescriptive solutions, however, our research often indicates that disasters, efforts at disaster prevention, and remnants from the past can intersect in unpredictable ways. Effective responses can often be unexpected, creative, and immaterial.

Material and Meaning: *Volcanic Winter/Nuclear Winter*

In my research, I have a long-standing desire to comprehend the incommensurate timescales of the geological/planetary and the human. I try to understand the interlinkage of those timescales in contexts of climate change and catastrophes. In past work, for example, I have drawn on concepts of disaster, material culture, and the archaeology of "unthinkable" volcanic eruptions to query our relationships with environments that can change radically (e.g., Holmberg 2005, 2007, 2013). I also wonder how we can best convey scientific data and concepts outside of the academy. When offered the chance to collaborate in 2011 with a contemporary artist (Keith Edmier) on a work that would be publicly accessible in New York City, then, I was happy to do so. I was teaching at Stanford University at the time and used the opportunity to materialize some of the issues I was thinking about regarding disaster, volcanism, climate change, and technology. *The Natural Contract* by Michel Serres (1995) had long been influential for me in its persuasive argument that global environmental change forces us to reconsider our relationship with nature. The recently published complement to that book by Serres, *Malfeasance* (2011, 66), contained a line that was very evocative for me: "Volcanic eruptions can bring about nuclear winters." Inspired by this, Edmier and I quickly put ideas together for an art piece I titled *Volcanic Winter/Nuclear Winter* embodied by a hybrid volcano-post-eruption/nuclear-tower-post-meltdown made of ice blocks.

On multiple levels, *Volcanic Winter/Nuclear Winter* was unsuccessful in conveying the intention behind its creation. The artwork was made of ice, and this had its own component of meaning per the loss of po-

a

b

Illustrations 2.1a–b. *Volcanic Winter/Nuclear Winter* ice-block structure under construction with the author in forefront (a) and as backdrop for a model (b), piece by artist Keith Edmier. Photos by Keith Edmier and author. Used with permission, courtesy of the artist Keith Edmier and Petzel Gallery, © Keith Edmier.

lar ice caps and sea-level rise. The ephemerality of the piece was something we anticipated through using ice as a medium; the transience of its meaning, though, was disappointing. The work—displayed on an ice rink used during Fashion Week in New York—became both backdrop and centerpiece (depending on the moment) of a fashion show that involved freezing fashion models, professional ice skaters, and Olympic medalist Johnny Weir. Any monumentality of scale intended in its form was lost. The sculpture was a perplexing addition to the pounding music and glittering clothes and faces that were more organic to the context. The fashion show took place on 12 February 2011. At the time, I was teaching about nuclear catastrophes. Even though I drew from well-written pieces on nuclear disasters such as that by Adelson et al. (2008) that clearly and explicitly discuss the future in both the text and title, the students and I studied the events at Three Mile Island and Chernobyl as historical pieces from what felt like a relatively distant past. As often happens, the past can become unexpectedly contemporary. Only a month later, on 11 March 2011, a high-magnitude earthquake and tsunami caused an unprecedented triple-reactor meltdown at the Fukushima Daiichi nuclear power station. The physical and emotional recovery from the disaster and its containment, decontamination, and reconstruction will last for generations.

Nuclear Power and the Ring of Fire

The Fukushima Daiichi Nuclear Meltdown

In response to the Fukushima Daiichi disaster, the International Atomic Energy Agency issued an action plan to strengthen the global nuclear safety framework (IAEA 2011). They additionally created the "Knowledge Management Portal on Observations and Lessons from the Fukushima Daiichi Accident" (IAEA 2015). The intention of this searchable portal is to allow the catastrophic past event to inform an array of users to make better decisions in the future. These users include emergency preparedness and response personnel, governments, NGOs, nuclear education and training organizations, regulatory bodies, security staff, technical and scientific organizations, users of radiation sources, vendors of nuclear equipment, and the press or relevant stakeholders. The question of who else constitutes a relevant stakeholder is one to which I will return at the end of this paper, but for now let me state that I believe archaeologists most certainly are; in such a context of broad impacts, we most certainly *all* are stakeholders.

Taking the Volcano to Muhammad: The Muria Nuclear Reactor on Java

Current policy and regulations rarely consider the fact that even regions with a perceived low chance of volcanic eruption in the human timescale still have a significant risk of eruption and unrest in the geological timescale in which nuclear waste materials remain toxic (C. Connor et al. 2009; S. Connor 2009; Hill et al. 2009; Mahoney et al. 2009). Despite the lack of policy response, the Fukushima Daiichi meltdown understandably added public resistance to the already contentious discussions of nuclear plant construction in Indonesia (Fauzan and Schiller 2011). Many Indonesians not only worry about the dangers posed to nuclear plants by tsunamis, earthquakes, and volcanic eruptions, but also harbor concern that authorities are not capable of implementing and enforcing safeguards against catastrophes (McBeth 2018; Sukma 2007). Residents of nearby countries such as Singapore and Australia share these concerns (Hyland 2007; McBeth 2018).

The Indonesian government created a national atomic energy agency (BATAN) in 1954. Because of serious questions regarding the safety of building nuclear reactors in the circum-Pacific seismic belt (or Ring of Fire), however, only three small research reactors have been built to date (WNA 2018). These include a thirty-megawatt facility in Serpong, Banten, on the outskirts of Jakarta built in the late 1980s; a two-megawatt reactor at Bandung, west Java; and a one-hundred-kilowatt reactor in Yogyakarta.

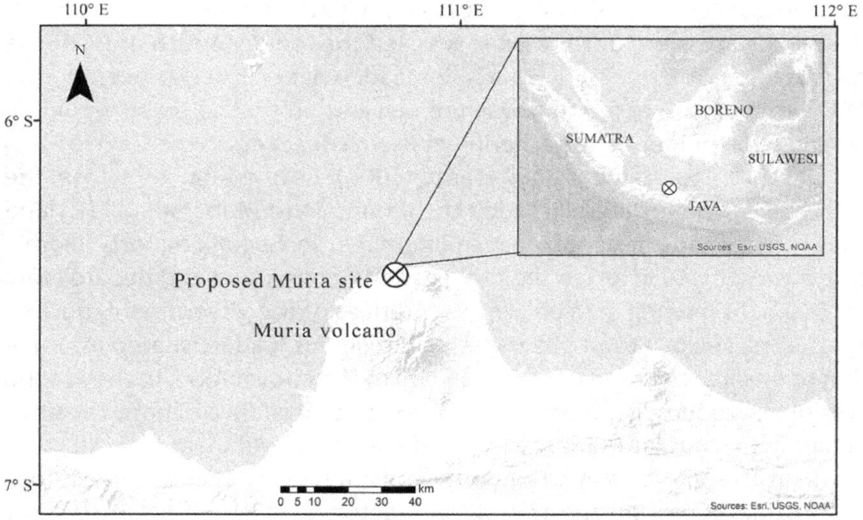

Figure 2.1. The Muria volcano complex and proposed location of the nuclear reactor. Data for the base map is from ESRI, USGS, and NOAA; data for the location of the nuclear reactor from the Indonesian Nuclear Energy Agency (BATAN).

Indonesia was under strict authoritarian rule during Suharto's New Order regime, yet challenges to the regime did exist, and intellectuals, students, and NGOs did attempt to resist nuclear power plant construction (Heryanto and Hadiz 2005; Fauzan and Schiller 2011). Scientifically, there certainly was reason for anxiety regarding the choice of Muria for nuclear reactors. As Tanter and Imhoff (2009) point out, not only is the area volcanically active, but government claims to the contrary were not supported by the few public scientific reports available; most scientific reports from the past thirty years were not made public. One report created with access to the nonpublic reports noted the significant methodological and data limitations of them as well as the reliance on earthquake resistance standards from earlier Japanese contexts that are very different from the geological context on Java (Tanter and Imhoff 2009). Further, the Japanese themselves no longer use those safety standards, having rewritten them substantially following the 2007 Chuetsu earthquake, which damaged a reactor in Nigata (Tanter and Imhoff 2009). Challenges to the Muria site choice as being "safe" were well established already in the 1990s, most especially through the threat of a hunger strike by the national chairman of Nahdlatul Ulama (NU), Indonesia's largest Islamic organization (Fauzan and Schiller 2011).

When the New Order fell in 1998, antinuclear demonstrations and organizations focused upon environmental issues increased dramatically (Fauzan and Schiller 2011, 15; Ichihara 2010). Scientists, environmental activists, and politicians were not the ones who led the movement to prevent the construction of a reactor at Muria. Instead, what uniquely prevented the Muria reactor's construction was the declaration that to do so would be *haram*, or forbidden, by a gathering of Islamic teachers in the town of Jepara, Java, on 1 September 2007 (Tanter 2007). As one reporter wrote, the clerics and scholars literally "took the mountain to Muhammad" (Hyland 2007). Thousands of people made pilgrimage, some walking forty kilometers overnight, to listen to the two sessions of dialogue and debate (Tanter 2007). In the first session, representatives of the government, nuclear specialists, sociocultural observers, and religious leaders shared information to ensure that the public had access to the information. In the second session, law specialists from various parts of central Java debated positive and negative outcomes of the planned nuclear power plant.

After listening to government officials, advisors, and scientists both supporting and opposing the Muria reactor, over a hundred *ulama*, or Islamic teachers, issued a fatwa against its construction, as the risks and negative outcomes outweigh the positive. Four particular concerns they noted were the long-term safe disposal and storage of radioactive waste, the local and regional environmental consequences of the plant, the lack of financial transparency, and the dependence upon foreign technology and fuel (Tanter 2007). As Fealy, Hooker, and White (2006, 48; see also Tanter 2007) state, "The movement was 'cultural' in that it eschewed formal political activity and sought to advance the interests of Muslims through intellectual, educational, social and artistic means . . . in an unprecedented and highly creative way."

Scientists, politicians, environmental activists, planners, first responders, and all other relevant stakeholders in decisions regarding risk mediation and catastrophes should take note. A group of clerics working in an innovative, creative way produced more tangible results than years of environmental activism and statements by Greenpeace regarding the feasibility of nuclear waste containment in the geologically hyperactive Ring of Fire (e.g., ABC 2007). Archaeologists, too, should take note that one of the significant reasons the area was of interest to the Muslim clerics is because it contains heritage landmarks, including the graves of saints (*wali*) who brought Islam to Java (Fauzan and Schiller 2011; Tanter 2007). The blockage of the long-proposed series of reactors proposed near the Muria volcano complex on central Java was the product of a complex entanglement of cultural, scientific, religious, financial, and political components over the course of several decades. The use of fatwa declaration as a political force, in particular, is an important component of the contemporary context that is specific to the Islamic context (Fudge 2019). I think that there is a great deal for us to learn, however, that is applicable and important in any context through the creative reworking of nonmaterial components of the past in ways unanticipated by their creators to effect change.

The Current and Future Energy Landscape in Indonesia

Indonesia's population of roughly 260 million people is served by power generation capacity of fifty-eight gigawatt electric as of 2016, with 56 percent of this from coal, 25 percent from natural gas, 9 percent from oil, 6 percent from hydroelectric, and 4 percent from geothermal (WNA 2018). Roughly 10 percent of the population lack access to electricity altogether, and blackouts are frequent for those who are on the grid. The government faces considerable challenges to meet its goals of universal access to electricity by 2025 (WNA 2018). Additionally, the Indonesian government pledged in the Paris Agreement of 2016 to decrease carbon emissions. Information that I accessed in 2015 stated that the Indonesian government desired to extend access to power while reducing carbon emissions by 26 percent before 2020 (BATAN 2014; Information Library 2014). More recent data, accessed in 2018, now lists the carbon emission decrease goal as 29 percent by 2030 (WNA 2018). In the meantime, however, Indonesia is actually increasing its use of coal (Climate Action Tracker 2018).

This is counter to the data (updated 30 April 2018) presented by the Climate Action Tracker website (2018), which states:

> Indonesian energy policy is going against the global trend where renewable capacity additions have overtaken coal. Indonesia's new updated energy plan, released in 2018, foresees overall lower capacity additions than previously, but still adds 27 GW of coal-fired power in the next ten years and only 15 GW of renewables over the same period. Planned capacity additions for both gas and renewables have been slashed in favour of coal, and most of the planned renewables come in well after 2020, while a significant share of the planned coal will be commissioned in the next five years. Over the past five years, Indonesia's coal capacity has already increased by 13.6 GW compared to 1.8 GW of renewable energy.

Indonesia is currently ranked as the eighth highest global emitter of carbon (Tacconi 2018). Under its current policies, Indonesia will not meet the nationally determined contribution (NDC) that it submitted in November 2016, which set a target for renewable energy to be 23 percent of its total energy supply by 2025 (Climate Action Tracker 2018). Making that context worse, Indonesia's most recent communications and figures—submitted to the United Nations in 2017—present serious inconsistencies and a lack of transparency about their intended contributions (Tacconi 2018). Indonesia needs to do *something*. Despite the cancellation of the nuclear power plant at Muria, the Indonesian government still has nuclear ambitions.

Nuclear Plans in Indonesia

From the data available (WNA 2019), varied nuclear possibilities are actively promoted in Indonesia as the way the country will decrease its carbon emissions while increasing access to electricity.

In August 2015 BATAN signed a cooperation agreement for floating nuclear power plants, built and serviced by Russia, to provide power to smaller islands. The province of Gorontalo on Sulawesi is reportedly considering a floating plant. The first of these mobile plants, the Akademik Lomonosov, was memorably termed a "nuclear Titanic" by Greenpeace (Haverkamp 2018) and a "floating Chernobyl" by other sources (Wootsen 2018), though this had little impact on the continued development of this form of energy production. These floating plants, if located far from the coast, can ostensibly lessen the risk from earthquakes and tsunamis.

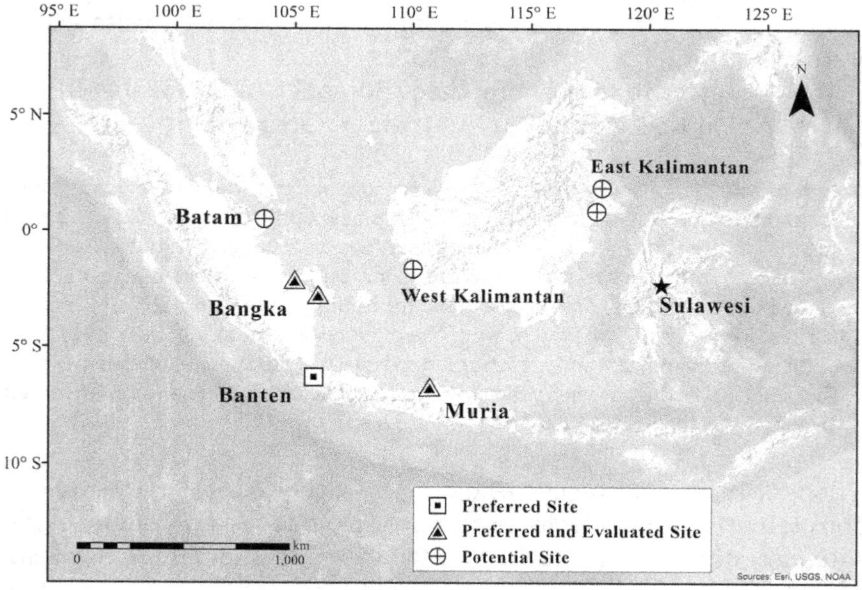

Figure 2.2. Some of the major locations proposed for nuclear power reactors in Indonesia; all are located in coastal sites for accessibility of water for cooling and thus are particularly vulnerable to tsunamis as well as volcanic and earthquake hazards (IAEA 2018). Courtesy National Nuclear Energy (BATAN).

In October 2015 a United States company, Martingale, signed an agreement with an Indonesian consortium of state-owned companies to build a thorium salt reactor. This untested form of nuclear energy is attractive both because Indonesia has ample thorium resources and because the molten salt within a bath of liquid fluoride is designed to be safer than the traditional water bath needed for uranium rod reactors (Banerjee and Prakash Gupta 2019; Kakodkar and Degweker 2016). The reaction can occur under normal atmospheric pressure, so does not need thick walls and is presumably less likely to explode (Freischlad 2018). A preliminary feasibility study, completed in March 2017, anticipated a 250-megawatt reactor commissioned in the 2020s pending approval from BATAN. If permitted, the plant anticipates a 2025 operation date. If opened, this will be the first full-sized nuclear power plant in Indonesia. The location of this construction is not listed (WNA 2019).

Multiple research and design test plans for various high-temperature reactors are ongoing by BATAN. In August 2016 BATAN signed a cooperation agreement with the China Nuclear Engineering Corporation to develop high-temperature pebble-bed reactors, which are supposedly safer, cheaper, and more efficient than other nuclear reactor designs (Kugeler and Zhang 2019). Planned construction of these will begin on Kalimantan and Sulawesi for completion by 2027. Following the successful construction of these high-temperature reactors, BATAN envisions the construction of large reactors on the populous islands of Bali, Java, Madura, and Sumatra.

Sulawesi: A Safe Location (Until It Was Not)

The Indonesian island of Sulawesi was one of the sites designated safe enough in prior plans for both a floating nuclear plant and a research and design high-temperature nuclear reactor before building larger reactors on more populated islands. On 2 October 2018, a 7.5 magnitude earthquake hit Sulawesi, decimating in particular the provincial capital of Palu. The next day, a volcano, Soputan, began erupting on Sulewesi. At least two thousand people died and five thousand were missing from the tsunami, landslides, liquefaction, and earthquake collapses in the weeks following the disaster. If a nuclear reactor was operating in the affected area, obviously, the catastrophe could have been exponentially worse and affected a far larger number of people. It is easily foreseeable that the terrestrial Indonesian nuclear power plants, planned for operation start dates in 2025 (while floating versions may be ready sooner), are plausible sites of future disaster. In such a sense, they are ruins in the making even prior to their construction.

Nuclear Material and Archaeological Assemblages

While a nuclear power plant can generate electricity for forty to fifty years, the waste it creates can threaten the health of the humans, plants, and animals near it for centuries or millennia. The presence of this waste in the Ring of Fire, long after the life span of the reactor, certainly entails what Schlanger et al. (2016, 421) describe in their heritage discussion of Fukushima in that it evokes an archaeology of anticipation or an "archaeology of the contemporary future." This echoes and builds upon the archaeology of the "contemporary past" (Buchli and Lucas 2001; Harrison and Schofield 2010).

The methods and metaphor of archaeology are very potent in the conjoined issues of the past, the future, and nuclear materials. "Nuclear archaeology," unbeknownst to many archaeologists, was declared a new field in the early 1990s (Fetter 1993; Wood et al. 2014). It is an endeavor I would classify more as forensics, however, in its attempt to account for the past production of fissile materials (highly enriched uranium and separated plutonium) to determine the quantity of materials present but unreported by various countries as an ostensible step toward nonproliferation and disarmament. At least per the 2014 special issue "The Future of Nuclear Archaeology" in *Science and Global Security*, progress is ongoing in detecting plutonium production, but we are still unable to detect highly enriched uranium. Estimating enriched uranium production "is both more technically demanding and far less experimentally mature" (Wood et al. 2014, 8). Archaeology, too, is less experimentally mature in considering its importance to the future than it is to the study of the past, but a number of projects are adding importantly to the discussion of archaeology's role in such discussions.

An increasing array of archaeologists are considering nuclear energy and nuclear waste (e.g., Holtorf and Högberg 2014; Joyce 2015, 2016a, 2016b, 2020; Schlanger, Nespoulous, and Demoule 2016). This focus is appropriate and in fact requisite. There is a recent trend among generally past-centric fields such as history to look at the future; these include works such as *The History Manifesto* by Guldi and Armitage (2014) or the final chapter of *The Shock of the Anthropocene* (Bonneuil and Fressoz 2016), which is titled "Surviving and Living in the Anthropocene." Bonneuil and Fressoz (2016, 21) firmly seek to draw their historical work into the realm of archaeology and its larger timescales and focus on materiality by stating that "the traces of our urban, industrial, consumerist, chemical and nuclear age will remain for thousands or even millions of years in the geological archives of the planet." It is only archaeology, however, that gives us access to the material remains of past disasters and permits considerations of the larger time frames required to consider geological events, radiation half-lives, and the deep future. I suggest that more archaeologists need to think about how our work intersects with the catastrophes of the future.

I agree with Shannon Dawdy (2006) that the methodological materialism of archaeology permits us to show that catastrophes are rarely, if ever, terminal and that they are recurrent and multi-scalar. These concepts work in tandem with work by Rosemary Joyce, whose research for me represents the most thoughtful engagement that archaeology has with nuclear landscapes (Joyce 2015, 2016a, 2016b, 2020). Joyce urges us to look at the perception of nuclear environments over time rather than the simple visual marker of a cultural heritage perspective that can be overly static and deterministic. She importantly offers critique of the way that archaeological sites as heritage—particularly through monumental sites like Stonehenge or the Acropolis—are mobilized in concepts of marking nuclear waste deposit sites as analogs of what to build and the amount of time they can be expected to function. This effectively results in the desire to create present-day ruins or a premade cultural heritage site with a progressivist bias that seeks to improve on ancient analogs. The behavior of actual archaeological assemblages, though, is prone to vary—often widely—from the intentions of the original creators of the material.

Even in our own personal experience and contexts, of course, the later meanings and reuse of materials we create are often unanticipated. The

a

b

Illustrations 2.2a–b. The maquette for the *Volcanic Winter/Nuclear Winter* piece by artist Keith Edmier. Courtesy of the artist, Keith Edmier.

Volcanic Winter/Nuclear Winter art piece certainly reflects this for me. In its original form, its monumentality underwhelmed not only in scale but also in longevity. The ice melted almost immediately. The maquette for the piece now sits on a shelf in my apartment in New York City though, as a gift from the artist. The work itself no longer exists, but the preliminary model for it does. The irony, given the environmental statement intended by the work, is that the maquette is made of polyurethane resin. It is not a genuine resin like the ancient ones that archaeologists might encounter (amber, balsam, copal), but a synthetic resin based on fossil fuels. What is worse? I inserted an electric light in it for display. The maquette will likely last for a century or more and will have a life span that exceeds my own. The energy to illuminate the maquette derives from a mix of fuels, each of which has their own risks.

Risky Business in New York City

The Current New York City Power Grid

New York City's electricity is the product of energy from nuclear power, hydroelectric plants, natural gas, wind, and some coal. The current energy grid for New York City is highly inefficient and outdated. "It's like a mainframe computer in the age of cloud computing," according to the state's energy czar (Rueb 2017). By 2030 the intention is for half of that energy to be from renewable energy sources. Fears of terrorism and contamination, though, are forcing the closure of the nearby Indian Point nuclear plant, in operation for fifty years, by 2021 (McGeehan 2017). This closure will require removal of the spent fuel from that plant as well as the fuel from a different plant closed in 1974 that has been stored there since the 1970s. Reference to Chernobyl-like consequences are frequent components of discussions of the proximity of Indian Point to New York City.

As a former chairman of the US Nuclear Regulatory Commission (NRC) states, it is "an agency overwhelmed by the industry it is supposed to regulate and a political system determined to keep in that way" (Jaczko 2019). The NRC routinely fails to enforce its own safety codes at nuclear power plants, and "it's the US's most extreme example of regulatory capture, rivalling Japan's 'nuclear village' of crony agencies and feeble regulation that led to the Fukushima disaster. How long can it be before the US experiences another nuclear catastrophe?" (Gunter 2016, 71; Jaczko 2019). It is, of course, not possible to make reactors "impervious to catastrophic releases of radiation" (Jaczko 2019, 116). Safety or the possibility of finding a fully "safe" energy source is an illusion at this point in history, and nuclear disasters will occur again in the United States and elsewhere.

Former mayor of New York City Michael Bloomberg is cofounder of an online climate change initiative called Risky Business (Bloomberg, Paulson, and Steyer 2013). Energy forms the integral focus of this website and initiative, with reports like "From Risk to Return: Investing in a Clean Energy Economy." Images of the iconic bull sculpture on Wall Street flash against wind turbines on its web page. The intersection of energy, economics, and the basic form of our governmental systems is in a state of flux. This offers a glimmer of possibility.

Unexpected Use of the Past

Environmental activism can take creative forms and the reutilization of Islamic jurisprudence and concepts of religious heritage in the Muria nuclear power plant protest is one example of how this can be effective. In looking for examples from recent New York City contexts that could indicate an ability to follow the example of Muria, I became interested in a law from 1899—the Refuse Act Bounty—that was invoked in 1968 by the Hudson River Fisherman's Association to successfully sue Penn Station Railroad for dumping oil into the river (New-York Historical Society 2019). This was the first of a series of lawsuits resulting in bounties that were utilized for the protection of the Hudson River as a landmark event following the publication of *Silent Spring* by Rachel Carson (1962). Rather than wait for new environmental legislation to address new environmental problems, attorneys working with citizen activists redirected attention to an overlooked existing law and had a significant impact on the industrial community in the 1960s and 1970s (Franz 2009). Creative reuse of the immaterial past had tangible, material impact in both the Muria and the New York City contexts. The creation of new "material" or technological fixes for the environmental issues we face feels uncomfortably inadequate. We also cannot pretend to understand or control the future contexts of them.

Ending Thoughts, Not End of Times

Fossils and Volcano-Sized Risks

Nothing embodies the awkward connection between the deep past and an uncertain future for biodiversity and the human presence on our planet more literally than fossil fuels and the carbon released from them; burnt, extinct life endangers future and yet-to-exist life. I wish that fossils could indeed speak, as Kathryn Yusoff (2013, 779) has them do as an intellectual exercise to "unlock this life-death, time-untimely, corporeal-incorporeal equation" for us. We do not seem able to do it on our own. Nuclear energy, seen by some (e.g., Nordhaus and Shellenberger 2007) as the solution to fossil fuel use, entails its own entrapment through the invisible yet potent harm of radiation. The volcano formed the metaphor for how nature endangers culture throughout the modern era through the resonance of the Vesuvius-Pompeii relationship; we are now in need of a new metaphor (Holmberg 2020). Nuclear disaster is a new intersection between human

a

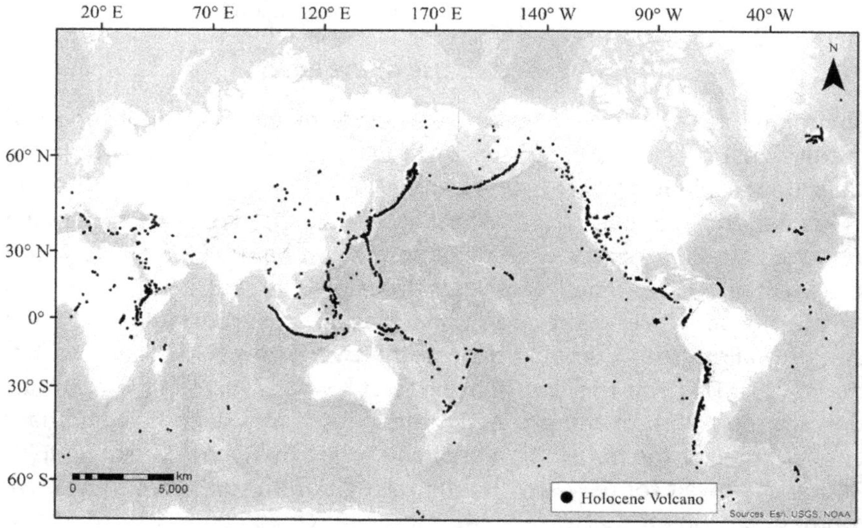

b

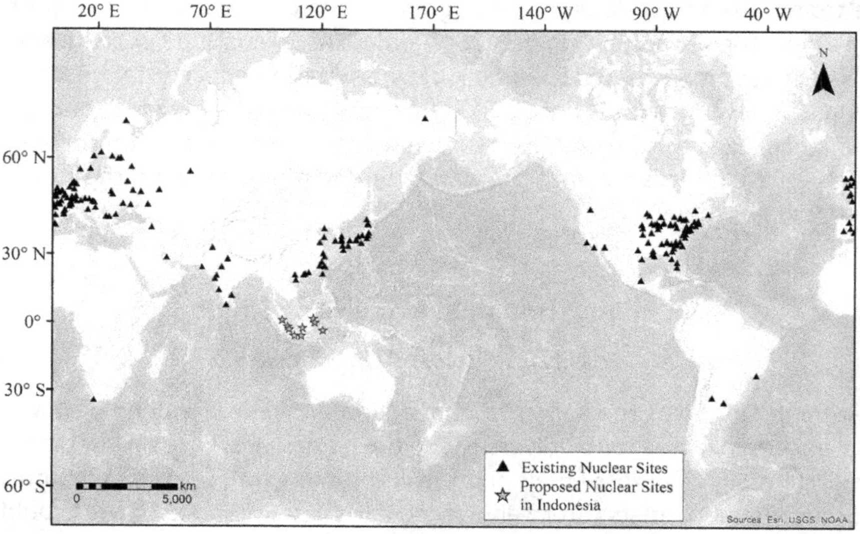

Figures 2.3a–b. Global distribution of Holocene volcanoes (a) and the existing and proposed nuclear power plants (b). Data from Venzke (2013) and IAEA.

life and environmental risk that we are still trying to comprehend, and we have no appropriate metaphor for it. The idea of a nuclear disaster and volcanic disaster overlapping is a very real possibility given the worldwide distribution of nuclear power plants in proximity to volcanoes that have been active in the Holocene period and hence could erupt again.

We should remember that nuclear disasters can take many forms though, including economic disparities in the way that production of nuclear materials divides cultural groups (Brown 2013). We are also aware that the state, particularly in the Global North, seeks to retain the status quo through deepening patterns of production and consumption (Brand and Wissen 2018). Most discussions of energy transition focus on technical innovation and efficiency in either economic or thermodynamic efficiency but a shift in technologies also provides a chance for "a just reorientation of society's production powers" (Huber 2009, 113).

Regulatory power is also in need of a shift as well if we are serious about minimizing risk. The nuclear waste stored at Indian Point near New York City does not require an act of terrorism—a great fear in the city since 11 September 2001—to become dangerous. Regulatory decisions are capable of doing that on their own. In 1984 the US Nuclear Regulatory Commission (NRC) published the "Waste Confidence Rule," which removed all consideration of used (spent) nuclear fuel from licensing decisions by placing "confidence" in the long-term safety of storing spent nuclear fuel and the eventual procurement of a federal geologic repository. The rule allowed the agency to say that they're confident that something will be done one day with this dangerous waste, so there's no need to consider it (or the concerns of the public about it) during licensing decisions (Gilhooly 2018). The NRC, as an agency, is overwhelmed by the industry it is supposed to regulate and the political system within which it operates to a level that it is impossible to make reactors that are safe (Jaczko 2019). The layers of risk are myriad.

Immaterial and Hopeful Imaginations

We are currently living in a "radically changing environment that is the unintended cumulative legacy of capitalism, militarism, and industrialism, which together are radically remaking the force of history as well as the established logics of periodization" (Masco 2015, 137–38). Fallout, per Masco (2015) occurs from more than just nuclear disasters; we are all living in an age of disintegrating structures and forms that no longer suit our historical moment or environmental realities. This does potentially offer some optimism to create positive change. I do not think that a new technology or anything material will be the source of that change.

One historical example of this to which we can potentially look is the gathering of international law scholars at the Bandung Conference in Indonesia in 1955. The Bandung Conference, attended by representatives of twenty-nine African and Asian nations, was a starting point for a new world order following the imperial order left behind by colonialism and neocolonialism (Eslava, Fakhri, and Nesiah 2017a). I am not romanticizing or mythologizing the Bandung Conference, which some historiography designates as a failure due to the lack of tangible, long-term impact (Eslava, Fakhri, and Nesiah 2017b, 7). The fascinating play between past and future represented by Bandung is worth remembering though, as is the new platform it provided for new conversations and voices.

Reflecting on the Bandung Conference and its promise through its material artifacts at the Museum of the Asia-Africa Conference in Bandung, Anna Tsing states, "As the future has shifted, the past contorts, confused" (Tsing 2005, 84). Archaeologists are most comfortable working with material culture via artifacts, but we can also acknowledge the deep importance of the immaterial and intangible. International law and its myths "give people a platform to dream of alternative futures and enable one to speak to the world" and can help to create "new spaces of unity and collective action that defy and transfigure concepts of nations and states" (Eslava, Fakhri, and Nesiah 2017b, 32). In stemming the power of seeming giants, actions like the Bandung Conference represent "sites for reclaiming the dream space of the globe" (Tsing 2005, 84). How can this play out in diverse times and different moments? The supposed superpowers of the world seem impotent in the search for better sources of energy or consumption patterns. Simultaneously, Bhutan prides itself on being "carbon neutral" or even "carbon negative" (Climate Action Tracker 2019b). Countries like Costa Rica aim for carbon neutrality in the near future (Climate Action Tracker 2019a). These examples seem truer sources of leadership and power in the twenty-first century than highly industrialized nations wield.

Meaning without Material: The Blue *by Hanae Utamura*

On 27 April 2019, during a semester in which she was auditing my courses at New York University, Japanese performance artist Hanae Utamura premiered a piece she called *The Blue* at the Big Orbit Gallery in Buffalo, New York. Utamura is the daughter of a nuclear scientist who worked for the Hitachi Company, which participated in designing the Fukushima nuclear plant. Her piece draws upon imagery from the Tokaimura nuclear accident on 30 September 1999 in which a worker mixing liquid uranium, Hisashi Ouchi, recalled seeing the color blue in the moment the radiation exposed his retina. This blue flash was potentially the result of Cherenkov radiation or electromagnetic radiation emitted when a charged particle travels at a speed higher than the phase velocity of light. Ouchi began to vomit immediately and lost consciousness several minutes later in the decontamination room. He suffered radiation burns to most of his body, serious internal organ damage, and almost a complete loss of white blood cells. He died on 21 December 1999. The "criticality accident" is attributed entirely to human error (US Nuclear Regulatory Commission 2000).

As Edmier and I did in *Volcanic Winter/Nuclear Winter*, Utamura used ice. She asked the audience, though—with eyes closed and standing—to make a circle as she handed ice to them to pass. They heard ice falling around them, and she read them a "Letter from Future Past" that referenced "a hundred, a million, a billion years." The piece explores the human desire to conquer and extract energy from nature, new social bodies after nuclear fallout, and the constant renegotiation between humans and the environment. Utamura said that she wanted to make the past, present, and future collide (personal communication, 31 May 2019). Her piece, for me, attains the intentions that *Volcanic Winter/Nuclear Winter* did not. I think that the fact that it was performance, not a material object, is significant. It signifies movement and action, which matters.

Illustration 2.3. Photo taken during the performance of *The Blue* by Japanese performance artist Hanae Utamura on 28 April 2019 at the Blue Orbit art gallery in Buffalo, New York. The performance piece is about the Tokaimura "criticality accident," an uncontrolled nuclear fission chain reaction on 30 September 1999. Permission to use courtesy Hanae Utamara and Lauren Tent and Cepa Gallery. Photo by Lauren Tent.

For Utamura, *The Blue* is about the impossible questions of scientific interpretation and representation of human life; the piece touches upon questions of progress and impossibility (personal communication, 31 May 2019). Creative responses can contribute to environmental understanding and adaptation, and climate change is a social as much as scientific event (Yusoff and Gabrys 2011). The intention of the searchable portal created after the Fukushima disaster was to allow the catastrophic past event to inform an array of users to make better decisions in the future. Who are these stakeholders? We all are. There is not a person currently on the planet who should not consider themselves a stakeholder. Nuclear radiation fallout can travel exceptionally long distances and unexpected paths. Fossil fuels form the basis of our economic and political systems globally. Everyone needs to have the agency to contribute to the discussions of what comes next. The archaeological capacity to consider temporality and materiality of nuclear waste and radiation certainly means that we should add to discussions. We should all, however, be a part of those discussions.

Acknowledgments

Shanti Escalante was invaluable in the preparation of maps for this chapter. My thanks to her and to the Gallatin Research Scholars program.

Karen Holmberg is a visiting assistant professor of environmental science at the Gallatin School, New York University. She serves as principal investigator of a National Geographic–funded project that studies a prehistoric rock art cave in Patagonia near the Chaiten volcano, which erupted unexpectedly in 2008. The transdisciplinary project examines the cultural and geological heritage of the cave in relation to contemporary post-disaster resettlement. She has prior awards from Fulbright, Wenner-Gren, Creating Earth Futures, and Make Our Planet Great Again. She is beginning new work with humanities, arts, and science collaborations for hazards reduction at Campi Flegrei in Naples, Italy.

References

Adelson, Glenn, James Engell, Brent Ranalli, and K. P. van Anglen. 2008. "Nuclear Power: Three Mile Island, Chernobyl, and the Future." In *Environment: An Interdisciplinary Anthology*, 83–116. New Haven: Yale University Press.

Banerjee, Srikumar, and Hari Prakash Gupta. 2019. "Nuclear Power from Thorium: Some Frequently Asked Questions." In *Thorium—Energy for the Future*, edited by A. K. Nayak and Bal Raj Sehgal, 11–26. Singapore: Springer Nature.

BATAN. 2014. "Perencanaan Energi—Indonesia Energy Scenario 2010–2050." Sistem Informasi Energi Nuklir (SIEN): Pusat Kajian Sistem Energi Nuklir. Retrieved 24 October 2014 from http://183.91.67.14/sien/index.php/menuutama/english#slide-2-1-1.

Bloomberg, Michael, Hank Paulson, and Tom Steyer. 2013. Risky Business website. Retrieved 16 May 2020 from https://riskybusiness.org/.

Bonneuil, Christophe, and Jean-Baptiste Fressoz. 2016. *The Shock of the Anthropocene: The Earth, History and Us*. Translated by David Fernbach. London and Brooklyn: Verso, New Left Books.

Brand, Ulrich, and Markus Wissen. 2018. *The Limits to Capitalist Nature: Theorizing and Overcoming the Imperial Mode of Living*. London and New York: Rowman & Littlefield International.

Brown, Kate. 2013. *Plutopia: Nuclear Families, Atomic Cities, and the Great Soviet and American Plutonium Disasters*. Oxford: Oxford University Press.

Buchli, Victor, and Gavin Lucas. 2001. *Archaeologies of the Contemporary Past*. London: Routledge.

Carson, Rachel. 1962. *Silent Spring*. Boston: Houghton Mifflin.

Climate Action Tracker. 2018. "Country Summary: Indonesia." Retrieved 31 May 2019 from https://climateactiontracker.org/countries/indonesia/.

———. 2019a. "Country Summary: Costa Rica." Retrieved 31 May 2019 from https://climateactiontracker.org/countries/costa-rica/.

———. 2019b. "Country Summary: Bhutan." Retrieved 31 May 2019 from https://climateactiontracker.org/countries/bhutan/.

Connor, C. B., R. S. J. Sparks, M. Díez, A. C. M. Volentik, and S. C. P. Pearson. 2009. "The Nature of Volcanism." In *Volcanic and Tectonic Hazard Assessment for Nuclear Facilities*, edited by C. B. Connor, N. A. Chapman, and L. J. Connor, 74–115. Cambridge: Cambridge University Press.

Connor, Steven. 2009. Introduction to *The Five Senses: A Philosophy of Mingled Bodies*, by Michel Serres, 1–16. London and New York: Continuum.

Crain, Rhiannon, Caren Cooper, and Janis L. Dickinson. 2014. "Citizen Science: A Tool for Integrating Studies of Human and Natural Systems." *Annual Review of Environment and Resources* 39 (1): 641–65.

Davenport, Coral. 2018. "Major Climate Report Describes a Strong Risk of Crisis as Early as 2040." *New York Times*, 7 October. https://www.nytimes.com/2018/10/07/climate/ipcc-climate-report-2040.html.

Dawdy, Shannon Lee. 2006. "The Taphonomy of Disaster and the (Re)formation of New Orleans." *American Anthropologist* 108 (4): 719–30.

Donovan, Amy R., and Clive Oppenheimer. 2015. "Modelling Risk and Risking Models: The Diffusive Boundary between Science and Policy in Volcanic Risk Management." *Geoforum* 58: 153–65.

Eslava, Luis, Michael Fakhri, and Vasuki Nesiah, eds. 2017a. *Bandung, Global History, and International Law: Critical Pasts and Pending Futures*. New York: Cambridge University Press.

———. 2017b. "The Spirit of Bandung." In *Bandung, Global History, and International Law: Critical Pasts and Pending Futures*, edited by Luis Eslava, Michael Fakhri and Vasuki Nesiah, 3–32. New York: Cambridge University Press.

Fauzan, Achmad Uzair, and Jim Schiller. 2011. *After Fukushima: The Rise of Resistance to Nuclear Energy in Indonesia*. Essen, Germany: ADB-Project of the German Asia Foundation/Asia House. http://www.lebret-irfed.org/IMG/pdf/resistance-in-indonesia-after-fukushima.pdf.

Fealy, Greg, Virginia Hooker, and Sally White. 2006. "Indonesia." In *Voices of Indonesian Islam: A Contemporary Source Book*, edited by Greg Fealy and Virginia Hooker, 39–40. Singapore: Institute of Southeast Asian Studies.

Fetter, Steve. 1993. "Nuclear Archaeology: Verifying Declarations of Fissile-Material Production." *Science and Global Security* 3 (3–4): 237–59.

Franz, Andrew. 2009. "Crimes against Water: The Rivers and Harbors Act of 1899." *Tulane Environmental Law Journal* 23: 255–78.

Freischlad, Nadine. 2018. "In a Country Long Wary of Nuclear, an Indonesian Chases the Thorium Dream." *Mongabay: News and Inspiration from Nature's Frontline*, 12 June. https://news.mongabay.com/2018/06/in-a-country-long-wary-of-nuclear-an-indonesian-chases-the-thorium-dream.

Fudge, Bruce. 2019. "Islam after Salman." *Aeon*, 21 February. https://aeon.co/essays/can-there-ever-be-another-novel-like-the-satanic-verses?utm_source=Aeon+Newsletter&utm_campaign=2fc4891ee2-EMAIL_CAMPAIGN_2019_02_25_03_18&utm_medium=email&utm_term=0_411a82e59d-2fc4891ee2-68668341.

Gilhooly, Rob. 2018. "Fukushima Heroes on Both Sides of the Pacific Still Fighting Effects of Radiation, Stress and Guilt." *Post Magazine*, 24 January. https://www.scmp.com/magazines/post-magazine/long-reads/article/2130359/fukushima-heroes-both-sides-pacific-still.

Guldi, Jo, and David Armitage. 2014. *The History Manifesto*. Cambridge: Cambridge University Press. http://historymanifesto.cambridge.org/files/6114/1227/7857/historymanifesto.pdf.

Gunter, Linda Pentz. 2016. "US Nuclear Regulatory Commission's 'Enforcement' Is as Fierce as the Comfy Chair." *Ecologist: The Journal for the Post-Industrial Age*, 2 August. https://theecologist.org/2016/aug/02/us-nuclear-regulatory-commissions-enforcement-fierce-comfy-chair.

Harrison, Rodney, and John Schofield. 2010. Introduction to *After Modernity: Archaeological Approaches to the Contemporary Past*, 1–18. Oxford: Oxford University Press.

Haverkamp, Jan. 2018. "Five Reasons Why a Floating Nuclear Power Plant in the Arctic Is a Terrible Idea." *Greenpeace*, 7 October.

Heryanto, A., and V. R. Hadiz. 2005. "Post-authoritarian Indonesia, a Comparative Southeast Asian Perspective." *Critical Asian Studies* 37 (2): 251–75.

Hill, B. E., W. P. Aspinall, C. B. Connor, A. R. Godoy, J.-C. Komorowski, and S. Nakada. 2009. "Recommendations for Assessing Volcanic Hazards at Sites of Nuclear Installations." In *Volcanic and Tectonic Hazard Assessment for Nuclear Facilities*, edited by C. B. Connor, N. A. Chapman, and L. J. Connor, 566–92. Cambridge: Cambridge University Press.

Holmberg, Karen. 2005. "The Voices of Stones: Unthinkable Materiality in the Volcanic Context of Western Panamá." In *Archaeologies of Materiality*, edited by Lynn Meskell, 190–211. Malden, MA: Blackwell.

———. 2007. "Beyond the Catastrophe: The Volcanic Landscape of Barú, Western Panamá." In *Living Under the Shadow: Cultural Impacts of Volcanic Eruptions*, edited by John Grattan and Robin Torrence, 274–97. Walnut Creek, CA: Left Coast Press.

———. 2013. "An Inheritance of Loss: Archaeology's Imagination of Disaster." In *Humans and the Environment: New Archaeological Perspectives for the 21st Century*, edited by Matthew Davis and Freda Nkirote, 197–209. Oxford: Oxford University Press.

———. 2020. "Inside the Anthropocene Volcano." In *Critical Zones: The Science and Politics of Landing on Earth*, edited by Bruno Latour and Peter Weibel, 56–71. Cambridge, MA: MIT Press.

Holtorf, Cornelius, and Anders Högberg. 2014. "Communicating with Future Generations: What Are the Benefits of Preserving for Future Generations? Nuclear Power and Beyond." *European Journal of Post-Classical Archaeologies* 4: 343–58.

Huber, Matthew T. 2009. "Energizing Historical Materialism: Fossil Fuels, Space and the Capitalist Mode of Production." *Geoforum* 40 (1): 105–15.

Hyland, Tom. 2007. "Nuclear Reactor Plan on Shaky Ground." *The Age*, 14 October. https://www.theage.com.au/environment/nuclear-reactor-plan-on-shaky-ground-20071014-ge61p4.html?page=fullpage.

IAEA. 2011. "IAEA Action Plan on Nuclear Safety." International Atomic Energy Agency. https://www.iaea.org/topics/nuclear-safety-action-plan.

———. 2015. "Knowledge Management Portal on the Observations and Lessons from the Fukushima Daiichi Accident." International Atomic Energy Agency; Global Nuclear Safety and Security Network. https://gnssn.iaea.org/FukushimaLessonsLearned/SitePages/default.aspx.

———. 2018. "Country Nuclear Power Profiles: Indonesia." International Atomic Energy Agency. https://cnpp.iaea.org/countryprofiles/Indonesia/Indonesia.htm.

Ichihara, M. 2010. "Information Availability and NGO advocacy." *Josef Korbel Journal of Advanced International Studies* 2: 45–60.

Information Library. 2014. "Nuclear Power in Indonesia." World Nuclear Association. Accessed 24 October 2014. http://www.world-nuclear.org/info/Country-Profiles/Countries-G-N/Indonesia/.

IPCC. 2018. "Global Warming of 1.5 Degrees Celsius: An IPCC Special Report." Intergovernmental Panel on Climate Change. http://www.ipcc.ch/report/sr15/.

Jaczko, Gregory. 2019. *Confessions of a Rogue Nuclear Regulator*. New York: Simon & Schuster.

Joyce, Rosemary. 2015. "Traces That Endure." Theoretical Archaeology Group, New York, paper presented at the symposium "Archaeology of the Future (Time Keeps on Slipping)," 23 May 2015.

———. 2016a. "Failure? An Archaeology of the Architecture of Nuclear Waste Containment." In *Elements of Architecture: Assembling Archaeology, Atmosphere and the Performance of Building Space*, edited by Mikkel Bille and Tim Flohr Sørensen, 424–38. London: Routledge.

———. 2016b. Keynote lecture, "Visions of Nuclear Landscapes: Seeing from the Perspectives of Art, Cultural Heritage, and Archaeology." Theoretical Archaeology Group, Southampton, UK.

———. 2020. *A Past for Nuclear Waste*. Oxford: Oxford University Press.

Kakodkar, Anil, and S. B. Degweker. 2016. "Towards Sustainable, Secure, and Safe Energy Future: Leveraging Opportunities with Thorium." In *Thorium Energy for the World*, edited by Jean-Pierre Revol, Maurice Bourquin, Yacine Kadi, Egil Lillestol, and Jean-Christophe de Mestral, 29–36.

Kugeler, Kurt, and Zuoyi Zhang. 2019. "General Aspects of High-Temperature Reactors." In *Modular High-Temperature Gas-Cooled Reactor Power Plant*, 1–22. Berlin and Heidelberg: Springer Berlin Heidelberg.

Mahoney, S. H., R. S. J. Sparks, L. J. Connor, and C. B. Connor. 2009. "Exploring Long-Term Hazards Using a Quaternary Volcano Database." In *Volcanic and Tectonic*

Hazard Assessment for Nuclear Facilities, edited by C. B. Connor, N. A. Chapman, and L. J. Connor, 326–45. Cambridge: Cambridge University Press.

Masco, Joseph. 2010. "Bad Weather: On Planetary Crisis." *Social Studies of Science* 40 (1): 7–40.

———. 2015. "The Age of Fallout." *History of the Present: A Journal of Critical History* 5 (2): 137–68.

McBeth, John. 2018. "Is Indonesia Preparing to Go Nuclear?" *Asia Times*, 26 June. http://www.atimes.com/article/is-indonesia-preparing-to-go-nuclear/.

McGeehan, Patrick. 2017. "Cuomo Confirms Deal to Close Indian Point Nuclear Plant." *New York Times*, 9 January. https://www.nytimes.com/2017/01/09/nyregion/cuomo-indian-point-nuclear-plant.html.

Mickelson, Karin, and Usha Natarajan. 2017. "Reflections on Rhetoric and Rage." In *Bandung, Global History, and International Law: Critical Pasts and Pending Futures*, edited by Luis Eslava, Michael Fakhri, and Vasuki Nesiah, 465–80. New York: Cambridge University Press.

Mitchell, Timothy. 2011. *Carbon Democracy: Political Power in the Age of Oil*. London and New York: Verso.

New-York Historical Society. 2019. *Hudson Rising*. Exhibit, New York City, 1 March–2 August.

Nordhaus, Ted, and Michael Shellenberger. 2007. *Breakthrough: From the Death of Environmentalism to the Politics of Possibility*. New York: Houghton Mifflin.

Rueb, Emily. 2017. "How New York City Gets Its Electricity." *New York Times*, 10 February. https://www.nytimes.com/interactive/2017/02/10/nyregion/how-new-york-city-gets-its-electricity-power-grid.html.

Schlanger, Nathan, Laurent Nespoulous, and Jean-Paul Demoule. 2016. "Year 5 at Fukushima: A 'Disaster-Led' Archaeology of the Contemporary Future." *Antiquity* 90 (350): 409–24.

Serres, Michel. 1995. *The Natural Contract*. Translated by Elizabeth MacArthur and William Paulson. Ann Arbor: University of Michigan Press.

———. 2011. *Malfeasance: Appropriation through Pollution?* Translated by Anne-Marie Feenberg-Dibon. Stanford, CA: Stanford University Press.

Sukma, Rizal. 2007. "Indonesia's Energy Plan: Is Nuclear Power Really the Only Option?" *Wild Singapore*, 28 February. http://www.wildsingapore.com/news/20070708/070720-1.htm.

Tacconi, Luca. 2018. "Indonesia's NDC Bodes Ill for the Paris Agreement." *Nature Climate Change* 8 (10): 842–42.

Tanter, Richard. 2007. "Nuclear Fatwa: Islamic Jurisprudence and the Muria Nuclear Power Station Proposal." *APSNet Policy Forum*, 28 February. https://nautilus.org/apsnet/nuclear-fatwa-islamic-jurisprudence-and-the-muria-nuclear-power-station-proposal/."

Tanter, Richard, and Arabella Imhoff. 2009. "The Muria Peninsula Nuclear Power Proposal: State of Play." *APSNet Policy Forum*, 28 February. https://nautilus.org/apsnet/muria-nuclear-power/.

Tsing, Anna Lowenhaupt. 2005. *Friction: An Ethnography of Global Connection*. Princeton and Oxford: Princeton University Press.

US Nuclear Regulatory Commission. 2000. *NRC Review of the Tokai-Mura Criticality Accident*. NRC Division of Fuel Cycle Safety and Safeguards, Office of Nuclear Material Safety and Safeguards. https://www.nrc.gov/reading-rm/doc-collections/commission/secys/2000/secy2000-0085/attachment1.pdf.

Venzke, Edward. 2013. *Volcanoes of the World*. Vol. 4.8.4., edited by Global Volcanism Program. Smithsonian Institution.

Waddington, Richard. 2014. "Scientists Needed for Risk Reduction," 7 October 2014. Madrid: European Forum for Disaster Risk Reduction, Spanish Chairmanship. Retrieved 16 May 2020 from *http://www.unisdr.org/archive/39688*.

WNA. 2018. "Country Profiles: Nuclear Power in Indonesia." World Nuclear Association. http://www.world-nuclear.org/information-library/country-profiles/countries-g-n/indonesia.aspx.

———. 2019. "Country Profiles: Nuclear Power in Indonesia." World Nuclear Association. http://www.world-nuclear.org/information-library/country-profiles/countries-g-n/indonesia.aspx.

Wood, Thomas, Bruce Reid, Christopher Toomey, Kannan Krishnaswami, Kimberly Burns, Larry Casazza, Don Daly, and Leesa Duckworth. 2014. "The Future of Nuclear Archaeology: Reducing Legacy Risks of Weapons Fissile Material." Special issue, *Science and Global Security* 22 (1): 4–26. http://scienceandglobalsecurity.org/editorial/2014/02/the_future_of_nuclear_archaeol.html.

Wootsen, Cleve. 2018. "Russia Says Its Sea-Based Nuclear Power Plant Is Safe: Critics Call It a 'Floating Chernobyl.'" *Washington Post*, 1 May.

Yusoff, Kathryn. 2013. "Geologic Life: Prehistory, Climate, Futures in the Anthropocene." *Environment and Planning D: Society and Space* 31 (5): 779–95.

Yusoff, Kathryn, and Jennifer Gabrys. 2011. "Climate Change and the Imagination." *Wiley Interdisciplinary Reviews: Climate Change* 2 (4): 516–34.

CHAPTER 3

Do Disasters Always Enhance Inequality?

PAYSON SHEETS

Summary for Stakeholders

I believe there are things we have learned in comparing disasters and human responses of ancient societies in Mexico through Central America, as well as some more recent disasters, that could be applied to modern societies. Those societies were successful in adapting to hazardous environments by learning from disasters. Ancient Mesoamericans used performances and reiterations to maintain knowledge of past disasters. By maintaining oral history over centuries or millennia, people remained aware of and could prepare for future disasters. Today we could enhance training beyond first responders, making sure that at least a few people in each neighborhood know how to take rapid action to mitigate the intensity of extreme event impacts and help neighbors cope. A model is the social networks of Hispanic households during the terrible heat wave in Chicago in 1995. They survived much better than white and black households of equivalent resources because they provided mutual assistance. They avoided a passive reliance on federal, state, or city authorities to come to their aid, by taking direct action as the extreme event ensued.

Training individuals in neighborhoods can provide prompt activities and enhance communication with first responders and agencies such as FEMA in the United States and National Recovery Guidance in the United Kingdom, even when landlines and cell phones fail. Localized decision-making can be much more efficient than waiting for a complex bureaucracy to respond.

The example of ancient communities in Costa Rica facing quite different hazards and sharing a cemetery illustrates the advantages of preparing a refuge area when disaster strikes. The village on the eastern side of the continental divide suffered from explosive eruptions of Arenal Volcano, while the western village suffered from occasional droughts. Intermarriage must have occurred, because village populations were so small, cementing relationships for future emergencies. Houston, Texas, was accommodating to refugees from New Orleans after Hurricane Katrina devastated it, but Gulf Coast cities were not as helpful when Hurricane Harvey flooded Houston. If Gulf Coast cities anticipated and organized for future such events, mutual aid could mitigate some suffering and facilitate recovery when the next hurricane strikes. Such agreements among hazard-prone cities could at least slightly decrease the enhanced inequality that so commonly results from disasters in the United States today. Effective programs and legislation to actually mitigate the increased inequality following disasters would require bipartisan efforts by courageous politicians at the national and state levels. Another way in which ancient Costa Ricans mitigated the stresses of explosive volcanic eruptions is in having access to abundant food and water in their refuge areas. We could encourage households or neighborhoods to store food and water to help them get through the initial days of waiting for the bureaucracy to become effective. Tax breaks or direct governmental assistance could provide both support and incentives for storage.

Introduction

This chapter begins with examinations of recent and presently ongoing disasters, involving hurricanes and flooding, as of this writing, December of 2018, to explore how people or institutions with a wide range of resources, from meager to considerable, cope with sudden stress. In such extreme-event situations, the individual agents are discernible in ways that are unavailable in the archaeological record. Lacking in these current disasters are the long-term implications. Archaeology provides that expansive time framework, and ancient cases and interpretations occupy the remainder of this chapter.

In disaster cases where detailed documentation is available, two phases can be identified (Driessen 2018). The first is the emergency, where people and institutions are attempting to save lives and facilities. The second is rehabilitation, which may be differentially successful in more complex societies. Both phases can be examined in recent disasters, but both are more challenging to reconstruct in detail with archaeological cases. Disasters often act as intensifiers of economic, social, and political aspects of societies, particularly in more complex societies where pre-disaster inequalities existed. They also can act as catalysts for innovations in political, economic, or social domains (Gibbs 2003). As will be presented toward the end of this chapter, smaller societies can rehabilitate without an increase in inequality.

The concepts of resilience and vulnerability are important to apply to the recent and ancient cases. Resilience refers to the abilities of communities to weather the stresses of extreme events, to maintain a high degree of cultural continuity, and in many cases to make creative adjustments with an eye to mitigate future disasters. Vulnerabilities are the socially constructed elements of communities including inequalities, factionalism, bureaucracies, traditions, and other internal factors.

An obvious clear difference in how societies explain why the disaster occurred is between ancient and modern cases. During the past few centuries, more people tend to explain geophysical extreme events in scientific terms. This is not true for many traditional areas today, for instance in Java (Dove 2008). In ancient disasters, people ascribe the forcing mechanism to supernatural beings and often, by extension, to the elites who supposedly had preferential access to those beings.

Ongoing and Recent Disasters

This section examines some recent and ongoing disasters in the United States and other countries where inequality increased. That is followed by ancient cases where inequality similarly increased. The final section presents two cases where extreme events did not increase inequality. The differences are examined to make policy suggestions for stakeholders today.

Recent and presently ongoing disasters often provide opportunities for people of means to take advantage of people adversely affected, resulting in increased economic inequality (Scanlon 1988). Not only is this a recent phenomenon, but analogous cases of increased inequality also occurred in antiquity. As more affluent people use their resources to enhance their wealth, the poor get poorer. Natural disasters almost always result in socioeconomic disasters for those with less resources. Often the poor live in more hazardous areas than the affluent, and in less substantial housing, therefore increasing their risk. Here I explore some ongoing, recent, and ancient natural disasters that did facilitate increased inequality. I also provide cases in which inequality did not result. The reasons inequality was not enhanced by the extreme events are of great importance. Might they provide suggestions for contemporary societies, if decisions or policies prior to the stresses were implemented to decrease the intensity of inequality enhancement?

Hawaii's Kilauea volcano is presently erupting large amounts of lava, destroying hundreds of homes. A total of seven hundred homes have been destroyed as of July 2018, according to National Public Radio. It previously erupted effusively in 1983, destroying sixteen homes, and then in 1990 another effusive eruption destroyed over one hundred homes. The cost to private insurers was so much that they stopped insuring property in Lava Flow Hazard zones 1 and 2. Why would so many people choose to live on the slopes of an active volcano, with two documented recent records of destruction? The Hawaii State Legislature created a "perverse incentive" for people to live in such a hazardous location (Akina 2018). As Akina states, "Hawaii's lawmakers put citizens in danger by giving them an incentive to live in an area that the market had deemed too risky to insure." People bought homes at unusually low prices for Hawaii, hoping to avoid destruction, but now have lost their homes. This is an obvious case of a legally and socially produced vulnerability, particularly for lower-income households. Developers profited greatly.

Hurricane Harvey devastated Houston in 2017 by dumping almost fifty inches of rain, thus flooding many areas (Romero 2018). That extreme event allowed affluent speculators to buy many of the thousands of flooded houses at low cost and then resell them at higher cost, making considerable profits, sometimes in the same day (Romero 2018). Speculators often paid about half of the pre-flood value of damaged or destroyed homes, leaving former residents so impoverished that they were unable to afford another suitable residence. The history of the Canyon Gate subdivision illustrates how state and private interests combined to create this social catastrophe, this socially produced vulnerability. The Canyon Gate subdivision is in the low-lying reservoir designed to receive floodwaters during extreme weather events so that central Houston is less flood-prone. There is a history to the creation of this reservoir. Downtown Houston flooded badly in 1935, and in response, during the 1940s authorities built flood-control reservoirs to protect the downtown. These reservoirs were not intended to contain housing—they were reservoirs intended to operate in extreme weather events. But in the 1990s massive housing projects were built right in the area that fifty years earlier had been engineered to flood. And flood it did in 2017. In August 2018, exactly one year after Harvey flooded Houston, Mimi Swartz (2018) noted how pitifully little federal or state funding had been offered to assist the most devastated families. She feared the lack of planning was creating great risks for the next hurricane.

A survey of Houstonians a year after Harvey revealed the unsurprising evidence that low-income and minority residents were having more difficulty recovering than more-affluent white residents (Fernandez 2018). The survey by the Kaiser Family Foundation and the Episcopal Health Foundation showed that 27 percent of Hispanic Texans with badly damaged homes reported that those homes remained unsafe to live in, compared to 20 percent of blacks and only 11 percent of whites. There were similar disparities by income: 50 percent of lower-income respondents said they were not getting the help they needed, compared to 32 percent of those with higher incomes. Clearly a part of the problem is that $5 billion in federal Community Development Block Grant (CDBG) disaster-recovery funds were approved for Texas, but Houston had yet to receive them as of mid-2018. Kurt Pickering, a spokesperson for FEMA in Texas, said the agency had seen no evidence that low-income areas were receiving less support from the agency. He said that federal assistance is not intended to make a family whole after a disaster, but to help start the recovery process. "FEMA does everything possible to assist every family in every way," within the bounds of its regulations, he said.

Insurance companies like to emphasize the great amounts of money they hand out after a disaster, and Harvey is an example. Allstate's catastrophic losses for 2017 totaled $3.23 billion (Sun and Scism 2018), a seemingly overwhelming amount for them to pay out. In spite of that, Allstate posted a profit of $3.07 billion that year. Altogether, the US property-casualty industry had $752.5 billion in surplus in December 2017, an increase of over 7 percent from the previous year, in spite of the increase in disaster damages from the previous year of 2016. Insurance companies can label disaster agents as "acts of God" and thus provide themselves with an easy way out. The households with more resources can afford more insurance and thus can recover more readily than the poor.

Hurricane Florence struck the Carolinas in September 2018, creating record flooding. The conditions shortly after the extreme event seem to be a setup for limited payments on claims filed after the disaster is over. According to the *Wall Street Journal* (14 September 2018), about $14 billion in catastrophe bonds ("cat bonds") could be exposed to the hurricane damage (Friedman 2018). According to Friedman, wealthy families and investors have invested billions in the cat bonds to diversify their investments in order to receive higher returns. The bonds benefit insurance companies by decreasing their exposure to claims. Homeowners' insurance policies usually cover hurricane wind damage but not flooding. If homeowners have sufficient funds and judge the cost worthwhile, they can purchase separate flood insurance from FEMA's National Flood Insurance Program (NFIP). FEMA's cat bond would pay out up to $500 million per disaster, but only if total losses exceed $5 billion. The insurance domain has an "oversupply of capital . . . resulting in minimal risk that insurers will run out of money to pay claims" (Friedman 2018). Flood damages could be well over 95 percent of the total losses from this disaster. The homeowners with the least resources, and without separate flood insurance, will suffer dearly.

Walsh (2018) reported that only 335,000 homes in the Carolinas have flood insurance (2018). The US census lists the Carolinas with 6,967,279 housing units, so one can calculate that only 4 percent have flood insurance. Walsh claims most of those with flood insurance are along the coast, where they expect flooding more than do people living inland, and most of them are relatively affluent homeowners. Most of the flooding from Florence was inland, where few people anticipated it. The system certainly is not weighted in favor of most households, and inequality is exacerbated.

Just a few weeks after Hurricane Harvey in Houston, hurricanes Irma and Maria devastated islands in the Caribbean. Maria completely wiped out the entire electrical system of Puerto Rico, devastated homes and businesses, and set up the opportunities for those with wealth or power to take advantage of the dispossessed. The Puerto Rican economy was in poor condition prior to the hurricane. A federal board established by the US Congress in 2016 oversees the commonwealth's economy. It was created after a recession that pushed the island into a "debt restructuring" akin to bankruptcy (Campo-Flores and Scurria 2018). Goodell (2018) notes the island has $70 billion in debt and 44 percent of people living in poverty, compared to 12 percent in the United States. Puerto Rico had a Gini coefficient—a summary measure economic inequality—that was among the ten worst in the world before the hurricanes (Brown et al. 2018). Many residents had their houses destroyed or damaged, and many lost their jobs. Brown describes drug-manufacturing companies rebuilding their facilities, taking advantage of dispossessed people earning the minimum wage. Had the island not been in such poor financial condition, of course, recovery could have begun from a better base condition.

Robles (2018) reported on FEMA-supported repairs to homes in Puerto Rico, about a year after Hurricane Maria devastated the island. The program is called Tu Hogar Renace (Your Home Reborn). FEMA is spending $1.2 billion to repair up to 120,000 homes, the largest sum that FEMA has ever spent for any disaster. None of the money was for destroyed houses, only for those that needed specific repairs. Unfortunately, over 60 percent of the money is going to multiple layers of middlemen and contractors instead of paying for roofs, windows, and doors. The housing department hired seven contractors to do the repairs. Those companies hired subcontractors, who then hired various companies to actually do the repairs. Contractors charged FEMA $3,700 each for 12,400 generators. The contractors purchased each generator for $800. The markup was 4.6 times the purchase price. The "Renace" certainly applies to the bank accounts of the middlemen and the contractors more than the homeowners (Robles 2018).

Comparing inequality among households, before and after the extreme event, is the focus of much research. In contrast, Durana (2017) considers intra-household enhanced inequality in her article "Gender Inequality in Puerto Rico Is about to Get Worse." She argues that the gender inequality that was deeply set in the island before the hurricane would intensify because of the stress. The devastation eliminated many jobs held by women, so many had to fall back into worse-paying jobs in the informal economy. Most of the construction jobs in the recovery effort go to men.

Yet another underreported aspect of natural disasters is the aftermath for nature itself. Most of the disaster literature focuses on infrastructure devastation and human impacts, followed by recoveries to varying degrees of success. Hurricane Maria devastated the tropical rainforest on the island, and ecological recovery is in doubt (Amandolare 2018). Because tropical forests contain more than two-thirds of the earth's terrestrial plant biomass, studies of conditions in El Yunque National Forest are of great importance. Global warming may stress many forests prior to hurricanes, generate more intense hurricanes, and inhibit recoveries of the biomass and biodiversity. Prior to the hurricane, multiple ecosystem services were provided by the rainforest, and that certainly happened in ancient times, as detailed below in prehistoric Costa Rica.

Two category 5 hurricanes struck the Cancun area of Mexico, Gilbert in 1988 and Wilma in 2005. Wilma was a category 5, the most powerful hurricane recorded to 2014. Prior to them, tourists went from their scattered hotels into the town to restaurants, markets, and stores, benefiting local Maya/Mexican residents. Both hurricanes created massive devastation, and both received considerable federal assistance to recover and construct new tourist facilities. There was very little assistance to individual families or small businesses in the city, and recoveries were uneven and slow. Following the hurricanes, government officials and developer-investors made radical changes by building all-inclusive destination hotels, thus cutting off local residents from contact with tourists staying there (Cordoba, Baptista, and Dominguez Rubio 2014). Tourists pay in advance, covering room, board, drinks, entertainment, and often other things and thus have little incentive to leave the walled premises of their inclusive venue. Following Hurricane Wilma, large time-share condominiums with gated access and de facto privatization of the beaches were constructed along the waterfront, further isolating tourists from local residents. The authors call this "enclosures within enclosures" to indicate domains and boundaries, supposedly deployed to improve security, economic growth, and the public good. The "enclosure" of the resort is within the "enclosure" of the Hotel Zone, which after the disasters became more isolated from the city. Economic benefits did occur, but far away from Cancun. Most big establishments were owned by large corporations in the United States or Europe, such as the Marriott Vacation Club Timeshare Resort

Cancun. It has three massive towers of thirteen or more stories each and land closures with guards that block beach access to those not staying within. Privatization of formerly public beaches occurred widely, even though it was prohibited by law. Elites with resources benefited by cutting tourists off from locals, to the detriment of the latter. Small local businesses suffered by being cut off from tourists.

Today the poor often live in more hazardous locations than the wealthy, and the latter often take advantage of the poor to enhance their own wealth. Might similar situations have occurred in the ancient past? Or are the recent cases considered above phenomena unique to capitalism? The information for most of the above cases was obtained from newspapers and magazine accounts of these current events, rather than from the academic literature. These recent and ongoing cases can serve as heuristic entryways into the in-depth consideration of archaeological cases. That is followed by a return to present hazard preparedness conditions toward the end of the chapter.

Sixth-Century Archaeological Cases: Effects and Inequality Compared, Pre- and Post-disasters

The examples that follow describe societies stressed to varying degrees by the most severe climatic downturn of the past twenty-five hundred years (Sigl et al. 2015). The cause was two closely spaced immense Plinian explosive volcanic eruptions, in 535 and 539 CE. The first was from at a high latitude in the northern hemisphere, from a yet-unknown source. The second was even greater, slightly north of the equator, evidently from the Ilopango Volcano in El Salvador (Oppenheimer 2011), an eruption I first discovered in 1969 in Chalchupa, El Salvador (Sheets 1976). The two eruptions caused great dislocations in atmospheric circulation, the water cycle (evaporation from water and falling precipitation), and cooling of the earth by fine volcanic ash reflecting sunlight and especially by sulfur aerosols. The strongest effects lasted a decade or two and gradually diminished. Some societies with dense populations living in marginal areas and relying on frost-sensitive crops suffered greatly and collapsed—for example, Teotihuacan, and the Wei dynasty in China (Houston 2000). Others survived but were fundamentally altered, such as Scandinavia (see chapter 4 in this volume, and Graslund and Price 2012). Societies in tropical areas were weakened to different degrees, allowing the slightly stronger to take advantage of the weaker and to prosper (e.g., various Maya city-states). Here, I explore the effects of these extreme environmental downturns on ancient societies in different parts of the world. I show how they coped with the stresses with quite different degrees of success or failure and emphasize the implications for inequalities in social, economic, and political domains.

The proximal, distal, and worldwide effects of the greatest of explosive eruptions bear consideration here (Oppenheimer 2011). Most explosive eruptions have the most intensive impacts closest to the volcano and diminish with distance, usually within a few kilometers to dozens of kilometers, taking into account wind direction. Their negative impacts are proximal. Near the volcano, lava flows, pyroclastic flows, lahars (debris flows), and deep deposits of airfall volcanic ash can be highly destructive to flora, fauna, people, and their livelihoods. Winds bias the density of volcanic ash, as they push the eruptive column downwind. The ejecta of most explosive eruptions do not push vertically above the tropopause (the boundary between the lower atmosphere and the stratosphere), often at about ten kilometers in height.

In contrast, the colossal explosive eruptions, such as the two under consideration here, blast great amounts of fine volcanic ash and sulfur aerosols above the tropopause and into the stratosphere (Oppenheimer 2011). Once in the stratosphere, the tephra and sulfur circulate around the world. Latitude is a crucial variable. If the volcano is located at high latitude, exemplified here with the 535 CE eruption (Sigl et al. 2015), then the distal distribution stays in that hemisphere. If the eruption is tropical in latitude, the worldwide distribution is in both hemispheres, as happened in the 539 CE eruption. The relative amounts of sulfur in ice cores in Antarctica versus Greenland from a tropical mega-eruption can indicate whether the source is north or south of the equator. The sulfur spike from the 539 CE eruption is slightly stronger in Greenland than in Antarctica, indicating a source somewhat north of the equator (Sigl et al. 2015). What is important here is that proximity to the source is not the relevant factor for how intense the stress was for a society anywhere in the world. Rather, a society thousands of miles away in a semi-arid environment relying on crops that are frost sensitive prior to the eruption would have been highly vulnerable. In contrast, a society in a wet tropical environment only hundreds of miles away can suffer a similar decline in temperature and moisture, but not to the point of devastating food production.

The former, in a climatically vulnerable environment, applies to Teotihuacan's semi-arid environment, above seven thousand feet in elevation, just below the usual frost line. The former also applies to the collapse of the Wei dynasty in northern China in the mid-sixth century (Houston 2000). The Wei dynasty was similar to Teotihuacan in having a dense population in a semi-arid environment vulnerable to cold summers. The latter, the buffered environment, applies to the lowland Maya of the Yucatan

Peninsula. Although the Maya lowlands are much closer to Ilopango Volcano, they did not suffer from the direct proximal effects of deep tephra deposits, and they were only moderately stressed by the climatic downturn. Their lowland tropical moist climate buffered the worldwide stresses of cold and diminished precipitation, while Teotihuacan's precariousness led to its demise. Although the stresses were essentially the same among Maya city-states in the central Maya lowlands, they did not all react in the same way, with markedly different consequences. None of the three Maya cities collapsed like Teotihuacan or the Wei, but they did not handle the stresses equally, for discernible reasons. After dealing with Teotihuacan, I look at three city-states, Tikal, Caracol, and Calakmul. All three were in warm, wet tropical lowland environments, and therefore a lowering of temperature and precipitation would not have been as drastic as the effects that devastated Teotihuacan. However, the differences in adaptations among the three led to very different outcomes, as documented by Dahlin and Chase (2014). After describing these outcomes, I then explore changes in inequalities among the Maya.

Teotihuacan was the biggest and most highly organized ancient city in the early first millennium in Mesoamerica, and even the New World, from about 100 BCE to 550 CE (Cowgill 2015, 1). Its population was somewhere between 100,000 and 200,000, with an additional 300,000 people under its control or influence in the general area. It was organized in a grid system of roads oriented on a major avenue lined with dozens of pyramids with temples on top. The wealthier homes near the major avenue were luxurious and richly frescoed. The residences of the majority of the common people consisted of thousands of substantial, well-built apartment complexes. Insubstantial structures housed less than 15 percent of the people (Cowgill 2015, 246). The nature of rulership in Teotihuacan has been a puzzle for archaeologists for decades, because it apparently was so different from most Mesoamerican civilizations. In contrast to the Maya, there are no sculptures or depictions of individual rulers. Of course, there must have been rulers, but they did not commemorate themselves in any durable medium. The influence of Teotihuacan stretched from western through southern Mexico and Yucatan into Guatemala, Belize, Honduras, and even into El Salvador (Cowgill 2001).

Teotihuacan had strikingly low wealth disparities prior to the sixth-century climatic crisis, but following its collapse, later societies displayed dramatic inequality. Smith (2018) argues that Teotihuacan had no underclass, in his slightly exaggerated article titled "In This Ancient City, Even Commoners Lived in Palaces." The article argues that the inequalities within the city were minimal. The vast majority of people lived in substantially constructed apartments with white lime-plastered floors, ornamented roofs, and spacious rooms with porches. Smith (2018) convincingly states that the city's residents lived far more economically equal lives than in any other Mesoamerican civilization. A normal Teotihuacan family dwelling was about 200 square meters (2,153 square feet), while during the later Aztec period (1450–1500 CE) a commoner house was only about 25 square meters (215 square feet). To quantify wealth inequality, Smith uses the Gini index, which ranges from 0, meaning complete equality, to 1, indicating all wealth is concentrated in only one household or segment of society. Teotihuacan's Gini index was 0.12, an extraordinarily low level of wealth inequality for any civilization past or present. It compares to the Aztecs at 0.3 to 0.4. Mexico today lies at 0.75 and the United States at 0.8 (see Kohler and Smith [2018] for a detailed explanation of the use of Gini coefficients to describe wealth disparities in the past).

The period following the collapse of Teotihuacan is called the Epiclassic, from about 550 to 850 CE (Cowgill 2015, 239). Although remnant populations still lived in the city, the powerful state had dissolved, and the remaining people created no new civic or ceremonial structures (Cowgill 2015, 240). There are insufficient data to assess the degree of inequality in this small remnant group.

Following the collapse of Teotihuacan, Tula was the next dominant city in the Basin of Mexico area. Tula began during the Epiclassic period, about when Teotihuacan was collapsing, and grew to its apex about four centuries later (Healan 2001, 776). Tula was a sizable city. It reached its peak population from 900 to 1200 CE, with a population perhaps as high as sixty thousand (Healan 2001, 776). Although a Gini index has not been calculated for Tula Grande, wealth disparities are quite evident. Healan (1989) notes the elegance of the central palace Palacio Quemado and the humble architecture of the commoners. The relationship between the demise of Teotihuacan and the rise of Tula is not clear, but the end result is. Following Tula, the wealth disparities of the Aztecs are many times greater than that of Teotihuacan, and they increased even more significantly in the colonial period, after the Spanish conquest. Inequality in Mexico today continues to increase, almost to that of the United States.

Prior to the sixth century Tikal was tremendously successful as the dominant city-state in the central lowlands of Guatemala's Peten (Harrison 2001). It thrived as a trading center and developed monumental architecture, sculpture, an innovative art style, hieroglyphics, and calendric notations. The mid-sixth-century climatic downturn presumably lowered both temperature and precipitation, but not so much that agricultural productivity failed, although it would have declined substantially. There is no evidence that Tikal responded to the stresses in an organized or systematic way (Dahlin and Chase 2014). They did not adjust their adaptation by terracing hill slopes to increase moisture retention, initiating marketing systems, or increasing alliances. Tikal had large intra-site causeways linking pyramid complexes, but no causeways extending out of the site's center that could have been used for food transport and material exchanges. Tikal lost the nearby city-state of Naranjo as an ally just a few years into the environmental downturn (Dahlin and Chase 2014), a sign of the difficulties to come. A little more than two decades after the downturn began, in 562 CE Tikal was defeated by their rivals Caracol and Calakmul (Dahlin and Chase 2014, 137). Tikal lost political independence, as the conquerors occupied the city and turned it into a vassal state for over a century. When Tikal regained its independence, its royals commissioned great construction of pyramids, temples, causeways, and palaces of unprecedented size. Haviland's (1967) analysis of skeletal material showed that commoners' diets worsened dramatically in the centuries after the environmental downturn, which I interpret as a proxy for increased inequality.

Dahlin and Chase (2014) argue that in contrast to Tikal, Caracol and Calakmul responded in innovative ways to the stress. Caracol improved food production by constructing water storage and distribution facilities, increased terracing, and constructed an elaborate road network to facilitate communication and transport. Terracing hillsides decreases erosion and increases water infiltration. Caracol was a relatively small center until it gained independence from Tikal by the time of the Star War of 562 CE. By the mid-seventh century it had increased in population by some five times (Dahlin and Chase 2014, 140). Both Caracol and Calakmul had centrally directed solar marketing systems that facilitated redistribution of goods (Dahlin and Chase 2014). There is no evidence that Tikal had such a system. In addition to three intra-site causeways, Calakmul had long inter-site causeways reaching dozens of kilometers in various directions. They would have been useful in transporting agricultural production from surrounding areas into the central site and its marketplace. The network of roads would have provided access to perennial wetlands to the northeast and northwest that would have been less affected by drought than upland areas. Calakmul perhaps gained access to or control of the Rio Hondo, an important river and floodplain nearby. If they did, that would have opened rather easy access to the productivity of raised fields near the Caribbean (Dahlin and Chase 2014, 151). Calakmul also became more aggressive in conquering nearby settlements or pressuring them to provide tribute. Calakmul's road system was more regional, while that of Caracol was more internal. The differing responses to the same powerful stresses are revealing lessons of the importance of leadership, and the nature of social and infrastructural networks, when disaster strikes. A simple physical cause and cultural effect model is insufficient and inappropriate. The three cities shared the same basic culture and cultigens, but significant variations played major roles in their divergent paths under the stress. Tikal had a socially produced vulnerability to the extreme event, while the other two cities had or created buffering mechanisms.

Looking internally at Calakmul and Caracol, the disparities of wealth increased by the mid-sixth century, as populations grew and the royals needed larger elite bureaucracies for administration, construction, and religious purposes. Tikal followed that same increase in inequality, but it was delayed for a century, until it achieved independence.

The impact of the sixth-century climatic crisis on Scandinavia was considerable. Fortunately, much is known about local conditions prior to the mid-sixth century and for centuries afterward. Viewed from the south, the late Roman Empire feared the "barbarians" threatening them from northern Europe (Noble 2006) and sent considerable amounts of gold to placate them. The Scandinavian gold hoards have been explained in two different ways: as caches hidden temporarily and intended for future use, and as supernatural means of connecting with the gods (Hedeager 2008). I suspect some of them were emergency caches when people realized they could not continue in their households under the extreme stress but hoped to return if conditions ameliorated. The fifth and sixth centuries are within the Migration period, when massive ethnolinguistic populations were on the move in Eurasia, and especially Germanic peoples in northern Europe (Noble 2006). Scandinavia prior to the mid-sixth-century stress had only slight disparities in wealth among households, as all engaged in cultivation of seed crops and animal husbandry involving cattle, sheep, and pigs (Graslund and Price 2012). However, the crisis allowed the slightly more wealthy households to take over the poorer ones. Graslund and Price (2012) document the Scandinavian case in detail and in the long time range. The numbers of households increased slowly from 2000 BCE until the first century BCE and then more rapidly until the sixth century CE. Then, about 75 percent of the villages in Sweden were abandoned during the mid-sixth century, constituting "the greatest change in settlement patterns in Sweden for 6000 years" (Graslund and Price 2012, 432). They argue that the "new structures of power" and the great expansion of land owned by elites in the Scandinavian late Iron Age derived from people taking advantage of the sixth-century climatic crisis. The demographic decline was even greater in areas of southern Norway, where the dated burials after the stress ameliorated diminished by 90 to 95 percent. The authors ingeniously relate the devastating stresses to the Norse mythology of the "Fimbulwinter," which describes severe winter with no summer that lasted for years. The Fimbulwinter serves as the warning of the "Ragnarok," which is the destruction of the entire world and all its inhabitants, even including the gods (Löwenborg 2012; Price and Graslund 2015).

Arenal, Costa Rica, and the Lack of Inequalities

Is there a case where disasters did not enhance socioeconomic inequality? The answer is yes, there is one in western Costa Rica with the multiple eruptions of Arenal Volcano and the residents affected, with their responses (Sheets and McKee 1994). Societies were egalitarian before and after the ten big eruptions that affected our research area, some twenty to thirty kilometers downwind to the east of the volcano. I will explore how and why these early hunter-gatherers and later villagers avoided disparities in wealth, power, and social prestige for sixty-five hundred years. The coping behaviors and long-term results are so dramatically different from the abovementioned ancient and modern cases that the interactions among the natural environment, volcanism, and the ancient cultures warrant detailed consideration here.

Polly Wiessner (2002) provides insights into how cultures can maintain egalitarian structures for hundreds of years. She studied 110 Enga tribes in Papua New Guinea and found that they varied considerably in how the maintained their egalitarian organizations over many generations. Wiessner explains how the sophisticated egalitarian structures benefit small-scale societies politically and economically. She notes the ethos of egalitarian societies rests in redistribution and measured generosity while discouraging differential accumulations of wealth. In addition, she documented the introduction of the sweet potato and how it greatly increased pig production, human demographic growth, overpopulation, and ultimately the institutionalization of inequality.

Wiessner's insights into how small-scale societies can maintain egalitarian organizations over long periods of time may apply well to thousands of years of human occupation of the Arenal area of Costa Rica. In the beginnings of my research to study human-volcanological interactions in the early 1980s, I quickly discovered that archaeology would be inhibited by working too close to Arenal Volcano, because the tephra layers were so thick we would have to excavate many meters down to encounter cultural remains. I also quickly learned that volcanology would be inhibited by working too far away, even though the archaeological discoveries would be abundant. At distances beyond thirty kilometers, the tephra layers are thin, mixed, or nonexistent, thus inadequate to study volcanic-human interactions. The "sweet zone" to integrate volcanology with archaeology turned out to be from fifteen to thirty kilometers west and downwind from the volcano. Many of the biggest eruptions left identifiable tephra layers intermixed with cultural materials and paleosols in that zone, yet were accessible by excavations in the range of two to four meters deep. Had we decided to focus our research to the northwest or southwest of the volcano, the "sweet zones" would have been much closer to Arenal Volcano, probably less than ten kilometers, due to the consistency of the winds from the east (figure 3.1).

The research area drapes over the continental divide, to include Laguna Arenal and Arenal Volcano on the Caribbean drainage to the east and the Pacific drainage to the west (figure 3.1). Current meteorological conditions seem to be similar to ancient ones (Sheets and McKee 1994). Presently the area around the volcano receives a mean of over 6,000 millimeters of annual precipitation (giving new meaning to the term "mean" precipitation), while at Cañas on the other end of the area, in the Pacific drainage, only 1,300 millimeters of precipitation falls annually on average. At ten degrees north of the equator and with the variable topography, the hot and dry area around Cañas is marginal for agriculture without irrigation. Above that area in elevation, the range of mean precipitation is 1,400 to 2,000

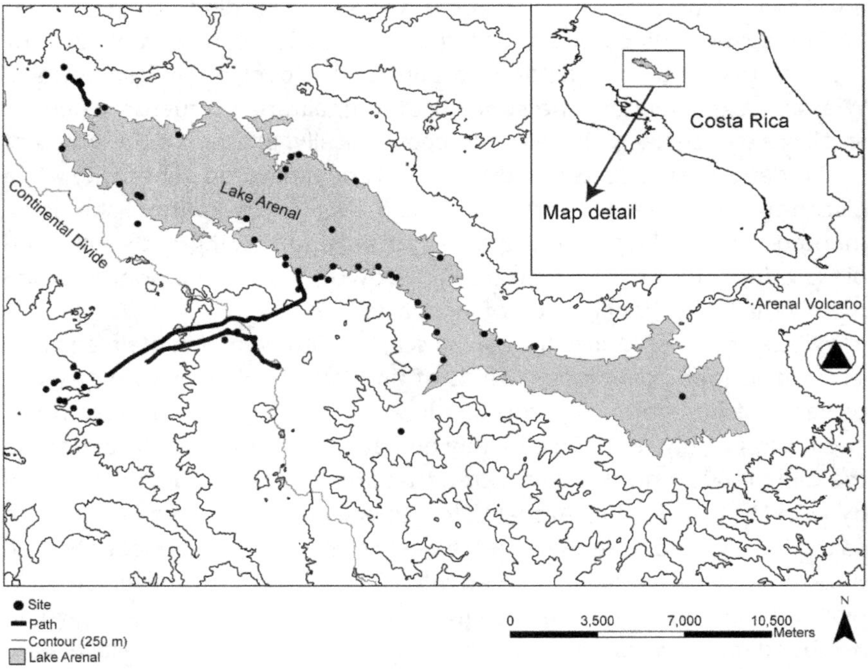

Figure 3.1. Map of the Arenal research area. Each dot is a confirmed and recorded archaeological site. The site in the middle of the lake is an island used for burials. Map by and provided courtesy of Rachel Egan.

millimeters and is suitable for seed crop agriculture without irrigation. However, on the Caribbean side of the divide, in the wetter areas, the precipitation exceeds evapotranspiration for many months. Therefore, the soils are saturated and hence anaerobic and not suited for most cultigens. Malanga (*Xanthosoma*) does grow well in saturated soils, but seed crops do not. An important caveat here is that even during the Silencio phase (see below), when one could expect seed crop agriculture to be at its peak, maize composed less than 12 percent of the diet (Sheets and McKee 1994, 321). This indicates that people in their settled villages continued to exploit the abundant wild foods of their tropical rainforest environment for the bulk of their diets.

Melson (1994) began studying the 1968 explosive eruption of Arenal Volcano shortly after it occurred, and he related it to the major explosive eruptions in the ancient past. The volcanic record of Arenal is summarized on the webpage of the Smithsonian Institution, National Museum of Natural History ("Global Volcanism Program" 2018). A total of twenty-eight explosive eruptions have been documented over a span of 7,000 years, for an average periodicity of 250 years. All have VEIs (volcanic explosivity index) of 4, of considerable magnitude, unless otherwise stated here. Arenal Volcano did not exist prior to 5000 BCE, making it one of the world's younger and more active volcanos. An unknown number of smaller eruptions must have occurred, but no tephra deposits have yet been identified and dated.

Following is an integration of the phases of human occupation in the Arenal-Tilaran research area with the explosive eruptions of Arenal Volcano and the soils that developed between eruptions. The Clovis style projectile point found along the Laguna Arenal shore is evidence of human occupation at about 11,000 BCE (Sheets and McKee 1994), about six millennia before Arenal Volcano erupted for the first time. Apparently, hunter-gatherers continued to occupy the area throughout the Paleo-Indian and Archaic periods. The two earliest Arenal eruptions, about 5060 and 4450 BCE ("Global Volcanism Program" 2018) would have severely impacted flora and fauna and required surviving people to evacuate, at least for a few decades. As the evacuees had been exploiting wild food resources, with few domesticated species, their relocation would not have been onerous. Population densities apparently were very low.

The earliest evidence we have for Archaic occupation is the Fortuna phase, 4000–3000 BCE, for which we found a campsite with two hearths, evidence of stone tool manufacture, volcanic stones used for boiling, and surface finds of lithics (Sheets and McKee 1994). During that millennium, Arenal erupted twice, 3900 and 3350 BCE, and the adjoining Cerro Chato erupted once, at 3190 BCE. Although we do not have direct stratigraphic associations of tephra with the excavated site, we can be confident that all three eruptions necessitated abandonments because of devastated life support capacity of the environment, even though by this time a slight reliance on a domesticated species or two may have emerged.

Our archaeological record has an unfortunate gap from 3000 to 2000 BCE, during which the transition from the high mobility of the Archaic hunter-gatherers shifted to Formative villages with ceramics. Because ceramics are heavy and fragile, I believe the villages were largely to completely sedentary. Arenal contributed two eruptions, 2800 and 2250 BCE, with predictable consequences, but during this span, we have no detailed cultural data.

The Tronadora phase dates from 2000 to 500 BCE. The Tronadora Vieja site provided numerous circular houses, both prior to and after Arenal's Unit 61 eruption of 1450 BCE (Sheets and McKee 1994, 314). Recovery from the eruption apparently was rapid, perhaps a few decades, and there are no indications of inequality in housing or artifacts, either before or after the eruption. A very black, humic-rich soil developed out of and on top of that eruption in the centuries before the next eruption. Ceramics were sophisticated and decorated by incising and painting, with *tecomate* shapes predominating. No changes in architecture or artifacts were detected, indicating the possibility that the descendants of the pre-eruption villagers were the ones who moved back in. However, there is no definitive evidence for this. Burials were secondary, in small rectangular pits outside the houses.

The Arenal phase began at 500 BCE and ended at 600 CE (Sheets and McKee 1994). It marked the densest populations in the research area, with about ten people per square kilometer. However, compared to populations in chiefdoms in Panama–Costa Rica, and especially with the states in Mesoamerica, this population density is low indeed. Arenal Volcano erupted five times during the phase (380 BCE, 270 BCE, 170 BCE, 400 CE, and 550 CE). The tephra deposits from the earlier four eruptions were not thick enough in our area to be individually discernable. Bioturbation and soil formation were sufficient to mix them. Each of them probably did not necessitate an outmigration of inhabitants seeking refuge from this area, although the ashfalls would have been stressful for flora, fauna, and people. Excavations a few kilometers closer to the volcano would probably reveal the individual tephra layers and would be areas sufficiently devastated to require outmigration until ecological recovery occurred. One of the more prominent paleosols in the sequence (Unit 54) developed at the end of this phase, in the four centuries up to 650 CE, when it was buried by a tephra (see below). Individual villages are about the same size as those in the preceding phase, of about fifty to one hundred people. The number of sites has doubled, but the sizes of them, and their egalitarian natures, have not changed.

Certainly, the most significant religious culture change in the entire occupation sequence occurred at about 500 BCE. That change does not correlate with any eruption. Instead of burying their dead adjacent to their homes, the villages initiated communal graveyards and situated them at a distance. The distances varied from about one to fourteen kilometers. People traveling to and from cemeteries walked a precise and straight-as-possible procession route, in spite of topography. They walked single file, as the actual path surface was only a half meter wide. On slopes where path erosion occurred, the decades and centuries of use entrenched the paths, often to a few meters deep. If an ethnographic analog might be relevant, the traditional Cuna of Panama bury their dead at a distance from their village and make pilgrimages when they need to get in contact with the spirit of the deceased (Sheets 2009). The Cuna believe the spirits are bothered by barking dogs and crying babies and therefore appreciate the quiet that comes from the distance. The spirits are powerful and therefore are best dealt with when people want or need to take the trip, instead of having them around their home all the time and having to deal with them when they would rather not.

Other culture changes are detectable from the previous phase but are modest, as *tecomate*-shaped vessels declined, while necked jars increased. Styles of decoration changed somewhat, from deeply incised borders of bichrome painting and some shell impressions, to finer incising with black-on-red painting, and some resist decoration. Housing did not change from the Tronadora phase, nor within the Arenal phase. Houses remained circular, and people continued to use boiling stones and some ceramic vessels in cooking. Ground-stone artifacts became more common and include three-legged metates and overhanging bar manos, and celts. What is important here is that no differentiation/inequality has been found in housing, artifacts, or burials within this period.

In the previous Tronadora phase, no clear evidence was discovered to ascertain if the re-settlers after an evacuation were descendants of the original occupants of a village or simply were opportunistic people in search of a suitable village location. Fortunately, excavations at the Arenal phase Cañales site encountered evidence that the re-settlers were descendants of the earlier residents (Sheets 2008). The egalitarian village on the south shore of Laguna Arenal was struck by a particularly deep deposit of volcanic ash during the Arenal phase, which would have necessitated abandonment. The stratigraphy presented in three illustrations (figures 2, 3, and 4 in Sheets 2008) indicate that the processional path to the communal graveyard was used for hundreds of years before and then after the eruption. The path extends from the village at 540-meter elevation, up over mountainous terrain at 970 meters, and then down through dissected topography to the graveyard at 500 meters, for a distance of 11 kilometers. Reuse of the path also occurred after the smaller eruptions. All eruptions would obscure the path by a new blanket of volcanic ash, and this is especially true of the biggest of eruptions. For someone not already familiar with the path, it would be challenging to locate it. Moreover, and most importantly, if the re-settlers were mere opportunists without relationships to the former villagers, they would not conduct pilgrimages to a cemetery that had nothing to do with their ancestors. The re-settlers must have been kin to the earlier residents. And it is possible that reconnecting with the spirits of their ancestors was a primary motivation to re-occupation of their village (Sheets 2008). Project members examined all architectural and artifactual categories for evidence of inequality and found none, with only one exception. In the Sitio Bolivar cemetery, burial practices were identical throughout, with the exception of complete vessels being sacrificed atop and already broken vessels scattered over the graves slightly downslope (Hoopes and Chenault 1994). At most, this could indicate some intra-community differentiation. Yet, the overall assessment is that the society was fundamentally egalitarian.

The Silencio phase (600–1300 CE) witnessed a decline in population to about half of that of the previous period, that is, back to about the population of the Tronadora phase (Sheets and McKee 1994). The principal change in ceramics is the introduction of polychromes. Chipped and ground stone assemblages showed virtually no change. The tradition of villages establishing communal cemeteries at considerable distances con-

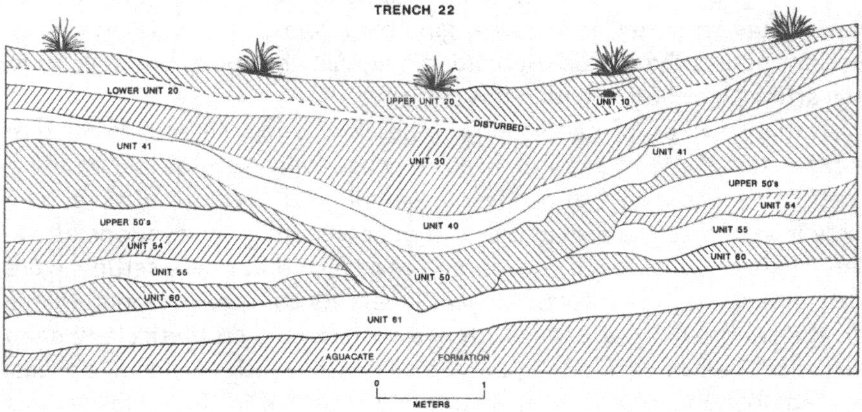

Figure 3.2. Volcanic and soils stratigraphy in Trench 22, with processional footpath eroded into the layers of volcanic ash and soils. Figure created by the author.

tinued. The style of inhumations changed considerably from the primary burial covered with river rocks in the Arenal phase to more deep burials and creating a stone cist or box for the primary burial. The stones used were the flat-fracturing *lajas* that occurred in a few places at significant distances from cemeteries. Those distances were traversed single file along set pathways that stretched many kilometers. The processional pathways from the Silencio cemetery extend to villages well to the west and southwest and well to the east. It is of great significance that villages shared the same cemetery, even though they lived separated by considerable distances. The principal hazard of an eastern village is an eruption from Arenal volcano, as that village would be only about fifteen kilometers away. The principal hazard of a village well down on the Pacific drainage would be drought. The relationships formed from communal use may have assisted people from one end under stress to take refuge in a village at the other end, an example of sophisticated risk perception and management. Cemetery associations provided a form of insurance or assurance in case of disaster. Because villages are so small, they could not be endogamous for many generations, and the extended ceremonies in the shared Silencio cemetery must have provided opportunities for liaisons to form.

Arenal Volcano erupted five times during the Silencio phase (650, 700, 750, and twice in quick succession ca. 1100 and 1250 CE). Three paleosols developed during that sequence, one early (Unit 53), and two prominent

Illustration 3.1. Tom Sever (*left*) and Payson Sheets pointing out two ancient footpaths descending a hill. They date to 600–1300 CE. Photo by the author.

ones later (Units 50 and 30). Cemetery and path use were well established prior to that double eruption, but they must have had sufficient impact that at least villagers living east of the cemetery had to flee and seek refuge to the west, likely in their partner village and perhaps to other areas. Those eruptions were so closely spaced that we do not detect even the beginnings of a soil forming atop the first one. Their combined thicknesses indicate that villages in the "sweet zone" would also have to be abandoned, perhaps for a few decades. Both cemetery use and path use were resumed after the eruption. The re-occupants in the eastern village resumed use of the exact same path to the cemetery, in spite of it having been deeply buried by the tephras and therefore difficult to detect. As with the above example with the Cañales village, I believe this is reliable evidence that the people returning to that eastern village were the same people who abandoned it or perhaps a generation later. If people reestablishing a village had no relation to former residents, but simply decided that would be a nice location in which to settle, they would not find and follow a processional path to a cemetery that did not contain their deceased and the spirits of their deceased. The determination to reoccupy a devastated area is reminiscent of community resilience after the Paricutin eruption in Mexico (Nolan 1979).

The Tilaran phase (1300–1500 CE) marks the final pre-Columbian occupation of the area. It witnessed a considerable decline in population, as the main settlement unit shifted from villages to hamlets widely dispersed across the countryside (Sheets and McKee 1994). The dominant cultural affiliations indicated by ceramics during the earlier phases was to the Pacific side, but those changed in this phase toward the central highlands and Caribbean drainage. The quality of ceramics in techniques and in decoration has deteriorated, and nothing is known from this area in interments. It appears the area was largely depopulated prior to the arrival of the Spanish. Arenal Volcano erupted in a big way about 1500 CE (Unit 20) and then with a relatively small eruption a few decades later. That thick tephra layer is very useful throughout the area, as it stratigraphically isolates pre-Columbian phenomena from colonial and later phenomena.

The multiple eruptions of Arenal over thousands of years brings up the question of oral history. Are the time gaps between eruptions too long for people to have maintained knowledge about the hazards? Russell Blong (1982) documented the oral histories of peoples in Papua New Guinea passing down strikingly detailed accounts of a volcanic eruption three hundred years earlier. That would be over some fifteen generations. The groups called it a "time of darkness," because the tephra blocked sunlight for days. People even remembered the depths of tephra quite accurately. Patrick Nunn's book (2018), *The Edge of Memory*, documents the rise in sea levels in twenty-one places around Australia some seven thousand years ago. Landmarks and sacred places were inundated, yet the knowledge about them was maintained by song, dance, and public performance for hundreds of generations. Krajick (2005) summarized many cases of societies maintaining knowledge of precursors, extreme events, and suitable anticipatory behavior around the world, for hundreds and thousands of years. Most often, the explanations of the extreme events were supernatural. For example, a battle between the sky deity (thunderbird) and the sea deity (whale) causes a tsunami on the coast near Seattle, and people should avoid shore locations where devastations had occurred in the past. In light of these publications, the abilities of ancient Arenal peoples to maintain accurate geo-ecological knowledge during their occupation of the impacted area should not be in doubt. That presumed sophistication was maintained within an egalitarian social order, with minimal inequality, for thousands of years. That success ended abruptly in the Arenal area, as with so many other areas of the world, when European colonists arrived (Riede 2017).

The native population densities in the Arenal area declined considerably in the centuries prior to the Spanish Conquest, to the point that very few settlements dating to the final Tilaran phase could be found in the area (Sheets and McKee 1994). Not only are the numbers of settlements drastically reduced, they no longer are villages, but just dispersed households. Diseases introduced by the Spanish further reduced native populations to about zero, and the area remained depopulated during the seventeenth to nineteenth centuries. Costa Ricans, of European descent, colonized the area during the late nineteenth and early twentieth centuries, largely for ranching. Geologists in the twentieth century knew that Arenal was a volcano, but the local Costa Ricans did not, and they were greatly surprised by the explosive eruption of 1968 (Melson 1994; "Global Volcanism Program" 2018). Because the precursors were not understood, nearby settlers remained in their homes and were killed by lava bombs and pyroclastic flows. More distant Costa Ricans drove jeeps into the area to try to help people, but they also did not understand the dangers, and many were killed by pyroclastic flows. They were asphyxiated and burned, and their gas tanks exploded. The loss of native traditional environmental knowledge resulted in almost a hundred deaths.

Can a Society Become Less Unequal (More Equal) after an Extreme Event?

I believe the Ancient Puebloans in the US Southwest provide an answer of yes. Ancient Puebloans in the Four Corners area began living sedentary lives in agriculturally based tiny to large villages in the Basketmaker III period (Lekson 2008, 65). Puebloan settlements evinced no evidence of hierarchical organizations, political or economic, in this period, from about 400 to about 750 CE. They were egalitarian in organization (my interpretations of data in Kantner 2008 and Lekson 2008). The environment then, and now, is semi-arid and relatively high in elevation (4,000–7,000 feet). Droughts are common in the area, and extended droughts have, and had, deleterious effects on rain-fed agriculture.

The subsequent period, Pueblo I, 700–900 CE, was a particularly dynamic one in the Southwest (Kantner 2008). Moderate to quite large villages, with up to 150 structures, formed and were occupied for short periods of one to two generations (Lekson 2008). Some of the larger villages evidently evince nascent hierarchy in the form of a larger residential structure of a leader, the beginnings of ranking in society.

It is during the Pueblo II period (900–1150 CE) that the Puebloan Southwest reached its apex in size of settlements and in political, economic, and social inequality. The massive multistory structures in Chaco Canyon and the dozens of Great House outliers burst upon the scene. Lekson (2008, 205) considers it a city with elites living in palaces. The Great Houses probably were subsidiary elite palaces and were widely scattered across a vast landscape. The prehistoric Southwest had never seen such inequality in Puebloan society—political, economic, or social—and it was never seen to that degree later.

During the Pueblo III period (1150–1300 CE) the largest sites were significantly smaller than the huge ones in the previous period (Lekson 2008), but they were impressive and clearly non-egalitarian. Levels of violence escalated as villages attacked other villages, cannibalism was practiced, and elites lost their power to maintain the social order (Lekson 2008, 160). As Lekson notes, some migrations from the Four Corners region southward to the Rio Grande area of northern New Mexico occurred throughout the period.

The Pueblo IV period that begins in 1300 CE followed four centuries of hierarchical settlements exemplified by Chaco and its regional system and then Aztec in New Mexico. Lekson (2008, 190–200) argues that Pueblo IV peoples deliberately organized against such hierarchy. He states (Lekson 2008, 197), "During Pueblo IV, people made hard decisions to re-form their societies after a history of unhappiness, war, hierarchies, and environmental catastrophes. They created societies that avoided hierarchy." The remaining people living in the Four Corners area abandoned it, as people made a smart move into New Mexico, along the Rio Grande, which provided reliable water. The great drought during the last two decades of the thirteenth century (Kantner 2004, 200) was too much of an additional stressor, a natural disaster, for the Ancestral Puebloans relying on rainfall. Cordell (1984, 384) notes that the drought from 1276 to 1299 "corresponds strikingly well with the abandonment of the Mesa Verde region." Kantner (2008, 200) describes the drought as "a precipitous drop in rainfall the likes of which had no precedent in the region's human history." Puebloans made deliberate decisions to decrease inequality, to avoid past experience with hierarchical society, and that decision has stuck. Abundant oral history of the terrible times, and the need to avoid hierarchy, still exists among Puebloans today (Kantner 2008; Lekson 2008).

Conclusions

In a discouraging number of examples above, when extreme events cause stresses on societies, those people who survive them with more resources take advantage of those with less. This applies to capitalist and non-capitalist societies, in recent and ancient times. Today, it would take a politician with extraordinary courage to initiate legislation prior to extreme events to ensure that resources would be equitably distributed. For a bill to pass in the US House and the Senate, a majority would be necessary in both chambers, and that is not foreseeable even in the far distant future.

The late eighteenth-century adage that "all men are created equal" is inspirational if it were true. However, considerable disparities in wealth and power existed at that time and have continued to the present day. At that time "men" referred to whites, did not include women, and obviously excluded all men and women brought from Africa as slaves, as well as all native populations already in the New World. Thus, the social inequality that exists prior to disasters is enhanced by the extreme events, in striking contrast to the egalitarian villagers of ancient Costa Rica. Therefore, in our deeply stratified contemporary societies, socially, politically, economically, and in terms of classes, new forms of disaster planning, political organization, and neighborhood functioning could be salutary to the coming disasters. If accompanied by less emphasis on technological fixes and efforts to rebuild in place, then future disasters can be less impactful.

In our decades of research in the Tilaran-Arenal area, we have sought evidence of socioeconomic-political inequalities. We found none in the early phases of occupation by hunter-gatherers in Paleo-Indian and Archaic times. Even when sedentary village life existed, for some four millennia, inequalities were miniscule to undetectable, and the egalitarian structure of society continued.

So what are the factors that contributed to Arenal people's resilience to many volcanic disasters, without enhanced inequality? An obvious one is the egalitarian organization for more than ten thousand years, from Paleo-Indian times all the way to the Spanish Conquest. Probably inherent in the egalitarian organization were wealth and power leveling mechanisms that were not present in the abovementioned examples. They would have had to be overcome for inequalities to increase following eruptions and their effects and adjustments. The differentials were not inherent in natives prior to any of the disasters, during their need to take refuge, or among the recolonizations. An element of such hunting-and-gathering bands or the later villages that dotted the countryside for some four thousand years is that decision-making was local. The perception of the disaster and the decision to take refuge was at the household level or the band or village, in contrast to complex societies. With the Maya, for instance, major decisions were made by the royals and their elites, and that can take time for the orders to be disseminated and acted upon. Because the royals were the principal liaisons with the deities, a huge natural disaster could be interpreted as a failure of religious belief and the supernatural efficacy of the royals. The loss of the "Mandate of Heaven" by the emperor of the Wei dynasty in mid-sixth-century China is a good example (Houston 2000).

Another key factor in the resilience of Arenal people was their experiencing frequent explosive eruptions. The average periodicity of Arenal's biggest eruptions is 250 years, and that does not include an unknown number of smaller eruptions. The time gaps between eruptions are small enough for oral traditions—that is, traditional ecological knowledge—to be passed on for generations and must have been sufficient to inform people as to coping mechanisms to be put into effect right away. Herein is an element that could be applied to present-day complex societies. Today many people are trained to wait for government-sponsored expert help, which during Hurricane Katrina did not materialize. Fortunately, there are some exceptions, where local agencies encourage people to be their own first responders, and this should be greatly expanded. Local training of people who are potentially in harm's way for hurricanes, floods, heat waves, volcanic eruptions, earthquakes, tornadoes, or other extreme events can go a long way in reducing injuries or deaths. This is training beyond that of first responders. It is training of at least some people on a per-neighborhood basis. This neighborhood training is analogous to oral histories of nonliterate groups, where people familiarize themselves with a hazard, an extreme event, and successful reactions to it.

An example that sticks in my mind, which also includes the topic of communication, occurred during the Katrina hurricane disaster in New Orleans. Hundreds of people took refuge on highway overpasses because all areas around them were flooded. When President Bush and FEMA officials flew over them in helicopters, the refugees looked upward but could not communicate because cell phones were out of electricity and the network was down. They desperately needed food and water but were unable to send that message. A miniscule of training could have resolved it: one person could organize a few people to spell out the message "DROP WATER" or "DROP FOOD" by means of their bodies lying down. Had TV footage of that been broadcast worldwide, US officials would have had to respond, promptly. Rather, officials did nothing beyond looking out of the window.

The only skeletal material recovered from our work on the Arenal Project was from the Silencio phase, as that was the only time people were buried in protective stone tombs. The mild acidity of the tropical soils removed all human remains from the other phases. Isotopic analyses indicated maize was only 12 percent of the diet at most, which suggests seed crop agriculture played a minor part of the diet. Most root crops would not have produced well because of soil saturation for so many months. It appears that during the millennia of sedentary villages, people relied heavily on the biodiversity of wild food resources of the tropical rainforest. That must have been advantageous when a village took refuge at a distance, as they could rely heavily on wild foods until they could reoccupy their abandoned villages. Here the obvious lesson for the present is for people to stockpile food and water to be self-sufficient for days or weeks.

Another factor is the low population densities during all phases of occupation, so the numbers of refugees would not drastically swamp the life-support capability of areas surrounding the disaster. Yet another aspect assisting in hazard preparedness is having a social network. An example is provided by the evident alliance between at least two Costa Rican villages facing quite different risks and sharing the Silencio cemetery. The alliances presumably functioned to facilitate refuge from extreme events by distant villagers. Might there be a suggestion for hurricane-prone areas of the US Gulf Coast? Cities such as Gulfport, Tallahassee, Houston, New Orleans, and Corpus Christi could enter into cooperative agreements to house refugees and provide quick and organized disaster relief, instead of doing it on an ad hoc basis. Houston was gracious to New Orleans refugees after Katrina, but Houstonians received little support from other cities after Hurricane Harvey.

Social networks have documented success in providing assistance during extreme events. The intense heat wave that lasted for five days in Chicago in July 1995 did not uniformly kill people of different ethnicities. While controlling for wealth, of the approximately eight hundred people who died, Klinenberg (2002) found that the death rate for Hispanics was markedly less than for whites or blacks. His explanation is that Hispanics had more formal and fictive kin relationships that were of assistance than did whites or blacks. The Hispanics checked on each other to deliver water, food, or fans or provide other assistance.

An important factor in the emergency phase of a disaster is the locus of authority. Centralized authority in complex societies can involve layers of decision makers who often are at significant distances from the actual disaster. The result often is delayed response, inappropriate assistance, or other problems. Small-scale societies such as the Ancient Puebloans and Arenal peoples are decentralized political groups. They can react to the sudden crisis more rapidly because of proximity, political autonomy, and knowledge of local actors and resources (Edwards 2015, 836).

Acknowledgments

I am greatly appreciative of my Colorado colleagues in giving careful reviews of an earlier draft of this chapter. Cathy Cameron, Scott Ortman, and Arthur Joyce were particularly helpful. I am immensely grateful to Felix Riede for all his efforts to organize this book's contributors, for his very useful comments on this essay, and for his skill in editing the chapters in the final volume.

Payson Sheets earned his PhD at the University of Pennsylvania. He is a professor in the Department of Anthropology at the University of Colorado in Boulder. His lifelong research has focused on the interrelationships among human societies and volcanic activity in ancient Central America. His studies include the full range of social complexities, from small-scale egalitarian groups, through ranked societies, to complex civilizations. Societies reacted very differently to the massive sudden stresses of explosive volcanic eruptions in areas proximal to the eruption and in distal areas.

References

Akina, Keli'i. 2018. "A Housing Boom, Then a Volcanic Eruption." *Wall Street Journal*, 20 May 2018. Retrieved 21 May 2018 from https://www.wsj.com/articles/a-housing-boom-then-a-volcanic-eruption-1526841109.

Amandolare, Sarah. 2018. "Windfall: A Catastrophic Hurricane Gave Scientists a Rare Chance to Study How Tropical Forests Will Fare in a Warmer, Stormier Future." *Science* 361 (6407): 1064–65.

Blong, Russell. 1982. *The Time of Darkness*. Seattle: University of Washington Press.

Brown, Phil, Carmen Veliz, Colleen Murphy, Michael Welton, Hector Torres, Zaira Rosario, Akram Alshawakbeh, Jose Cordero, Ingrid Padilla, and John Meeker. 2018.

"Hurricanes and the Environmental Justice Island: Irma and Maria in Puerto Rico." *Environmental Justice* 11 (4): 148–153.

Campo-Flores, Arian, and Andrew Scurria. 2018. "Puerto Rico Recovery Has Long Way to Go." *Wall Street Journal*, 21 September, A3. Retrieved 15 February 2019 from https://blendle.com/i/the-wall-street-journal/puerto-rico-recovery-has-long-way-to-go/bnl-wallstreetjournal840-20180921-3_1?sharer=eyJ2ZXJzaW9uIjoiMSIsInVpZCI6InNoZWV0c3AiLCJpdGVtX2lkIjoiYm5sLXdhbGxzdHJlZXRqb3VybmFsODQwLTIwMTgwOTIxLTNfMSJ9 .

Cordell, Linda. 1984. *Archaeology of the Southwest*. San Diego: Academic Press.

Cordoba Azcarate, Matilde, Idalina Baptista, and Fernando Dominguez Rubio. 2014. "Enclosures within Enclosures and Hurricane Reconstruction in Cancun, Mexico." *City and Society* 26 (1): 96–119.

Cowgill, George. 2001. "Teotihuacan." In *Archaeology of Ancient Mexico and Central America: An Encyclopedia*, edited by Susan Evans and David Webster, 722–31. New York: Garland.

———. 2015. *Ancient Teotihuacan: Early Urbanism in Central Mexico*. Cambridge: Cambridge University Press.

Dahlin, Bruce, and Arlen Chase. 2014. "A Tale of Three Cities: Effects of the AD 536 Event in the Lowland Maya Heartland." In *The Great Maya Droughts in Cultural Context: Case Studies in Resilience and Vulnerability*, edited by Gyles Iannone, 127–55. Boulder: University Press of Colorado.

Dove, Michael R. 2008. "Perception of Volcanic Eruption as Agent of Change on Merapi Volcano, Central Java." *Journal of Volcanology and Geothermal Research* 172 (3–4): 329–37.

Driessen, Jan. 2018. "Santorini Eruption: An Archaeological Investigation of its Distal Impacts on Minoan Crete." *Quaternary International* 499 (April). Retrieved 26 December 2018 from https://www.researchgate.net/publication/324681445_The_Santorini_eruption_An_archaeological_investigation_of_its_distal_impacts_on_Minoan_Crete.

Durana, Alieza. 2017. "Gender Inequality in Puerto Rico Is about to Get Worse." *Slate*, 12 October. Retrieved 25 October 2018 from https://slate.com/human-interest/2017/10/gender-inequality-in-puerto-rico-is-going-to-get-worse-after-hurricane-maria.html.

Edwards, J. H. Y. 2015. "The Structure of Disaster Resilience: A Framework for Simulations and Policy Recommendations." *Natural Hazards and Earth System Sciences* 15: 827–41.

Fernandez, Manny. 2018. "A Year after Hurricane Harvey, Houston's Poorest Neighborhoods Are Slowest to Recover: Texas Has Made Progress Recuperating from Hurricane Harvey, but Low-Income and Minority Residents Have Had a Much Harder Time." *New York Times*, 3 September. Retrieved 3 September 2018 from https://www.nytimes.com/2018/09/03/us/hurricane-harvey-houston.html?action=click&module=Top percent20Stories&pgtype=Homepage.

Friedman, Nicole. 2018. "Florence Exposes Billions of 'Cat Bonds." *Wall Street Journal*, 14 September, B10.

Gibbs, M. 2003. "The Archaeology of Crisis: Shipwreck Survivor Camps in Austalasia." *Historical Archaeology* 37: 128–45.

"Global Volcanism Program." 2018. Smithsonian Institution. Retrieved 4 September 2018 from http://volcano.si.edu/volcano.cfm?vn=345033.

Goodell, Jeff. 2018. "The Perfect Storm: How Climate Change and Wall Street Almost Killed Puerto Rico." *Rolling Stone*, 12 September. Retrieved 17 October 2018 from https://www.rollingstone.com/politics/politics-features/puerto-rico-hurricane-maria-damage-722570/.

Graslund, Bo, and Neil Price. 2012. "Twilight of the Gods? The 'Dust Veil Event' of AD 536 in Critical Perspective." *Antiquity* 86: 428–43.

Harrison, Peter. 2001. "Tikal." In *Archaeology of Ancient Mexico and Central America: An Encyclopedia*, edited by Susan Evans and David Webster, 748–55. New York: Garland.

Haviland, William. 1967. "Stature at Tikal, Guatemala: Implications for Ancient Maya Demography and Social Organization." *American Antiquity* 32: 316–25.

Healan, Dan. 1989. *Tula of the Toltecs: Excavations and Survey*. Iowa City: University of Iowa Press.

———. 2001. "Tula de Hidalgo." In *Archaeology of Ancient Mexico and Central America: An Encyclopedia*, edited by Susan Evans and David Webster, 774–77. New York: Garland.

Hedeager, Lotte. 2008. "Scandinavia before the Viking Age." In *The Viking World*. Routledge Handbooks Online. Retrieved 18 December 2018 from https://www.routledgehandbooks.com/doi/10.4324/9780203412770.ch1.

Hoopes, John, and Mark Chenault. 1994. "Excavations at Sitio Bolivar: A Late Formative Village in the Arenal Basin." In *Archaeology, Volcanism, and Remote Sensing in the Arenal Region, Costa Rica*, edited by Payson Sheets and Brian McKee, 87–105. Austin: University of Texas Press.

Houston, Margaret. 2000. "Chinese Climate, History, and State Stability in AD 536." In *The Years without Summer: Tracing AD 536 and Its Aftermath*, edited by Joel Gunn, 71–78. BAR International Series 872. Oxford: British Archaeological Reports.

Kantner, John. 2008. *Ancient Puebloan Southwest*. Cambridge: Cambridge University Press.

Klinenberg, Eric. 2002. *Heat Wave: A Social Autopsy of Disaster in Chicago*. Chicago: Chicago University Press.

Kohler, Timothy, and Michael Smith, eds. 2018. *Ten Thousand Years of Inequality: The Archaeology of Wealth Differences*. Tucson: University of Arizona Press.

Krajick, Kevin. 2005. "Tracking Myth to Geological Reality." *Science* 310: 762–64.

Lekson, Stephen. 2008. *A History of the Ancient Southwest*. Santa Fe: School for Advanced Research.

Löwenborg, Daniel. "An Iron Age Shock Doctrine—Did the AD 536–7 Event Trigger Large-Scale Social Changes in the Mälaren Valley Area?" *Journal of Archaeology and Ancient History* 4 (2012): 1–29.

Melson, William. 1994. "The Eruption of 1968 and Tephra Stratigraphy of Arenal Volcano." In *Archaeology, Volcanism, and Remote Sensing in the Arenal Region, Costa Rica*, edited by Payson Sheets and Brian McKee, 24–47. Austin: University of Texas Press.

Noble, Thomas. 2006. *From Roman Provinces to Medieval Kingdoms*. London: Routledge.

Nolan, Mary Lee. 1979. "Impact of Parícutin on Five Communities." In *Volcanic Activity and Human Ecology*, edited by Payson D. Sheets and Donald K. Grayson, 293–337. New York: Academic Press.

Nuun, Patrick. 2018. *The Edge of Memory: Ancient Stories, Oral Tradition and the Post-Glacial World*. London: Bloomsbury.

Oppenheimer, Clive. 2011. *Eruptions That Shook the World*. Cambridge: Cambridge University Press.

Price, Neil, and Bo Gräslund. 2015. "Excavating the Fimbulwinter? Archaeology, Geomythology and the Climate Event(s) of AD 536." In *Past Vulnerability: Volcanic Eruptions and Human Vulnerability in Traditional Societies Past and Present*, edited by Felix Riede, 109–32. Aarhus: Aarhus University Press.

Riede, Felix. 2017. "Past-Forwarding Ancient Calamities: Pathways for Making Archaeology Relevant in Disaster Risk Reduction Research." *Humanities* 6 (4): 79.

Robles, Frances. 2018. "$3,700 Generators and $666 Sinks: FEMA Contractors Charged Steep Markups on Puerto Rico Repairs." *New York Times*, 26 November. Retrieved 26 November 2018 from https://www.nytimes.com/2018/11/26/us/fema-puerto-rico-housing-repairs-maria.html.

Romero, Simon. 2018. "Houston Speculators Make a Fast Buck from Storm's Misery: A New Economy Has Arisen in the Suburbs of Houston Battered by Storms: The Buying and Selling of Flooded Homes." *New York Times*, 23 March. Retrieved 4 September 2018 from https://www.nytimes.com/2018/03/23/us/flooding-canyon-gate-hurricane-harvey.html?hp&action=click&pgtype=Homepage&clickSource=nytmm_FadingSlideShow_item&module=photo-spot-region&region=top-news&WT.nav=top-news.

Scanlon, Joseph. 1988. "Winners and Losers: Some Thoughts about the Political Economy of Disaster." *International Journal of Mass Emergencies and Disasters* 6 (1): 47–63

Sheets, Payson. 1976. *Ilopango Volcano and the Maya Protoclassic.* University Museum Studies 9. Carbondale: Southern Illinois University Museum.

———. 2008. "Memoria Social Perdurable: A Pesar de Desastres Volcanicos en el Area de Arenal." *Vinculos* 31: 1–26.

———. 2009. "When the Construction of Meaning Preceded the Meaning of Construction: From Footpaths to Monumental Entrances in Ancient Costa Rica." In *Landscapes of Movement: Trails, Paths, and Roads in Anthropological Perspective*, edited by James Snead, Clark Erickson, and Andrew Darling. Philadelphia: University of Pennsylvania Museum.

Sheets, Payson, and Brian McKee, eds. 1994. *Archaeology, Volcanism, and Remote Sensing in the Arenal Region, Costa Rica.* Austin: University of Texas Press.

Sigl, M., M. Winstrup, J. R. McConnell, K. C. Welten, G. Plunkett, F. Ludlow, U. Büntgen, M. Caffee, N. Chellman, 2015. "Timing and Climate Forcing of Volcanic Eruptions for the Past 2,500 Years." *Nature* 523 (7562): 543–49. Retrieved 10 December 2018 from https://www.nature.com/articles/nature14565.

Smith, Michael. 2018. "In This Ancient City, Even Commoners Lived in Palaces." *Slate*, 3 April. Retrieved 30 August 2018 from https://slate.com/technology/2018/04/teotihuacn-the-ancient-city-upending-archaeologists-assumptions-about-wealth-inequality.html.

Sun, Mengqu, and Leslie Scism. 2018. Insurers Ready to Take On Storm Season. *Wall Street Journal*, 2 July, B1.

Swartz, Mimi. 2018. "What Houston Didn't Learn from Harvey." *New York Times*, Opinion section, 24 August.

Walsh, Mary Williams. 2018. "Millions of Carolina Homes Are at Risk of Flooding: Only 335,000 Have Flood Insurance." *New York Times*, 19 September. Retrieved 19 September 2018 from https://www.nytimes.com/2018/09/19/business/flood-insurance-florence.html .

Wiessner, Polly. 2002. "The Vines of Complexity: Egalitarian Structures and the Institutionalization of Inequality among the Enga." *Current Anthropology* 43 (2): 233–69.

CHAPTER 4

Political Participation and Social Resilience to the 536/540 CE Atmospheric Catastrophe

PETER NEAL PEREGRINE

Summary for Stakeholders

In this chapter I discuss research I have been conducting for the past five years. I have used archaeological data to look across time at social and political traits that fostered resilience to catastrophic climate-related disasters in ancient societies. Looking across time in this way has allowed me to empirically examine change caused by specific disasters, comparing social and political traits before and after the disaster to explore how they affect resilience. What I have found is that societies allowing greater political participation tend to be more resilient to catastrophic climate-related disasters. I suggest that this finding supports current approaches in disaster prevention and management that focus on creating social capital and community engagement. I argue that such efforts should continue to be emphasized as we prepare for more severe climate conditions as a result of global warming. Such efforts might include expanding FEMA's "Whole Community" approach to disaster response and management, perhaps placing a stronger focus on community engagement in disaster planning and the community's role in implementing and evaluating disaster response and management policy. Effort might also be put into social and technological innovations to improve communication between local stakeholders and disaster responders. Finally, these efforts might encourage government, foundation, and stakeholder investment in community-based organizations through both direct funding and the support of innovative approaches to community engagement such as time banking.

Introduction

In previous work I have argued that greater political participation provides a society with greater resilience to climate-related disasters (Peregrine 2017, 2018a, 2018b). In that work I employed data from archaeologically known societies to examine resilience diachronically—that is, comparing social conditions before and after a given disaster. The work was not unique in using archaeological data to examine the societal impact of natural disasters or mechanisms of social resilience (e.g., Cooper and Sheets 2012; Fisher, Hill, and Feinman 2009; Hegmon et al. 2008; Redman 2005), but was unique in doing so using cross-cultural comparison of ancient societies throughout the world. I argued that a strength of cross-cultural comparison using archaeological data is that it allows one to test whether an assumed predictive condition actually precedes its assumed effects—that is, whether a society with the predictive condition empirically changes in the predicted manner over time (Peregrine 2001, 2004; Smith and Peregrine 2012). I suggested that if a predictor of social resilience to climate-related disasters could be identified and applied to societies of varying scales and complexities throughout human history, then there is good reason to believe that it could be used to create interventions applicable today (see also Cooper and Sheets 2012; Hegmon et al. 2008; Redman 2012; Redman and Kinzig 2003; Van de Noort 2011).

The issues I examine in my work are the social conditions that provide the greatest resilience to disaster. Social resilience as I employ the concept refers to the ability of a social system to absorb disturbances while retaining the same basic structures and abilities to respond to further disturbances (see Parry et al. 2007, 37; also Holling 1973, 17). There are many other definitions of resilience or processes involved in resilience (Davidson et al. 2016; see also chapter 8 in this volume). The definition I use is commonly called "resistance" or "adaptability," which refers to the capacity of a social system "to successfully avoid crossing into an undesirable system regime, or to succeed in crossing back into a desirable one" following a disaster (Walker, Holling, Carpenter, and Kinzig 2004). This is opposed to "transformative resilience," which refers to the capacity of a social system "to create a fundamentally new system" following a disaster (Walker, Holling, Carpenter, and Kinzig 2004). A social system with adaptive resilience will tend to return to a state of equilibrium following a disaster similar to that which existed before the disaster (but not identical to it, as a resilient system will change to reduce future risk—see Wisner and Kelman 2015). A social system with transformative resilience will fundamentally change its pre-disaster social system in order to achieve a new equilibrium state.

It must be noted that scalar issues are important to these definitions of resilience, as change is always occurring in social systems. These two forms of resilience focus on what occurs at the system level—does the system change in order to maintain fundamental social structures, or are those structures fundamentally transformed in order to allow the system to continue (Redman and Kinzig 2003)? An assumption I make is that adaptive resilience is preferable to transformative resilience in social systems because adaptive resilience tends to retain existing social structures and relationships (Turner 2010). Thus, adaptive resilience is the focus of my work.

In addition, my work focuses on catastrophic disasters defined by Lorenz and Dittmer (2016, 37) as "devastating events which encompass entire societies," as opposed to less far-reaching "disasters" or localized "emergencies." In the modern world, a "catastrophic" event would be something like Typhoon Haiyan, which hit the Philippines in November of 2013, devastating infrastructure throughout the Visayan Islands, choking the economy of the entire nation, and threatening the stability of the Aquino government (Salazar 2015). In the ancient world, similar impacts might be seen among states, but in the smaller-scale chiefdoms and village societies included in my sample, a "catastrophic" event might be far more localized, impacting only the area of chiefly control or individual villages and their immediate neighbors. This focus on "catastrophic" events is due to the limitations of the archaeological and paleoenvironmental records.

In the next section I offer a review of literature pertinent to the hypothesis that higher levels of political participation provide a heightened level of resilience to catastrophic disasters and a summary of my efforts to test this hypothesis.

Resilience and Political Participation

Two major themes have become the subject of increasing discussion in the literature on social resilience to disasters. The first is the importance of "vulnerability"—that the impact of a disaster is in part socially created because societies frequently build structures (both social and physical) that exacerbate the impact of disaster (e.g., Comfort, Boin, and Demchack 2010; Tierney 2014; Wisner, Blaikie, Cannon, and Davis 2004; see also chapter 5 in this volume). The second is that more "flexible" social structures (again, both social and physical) are more resilient to disasters than more "rigid" social structures (e.g., Aldrich 2012; Holling, Gunderson, and Peterson 2002; Kahn 2005; Paton 2006)—a perspective that I refer to as "flexibility theory." Both of these themes suggest that flexibility or freedom to adapt is a key to social resilience to climate-related disasters (Hegmon et al. 2008; Redman 2005; Redman and Kinzig 2003). This is particularly true for adaptive resilience, as flexibility is one of the features that allows societies to adapt rather than transform.

Measuring flexibility in social systems is difficult (Lebel et al. 2006). I use political participation as a measure of flexibility, as proxied through the corporate/exclusionary model. The corporate/exclusionary model developed through efforts to explain an archaeological puzzle: when looking at ancient polities of equivalent scale and complexity, there is a marked difference in the visibility of political leaders. Some ancient polities, such as those of the Sumerian Empire, have leaders who are clearly identified and often glorified, even to the extent of being considered divine. Others, even contemporary ones in regular contact, such as the Harappan Empire of the Indus Valley (which had important ties to the Sumerian Empire) are "faceless," having no clearly identified leaders. A similar situation can be seen in Mesoamerica, where the civilization centered at Teotihuacan had no visible rulers, while the contemporary Maya had rulers whose achievements were recorded on prominent stelae on public view.

Blanton and colleagues (1996) theorized that this puzzling difference stems from the strategies leaders employ to implement and maintain authority, and they found broad regularities that break down into a continuum with two poles. One end of the continuum is characterized by exclusionary strategies in which leaders tightly control access to political participation and legitimize their authority through a cult of personality and ties to both local and foreign elites whose loyalty they sustain through control over esoteric goods and knowledge (see Helms 1976). The other end of the continuum is characterized by corporate strategies in which leaders encourage political participation and legitimize their authority through their generosity, often displayed in feasts, and an appeal to their being "first among equals" (see Leach 1954).

The corporate/exclusionary model has been widely employed in archaeology and has been developed along several lines, including cultural evolutionary theory (e.g., Peregrine 2012) and collective action theory (Blanton and Fargher 2008; Feinman 2016). The model has also been applied to the contemporary world (e.g., Feinman 2010) and has obvious parallels to regime models (e.g., autocratic versus democratic) used widely in other areas of the social sciences (e.g., Marshall, Gurr, and Jaggers 2016; also Blanton 1998). It is important to note that the corporate/exclusionary model does not describe polity types but rather a continuum of political strategies that change over time as leaders respond to different challenges and opportunities.

The corporate/exclusionary model holds an explicitly top-down view of political processes but in doing so does not deny that a complex dialectical relationship exists in all societies between rulers and citizens, nor does it assume that the perception and reality of power are isomorphic (Feinman 2016). Rather, the corporate/exclusionary model posits that the way power is wielded by authority is what shapes both how power is perceived and the manner in which power can be co-opted or resisted by citizens (Peregrine 2012). And while the citizens' perception of their access to power is important, it is virtually impossible to "see" archaeologically (Fargher 2016). What we can see is the degree to which leaders allow or limit access to political decision-making, and that is the key concept I use to measure social flexibility.

The link between participation in political decision-making and social flexibility is well established in the disaster resilience literature through the concept of "participative capacity." Participative capacity refers to the ability of local actors to influence decision-making (Lorenz and Dittmer 2016, 47–48). As Redman (2005, 72; also Redman and Kinzig 2003) put it, "Management has to be flexible, working at scales that are compatible with the scales of critical ecosystem and social functions." Because those scales range from local to societal, participation has to be equal at all those levels. A key element in participative capacity is control and flow of information. In more resilient social systems, horizontal (that is, between individuals operating on similar scales) information flow appears more important than vertical flow so that control of information at high levels in a hierarchical system may lead to less resilience (Redman and Kinzig 2003; also Inkpen and Tsang 2005). Because key definitional elements of the corporate/exclusionary model focus on both these features—participation in decision-making and control over information and material flows—I argue that the corporate/exclusionary model provides a good proxy for societal flexibility.

The primary independent variable I examine is the corporate/exclusionary index. The index consists of the average standardized scores on the five variables listed in table 4.1 (described in more detail by Peregrine 2008, 2012; and Peregrine and Ember 2016). In brief, the index measures the degree to which political agents encourage or discourage political participation and interaction with external polities. In more-corporate societies, which score lower on the scale, agents encourage members of the society to participate in political activities, share authority broadly, and allow greater interaction with outsiders. The opposite is true in more-exclusionary societies, where agents control access to political authority, share it only among a small group of peers, and prevent most members of society from interacting with outsiders. The corporate/exclusionary index has been used to code archaeological data in several previous research projects that have produced statistically robust results (Peregrine 2008, 2012; Peregrine and Ember 2016) and is itself statistically robust, with an alpha of .978 (five items) and all the variables comprising it correlating to a single factor explaining 92 percent of the variance (Peregrine 2018a).

The dependent variables I examine reflect the social impact of a specific catastrophic climate-related disaster on seven areas: population, health and nutrition, conflict, household organization, village organization, re-

Table 4.1. Corporate/exclusionary index codes. These variables were coded following coding details given in Peregrine (2012).

Differentiation among Leaders and Followers

0 = egalitarian/no formal leaders
1 = none
2 = leaders have some privileges and/or access to resources others do not
3 = leaders have extensive privileges and access to resources others do not, including special housing and sumptuary goods
4 = leaders have exclusive privileges and exclusive access to special housing, resources, and sumptuary goods

Leader Identification

0 = egalitarian/no formal leaders
1 = none
2 = leaders are identified by treatment or appearance
3 = leaders are identified by recognized symbols of power or special behaviors
4 = individual aggrandizement and/or cult of leaders

Sharing of Authority

0 = egalitarian/no formal leaders
1 = leaders share power extensively with others
2 = leaders share power with a large cadre of other leaders
3 = leaders share power with a few other leaders
4 = leaders exercise exclusive power

Emphasis of Authority

0 = egalitarian/no formal leaders
1 = emphasis placed on group solidarity and group survival
2 = emphasis shared between group and leader, with greatest importance given to group survival
3 = emphasis shared between group and leader, with greatest importance given to leader survival
4 = emphasis placed on leaders as the embodiment of the group

External Contacts (Excluding Warfare)

0 = egalitarian/no formal leaders
1 = few or unimportant
2 = external contacts are part of leaders' authority, but not exclusive
3 = external contacts are key to leaders' authority, but not exclusive
4 = external contacts are exclusively controlled by leaders

gional organization, and communal ritual, all coded on a five-point scale from significant decrease to significant increase. These are coded based on the change observed in related variables coded for the time period before the climate-related disaster versus those for the time period following. Greater stability in the dependent variables is assumed to indicate adaptive resilience, following the definition presented earlier. I have usually employed these variables in a recoded none-some-much form, since the hypotheses I examine are related to stability and not the direction of change.

The sample used in my previous research is based on catastrophic climate-related disasters rather than disasters involving geological processes, human-induced environmental degradation, or the like. Within an archaeological context this may reflect a period of repeated climate-related disasters (e.g., sequential years of drought or flooding) and not just a single event. Not all societies have experienced a catastrophic climate-related disaster, and not all of those have been the focus of archaeological research that provides adequate data for coding the variables I am interested in, so the sample had to be selected based on predefined criteria rather than on random sampling. Those criteria were a specific region or site that (1) has been the focus of extensive archaeological research; (2) has been subjected to at least one catastrophic climate-related disaster that can be clearly identified in both the geological and archaeological records (and, again, what is visible in the archaeological and geological records is often a time period of repeated climate-related disasters rather than a single catastrophic event); and (3) is spatially and culturally distinct from other cases in the sample in order to minimize the likelihood of autocorrelation.

To address the first sampling criterion, preference was given to cases included in *eHRAF Archaeology* (ehrafarchaeology.yale.edu), a repository of primary and secondary source documents that have been indexed for content to the paragraph level and thus provides rapid access to specific information in the repository documents. To address the second sampling criterion, only cases that have been discussed in the archaeological literature as having been subjected to one or more catastrophic climate-related disaster were considered. And to address the third sampling criterion, cases were sought from different culture areas of the world. Because the cases are from different culture areas and are spatially and chronologically segregated, autocorrelation should be minimized. In the end, twenty-two distinct catastrophic climate-related disasters impacting societies in nine regions were selected for coding (figure 4.1). Individual cases consisted of those archaeologically known societies inhabiting a specific region impacted by the disaster, with one case representing the time period within

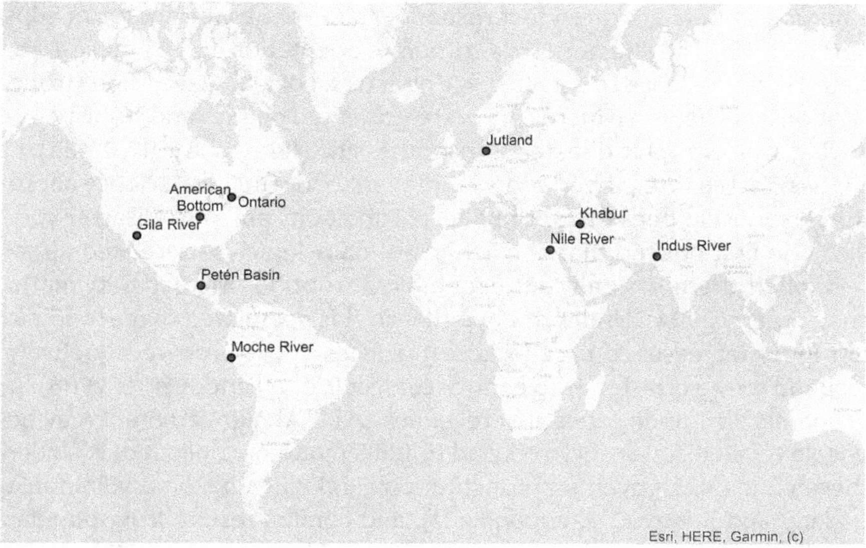

Figure 4.1. Location of focal regions coded for social resilience to catastrophic climate-related disasters. Figure created by the author.

one hundred years before the disaster and another the time period within one hundred years after the disaster. The sample cases are listed in Peregrine (2018a) along with the focal communities and time periods as typically defined in local chronologies (the time periods coded are within these local chronological periods) and the catastrophic climate-related disasters that impacted the cases.

Using the corporate/exclusionary index as the independent variable, and accepting the definition of adaptive social resilience put forward above, the main hypothesis I have been examining is that societies with more corporate political strategies are more resilient to catastrophic disasters. I found support for this hypothesis in two ways. First, I tested the hypothesis against a competing one that posits that strong adherence to social norms is key to social resilience. This idea comes from the work of Michele Gelfand and colleagues (Gelfand et al. 2011; Harrington and Gelfand 2014), who have found evidence that what they term "tighter" societies—those with strong social norms that are rigidly adhered to—are significantly more common in both world nations and states within the United States where disasters are more common. They theorize that such societal tightness creates strong social bonds that provide resilience. I found no support for this theory in the archaeologically known societies I examined. I have suggested elsewhere (Peregrine, forthcoming) that societal tightness may be associated with resilience to localized disasters where neighbors are often first responders and are a vital source of support following the disaster, while corporate orientation may be more associated with resilience to catastrophic disasters. I did, however, find strong relationships between more corporately oriented polities and stability following a catastrophic disaster, as hypothesized (Peregrine 2017, 2018a).

I also tested three theories drawn primarily from political science about the relationship between sociopolitical conditions and post-disaster conflict. The first posited that conflict arises following climate-related disasters when there is significant economic disruption (Miguel, Satyanath, and Sergenti 2004). Under this hypothesis, it is postulated that economic disruption increases conflict because it reduces a polity's power to actively respond to the disaster or to control conflict (Cohen and Werker 2008). If economic disruption causes tax revenues to fall, the government may be unable to aid disaster survivors and to fulfill monetary obligations. Under these conditions government institutions and elites become vulnerable (Hsiang and Burke 2014, appendix D), and conflict results from popular uprisings or between competing elites (Burke 2012; Apodaca 2017).

The second hypothesis emphasizes differences in access to resources and posits that conflict is more likely to arise following a climate-related disaster where there are existing high levels of social and economic inequality (Hsiang and Burke 2014, appendix D; Wisner et al. 2004). It is assumed that economic stress following a climate-related disaster exacerbates existing inequalities, leading those in lower socioeconomic conditions to revolt against the government (Miguel, Satyanath, and Sergenti 2004; Nel and Righarts 2008). Such revolts occur when the benefits of revolt are perceived to outweigh the benefits of accepting inequality (Apodaca 2017).

The third hypothesis about the relationship between climate-related disasters and conflict I tested was that conflict arises because of migration out of disaster zones (Hsiang and Burke 2014, appendix D). Under this hypothesis, migration is postulated to create conflict as people from different ethnic groups (some with a history of conflict) are forced into close proximity, for example in refugee camps, but perhaps more significantly in established communities where refugees disrupt daily life. Not only does this heighten existing differences and disagreements, but also increased population density creates a host of problems (e.g., disease, famine, social disruption), any of which might foster conflict (Schleussner et al. 2016; Zhang et al. 2011).

Using multiple regression, I found that none of these models produced statistically significant results, but that a model based on the corporate/exclusionary index and the number of levels of political integration indicated that more exclusionary societies suffer more post-disaster conflict than others (Peregrine 2018b; also Peregrine and Ember 2016). From this I concluded that the strategies employed by political leaders to legitimate and maintain authority, which is perhaps similar to what is termed regime type in the political science literature on modern states, seems the key variable predicting post-disaster conflict (see also Goldstone et al. 2010; Omelicheva 2011; Tselios and Tompkins 2017)

These results suggested that societies with more-inclusive political structures tend to be more resilient to disasters and thus support the basic tenants of "flexibility theory" (e.g., Lebel et al. 2006; Norris et al. 2008). In the next section I describe my current research, which is intended to further test the hypothesis that more-corporately oriented societies are more resilient to natural disasters.

Extending the Hypothesis to the 536/540 CE Atmospheric Catastrophe

In June 536 CE something extraordinary happened: the sky darkened, the weather cooled, and for the next eighteen months the sun "shone for about four hours, and still this light was only a feeble shadow" (John of Ephesos, quoted in Arjava 2005). The result was widespread famine, social unrest, and perhaps the root cause of the Plague of Justinian. The climate did not recover from this event for nearly ten years, and by that time many societies in the Northern Hemisphere had experienced profound (and in some cases irreversible) disruption (see, e.g., Graslund and Price 2012; Lowenborg 2012).

Tree-ring data provide physical evidence of a dramatic climatic downturn beginning in 536 CE and continuing until roughly 545 CE. Tree rings throughout the Northern Hemisphere—from northern Europe to the Yucatan—show constricted growth during this period (described in detail in Gunn 2000), indicating that the climate had grown colder and potentially drier. It is unknown what caused this dramatic climatic cooling or the "dry fog" that is reported to have accompanied it, although the most probable culprit is a massive volcanic eruption that sent a large volume of dust and smoke into the upper atmosphere (Rigby, Symonds, and Ward-Thompson 2004; Gibbons 2018). A second eruption in 540 CE may have contributed to the long period of climatic downturn that is evidenced by the tree-ring data (Toohey et al. 2016).

Figure 4.2 represents the "classic" model of resilience under which my previous work was conducted. Here a given hazard interacts with vulnerability to create risk for disaster. I saw resilience in this model as related to lowering risk. Since climate-related hazards cannot be easily reduced, the key to increasing resilience lies in lowering vulnerability. Under this model,

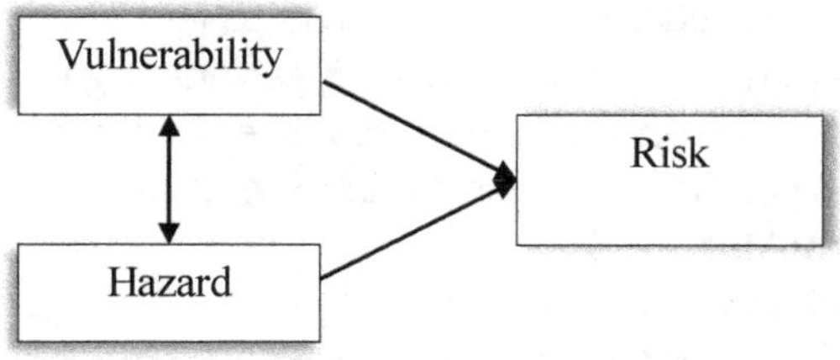

Figure 4.2. General model of disaster impact. Figure created by the author.

I found that high degrees of political participation appear to lower vulnerability. That is a very simplistic model; it does not directly relate to resilience, and it does not take into account important control variables or differing forms of vulnerability. Indeed, in my study of post-disaster conflict I added levels of political integration to the regression models as a control variable (Peregrine 2018b).

Figure 4.3 presents the model under which I am working now. Here two mediating variables are present: levels of political integration (political integration) and the diversity of available natural resources (natural environment) as measured by ecosystem regime, agricultural potentials and restrictions, and diversity of wildlife. The natural environment control variable is here because it is widely accepted that subsistence diversity, which is mediated by the natural environment, has significant impact on resilience (e.g., Lin 2011; Mijatović et al. 2013). This is also why subsistence economy is included in the model.

Infrastructure has been a focus of the resilience literature from its beginning, particularly in the form of engineering hazardous environments

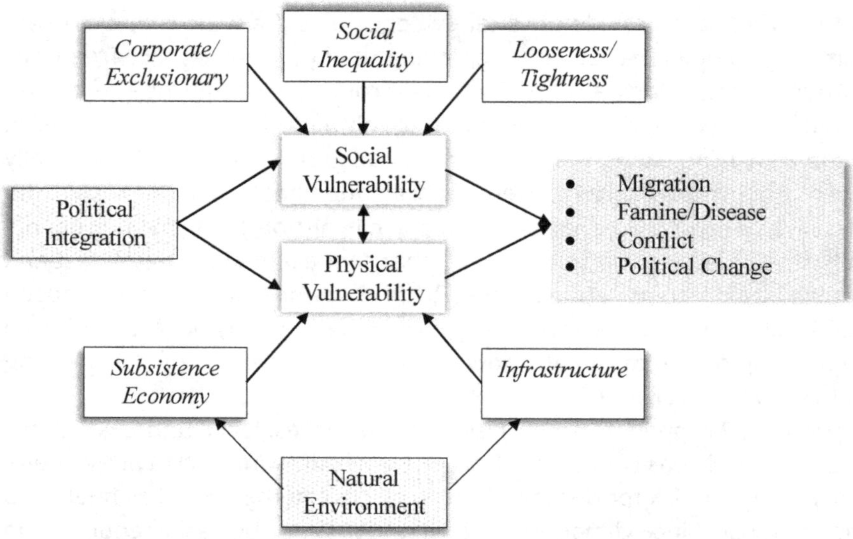

Figure 4.3. Expanded model of disaster impact. Figure created by the author.

to reduce risk (through dams and levees, for example) (Paton 2006). However, there is a greater need to include infrastructure in a model of resilience, especially when considering a wide range of human societies with greatly varying technological capabilities and political integration, and that is because humans are niche constructors and use infrastructure extensively in the creation of beneficial niches (Laland, Boogert, and Evans 2014). In arid regions, for example, complex irrigation systems were developed in order to adopt agricultural subsistence regimes. These irrigation systems, therefore, allowed humans to construct an agricultural niche in an environment where it would otherwise be impossible. Creating a resilient irrigation system is thus essential to creating a resilient society in such an environment.

Subsistence economy and infrastructure are both aspects of what I call physical vulnerability, or those material structures and processes that are necessary to maintain a society. As noted earlier, this physical vulnerability has been a focus of resilience literature for many years. However, physical vulnerability is only one aspect of vulnerability, as more recent research (including my own) has demonstrated. There is also a growing literature on "social capital" and "participative capacity" as important elements of resilience (Cretney 2016; Kasdan 2016). I have already discussed the relationship between participative capacity (in the form of political participation) and the corporate/exclusionary model. And although, as I discussed above, I found no relationship between the tightness/looseness model and social resilience, its similarity to the concept of social capital makes it an important element to include in the model; after all, societal tightness has been shown to provide resilience in modern nations and within the United States, and the fact that my work did not support that hypothesis does not mean it is not important in other contexts (see Peregrine 2018a). As noted earlier, I have suggested elsewhere (Peregrine, forthcoming) that tightness creates bonds that aid resilience in the context of localized disasters (such as tornadoes or localized floods) because neighbors and other nearby community members not affected by the disaster provide vital support in response and recovery efforts.

A key element of social capital is simply access to resources. Current research is showing convincingly that individuals or groups with greater access to resources are more resilient to disasters (Kahn 2005). The reasons for this are obvious: those with greater access to resources are able to stockpile them before a disaster strikes, to obtain them after a disaster, to move elsewhere either before or after a disaster, and to rebuild their lives more quickly and easily in the wake of a disaster than those who have limited access to resources. Thus social inequality must be part of any model of resilience. Together the corporate/exclusionary model, the tightness/looseness model, and social inequality combine to create social vulnerability, a form of vulnerability quite different from physical vulnerability, but no less important.

There are four aspects of resilience that seemed most important to consider from previous research. These are migration, famine or disease, conflict, and political change. I am using the same variables as I have previously but have revised them in order to better focus on these four aspects of stability and change. Migration seems important because it marks the dissolution of a society, the separation of the people from their communities and lands. Famine and disease can be devastating to any society, breaking social bonds through the cessation of sharing and mutual care as well as through deaths. Conflict can obviously cause a breakdown of society and can lead to political change as well (or, indeed, total regime change). In addition, political change marks political breakdown or conquest. Thus, these four dependent variables seem key to measuring social resilience.

Why apply this more detailed model of resilience to the 536/540 CE atmospheric catastrophe? Several reasons led me to examine this particular event. First, it is well-documented and has been suggested as the cause of major social disruptions in a number of equally well-documented cases. Second, I assumed that the data were much better than those I employed in my previous research. In that assumption I was not fully correct. The time period of 536/540 CE marks a transition in Europe between Late Antiquity and the Dark Ages. In the aftermath of Roman occupation, both the archaeological and historical records become limited (from which the term "Dark Ages" arises—as there is relatively little information in comparison with the Roman and High Middle Ages). However, the time period has become better known through focused excavation and historical research, and adequate, though not abundant, data are available. The situation is better in the Americas and East Asia, where the archaeological (Americas) and historical (East Asia) records are relatively good. Elsewhere the situation is mixed.

Finally, I assumed that access to data would be facilitated by my affiliation with the Seshat: Global History Databank project (Turchin et al. 2015, François et al. 2016). In this assumption I was correct. Seshat has been under development since 2011. Its focus is to provide data to allow scholars to examine cultural evolution between the Neolithic period and the nineteenth century. The initial sample, which is the most comprehensively coded, includes thirty locations across the globe, stratified by the world region and the antiquity of complex societies (Turchin et al. 2018). The sampling procedure and focus of coding have been described elsewhere (Turchin et al. 2018), so I will provide only a brief summary here.

In the development of Seshat, the world was divided into ten major regions, within each of which three differing natural geographical areas (NGAs) were selected, areas defined by naturally occurring geographical features (for example, river basins, coastal plains, valleys, and islands). The extent of the NGAs does not change over time, so the NGAs are fixed points within which data are collected on a specific polity for time periods of roughly one hundred years (adjusted by logical break points such as changes in long-standing regimes, conquest, etc.). The selection criteria for NGAs included a desire to represent a wide range of sociopolitical forms, so that information would be coded for as wide a range of societies as possible. This was determined by considering the time period when political complexity first emerged and selecting one society where political complexity is ancient, one recent, and one in between. The initial sample, thus, included thirty locations across the globe, stratified by the world region and the antiquity of the complex societies within it (see Turchin et al. 2018 for more detail).

Twelve Seshat cases were available for the 536/540 CE time period within the area that is thought to have been significantly impacted by the event. Three cases I had already coded for my previous research were also within the time period and location to be used. And I added five additional cases so that the areas most impacted by the event would be well represented (these cases are all in Eurasia). Thus, I am coding twenty cases, at least initially. These are listed in table 4.2 and are shown in figure 4.4.

The variables are similar to those I employed previously, though many have been replaced with similar or identical Seshat variables. This allows me to populate a large percentage of my code sheets automatically by drawing the information from Seshat. That information includes coded values and, more importantly, direct quotes from authoritative sources, so that I am able to evaluate the coding based on those source documents. I am also able to add source materials for all the variables, including those already coded by Seshat researchers. All those sources will be available to future researchers through Seshat, as will all the coded values and justifications for those codes. Where scholars disagree, all alternate codings are presented, so that researchers can consider the scholar's justification for the code and the source documents upon which they based that justification.

Seshat also takes advantage of developments in computer science that provide new ways of harvesting, storing, and retrieving data. Seshat is built on Dacura, a data curation platform that uniquely reflects three of these developments: (1) a data model based on a knowledge graph (as opposed to the standard column and row data structure), (2) the use of Web Ontology Language (OWL) for data definition, and (3) an automated

Table 4.2. Atmospheric catastrophe cases, 536/540 CE.

North America

ARO-1. Point Peninsula Complex (Ontario Peninsula IBSS) 300 BCE–700 CE
ARO-2. Mund Phase (Cahokia NGA/IBSS) 450–600 CE
ARO-3. Pioneer/Formative Phase (Gila River IBSS)
ARO-4. Monte Alban IIIB and IV (Oaxaca NGA) 500–900 CE
ARO-5. Early Classic (Tikal IBSS) 250–600 CE

Europe

ARO-6. Early Merovingian (Paris Basin NGA) 486–543 CE
ARO-7. Ostrogothic Kingdom (Latium NGA) 489–554 CE
ARO-8. Migration Period (Southern Jutland ARO) 500–700 CE
ARO-9. Brega (Ireland ARO) Reign of Túathal Máelgarb 533–544 CE
ARO-10. Toledo (Central Spain ARO) Reign of Theudis 531–548 CE

Eastern Asia

ARO-11. Rouran Khaganate (Orkhon Valley NGA) 300–555 CE [Mongolia]
ARO-12. Hephthalites (Sogdiana NGA) 408–561 CE [Central Asia]
ARO-13. Kofun (Kansai NGA) 250–710 CE [Japan]
ARO-14. Early Imperial Period (Middle Yellow River NGA) 200 BCE–900 CE
ARO-15. Liang (Lower Yangtze River Valley ARO) Emperor Wu, 502–549 CE

Southern Asia

ARO-16. Sasania Period (Susiana NGA) 224–642 CE
ARO-17. Kadamba Empire (Deccan NGA) 354–540 CE
ARO-18. Gupta Empire (Ganges ARO) Kumaragupta III ca. 530–540 CE

Northern Africa

ARO-19. Byzantine Empire (Upper Egypt NGA) 395–631 CE
ARO-20. JennE–jeno III (Lower Niger River NGA) 400–900 CE

process based on sematic reasoning for weeding out the thousands of online and database hits not directly related to a problem of interest and/or of dubious accuracy (Peregrine et al. 2018). Dacura was built in tandem with the Seshat databank, so was specifically designed for the type of research I am doing.

Initial results appear to support the findings of my previous studies. Although only the first ten cases (North American and Europe) have been coded to date, they demonstrate some statistically significant associations (table 4.3). When controlling for political integration, there are significant associations between political participation, change in population, and change in regional organization and a marginally significant (though statistically significant one-tailed, which is appropriate for this analysis since the hypothesis is directional) association between political participation and change in community organization. All the Pearson correlation coefficients are relatively high, especially for there being so few cases. Having

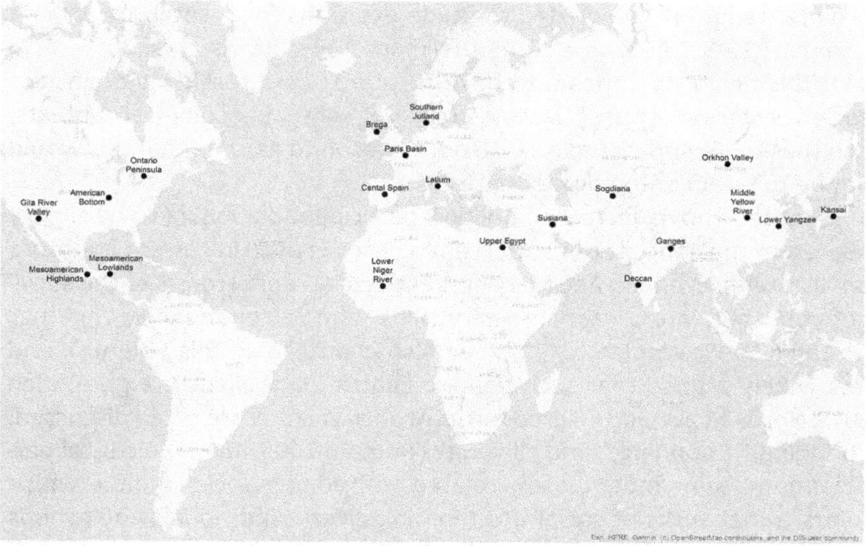

Figure 4.4. Location of 536/540 CE atmospheric catastrophe cases. Figure created by the author.

Table 4.3. Pearson correlations and two-tailed probability values controlling for political integration.

	Change in Population	**Change in Village Organization**	**Change in Regional Organization**
Corporate/ exclusionary index	*r* = .727 *p* = .026	*r* = .624 *p* = .072	*r* = .691 *p* = .039

only ten cases, I have not attempted any higher-level analyses, but that ten cases show patterns similar to those found in my previous studies is encouraging. It would appear that political participation does foster social resilience.

Conclusions

Humans have faced catastrophic disasters many times and will face such disasters many times in the future. The results of my work suggest that to become more resilient, societies should promote policies that encourage citizens to actively participate in governance and decision-making (Lebel et al. 2006). Such policies would appear to provide greater flexibility in decision-making, the ability to communicate information and responses at appropriate scales, and perhaps the entire response system with a broader range of knowledge to guide decisions (also see Brugger and Crimmins 2015; Dilling et al. 2015; Heijmans 2004; Norris et al. 2008, 142–44). This flexibility appears to have fostered social resilience in ancient societies at a variety of scales and in a variety of socio-ecological contexts, and thus there appears to be no *a priori* reason to assume that this would not be true for contemporary societies.

As noted above, increased political participation appears to be closely related to the concept of "social capital" as it is used in current literature on disaster prevention and management. Social capital refers to the social networks and interpersonal relationships that tie communities together (Putnam 1995; Woolcock 1998; see also chapter 7 in this volume), and it is widely argued that such ties are central to resilience (e.g., Aldrich 2012; Norris et al. 2008). Three forms of social capital are often discussed: "bridging," "bonding," and "linking" (Putnam 2000, 18–24). Political participation seems most closely related to bridging social capital, which refers to networks of social ties that link diverse individuals and groups together across a community. Indeed Putnam (2000, 31–47) includes political participation in the form of voting, interest in public affairs, and participation in political and civic organizations as measures of bridging social capital (also Onyx and Bullen 2000). Bonding social capital, in contrast, are inter-relational ties that bond together individuals within social groups. Bonding social capital seems quite similar to the idea of societal tightness, as discussed above. Finally, linking social capital refers to ties that connect individuals, organizations, and communities to higher-level structures, such as local or regional governments.

Bridging social capital has been associated with resilience following unpredictable catastrophic disasters, such as those experienced by the societies I have examined in my research, while bonding social capital seems more effective in societies where smaller natural disasters are frequent (Jordan 2014; Masoud-All-Kamal and Hassan 2018). This appears to occur because bridging social capital, by providing a network of ties that link individuals and organizations across a community, allows communities to prepare well for major disasters and to have effective, coordinated response and recovery plans and practices in place. Bonding social capital is more effective in situations where there are frequent smaller disasters because neighbors and family are typically the first responders in any disaster situation. Where disasters are common, strong bonds among individuals in a community provide for rapid response and reconstruction (Jordan 2014). Linking social capital, however, appears not always to be helpful in disaster response and recovery, as higher-level organizations sometimes direct efforts toward more politically powerful communities, and ranking officials may misappropriate funds and materiel for personal gain (Masoud-All-Kamal and Hassan 2018).

The major implication of my work, I suggest, is that to limit the impact (in terms of change) of catastrophic natural disasters, policy makers should work to encourage political participation and, in doing so, increase the value of bridging social capital in local communities. That is a broad and, quite honestly, largely un-actionable conclusion. However, there are more focused and actionable conclusions that can be drawn from my work. Here I suggest three.

First, policy makers should encourage stakeholders at the local level to participate in decision-making about disaster response and management (Aldrich and Meyer 2015; Burby 2003). In practice this may mean that town or city boards and local disaster management officials hold regular community forums, and even regular meetings should be open to public attendance and participation (White et al. 2015). This should go beyond simply opening meetings to obtain stakeholder input, but rather officials should actively seek input by directly inviting stakeholders to meetings and forums. Officials should undertake an active approach to gaining input, contacting the community of stakeholders directly to encourage them to give input at meetings and forums (Horney et al. 2016).

Some governments are already putting policies that stress inclusion of local stakeholders into practice. For example, the United States Federal Emergency Management Agency (FEMA) is implementing a "Whole Community" approach to disaster response and management (FEMA 2011) as part of the national strategy for disaster preparedness (FEMA 2013). The Whole Community approach is rooted in the idea that local participation in decisions about disaster response and management creates more resilient communities. The effort focuses on three areas: (1) understand and meet the actual needs of the whole community; (2) engage and empower all parts of the community; and (3) strengthen what works well in communities on a daily basis (FEMA 2013, 4–5). To implement the Whole Community approach, FEMA expects local emergency managers to focus their efforts on creating engagement strategies and programs on the specific characteristics and needs of the community. Emergency managers are expected to work directly with community leaders and organizations to empower community action and collective solutions. As FEMA puts it, "Empowering local action requires allowing members of the communities to lead—not follow—in identifying priorities, organizing support, implementing programs, and evaluating outcomes" (FEMA 2013, 14); in short, political participation needs to be fostered to encourage bottom-up agency within communities.

Second, policy makers should encourage regular communication between local decision makers, emergency and disaster response personnel, and disaster response organizations to ensure smooth communication at appropriate levels during a disaster response. Smooth communication has both technological and interpersonal aspects (White et al. 2015). The technological ones include devices (radio, telephone, etc.) that allow communication among all the response groups; redundancy so that if one communication technology is made unworkable by the disaster, others can be used in its place; and regular training to ensure all users are up-to-date on the active technology. The interpersonal aspects are more complicated and difficult to implement. They include things like simply knowing one another, knowing whom to call given a particular need during response, and knowing the specific responsibilities of each person and each agency or organization (Aldrich 2010; Aldrich and Meyer 2015). These two aspects of communication can be combined through shared training and planning sessions, but as with political participation, this needs to be done actively by decision makers developing and implementing specific plans and purchases to build an overlapping, redundant communication technology and to ensure that strong interpersonal relationships are built among disaster and emergency response personnel.

Better communication between local stakeholders and disaster response and management agencies is obviously part of what FEMA is trying to accomplish with its Whole Community approach. A more direct approach, however, is one developed by the Asian Disaster Preparedness Center called community-based disaster risk management (CBDRM) (Abarquez and Murshed 2004). A central part of the CBDRM is building rapport and trust between government disaster management officials and local communities. To accomplish this, the CBDRM approach specifically instructs government officials to spend time "building the relationship and trust with the local people" (Abarquez and Murshed 2004, 16) in order to better understand local social, political, and economic conditions, especially those that impact vulnerable members of the community. Government officials are expected to live in the community for which they are responsible and to facilitate community discussions about disaster prevention and management. They are also tasked with developing a community organization focused on disaster prevention and management to function alongside government agencies (Abarquez and Murshed 2004). Members of this organization not only review and update disaster plans, but also are trained in disaster response, including intercommunity conflict management and external communication technologies. Both are intended to ensure that clear and effective communication is maintained both within and outside the community. While the CBDRM approach is designed with small and remote communities in mind, I suggest it is one that provides a model that could be useful anywhere.

The third conclusion derived from my work is that policy makers should actively support community-based organizations that build capacity for political participation (Aldrich 2012). A community organization specifically focused on disaster management, as suggested by the CBDRM approach discussed above, is an excellent idea, but how would one go about developing such a community-based organization in a large community, particularly one in places like the United States, where political and community participation has been declining for decades (Putnam 2000)? One possibility is "time banking," which provides incentives, such as gift certificates, for citizens who volunteer with community-based organizations (Collom and Lasker 2012). This serves to engage citizens who might otherwise not participate in community organizations and may create a "virtuous cycle" of community engagement and mutual aid (Aldrich and Meyer 2015). Support should include both active promotion and political support and, perhaps more importantly, financial aid to ensure these community-based organizations can sustain themselves over the long term (White et al. 2015).

The fact that the findings from the past reaffirm contemporary practices in disaster prevention and management is extremely important, for it shows that these practices have empirically served to provide resilience to societies over long periods of time. These findings reinforce existing policy suggestions and indeed empirically demonstrate that efforts to build social capital, as is emphasized in the current disaster prevention and management literature, will result in significant benefits to society. Those social benefits—and specifically resilience to natural disasters—is what all the authors in this volume seek to foster. I hope my work contributes in some way to that important effort.

Acknowledgments

I must thank Felix Riede and Payson Sheets for their valuable suggestions on this chapter. Carol R. Ember, Michele Gelfand, and Eric Jones have provided ongoing advice and encouragement as my projects have developed. As always, any flaws or errors the reader might find remain solely my own.

Research presented here was supported by the National Science Foundation (Award #SMA-1416651) and the Army Research Office (Contract Number W911NF-17-1-0441). The views and conclusions contained in this chapter are those of the author and should not be interpreted as representing the official policies, either expressed or implied, of the Army Research Office or the US government. The US government is authorized to reproduce and distribute reprints for government purposes notwithstanding any copyright notation herein. Both awards are administered through the HRAF Advanced Research Center (hrafARC) at Yale University.

Peter Neal Peregrine earned a PhD in anthropology from Purdue University. He is a registered professional archaeologist who specializes in the remote sensing of near-surface archaeological features using geophysical techniques, and he has used these techniques to do fieldwork on every continent over nearly forty years as a practicing archaeologist. Peregrine also pioneered the field of cross-cultural comparative archaeology, authoring the *Atlas of Cultural Evolution*, coediting the nine-volume *Encyclopedia of Prehistory*, and providing ongoing expertise for the eHRAF Collection of Archaeology. In previous work he has used the cross-cultural method to examine patterns and processes of cultural evolution, and in his current research he employs the cross-cultural method to explore social resilience to climate-related disasters. He is a founding member of the Cultural Evolution Society and the Society for Anthropological Sciences and is a Fellow of the American Association for the Advancement of Science.

References

Abarquez, I., and Z. Murshed. 2004. *Community Based Disaster Risk Management Field Practitioner's Handbook*. Klong Luang, Thailand: Asian Disaster Preparedness Center.

Aldrich, D. 2010. "Power of the People: Social Capital's Role in Recovery from the 1995 Kobe Earthquake." *Natural Hazards* 56 (3): 595–611.

———. 2012. *Building Resilience: Social Capital in Post-disaster Recovery*. Chicago: University of Chicago Press.

Aldrich, D., and M. Meyer. 2015. "Social Capital and Community Resilience." *American Behavioral Scientist* 59 (2): 254–69.

Apodaca, C. 2017. *State Repression in Post-disaster Societies*. New York: Routledge.

Arjava, Antti. 2005. "The Mystery Cloud of 536 C.E. in the Mediterranean Sources." *Dumbarton Oaks Papers* 59: 73–94.

Blanton, R. E. 1998. "Beyond Centralization: Steps toward a Theory of Egalitarian Behavior in Archaic States." In *Archaic States*, edited by G. M. Feinman and J. Marcus, 135–72. Santa Fe, NM: School of American Research.

Blanton, R. E., and L. Fargher. 2008. *Collective Action in the Formation of Pre-modern States*, New York: Springer.

Blanton, R. E., S. Kowalewski, G. Feinman, and P. Peregrine. 1996. "A Dual-Processual Theory for the Evolution of Mesoamerican Civilization." *Current Anthropology* 37 (1): 1–14.

Brugger, J., and M. Crimmins. 2015. "Designing Institutions to Support Local-Level Climate Change Adaptation: Insights from a Case Study of the U.S. Cooperative Extension System." *Weather Climate and Society* 7 (1): 18–38.

Burby, R. 2003. "Making Plans That Matter: Citizen Involvement and Government Action." *Journal of the American Planning Association* 69 (1): 33–49.

Burke, P. 2012. "Economic Growth and Political Survival." *B.E. Journal of Macroeconomics* 12: article 5.

Cohen, C., and Werker, E. 2008. "The Political Economy of 'Natural' Disasters." *Journal of Conflict Resolution* 52 (6): 795–819.

Collom, E., and J. Lasker. 2012. *Equal Time, Equal Value: Community Currencies and Time Banking in the US*. London: Routledge.

Comfort, L., A. Boin, and C. Demchack. 2010. *Designing Resilience: Preparing for Extreme Events*. Pittsburgh: University of Pittsburgh Press.

Cooper, J., and P. Sheets. 2012. *Surviving Sudden Environmental Change: Answers from Archaeology*. Boulder: University Press of Colorado.

Cretney, R. M. 2016. "Local Responses to Disaster: The Value of Community-Led Post-disaster Response Action in a Resilience Framework." *Disaster Prevention and Management* 25 (1): 27–40.

Davidson, J. L., C. Jackson, A. Lyth, A. Dedekorkut-Howes, C. Baldwin, et al. 2016. "Interrogating Resilience: Toward a Typology to Improve Its Operationalization." *Ecology and Society* 21 (2): article 12.

Dilling, L., K. Lackstrom, B. Haywood, K. Dow, M. Lemos, J. Berggren, and S. Kalafatis. 2015. "What Stakeholder Needs Tell Us about Enabling Adaptive Capacity: The Intersection of Context and Information Provision across Regions of the United States." *Weather Climate and Society* 7 (1): 5–17.

Fargher, L. 2016. "Corporate Power Strategies, Collective Action, and Control of Principals: A Cross-Cultural Perspective." In *Alternative Pathways to Complexity*, edited by L. F. Fargher and V. Y. Heredia Espanosa, 309–26. Boulder: University Press of Colorado.

Feinman, G. 2010. "A Dual-Processual Perspective on the Power and Inequality in the Contemporary United States." In *Pathways to Power*, edited by T. D. Price and G. M. Feinman, 255–88. New York: Springer.

———. 2016. "Variation and Change in Archaic States: Ritual as a Mechanism of Sociopolitical Integration." In *Ritual and Archaic States*, edited by J. M. A. Murphy, 1–22. Gainesville: University of Florida Press.

FEMA (Federal Emergency Management Agency). 2011. *A Whole Community Approach to Emergency Management: Principles, Themes, and Pathways for Action*. Washington, DC: Federal Emergency Management Agency.

———. 2013. *National Strategy Recommendations: Future Disaster Preparedness*. Washington, DC: Federal Emergency Management Agency.

Fisher, C. T., J. B. Hill, and G. M. Feinman. 2009. *The Archaeology of Environmental Change: Socionatural Legacies of Degradation and Resilience*. Tucson: University of Arizona Press.

François, P., J. Manning, H. Whitehouse, R. Brennan, et al. 2016. "A Macroscope for Global History: Seshat Global History Databank." *Digital Humanities Quarterly* 10 (4).

Gelfand, M., J. L. Raver, L. Nishii, L. Leslie, J. Lun, et al. 2011. "Differences between Tight and Loose Cultures: A 33-Nation Study." *Science* 332 (6033): 1100–1104.

Gibbons, A. 2018. "Eruption Made 536 'the Worst Year to Be Alive." *Science* 362 (6416): 733–34.
Goldstone, J., R. Bates, D. Epstein, T. Gurr, M. Lustik, M. Marshall, J. Ulfelder, and M. Woodward. 2010. "A Global Model for Forecasting Political Instability." *American Journal of Political Science* 54 (1): 190–208.
Graslund, Bo, and Neil Price. 2012. "Twilight of the Gods? The 'Dust Veil Event' of A.D. 536 in Critical Perspective." *Antiquity* 86 (332): 428–43.
Gunn, Joel D., ed. 2000. *The Years without Summer: Tracing A.D. 536 and Its Aftermath.* Oxford: Archaeopress.
Harrington, J., and M. Gelfand. 2014. "Tightness-Looseness across the 50 United States." *PNAS* 111 (22): 7990–95.
Hegmon, M., M. Peeples, A. Kinzig, S. Kulow, C. Meegan, and M. Nelson. 2008. "Social Transformations and Its Human Costs in the Prehispanic U.S. Southwest." *American Anthropologist* 110 (3): 313–24.
Heijmans, A. 2004. "From Vulnerability to Empowerment." In *Mapping Vulnerability: Disasters, Development, and People,* edited by G. Bankoff, G. Frerks, and D. Hilhorst, 115–27. London: Earthscan.
Helms, M. 1976. *Ancient Panama: Chiefs in Search of Power.* Austin: University of Texas Press.
Holling, C. S. 1973. "Resilience and Stability of Ecological Systems." *Annual Review of Ecology and Systematics* 4: 1–23.
Holling, C. S., L. Gunderson, and G. Peterson. 2002. "Sustainability and Panarchy." In *Panarchy: Understanding Transformations in Human and Natural Systems,* edited by L. Gunderson and C. S. Holling, 63–102. Washington, DC: Island Press.
Horney, J., D. Spurlock, S. Grabich, and P. Berke. 2016. "Capacity for Stakeholder Participation in Recovery Planning." *Planning Practice & Research* 31 (1): 65–79.
Hsiang, S., and Burke, M. 2014. "Climate, Conflict, and Social Stability: What Does the Evidence Say?" *Climatic Change* 123 (1): 39–55.
Inkpen, A. C., and E. W. K. Tsang. 2005. "Social Capital, Networks, and Knowledge Transfer." *Academy of Management Review* 30 (1): 146–65.
Jordan, J. 2014. "Swimming Alone? The Role of Social Capital in Enhancing Local Resilience to Climate Stress: A Case Study from Bangladesh." *Climate and Development* 7 (2): 110–23.
Kahn, M. 2005. "The Death Toll from Natural Disasters: The Role of Income, Geography, and Institutions." *Review of Economics and Statistics* 87 (2): 271–84.
Kasdan, D. O. 2016. "Considering Socio-cultural Factors of Disaster Risk Management." *Disaster Prevention and Management* 25 (4): 464–77.
Laland, Kevin, N. Boogert, and C. Evans. 2014. "Niche Construction, Innovation and Complexity." *Environmental Innovation and Societal Transitions* 11: 71–86.
Leach, E. 1954. *Political Systems of Highland Burma.* London: G. Bell and Son.
Lebel, L., J. Anderies, B. Campbell, C. Folke, S. Harfield-Dodds, T. Hughes, and J. Wilson. 2006. "Governance and the Capacity to Manage Resilience in Regional Social-Ecological Systems." *Ecology and Society* 11 (1): article 19.
Lin, Brenda. 2011. "Resilience in Agriculture through Crop Diversification: Adaptive Management for Environmental Change." *BioScience* 61 (3): 183–93.
Lorenz, D., and C. Dittmer. 2016. Resilience in Catastrophes, Disasters, and Emergencies." In *New Perspectives on Resilience in Socio-economic Spheres,* edited by A. Maurer, 25–59. Leiden: Springer VS.

Lowenborg, Daniel. 2012. "An Iron Age Shock Doctrine: Did the A.D. 536–7 Event Trigger Large-Scale Social Changes in the Malaren Valley Area?" *Journal of Archaeology and Ancient History* 4: 1–29.

Marshall, M., T. Gurr, and K. Jaggers. 2016. *Polity IV Project Dataset User's Manual*. Vienna, VA: Center for Systematic Peace.

Masoud-All-Kamal, M., and S. M. Hassan. 2018. "The Link between Social Capital and Disaster Recovery: Evidence from Coastal Communities in Bangladesh." *Natural Hazards* 93 (3): 1547–64.

Miguel, E., S. Satyanath, and E. Sergenti. 2004. "Economic Shocks and Civil Conflict: An Instrumental Variable Approach." *Journal of Political Economy* 112 (4): 725–53.

Mijatović, Dunja, Frederik Van Oudenhoven, Pablo Eyzaguirre, and Toby Hodgkin. 2013. "The Role of Agricultural Biodiversity in Strengthening Resilience to Climate Change: Towards an Analytical Framework." *International Journal of Agricultural Sustainability* 11 (2): 95–107.

Nel, P., and M. Righarts. 2008. "Natural Disasters and the Risk of Violent Conflict." *International Studies Quarterly* 52 (1): 159–85.

Norris, F., S. Stevens, B. Pfefferbaum, K. Wyche, and R. Pfefferbaum. 2008. "Community Resilience as a Metaphor, Theory, Set of Capacities, and Strategy for Disaster Readiness. *American Journal of Community Psychology* 41 (1–2): 127–50.

Omelicheva, M. 2011. "Natural Disasters: Triggers of Political Instability?" *International Interactions* 37 (4): 441–65.

Onyx, J., and Bullen, P. 2000. "Measuring Social Capital in Five Communities." *Journal of Applied Behavioral Science* 36 (1): 23–42.

Parry, M. L., O. F. Canziani, J. P. Palutikof, P. J. van der Linden, and C. E. Hanson. 2007. *Contribution of Working Group II to the Fourth Assessment Report of the Intergovernmental Panel on Climate Change*. Cambridge: Cambridge University Press.

Paton, D. 2006. "Disaster Resilience: Building Capacity to Co-exist with Natural Hazards and Their Consequences." In *Disaster Resilience: An Integrated Approach*, edited by D. Paton and D. Johnston, 3–10. Springfield, IL: Charles Thomas.

Peregrine, P. N. 2001. "Cross-Cultural Comparative Approaches in Archaeology." *Annual Review of Anthropology* 30: 1–18.

———. 2004. "Cross-Cultural Approaches in Archaeology: Comparative Ethnology, Comparative Archaeology, and Archaeoethnology." *Journal of Archaeological Research* 12 (3): 281–309.

———. 2008. "Political Strategy and Cross-Cultural Variation in Games." *Cross-Cultural Research* 42 (4): 386–92.

———. 2012. "Power and Legitimation: Political Strategies, Typology, and Cultural Evolution." In *Comparative Archaeology of Complex Societies*, edited by M. E. Smith, 165–91. Cambridge: Cambridge University Press.

———. 2017. "Political Participation and Long-Term Resilience in Pre-Columbian Societies." *Disaster Prevention and Management* 26 (3): 314–29.

———. 2018a. "Social Resilience to Climate-Related Disasters in Ancient Societies: A Test of Two Hypotheses." *Weather, Climate, and Society* 10 (1): 145–61.

———. 2018b. "Reducing Post-Disaster Conflict: A Cross-Cultural Test of Four Hypotheses Using Archaeological Data." *Environmental Hazards* 18 (2): 93–110.

———. Forthcoming. "Social Resilience to Climate Change During the Late Antique Little Ice Age: A Replication Study." *Weather, Climate, and Society*.

Peregrine, P. N., R. Brennan, T. Currie, K. Feeney, P. François, P. Turchin, and H. Whitehouse. 2018. "Dacura: A New Solution to Data Harvesting and Knowledge Extraction for the Historical Sciences." *Historical Methods* 51 (3): 165–74.

Peregrine, P. N., and C. R. Ember. 2016. "Network Strategy and War." In *Alternative Pathways to Complexity*, edited by L. Fargher and V. Heredia Espinoza, 259–69. Boulder: University Press of Colorado.

Putnam, R. 1995. "Bowling Alone: America's Declining Social Capital." *Journal of Democracy* 6 (1): 65–77.

———. 2000. *Bowling Alone: The Collapse and Revival of American Community*. New York: Simon & Schuster,

Redman, C. L. 2005. "Resilience Theory in Archaeology." *American Anthropologist* 107 (1): 70–77.

———. 2012. "Global Environmental Change, Resilience, and Sustainable Outcomes." In *Surviving Sudden Environmental Changes: Answers from Archaeology*, edited by J. Cooper and P. Sheets, 237–44. Boulder: University Press of Colorado.

Redman, C. L., and A. P. Kinzig. 2003. "Resilience of Past Landscapes: Resilience Theory, Society, and the Longue Durée." *Conservation Ecology* 7 (1): article 14. Retrieved 14 May 2020 from http://www.consecol.org/vol7/iss1/art14/.

Rigby, E., M. Symonds, and D. Ward-Thompson. 2004. "A Comet Impact in A.D. 536?" *Astronomy and Geophysics* 45 (1): 23–26.

Salazar, L. 2015. "Typhoon Yolanda: The Politics of Disaster Response and Management." *Southeast Asian Affairs* 2015: 277–301.

Schleussner, C.-F., J. Donges, R. Donner, and H. Schellnhuber. 2016. "Armed-Conflict Risks Enhanced by Climate-Related Disasters in Ethnically Fractionalized Countries." *PNAS* 113 (33): 9216–21.

Smith, M. E., and P. N. Peregrine. 2012. "Approaches to Comparative Analysis in Archaeology." In *The Comparative Archaeology of Complex Societies*, edited by M. E. Smith, 4–20. Cambridge: Cambridge University Press.

Tierney, K. 2014. *The Social Roots of Risk: Producing Disasters, Promoting Resilience*. Stanford: Stanford University Press.

Toohey, M., K. Krüger, M. Sigl, F. Stordal, and H. Svensen. 2016. "Climatic and Societal Impacts of a Double Volcanic Event at the Dawn of the Middle Ages." *Climatic Change* 136 (3–4): 401–12.

Tselios, V., and E. Tompkins. 2017. "Local Government, Political Decentralization and Resilience to Natural Hazard-Associated Disasters." *Environmental Hazards* 16 (3): 228–52.

Turchin, P., R. Brennan, T. Currie, K. Feeney, et al. 2015. "Seshat: The Global History Databank." *Cliodynamics* 6 (1): 77–107

Turchin, P., T. Currie, H. Whitehouse, P. Francois, et al. 2018. "Quantitative Historical Analysis Uncovers a Single Dimension of Complexity That Structures Global Variation in Human Social Organization." *PNAS* 115 (2): E144–51.

Turner, B. L. 2010. "Vulnerability and Resilience: Coalescing or Paralleling Approaches for Sustainability Science?" *Global Environmental Change* 20 (4): 570–76.

Van de Noort, R. 2011. "Conceptualizing Climate Change Archaeology." *Antiquity* 85 (329): 1039–48.

Walker, B., C. S. Holling, S. Carpenter, and A. Kinzig. 2004. "Resilience, Adaptability and Transformability in Socio-ecological Systems." *Ecology and Society* 9 (2): article 5. http://www.ecologyandsociety.org/vol9/iss2/art5.

White, R., W. Edwards, A. Farrar, and M. J. Plodinec. 2015. "A Practical Approach to Building Resilience in America's Communities." *American Behavioral Scientist* 59 (2): 200–19.

Wisner, B., P. Blaikie, T. Cannon, and I. Davis. 2004. *At Risk: Natural Hazards, People's Vulnerability, and Disasters*. London: Routledge.

Wisner, B., and I. Kelman. 2015. "Community Resilience to Disasters." In *International Encyclopedia of the Social Sciences*, edited by J. D. Wright, 354–60. New York: Elsevier.

Woolcock, M. 1998. "Social Capital and Economic Development: Toward a Theoretical Synthesis and Policy Framework." *Theory and Society* 27 (2): 151–208.

Zhang, D., H. Lee, C. Wang, B. Li, Q. Pei, J. Zhang, and Y. An. 2011. "The Causality Analysis of Climate Change and Large-Scale Human Crisis." *PNAS* 108 (42): 17296–301.

CHAPTER 5

Collapse, Resilience, and Adaptation

An Archaeological Perspective on Continuity and Change in Hazardous Environments

ROBIN TORRENCE

Summary for Stakeholders

Archaeological research based on numerous observations spread over long periods of time contributes to contemporary policy by identifying social behaviors that have consistently mitigated the destructive effects of past natural disasters. In the face of five high-magnitude (VEI 4–6) volcanic eruptions over ten thousand years, the cultural strategies adopted by communities in the Willaumez Peninsula, Papua New Guinea, could also benefit modern communities. Although some cultural traits disappeared after these extreme environmental perturbations, the retention of other practices demonstrates a measure of resilience. Maintaining social connectedness over long distances was an essential component of effective recovery. The archaeological data imply that experiences from previous disasters were mobilized effectively, enabling people to flee the impacted area safely. These ancient populations found secure refuge with exchange partners who supported them over the significant length of time required for the impacted environment to recover enough to sustain self-sufficient groups. Subsequently, they recolonized their homelands successfully because memories about places had been maintained over multiple generations, probably through oral history and mythology supported by occasional visits. Over time, the adoption of increasingly more intensive agricultural practices shortened the time required for refuging.

Findings from archaeological research indicate that effective disaster management would ensure that (1) knowledge gained from past experiences is valued and passed on through cultural practices such as mythology, storytelling, and oral history; (2) communities actively maintain strong social connections with relatives, friends, and trading partners who reside outside potentially impacted regions; (3) authorities leverage the ability of local groups to make sensible decisions; and (4) following an event, innovations in agricultural (and other) practices that support and increase the speed of recolonization are encouraged and fostered. Research in Papua New Guinea demonstrates that actions inspired and driven by the community (bottom-up rather than top-down) can lead to successful enduring solutions.

Introduction

In the very early hours of the morning on 19 September 1994, two volcanoes on opposite sides of Rabaul Harbor (New Britain Island, Papua New Guinea) erupted simultaneously. Government authorities had not yet issued instructions to evacuate, fearing the mass exodus of people under darkness was too dangerous, but local communities concerned by the increased earthquake activity throughout the previous day had already taken it upon themselves to abandon their homes and seek safety. The spontaneous evacuation was largely stimulated by memories of the massive destruction and large death toll resulting from the 1937 eruption (Johnson 2013, 283–84; Neumann 1996). In contrast, the self-organized departure of thousands of people in 1994 was undoubtedly responsible for the low number of fatalities. Miraculously, no one was killed by the substantial ejecta or pyroclastic flows from this large-scale (VEI 4) eruption. The Rabaul experience raises important issues about the impact of extreme environmental events on human history. Do communities living in areas with relatively frequent volcanic events actively build on past experiences and cultural memories to increase their likelihood of survival? Or, put another way, have some human groups adapted to hazardous environments, and if so, can the same strategies they have developed be used to mitigate natural disasters in the modern world?

Archaeology is an ideal discipline for addressing these questions because most research projects encompass the substantial time frames required for comparative analysis of multiple events. Long archaeological timescales are also especially valuable for research on disasters because the vulnerability of populations is neither an independent nor an absolute property. Since humans have a propensity for learning from their experiences (i.e., building on knowledge of what past coping strategies worked and what did not) and have the ability to pass knowledge on through multiple generations, the way people cope with the impacts of an extreme environmental event at a specific time and place will undoubtedly be affected by their experiences of previous incidents.

In addition to selecting relevant timescales for analysis, it is also critical to examine the impacts of natural disasters over a geographical area large enough to incorporate the networks of social relations common among human groups. Tracking responses across the entire social network impacted by a natural disaster requires the spatial scale of the analysis to be framed around the social landscape, rather than concentrated at a single site.

Since it has experienced a long history of interaction between human societies and volcanism, the Willaumez Peninsula (WP) on New Britain Island, located approximately 250 kilometers west of Rabaul (figure 5.1), is ideal for exploring questions about the nature of cultural adaptability within a hazardous environment. After people first settled in this relatively small region (ca. 750 square kilometers) at least forty thousand years ago, they experienced at least twenty-seven volcanic events (table 5.1). The environmental consequences of most of the explosive eruptions were so severe that survivors would have been forced to leave their homes for significant lengths of time, in the order of at least several generations. Some locations would have been so drastically altered that reoccupation was impossible. For example, at various times lava flows of molten volcanic rock permanently reshaped part of their homelands. Tracing the

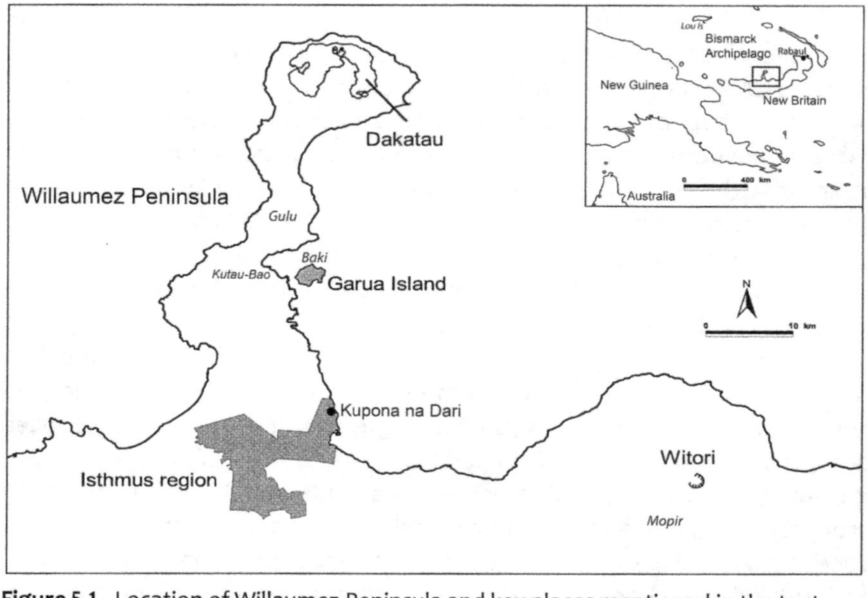

Figure 5.1. Location of Willaumez Peninsula and key places mentioned in the text. Names in italic are obsidian sources. Illustrated by Peter White and Nerida Little.

Table 5.1. Volcanic activity in the Willaumez Peninsula experienced by human groups. Ages are based on AMS radiocarbon determinations except (a) thermoluminescence dating and (b) fission track dating. For details see Machida et al. (1996, 71, figure 4), McKee et al. (2005, 2011), Neall et al. (2008), Petrie and Torrence (2008), and Torrence et al. (2004, 2009).

Volcanic Event	Type	VEI	BP Date
HOLOCENE			
W-H6	Plinian, subplinian	4	<500
W-H5	Phreatomagmatic	4	<500
W-H4	Plinian	4/5	<500
W-H3	Phreatomagmatic	4	<500
W-K4	Phreatomagmatic, plinian, ignimbrite forming	5	1310–1170
Dk	Phreatomagmatic, plinian, ignimbrite forming	5	1350–1280
W-K3	Plinian	5	1740–1540
Garbuna	Pyroclastic flow	?	ca. 1800
W-K2	Phreatomagmatic, plinian, ignimbrite forming	5	3480–3160
Unknown, east of Garbuna	Pyroclastic flow	?	ca. 4200
W-K1	Plinian, ignimbrite forming	5/6	6160–5740
Kulu tuff	Subplinian, phreatomagmatic	?	>W-K1
Numundo Maar	Subplinian, phreatomagmatic	?	<7500
PLEISTOCENE			
Tephra H: Kupona na Dari	Long period with small dustings of airfall tephra	?	23,200 ± 6,100[a]
Tephra G: Kupona na Dari	Long period with small dustings of airfall tephra	?	
Tephra F: Kupona na Dari	Long period with small dustings of airfall tephra	?	
Kutau-Bao obsidian	Rhyolitic flow	?	12,000–27,000[a]
Tephra Lower E: Kupona na Dari	Local subplinian or distal plinian	?	39,8000 ± 5,200[a]; 38,000 ± 10,4000[a]
Tephras D1 and D2: Kupona na Dari	Subplinian eruption	?	
Tephra Upper C: Kupona na Dari	Long period with small dustings of airfall tephra	?	
Tephra Middle C: Kupona na Dari	Long period with small dustings of airfall tephra	?	
Tephra C: Kupona na Dari	Plinian eruption	?	

(continued)

Table 5.1. continued

Volcanic Event	Type	VEI	BP Date
Tephra B: Kupona na Dari	Long period with small dustings of airfall tephra	?	
Tephra B1: Kupona na Dari	Long period with small dustings of airfall tephra	?	
Tephra A: Kupona na Dari	Series of eruptions in quick succession culminating in a plinian eruption	?	36,000 ± 3,900[a]
Gulu obsidian	Rhyolitic flow	?	21,000–27,000[b]; 138,000[b]
Baki obsidian	Rhyolitic flow	?	30,000[b]; 232,000[b]

patterns of human settlement and cultural practices during the most recent ten thousand years, during which the region experienced five major eruptions, provides an opportunity to investigate whether and how societies living in an area with relatively frequent natural disasters developed coping strategies that enabled survival. It is also crucial to consider what insights the experiences of these ancient societies can offer for improving the way contemporary groups in risk-prone environments cope with very large scale, catastrophic events.

Frameworks for Analysis

In modeling the effects of ancient disasters, it is useful to consider the range of responses glossed here as "collapse," "resilience," or "adaptation" (Torrence 2019). Viewed over a significantly long timescale, some aspects of culture might not survive a major environmental impact. The loss of cultural practices will be considered here as a kind of "collapse." When a collapse has occurred after each of several subsequent volcanic events, the temporal pattern is characterized as "chaotic." In contrast, continuity or persistence in behavior (i.e., a return to the former state) is a form of "resilience," as defined by Holling (1973). Another possibility is that through learning from previous experiences or due to innovations (either intentional or accidental), a society may respond to volcanic disasters in ways that decrease the force of the impacts and reduce the time it takes to recover, a response I term "adaptation." In examining archaeological case studies as a potential guide for modern disaster management, it is especially productive to focus on cultural behaviors that assisted resilience or adaptations that led to more effective responses subsequently.

Sampling Volcanic History

Located in an area aptly described as "a unified tangle of interconnecting tectonic plate boundaries and volcanic provinces of remarkable complexity" (Johnson 2013, 10), the island of New Britain has an impressive suite of fifteen active volcanoes spread along five hundred kilometers of the north coast (Johnson 2013, xxiii; McKee et al. 2011, figure 1). Within the Willaumez Peninsula—comprised of another string of volcanoes jutting out northward from the mainland—interdisciplinary fieldwork has recognized multiple high-magnitude volcanic events that must have had deleterious impacts on human groups (table 5.1). Archaeological research has identified an intriguing mix of chaos, resilience, and adaptation in the way ancient groups have responded to these events. This long historical record may offer clues about the kinds of cultural practices that could help future communities deal effectively with large volcanic eruptions.

Remnants of early human occupation in New Britain are preserved at the Kupona na Dari site (figure 5.1), where chipped stone tools made from the volcanic glass obsidian were found interbedded within a stratified sequence of eleven airfall tephras dating between approximately forty thousand and twenty thousand years ago. Besides having to deal with the significant risks implied by these volcanic deposits, early island colonizers also had to cope with rhyolitic lava flows that created the Kutau-Bao, Gulu, and Baki obsidian sources (figure 5.1) (Torrence et al. 2004). Although the immediate risks to human life may not have been high when compared to the explosive eruptions, these lavas would have completely obliterated people's homelands, thereby necessitating abandonment and subsequent renegotiations of territorial claims. On the positive side, obsidian extruded in the rhyolitic eruptions became a valued resource that was used for making tools and creating social links through exchange. In particular, raw material from the youngest obsidian source, Kutau-Bao, seems to have been the most highly prized and widely distributed, although its physical properties are identical to the other local obsidians (e.g., Summerhayes 2009; Torrence et al. 1992; Torrence 2004). Perhaps the harrowing experience of witnessing the emergence of a new, shiny, and attractive raw material, in the midst of what would have otherwise been a significant disaster, contributed to the high cultural value of this stone, one that lasted over tens of thousands of years.

The Pleistocene record of human settlement is difficult to track in this region. The highly weathered tephras are very deeply buried, and the original distinctive physical traits and mineral compositions have been completely altered. The long archaeological sequence at the Kupona na Dari site shows that human groups persisted through periods of frequent, small dustings of tephra, but the area had to be abandoned after large eruptions (Neall et al. 2008; Torrence et al. 2004). The density of artifacts and remains of earth ovens indicate the site was repeatedly occupied for reasonably long periods, but the nature of the chipped stone cores and tools implies that local groups practiced a mobile lifestyle. Obsidian tools made from raw material brought from sources located both to the east (Mopir) and west (Baki, Gulu, and late in the sequence, Kutau-Bao) suggest human groups regularly ranged over fairly large areas and were probably aware of alternative resources that could be accessed when their territory was impacted by volcanic activity (figure 5.1).

A much more detailed picture of human interaction with volcanism can be gained from archaeological sites dated to the more recent Holocene period. During the past ten thousand years local communities would have experienced five large-magnitude plinian (i.e., explosive) eruptions measuring VEI 5/6 (W-K1–4 and Dk in table 5.1). The four W-K events emanated from the Witori caldera complex, located to the east, whereas the Dakataua volcano, whose current lake-filled caldera occupies the northern end of the WP, was responsible for the DK event (figure 5.1). The human impacts of the smaller eruptions from Witori (W-H series) during the last millennium are more difficult to monitor because preservation of the thin tephras has a patchy distribution. The DK (1350–1280 BP) and W-K4 (1310–1170 BP) events were so closely spaced in time, they can be considered together. The major impacts of each would have been felt near their source volcanoes, with the thick DK tephra only present in the northern part of the WP, and W-K4 only clearly expressed in the south (Machida et al. 1996; Torrence, Neall, and Boyd 2009). Also relevant is the close timing of the W-K4 and DK events, with a major eruption at Rabaul dated to approximately 1283–1251 BP (McKee et al. 2015; table 5.1). This additional disaster would have greatly reduced the potential areas where people impacted by DK and W-K4 could seek refuge, thereby substantially increasing the severity of their combined impacts.

Each of the Holocene eruptions produced high volumes of material that buried the entire region under thick layers of airfall tephra (table 5.2; Machida et al. 1996; Torrence et al. 2009). The emplacement of the tephras often led to further subsequent impacts that radically altered access to natural resources. For example, following the W-K2 event, a large tidal embayment on the southwestern side of the peninsula was completely inundated by sediments, probably after a dam built up by the accumulation of airfall tephra burst open, leading to massive flooding and the redeposition of thick beds of sediments downstream (Neall et al. 2008; Torrence et al. 2009). On the east side of the WP, the accumulation of airfall tephras from the W-K events gradually converted swampy areas into dry land, which

Table 5.2. Comparison of extant, preserved depth of airfall tephra with the modal length of abandonment for Garua Island and the Isthmus region of the Willaumez Peninsula. See Machida et al. (1996); Petrie and Torrence (2008); Torrence et al. (2009); Torrence fieldnotes.

Eruption	Garua Island		Isthmus Region	
	Tephra Depth (mm)	Modal Length of Abandonment (years)	Tephra Depth (mm)	Modal Length of Abandonment (years)
W-K4	Not observed		100–500	105
DK	600–900	235	Trace	0
W-K3	150	95	400–700	55
W-K2	600–800	140	500–900	155
W-K1	Unknown	120	500–900	1,710

had the benefit of considerably expanding the area available for human settlement (Parr et al. 2009).

The widespread deposition of the tephras has proved to be a huge advantage for archaeological research, since each distinctive layer comprises a reliable temporal marker horizon that can be traced across the entire peninsula (illustration 5.1). This is especially important in this tropical area with high temperatures and rainfall, because charcoal and other organic

Illustration 5.1. Typical archaeological test pit showing tephra layers. Photograph by Robin Torrence.

remains normally used for chronometric dating are poorly preserved. Systematic archaeological field research has been conducted in two areas. Garua Island is situated just offshore from the western side of the WP and the Isthmus region was arbitrarily chosen (figures 5.2a–b). The swampy area of the transformed tidal embayment was not sampled. In both study areas, one-meter-square test pits, distributed as widely as possible, were excavated to a depth of twenty centimeters below the W-K1 tephra, if preserved, or at least twenty centimeters into the clay beneath the W-K2 tephra. The resulting landscape sample comprises sixty-seven square meters on Garua Island (Torrence 2002) and sixty-nine square meters in the Isthmus (Torrence and Doelman 2007, 49, 57).

Collapse and Innovation as Reflections

For small scale, premodern societies, collapse would seem an inevitable consequence of exposure to high-magnitude volcanic hazards. Outside the immediate environs of the volcano, the accumulation of airfall tephra probably had very few, if any, immediate lethal effects. On the other hand, faced with the total destruction of houses under the weight of the tephra, the burial of gardens, severe damage to the forest through the loss of branches, the fouling of water, and health risks caused by breathing the abrasive and dusty tephra, residents must have been forced to abandon the region for substantial lengths of time after each major eruption. It would only be sensible to return when the environment was safe and stable and, perhaps, not until the tephra had broken down enough to form soil necessary for forest regeneration and/or for gardening. Consequently, the resulting history of human occupation fits a chaotic pattern with repeated cycles of collapse and recovery (table 5.2).

Since the archaeological excavations comprise a very small sample of the total surface area, it is unlikely that the exact date of the "first footsteps" of the people who returned after each volcanic event has been discovered. Given the relatively large number of radiocarbon determinations obtained (Petrie and Torrence 2008), however, we can assume that the oldest dates obtained for the layer directly on top of each tephra provides a reasonable approximation of when people began to recolonize the region. Not surprisingly, given the large depths of tephra, the Holocene temporal record of human settlement on the WP has substantial periods lacking human occupation (table 5.2). After each event, the population was forced to flee the region and was unable to return for long periods of time, roughly in the order of one to two centuries or about five to ten generations. In both study areas there is also a close correlation between

a

b

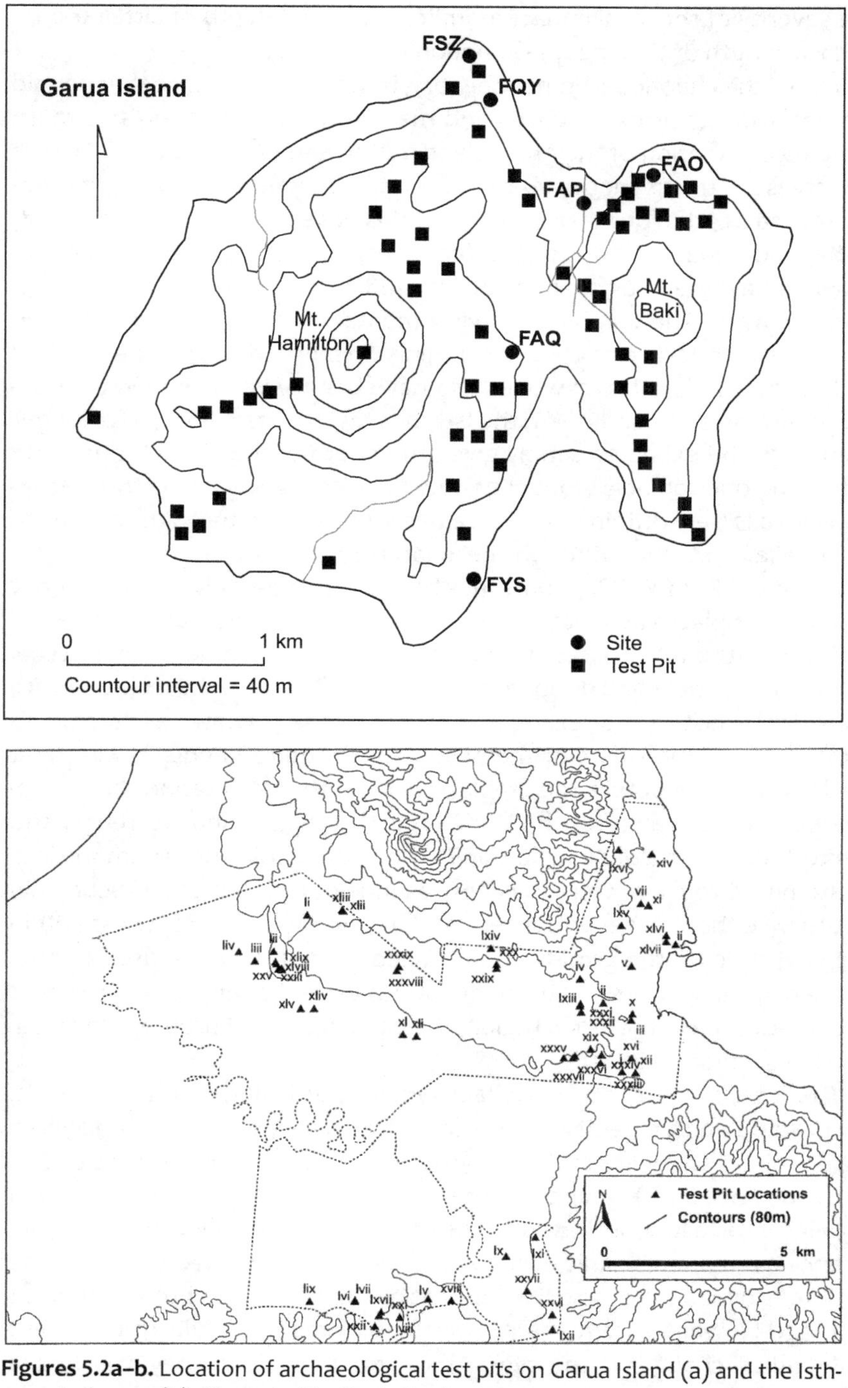

Figures 5.2a–b. Location of archaeological test pits on Garua Island (a) and the Isthmus study area (b). Illustrated by Trudy Doelman.

the severity of the local impact as indicated by the depth of airfall tephra and the length of time people abandoned the region.

Within the chaotic settlement history, is there any evidence that people learned from their experiences and made innovations to assist a more rapid recolonization of their homelands? Between W-K1 and W-K3 there is a decrease in the abandonment period in the Isthmus region, despite similar tephra depths for these events, but the close contemporaneity of DK, W-K4, and Rabaul clearly constituted a very significant disaster, because it would have been difficult to recover sufficiently before the next eruption occurred. The combined environmental hazards would have been exacerbated because relatives or trading partners who could be reached within several days travel would also have been severely impacted. Consequently, after DK and W-K4, the Isthmus region was deserted for longer than might be expected simply given the depth of the airfall tephra. Furthermore, one can only wonder at how the close timing of the three eruptions across New Britain might have been interpreted through the lens of local belief systems. Although these later eruptions were of less magnitude than W-K1 or W-K2, people may have been extremely cautious about returning to places associated with repeated environmental calamities.

Tracking the punctuated occupation history, key elements of material culture also appear and disappear in a "chaotic" pattern in synchrony with the volcanic history. For example, obsidian artifacts known as "stemmed tools" (due to the shape of the protrusions used as handles), were first made some time before the emplacement of the W-K1 tephra but disappeared immediately after the W-K2 eruption (e.g., Araho, Torrence, and White 2002; Torrence, Kelloway, and White 2013). Coincident with the loss of stemmed tools, pottery making was introduced, but this practice did not survive the W-K3 event. After W-K4, or perhaps even as late as within the W-H series, large ground and polished stone axes composed of fine-grained volcanic rocks and used for various woodworking tasks were first widely adopted in the study region and persisted until European colonization (illustrations 5.2a–c).

The losses of significant artifact types—particularly stemmed tools, decorated Lapita ceramics, or ground stone axes, all of which played a major role in social life and ceremony (e.g., Specht 2005; Torrence et al. 2013; Torrence 2016)—might be inferred to signal cultural "collapses" and highlight the failure of these societies to deal successfully with the consequences of major volcanic events. Certainly, such a marked change in the kinds of objects used in social negotiations is significant, but it is difficult to judge to what extent the new classes of material culture represent truly radical changes in the overall structure of society. They might have been straight replacements that merely signify changes in fashion rather

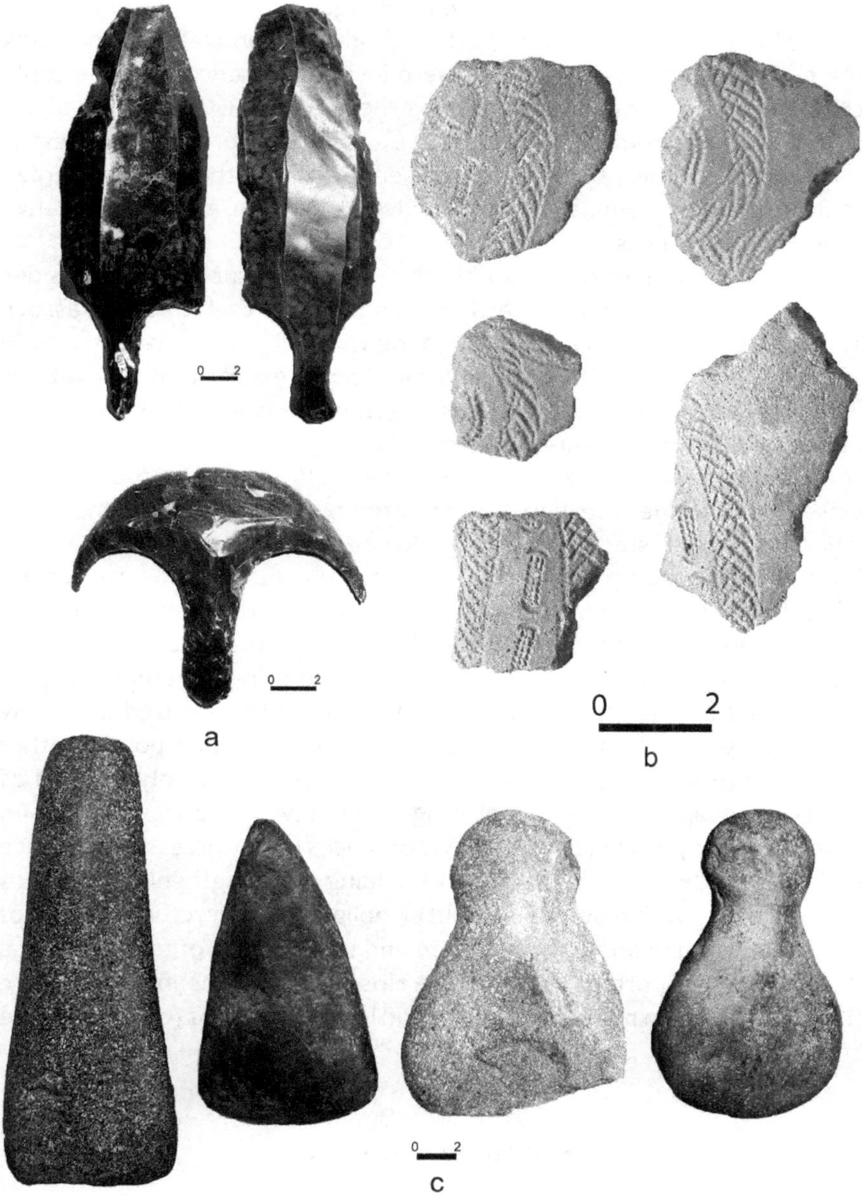

Illustrations 5.2a–c. Primary artifact types recovered from archaeological excavations in the Willaumez Peninsula: obsidian stemmed tools (a), Lapita pottery (b), ground stone ax blades (c). The scale bar is two centimeters. Photographs by Robin Torrence, Peter White, and Jim Specht.

than a restructuring of social and political organization. Rather than focus on the losses, however, it is important to identify innovations. Following the eruptions, new artifact types were invented or adopted. One could conceptualize changes like these along the lines of the Greek myth about a phoenix rising from the ashes or, to use another expression, "necessity is the mother of invention." Although people living in the WP were forced to flee from their homelands, they survived, persisted, and made creative changes to their lives.

Collapse and innovation can be usefully conceptualized as flip sides of the same coin. The novel artifacts and the cultural practices associated with them show that despite experiencing substantial damage, social organization in the WP remained intact to the extent that innovations were implemented. In fact, the loss of some practices may have created opportunities for previously disenfranchised groups to take charge and stimulate change. For example, Torrence (2016) proposes that the collapse of the former prestige system based on the production and circulation of obsidian stemmed tools, which occurred immediately following the W-K2 disaster, provided the necessary stimulus for the introduction of Lapita pottery. Previous leaders lost their authority because they had been driven away from the sources of obsidian by the eruption and were unable to continue ceremonial practices while living in refugee camps. Capitalizing on the weakness of the old guard, others seized on a new ideology signified by the elaborate decorations on Lapita pots. In other words, cultural changes following a disaster need not only be read as failure or collapse. They might also signify creative responses to stressful times. It is also possible that the novel practices led to increased resilience in the future through, for example, extending or strengthening social ties with distant communities who would be obliged to offer refuge in times of need. Rather than adopting a "gloom and doom" view of environmental disasters, it is important to look more closely at just who in society were the losers and who might have converted losses into gains (cf. Grattan and Torrence 2007).

Persistence of Places

Alongside the material culture changes and punctuated settlement history, both of which track the high-magnitude events, there are also remarkable hints in the WP archaeological record that some behaviors persisted. These confirm that people survived the volcanic hazards and over time developed a measure of resilience to the effects of these large-scale catastrophes. Unfortunately, due to the paucity of archaeological research in the surrounding regions, it is not yet possible to track the places where survivors of the volcanic eruptions in New Britain sought refuge. With regard to post W-K1 and W-K2, it is worth noting that stemmed tools made from WP obsidian have been found over a very wide area stretching as far east as Bougainville, west to West Papua, Misima Island to the south, and also including mainland New Guinea, East New Britain, Uneapa Island, and New Ireland. Torrence et al. (2013) argued that the widespread distribution of these distinctive artifacts is a consequence of the material consequences of long-distance social networks, but another plausible interpretation is that these highly prized possessions were carried away by refugees fleeing the eruptions. Unfortunately, none have yet been recovered from dated archaeological contexts.

There are convincing indications that after each high-magnitude volcanic event, a significant number of people found safe refuge. Based on the preservation of cultural traits, their descendants were among those who recolonized the impacted area generations later. Obsidian stemmed tools reappear after the W-K1 event (Araho et al. 2002; Torrence et al. 2013) and again following W-K2, although these later survivals are smaller and less abundant (Kononenko, Specht, and Torrence 2010). There is, however, continuity through time in the practice of obsidian exchange (Torrence 2004) and the use of obsidian tools for tattooing (Kononenko 2012; Torrence et al. 2018).

After each eruption, people repeatedly returned to locations previously used even if they had been radically altered by the emplacement of tephra deposits as much as a meter thick (table 5.2; Torrence et al. 2009; Torrence and Doelman 2007). For instance, data presented in table 5.3 show that a high percentage of samples in the Isthmus area were reoccupied after each of the eruptions. From 130 sample pits, 98 (75 percent) were occupied in consecutive periods. To take one example, the high densities of stone tools and remains of earth ovens recovered from excavations on hilltops situated around the southern edge of the shallow bay on the west side of the peninsula show that prior to the W-K2 eruption these were favored places used relatively intensively. Following the massive flooding resulting from W-K2 tephra accumulation, the bay was converted to a swamp (Torrence et al. 2009). Despite this significant environmental change, these hills were among the earliest places that people returned to roughly seven or eight generations later (Specht and Torrence 2007, 80–81). The large quantities of stone tools and the newly adopted Lapita pottery found at these sites indicate intense use rather than casual visits. Clearly, when people returned to the region many generations after the volcanic disaster, places that had special significance in the past were still remembered. The reuse of locales suggests that refugees retained knowl-

Table 5.3. Frequency of places in the Isthmus study area (figure 5.1) that were reoccupied following each of the high-magnitude volcanic events.

Eruption	W-K1	W-K2	W-K3	W-K4/Dk
Abandonment length (years)	1,710	155	55	105
Prior to eruption (sample pits)	12	49	46	23
Post-eruption (sample pits)	12	38	22	26
Reoccupation rate (%)	100	78	48	88

edge of their traditional lands over many generations, perhaps through oral history, myth, and ceremony. It is also possible that while they were still refugees, people made special trips to monitor these highly valued settings, in the same way as ancient groups in Costa Rica revisited their cemeteries after a volcanic disaster (Sheets 2016).

The persistence of memory is also implied by the continued use of Mopir obsidian (figure 5.1). Obsidian from the Mopir source occurs throughout the Kupona na Dari site and was relatively common in stone tool assemblages in the WP until it dropped out after the W-K2 event (Torrence 2004). The disappearance of Mopir obsidian is not surprising given the outcrops are situated in the area that suffered the most severe impacts from the Witori volcano. More importantly, pyroclastic flows from the W-K2 eruption blocked off the coastal access to the Mopir obsidian outcrops and left them landlocked (Torrence et al. 1996). Faced with a completely remodeled terrain, those who had previously reached the resource by sea may have had great difficulty in relocating it. The first people to return to Mopir probably approached it from the south coast along a familiar inland route (Summerhayes et al. 1988). It seems most plausible that the memory of Mopir could be retained by those for whom the landscape was least impacted and where trails could still be recognized. The history of the Mopir obsidian source illustrates both the potential power as well as the limitations of memory within a volcanically altered landscape.

I was once offered the opportunity to examine village sites near the Kutau-Bao obsidian source that had not been occupied for several generations. My guide was showing a kinsman places central to the oral history of their clan. His companion knew the stories and the place names, but he had never seen the actual physical locations because the area was abandoned in colonial times. For both men, the trip was not just about seeing the village sites. It was also about claiming ownership of these locales. It is through this combination of oral history and tutored visits that knowledge can be passed on effectively, even if the locations are only visited on rare occasions. It is plausible that a similar use of oral history helped ancient groups retain memory of places long after volcanic activity had forced their ancestors to flee their homelands.

Adapting Cultivation

A possible motivation for the retention of place knowledge, as indicated by the high rate of reoccupation in the study area, might have been the need to actively defend territorial rights to resources. Certainly, modern Papua New Guinea communities are very concerned about protecting ownership claims over land, even if immediate reoccupation after a volcanic event is difficult or impossible given the extent of damage (e.g., Johnson 2013; Torrence 2012). Consequently, while seeking refuge elsewhere, people revisit their old home sites, put up territorial markers, and plant gardens to enforce a claim over land (e.g., Lentfer and Boyd 2001, 51, 55; Martin 2013; Torrence 2012, 154, figure 4). It therefore seems reasonable to assume that competition over resources (perceived or real) could be a powerful stimulus for speeding up recolonization of an impacted region (cf. Crittenden and Rodolfo 2002).

In the case of the WP, there is tantalizing evidence that through time people devised a more intensive system of cultivation that enabled them to return to their homelands more quickly, rather than wait until the forest had regenerated. The data are based on the kinds and frequencies of phytoliths (diagnostic silica parts of plants that preserve over long periods) and plant charcoal extracted from systematic "column sampling" of sediments down the walls of the excavations. Changes in the relative numbers of these indicators show that the practice of shifting cultivation became more intensive. In the periods prior to W-K2, the composition of the plant fossils indicates that after an eruption people did not return until the forest had regrown. After W-K2, however, there is evidence for an increase in the amount of active intervention through landscape burning to clear land for gardens. In other words, human interference in the natural pattern of forest regeneration began increasingly earlier in the cycle (Lentfer and Torrence 2007; Lentfer, Pavlides, and Specht 2010; Parr et al. 2009). People reduced the length of time that plots were left to lie fallow before they were planted again. By adopting a more active and intensive form of cultivation, they could return to the region more quickly.

Supporting evidence for a change to more intensive gardening practices is also found in the distribution of activities across space, based on the incidence of stone tools in the sample pits. Beginning with a reasonably even spread over the entire Isthmus study area, around five hundred to a thousand years ago there is a gradual shift to a more clustered pattern of activities. The most intensive use of the landscape became focused on the flatter coastal areas and the periphery of swampy areas along the river, where intensive gardening would have been most productive (Torrence and Doelman 2007, 155–56, figures 5 and 6). On Garua Island the change to a more tightly clustered pattern (larger numbers of artifacts at fewer places) is even more pronounced, particularly after the DK event (Torrence 2002). One possibility is that rather than wait for the forest to regenerate, people took advantage of the natural clearance of the forest caused by the tephra falls and established gardens as soon as they could. They then extended the cropping period by intensive weeding and mulching to keep the forest at bay for longer periods (Lentfer et al. 2010; Lentfer and Torrence 2007; Torrence 2012).

The gradual intensification of land use over thousands of years can be interpreted as an adaptation to volcanic activity. Through time, cultivators increasingly took advantage of the reduction of forest cover following volcanic events. They also reinforced their control and ownership of their territories through longer-term and more-intense occupation. The case study shows that despite occupying risk-prone landscapes, human societies can find ways to increase their success. Refuging after high-magnitude disasters may always be a necessity, but future research should look for innovations that helped decrease the time needed for refuge and/or otherwise assisted and sped up the process of recolonization.

Resilient Social Ties

Underlying the previous arguments highlighting aspects of resilience and adaptation in the long history of the WP is the assumption that the re-colonizers were descendants of people who had survived the volcanic hazards. To support this premise, it is important to identity the strategies used by groups to ensure they could maintain themselves outside the critically affected areas for considerable lengths of time. As illustrated in recent case studies of volcanic disasters in Papua New Guinea, the problem of obtaining secure refuge over long periods is often not satisfactorily achieved. Furthermore, inappropriate solutions can lead to significant mortality, for instance due to poor nutrition or disease (Johnson 2013; Martin 2013). Currently, there is no archaeological evidence outside the WP for an influx of refugees from volcanic disasters, with the exception that the recolonization of the Siassi Islands following a period of abandonment might be coincident with the W-K3 eruption (Lilley 2004).

The absence of data is perhaps not surprising because very little archaeological research has been conducted in neighboring regions where refugees would have been most likely to have fled. Although it is plausible that the descendants of people affected by the W-K2 eruption had still not found a secure refuge several hundred years later and so stimulated the migration of people into the remote Pacific region approximately three thousand years ago, the gap in time after the disaster seems too long. Origin stories collected in the 1970s from inhabitants of the Witu Islands, located to the north of New Britain, describe a massive eruption of the Dakataua volcano as the cause for the formation of their island and claim that the first inhabitants came from the west coast of the WP (Rhoads and Specht 1980). Possibly the oral history records a causal connection between the Dk event and the arrival of refugees.

As an alternative to finding the actual places where people found refuge, it is useful to consider potential mechanisms that would have enabled people fleeing the region to be accepted into foreign villages and subsequently allowed to stay for a considerable length of time. The most important factor would have been social ties created and maintained through the practice of customary exchange. There is considerable evidence from oral history, ethnography, and archaeology for extensive trade networks in the recent past between the WP and places to the west, north, and east (e.g., Blythe and Fairhead 2017; Chowning 1978; Pengilley et al. 2019; Specht 1981). In addition, archaeological data show that exchange links both within and outside the local area have been a part of life in this area for thousands of years (e.g., Summerhayes 2009; Torrence et al. 2013). The preservation of these ties over time is an excellent example of the kinds of mechanisms used to foster resilience among groups in disaster-prone environments.

The strongest evidence for social connections leveraged in times of need is the widespread spatial distribution of stone tools made from the volcanic glass obsidian. Since each outcrop of obsidian has a relatively unique chemical composition, it is possible to attribute artifacts found at archaeological sites to their geological source. Extensive studies have shown that throughout the entire history of human settlement in the WP, obsidian was moved from four spatially discrete outcrops to consumers located across the local region (e.g., Summerhayes et al. 1988) (figure 5.1). The mix of sources found at each locality is unique, indicating that residents were maximizing their "lifelines" to external communities through personalized social links stretching in several directions (Torrence 2004). Beginning in the Late Pleistocene and lasting into the recent period, obsidian was transported as much as thirty-three hundred kilometers both to the east and west of the sources on New Britain. To the west it is found on sites on the mainland of Papua New Guinea and stretching into Indonesia, whereas to the east it occurs in archaeological contexts in New Ireland and the Solomon Islands, and all the way to Fiji (Galipaud et al. 2014; Summerhayes 2009; Torrence et al. 2013). The changes through time in the dominance of particular sources or in the form in which obsidian was moved, as finished tools or as raw material, suggest the particular social mechanisms have varied, but the persistence of obsidian exchange confirms that WP residents have been continually reaching out to make ties with communities who could offer safe refuges in times of stress. In addition, the persistence of obsidian trade (and, by implication, return exchange of perishable items not preserved in the archaeological record) suggests this practice has assisted communities to find a safe haven following environmental disasters.

Vulnerability and Disaster Management

When thinking about how to use the past to help benefit the future, it is important to first recognize that responses to current natural disasters can be heavily influenced by long-term interactions between environmental processes and human histories. As illustrated by the WP case study, archaeological research raises important issues relevant for designing effective ways to prepare for and manage future events. The most important point is that knowledge about previous human interactions with hazards is essential for accurately predicting the vulnerability of current communities, because the potential for social groups to recover from a volcanic disaster can be radically affected by prior experience. As such, it is productive to think in terms of the pasts, presents, and futures of disasters (Oliver-Smith and Hoffman 2002, 12; Torrence 2019). The present tense, which represents the initial impact of the hazard, is generally envisaged in terms of a social group's vulnerability, which is usefully conceived as the capacity "to anticipate, cope with, resist and recover" (Blaikie et al. 1994, 9). I prefer this more dynamic definition of vulnerability rather than the more passive characterization of vulnerability as "susceptibility to harm" (Gallopin 2006, 295). Vulnerability cannot be accurately measured by simply considering the contemporary period. Cultural groups whose history has been entangled with natural hazards might have the capacity to cope more effectively with environmental forcing agents than those with no previous exposure. Archaeological research in the WP shows that humans are creative and have the potential to adapt through developing innovative behavior that could increase their ability to withstand future environmental perturbations. Following on from this observation, encouragement and support of local, creative solutions to the problems caused by natural disasters, ones that may have developed and been maintained over long periods of time, could play important roles in successful disaster management.

To illustrate these points, it is useful to turn to a sister science of archaeology: geology. As a basis for predicting future volcanic risks in a specific region, earth scientists use geological data from field studies to reconstruct the history of past volcanic activity, in the order of tens of thousands of years. By examining a long series of volcanic events, geologists first identify repeated patterns. These are then compared with theories relating to the nature of plate activity in order to fine-tune current understandings of the relationship between general crustal behavior and specific landscape configurations. For example, Johnson (2013) has created a risk profile for each volcanic center in Papua New Guinea by bringing together theory about plate tectonics with knowledge about the specific trajectories of each particular place, based on extensive geological field research and informed by several hundred years of historical and oral history accounts. Contemporary hazard managers might benefit from adopting a similar approach in which theory about human behavior is combined with detailed information about how societies resident in a high-risk area have previously coped with rapid environmental changes over many centuries. What memories or oral history can be brought to bear to ensure rapid decision-making and effective evacuation? How can groups be supported to operationalize or extend social ties and obligations that could assist with ensuring long-term refuge? Following this approach, knowledge from archaeological and historical research about patterns of behavior during engagements with volcanic hazards could usefully supplement general concepts about how societies cope with crisis conditions.

Unfortunately, in contrast to the geological model, much archaeological research has targeted a single volcanic event and been directed solely at the immediate aftermath, using timescales in the order of one or two generations. The downside of framing a study of human interactions with volcanic activity in terms of small blocks of time is that the initial impact is inevitably followed by failures and collapses. These capture all the attention, leaving very little space for consideration of how in the longer run populations might have dealt with, innovated, or even benefited. Within this short-term, disaster-oriented mindset, there is little room for learning about whether or how societies might have leveraged coping strategies or developed creative solutions, processes that often unfold over years and decades.

Archaeological research should play a much more important role than simply documenting short-term events and catastrophes. The comparison of the archaeological record of human activity before and after five major volcanic events (ca. ten thousand years) in the WP shows that in the face of very high magnitude volcanic eruptions, populations unable to sustain themselves in the short term can nevertheless develop strategies that ensure their survival as refugees until they could safely return and reoccupy their ancestral lands. While maintaining memory and knowledge of their homelands, these refugees modified old ways or created new social practices, as evidenced by novel items of material culture and changes in the spatial distribution of activities. Some innovations, such as the adoption of decorated pottery or stone axes, may have bolstered their resilience to future events through strengthening cultural ties with people who could offer refuge in time of need. In addition, over time the WP populations developed increasingly more intensive strategies of land management that enabled them to reoccupy their homelands more quickly.

Since ancient lives in the WP are very distant from the modern world, it is appropriate to ask how insights derived from archaeology can inform modern disaster management. To begin with, it is useful to think in terms of the problems faced and the solutions found. Firstly, people need to be aware of the warning signs—such as earthquakes, sounds, initial tephra falls, etc.—and then take action quickly before the level of risk increases and escape is made difficult, for example, as a consequence of pyroclastic flows or lahars. Oral history could play a major role in guiding appropriate action. The role of memory is evidenced by the return of populations to places previously occupied despite major changes in the landscape. Many societies that occupy risky environments preserve stories about previous natural disasters, and these help keep people away from dangerous areas or guide appropriate action once an event has been initiated (e.g., Blong 1982; Cronin and Cashman 2007; Cashman and Cronin 2008; Chester and Duncan 2007; Walshe and Nunn 2012; Troll et al. 2015). Not only do these stories help modern-day earth scientists reconstruct past events, but since they are often incorporated into ceremony and practice, they are widely shared and retained. Information about appropriate action for how to seek safety is often present in myths and legends passed on through generations, but as the 1994 Rabaul case that opened this chapter shows, useful knowledge can also be embedded within more recent memories and stories shared within the family or wider group. Information can be effectively transmitted through existing cultural channels, for example by encouraging storytelling using existing mythology, oral history, and memories of recent disasters.

If knowledge about how to act in times of crisis is widespread and embedded in local culture, then it is more likely that people will recognize warning signs and act sensibly.

The ancient communities in the WP were largely egalitarian and self-sufficient. Consequently, most decisions would have been made at the individual or family level and could be implemented very quickly. People would have been accustomed to looking after themselves and would not wait for others to give advice or orders about leaving a dangerous area. More likely, they would follow their own instincts based on traditional knowledge passed on over generations. There is additional evidence from modern Papua New Guinea that nonurban communities still operate in a similar manner. Johnson's (2013, 363–64) extensive study of all the volcanic disasters in Papua New Guinea since 1937 found that in nine of thirteen cases, villagers moved themselves away from danger without waiting for instructions from government authorities. In four incidents people did not wait until an eruption began, but they were concerned enough by warning signs to evacuate. He concludes that in poor countries lacking access to sustainable, sophisticated monitoring instruments, the most practical option is to build and support "well-informed, resilient, and self-sufficient communities" (Johnson 2013, 376).

> Communities at risk from volcanic eruptions in Papua New Guinea are commonly self-reliant when decisions have to be made about their own safety and the need for possible evacuations. Such community decisions typically can be made promptly, responses can be rapid, and the evacuation communities can be remarkably mobile, as long as authorities do not interfere negatively with the spontaneity of the process. . . . "Spontaneous" evacuations such as these can, in many circumstances, be a more effective way of volcanic-threat avoidance, compared with waiting for instrument-based early warnings of eruptions from cautious, distant authorities. (Johnson 2013, 376)

This sentiment is echoed by Chester, Duncan, and Sangster's (2012) extensive study of responses to threat among farming villages in Sicily.

Once they have avoided the initial impacts of the disaster by leaving the affected area, the second hurdle for survivors is to find a safe place for temporary refuge. When the immediate threat is over and the full extent of the damage has been assessed, a longer-term solution may be required until it is feasible to return home. I think the problem of refuge for displaced groups in ancient times was overcome by enlisting long-distance social ties that had been forged and curated over millennia through exchange, as indicated by the widespread distribution of obsidian and the reinstatement of the Mopir source after the W-K2 event (Summerhayes 2009; Torrence 2004; Torrence et al. 1996). The broader importance of archaeological research is that modern groups at risk need to actively seek and foster strong, binding, and long-term social connections with others who reside outside the potential impact zone. Just knowing where to go is not adequate protection. People also need to leverage strong and durable support networks.

For communities at risk, government agencies could assist in ensuring the maintenance of strong social ties through creating occasions for social links to be built up (e.g., ceremonies, sporting events, church activities) and by actively supporting new or established long-distance linkages by providing transport. In Papua New Guinea, for example, government-sponsored dance or "mask" festivals held around the country often bring people together from many different cultural and language groups. Some might have been connected in the past through established trading routes, but these have faded. The memories of past cultural activities and voyages are still there, however, so that resurrecting and building on ancient social ties has great potential for ensuring refuges for communities affected by future volcanic disasters. Rekindling and building on existing social ties over long distances should be integral to current disaster management plans.

A third problem faced by refugees is how to recolonize their ancestral lands as soon as it is safe to do so, especially to maintain territorial rights over land essential for self-sufficiency and protection of sacred sites. I suspect there is a high likelihood of a conflict between the desire and need of refugees to return and the concern of authorities to protect citizens from danger, as described by Johnson (2013, 326–30) for people affected by volcanic activity on Manam Island in Papua New Guinea. In this case refugees from ongoing eruptions have experienced conflict with their hosts over access to the land needed for gardens, leading to high mortality in care centers on the mainland. Archaeological data from the WP do not provide answers for how refuging is best handled. The findings do, however, indicate that people are likely to experiment with subsistence practices to support a rapid return. Applying this observation in the contemporary world, governments might assist by conducting research on intensive farming methods suitable for areas affected by airfall tephra and being prepared to assist affected communities to adopt appropriate strategies or to support their experiments so they can develop new solutions themselves.

Archaeology of Volcanic Disasters

As illustrated by the Willaumez Peninsula case study, archaeological research shows the value of contextualizing disasters within a broader, long-term history that considers events and processes before, during, and after the events. How a group will respond is partially dependent on prior experience, which may entail hundreds of years during which a record of observations is built up and passed on through oral history and ceremony. Knowledge gained from the past may be put to good use in the future when the community experiences a severe hazard. It is also important to realize that in environments that have experienced disasters fairly frequently, some groups will have developed means for coping with them—for example, by recognizing warning signs, fleeing the area prior to the impact, leveraging social ties to secure refuge among other groups, and intensifying land use practices to speed up their return. Understanding how and to what extent societies adapt to environments characterized by relatively frequent hazards merits further comparative archaeological research in other areas of the world.

Acknowledgments

Archaeological research in the Willaumez Peninsula was funded by the Australian Research Council, Australian Museum, New Britain Palm Oil Palm Ltd., Pacific Biology Foundation, Australian and Pacific Foundation, and Earthwatch Institute and supported by the National Museum and Art Gallery of Papua New Guinea, West New Britain Cultural Centre, Walindi Plantation and Resort, Mahonia Na Dari Research Institute, and Kimbe Bay Shipping Agencies. I am indebted to long-term collaborators Jim Specht, Peter White, Vince Neall, Nina Kononenko, Bill Boyd, Carol Lentfer, Trudy Doelman, Chris McKee, and Hugh Davies and a host of volunteers from around the world. Comments from Payson Sheets helped sharpen my arguments.

Robin Torrence is a senior research fellow at the Australian Museum in Sydney. She received the Society for American Archaeology's award for "Excellence in Archaeological Analysis" for her research in stone tool studies, including her book *Production and Exchange of Stone Tools* and edited books *Time, Energy and Stone Tools* and *Ancient Starch Analysis*. Her edited books with John Grattan, *Natural Disasters and Cultural Change* and *Living Under the Shadow: The Cultural Impacts of Volcanic Eruptions*, highlight complex interrelationships between human societies and natural disasters. Her current archaeological research focuses on Papua New Guinea.

References

Araho, Nick, Robin Torrence, and J. Peter White. 2002. "Valuable and Useful: Mid-Holocene Stemmed Obsidian Artefacts from West New Britain, Papua New Guinea." *Proceedings of the Prehistoric Society* 68: 61–81.

Blaikie, Piers, Terry Cannon, Ian Davis, and Ben Wisner. 1994. *At Risk: Natural Hazards, People's Vulnerability, and Disasters*. London: Routledge.

Blong, Russell J. 1982. *The Time of Darkness: Local Legends and Volcanic Reality in Papua New Guinea*. Seattle: University of Washington Press,

Blythe, Jennifer, and James Fairhead. 2017. "The Spirit and the Gifts: Dako, Benjamin Morrell and Cargo in the Vitiaz Trading Area, New Guinea." *Oceania* 87 (1): 21–37.

Cashman, Katherine V., and Shane J. Cronin. 2008. "Welcoming a Monster to the World: Myths, Oral Tradition, and Modern Societal Response to Volcanic Disasters." *Journal of Volcanology and Geothermal Research* 176 (3): 407–18.

Chester, David K., and Angus M. Duncan. 2007. "Geomythology, Theodicy, and the Continuing Relevance of Religious Worldviews on Responses to Volcanic Eruptions." In *Living Under the Shadow: The Cultural Impacts of Volcanic Eruptions*, edited by John Grattan and Robin Torrence, 203–24. Walnut Creek, CA: Left Coast Press.

Chester, David K., Angus M. Duncan, and Heather Sangster. 2012. "Human Responses to Eruptions of Etna (Sicily) During the Late Pre-Industrial Era and Their Implications for Present-Day Disaster Planning." *Journal of Volcanology and Geothermal Research* 225–26: 65–80.

Chowning, Ann. 1978. "Changes in West New Britain Trading Systems in the Twentieth Century." *Mankind* 11 (3): 296–307.

Crittenden, Kathleen S., and Kelvin S. Rodolfo. 2002. "Bacolor town and Pinatubo Volcano, Philippines: Coping with Recurrent Lahar Disaster." In *Natural Disasters and Cultural Change*, edited by Robin Torrence and John Grattan, 43–65. London: Routledge.

Cronin, Shane J., and Katherine V. Cashman. 2007. "Volcanic Oral Traditions in Hazard Assessment and Mitigation." In *Living Under the Shadow: The Cultural Impacts of Volcanic Eruptions*, edited by John Grattan and Robin Torrence, 175–202. Walnut Creek, CA: Left Coast Press.

Galipaud, Jean-Christophe, Christian Reepmeyer, Robin Torrence, Sarah Kelloway, and Peter White. 2014. "Long Distance Connections in Vanuatu: New Obsidian Characterisations for the Makué site, Aore Island." *Archaeology in Oceania* 49 (2): 110–16.

Gallopin, Gilberto C. 2006. "Linkages between Vulnerability, Resilience, and Adaptive Capacity." *Global Environmental Change* 16 (3): 292–303.

Grattan, John, and Robin Torrence. 2007. "Beyond Gloom and Doom: the Long-Term Consequences of Volcanic Disasters." In *Living Under the Shadow: The Cultural Impacts of Volcanic Eruptions*, edited by John Grattan and Robin Torrence, 1–18. Walnut Creek, CA: Left Coast Press.

Holling, Crawford Stanley. 1973. "Resilience and Stability of Ecological Systems." *Annual Review of Ecology and Systematics* 4: 1–23.

Johnson, R. Wally. 2013. *Fire Mountains of the Islands: A History of Volcanic Eruptions and Disaster Management in Papua New Guinea and the Solomon Islands*. Canberra: ANU E Press.

Kononenko, Nina. 2012. "Middle and Late Holocene Skin-Working Tools in Melanesia: Tattooing and Scarification?" *Archaeology in Oceania* 47 (1): 14–28.

Kononenko, Nina, Jim Specht, and Robin Torrence. 2010. "Persistent Traditions in the Face of Natural Disasters: Stemmed and Waisted Stone Tools in Late Holocene New Britain, Papua New Guinea." *Australian Archaeology* 70 (1): 17–28.

Lentfer, Carol, and William E. Boyd. 2001. *Maunten Paia: Volcanoes, People and Environment: The 1994 Rabaul Volcanic Eruptions*. Lismore, NSW: Southern Cross University Press.

Lentfer, Carol, Christine Pavlides, and Jim Specht. 2010. "Natural and Human Impacts in a 35,000 Year Vegetation History in Central New Britain, Papua New Guinea." *Quaternary Science Reviews* 29 (27–28): 3750–67.

Lentfer, Carol, and Robin Torrence. 2007. "Holocene Volcanic Activity, Vegetation Succession, and Ancient Human Land Use: Unravelling the Interactions on Garua Island." *Review of Palaeobotany and Palynology* 143 (3–4): 83–105.

Lilley, Ian. 2004. "Trade and Culture History across the Vitiaz Strait, Papua New Guinea." In "A Pacific Odyssey: Archaeology and Anthropology in the Western Pacific; Papers in Honour of Jim Specht," edited by Val Attenbrow, and Richard Fullagar. Supplement, *Records of the Australian Museum Supplement* 29: 89–96.

Machida, Hiroshi, Russell J. Blong, Jim Specht, Robin Torrence, Hiroshi Moriwaki, Yukio Hayakawa, Ben Talai, David Lolok, and Colin F. Pain. 1996. "Holocene Explosive Eruptions of Witori and Dakataua Caldera Volcanoes in West New Britain, Papua New Guinea." *Quaternary International* 34–36: 65–78.

Martin, Keir. 2013. *The Death of the Big Men and the Rise of the Big Shots: Custom and Conflict in East New Britain*. New York: Berghahn Books.

McKee, Chris O., Michael G. L. Baillie, and Paula J. Reimer. 2015. "A Revised Age of AD667–699 for the Latest Major Eruption at Rabaul." *Bulletin of Volcanology* 77 (7).

McKee, Chris O., Vince Neall, and Robin Torrence 2011. "A Remarkable Pulse of Large-Scale Volcanism on New Britain Island, Papua New Guinea." *Bulletin of Volcanology* 73 (1): 27–37.

McKee, Chris O., Herman Patia, John Kuduon, and Robin Torrence. 2005. "Volcanic Hazard Assessment of the Krummel-Garbuna-Welcker Volcanic Complex, Southern Willaumez Peninsula, WNB, Papua New Guinea." *Geological Survey, Papua New Guinea*, report 2005/4.

Neall, Vince, R. Clelland Wallace, and Robin Torrence. 2008. "The Volcanic Environment for 40,000 Years of Human occupation on the Willaumez Isthmus, West New Britain, Papua New Guinea." *Journal of Volcanology and Geothermal Research* 176: 330–43.

Neumann, Klaus 1996. *Rabaul: Yu Swit Moa Yet: Surviving the 1994 Volcanic Eruption*. Oxford: Oxford University Press.

Oliver-Smith, Antony, and Susanna M. Hoffman. 2002. "Why Anthropologists Should Study Disasters." In *Catastrophe and Culture: The Anthropology of Disaster*, edited by Antony Oliver-Smith, and Susanna M. Hoffman, 3–22. Sante Fe: School of American Research Press.

Parr, Jeff, William E. Boyd, Vicki Harriott, and Robin Torrence. 2009. "Human Adaptive Responses to Catastrophic Landscape Disruptions during the Holocene at Numundo, PNG." *Geographical Research* 47 (2): 155–74.

Pengilley, Alana, Christabel Brand, James Flexner, Jim Specht, and Robin Torrence. 2019. "Detecting Exchange Networks in New Britain, Papua New Guinea: Geochemical Comparisons Between Axe-Adze Blades and In Situ Volcanic Rock Sources." *Archaeology in Oceania* 54 (3): 200–213.

Petrie, Cameron, and Robin Torrence. 2008. "Assessing the Effects of Volcanic Disasters on Human Settlement in the Willaumez Peninsula, Papua New Guinea: A Bayesian Approach." *The Holocene* 18 (5): 729–44.

Rhoads, Jim, and Jim Specht. 1980. "Aspects of the Oral History of the Bali-Witu Islands, West New Britain Province." *Oral History* 8 (8): 10–22.

Sheets, Payson. 2016. "Thoughts and Observations on Volcanic Activity and Human Ecology." *Quaternary International* 394: 152–54.

Specht, Jim. 1981. "Obsidian Sources at Talasea, West New Britain, Papua New Guinea." *Journal of the Polynesian Society* 90 (3): 337–56.

———. 2005. "Stone Axe Blades and Valuables in New Britain, Papua New Guinea." In *A Polymath Anthropologist: Essays in Honour of Ann Chowning*, edited by Claudia Gross, Harriet D. Lyons, and Dorothy A. Counts, 15–22. University of Auckland Research in Anthropology and Linguistics Monograph 8. Auckland: Department of Anthropology, University of Auckland.

Specht, Jim, and Robin Torrence. 2007. "Lapita All Over: Land-Use on the Willaumez Peninsula, Papua New Guinea." In *Oceanic Explorations: Lapita and Western Pacific Settlement*, edited by Stuart Bedford, Christophe Sand, and Sean Connaughton, 71–96. Terra Australis 26. Canberra: ANU E-Press.

Summerhayes, Glenn R. 2009. "Obsidian Network Patterns in Melanesia—Sources, Characterization and Distribution." *Bulletin of the Indo-Pacific Prehistory Association* 29: 109–24.

Summerhayes, Glenn R., J. Roger Bird, Richard Fullagar, Chris Gosden, Jim Specht, and Robin Torrence. 1988. "Application of PIXE-PIGME to Archaeological Analysis of Changing Patterns of Obsidian Use in West New Britain, Papua New Guinea." In *Archaeological Obsidian Studies*, edited by Steven Shackley, 129–58. New York: Plenum.

Torrence, Robin. 2002. "Cultural Landscapes on Garua Island, Papua New Guinea." *Antiquity* 76 (293): 766–76.

———. 2004. "Now You See It, Now You Don't: Changing Obsidian Source Use in the Willaumez Peninsula, Papua New Guinea." In *Explaining Social Change: Studies in Honour of Colin Renfrew*, edited by John F. Cherry, Chris Scarre, and Stephen Shennan, 115–25. Cambridge: McDonald Institute for Archaeological Research.

———. 2012. "Volcanic Disasters and Agricultural Intensification: A Case Study from the Willaumez Peninsula, Papua New Guinea." *Quaternary International* 249: 151–61.

———. 2016. "Social Resilience and Long-Term Adaptation to Volcanic Disasters: The Archaeology of Continuity and Innovation in the Willaumez Peninsula, Papua New Guinea." *Quaternary International* 394: 6–16.

———. 2019. "Social Responses to Volcanic Eruptions: A Review of Key Concepts." *Quaternary International* 499: 258–65.

Torrence, Robin, and Trudy Doelman. 2007. "Problems of Scale: Evaluating the Effects of Volcanic Disasters on Cultural Change in the Willaumez Peninsula, Papua New Guinea." In *Living Under the Shadow: The Cultural Impacts of Volcanic Eruptions*, edited by John Grattan, and Robin Torrence, 42–66. Walnut Creek, CA: Left Coast Press.

Torrence, Robin, Sarah Kelloway, and Peter White. 2013. "Stemmed Tools, Social Interaction, and Voyaging in Early-Mid Holocene Papua New Guinea." *Journal of Island and Coastal Archaeology* 8 (2): 278–310.

Torrence, Robin, Nina Kononenko, Peter Sheppard, Melinda Allen, Stuart Bedford, Patrick V. Kirch, and Matthew Spriggs. 2018. "Tattooing Tools and the Lapita Cultural Complex." *Archaeology in Oceania* 53 (1): 58–73.

Torrence, Robin, Vince C. Neall, and William E. Boyd. 2009. "Volcanism and Historical Ecology on the Willaumez Peninsula, Papua New Guinea." *Pacific Science* 63 (4): 507–35.

Torrence, Robin, Vince C. Neall, Trudy Doelman, Ed Rhodes, Chris McKee, Hugh Davies, Roberto Bonetti, Alesandra Guglielmetti, Alberto Manzoni, Massimo Oddone, Jeff Parr, and R. Cleland Wallace. 2004. "Pleistocene Colonization of the Bismarck Archipelago: New Evidence from West New Britain." *Archaeology in Oceania* 39 (3): 101–130.

Torrence, Robin, Jim Specht, Richard Fullagar, and J. Roger Bird. 1992. "From Pleistocene to Present: Obsidian Sources in West New Britain Province, Papua New Guinea." *Records of the Australian Museum* 42: 83–98.

Torrence, Robin, Jim Specht, Richard Fullagar, and Glenn R. Summerhayes. 1996. "Which Obsidian Is Worth It?" In *Oceanic Culture History: Essays in Honour of Roger Green*, edited by Janet M. Davidson, Geoffrey Irwin, B. Foss Leach, Andrew Pawley, and Dorothy Brown, 211–24. Dunedin: New Zealand Journal of Archaeology Special Publication.

Troll, Valentin R., Frances M. Deegan, Fester M. Jolis, David A. Budd, Bőrje Dahren, and Lothar M. Schwarzkopf. 2015. "Ancient Oral Tradition Described Volcano-Earthquake Interaction at Merapi Volcano, Indonesia." *Geografiska Annales, Series A, Physical Geography* 91 (1): 137–66.

Walshe, Rory A., and Patrick A. Nunn. 2012. "Integration of Indigenous Knowledge and Disaster Risk Reduction: A Case Study from Baie Martelli, Pentecost Island, Vanuatu." *International Journal of Disaster Risk Science* 3 (4): 185–94.

CHAPTER 6

Continuity in the Face of a Slowly Unfolding Catastrophe

The Persistence of Icelandic Settlement Despite Large-Scale Soil Erosion

ANDREW DUGMORE, ROWAN JACKSON, DAVID COOPER, ANTHONY NEWTON, ÁRNI DANÍEL JÚLÍUSSON, RICHARD STREETER, VIÐAR HREINSSON, STEFANI CRABTREE, GEORGE HAMBRECHT, MEGAN HICKS, and THOMAS H. MCGOVERN

Summary for Stakeholders

Within Europe, Iceland has suffered from more soil erosion than any other country. It provides an instructive case study to evaluate the long-term consequences of a slowly unfolding environmental catastrophe that impacts a primary means of food production for an entire nation. Animal husbandry, the basis of the land-based economy in Iceland since the ninth century, coupled with the cumulative effects of land management, climate change, and volcanic impact have led to the loss of about fifteen thousand to thirty thousand square kilometers of vegetation and soil cover from the Icelandic landmass. This catastrophic geomorphological change represents a fundamental alteration to some 15–30 percent of the island's total surface area. Due to the sensitivities of the landscape, soil erosion cannot be reversed by a simple return to the conditions existing immediately before it began and thus has continued for centuries. Halting erosion requires a fundamental reset in terms of land use, and that is hard to do—especially when the opportunity cost of changing subsistence practices is too great. Buffered by the sufferings of regions of Iceland, individual farms, and particular social groups, Icelandic society as a whole endured mostly through flexible subsistence, intensified social inequalities, and the ability to tap into larger marine and overseas provisioning and economic networks. This case demonstrates how an adaptable society can confront challenges through social organization and by diversifying the ways they impact the ecosystem. In the medium term—the past thousand years or so—this can be an effective, if costly, strategy, but it constrains future options and may fatally undermine human security in the future. A country can be highly eroded, yet still support a resilient agricultural system and develop to support a sophisticated urban society. But the scale of soil loss will generate issues for long-term local food security as the potential for future agriculture is limited by the soil erosion of the past. These limitations of local potential currently occur against the background of unprecedented global change and increasing international uncertainty, both of which could dislocate the international networks on which Iceland is heavily dependent. The Icelandic human ecodynamics story is far from over, and the next century will certainly see profound global change and many unanticipated outcomes. The slow catastrophe of Icelandic soil erosion is still unfolding; with the perspective of the *longue durée* it is evident that decisions made in the Viking Age and medieval period still resonate, constraining future options for resilience and adaptive flexibility. Management decisions today will create the landscape heritage of the future. Planners need to be aware that trade-offs among options for enhancing short-term resilience can have severe long-term consequences in the context of slowly evolving catastrophic outcomes.

Introduction

In 2009 Sveinn Runólfsson, director of the Soil Conservation Service, Iceland, remarked that "the strong link between the health of the land and human living conditions has been amply demonstrated over the 1,100 years of Icelandic history. . . . Massive land degradation and soil erosion contributed to the collapse of a once prosperous nation" (Runólfsson 2009). Runólfsson neatly captures a common view of the consequences of soil erosion in Iceland and elsewhere (e.g., Diamond 2005), views that we explore in this chapter.

Soil erosion in Iceland provides a unique case to evaluate the consequences of a slowly unfolding environmental catastrophe that affected and is affecting the primary means of subsistence for a whole society. In Iceland, animal husbandry—the raising of cattle, horses, sheep, and goats and, in the early centuries of settlement, pigs—has been the basis of terrestrial subsistence and land-based trade from initial settlement of the island in the ninth century (*Landnám*) to early modern times. Over the same period, the cumulative effects of land management, climate change, and volcanic impact have led to the loss of about fifteen thousand to thirty thousand square kilometers of vegetation and soil cover (Arnalds et al. 2001; Arnalds and Barkarson 2003; Crofts 2011; Streeter et al. 2015). This catastrophic geomorphological change represents a fundamental alteration to some 15–30 percent of the island's total surface area and, as about 10 percent of the island is ice covered, a higher proportion of its usable soils and continuous vegetation cover. Soil erosion in Iceland is in most cases a gradual and cumulative process, developing over multiple decades, if not centuries. Thus, it is not a disaster "event" as such, but a slowly unfolding catastrophe. The triggering and rate of soil erosion are heavily influenced by the intensity of geophysical and meteorological processes (Arnalds 2000; Ólafsdóttir, Schlyter, and Haraldsson 2001). However, since the introduction of domestic animals to this sensitive subarctic environment, animal husbandry and the management of grazing have had the greatest influence on composition, health, and extent of vegetation and soil cover (Runólfsson 1978; Thorsteinsson 1986; Arnalds 2000, 2004; Streeter et al. 2015). Historical and paleoenvironmental evidence of landscape-scale change has been central to understanding the rate and scale of erosion in Iceland. However, the relationship between soil erosion and social vulnerability has received less attention. What were the overall effects of soil loss on Icelandic society?

Soil is the foundation of agriculture, and in Iceland's case, healthy grazing lands are vital for successful animal husbandry. Thus, we might assume that the extreme nature of Icelandic soil erosion has also been a primary driver of large-scale social change (Diamond 2005; Montgomery 2012). From an environmentally deterministic perspective we might infer a connection between large-scale soil erosion and acute social stress, but this is not necessarily so, because societies may choose to innovate and adapt. Icelandic society as a whole has been highly resilient over multi-century timescales, avoiding the fate of the neighboring Norse colonies in Greenland, despite the compounding effects of sociopolitical and economic change, environmental degradation, climate change, volcanic eruptions, and outbreaks of disease (Karlsson 2000; Dugmore et al. 2012). Icelandic society has experienced acute social pressures in the centuries since settlement. There have been prolonged limits to population growth and long periods of profound inequality, where substantial proportions of the population were insecure, marginalized, and vulnerable, especially during the variable climates of the fourteenth to nineteenth centuries (Vasey 1996; Karlsson 2000). Individual farms have failed as a result of soil erosion, but Icelandic society has endured despite the massive environmental change and in the nineteenth century entered a prolonged period of growth, increasing human security and wealth, despite rapidly eroding soils and the cumulative effects of a millennium of soil erosion (Karlsson 2000; Crofts 2011) (see figure 6.1).

Figure 6.1 gives a very good impression of the extent of settlement in the early modern period before the population increases of the nineteenth century and mechanization. Island-wide, cumulative soil erosion has a very limited effect on home field areas vital for most terrestrial food production in medieval and early modern times. Degraded areas can be effectively utilized for extensive sheep grazing in the summertime and wool production, even though this will exacerbate their deterioration. We argue that persistence of settlement in Iceland was the outcome of adjustments made to the initial subsistence system and subsequent landscape learning that allowed the Norse to take advantage of new opportunities offered by resource systems across Iceland during the Viking Age. Societal resilience in later medieval Iceland was also a product of social structures that enshrined inequalities, a flexible response to political and environmental change, and the ability to both tap into marine food webs and to capitalize on external economic opportunities. The basis of Icelandic

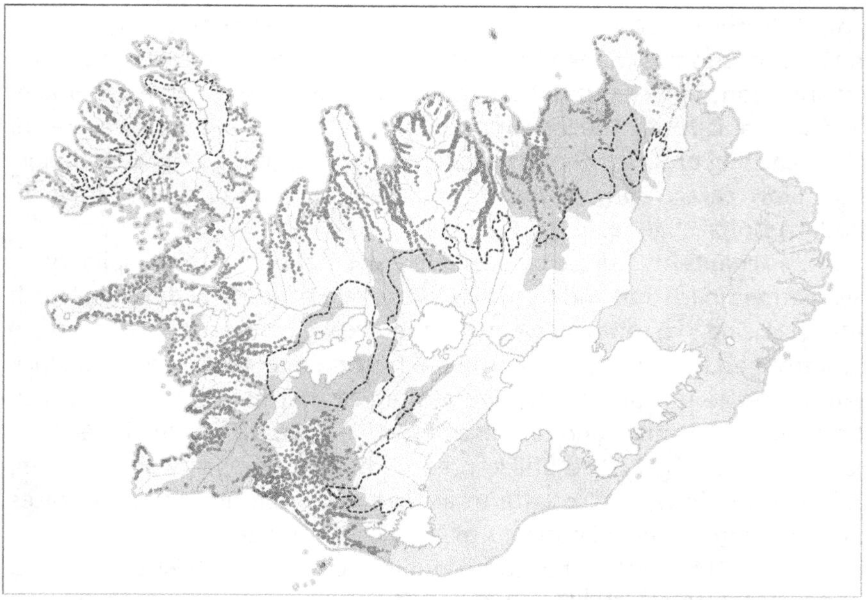

Figure 6.1. The dots represent settlement sites from the 1703 "Book of Farms" (data for the southeastern part of the island does not survive). Shaded areas represent districts with significant late twentieth-century rangeland degradation, soil erosion, and development of *rofabarð* erosion scarps (Arnalds 2000). The dotted lines mark the early twenty-first-century upland extent of major areas of very sparsely vegetated zones of poorly weathered vitrisols and lithosols that contain less than 1 percent organic carbon and are infertile (Agricultural University of Iceland 2001; Arnalds 2008).

societal resilience (from both engineering and ecological perspectives) was the ability to mitigate impacts of environmental degradation through social and political networks that created flexible resource-use strategies for land, rivers, lakes, and sea (Jackson et al. 2018). By displacing vulnerabilities spatially, temporally, and socially, the controlling social groups could promote their own resilience, with the costs borne by multiple landscapes and lower-ranking Icelanders.

Today, societies are also facing another type of slowly unfolding catastrophe driven by anthropogenic climate change. As global average temperatures increase, we are aware of the potential for future problems now, but increasingly severe impacts are only likely in generations to come, and the cumulative effects may be exacerbated by the displacement of vulnerabilities within the entire global system. Global disparities in wealth, access to resources, and exposure to the impacts of climate change are likely to widen the capabilities gap in the future (Leichenko and O'Brien 2008). Ecological damage has also become a major threat to global food security. Deforestation and soil erosion are strongly associated with unsustainable land management through intensive grazing and monocultures in many modern contexts (e.g., Foley et al. 2005). Such is the rate of land-use change that the United Nations Food and Agriculture Organization suggests that there may be as few as sixty harvests remaining (Arsenault 2014). The loss of nutrient-rich topsoils is thus a long-term, wide-reaching problem connecting current global change to the Icelandic case. Slow catastrophes visible in the Icelandic past may shed light on modern global change.

In this chapter we draw on sustained international interdisciplinary investigations in Iceland and from across the rest of the Scandinavian North Atlantic. Using a historical ecology framework, we combine landscape-scale data from archaeology, environmental history, and geosciences to elucidate evidence of human adaptive strategies that built redundancy into the subsistence and economic base of the Icelanders (Crumley 1994, 2017; Hartman et al. 2017). We utilize records of contemporary soil erosion, tephrochronology, and long-term aeolian sediment accumulation rates (SeAR) to infer detailed patterns of landscape change over multi-century timescales. This work is based on published and unpublished sources, reinterpretation of established knowledge, and a nuanced philosophical approach to the role of environmental change in human affairs. We do not focus on a single discovery and its implications, an approach that can encourage monocausal and environmentally deterministic emphasis to explanation (Dugmore et al. 2012; cf. Diamond 2005). A belief in reductionism and determinism expresses the view that our future is determined by irresistible forces (Hulme 2011)—that there is indeed "a divinity that shapes our ends, rough hew them how we may" (William Shakespeare, *Hamlet*, act 5, scene 2). Instead, we choose to evaluate the interplay between the constraints and opportunities presented by the environment, human actions, and their consequences. We use a historical perspective to understand how situations developed, with the recognition that alternative outcomes were possible and that lessons may be learned from the past that can inform contemporary debates about future actions.

The Peopling of an Island

The colonization of Iceland by the Norse in the late ninth century marked the initial occupation of one of the last settled places on Earth. Before the arrival of the Norse, the only land mammal on the island was the arctic fox. There were no indigenous herbivorous mammals. The depauperate, boreo-temperate vegetation of the island was a subset of that of northwest Europe and lacked endemic species (Dugmore et al. 2005). Woodlands of birch, willow, and juniper covered the sheltered and geomorphologically stable areas of the lowlands. Heath lands extended into favorable areas of the central highlands, which were, and still are, dominated by a series of icecaps that cover about 10 percent of the island. There is good evidence for a population of over twenty thousand people arriving in Iceland in less than a generation and transforming lowlands and uplands landscapes within this timescale (Vésteinsson and McGovern 2012). Settlement rapidly spread to cover the lowlands up to approximately four hundred meters above sea level (Schmid et al. 2017). The first settlers introduced cattle, horses, sheep, goats, and pigs to form the basis of their farming economy; they cleared woodlands and created field systems to produce fodder and grazing; and they organized a shieling system for seasonal grazing between lowland and upland pastures. Upland pastures were used during the summer months, and specific upland areas were utilized as commons grazing land corresponding to each rural municipality (Icel. *hreppur*), while lowland pastures more often had rights connected with specific farms. Historically, sheep have been taken down to lowland pastures in early September and were taken into barns as fall and winter progress. Although the Norse settlement was based on farms and a farming identity, the early settlers also exploited wild birds, walrus, and seal colonies, with marine and freshwater fish providing an increasingly important supplement to the farming economy (Perdikaris and McGovern 2008; Lawson et al. 2007).

The Anatomy of an Environmental Catastrophe

The scale of soil degradation and desertification in Iceland over the last millennia, which has been identified from paleoenvironmental evidence, is without parallel in the wider North Atlantic region (northern Europe, the other North Atlantic islands, and the eastern part of North America). Iceland is probably the most eroded country in northern Europe, despite its late settlement by people, and the processes that drive Icelandic soil erosion are well known (Arnalds 2000, 2004, 2008).

In modern Icelandic, the noun *uppblástur* is the most common word for wind erosion. It is derived from the Old Icelandic terms for this phenomenon: the verb *blása* (to blow), and the past participle or adjective form *blásinn* (blown). This indicates that wind was considered a primary cause of erosion and that it was well known in the medieval period. The terms *blása/blásinn* appear a number of times in medieval and pre-Reformation texts in different contexts: accounts of Iceland's settlement, sagas, legends, and official documents. The multiple references to wind erosion across a number of sources indicates that there was a general awareness of the problem of deflation. However, when viewed in the context of the widespread environmental evidence for soil erosion, references are perhaps less frequent than might be expected.

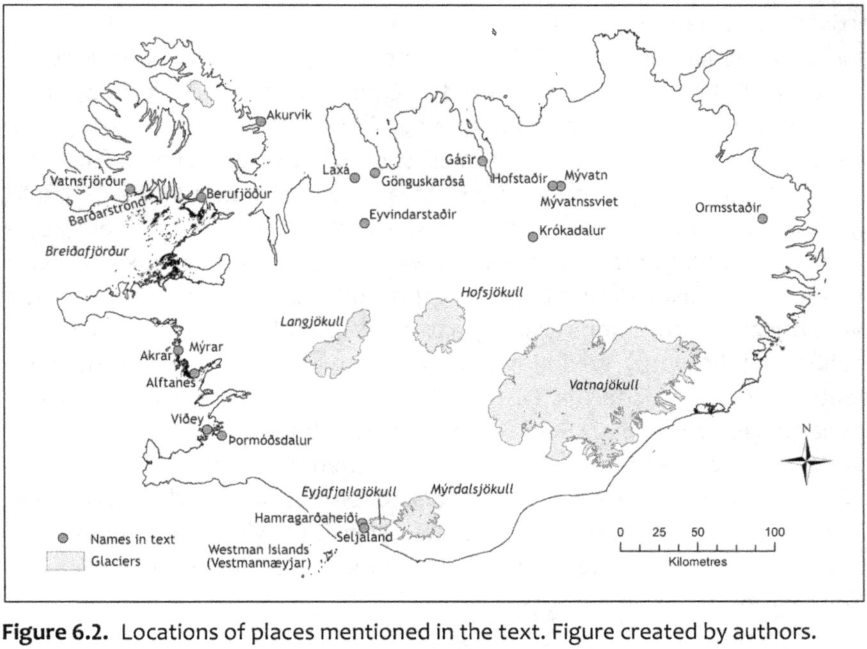

Figure 6.2. Locations of places mentioned in the text. Figure created by authors.

One example of an early written reference to soil erosion can be found in the *Hauksbók* version of *Landnámabók* (*The Book of Settlements*), compiled by Haukur Erlendsson in the early fourteenth century. This text says that Ormur Auðgi, son of Herjólfur, the first settler of the Westman Islands (see figure 6.2), "*bio a Orms stoðvm við Hamar niðri þar sem nv er blasit allt*" (lived in Ormsstaðir down by Hamar where it is all eroded now) (*Hauksbók*, p. 105). In a version of Örvar-Odds saga dated shortly before 1300, erosion appears in an interesting existential or philosophical context, underlining or symbolizing the passing of time (Pálsson and Edwards 1985). When Odd was a young man, a sorceress predicted that he would become three hundred years old, but the skull of the horse Faxi would eventually be the cause of his death. Odd killed the horse and dug it very deep in the ground. After that he traveled all around the world and did not return until three hundred years later to Berurjóður, where he had grown up. "*Þar var þá víða blásit ok jǫrvi, er þá váru hlíðir fagrar*" (it was widely eroded there, and gravel was where there used to be beautiful slopes), and a snake came out of the eye of the weathered skull of Faxi and bit Oddur, who then died. An eroded grave mound appears in the saga of Saint Olaf (ca. 1350–75), where strong wind had blown the soil off some silver (Johnsen and Helgason 1941). "*Blásinn*" appears once in the *Diplomatarium Islandicum*, in a document about the Viðey monastery purchasing the abandoned farm Þormóðsdalur in Mosfellssveit (near Reykjavík), "*var jordin adr blasin ok langa tima i eyde. sa þar litil merki til tvna ok tofta oc spiltt at ollv*" (The land was eroded earlier and abandoned for a long time. There were little remains of a home field and ruins and damaged in every way) (*Diplomatarium Islandicum* VII, 584–85).

Soil is mobilized when vegetation cover is lacking or breeched and erodible sediment is exposed to the action of frost, trampling by animals, wind, and the action of running water. There are, however, significant differences of opinion over the relative importance of different drivers of vegetation disruption that can lead to soil erosion. The drivers broadly fall into two categories: human impacts, such as deforestation and the (mis)management of domestic animals; and natural processes, such as ashfall from volcanic eruptions, drifting sand, flooding, low temperatures, high rainfall, and strong winds (Arnalds and Barkarson 2003; Simpson et al. 2001; Greipsson 2012). Broadly, opinions may be divided into those who think that people are primarily to blame, those who attribute the scale of change primarily to natural forces (while acknowledging some role for human impact), and those who would argue for combined synergistic effect of human actions and natural drivers. Crucially, the importance of different drivers of soil erosion has varied through time and across different regions of Iceland (Streeter and Dugmore 2014).

While authors debate the relative importance of triggers and drivers of soil erosion, the characteristics of Icelandic soils that make them vulnerable to erosion are generally agreed upon. The soils of Iceland are dominated by loessial andosols, which are derived from volcanic sediments (Arnalds 2015). Discrete layers of volcanic ash (tephra) augment most Icelandic soils. These are the soils subject to greatest erosion. The rapid weathering of fine-grained basaltic tephra (due to a high surface to volume ratio) results in the formation of poorly crystalline clay minerals, such as allophane and imogolite (Arnalds 2015), which lack the cohesive properties of phyllosilicate clay minerals. The ready aggregation of these clay minerals to form stable silt-sized particles means that Icelandic andosols are particularly vulnerable to wind erosion. In addition, other properties such as high water retention and very low plasticity mean loessial andosols are vulnerable to erosion by rain splash, running water, frost heave, and slope failure (Arnalds 2000). Icelandic andosols began to form soon after the decay of the last inland ice sheet, and over the course of the last eight thousand years soil profiles have been thickened through the addition of aeolian sediments derived from unstable sandy areas (Arnalds 2004; Ólafsdóttir and Guòmundsson 2002). Source areas for these wind-borne sediments include the highland deserts, pro-glacial areas, and the great outwash plains. In addition, volcanic ash (tephra) from eruptions (in some cases up to several cubic kilometers) has been spread over large parts of Iceland several times a century on average. These tephra layers have provided additional sources of fine-grained sediment that may be picked up by the wind and added to soils elsewhere on the island (Larsen and Eiríksson 2008; Larsen and Thórarinsson 1977; Larsen 2000; Thórarinsson 1967, 1975). Island-wide there are two main trends in soils thickness and composition. First, thicker soil profiles will tend to contain more tephra layers than thinner soils, because prevailing wind patterns and proximity to active volcanic systems shape the distributions of both aeolian soils and tephra. Second, soil cover is older and generally thicker in lowland areas, becoming thinner and younger in higher, more inland locations (Ólafsdóttir and Guòmundsson 2002).

Un-vegetated Icelandic soils are readily eroded by the wind and may be transported locally and regionally. The eroded sediment can be redeposited in the surviving areas of soils and vegetation. This means that aeolian sediment accumulation rates (SeAR) can be used as proxy records of the erosion intensity in the surrounding area (Thórarinsson 1961; Dugmore and Buckland 1991; Streeter, Dugmore, and Vesteinsson 2012). This is important, as soil erosion in Iceland often leads to the loss of the entire soil thickness, down to the bedrock or lag deposits (Arnalds 2000). Therefore, enhanced off-site accumulation is the only means of measuring the rates of erosion. Thórarinsson (1961) pioneered the use of tephrochronology to track changes in SeAR, and this approach can be used to precisely and accurately track variations in SeAR temporally and spatially, and thus infer the intensity and scale of erosion (e.g., Dugmore and Erskine 1994; Dugmore et al. 2009; Streeter and Dugmore 2014).

Thórarinsson (1961) first highlighted the dramatic environmental changes that occurred following the settlement of Iceland, which triggered a shift from an island-wide system characterized by extensive lowland birch forests and low regional rates of sediment accumulation, to one characterized by very limited birch woodland and high regional rates of sediment accumulation (Streeter et al. 2015). In addition to large-scale, island-wide changes, more localized trends exist in the data collected from soil sections. This is because rates of accumulation at any one location represent an amalgamation of the local aeolian sediment flux, which reflects the immediate geomorphological setting, and the regional aeolian sediment flux, which reflects the soil erosion over a wider area. Rates of accumulation will increase, often dramatically, as aeolian erosion develops in the local area (Dugmore and Erskine 1994). The main reasons for the large increase observed in some locations are (1) increasing proximity to eroding slopes, (2) increasing erosion of nearby, deeper, lowland soils, and (3) a location downwind of actively eroding areas. As proximity to an eroding slope increases, so will accumulation rates, and sites downwind and downslope of eroding slopes will capture more material than sites upwind and upslope (Dugmore et al. 2009). The erosion of shallow soils will generate a comparatively limited sediment flux, but the erosion of deep soils can generate a very large sediment flux (Dugmore et al. 2009). Changes in absolute, normalized, and relative SeAR within and between soil sections indicate patterns of nearby erosion (Dugmore and Erskine 1994; Streeter and Dugmore 2014). Increased spatial variability between accumulation rates in soil sections indicates increased levels fragmentation within the landscape, and relative variations of SeAR within a soil section revealed by tephrochronology are important indicators of local change (Streeter et al. 2012; Streeter and Dugmore 2014).

Soil erosion typically begins with the development of small breaks within vegetation cover, known as erosion spots (Gísladóttir 1998, 2001; Arnalds, Aradóttir, and Thorsteinsson 1987; Arnalds 2000; Dugmore et al. 2009). Either these spots of exposed soil may be recolonized by plants, or they may erode further, creating persistent deflation patches. These patches will tend to deepen until the resistant underlying substrate is exposed. The denuded areas expand as the eroding fronts eat into the surrounding areas of soil and vegetation, ultimately stripping the landscape of its primary soil cover (Ólafsdóttir 2002). These eroding soil slopes on the margins of vegetated land are a common feature of many parts of the Icelandic landscape, and they are named *rofabarðs* in Icelandic (Arnalds 2000). *Rofabarðs* form a semipermanent feature of the landscape, as they move at a pace of centimeters per year or meters per century. While the rate of back wearing of the exposed soil slope is an important determinant of the pace of soil cover loss, the most important factor in Iceland is the density of eroding spots or the length of *rofabarðs* per hectare (Fridriksson and Gudbergsson 1995).

The morphology of eroding soil slopes and their vulnerability to degradation will have changed through time (figures 6.3a–b). We have good evidence that the rate of soil cover loss was greater in the past than it is today, and yet SeAR are higher now than then (Arnalds et al. 1987; Dugmore et al. 2009). This mismatch can be explained by an early phase of

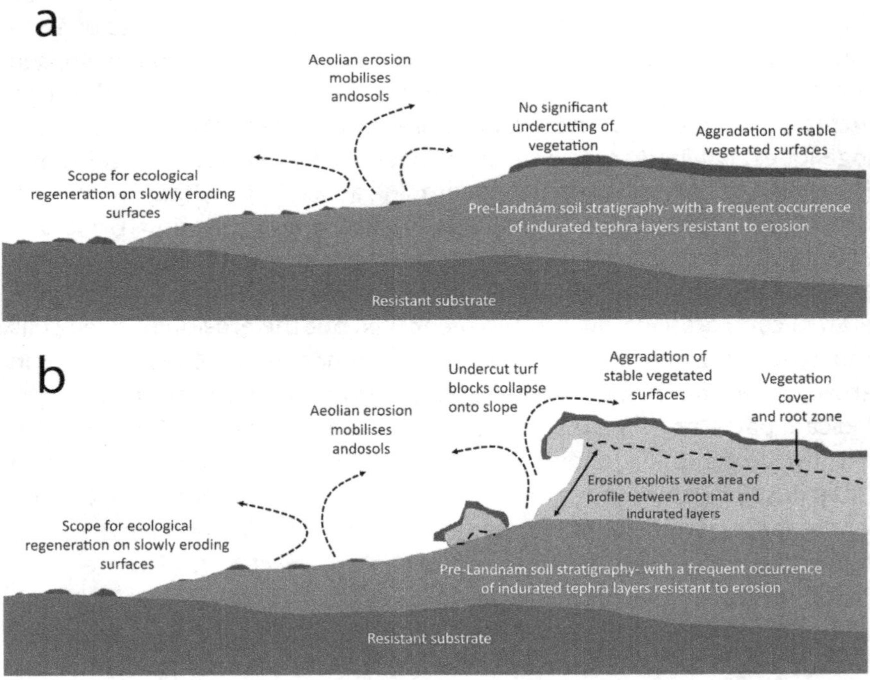

Figures 6.3a–b. Once *rofabarðs* form, feedback mechanisms can reinforce their development, leading to a slowly unfolding catastrophe. As andosols erode (a), the surviving soil profile thickens (b), and its resistance to erosion changes; thicker soils separate roots from the resistant underlying substrate and create zones more susceptible to back wearing that are formed from more rapidly accumulated, more easily erodible sediment that lacks binding roots. This creates the potential to unzip the soil cover, a process exacerbated by livestock seeking shelter beneath overhanging turf blocks.

rapid areal loss of thin soils in more marginal upland areas, probably due to a high density of erosion spots across these parts of the landscape and a resulting high density of *rofabarðs*. More recently, particularly in the last few centuries, the erosion of thick soils in lowland areas has generated much higher levels of SeAR, but because it involves a lower density of *rofabarðs* per hectare, it results in lower rates of soil cover loss.

Different parts of the eroding slope have varying susceptibilities to erosion depending on the overall thickness of the soil profile, the frequency and degree of weathering of tephra layers contained within the soil, and the depth of the root mat. The basal part of soil profiles may have significant resistance to soil erosion, resulting in low islands of remnant soil scattered across a landscape stripped of soil. This is because pre-*Landnám* andosols have comparatively low rates of aeolian sediment accumulation (Thórarinsson 1961; Dugmore and Buckland 1991; Streeter et al. 2015). As a result, tephra layers tend to be closer together, and where these tephra are basaltic in composition they are often weathered to form semi-lithified (indurated) layers with a lower susceptibility to erosion. This development of semi-lithified tephra layers within andosol profiles is a function of the presence of tephra layers and their age, but it is also heavily dependent on the weathering environment, which is influenced by rates of profile aggradation. In southern Iceland, we have noticed that where rates of accumulation are low, weathering of basaltic tephra layers is more developed and vice versa.

The presence of semi-lithified tephra layers in the basal parts of soil profiles slows the lateral movement of *rofabarðs*, resulting in low-angle slopes that are more resistant to erosion (figures 6.3a–b). Within the upper parts of the soil profile, the root mat offers significant resistance to erosion by wind and water. This is especially true of the dense and thick root mats that develop under well-grazed forb meadows. If the dense root mat penetrates to levels that include semi-lithified tephra layers, overall erosion rates are inhibited. Because of anthropogenic soil erosion, however, the upper parts of surviving post-*Landnám* soils profiles are characterized by faster accumulation rates than those formed before settlement, and the surface root mat is lifted away from both the underlying substrate and the semi-resistant pre-*Landnám* soil layers. When this happens, the upper parts of the eroding slopes can be undercut, and the advance of *rofabarðs* is dominated by rapid back wearing and turf block collapse. This "unzipping" of the landscape is difficult to stop, without a physical reshaping of the exposed slopes and proactive revegetation.

While certain combinations of ecology, grazing regime, and climate will lead to breaks in vegetation cover and initiate soil erosion at a particular place, a partial amelioration of those triggering conditions will not necessarily stop that erosion. This is because the vegetated soil surface and the exposed, persistently eroding soil surface represent alternative states that are reinforced by biophysical feedbacks and that can exist under the same external environmental conditions (Marston 2010). While a stable vegetation cover enables plants to grow, and thus perpetuates stability, surface instability inhibits plant growth, and that lack of plant growth enhances continued instability. Once *rofabarð* erosion begins, it will tend to be enhanced as the surviving soils are thickened with locally eroded materials, eroding slopes become more exposed and steeper, and the processes of erosion reinforced (Arnalds et al. 1987). This is an example of the positive feedbacks that exist within the Icelandic soil system that promote high and continuing rates of erosion. Very low levels of grazing disturbance reinforced by positive feedback loops can maintain the eroding surface. For example, needle ice formation and cryoturbation in areas of exposed sediments, which disrupt the establishment of seedlings, make it hard for plants to revegetate these areas (Arnalds 2015). Thus, the development of *rofabarðs* represents a cusp bifurcation (Streeter and Dugmore 2013).

Once past land management (or indeed mismanagement) led to the creation of eroding surfaces, the prevailing climate became the dominant factor determining the pace of geomorphological change, as this is driven by a combination of earth surface processes such as aeolian erosion, needle ice formation, raindrop impacts, overland flow, rill formation, and gullying (Arnalds 2000). The life span of *rofabarðs* will depend on their spacing in the landscape and rate of movement, but where they have become established tens to hundreds of meters apart in thick soil profiles, they can persist over multi-century timescales. Close to the farms of Seljaland in south Iceland, for example, changes in the spatial patterns of SeAR coupled with coarse sediment transported by overland flow indicates that the *rofabarðs* present on hillsides today initially formed in the fourteenth century (Dugmore and Erskine 1994).

The spatially complex interplay of grazing impacts and earth surface processes is illustrated by recent *rofabarð* development on the sheltered slopes of Hamragarðaheiði in southern Iceland (figures 6.4a–d). Here, at about two hundred meters above sea level, *rofabarðs* consist of prominent upstanding patches of soil and vegetation tens of meters across, separated by lower-lying denuded areas of approximately the same scale. Locally, grazing intensity has declined since the late twentieth century, reflecting national trends. On Hamragarðaheiði, vegetation growth during the summers of 2014 to 2017 was strong, which combined with modest grazing allowed a lush and deep herbaceous ground cover to grow each year. A partial recolonization of some bare soil slopes has taken place, with the seasonal appearance of "horsetails," *Equisetum* spp. Despite signs of ecological recovery on slopes facing the west and south, *rofabarð* slopes facing the east continued to retreat at rates of centimeters per year over this period. This is probably because of prevailing easterly winds that dry exposed soils and then erode exposed particles (figure 6.4b). This effect is probably enhanced as these winds pass over the nearby mountain ice cap of Eyjafjallajökull. The pattern of change on Hamragarðaheiði illustrates how environmental drivers can maintain active areas of soil erosion centuries after the erosion was originally triggered, despite modern grazing pressures that are in of themselves currently sustainable.

In addition to the *environmental* feedbacks that act to maintain soil erosion once it has been initiated, *social and cultural* drivers have also been important in maintaining as well as triggering soil erosion. Traditions of land use, vested interests, and displaced impacts have also acted to reinforce established grazing practices, even when changing circumstances may have rendered them unsustainable and environmentally destructive. For example, revealing details about the management of the uplands and the drivers to maintain grazing there despite environmental degradation are contained in documents from the fifteenth and sixteenth centuries and references to events of the fourteenth century.

> *2. okt. 1464 á Svínavatni. ". . . Kærði Egill það til Magnús að hann hefði ekki rekið lambfé sitt á Eyvindarstaða heiðar eður toll goldið eftir gömlum vana . . . nefndur Egill lét lesa þar transkriptarbréf af úrskurði Einars Gilssonar lögmanns norðan og vestan á Íslandi með heilum og ósködduðum góðra manna innsiglum svo látanda að fyrr nefndur Einar hefði úrskurðað alla bændur í milli Gönguskarðsár í Skagafirði fyrir vestan vötn og Laxár á Skagaströnd fyrir norðan Blöndu þá sem eiga tíu lömb eður fleiri frjálslega í heimild að reka sinn lambfénað um sumar á Eyvindastaðaafrétt en lúka að hausti eitt lamb af rekstri Eyvindarstaðamönnum er af fjalli kemur svo fram sem þeir vilja forðast . . . sekt."* (*Diplomatarium Islandicum* V: 433)

> 2 October 1464 at Svínavatn. ". . . Egill charged Magnús for not driving his lambs to Eyvindastaðir heath or paying tax according to custom. . . . The aforementioned Egill had a transcripted letter read aloud there, the ruling of Einar Gilsson lawman in North and East Iceland with whole and undamaged seals of good men saying that the aforementioned Einar had ruled that all farmers between Gönguskarðsá in Skagafjörður west of the rivers and Laxá in Skagaströnd north of Blanda, those who had ten lambs or more free to drive their flock of lambs during the summer to Eyvindastaðaafrétt but paying in fall one lamb of the flock to the Eyvindarstaðir farmers when the lambs are driven from the mountain if they want to avoid a fine." (*Diplomatarium Islandicum* V: 433)

This passage refers to a court order from Einar Gilsson, lawman of Iceland 1367 to 1369. The order requires all farmers between Gönguskarðsá in Skagafjörður west of the water divide and Laxá in Skagaströnd north of the Blanda river who owned ten or more lambs to drive all their lambs to

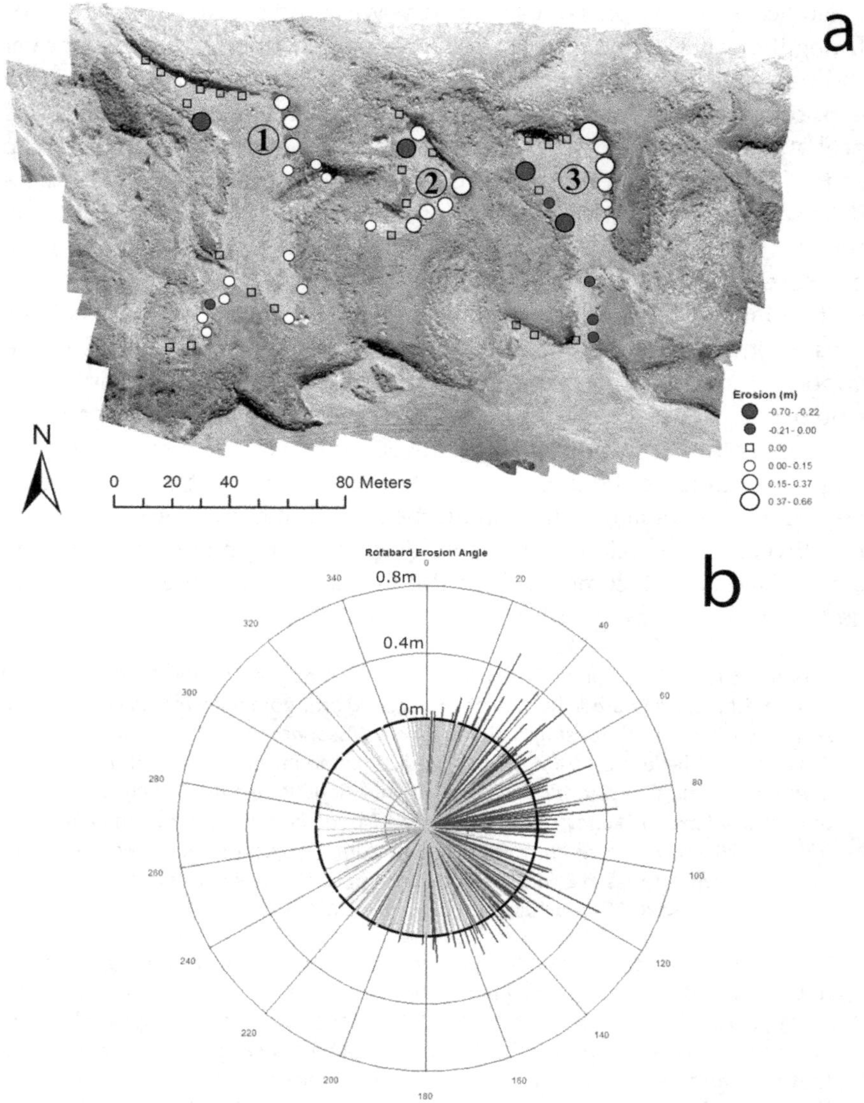

Figures 6.4a–d. Analysis of *rofabarð* erosion over a two-year period using aerial imagery. Orthophotos and digital elevation models were derived using UAV photography, corrected with differential GPS, via the structure from motion software Agisoft Photoscan. *Rofabarð* margins for 2015 and 2017 are delineated and differences measured manually using ArcGIS v10.1 (measurement accuracy ~0.05 meter), to indicate erosion (white circles) and accretion (black circles) (a). The aspect of each *rofabarð* margin and its associated level of erosion/accretion (b) are compared to the prevailing wind direction (data from nearby Vestmannaeyjar) (c). A topographic representation of the site is shown (d) that displays the transect used for creating profiles of *rofabarðs* (1), (2), and (3). The *rofabarð* cross profiles are created using ArcGIS 3D analyst.

c

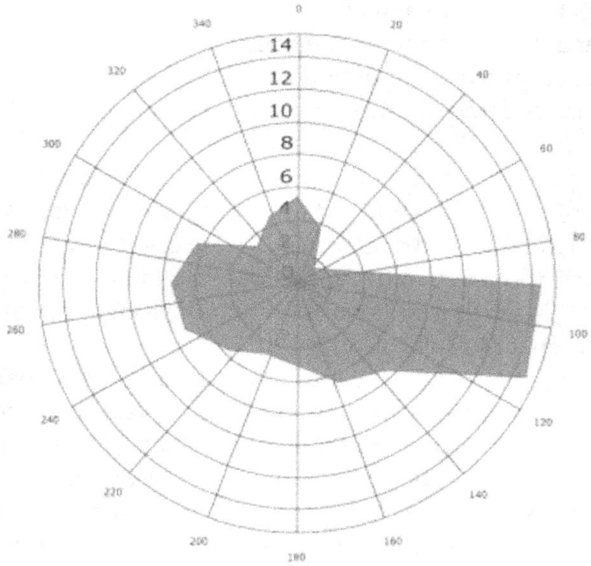
0
20
40
60
80
100
120
140
160
180
200
220
240
260
280
300
320
340
14
12
10
8
6

d

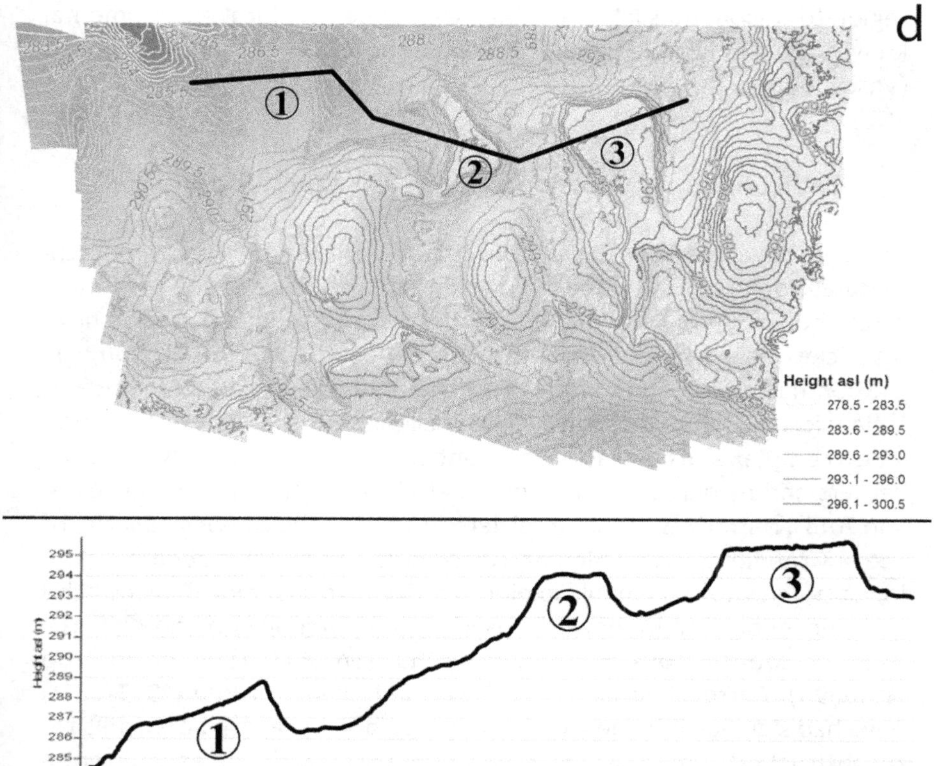
①
②
③
Height asl (m)
278.5 - 283.5
283.6 - 289.5
289.6 - 293.0
293.1 - 296.0
296.1 - 300.5
Height asl (m)
Distance (m)
Rofabard Profile 2017

Eyvindarstaðaheiði (an area of upland grazing) and pay a fee of one lamb to the farmer at Eyvindarstaðir or be fined if they failed to do so. There are several court cases from the period after 1500 where farmers in various areas were also ordered to drive their lambs into the highlands or be fined for failing to do so. In these circumstances the farmers who owned access rights had a powerful incentive (backed by law) to require a continued use of the uplands, even though the grazing quality was failing due to changing climates and land degradation. In the case of Eyvindarstaðaheiði, it was not until the nineteenth century that the landowners were able to restart mountain grazing by tenants and profit from it, but at the cost of enhanced soil erosion (Júlíusson 2019).

In the early modern period widespread tenancy, combined with insecure leases, did nothing to promote practices of landscape conservation and probably acted to greatly exacerbate impacts (Jónsson 1993). Short leases of one to two years, combined with widespread tenancies at will and no incentives or rewards for investing in the land, encouraged tenants to focus their meager resources in livestock and maximize offtake rather than tackling soil erosion. In addition, tenants moved frequently from region to region, thus inhibiting the development of local environmental knowledge and nuanced understanding of how best to manage the land (Vasey 1996).

Environmental Catastrophe versus Societal Resilience

So far we have discussed the anatomy of the slowly unfolding environmental catastrophe following the rapid colonization and expansion of farming throughout Iceland, but what effects did deforestation and erosion have on society as a whole? For Jared Diamond and Sveinn Runólfsson, soil erosion had devastating impacts on the prosperity and subsistence of Icelandic society. Studies have since challenged these narratives to provide a complex and contrasting account of the relationship between early settlers and resource use (McGovern et al. 2007; Kristinsson and Júlíusson 2016). Narratives of Norse settlers surpassing the carrying capacity of the environment, overexploiting common resources, or indeed developing strategies to sustainably exploit resources to meet local needs echo broader theoretical frameworks used to study population and resource use. The contributions of Thomas Malthus (1766–1834), Ester Boserup (1910–99), Garrett Hardin (1915–2003), and Elinor Ostrom (1933–2012) have had significant influence on contemporary research frameworks for reconstructing human resource use in the past—and studies of environmental degradation in particular.

Malthus (1798) observed a cyclical relationship between population growth and food production: as population increased, a greater number of laborers were available to utilize resources, but this growing population would eventually surpass the capacity of the environment to support subsistence. Critically, Malthus observed that human population grows geometrically—or exponentially—whereas food production follows an arithmetic—or linear—growth trajectory (Rowley-Conwy and Leyton 2011). This has informed so-called neo-Malthusian fears that exponential population growth, coupled with overconsumption and the degradation of common-pool resources, will eventually surpass the carrying capacity of the planet (Hardin 1968). Others argue that a global food shortage could even trigger the collapse of global civilization (Ehrlich and Ehrlich 2013; Diamond 2005).

Adopting a neo-Malthusian view, Diamond (2005) outlines a general framework for population overshoot and collapse. The rapid colonization of Iceland and the increasing utilization of marginal lands as the population increased, coupled with the degradation of vegetation cover, soil erosion, conflict, and disease, appear to follow this "grand narrative" closely. The problem with Diamond's account is that he does little to explain how the Norse adapted subsistence strategies in light of terrestrial environmental degradation. Rather than blindly persisting with their initial strategies, they intensified their subsistence system, utilizing wild resources to supplement shortfalls from animal husbandry and to capitalize on opportunities to trade wool and dried fish overseas.

As Kristinsson and Júlíusson (2016) explain, there is limited evidence to suggest the Norse Icelanders diminished their resource base in the upland region through deforestation and overgrazing. Estimates from settlement surveys also indicate that the population was not close to carrying capacity at any time between the twelfth and fifteenth centuries (Karlsson 2000). The human population has declined at various times in Iceland, but it has always remained above thirty thousand people (Vasey 1996). There have been acute but comparatively short-lived demographic contractions, most notably following the fifteenth-century plagues, the smallpox epidemics, and the early eighteenth- and late eighteenth-century famines that were driven by impacts of climate cooling (in 1755) and volcanism (in 1783) (Vasey 1996). Yet even after the eighteenth century—also known by historians as the "century of misery"—the Icelandic population was able to recover after each of these shocks. A younger recovering population is likely to have taken on farms that had been abandoned throughout the famine and disease of the 1780s (1783–86); annual population growth averaged 1.32 percent from 1791 to 1795 and increased to 1.67 percent in the late 1790s. By the 1801 census, the population had recovered to 47,240—an increase of 8,000 on late 1780s levels (Karlsson 2000).

Characterizations of early Icelandic agricultural systems as rigid or conservative seem misplaced. Kristinsson and Júlíusson (2016) argued that Icelandic agriculture should be viewed through the Boserupian theoretical framework. In contrast to Malthusian and neo-Malthusian approaches, Boserup (1965) argued that population growth is likely to stimulate technological and adaptive innovations that allow the population to increase food production. This does not, however, rely on an exponential trajectory of innovation in the techno-optimist sense. Rather, population pressure is eventually felt by a law of diminishing returns. A well-known application of this model in archaeology is Tainter's (1988) seminal work, *The Collapse of Complex Societies*. As he argued, societies collapse in a cyclical process of complex buildup—investment in sociopolitical complexity required to managing societal problems—and fragmentation—complexity leads to marginal returns and the destabilization, decline, and fragmentation of sociopolitical institutions. This follows the Boserupian law of diminishing returns, as the increasing complexity of an expanding society demands increasing energy to sustain its size and complexity. This model fits the Icelandic system in the sense that the Norse settlers demonstrated adaptiveness, but there is increased hierarchy with the emergence of magnates and the demise of independent farmers.

Unlike the Scandinavian colonies in Greenland, settlement in Iceland has endured and survived the multiple environmental, political, economic, and social challenges of the last millennium (Dugmore et al. 2007, 2012, 2013). Despite the demonstrable scale and acute local impacts of soil erosion, in Iceland there was no societal collapse, in either a Diamond-esque or Tainter-esque sense. It should be acknowledged that long-term vulnerability to acute climate variation does increase in the mid-fourteenth century especially and has been associated with the abandonment of multiple upland farms in the northern highland valley of Krókdalur, for example (Vésteinsson et al. 2014; Nelson et al. 2016). This would suggest that many settlers walked a fine line between resilience and (household) collapse, but at the island-wide scale the population managed the potential impacts of political-economic complexity and environmental overshoot. Missing from these models is the identification of resource flexibility and governance required to endure times of hardship. Kristinsson and Júlíusson (2016) emphasize that strategic subsistence adaptations were essential to survival in Iceland.

The Boserupian model can be taken further, however, using Ostrom's influential economic model for managing common-pool resources and assessing the sustainability of socio-ecological systems (Ostrom 2015, 2009).

Ostrom, who builds on Malthus, Hardin, and Boserup, saw value in each of their theories of resource use but argued that they largely focused on extremes rather than the various modes of collective action, cooperation, and trust that are observed in all societies (Ostrom 2015). This approach can be summarized in Ostrom's (2009) framework for analyzing sustainable socio-ecological systems and incorporates four subsystem elements: resource units, the resource system, systems of governance, and users. The resource system and units comprise what resources fall within the system that are utilized by user groups and over what timescales and spatial extents they are abundant. Governance and users include how human resources are organized and what rules are imposed on exploiting the resource system (Ostrom 2005, 2007, 2009). Understanding the relationship between each of these subsystems can provide a clearer understanding of how the medieval Icelandic political economy functioned over the *longue durée* and what impacts the organization of social groups and collective and private resource had on resource use and local environmental change.

Sustained research in the north and central uplands of Iceland have challenged existing narratives that assumed the early settlers had "immediate and severe" impacts on the local environment through deforestation and intensive grazing of highland pastures (McGovern et al. 2007). While insufficient settlers' knowledge of the sensitivity of Icelandic ecosystem and volcanic soils in particular could have triggered some episodes of erosion (Dugmore et al. 2005), these knowledge limits do not apply to all settlements (cf. Vésteinsson et al. 2014).

The Medieval Subsistence Economy of Iceland

With the possible exception of some very minor short-lived settlement by Irish hermits before the early eighth century, Norse settlers would have arrived in a culturally blank landscape. Settlement and organization of subsistence was therefore based entirely on an imported agricultural niche from the Scandinavian homelands to the east (Jackson et al. 2018; Vésteinsson McGovern, and Keller 2002; Vésteinsson 2000). To accommodate the Norse agricultural economy, birch and willow scrub were removed to create grasslands for animal grazing, and prime land was reserved to produce hay fodder for stalled winter livestock (Amorosi et al. 1997). The accumulation of environmental knowledge about wild resources would have been an essential strategy from the outset of settlement (Amorosi et al. 1997; Dugmore et al. 2007). In the highland region of Mývatn, extensive multi-disciplinary investigation has revealed a diverse seasonal resource strategy that incorporated animal husbandry with the hunting and gathering of a wide range of local wild resources (McGovern et al. 2007). This has existed from the early tenth century and involved the integration of long-distance economic networks linking inland farms with winter fishing stations on the coast (Perdikaris and McGovern 2009).

The rapid settlement of Iceland is likely to have been sustained by an influx of settlers seeking wealth and status on newly available lands at a time when west Norwegian chieftains were losing power to King Harald Finehair (Fitzhugh 2000; Raffield et al. 2017). Settlers could make a name for themselves by claiming land in Iceland and awarding land to a loyal following (Vésteinsson et al. 2002). This strategy is captured in accounts of early settlers such as Skallagrim, in *Egil's Saga*:

> Skallagrim was an industrious man. He always kept many men with him and gathered all the resources that were available for subsistence, since at first they had little in the way of livestock to support such a large number of people. Such livestock as there was grazed free in the woodland all year round. . . . There was no lack of driftwood west of Myrar. He had a farmstead built on Alftanes and ran another farm there, and rowed out from it to catch fish and cull seals and gather eggs, all of which were there in great abundance. . . . Whales beached there, too, in great numbers, and there was wildlife there for the taking at this hunting post; the animals were not used to man and would never flee. He owned a third farm by the sea on the western part of Myrar. . . . And he planted crops there and named it Akrar (Fields). . . . Skallagrim also sent his men upriver to catch salmon. He put Odd the hermit by Gljufura to take care of the salmon fishery there. . . . When Skallagrim's livestock grew in number, it was allowed to roam the mountain pastures for the whole summer. Noticing how much better and fatter the animals were that ranged on the heath, and also that the sheep which could not be brought down for the winter survived in the mountain valleys, he had a farmstead built up on the mountain, and ran a farm there where his sheep were kept. . . . In this way, Skallagrim put his livelihood on many footings. (*Egil's Saga*, 1997, chapter 29)

This is a model strategy; Skallagrim took claim of land from the uplands down to the sea. He grants land to his kin as a retainer of resourceful land, and he then exploits multiple resource spaces for seasonal grazing, haymaking, and fishing (Vésteinsson et al. 2002). This is in stark contrast to the account of Raven Floki, who fails to utilize a range of resources upon settlement in Iceland.

> Floki and his crew sailed west across Breidafjord and made land at Vatnsfjord in Bardastrand. At that time the fjord was teeming with fish, and they got so caught up with the fishing they forgot to make hay, so their livestock starved to death the following winter. (*Landnámabók: The Book of Settlements*, 1972, chapter 5)

These contrasting narratives can be understood as allegories for sustainable subsistence. The strategy of organizing a communal labor force that could be pooled to utilize seasonally abundant resources provided a diversity of resources, building redundancy into the system to buffer against less productive years.

There is evidence of farm abandonment across marginal areas in Iceland—possibly as a result of localized environmental degradation and isolation from supplementary resources—but far from being viewed as examples of failure, recent research has suggested that attempts to occupy marginal land should be viewed as opportunities to create social capital. As Vésteinsson and colleagues (2014) have explained, the occupation of marginal upland environments, such as Krókdalur, should be viewed in the context of the Norse status system. The availability of land in the uplands would have allowed settlers to increase livestock and with this their reproductive rights and social status (Vésteinsson et al. 2014). In other upland areas, such as Mývatnssveit, the early subsistence system is understood to have been sustainable and resilient. Initially, subsistence farming was buffered by marine resources and then, after the fourteenth century, by a wider network of external trade and exchange. So, while conventional narratives viewed upland areas like Mývatnssveit as marginal, archaeological and paleoenvironmental evidence has revealed a diverse and sustainable strategy that placed rules on exploitation and networked between different resource areas (McGovern et al. 2007).

From the ninth to eleventh centuries, subsistence was largely organized at the household scale, in a peasant mode of production that yielded a minimal surplus that could be stored for hard times or shared with other farms in the district (Wickham 2005; Jakobsson 2013). Inland farms utilized marine resources of fish, marine mammals, and sea birds from the earliest times. Chieftains maintained status not through coercive control akin to feudalism but through honor and loyalty delivered by an allied following. Medieval Iceland underwent a political and economic transformation in the twelfth and thirteenth centuries. In this time, the economy transitioned from a peasant mode of production to a manorial tenant system comprising greater taxation and commercial exports (Jakobsson 2013). The transition to a manorial tenant system is significant because it moves the population from a more even distribution of resilience to a generally resilient population, but with significantly more uneven distribution. Izdebski, Mordechai, and White (2018) describe this observed historical phenomenon as the social burden of resilience. This is an outcome of the reorganization of the economy from reciprocity (more sharing) under a peasant mode of production to redistribution (less sharing from elite to lower social classes) under the new manorial system of accumulated power by the church and elite families.

This transition in political and economic power also leads to a reorganization of control over the means and spatial organization of production.

Vésteinsson (2016) argues that this transition from a political economy of reciprocity to a manorial system where magnates and the church-controlled surplus production could be a key factor in the expansion of commercial stock fishing in the thirteenth century. Under this system, the elite received their status from the support of the Norwegian royal court rather than a loyal following (Jakobsson 2013). By controlling land and the means of production—and therein its surplus—the elite could maintain a lifestyle that would have included obtaining status goods from abroad and attending the royal court in Norway (Karlsson 2000; Vésteinsson 2016). This entailed the specialization of existing elements of the Norse production system. Extensive research at Hofstaðir and the surrounding farms in the Mývatnssveit reveals an early connection between inland farms and coastal fishing stations (McGovern 2009; McGovern et al. 2007). From the fourteenth century, bulk staple goods including dried cod (stockfish) and woollen cloth (*vaðmál*) were being exported from Iceland to the European sites. Seasonal trade centers, such as the northeastern site of Gásir

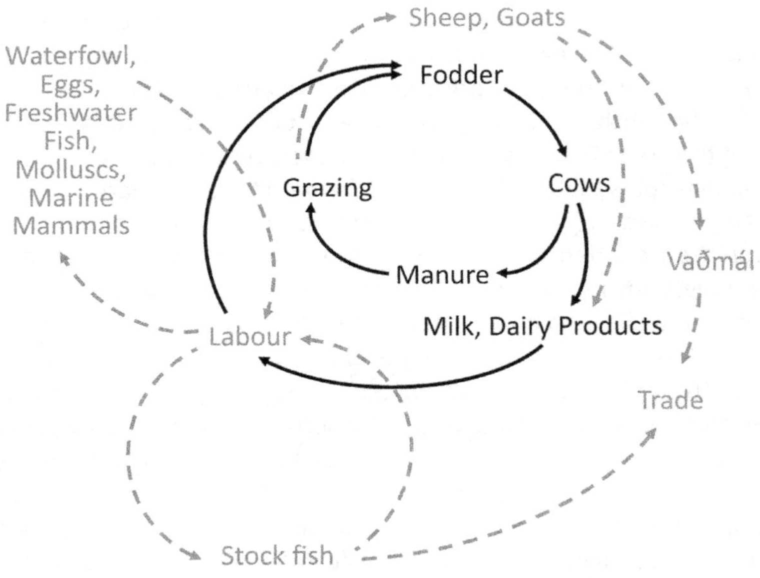

Figure 6.5. Thomas Malthus's (1798) example of the cyclical relationship between resources, labor, and productivity in Alpine Switzerland (solid lines, based on a schematic in Rowley-Conwy and Layton 2011). The population will reach a dynamic equilibrium as population is balanced against the available resources and productivity. Overgrazing through mismanagement—which could be related to population growth—will cause environmental degradation and thus reduce the productivity of the environment. However, broader subsistence networks (dotted lines), including hunting and gathering strategies, would allow the utilization of resources between upland and lowland grazing areas and marine resources.

in Eyjafjördur, became points of cultural contact between Icelanders and European traders (Harrison, Roberts, and Adderley 2008). This entailed the specialization of cloth production from artisanal production (ninth to thirteenth centuries) to standardization and specialization from the thirteenth to fourteenth centuries onward (Hayeur Smith 2014). Sites such as Akurvík and Gásir show evidence of the increased control and manipulation of stockfish markets by elite groups from the fourteenth century onward (Amundsen et al. 2005).

The transition from a relatively equal distribution of subsistence resources during the Viking Age to a system of tenancy, taxation, and specialization would have created higher levels of material inequality. The overall level of resilience across society as a whole would have remained relatively stable. But this masks the underlying vulnerability and inequalities that were created as powerful magnates exploited labor and rent from materially impoverished farms. In his research on the economy of the Skálholt bishopric in southern Iceland, Hambrecht (2011) demonstrated that the extraction of rents from their tenants by the bishopric in the form of food, driftwood, and other resources from a variety of environmental niches secured the elite site and buffered it from the significant environmental variability of the eighteenth century. This security would have come at the expense of impoverished farms that were already suffering the consequences of famine and smallpox.

A Sustainable Socio-ecological System?

Access to a diversity of resources would have allowed farms to modulate between sources of subsistence and trade depending on their seasonal and interannual availability. If we consider an inflexible agricultural system based solely on grazing, then as soon as erosion is triggered and the size of rangelands declines, there would be little option other than to intensify (figure 6.5, dotted lines). This would soon lead to an overshoot and abandonment scenario (cf. Diamond 2005). Many—including Diamond—have considered erosion in Iceland to be a significant challenge for the human population. However, this logic fails to take into account economic networks and modularity built into the Norse Icelandic subsistence system (figure 6.6). Broad subsistence networks, hunting and gathering strategies, and management of livestock numbers, plus developing local and regional networks, allowed the Norse to utilize resources across upland and lowland grazing areas and from the sea (figure 6.5, solid lines). The modularity and heterogeneity of the resource system meant the Norse were able to adapt to local stresses created by soil erosion (Scheffer et al. 2012). The upland areas also never reached carrying capacity, meaning

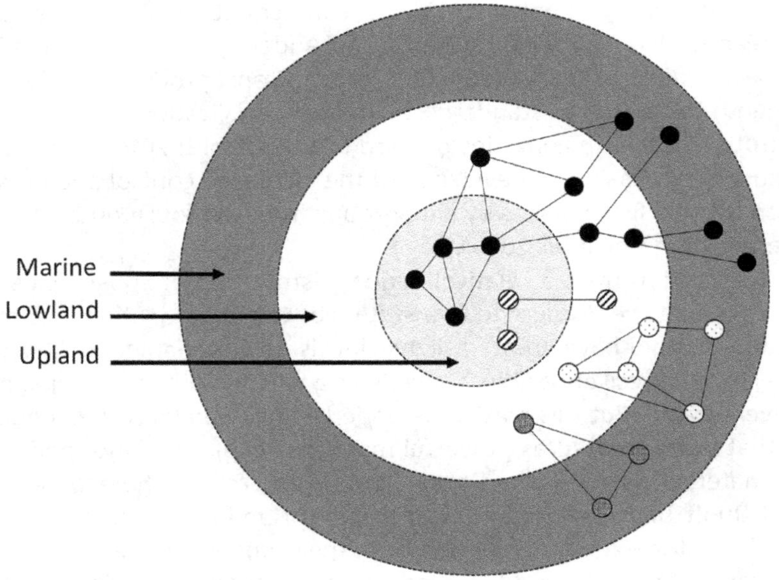

Figure 6.6. A conceptual diagram showing three different resource systems (upland, lowland, and marine) and four different economic networks in medieval Iceland. Farms are shown as small circles, and they are joined by lines representing resource networks. The ability to network across multiple resource spaces would have built redundancy into the subsistence system. Those with limited access to the full range of lowland, upland, and marine provisioning systems are more likely to fail and can fail in isolation. This provides scope for incremental changes, as opposed to a critical transformation of the whole system. In resilience thinking, redundancy allows resource users to modulate between areas where the resource system has been impacted and areas that remain unaffected.

erosion would have had little impact on livestock grazing other than in localized areas that were already marginal or slowly became overwhelmed by the scale of erosion.

From the earliest days of settlement, access to rich marine food webs provided buffering to climate and demographic shocks. The external trade and exchange that developed from the thirteenth century onward provided wider network linkages, but these were associated with elite management and increased hierarchy, and so, over the *longue durée*, landscape damage and social inequality were linked. In the face of soil erosion, the subsistence system remained resilient through a flexible resource-use strategy—rather than managing the variability of local resources (cf. Carpenter et al. 2014). In other words, the buffering capacity (i.e., resilience) of the seasonal round, plus their ability to tap into the large-scale food webs presented by marine resources (principally fish supplemented by marine mammals) and trade overseas (principally wool and stockfish), allowed them to maintain a large safe operating space through periods of environmental and climatological change. However, these buffering abilities came at a significant social cost of enhanced inequality and would only be available if stresses did not coincide. If marine resources did not arrive while other pressures were being felt, this would have had dramatic impacts on the Icelandic people. Attempts to mitigate erosion would have created huge opportunity costs because the erosion represents the crossing of a fold bifurcation (catastrophe cusp) and thus requires a nonlinear management response to reverse it—strict controls over grazing regimes and/or reductions in grazing intensity are required to promote ecological regeneration. An environmentally conservative strategy focused on minimizing soil erosion could have consumed significant domestic resources through investment of time and labor and promoted homogeneity and reduced the modularity of resource systems (i.e., diversity of alternative resources in the seasonal round). The implication is that rangeland soil erosion was not in of itself a critical problem in the resource system because the Norse were flexible in terms of their utilization of grazing animals (for meat and milk or wool production), access to wild resources, and the extent and diversity of the provisioning system and trade links.

The story of Norse farming should not, however, be viewed simply as a positive example of a resilient society that was impervious to the impacts of soil erosion. Redundancy was built into the Icelandic subsistence economy from the beginning of settlement, but the ability to overcome local impacts also set Icelandic society on a slow and unrelenting path toward the extensive soil erosion now found across Iceland and the depleted fish stocks in the North Atlantic today.

Implications and Lessons

Decoupled Socio-ecological Change in Medieval Iceland: A Caution in Resilience

Karl Butzer (2012) acknowledged contemporary society's pressing need to transform toward sustainability (see O'Brien 2012, Pelling 2011) but notes that historical examples are needed to offer a deep time basis to test resilience, with the caution that "what is logical in contemporary perspective may be unpredictable in light of good field, archival or other primary sources for historical time" (Butzer and Endfield 2012, E2032).

The declining quality and productivity of the Earth's biophysical systems is a "grand challenge" for society in the twenty-first century (National Research Council 2001). The search for parallel challenges in past societies has been plagued with erroneous monocausal and deterministic claims that "suck in" or "smear" historical data (Baillie 1991). "Grand narratives" of collapse are a case in point, often disregarding complex multiscale changes that contributed to societal stress (Butzer 2012; Butzer and Endfield 2012). The rate and scale of soil erosion in Iceland have been severe since the tenth century (Thórarinsson 1961; Crofts 2011; Streeter et al. 2015), but the impacts of environmental degradation on societal resilience have been overestimated. Large-scale and correlated impacts cannot be equated to simple cause-effect relationships (Oppenheimer 2015; Butzer 2012). Many researchers now caution overreliance on physical indicators that cannot show direct effects on human populations that could have been resilient to such changes (Redman 2005; McAnany and Yoffee 2010; Middleton 2017; Riede 2017).

We recognize that soil erosion in Iceland operates as a slow variable. It has persisted over the last eleven hundred years, albeit at varying rates (Dugmore et al. 2009). As we have discussed, societies such as Iceland have been and can be resilient to the impacts of soil erosion through the efficient and flexible subsistence strategies that tap into multiple resource systems combined with social systems that enshrined inequalities. Despite social and environmental costs, group survival was ensured. However, at a broader spatial scale and over longer periods of time the system is under threat, there is a significant danger in simply arguing that societies can be resilient to the effects of centuries of soil erosion without a cost. In the past, soil erosion may not have driven transformative change to Icelandic society, but at a broader scale, environmental degradation has destroyed natural capital of soils and vegetation that could prove to be vital in the future if Iceland is thrown back on its own terrestrial resources for food production. Societies may be so flexible and oblivious to costs that they fail to identify the slow decline of local resources and become increasingly dependent on resources brought in along extensive but increasingly destructive networks that erode other resources outside the system.

Conclusions

Iceland is an exemplar of the rate and scale of ecological impact that humans can cause to their environments. Over eleven hundred years, animal husbandry has unzipped the landscape—as localized threshold-crossing events exposed soils to erosion. Buffered by the sufferings of regions of Iceland, individual farms, and particular social groups, Icelandic society as a whole endured through subsistence flexibility, social inequalities, and the ability to tap into larger provisioning and economic networks.

Our case study from Iceland demonstrates how an adaptable society can confront challenges through social organization and by diversifying the ways in which they impact the ecosystem. In the medium term—the past thousand years or so—this can be an effective, if costly, strategy, in terms of both the environment and society. Without conservation and alternative resource-use strategies, revealed in archaeological and paleoenvironmental studies, the soils could have been even more eroded, and long-term effects may have further compounded vulnerabilities. With unchecked soil erosion, farming on Iceland would be compromised. Likewise, with increasing exploitation of marine resources, the marine food web could collapse, further amplifying exposure to risk.

Human exposure to risks can be studied as natural experiments of the past. By focusing on the biophysical processes of soil erosion and the changing social, economic, and political organization of Icelandic society, it is possible to map human vulnerability over space and time and between social groups. This of course requires the input of multiple disciplines to reconstruct an accurate account of the connections between sociocultural and environmental processes (Hartman et al. 2017). The past can be understood in this sense as a laboratory—revealing an experiment on the influence that soil erosion had on society (Curtis, Bavel, and Soens 2016). This permits a diachronic perspective, linking the evidence for vegetation change and soil erosion with the economic and legal history governing land use and the household/catchment-scale processes that show evidence of agricultural management (see, e.g., McGovern et al. 2007).

The Iceland case study shows that a country can be highly eroded and still support a resilient agricultural system and can develop a sophisticated urban society centered on modern Reykjavik and surrounding communities. While Iceland is today an internationally popular tourism destination and is ranked among the best places to live in the world, concerns remain about long-term food security (Bailes and Jóhannsson 2011). Soil conservation is now a national priority (Crofts 2011), woodland is returning, and climate warming is opening up more potentials for Icelandic arable agriculture, but future geographic expansion is limited by the soil erosion of the past. While Iceland is positioned to profit from new transpolar shipping enabled by melting sea ice, much of its modern infrastructure is near sea level and vulnerable to rising tides and increasing storminess. The Icelandic human ecodynamics story is far from over, and the next century will certainly see profound global change and many unanticipated outcomes. The slow catastrophe of Icelandic soil erosion is still unfolding; with the perspective of the *longue durée* it is evident that decisions made in the Viking Age and medieval period still resonate, constraining future options for resilience and adaptive flexibility.

Acknowledgments

The National Science Foundation of America provided financial support for this research through grants 1202692, "Comparative Island Ecodynamics in the North Atlantic," and 1249313, "Tephra Layers and Early Warning Signals for Critical Transitions." We are particularly thankful to the people of Rangárþing eystra, Rangárþing ytra, Mýrdalshreppur, Skaftárhreppur, and Skútustaðahreppur and gratefully acknowledge the permissions of landowners for our fieldwork and the long-term support of Kristján Ólafsson of Seljaland.

Andy Dugmore (PhD 1987, University of Aberdeen) is a physical geographer and professor of geosciences at the University of Edinburgh. His main research interests lie in understanding human-environment interactions, environmental change over timescales from decades to millennia, and the significance of both environmental and climate change for human society. A key theme is the development and application of tephrochronology, and he is working on North Atlantic Biocultural Organization (NABO) projects across the North Atlantic islands plus wider collaborations through the Santa Fe Institute, supported by the Coalition for Archaeological Synthesis.

Rowan Jackson is university teacher in environmental sustainability and director of the MSc Environmental Sustainability program at the University of Edinburgh. His current research explores human vulnerability, adaptation, and resilience in medieval Greenland and the application of archaeological data to contemporary human adaptation and vulnerability to climate change and natural hazards.

David Cooper (PhD 2019, University of Edinburgh) is a biogeographer and geographical information systems specialist. His main research interests lie in the interplay between long-term climatic variation and anthropogenic disturbance in shaping the modern distributions and phylogeographic patterns of big cat species. Currently he is working within the University of Edinburgh to develop commercial interests in satellite data procurement and analysis.

Anthony Newton (PhD 1999, University of Edinburgh) is a senior lecturer in the School of GeoSciences at the University of Edinburgh. He specializes in the application of tephrochronology to understanding environmental and geomorphological change and human-environment interactions. His research is mainly based in Iceland, but he has helped to establish tephrochronological frameworks in Scotland and Mexico, as well as study of ocean-transported pumice in the North Atlantic. He established the pioneering tephrochronological database Tephrabase in 1995 and is currently involved in NABO collaborations including the dataARC project, which aims to bring together a wide range of environmental, ecological, and archaeological data sets through a central portal.

Árni Daníel Júlíusson is an Icelandic historian. He has a PhD from the University of Copenhagen. He has written and edited several books, among them *Icelandic Historical Atlas* (three volumes, 1989), *Agricultural History of Iceland* (four volumes, 2013), and the monograph *Af hverju strái* (2018), about the environmental history of premodern Iceland. He is a specialist at the University of Iceland and is presently active in several international research projects on the environmental history of Iceland.

Richard Streeter (PhD 2011, University of Edinburgh) uses layers of volcanic ash (tephra) to date and reconstruct past environmental change. One of his main focuses over the last decade has been understanding past environmental change in Iceland, particularly the interaction between soil erosion, changing climate, and a fluctuating population. Recently, he has also started to use aerial images to quantify patterns of erosion in Iceland, with the aim of enhancing our understanding of the underlying biological and physical processes that control soil erosion patterns in order to better predict the response of Icelandic eroded landscapes to future global change.

Viðar Hreinsson has a Mag. Art degree in literary studies from the University of Copenhagen. He has lectured and published widely on Icelandic literary and cultural history, is the general editor of *The Complete Sagas of Icelanders*, volumes 1–5 (1997), and has written award-winning monographs: a biography of Icelandic Canadian poet Stephan G. Stephansson 2002–3 (English version, *Wakeful Nights*, 2012) and *Jón lærði og náttúrur náttúrunnar* (Jón the learned and the natures of nature, 2016), on the seventeenth-century conception of nature and the life of the autodidact Jón Guðmundsson the Learned (1574–1658).

Stefani Crabtree (PhD 2016, Washington State University; PhD 2017, Université de Franche-Comté) is the ASU-SFI Center for Biosocial Complex Systems Fellow at the Santa Fe Institute and assistant professor in social-environmental modeling at Utah State University. She has developed methods for assessing the human place in food webs, publishing on those in the American Southwest and the Western Desert of Australia. Director of the ArchaeoEcology project (funded by the Coalition for Archaeological Synthesis), she is leading efforts to understand human-centered ecological networks globally. In Iceland she is currently assessing responses to the tenth-century Norse settlement.

George Hambrecht (PhD 2011, Graduate Center of the City University of New York) is an assistant professor in the Anthropology Department of the University of Maryland, College Park. He is a zooarchaeologist whose work focuses on the relationships between humans and environmental change over the last millennium in the North Atlantic. He is participating in a number of NABO projects, as well as larger comparative projects that put North Atlantic data into wider global contexts. Alongside these projects he has also been active in the international community concerned with climate-change-based threats to cultural heritage.

Megan Hicks (PhD, City University of New York) is an assistant professor of archaeology in the Anthropology Department of Hunter College of the City University of New York. Her archaeological work has focused on the experiences of communities and ecologies in contexts of colonialism and capitalism, viewed through their long-term uses of animals and landscapes. Her current focus is on Iceland's rural communities and ecologies in the postmedieval period as part of larger Atlantic world economic formations. She has led excavations and maintained long-term interests in community collaboration and how environmentally focused archaeology can be applied in advocacy and supporting local decision-making in environmental management.

Thomas H. McGovern (PhD 1979, Columbia University) is a professor in the Anthropology Department of Hunter College of the City University of New York and directs the Hunter Zooarchaeology Laboratory. He serves as coordinator for the North Atlantic Biocultural Organization (NABO, www.nabohome.org), which is a research and education cooperative connecting across disciplines and communities in the region. He has worked on NABO collaborative projects in Norway, Scotland, Faroes, Iceland, and Greenland and is currently principal investigator on a US National Science Foundation international project in South Greenland responding to rapid loss of both science and heritage to climate change.

References

Agricultural University of Iceland. 2001. "Soils of Iceland." Retrieved 4 April 2019 from http://rangarvellir.ru.is/?page_id=198.

Amorosi, Tom, Paul Buckland, Andrew Dugmore, Jon H. Ingimundarson, and Thomas H. McGovern. 1997. "Raiding the Landscape: Human Impact in the Scandinavian North Atlantic." *Human Ecology* 25 (3): 491–518.

Amundsen, Colin, Sophia Perdikaris, Thomas H. McGovern, Yekaterina Krivogorskaya, Matthem Brown, Konrad Smiarowski, Shaye Storm, Salena Modugno, Malgorzata Frik, and Monica Koczela. 2005. "Fishing Booths and Fishing Strategies in Medieval Iceland: an Archaeofauna from the of Akurvík, North-West Iceland." *Environmental Archaeology* 10 (2): 141–98.

Arnalds, Andrés. 1987. "Ecosystem Disturbance and Recovery in Iceland." *Arctic and Alpine Research* 19: 508–13.

Arnalds, Ólafur. 2000. "The Icelandic 'Rofabard' Soil Erosion Features." *Earth Surface Processes and Landforms* 25 (1): 17–28.

———. 2004. "Volcanic Soils of Iceland." *Catena* 56 (1–3): 3–20.

———. 2008. "Soils of Iceland." *Jökull* 58: 409–421.

———. 2015. *The Soils of Iceland*. Dordrecht: Springer.

Arnalds, Ólafur, Asa L. Aradóttir, and Ingvi Thorsteinsson. 1987. "The Nature and Restoration of Denuded Areas in Iceland." *Arctic and Alpine Research* 19 (4): 518–25.

Arnalds, Óalfur, and Björn. H. Barkarson. 2003. "Soil Erosion and Land Use Policy in Iceland in Relation to Sheep Grazing and Government Subsidies." *Environmental Science & Policy* 6 (1): 105–13.

Arnalds, Ólafur, Elin Thorarinsdottir, Sigmar Metusalemsson, Asgeir Jonsson, Einar Gretarsson, and Arnor Arnason. 2001. *Soil Erosion in Iceland* (Tech. rept. English translation of original Icelandic publication from 1997). Reykjavik: Soil Conservation Service and Agricultural Research Institute.

Arsenault, Chris. 2014. "Only 60 Years of Farming Left If Soil Degradation Continues." *Scientific American*, 5 December. Retrieved 20 May 2020 from https://www.scientificamerican.com/article/only-60-years-of-farming-left-if-soil-degradation-continues/.

Bailes, Alyson J. K., and Orri Jóhannsson. 2011. "Food Security in Iceland 2011." *Stjórnmál & Stjórnsýsla* 2 (7): 491–509.

Baillie, Mike G. L. 1991. "Suck-In and Smear: Two Related Chronological Problems for the 90s." *Journal of Theoretical Archaeology* 2: 12–16.

Barclay, Rebecca. 2016. "Formation, Cultural Use and Management of Icelandic Wet Meadows—a Palaeoenvironmental Interpretation." PhD dissertation, University of Stirling.

Boserup, Ester. 1965. *The Conditions of Agricultural Growth: The Economics of Agrarian Change under Population Pressure*. Oxford: Earthscan.

Butzer, Karl W. 2008. "Challenges for a cross-Disciplinary Geoarchaeology: The Intersection between Environmental History and Geomorphology." *Geomorphology* 101 (1–2): 402–11.

———. 2012. "Collapse, Environment and Society." *Proceedings of the National Academy of Sciences* 109 (10): 3632–39.

Butzer, Karl W., and Georgina H. Endfield. 2012. "Critical Perspectives on Historical Collapse." *Proceedings of the National Academy of Sciences* 109 (10): 3628–31.

Carpenter, Stephen R., William A. Brock, Carl Folke, Egbert H. van Nes, and Marten Scheffer. 2014. "Allowing Variance May Enlarge the Safe Operating Space for

Exploited Ecosystems." *Proceedings of the National Academy of Sciences* 112 (46): 14384–389.

Crofts, Roger. 2011. *Healing the Land*. Soil Conservation Service of Iceland.

Crumley, Carole, ed. 1994. *Historical Ecology: Cultural Knowledge and Changing Landscapes*. Santa Fe: School of American Research Press.

Crumley, Carole L. 2017. "Historical Ecology and the Study of Landscape." *Landscape Research* 42 (sup1): S65–S73.

Curtis, Daniel R., Bas van Bavel, and Tim Soens. 2016. "History and the Social Sciences: Shock Therapy with Medieval Economic History as the Patient." *Social Science History* 40: 751–74.

Diamond, Jared. 2005. *Collapse: How Societies Choose to Fail or Succeed*. New York: Penguin.

Diplomatarium Islandicum. Diplomatarium Islandicum, Íslenzkt fornbréfasafn, sem hefur inni að halda bréf og gjörninga, dóma og máldaga, og aðrar skrár, er snerta Ísland eða Íslenzka menn. Edited by Jón Þorkelsson. Reykjavík Hið íslenzka bókmenntafélag, 1899–1902.

Dugmore, Andrew. J., and Paul C. Buckland. 1991. "Tephrochronology and Late Holocene Soil Erosion in South Iceland." In *Environmental Change in Iceland*, edited by J. Maizels and C. Caseldine, 147–59. Dordrecht: Kluwer.

Dugmore, Andrew J., Mike J. Church, Paul C. Buckland, Kevin J. Edwards, Ian Lawson, Thomas H. McGovern, Eva Panagiotakopulu, Ian A. Simpson, Peter Skidmore, and Guðrún Sveinbjarnardóttir. 2005. "The Norse Landnám on the North Atlantic Islands: An Environmental Impact Assessment." *Polar Record* 41 (216): 21–37.

Dugmore, Andrew. J., and Camilla C. Erskine. 1994. "Local and Regional Patterns of Soil Erosion in Southern Iceland." *Münchener Geographische Abhandlungen* 12: 63–79.

Dugmore, Andrew J., Guðrún Gísladóttir, Ian A. Simpson, and Anthony J. Newton. 2009. "Conceptual Models of 1,200 Years of Soil Erosion Reconstructed Using Tephrochronology." *Journal of the North Atlantic* 2: 1–18.

Dugmore, Andrew J., Christian Keller, and Thomas H. McGovern. 2007. "The Norse Greenland Settlement: Reflections on Climate Change, Trade and the Contrasting Fates of Human Settlements in the Atlantic Islands." *Arctic Anthropology* 44 (1): 12–37.

Dugmore, Andrew J., Thomas H. McGovern, Richard Streeter, Christian Koch Madsen, Konrad Smiarowski, and Christian Keller. 2013. "'Clumsy Solutions' and 'Elegant Failures': Lessons on Climate Change Adaptation from the Settlement of the North Atlantic." In *A Changing Environment for Human Security: Transformative Approaches to Research, Policy and Action*, edited by L. Sygna, K. O'Brien, and J. Wolf. London: Routledge.

Dugmore, Andrew J., Thomas H. McGovern, Orri Vésteinsson, Jette Arneborg, Richard Streeter, and Christian Keller. 2012. "Cultural Adaptation Compounding Vulnerabilities and Conjunctures in Norse Greenland." *Proceedings of the National Academy of Sciences* 109 (10): 3658–63.

Dugmore, Andrew J., Anthony J. Newton, Guðrún Larsen, and Gordon T. Cook. 2000. "Tephrochronology, Environmental Change and the Norse Settlement of Iceland." *Environmental Archaeology* 5: 21–34.

Egil's Saga. 1997. Translated by Bernard Scudder. In *The Complete Sagas of Icelanders*, edited by Viðar Hreinsson, vol. 1, chap. 29. Reykjavík: Leifur Eirikksson Publishing.

Ehrlich, Paul R., and Anne H. Ehrlich. 2013. "Can a Collapse of Global Civilization Be Avoided?" *Proceedings of the Royal Society B* 280 (1754): 20122845.

Fitzhugh, William W. 2000. "Puffins, Ringed Pins, and Runestones: The Viking Passage to America." In *Vikings: The North Atlantic Saga*, edited by W. W. Fitzhugh and E. I. Ward, 8–25. Washington, DC: Smithsonian University Press.

Foley, Jonathan A., Ruth DeFries, Gregory P. Asner, Carol Barford, Gordon Bonan, Stephen R. Carpenter, F. Stuart Chapin, Michael T. Coe, Gretchen C. Daily, Holly K. Gibbs, Joseph H. Helkowski, Tracey Holloway, Erica A. Howard, Christopher J. Kucharik, Chad Monfreda, Jonathan A Patz, Colin Prentice, Navin Ramankutty, and Peter K. Snyder. 2005. "Global Consequences of Land Use." *Science* 309 (5734): 570–74.

Fridriksson, Sturla, and Grétar Gudbergsson. 1995. "Rate of Vegetation Retreat at Rofbarðs (in Icelandic)." *Freyr* 1995: 224–31.

Gísladóttir, Guðrún. 1998. "Environmental Characterization and Change in South-Western Iceland." Department of Physical Geography, Stockholm University, Dissertation Series 10.

———. 2001. "Ecological Disturbance and Soil Erosion on Grazing Land in Southwest Iceland." In *Land Degradation: Papers selected from Contributions to the Sixth Meeting of the International Geographical Union's Commission on Land Degradation and Desertification, Perth, Western Australia, 20–28 September 1999*, edited by Arthur Conacher, 109–26. Dordrecht: Springer.

Greipsson, Sigurdur. 2012. "Catastrophic Soil Erosion in Iceland: Impact of Long-Term Climate Change, Compounded Natural Disturbances and Human Driven Land-Use Changes." *Catena* 98: 41–54.

Hambrecht, George. 2011. "Faunal Analysis of the Early Modern Bishop's Farm at Skalholt, Arnessysla Iceland." PhD dissertation, City University of New York.

Hardin, Garrett. 1968. "The Tragedy of the Commons." *Science* 162 (3859): 1243–1248.

Harrison, Ramona, Howell M. Roberts, and W. Paul Adderley. 2008. "Gásir in Eyjafjördur: International Exchange and Local Economy in Medieval Iceland." *Journal of the North Atlantic* 1 (1): 99–199.

Hartman, Steve, Astrid E. J. Ogilvie, Jón Hauker Ingimundarson, Andrew. J. Dugmore, George Hambrecht, and Thomas H. McGovern. 2017. "Medieval Iceland, Greenland and the New Human Condition: A Case Study in Integrated Environmental Humanities." *Global and Planetary Change* 156: 123–39.

Hauksbók. Hauksbók udgiven efter de arnamagnæanske håndskrifter no. 371, 544 og 675, 4°samt forskellige papirshåndskrifter. In *Det kongelige nordiske oldskrift-selskab 1892–1896*, edited by E. Jónsson and F. Jónsson Copenhagen.

Hayeur Smith, Michèle. 2014. "Thorir's Bargain: Gender, Vaðmál and the Law." *World Archaeology* 45 (5): 730–46.

Hicks, Megan. 2014. "Losing Sleep Counting Sheep: Early Modern Dynamics of Hazardous Husbandry in Mývatn, Iceland." In *Human Ecodynamics in the North Atlantic: A Collaborative Model of Humans and Nature through Space and Time*, edited by Ramona Harrison and Ruth Maher, 137–53. Lanham, MD: Lexington Books.

Hulme, Mike. 2011. "Reducing the Future to Climate: A Story of Climate Determinism and Reductionism." *Osiris* 26 (1): 245–66.

IPCC. 2014. *Contribution of Working Group II to the Fifth Assessment Report of the Intergovernmental Panel on Climate Change*. Cambridge: Cambridge University Press.

Izdebski, Adam, Lee Mordechai, and Sam White. 2018. "The Social Burden of Resilience: A Historical Perspective." *Human Ecology* 46 (3): 291–303.

Jackson, Rowan, Jette Arneborg, Andrew Dugmore, Christian Madsen, Thomas H. McGovern, Konrad Smiarowski, and Richard Streeter. 2018. "Disequilibrium,

Adaptation, and the Norse Settlement of Greenland." *Human Ecology* 46 (5): 665–84.

Jakobsson, Sverrir. 2013. "From Reciprocity to Manorialism: On the Peasant Mode of Production in Medieval Iceland." *Scandinavian Journal of History* 38 (3): 273–95.

Johnsen, Oscar A., and Jón Helgason. 1941. *Saga Óláfs konungs hins helga: Den store saga om Olav den hellige. Efter pergamenthåndskrift i Kungliga Biblioteket i Stockholm nr 2 4 to med varianter fra andre handskrifter* (The saga of King Olaf the Holy: The large saga of Saint Olaf. Based on the parchment manuscript in the Royal Library in Stockholm no. 2 with variants from other manuscripts). Oslo: Norsk historisk kjeldieskrift institut.

Jónsson, Gudmundur. 1993. "Institutional Change in Icelandic Agriculture, 1780–1940." *Scandinavian Economic History Review* 41 (2): 101–28.

Júlíusson, Árni D. 2019. "Vannýtt hálendi? Um nýtingu miðhálendisins til beitar á 15–18. öld." In *Nýtt Helgakver*, 149–67. Reykjavík: Sögufélag.

Karlsson, Gunnar. 2000. *Iceland's 1100 Years: The History of a Marginal Society*. London: C. Hurst.

Kristinsson, Axel, and Árni D. Júlíusson. 2016. "Adapting to Population Growth: The Evolutionary Alternative to Malthus." *Cliodynamics* 7: 37–75.

Landnámabók: The Book of Settlements. 1972. Translated, with introduction and notes, by Hermann Pálsson and Paul Edwards. Winnipeg: University of Manitoba Press.

Larsen, Guðrún. 2000. "Holocene Eruptions within the Katla Volcanic System, South Iceland: Characteristics and Environmental Impact." *Jökull* 49: 1–28.

Larsen, Guðrún, and Jón Eiríksson. 2008. "Holocene Tephra Archives and Tephrochronology in Iceland—A Brief Overview." *Jökull* 58: 229–50.

Larsen, Guðrún, and Sigurdur Thórarinsson. 1977. "H4 and Other Acidic Hekla Tephra Layers." *Jökull* 27: 28–46.

Lawson, Ian, Karen Milek, W. Paul Adderley, Andrew F. Casely, Mike C. Church, Luisa Duarte, Andrew J. Dugmore, Kevin J. Edwards, Frederick. J. Gathorne-Hardy, Garðar Gudmundsson, Stuart Morrison, Anthony J. Newton, and Ian A. Simpson. 2009. "The Palaeoenvironment of Mývatnssveit during the Viking Age and Early Medieval Period." In *Hofstadir: Excavations of a Viking Age Feasting Hall in North-Eastern Iceland*, edited by G. Lucas, 26–54. Reykjavík: Fornleifastofnun Íslands.

Lawson, Ian T., Frederick J. Gathorne-Hardy, Mike J. Church, Árni Einarsson, Kevin J. Edwards, Sophia Perdikaris, Thomas H. McGovern, Colin Amundsen, and Guðrun Sveinbjarnardóttir. 2004. "Human Impact on Freshwater Environments in Norse and Early Medieval Mývatnssveit." In *Dynamics of Northern Societies*, edited by Jette Arneborg and B. Grønnow, 375–83. Copenhagen: National Museum of Denmark

Lawson, Ian T., Frederick J. Gathorne-Hardy, Mike J. Church, Anthony J. Newton, Kevin J. Edwards, Andrew J. Dugmore, and Árni Einarsson. 2007. "Environmental Impacts of the Norse Settlement: Palaeoenvironmental Data from Mývatnssveit, Northern Iceland." *Boreas* 36 (1): 1–19.

Leichenko, Robin, and Karen O'Brien. 2008. *Environmental Change and Globalization: Double Exposure*. Oxford: Oxford University Press.

Malthus, Thomas. (1798) 2015. *An Essay on the Principle of Population*. Pelican Classics.

Marston, Richard A. 2010. "Geomorphology and Vegetation on Hillslopes: Interactions, Dependencies, and Feedback Loops." *Geomorphology* 116 (3–4): 206–17.

McAnany, Patricia, and Norman Yoffee, eds. 2010. *Questioning Collapse: Human Resilience, Ecological Vulnerability, and the Aftermath of Empire*. Cambridge: Cambridge University Press.

McGovern, Thomas H. 2009. "The Archaeofauna." In *Hofstadir: Excavations of a Viking Age Feasting Hall in North-Eastern Iceland*, edited by Gavin Lucas. Reykjavík: Fornleifastofnun Íslands.

McGovern, Thomas H., Ramona Harrison, and Konrad Smiarowski. 2014. "Sorting Sheep and Goats in Medieval Iceland and Greenland: Local Subsistence or World System." In *Human Ecodynamics in the North Atlantic: A Collaborative Model of Humans and Nature through Space and Time*, edited by Ramona Harrison and Ruth Maher, 153–77. Lanham, MD: Lexington Books.

McGovern, Thomas H., Orri Vésteinsson, Adolf Friðriksson, Mike Church, Ian Lawson, Ian A. Simpson, Arni Einarsson, Andrew Dugmore, Gordon Cook, Sophia Perdikaris, Kevin J. Edwards, Amanda M. Thomson, W. Paul Adderley, Anthony Newton, Gavin Lucas, Ragnar Edvardsson, Oscar Aldred, and Elaine Dunbar. 2007. "Landscapes of Settlement in Northern Iceland: Historical Ecology of Human Impact and Climate Fluctuation on the Millennial Scale." *American Anthropologist* 109 (1): 27–51.

Middleton, Guy D. 2017. *Understanding Collapse: Ancient History and Modern Myths*. 462 vols. Cambridge: Cambridge University Press.

Montgomery, David R. 2012. *Dirt: The Erosion of Civilizations*. Berkeley and Los Angeles: University of California Press.

National Research Council. 2001. *Grand Challenges in Environmental Sciences*. Washington, DC: The National Academies Press.

Nelson, Margaret. C., Scott E. Ingram, Andrew J. Dugmore, Richard Streeter, Matthew A. Peeples, Thomas H. McGovern, Michelle Hegmon, Jette Arneborg, Keith W. Kintigh, Seth Brewington, Katherine A. Spielmann, Ian A. Simpson, Colleen Strawhacker, Laure E. L. Comeau, Andrea Torvinen, Christian K. Madsen, George Hambrecht, and Konrad Smiarowski. 2016. "Climate Changes, Vulnerabilities, and Food Security." *Proceedings of the National Academy of Sciences* 113 (2): 298–303.

O'Brien, Karen. 2012. "Global Environmental Change II, from Adaptation to Deliberate Transformation." *Progress in Human Geography* 36 (5): 667–76.

Ólafsdóttir, Rannveig 2002. *Land Degradation and Climate in Iceland: A Spatial and Temporal Assessment*. Lund: Department of Physical Geography and Ecosystem Science, Lund University.

Ólafsdóttir, Rannveig, and Hjalti J. Guòmundsson. 2002. "Holocene Land Degradation and Climatic Change in Northeastern Iceland." *The Holocene* 12 (2): 159–67.

Ólafsdóttir, Rannveig, Peter Schlyter, and Hörður Haraldsson. 2001. "Simulating Icelandic Vegetation Cover during the Holocene: Implications for Long-Term Land Degradation." *Geografiska Annaler* 83A (4): 203–15.

Oppenheimer, Clive. 2015. "Eruption Politics." *Nature Geoscience* 8: 244–245.

Ostrom, Elinor. 2005. *Understanding Institutional Diversity*. Princeton: Princeton University Press.

———. 2007. "A Diagnostic Approach for Going Beyond Panaceas." *Proceedings of the National Academy of Sciences* 104 (39): 15181–187.

———. 2009. "A General Framework for Analysing Sustainability of Social-Ecological Systems." *Science* 325 (5939): 419–22.

———. 2015. *Governing the Commons*. Cambridge: Cambridge University Press.

Pálsson, Hermann, and Paul Edwards. 1985. "Arrow-Odd." In *Seven Viking Romances*, 25–137. London: Penguin.

Pelling, Mark. 2011. *Adaptation to Climate Change: From Resilience to Transformation*. London: Routledge.

Perdikaris, Sophia, and Thomas H. McGovern. 2008. "Codfish and Kings, Seals and Subsistence: Norse Marine Resource Use in the North Atlantic." In *Viking Voyagers*, edited by J. M. Erlandson and T. R. Rick, 187–14. Oakland: UCLA Press.

Raffield, Ben, Neil Price, and Mark Collard. 2017. "Male-Biased Operational Sex Ratios and the Viking Phenomenon: An Evolutionary Anthropological Perspective on Late Iron Age Scandinavian Raiding." *Evolution and Human Behaviour* 38 (3): 315–324.

Redman, Charles L. 2005. "Resilience Theory in Archaeology." *American Anthropologist* 107: 70–77.

Riede, Felix. 2017. *Splendid Isolation: The Eruption of the Laacher See Volcano and Southern Scandinavian Late Glacial Hunter-Gatherers*. Aarhus: Aarhus University Press.

Rowley-Conwy, Peter, and Robert Layton. 2011. "Foraging and Farming as Niche Construction: Stable and Unstable Adaptations." *Philosophical Transactions of the Royal Society B* 366: 849–62.

Runólfsson, Sveinn. 1978. "Soil Conservation in Iceland." In *The Breakdown and Restoration of Ecosystems*, edited by M. W. Holdgate and M. J. Woodman, 231–40. New York: Plenum Press.

———. 2009. "Soil Knowledge for a Sustainable Planet." Inaugural lecture to GlobalSoilMap.net New York.

Scheffer, Marten, Stephen R. Carpenter, Timothy M. Lenton, Jordi Bascompte, William Brock, Vasilis Dakos, J. van de Koppel, Ingrid. A. van de Lemput, Simon A. Levin, Egbert H. van Nes, Mercedes Pascual, and John Vandermeer. 2012. "Anticipating Critical Transitions." *Science* 338 (6105): 344–48.

Schmid, Magdalena. M. E., Andrew J. Dugmore, Orri Vésteinsson, and Anthony J. Newton. 2017. "Tephra Isochrons and Chronologies of Colonisation." *Quaternary Geochronology* 40: 56–66.

Simpson, Ian A., Andrew J. Dugmore, Amanda Thomson, and Orri Vésteinsson. 2001. "Crossing the Thresholds: Historical Patterns of Landscape Degradation in Iceland." *Catena* 42: 175–92.

Simpson, Ian A., Garðar Guðmundsson, Amanda M. Thomson, and Jonathan Cluett. 2004. "Assessing the Role of Winter Grazing in Historic Land Degradation, Mývatnssveit, Northeast Iceland." *Geoarchaeology: An International Journal* 19 (5): 471–502.

Streeter, Richard, and Andrew J. Dugmore. 2014. "Late-Holocene Land Surface Change in a Coupled Social-Ecological System, Southern Iceland: A Cross-Scale Tephrochronology Approach." *Quaternary Science Reviews* 86: 99–114.

Streeter, Richard, Andrew J. Dugmore, Ian T. Lawson, Egill Erlendsson, and Kevin J. Edwards. 2015. "The Onset of the Palaeoanthropocene in Iceland: Changes in Complex Natural Systems." *The Holocene* 25 (10): 1662–75.

Streeter, Richard, Andrew J. Dugmore, and Orri Vesteinsson. 2012. "Plague and Landscape Resilience in Premodern Iceland." *Proceedings of the National Academy of Sciences* 109 (10): 3664–69.

Streeter, Richard T., and Andrew J. Dugmore. 2013. "Anticipating Land Surface Change." *Proceedings of the National Academy of Sciences* 110 (15): 5779–84.

Tainter, Joseph. 1988. *The Collapse of Complex Societies*. Cambridge: Cambridge University Press.

Thomson, Amanda. M., and Ian A. Simpson. 2007. "Modeling Historic Rangeland Management and Grazing Pressures in Lanscapes of Settlement." *Human Ecology* 35 (2): 151–68.

Thórarinsson, Sigurður. 1961. "Wind Erosion in Iceland: A Tephrochronological Study (in Icelandic)." *Ársrit Skógræktarfélags Íslands 1961*: 17–54.

———. 1967. "The Eruptions of Hekla in Historical Times." *The Eruption of Hekla 1947–1948* 1: 1–170.

———. 1975. "Katla og annáll Kötlugosa (Katla and the Annals of Katla Tephras)." In *Árbók ferðafélags Íslands 1975*, 125–49.

Thorsteinsson, Ingvi. 1986. "The Effect of Grazing on Stability and Development of Northern Rangelands: A Case Study from Iceland." In *Grazing Research at Northern Latitudes*, edited by O. Gudmundsson, 37–43. New York: Plenum.

Vasey, Daniel E. 1996. "Population Regulation, Ecology, and Political Economy in Pre-industrial Iceland." *American Ethnologist* 23 (2): 366–92.

Vésteinsson, Orri. 2000. "The Archaeology of Landnám: Early Settlement in Iceland." In *Vikings: The North Atlantic Saga*, edited by W. W. Fitzhugh and E. I. Ward, 164–74. Washington, DC: Smithsonian Institution Press.

———. 2016. "Commercial Fishing and the Political Economy of Medieval Iceland." In *Cod and Herring: The Archaeology and History of Medieval Sea Fishing*, edited by J. H. Barrett and D. C. Orton. Oxford: Oxbow.

Vésteinsson, Orri, Mike Church, Andrew Dugmore, Thomas H. McGovern, and Anthony Newton. 2014. "Expensive Errors or Rational Choices: The Pioneer Fringe in Late Viking Age Iceland." *European Journal of Post-Classical Archaeologies* 4: 39–68.

Vésteinsson, Orri, and Thomas H. McGovern. 2012. "The Peopling of Iceland." *Norwegian Archaeological Review* 45 (2): 206–18.

Vésteinsson, Orri, Thomas H. McGovern, and Christian Keller. 2002. "Enduring Impacts: Social and Environmental Aspects of Viking Age Settlement in Iceland and Greenland." *Archaeologia Islandica* 2: 98–136.

Wickham, Christopher. 2005. *Framing the Middle Ages: Europe and the Mediterranean, 400–800*. Oxford: Oxford University Press.

CHAPTER 7

Coping through Connectedness

A Network-Based Modeling Approach Using Radiocarbon Data from the Kuril Islands of Northeast Asia

ERIK GJESFJELD and WILLIAM A. BROWN

Summary for Stakeholders

Small and remote islands present unique challenges for the reduction of disaster risk (Pelling and Uitto 2001). Some of these difficulties include (1) small geographic areas with correspondingly limited resources; (2) elevated disaster frequency and severity based on geography, geophysics, and topography; and (3) physical isolation from neighboring regions with more significant resources (Shultz et al. 2016). One recent recommendation for disaster risk reduction on small islands is to increase their connectedness to information management and knowledge sharing systems (UNESCO 2016). It is assumed that by increasing the connectivity of small islands to global infrastructure, they will be better able to access early warning signals, to efficiently distribute critical resources, to increase access to emotional and financial support, and to offer a greater range of options for temporary or permanent relocation. In other words, *connectedness* on small islands can be viewed as a form of community self-protection that operates independently of local, state, and federal governments (Wisner et al. 2004).

An important strategy for integrating local community networks with global information networks is to balance indigenous/folk/traditional knowledge accumulated by local populations with scientific knowledge that originates from global entities. It is well-documented that preindustrial societies encode strategies for disaster risk reduction within folk stories that are retold across generations and communities. However, the integration of traditional knowledge into global knowledge faces many challenges, as these two bodies of knowledge can present contradictory information or require individuals to dismiss the importance of their indigenous knowledge in favor of scientific knowledge (Agrawal 1995). Often, by increasing the connectivity of developing small-island states to global information hubs, indigenous knowledge can be lost as reliance on scientific knowledge becomes more prominent.

A few successful examples of disaster risk reduction in indigenous communities have come when local knowledge networks are intertwined with outside knowledge in order to create multiple forms of knowledge that are available to populations (Campbell 2006). For example, Yates and Anderson-Berry (2004) and Mercer et al. (2010) highlight that prior to the landfall of Cyclone Zoe in the Solomon Islands, only a few residents were able to receive and understand the early warning signal sent by Radio Australia. In reality, it was the local face-to-face communication network that served to transmit the warning message throughout the broader community. This was largely due to the aid of local runners who took the message to community members in their local language. A second example comes from the 2008 Wenchen earthquake in Sichuan, China, where local social networks were a vital mechanism that aided in search and rescue, social support, and the distribution of support resources (Zhao 2013). After television and local military officials, local social networks were a significant channel from which individuals received critical information about the relief efforts, with approximately 30 percent of survey respondents viewing their local social network as their most important support provider. Similar to predictions from our Information Networks model, Zhao (2013) highlighted that a more heterogeneous network structure with a combination of local (family and friends) and regional or distant ties (acquaintances) is the most effective network structure for receiving and disseminating information.

Building long-distance connections between small-island states and larger global hubs undoubtedly has benefits to small island communities, but it is critical to note that these same connections can create vulnerabilities if not properly managed. For example, in the recent tsunami that struck the island of Sulawesi on 28 September 2018, the network infrastructure trusted to relay information from global hubs to local communities severely malfunctioned. As reported by Singhvi, Saget, and Lee (2018), cell phone towers had broken down from the preceding earthquake, so no text warnings could be transmitted. In addition, nearly twenty-two water buoys had not been functional since 2012 due to vandalism and lack of routine maintenance. Even if the early warning signal had been transmitted, many community members did not know where to go or what to do had the sirens sounded. Based on our network models of past societies, it is evident that if social connections and regional or distant scales are not reinforced and reciprocated on a routine basis, they can easily deteriorate through time. The resulting loss of connections at different spatial scales can create community vulnerabilities and increase the susceptibility of communities to unpredictable hazard events. In this respect, the long-term maintenance of network connections is as important, if not more so, than simply creating networks of connection between small-island states. While maintaining connections between local populations on small islands and hubs of information in distant locations was likely a major challenge for preindustrial societies, it is becoming increasingly easy to establish and maintain connections given advancements in communication, transportation, and information technology. Overall, we agree with UNESCO that developing small-island states would greatly benefit from increased connectivity with global networks, but only if these are effectively connected to existing local support networks and knowledge bases that can be maintained over time. We argue that without a clear plan for the creation *and* maintenance of social and information connections, it is quite possible that when the next hazard event occurs, which it inevitably will, *connectedness* may do more harm than good.

Introduction

This chapter explores the adaptive role social support networks play in mediating the impact of disasters. We start from a general assumption that the variety of rights and obligations that connect individuals, households, and communities is a valuable mechanism for the bargaining and securing of resources during times of crisis (Agarwal 1990, 343; Wisner et al. 2004, 117). More specifically, these networks of social relationships function to reduce disaster stress by allowing individuals and communities access to resources and information beyond what is directly available to them, as well as physical area to relocate if it is less impacted than their local area (Whallon 2006).

We center our discussion on the ambiguous term "connectedness," whose equivocality encompasses a broad set of themes that can nevertheless be synthesized in a way that allows us to explore how communities respond to disasters in both the past and present. In the framework of social network analysis, connectedness gives name to relationships among individuals, institutions, and communities that aid in reducing disaster risk. In contrast, resilience theory applies this label to the rigidity of a system and a key factor in the long-term transition of a system between phases of growth and conservation (Bradtmöller, Grimm, and Riel-

Salvatore 2017). We attempt to connect these different concepts of connectedness through a methodological approach that translates trends in regional human population into models of *community connectedness* and *system connectedness*. An added value of our approach is the ability to estimate the social connections of past communities at fine-grained timescales, as well as long-term systemic changes in networks and their potential impact on how communities mitigate hazardous events.

The results of our work highlight several concerns for populations relying on diverse social connections, such as those living in marginal and isolated landscapes without consistent access to resources and information. We argue that it is imperative for communities living at the limits of marginality to overcome geographic limitations and develop connectedness at multiple, independent scales when confronting a likely increase in the global frequency and intensity of climatic natural hazards. While the construction and maintenance of networks connecting small and remote island communities requires substantial investment, these spatially diverse networks are critical components to the long-term safety and welfare of these communities.

Connectedness in Disaster Risk Reduction and Resilience Theory

The goal of disaster risk reduction (DRR) research is to identify and intervene on the mediating variables that modulate the risk that natural hazards will entail disastrous consequences (UNESCO 2019). Central to this goal is assessing community vulnerability—the degree to which "*the characteristics of a person or group and their situation that influence their capacity to anticipate, cope with, resist and recover from the impact of a natural hazard*" [italics in original] (Wisner et al. 2004, 11). This differs from the common use of the vulnerability as the susceptibility to harm, damage, or injury (Wisner et al. 2004; Adger 2006; Torrence 2016), which overemphasizes the negative outcomes of disaster events while downplaying how communities and social groups react to, innovate, and grapple with catastrophes (Torrence 2016). Accentuating the role that individual- and community-level characteristics play in modulating the degree of adversity reorients the research focus away from the magnitude of the hazard itself and toward the characteristics of social systems that influence disaster responses—class, occupation, ethnicity, gender, health status, age, and infrastructure (both physical and social), to name only a few (Wisner et al. 2004, 11).

One of the key characteristics of a community influencing its responsiveness to hazard events is its social infrastructure. The concept of social infrastructure broadly refers to the physical conditions that determine the social capital that emerges from network interactions between individuals and communities (Klinenberg 2018, 5). When social infrastructure is healthy, connections between individuals and communities are routinely strengthened, and social networks provide the support necessary in times of crisis. However, when the social infrastructure is degraded, interaction is discouraged, and social support is lacking, ultimately leading to poorer health and greater fatalities for individuals living in comparable socioeconomic conditions. At a local scale, social infrastructure is often fostered through face-to-face interaction in parks, social clubs, religious organizations, or any popular gathering place. More broadly, social infrastructure can also refer to physical structures that promote interaction. For example, transit networks themselves would not necessarily qualify as social infrastructure, but these hard infrastructures have been shown to increase social interactions such as the development of "transient communities," which consist of people who commute together regularly. While the shared daily experience of these individuals may not produce strong local friendships, they do contribute to a greater sense of community cooperation and trust (Klinenberg 2018, 18).

In this chapter, we broadly draw from the concept of social infrastructure to explore the degree to which social connections within and between communities at various spatial scales may influence responsiveness to hazard events. The general premise is that the more diverse and richly connected a community is, the lower its risk of experiencing disaster, as the community has a greater capacity to anticipate, cope, and recover. As Kelly M. Britt (chapter 8 in this volume) demonstrates, the robust infrastructure of social connections was key to the survival of many communities after Hurricane Sandy by providing access to basic provisions, shelter, and the help necessary to rebuild. Furthermore, these same community networks were instrumental in changing the way cultural organizations and institutions prepared, mitigated, responded to, and recovered from disasters (Britt, chapter 8 in this volume). We will refer to these snapshots of social networks as "community connectedness," a term we hope highlights the importance of social infrastructure, but can also dovetail with related, yet distinct concepts of connectedness used in resilience theory (RT).

One of the recent trends in the social sciences is the application of RT to frame our understanding of long-term change in human-environmental interactions. This body of theory was introduced to archaeology nearly fifteen years ago (Redman 2005; Redman and Kinzig 2003) after its application in ecology a decade earlier (Gunderson and Holling 2002; Folke et al. 2004). Since this time, the utility of RT to archaeological inquiry has been widely discussed and debated (see Bradtmöller, Grimm, and Riel-Salvatore 2017 for a review of archaeological research that uses RT). One domain of archaeological research in which RT has been particularly appealing is the archaeology of catastrophes and sudden environmental change (Cooper 2012; Cooper and Sheets 2012). At a conceptual level, the attraction of RT is obvious, as its emphasis on cycles of persistence punctuated by abrupt periods of transformation (Holling and Gunderson 2002; Walker et al. 2004) provides a model for framing how catastrophic events can influence socio-ecological systems. However, at a practical level, operationalizing RT within archaeological research on disasters has been slow to develop. Key limitations include analytical ambiguity (Fitzhugh et al. 2019), poor and often variable definitions, overemphasis on the stability of systems, minimization of discussion about political influences, and strong assumptions about the nature of communities and societies (Barrios 2016). As Peters and Zimmermann (2017, 43) suggest, "A state has been reached now, however, where a merely metaphorical use of the concept will not take the issue any further. The next step in the application of RT in archaeology has to involve clearly defined parameters and measurable proxy variables."

The operationalization of RT was a central theme in a special issue of *Quaternary International* (Bradtmöller, Grimm, and Riel-Salvatore 2017). The compilation of papers in this issue demonstrates one of the most extensive efforts to review, translate, and apply concepts of ecological resilience into archaeological practice. The approach taken by many of the authors was to bridge RT with empirical evidence by invoking the adaptive cycle (AC) model. This was often accomplished by developing analogies (Freeman, Hard, and Mauldin 2017) between patterns of change in the archaeological record and phases of the adaptive cycle such as growth, conservation, release, and reorganization.

One of the key parameters of the adaptive cycle is termed "connectedness." As defined by Gunderson and Holling (2002, 50), connectedness measures the strength of internal connections and their mediation of ecological dynamics. If a system demonstrates a high degree of connectedness, it is not strongly influenced by external perturbations but rather by the internal dynamics that mediate variability. More broadly, connectedness is viewed as a measure of the rigidity of a system and is a key factor in how the system moves between phases of growth and conservation (Bradtmöller, Grimm, and Riel-Salvatore 2017). Applying the concept of connectedness in archaeology has been challenging due to its abstractness, as is evidenced by its association with a diverse range of archaeological proxies, including the intensity of subsistence, mobility, and social organization (Bradtmöller, Grimm, and Riel-Salvatore 2017). Freeman, Hard, and Mauldin (2017, 85) insist upon greater clarity regarding the concept in their qualification that "one must show how the resilience of hunter-gatherer socio-ecological systems is affected by different forms of increasing connectedness (e.g., asymmetrical vs. symmetrical networks) and how the resilience and vulnerability of forager-resource systems changes in response to changes in climate and demographic populations."

RT favors the adoption of a long-term perspective on connectedness as an attribute of socio-ecological systems. For clarity, we refer to this attribute as "system connectedness." Community connectedness and system connectedness may on the surface appear to be in opposition to each other. For example, the system rigidity that characterizes high system connectedness is proposed to make the system more prone to harm from external disturbances, such as unpredictable natural hazards. Conversely, high community connectedness is often considered to be an asset that presents communities with diverse routes toward potentially lifesaving resources and information during times of crisis. It is important to acknowledge that the main difference between these concepts is a difference in scale: community connectedness emphasizes the web of historically ephemeral social connections, organizations, and places that help to reduce disaster risk, while system connectedness shifts focus to the long-term adaptive outcomes of these community connections—that is, whether such connections precipitate rigidity in the system of social infrastructure. In other words, the community connectedness concept draws attention to the structure of social connections at any given moment in time, whereas system connectedness emphasizes the dynamic patterns of these connections over time.

Operationalizing Community and System Connectedness Using Demography

Ideally, the archaeological record would offer multiple access points through which to engage both concepts of connectedness, as well as how they may have influenced past human responses to catastrophic events. However, balancing between archaeological evaluations of long-term systematic change and relatively short-lived social connections is a nontrivial task due the inherent biases of the archaeological record. Here, we attempt to bridge this divide by using demographic trends estimated from the archaeological record as a source of data that can further illuminate the relationship between our two kinds of connectedness (figure 7.1).

Archaeological demography can be broadly defined as the "investigation of the structure and dynamics of past human populations" (Cham-

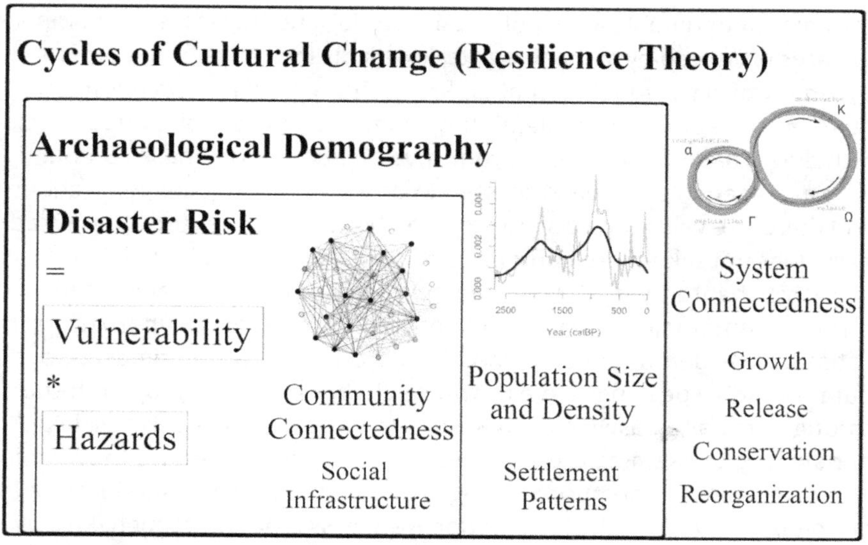

Figure 7.1. Conceptual model for linking community and system connectedness based on research in resilience theory and disaster risk reduction. Adaptive cycle image is adopted from Holling and Gunderson (2002) and created by Hernan De Angelis and used under the CC-BY-SA-4.0 license. All other images are created by the authors.

berlain 2009, 275). These changes in past populations are often viewed by estimating demographic parameters such as the size, structure, density, and spatial distribution of populations in combination with rates of fertility, mortality, and migration (Chamberlain 2009, 276). The utility of adopting a demographic perspective for bridging concepts of connectedness is that it affords empirically tractable expectations across multiple temporal scales, provided the necessary historical or archaeological evidence is available. Specifically, community vulnerability to catastrophic events and the disaster risk that such vulnerability entails may be assessed by monitoring the direction of demographic change over narrowly bounded temporal intervals. Conversely, we argue that long-run trends in population abundance monitor long-term cycles of resilience. For example, periods of sustained population growth punctuated by rapid periods of decline have been used to identify transitions between sequent phases of the adaptive cycle—for example, the transition between periods of collapse (Ω) and reorganization (α) (Peters and Zimmermann 2017).

The last decade has seen a substantial increase in efforts to estimate long-term changes in regional human population abundance based on the description of temporal distributions of radiocarbon-timestamped archaeological data sets. Broadly referred to as the "dates as data" approach (Rick 1987), this analytical framework rests on the premise that the amount of datable archaeological material, and therefore the number of dates produced by archaeologists, is broadly indicative of the temporal dynamics of past population abundance. The viability of such inference rests on the successful mitigation of numerous potential confounders, including creation, preservation, and investigation error. These confounders have been extensively discussed in other archaeological publications and therefore will not be discussed here, though the case study presented here does not take these confounders lightly (see Fitzhugh et al. 2016).

In this chapter, we introduce an approach to the simultaneous monitoring of community and system connectedness that builds upon our past estimates of demographic trends based on radiocarbon-timestamped data. Broadly speaking, we aim to use changes in demographic trends through time as a baseline from which we may simultaneously "scale up" our analysis to examine the dynamics of system connectedness and "drill down" to examine temporal changes in community connectedness. We do this by drawing on the Information Networks model (Fitzhugh, Phillips, and Gjesfjeld 2011) to formulate predictions about the structure of networks between communities living in hazard-prone landscapes. A central assumption of the Information Networks model is that individuals and communities routinely monitor environmental change and adjust their strategies to optimize their chances of survival, well-being, and reproductive success. Therefore, in landscapes that are prone to catastrophic hazards, one of most important adaptive strategies for small-scale societies is modifying their degree of community connectedness.

The Information Networks model views the structure of networks on a continuum that ranges from integrated to isolated (see table 7.1 and figure 7.2). Integrated networks have high community connectedness, with ties occurring at multiple spatial scales and between individuals, households, neighboring communities, and even distant communities. In contrast, isolated networks are characterized by low community connectedness, comprising social relationships that mostly occur at local scales and between closely related individuals who interact frequently. The integrated network structure proposed by the Information Networks model

Table 7.1. Expectations of system and community connectedness for integrated and isolated networks as defined in Fitzhugh, Phillips, and Gjesfjeld (2011).

Network Type	System Connectedness	Community Connectedness
Integrated	**Low:** flexible system that balances internal and external variability	**High:** spatially diverse connections between many communities
Isolated	**High:** rigid system where fate controlled by internal dynamics	**Low:** limited connections between only a few communities

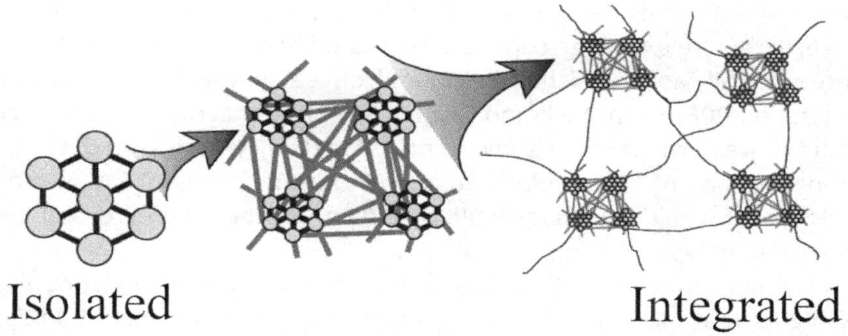

Figure 7.2. Example of network structures as predicted by the Information Networks model. Image modified from original publication in Fitzhugh, Phillips, and Gjesfjeld (2011) and used with permission from the Cotsen Institute of Archaeology Press.

has parallels to scale-free networks that are identified in many real-life settings (Barabási 2009). For the present chapter, this parallel is important because research has shown scale-free networks to be more robust against unpredictable perturbations (Albert, Jeong, and Barabási 2000; Allenby and Fink 2005; Ash and Newth 2007). This is due to the flexible connections of scale-free networks and their unique topological features, including a higher degree of clustering and modularity (Albert, Jeong, and Barabási 2000). In effect, scale-free networks provide high levels of connectivity between nodes by balancing nodes that are closely connected and central nodes that connect sub-networks or nodes that would otherwise be isolated. In stark contrast, isolated networks exhibit a low diversity of ties and can therefore more easily become rigid over time (i.e., high system connectedness).

The Community and System Connectedness of Small and Remote Islands

Anthropological research on small and remote islands has often highlighted the importance of connectedness. Previous discussions about connectedness in this context have focused on the potential for communities living on small and remote islands to overcome various degrees of spatial isolation and environmental constraints in order to maintain connectivity with communities on the mainland or other islands (Erlandson and Fitzpatrick 2006; Fitzpatrick and Anderson 2008; Fitzpatrick 2004). However, the remoteness of small islands is now more commonly viewed as a product of many interacting and mediating factors, including geography, demography, climate, technology, and ideology. For example, research on the small islands of the Pacific demonstrate that despite expansive geographic distance, extensive exchange connections existed between populations that were culturally and linguistically distinct from each other (Fitzpatrick and Anderson 2008; Fitzpatrick and Diveley 2004). Archaeological evidence from the western Aleutians shows a similar pattern, where even the most remote islands of the archipelago had strong traditions of inter-island contact that would have been vital for survival (Corbett, Lefevre, and Siegel-Causey 1997).

It is important to note that archaeological and historical evidence also highlights that increasing the social connections between communities living on small islands is not always beneficial. In the thirteenth century, the Faroe Islands of the North Atlantic became increasingly intertwined in Scandinavian trade networks, which subsequently led to the arrival of the Black Plague, killing as much as 70 percent of the population (Wylie 1987). The history of islands in the Caribbean also highlights how novel connections can rapidly decimate the ecology and demography of small-island environments as many of these islands suffered catastrophic losses (Curet and Hauser 2011). Even the famous collapse of Rapa Nui is now believed to be an outcome of epidemics brought by the first wave of Dutch explorers in 1722, ultimately devastating the population of the remote island in less than two generations (Hunt and Lipo 2009).

The Kuril Islands

The Kuril Islands serve as our case study for examining both kinds of connectedness on small and remote islands. The Kuril Archipelago comprises a string of volcanic islands stretching from the island of Hokkaido to the Kamchatka Peninsula in the western North Pacific (figure 7.3). The Kurils are similar to many other islands of the North Pacific in that they display a combination of frequent hazards and relatively insular geography. However, unlike many other islands of the Pacific, the Kuril Archipelago demonstrates a long history of cultural occupation that spans eight millennia (Fitzhugh et al. 2016).

The various natural hazards characterizing the Kuril Islands can be divided into three broad categories: volcanic eruptions, earthquakes and tsunamis, and weather or climatic events (see Fitzhugh 2012 for a more detailed discussion). The evidence of frequent volcanic eruptions is obvious across the Kuril landscapes, including intact tephra layers visible in geologic stratigraphies and massive calderas that dramatically shape the topography of many islands. Over the last two thousand years, at least fifty-eight major eruptions occurred, with 84 percent of these eruptions taking place north of the Bussol Strait (Nakagawa et al. 2009), which sep-

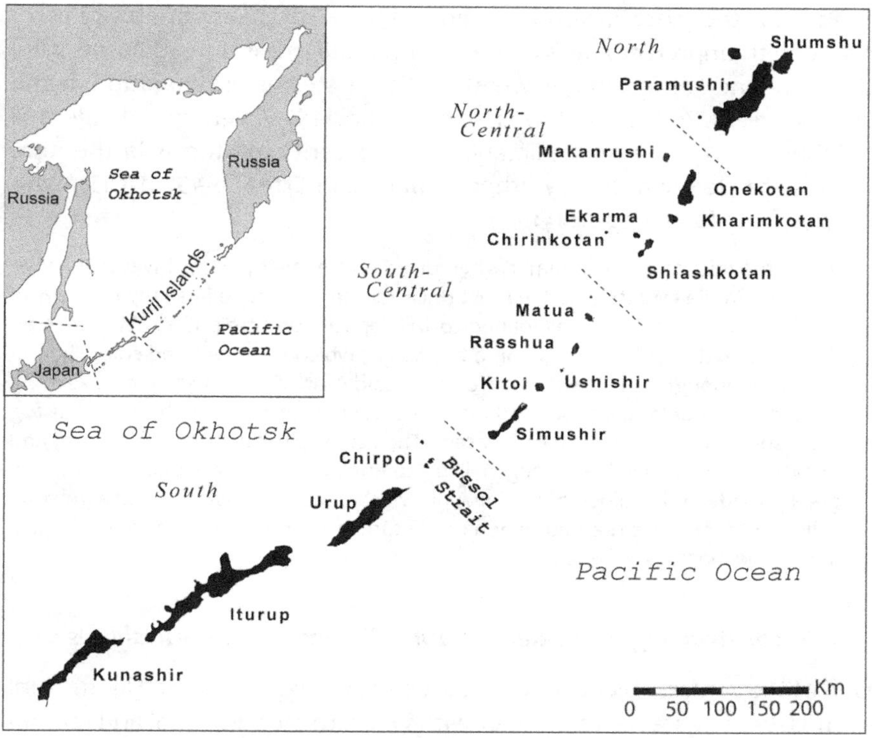

Figure 7.3. Map of the Kuril Islands with island names, selected site names, major straits, and geographic regions. Image is reprinted from Fitzhugh et al. (2016) with permission from Elsevier.

arates the larger southern islands from the small and remote islands of the central and northern regions. Six of these fifty-eight eruptions were considered large (Plinian or caldera-forming) and likely would have resulted in pyroclastic flows and locally significant ash deposits (Fitzhugh 2012). At the archaeological site of Rasshua 1, a fifteen-centimeter-thick layer of pumice ash was uncovered, which is likely associated with the caldera-forming eruption on the island of Ushishir, approximately twenty-five kilometers away.

Earthquakes were also a common feature of the Kuril paleoenvironment, but for the hunter-fisher-gatherer inhabitants of the Kuril Islands the direct impact of earthquakes was likely minimal. However, indirect earthquake effects such as landslides or tsunamis probably had a more significant impact on Kuril inhabitants and their ecosystem (Fitzhugh 2012). Geological research in the archipelago estimates that the interval of time separating large tsunamis (ten to thirty meters in elevation) is between about 150 and 500 years (MacInnes et al. 2016).

Perhaps the most hazardous events in the Kuril Islands are those associated with unpredictable weather and climatic transitions that intensify the frequency of inclement weather. Large storms are common in the archipelago, with winter storms being particularly violent and dangerous (Fitzhugh 2012). The unpredictability and severity of storms in the Kuril Islands are clearly noted by ethnographer Carl Etter (1949, 112–13), who recounts the following story:

> It was the middle of the summer when one might expect pleasant weather. However, the Kurile climate was the most uncertain thing I found in all my journeys in the Orient. . . . Our boat was loaded to full capacity and freight. . . . We went on deck and made our bed under some tarpaulins, which were wet and cold. The fog was thick enough to cut with a knife and a cold east wind blew all night, keeping us cold and unable to sleep. The Japanese crew that brought us through that fog must surely know these Kurilian waters. The sea was rolling mountains high, and our little craft seemed like an eggshell in a tempest. . . . There are tales in which the gods provided miraculous boats for Ainu who were in distress. I would almost be willing to admit that the boat in which I returned from Etorofu was one of those miraculous boats.

Reconstructing Paleo-demographic Trends in the Kuril Islands

One of the central objectives of recent archaeological research in the Kuril Islands was to establish a data set with which to model spatial and temporal variability of settlement (Fitzhugh et al. 2016). This goal was achieved by generating a cultural radiocarbon database consisting of 380 dates recovered from archaeological sites across the archipelago (Fitzhugh et al. 2016). As highlighted above, approaches to estimating paleo-population dynamics based on such data are predicated on the premise that larger populations will tend to deposit a greater amount of organic archaeological material than smaller populations (Rick 1987). It also assumes that various potential confounders, having both random and systematic components, have been acknowledged and, when necessary, mitigated. Strategies for mitigating such uncertainty in the Kuril Islands paleo-population model are discussed in detail in Fitzhugh et al. (2016).

Our Kuril paleo-population model suggests five major trends in the region's population history (Fitzhugh et al. 2016). The most significant are two pulses of marked population growth and decline, the first taking place between 2500 and 1300 cal BP, the second between 1300 and 650 cal BP (figure 7.4). The presence of diagnostic archaeological features, particularly pottery remains (Gjesfjeld 2014), strongly suggest that the first of these pulses is related to the Epi-Jomon (or Zoku-Jomon) culture, which is prevalent throughout Hokkaido around this same time period. This cultural designation is largely based on the ubiquity of cord-marked pottery

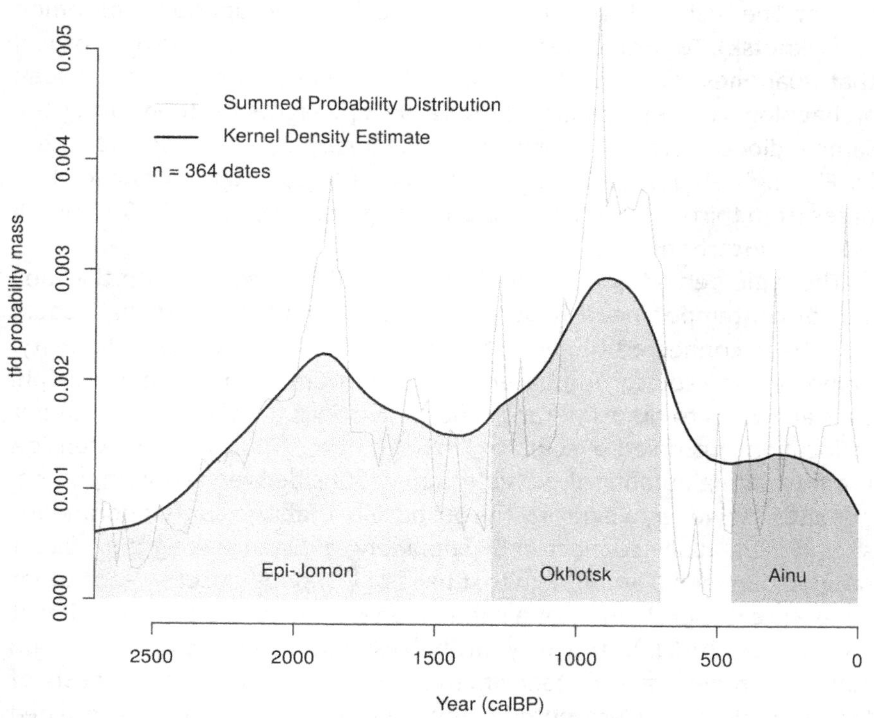

Figure 7.4. Temporal frequency distribution of radiocarbon dates from the Kuril Islands. The paleo-demographic model suggests two periods of population growth and decline associated with the Epi-Jomon and Okhotsk cultural traditions. Figure created by the authors.

at archaeological sites throughout the archipelago. The second period is associated with the broader Okhotsk migration and expansion throughout Northeast Asia between the sixth and twelfth centuries CE (Hudson 2004). The emergence and decline of the Okhotsk occupation in the Kurils is dramatic, marked by rapid growth between 1400 and 900 cal BP and even more rapid decline between 900 and 650 cal BP (figure 7.4).

Community Connectedness in the Kuril Islands

Previous efforts to estimate the community connectedness of Kuril communities have made use of a variety of data sources, particularly compositional data from pottery (Gjesfjeld 2014) and lithics (Phillips 2011). While this research provided insights into broad changes in network structure, the resolution of the lithic and ceramic record only permits the construction of one archaeological network per cultural occupation (Epi-Jomon and Okhotsk). To overcome this limitation, we introduce a novel protocol that quantifies the credibility of possible network connections between archaeological sites by placing probabilistic weights on them using the same radiocarbon data underlying the paleo-population model presented by Fitzhugh et al. (2016). These data comprise 330 cultural radiocarbon dates from thirty-two archaeological sites (see Fitzhugh et al. 2016 for full list of radiocarbon dates).

The logic behind our approach begins with the assumption that any pair of contemporaneously occupied sites within the island chain could have been connected to each other by virtue of their contemporaneity. Summarizing radiocarbon-based occupation timestamps from multiple sites allows us to draw inferences not only about the fluctuating number of locations occupied over time (Fitzhugh et al. 2016), but by extension the fluctuating number of possible connections between contemporaneous sites. However, we qualify the probability that two contemporaneous sites were actually connected by stipulating a distance-weighting factor ranging between 0 and 1, such that pairs of locations closer to each other have a greater probability of a connection (closer to 1) than more distant pairs (closer to 0). In this way, probabilistic assessments of occupation contemporaneity and distance-mediated connection form the basis of the network models presented below, informing temporally fine-grained measures of community connectedness at a regional scale.

The distance-based network models that our approach generates are advantageous because they can be constructed at fine-grained temporal intervals while remaining agnostic about underlying social infrastructure. Such network models are thus simplistic representations of social organization and do not capture the reality of how social infrastructure or other community-level characteristics actually mediated the human outcomes of catastrophic events. This limitation of our approach is not accidental; the models it generates are offered as containers for uncertainty about the true configuration of past community connections in the archipelago, due to the coarse-grained perspective on regional networks afforded by other lines of archaeological evidence.

Building Networks from Radiocarbon Data

The construction of network models from radiocarbon-timestamped archaeological data occurs in four steps. The first is the calculation of the probability of site occupation at uniformly spaced and fine-grained points along the timeline based on radiocarbon dates. Figure 7.5 describes time series of site occupation probabilities for two sites (left panel: Ainu Creek

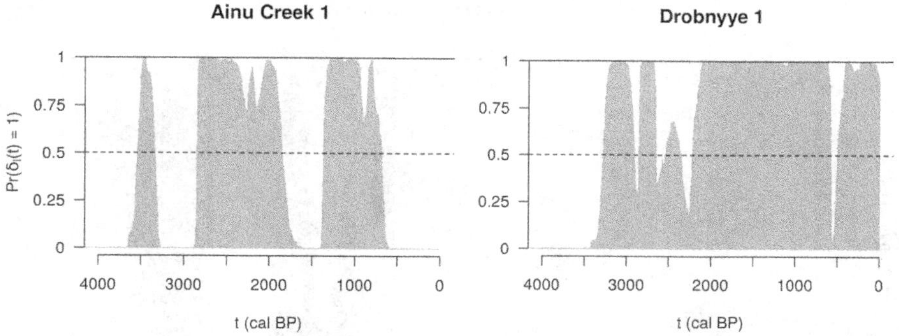

Figure 7.5. Time series of the probability $Pr(\delta_i(t) = 1)$ that Ainu Creek 1 and Drobnyye 1 were occupied at each five-year point between 4000 and 0 cal BP. Ainu Creek 1 exhibits a punctuated history, with three separate periods of occupation, whereas Drobnyye 1 tends toward a more continuous occupation history, especially between 2000 and 550 cal BP. Figure created by the authors.

1; right panel: Drobnyye 1), derived from the posterior probability distributions of all radiocarbon timestamp estimates available for each site (grain: five-year intervals). To control for chronometric uncertainty characterizing radiocarbon-based timestamp estimation, a symmetrical two-hundred-year buffer was placed around each timestamp drawn at random from each radiocarbon date's posterior distribution; points along the timeline falling within any of these buffers were assigned a value of 1, or 0 otherwise; and occupation probabilities were estimated as the average of all such 0–1 time series after a repeated and large number of draws (see Brown 2017 for a more formally explicit description of a similar simulation approach, composite kernel density estimation). We acknowledge that such estimates of site occupation history likely offer an incomplete picture, as not all cultural deposits from any given site could be dated, though the two-hundred-year buffers should mitigate this problem to a degree. In this analysis, 224 dates come from eight intensively sampled sites, while the remaining 106 dates come from the remaining twenty-four sites.

The second step of our approach is to calculate the probability of contemporaneous occupation for each pair of archaeological sites, accomplished by multiplying that pair of sites' time series of site occupation probabilities (see figure 7.6). This step implies that any two sites cannot have been contemporaneously occupied for any given point in time (i.e., show a contemporaneous occupation probability of 0) if the probability that either site was occupied at that time was also 0. Once again, we acknowledge that our inability to fully date all cultural deposits present at the thirty-two sites included in our analysis implies that probabilities of contemporaneous site occupation are underestimated for some intervals

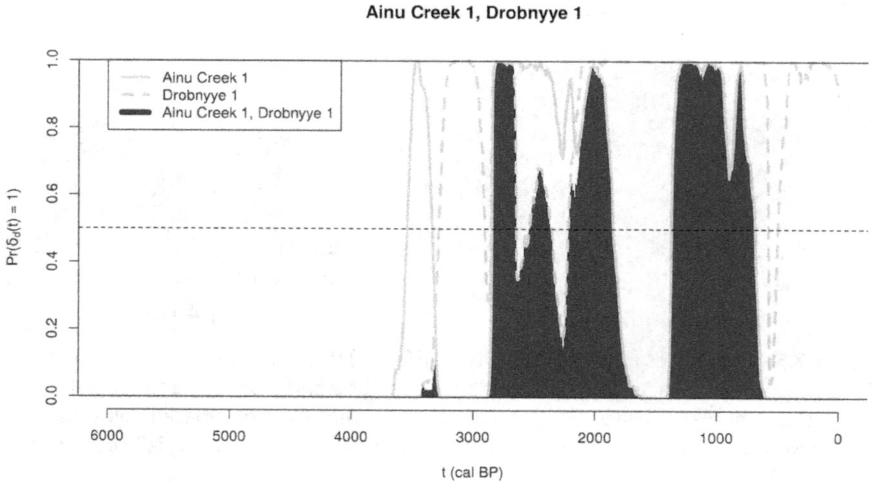

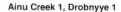

Figure 7.6. Time series of the probability $Pr(\delta_d(t) = 1)$ that the sites of Ainu Creek 1 and Drobnyye 1 were occupied contemporaneously (dark-shaded area) based on fifty-eight radiocarbon dates from the two sites. Solid and dashed lines represent the time series of probabilities of individual site occupations, as presented in figure 7.5. Figure created by the authors.

for some pairs of sites, though once again the buffers placed around each timestamp estimate should reduce this problem to a degree.

Third, a second network structure is constructed that weights the edge connecting each pair of sites in the database by the geographic distance separating that pair. As a first pass at distance weighting, we have adapted the two-parameter Weibull survival function and applied this to the great circle distance between each pair of sites. Repurposed as a distance decay model, this function has the desirable property of decreasing monotonically and asymptotically from 1 to 0, suitable for distance decay modeling. In the present analysis, we parameterized this model such that each archaeological site has a greater than 50 percent probability of connection with each other site provided that the two lie within a distance less than 120 kilometers from each other, decreasing from 50 percent for distances greater than this.

We acknowledge that the weighting of network edges by distance is simplistic and reductive, treating the degree of community connectedness at any given point in time as if determined solely by the spatial positioning of sites. Even so, the decision to introduce distance into our network models stems from the reality that geography exerts a strong influence on movement and transportation in the Kuril Islands. Three large open-water straits divide the island chain into subregions, often making movement within each region easier than between regions. In the future, productive refinements on how distance is incorporated in our network models would allow measures of distance or "remoteness" between each pair of sites to vary over time as a function of dynamic variables that influence the costliness of movement, including variables exogenous to human systems such as changes in storminess and sea ice regimes, as well as endogenous variables such as innovations in seafaring and way-finding technologies. Such refinements are expected to improve our ability to draw meaningful interpretations of network dynamics, at least to the degree that temporal variability in "remoteness" bears on the viability of long-distance social connections.

The fourth and final step of our approach is to multiply the static distance-weighted network (DW network) by the network of contemporaneous site occupation probabilities (CSO network). Their product is a distance-weighted contemporaneous site occupation network (DW-CSO network) (see figure 7.7 for examples).

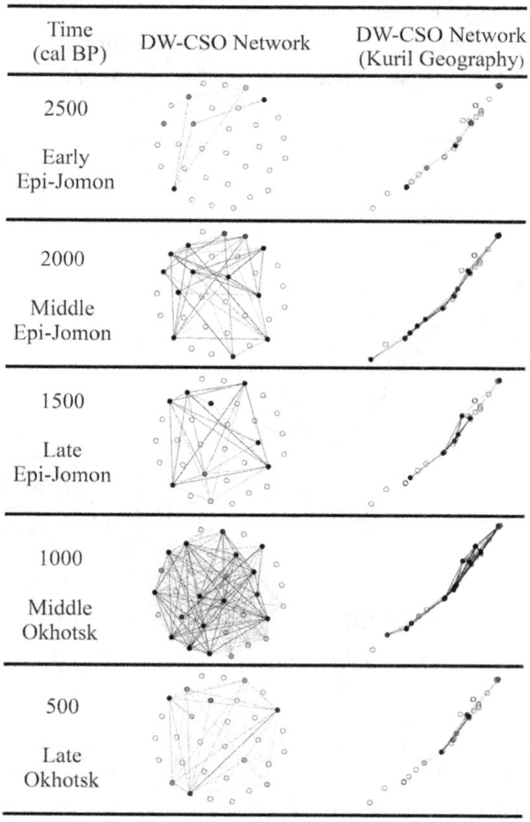

Figure 7.7. Graphical representation of distance-weighted contemporaneous site occupation models (DW-CSO) at various times throughout the main occupation periods in the Kuril Islands. Figure created by the authors.

Results of Network Modeling

An important advantage of constructing DW-CSO networks is the opportunity it affords to explore changes in network structure over time. To illustrate this utility, we extracted a time series of one hundred networks at twenty-five-year intervals between 2500 cal BP and 0 cal BP. The structure of each network in the time series was summarized by calculating a time series of mean tie distance between all dyadic connections. This graph-level measurement was favored over node-level indices (e.g., centrality) because the latter are sensitive to the manner in which our network graphs are constructive and therefore uninformative. Based on the Information Networks model, our assumption is that isolated networks will be characterized by a greater proportion of local ties, corresponding with a lower mean tie across the network. In contrast, integrated networks will tend toward a larger proportion of distant regional ties and therefore have a higher mean tie distance.

Figure 7.8 presents the mean tie distance time series. The most obvious trend is an overall decrease in mean tie distance from 2500 to 500 cal BP,

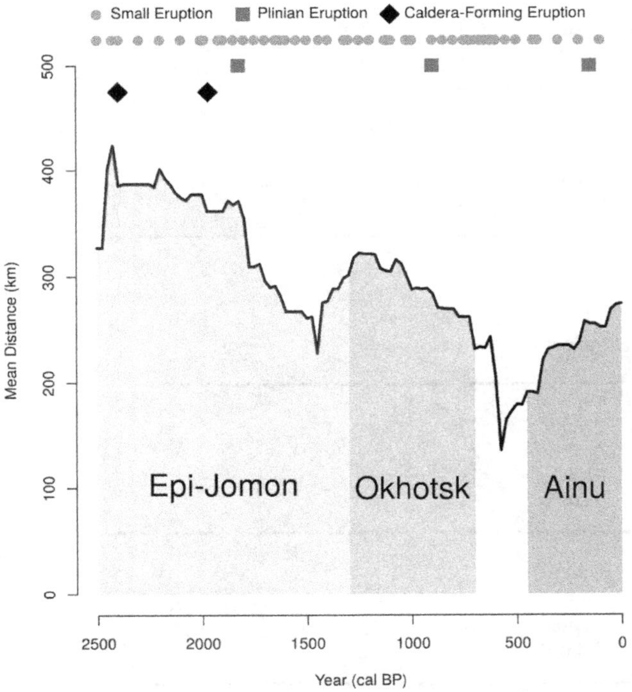

Figure 7.8. Mean tie distance for the Kuril DW-CSO network time series based on radiocarbon data. Also included are known volcanic eruptions in the Kuril Islands since 2500 cal BP (from Nakagawa et al. 2009). Figure created by the authors.

suggesting a shift from a relatively evenly spaced settlement pattern during the Epi-Jomon period to a clustered and insular settlement pattern during the Okhotsk period. After an episode of marked population decline of the archipelago between 700 and 500 cal BP, resettlement by Ainu hunter-gatherers appears to have corresponded with a more far-reaching network.

Community and System Connectedness in the Kuril Islands

As discussed above, community connectedness refers here to the degree and character of social connections, particularly regarding their capacity to facilitate the distribution of information and resources within and between communities during times of crisis. Unfortunately, the local connections within communities are often difficult to see directly in the archaeological record, and our analysis is no exception in this respect, but the network models we present at least provide general insights into the temporal dynamics of connectedness between communities in the Kuril Islands. The long-term trend toward diminishing mean tie distance of Kuril networks can be taken to suggest increasing spatial isolation, reaching a nadir around 600 cal BP. This inferred trend toward low community connectedness likely affected the ability for communities to anticipate and cope with the impacts of unpredictable and localized hazard events. One category of recurring hazard that may have been particularly harmful to these increasingly isolated Kuril communities was volcanic eruptions, which may have forced communities to vacate their settlements and move to neighboring islands or to the next nearest community. In particularly severe situations, such relocation may have been extensive enough to register in the mean tie distance of the DW-CSO networks.

A potential hypothesis for the dramatic decline in mean tie distance between 1050 and 550 cal BP is that a volcanic eruption, or a series of volcanic eruptions, eliminated habitable locations and drove populations into closer spatial proximity to each other, resulting in a lower mean tie distance and even greater spatial isolation. However, the timing of volcanic eruptions in the Kuril Archipelago does not indicate any single eruption that appears to have impacted either population abundance (Fitzhugh et al. 2016) or the network attribute of mean tie distance (figure 7.8). Neither Plinian nor caldera-forming eruptions that occurred within the Kuril Islands appear to coincide with the changes observed in network structure. An increase in the frequency of small eruptions is broadly coincident with a period of increasing isolation (750–550 cal BP), though any positive association between these trends would require additional research.

The temporal trend of community connectedness inferred from the DW-CSO network time series can also be interrogated to shed light on the long-run dynamics of system connectedness. The trend toward declining mean tie distance (i.e., greater spatial clustering) can be framed as a long-term process of marginalization, signaling that the system was becoming increasingly rigid (high system connectedness) by 600 cal BP, resulting in a diminished capacity of communities to cope with unexpected hazards. The process of Okhotsk marginalization and isolation has been previously discussed by Fitzhugh et al. (2016) and Hudson (2004), who both highlight evidence for Okhotsk populations inhabiting the Kuril Islands attempting, and perhaps failing, to incorporate into an emerging East Asia world system (Hudson 2004). A plausible scenario is that Okhotsk inhabitants of the Kuril Islands became more engaged in commodity and market-driven trading relationships with mainland Japan, exploiting connections with southern Okhotsk communities in Hokkaido. However, after the absorption of Hokkaido Okhotsk communities by Satsumon populations that moved into Eastern Hokkaido, the peripheral Kuril Okhotsk populations probably became increasingly marginalized from the trading economy over time. This process of marginalization may be indicated in the clustering of Okhotsk settlements and the declining proportion of distant network ties between 1000 and 550 cal BP.

Conclusion

Nearly all disasters, whether unpredictable volcanic eruptions or long-term droughts, impact communities at multiple spatial and temporal scales. Social networks provide one of the most flexible and adaptable mechanisms to disseminate information between individuals and communities and are therefore important means of reducing disaster risk. However, social networks, like any other system, are not static through time, and the degree of system flexibility can influence how capable communities are to respond to hazards when they arise. In this chapter, we have focused our attention on distinct but complementary concepts of connectedness in order to explore how social networks can be operationalized in fields such as disaster risk reduction (community connectedness) and resilience theory (system connectedness).

Our novel contribution is a methodological approach that uses spatio-temporal settlement data to estimate a time series of network models that help to illuminate changes in connectedness through time. Our case study illustrates this approach using radiocarbon-timestamped archaeological data from the Kuril Islands of Northeast Asia. The most significant outcome of this study was the demonstration of a temporal trend toward more insular networks with fewer long-distance ties. We conclude with the suggestion that this increasing isolation of communities in the Kurils increased their vulnerability and susceptibility to unpredictable hazards, although volcanic eruptions do not appear to have counted among these. This increasingly insular network structure, in combination with a changing climate and social order in mainland eastern Asia and Japan, marginalized the Okhotsk communities inhabiting the Kurils, precipitating a dramatic reduction in the archipelago's population. This example demonstrates that the long-term perspective on changes in social network structure afforded by archaeology may contribute a unique and valuable component to an interdisciplinary blueprint for the design of modern support networks and help reduce the disaster risk faced by many contemporary communities.

Erik Gjesfjeld is currently a Renfrew Fellow at the McDonald Institute for Archaeological Research at the University of Cambridge and a research fellow at Fitzwilliam College. He was educated at the University of Wisconsin–La Crosse (BA), University College London (MA, MA), and the University of Washington (MA, PhD). His main research interests include the application of archaeological and macroevolutionary approaches to explore how past communities managed the challenges of social and environmental change. He specializes in quantitative research methods, cultural evolution, hunter-gatherers, and the archaeology of Northeast Asia.

William A. Brown is a temporary lecturer in the Department of Statistics at the University of Washington. He received a BA in history and philosophy from Northwest Nazarene University, an MA in Near Eastern and Judaic studies from Brandeis University, and an MA and PhD in archaeology from the University of Washington. His research focuses on developing and refining probabilistic models and methods in quantitative and statistical archaeology, with a special emphasis on improving the reliability of statistical inference in the context of archaeological demography.

References

Adger, W. Neil. 2006. "Vulnerability." *Global Environmental Change* 16 (3): 268–81.

Agarwal, Bina. 1990. "Social Security and the Family: Coping with Seasonality and Calamity in Rural India." *Journal of Peasant Studies* 17 (3): 341–412.

Agrawal, Arun. 1995. "Dismantling the Divide between Indigenous and Scientific Knowledge." *Development and Change* 26 (3): 413–39.

Albert, Réka, Hawoong Jeong, and Albert-László Barabási. 2000. "Error and Attack Tolerance of Complex Networks." *Nature* 406 (6794): 378–82.

Allenby, Brad, and Jonathan Fink. 2005. "Toward Inherently Secure and Resilient Societies." *Science* 309 (5737): 1034–36.

Ash, J., and D. Newth. 2007. "Optimizing Complex Networks for Resilience against Cascading Failure." *Physica A: Statistical Mechanics and Its Applications* 380 (July): 673–83.

Barabási, Albert-László. 2009. "Scale-Free Networks: A Decade and Beyond." *Science* 325 (5939): 412–13.

Barrios, Roberto E. 2016. "Resilience: A Commentary from the Vantage Point of Anthropology." *Annals of Anthropological Practice* 40 (1): 28–38.

Bradtmöller, Marcel, Sonja Grimm, and Julien Riel-Salvatore. 2017. "Resilience Theory in Archaeological Practice: An Annotated Review." *Quaternary International* 446 (August): 3–16.

Brown, William A. 2017. "The Past and Future of Growth Rate Estimation in demographic Temporal frequency analysis: Biodemographic Interpretability and the Ascendance of Dynamic Growth Models. *Journal of Archaeological Science* 80: 96–108.

Campbell, John R. 2006. *Traditional Disaster Reduction in Pacific Island Communities.* GNS Science Report 38. Lower Hutt, NZ: GNS Science.

Chamberlain, Andrew. 2009. "Archaeological Demography." *Human Biology* 81 (3): 275–86.

Cooper, Jago. 2012. "Building Resilience in Island Communities: A Paleotempestological Perspective." In *Climates, Landscapes, and Civilizations*, edited by Liviu Giosan, Dorian Q. Fuller, Kathleen Nicoll, Rowan K. Flad, and Peter D. Clift, 43–50. Washington, DC: American Geophysical Union.

Cooper, Jago, and Payson Sheets, eds. 2012. *Surviving Sudden Environmental Change.* Boulder: University Press of Colorado.

Corbett, Debra G., Christine Lefevre, and Douglas Siegel-Causey. 1997. "The Western Aleutians: Cultural Isolation and Environmental Change." *Human Ecology* 25 (3): 459–79.

Curet, L. Antonio, and Mark W. Hauser. 2011. *Islands at the Crossroads: Migration, Seafaring, and Interaction in the Caribbean.* Tuscaloosa: University of Alabama Press.

Erlandson, Jon M., and Scott M. Fitzpatrick. 2006. "Oceans, Islands, and Coasts: Current Perspectives on the Role of the Sea in Human Prehistory." *Journal of Island & Coastal Archaeology* 1 (1): 5–32.

Etter, Carl. 1949. *Ainu Folklore: Traditions and Culture of the Vanishing Aborigines of Japan.* Chicago: Wilcox & Follett.

Fitzhugh, Ben. 2012. "Hazards, Impacts and Resilience among Hunter-Gatherers of the Kuril Islands." In *Surviving Sudden Environmental Change: Answers from Archaeology*, edited by Jago Cooper and Payson Sheets, 19–42. Boulder: University Press of Colorado.

Fitzhugh, Ben, Virginia L. Butler, Kristine M. Bovy, and Michael A. Etnier. 2019. "Human Ecodynamics: A Perspective for the Study of Long-Term Change in Socioecological Systems." *Journal of Archaeological Science: Reports* 23 (February): 1077–94.

Fitzhugh, Ben, Erik W. Gjesfjeld, William A. Brown, Mark J. Hudson, and Jennie D. Shaw. 2016. "Resilience and the Population History of the Kuril Islands, Northwest Pacific: A Study in Complex Human Ecodynamics." *Quaternary International* 419 (October): 165–93.

Fitzhugh, Ben, S. Colby Phillips, and Erik Gjesfjeld. 2011. "Modeling Variability in Hunter-Gatherer Information Networks: An Archaeological Case Study from the Kuril

Islands." In *Information and Its Role in Hunter-Gatherer Bands*, edited by Robert Whallon, William Lovis, and Robert K. Hitchcock, 85–115. Ideas, Debates and Perspectives 5. Los Angeles: Cotsen Institute of Archaeology Press.

Fitzpatrick, Scott M., ed. 2004. *Voyages of Discovery: The Archaeology of Islands*. Westport and London: Praeger.

Fitzpatrick, Scott M., and Atholl Anderson. 2008. "Islands of Isolation: Archaeology and the Power of Aquatic Perimeters." *Journal of Island and Coastal Archaeology* 3 (1): 4–16.

Fitzpatrick, Scott M., and Brian Diveley. 2004. "Interisland Exchange in Micronesia: A Case of Monumental Proportions." In *Voyages of Discovery: The Archaeology of Islands*, edited by Scott M. Fitzpatrick, 129–46. Westport and London: Praeger.

Folke, Carl, Steve Carpenter, Brian Walker, Marten Scheffer, Thomas Elmqvist, Lance Gunderson, and C. S. Holling. 2004. "Regime Shifts, Resilience, and Biodiversity in Ecosystem Management." *Annual Review of Ecology, Evolution, and Systematics* 35 (December): 557–81.

Freeman, Jacob, Robert J. Hard, and Raymond P. Mauldin. 2017. "A Theory of Regime Change on the Texas Coastal Plain." *Quaternary International* 446 (August): 83–94.

Gjesfjeld, Erik W. 2014. "Of Pots and People: Investigating Hunter-Gatherer Pottery Production and Social Networks in the Kuril Islands." PhD dissertation. Seattle: University of Washington.

Gunderson, Lance H., and C. S. Holling, eds. 2002. *Panarchy: Understanding Transformations in Human and Natural Systems*. Washington, DC: Island Press.

Holling, C. S., and Lance H. Gunderson. 2002. "Resilience and Adaptive Cycles." In *Panarchy: Understanding Transformations in Human and Natural Systems*, edited by Lance Gunderson and C. S. Holling, 25–62. Washington DC: Island Press.

Hudson, Mark J. 2004. "The Perverse Realities of Change: World System Incorporation and the Okhotsk Culture of Hokkaido." *Journal of Anthropological Archaeology* 23 (3): 290–308.

Hunt, Terry L., and Carl P. Lipo. 2009. "Revisiting Rapa Nui (Easter Island) 'Ecocide.'" *Pacific Science* 63 (4): 601–16.

Klinenberg, Eric. 2018. *Palaces for the People: How Social Infrastructure Can Help Fight Inequality, Polarization, and the Decline of Civic Life*. New York: Random House.

MacInnes, Breanyn, Ekaterina Kravchunovskaya, Tatiana Pinegina, and Joanne Bourgeois. 2016. "Paleotsunamis from the Central Kuril Islands Segment of the Japan-Kuril-Kamchatka Subduction Zone." *Quaternary Research* 86 (1): 54–66.

Mercer, Jessica, Ilan Kelman, Lorin Taranis, and Sandie Suchet-Pearson. 2010. "Framework for Integrating Indigenous and Scientific Knowledge for Disaster Risk Reduction." *Disasters* 34 (1): 214–39.

Nakagawa, Mitshuhiro, Yoshihiro Ishizuka, Takeshi Hasegawa, Akira Baba, and Ayumi Kosugi. 2009. "Preliminary Report on Volcanological Research of KBP 2007–2008 Cruise by Japanase Volcanology Group." Unpublished report on file with the Ben Fitzhugh (Project PI), University of Washington, Seattle.

Pelling, Mark, and Juha I. Uitto. 2001. "Small Island Developing States: Natural Disaster Vulnerability and Global Change." *Global Environmental Change Part B: Environmental Hazards* 3 (2): 49–62.

Peters, Robin, and Andreas Zimmermann. 2017. "Resilience and Cyclicity: Towards a Macrohistory of the Central European Neolithic." *Quaternary International* 446 (August): 43–53.

Phillips, S. Colby. 2011. "Networked Glass: Lithic Raw Material Consumption and Social Networks in the Kuril Islands." PhD dissertation. Seattle: University of Washington.

Redman, Charles L. 2005. "Resilience Theory in Archaeology." *American Anthropologist* 107 (1): 70–77.

Redman, Charles, and Ann Kinzig. 2003. "Resilience of Past Landscapes: Resilience Theory, Society, and the Longue Durée." *Conservation Ecology* 7 (1): 14.

Rick, John W. 1987. "Dates as Data: An Examination of the Peruvian Preceramic Radiocarbon Record." *American Antiquity* 52 (1): 55–73.

Shultz, James M., Madeline A. Cohen, Sabrina Hermosilla, Zelde Espinel, and Andrew McLean. 2016. "Disaster Risk Reduction and Sustainable Development for Small Island Developing States." *Disaster Health* 3 (1): 32–44.

Singhvi, Anjali, Bedel Saget, and Jasmine Lee. 2018. "What Went Wrong with Indonesia's Tsunami Early Warning System." *New York Times*, 2 October. Retrieved 19 April 2019 from https://www.nytimes.com/interactive/2018/10/02/world/asia/indonesia-tsunami-early-warning-system.html.

Torrence, Robin. 2016. "Social Resilience and Long-Term Adaptation to Volcanic Disasters: The Archaeology of Continuity and Innovation in the Willaumez Peninsula, Papua New Guinea." *Quaternary International* 394 (February): 6–16.

UNESCO. 2016. "Small Island Developing States: UNESCO's Action Plan." Sustainable Development Goals. Paris: UNESCO. Retrieved 16 April 2019 from https://unesdoc.unesco.org/ark:/48223/pf0000246082.

———. 2019. "Disaster Risk Reduction | United Nations Educational, Scientific and Cultural Organization." UNESCO. Retrieved 16 April 2019 from http://www.unesco.org/new/en/natural-sciences/special-themes/disaster-risk-reduction/.

Walker, Brian, Crawford S. Holling, Stephen Carpenter, and Ann Kinzig. 2004. "Resilience, Adaptability and Transformability in Social-Ecological Systems." *Ecology and Society* 9 (2): 5.

Whallon, Robert. 2006. "Social Networks and Information: Non-'Utilitarian' Mobility among Hunter-Gatherers." *Journal of Anthropological Archaeology* 25 (2): 259–70.

Wisner, Ben, Piers Blaikie, Terry Cannon, and Ian Davis. 2004. *At Risk: Natural Hazards, People's Vulnerability and Disasters*. 2nd ed. New York: Routledge.

Wylie, Jonathan. 1987. *The Faroe Islands: Interpretations of History*. Lexington: University Press of Kentucky.

Yates, Loti, and Linda Anderson-Berry. 2004 "The Environmental and Societal Impacts of Cyclone Zoë and the Effectiveness of the Tropical Cyclone Warning Systems in Tikopia and Anuta Solomon Islands: December 26–29, 2002." *Australian Journal of Emergency Management* 19 (1): 16.

Zhao, Yandong. 2013. "Social Networks and Reduction of Risk in Disasters: An Example of the Wenchuan Earthquake." In *Economic Stress, Human Capital, and Families in Asia: Research and Policy Challenges*, edited by Wei-Jun Jean Yeung and Mui Teng Yap, 171–82. Dordrecht: Springer Netherlands.

Section II
WATER

Freshwater is the stuff of life, and the sea the great connector of societies past and present. Humans cannot do without water, and from the earliest stages of the human career until this very day, settlements patterns and flows of people and information—networks—are contingent on waterways and water sources as routes and nodes. This dependency on water for basic biological and societal functioning also means, however, that when there is either too much or too little, disaster ensues, and lives and livelihoods are disrupted.

While the first part of this volume dealt with the hazards associated primarily with fire—especially the fire of volcanoes—the following section addresses watery hazards, at times in fateful combination with air, namely in the form of storms. Already the last chapters in the previous section demonstrated that the two often go hand in hand. Yet, water hazards—storms, floods, droughts—reveal, like no others, the foundational structures of communities and societies. Water is the ultimate and most non-negotiable requirement of life; it interacts with the physical structures and political structures of all societies. The chapters in the coming section make this abundantly clear. Indeed, chapter 8, by Kelly M. Britt, brings an archaeological perspective to bear on one of the most recent watery catastrophes, Superstorm Sandy (2012 CE) and the destruction it brought to the metropolis of New York. More so perhaps than any other city, New York epitomizes future visions of urban societies. Yet, the city struggles with a legacy of racial and class conflict that is manifest in its infrastructure. In interactions with extreme events such as Sandy, this legacy—this heritage—becomes evident. By the same token, this heritage also serves as a source of community resilience and, handled with care, can prove vital in building not a dystopian but a utopian New York.

Chapter 9, by Shannon Lee Dawdy, follows similar lines of investigation but focuses on the aftermath of Hurricane Katrina (2005 CE) and its impact on yet another iconic and variously dystopian or utopian city, New Orleans. In a remarkable intimate ethno-archaeological investigation of this modern-day catastrophe, Dawdy extends her earlier work (Dawdy 2016) to show how materials and materiality, monuments and monumentality play their roles in the making and unmaking of disasters. The vulnerability of New Orleans to hurricanes and associated flooding has been the subject of historical inquiry too (Rohland 2018a, 2018b), yet Dawdy's singularly archaeological perspective makes her study useful as an analytical "hinge" (cf. Pedersen and Nielsen 2013) for then considering case studies located deeper in time. This is precisely where Nicola Sharratt's study, in chapter 10, of the Tiwanaku state of thirteenth-century South America and its response to drought slots in. While she turns our gaze to water lack as the hazard, her detailed considerations of community responses rather than state- or society-level responses bring us close to the intimacy provided by Dawdy, albeit without the privilege of living informants. Sharratt stresses how drought interacts without facets of society and how multiple stressors interact to entrench inequality. She also very much underlines the importance of networks in causing vulnerability and in providing solutions.

Staying with the troubles of drought, in chapter 11, Timothy A. Kohler, Laura J. Ellyson, and R. Kyle Bocinsky offer a powerful analysis of the structural vulnerability of the pre-Hispanic Pueblo communities of 600–1280 CE. Sandwiched between the dire decades of the sixth century and their ultimate demise in the thirteenth, the ups and downs of ancient Pueblan society provide a tantalizing natural experiment of history for revealing causal relations between climate change, social inequality, and violence. Kohler and colleagues frame their analysis in an analytical paradigm and a terminology that should be familiar to, for instance, political scientists and indeed politicians. Their perhaps unsurprising yet deeply worrying conclusion is that production crises lead, all else equal, to violence—a relationship also flagged by other analyses of more recent historical periods (e.g., Parker 2014) but which remains controversial in relation to the contemporary (e.g., Hsiang, Burke, and Miguel 2013).

In chapter 12, Detlef Gronenborn and colleagues pursue a trajectory not dissimilar to Kohler et al., but push their perspective much further into the depths of time. They focus on a truly iconic period of human prehistory, the origin and spread of farming practices in mid-Holocene Europe. Traditionally, this narrative is one of biblical conquest (cf. Golitko and Keeley 2007; Petrasch 2001)—of land, of peoples, of animals, of plants—but Gronenborn et al. paint a more complex picture. Internal societal and external climatic variables, including drought, come together to produce flickering violence and politically volatile societal changes. Importantly, the authors of this chapter also ask whether the patterns and processes they see in deep time hold true of the present.

In chapter 13, Daniel H. Sandweiss and Kirk A. Maasch also consider, diachronically, the role of drought on complex societies, now of the Andes. Here, societies are vulnerable to the now infamous El Niño drought phenomenon. These droughts have influenced the fates of Andean communities from deep time to the present. Indeed, such droughts—especially the rare mega-droughts—have not only been shown to have strongly affected societies in this region and elsewhere, but they are now being used as geological markers for the most significant climate fluctuations of the recent millennia (Walker et al. 2012). Are such droughts and their societal—and hence material and stratigraphic—consequences also going to become the markers of the Anthropocene? The volume's final chapter, by Nick Shepherd, is suggestive of this. Immersed in the recent, or rather ongoing, Cape Town water crisis, Shepherd uses a suite of sources—all archaeological, really—to prognosticate the fate of a major contemporary urban center: coping or collapse. Shepherd's analysis powerfully reveals actors and structures—structures that, ironically in the absence of running water, become more fluent around the crisis event (cf. Sewell 1996). The analysis also reveals actors and actions in intricate and intimate detail, as well as oppositions and paradoxes. The situation is, like those in all the volume's chapters, complex. In contrast to all the complete natural experiments of history that make up the bulk of chapters, this final chapter is about pasts in the making, about a history that has yet to unfold. The disaster that is the water crisis reveals causalities and suggests future scenarios. In that way Shepherd's chapter connects richly with those by Riede and Jackson as well as Holmberg, which also, albeit in different ways, urge us to take the archaeological perspectives on the past more seriously in thinking through our futures.

References

Dawdy, Shannon Lee. 2016. *Patina: A Profane Archaeology*. Chicago: University of Chicago Press.

Golitko, M., and L. H. Keeley. 2007. "Beating Ploughshares Back into Swords: Warfare in the *Linearbandkeramik*." *Antiquity* 81 (312): 332–42.

Hsiang, Solomon M., Marshall Burke, and Edward Miguel. 2013. "Quantifying the Influence of Climate on Human Conflict." *Science* 341 (6151).

Parker, Geoffrey. 2014. *Global Crisis: War, Climate Change and Catastrophe in the Seventeenth Century*. New Haven: Yale University Press.

Pedersen, Morten Axel, and Morten Nielsen. 2013. "Trans-temporal Hinges: Reflections on an Ethnographic Study of Chinese Infrastructural Projects in Mozambique and Mongolia." *Social Analysis* 57 (1): 122–42.

Petrasch, J. 2001. "Seid fruchtbar und mehret Euch und füllet die Erde und machet sie Euch Untertan: Überlegungen zur demographischen Situation der bandkeramischen Landnahme." *Archäologisches Korrespondenzblatt* 31: 13–25.

Rohland, Eleonora J. 2018a. *Change in the Air: Hurricanes in New Orleans from 1718 to the Present*. Oxford: Oxford University Press.

———. 2018b. "Adapting to Hurricanes: A Historical Perspective on New Orleans from Its Foundation to Hurricane Katrina, 1718–2005." *Wiley Interdisciplinary Reviews: Climate Change* 9 (1): e488.

Sewell, William H. 1996. "Historical Events as Transformations of Structures: Inventing Revolution at the Bastille." *Theory and Society* 25 (6): 841–81.

Walker, Mike J. C., M. Berkelhammer, S. Björck, L. C. Cwynar, D. A. Fisher, Andrew J. Long, John J. Lowe, R. M. Newnham, Sune Olander Rasmussen, and Harvey Weiss. 2012. "Formal Subdivision of the Holocene Series/Epoch: A Discussion Paper by a Working Group of INTIMATE (Integration of Ice-Core, Marine and Terrestrial Records) and the Subcommission on Quaternary Stratigraphy (International Commission on Stratigraphy)." *Journal of Quaternary Science* 27 (7): 649–59.

CHAPTER 8

The Materiality of Heritage Post-disaster

Negotiating Urban Politics, People, and Place through Collaborative Archaeology

KELLY M. BRITT

Executive Summary for Stakeholders

It is the goal of this work to provide potential points of departure for a variety of communities that are involved with catastrophe preparedness, response, recovery, and mitigation. This includes but is not limited to those working in extremely localized spaces like community nongovernmental organizations to more political organized units of government at the state and federal level. I hope that some of the points discussed in the following chapter allow people to question the repetitive acts of engagement dictated through policy that keeps communities in a perpetual state of treading water to climate change, rather than truly responding to it. This chapter looks into collaborative efforts that were developed in response to Superstorm Sandy connecting publics to rebuilding efforts through shared heritage places and preservation efforts. The hope is that the theoretical points developed here provide a potential point of reference to more pragmatic and applied processes, with space for the thoughts presented here to transform into new practices as well. As these examples move from top-down political federal endeavors used in public policy to molded theoretical thoughts discussed in academic circles, I hope they will morph back again into the public arena from a more bottom-up approach, to be exposed, be critiqued, and include more nuanced collaborative responses that address particular needs of communities in response to disasters.

Introduction

Climate change has resulted in increased and intensified weather events across the globe, producing disasters and impacting nations, states, and local communities on a more frequent basis. Urban landscapes, many situated along water bodies, find themselves in a precarious and vulnerable position of being on the front line to tropical storms and impacts of sea-level rise. Particularly vulnerable communities are ones located on the waterfront, low-lying areas, or ones built on landfill. In New York City, many of these at-risk locations have also traditionally been residential and occupational areas for people of color and working-class communities. Many of these communities now find themselves displaced from the long-term governmental recovery efforts post-disaster, living in temporary housing or moving to new communities entirely. Recent storms that have impacted the northeast coast of the United States, particularly Superstorm Sandy of 2012, have illustrated that community-based networks are no longer supplemental to governmental response and recovery efforts, but are essential for communities to recover and survive. Therefore, displacement and gentrification not only break communities apart, but by disrupting these community connections and relationships, they exacerbate disaster response and recovery. Additionally, displacement separates communities from historic sites and heritage places as well. Heritage and history play an important part in establishing power relations and control as well as serve as sites of memory and healing. The physical creation or reconstruction of a heritage site serves as a place and space for mediation and social awareness with the community itself. This makes the heritage site formation or renovation process not divorced from the past disaster, but rather very much wedded to it in the present. Since many rebuilding and resiliency projects have acquired governmental funds, environmental and historic preservation laws play an instrumental part of the process of post-disaster urbanization and are mandated to include public coordination. But what does this coordination look like? Is it merely a tick in the checkbox, or are collaborative efforts of community-based networks connecting the public to these rebuilding projects and maintaining communities? Furthermore, disasters that affect urban areas influence ongoing urbanization; thereby, what role do heritage sites play in the urbanization process post-disaster? This chapter will explore these questions in the context of post-disaster urban recovery projects and the potential role archaeological collaboration has or can have in providing a space for collective community agency within the rebuilding process. Methodologically, the thoughts in this chapter were developed over my seven-year tenure from 2010 to 2017 as regional archaeologist at the Federal Emergency Management Agency

(FEMA), Region II, which incorporated the states of New York and New Jersey and the territories of Puerto Rico and the United States Virgin Islands (USVI). Information was gathered from my own personal experience and observations.

To ease the understanding of the various parts at play covered in this chapter, it will be divided into three main parts. Much like a playwright does before telling the narrative, background information must be drawn so the audience can fully understand the story. Therefore, part 1 is the playbill for the audience, noting the actors, the location, and the issue at the heart of the tale. This section will introduce the players and their roles, define the terminology, and break down US historic preservation laws, ordinances, and regulations that are essential for understanding the nature of the questions put forth in this chapter.

Once the setting is set, the story can begin with part 2. While I wish I could begin with "In a magical world, far far away . . .", this story takes place in New York City with catalyst Superstorm Sandy, far from any magical world. This section will discuss some of the key players in the rebuilding process, explore why heritage is so important in rebuilding, and discuss how Mayor Bloomberg's neoliberal policies, rebuilding, and new development projects have turned the once-known "Big Onion" into more of what I would call a "Golden Apple," an emerging western luxury destination for tourists and the top 1 percent. The materiality of heritage now finds itself caught between communities' heartstrings and the tourist gaze that has supported a new form of gentrification to the evolving urbanization of the city.

Finally, while some stories come to end, many continue on with an epilogue, and in this case, the epilogue is still being written. Part 3 will illustrate that the historic preservation laws that govern much of the heritage management post-disaster in the United States can and have been effective (in certain contexts) in moving beyond mere mandated public consultation to more collaborative projects, particularly with tribal nations. Therefore, additional communities can and should be part of the process. I will draw upon the work of Danny MacKinnon and Kate Driscoll Derickson (2013) on a "politics of resourcefulness" as a potential way forward in that process.

Part I: Exposition

Terminology and Definitions: Scientific, Political, and Popular Uses

The United States has recently experienced what seems to be an increase in disasters from human-induced ones, such as 9/11, to more "natural" ones, such as Hurricanes Katrina, Sandy, Irma, Maria, and Harvey, to name just a few. Even while I was writing early drafts of this chapter, the East Coast of the United States was paying close attention to Hurricane Florence as she inched closer to shore and communities prepared for a potential devastating and catastrophic impact to their social and physical worlds. Other chapters in this volume will explore the tangled network of effects coastal hazards and storms have on communities in various contexts, from deep time to the contemporary (see chapter 9 in this volume), but Hurricane Florence, as with other hurricanes like Sandy, is just that—a hurricane, a geophysical weather event. According to the United States National Oceanic and Atmospheric Administration (NOAA), hurricanes are tropical cyclones that reach a minimum seventy-four miles per hour sustained winds and are found in the Atlantic basin, which includes the Atlantic Ocean, Caribbean Sea, and the Gulf of Mexico. The United States uses the Saffir-Simpson Hurricane Wind Scale to rate hurricane wind capacity. As the wind capacity increases, the level or category of hurricane increases as well, on a scale from 1 to 5, with 5 being the highest and most destructive to humans and the built environment. Severe storms generally occur approximately twelve times a year, with an average of six turning into named hurricanes within each hurricane season, which is 1 June through 30 November (NOAA 2018; Trenberth et al. 2018). Recently, scholars have linked the higher ocean heat content and sea surface temperatures due to human-induced climate change with the increase in the number and intensification of hurricanes. Hence, these storms produce a greater impact on humanity and the environment, primarily through the longer periods of rain, leading to more overall flooding (Trenberth et al. 2018).

The Federal Emergency Management Agency (FEMA), the US agency responsible for assisting communities responding to, recovering from, as well as preparing for and mitigating both natural and human-made disaster events, produced a 928-page guide to emergency management, with related terms and definitions. This document has ten pages dedicated to the term "disaster" and its various meanings and exemplifies the complexity a mere definition can produce. Some definitions focus on the social aspect of the term, others the economic impact particularly relating to insurance claims and figures, and others to more political and legislative uses (Blanchard 2008). Despite the holistic shortcomings of this definition, for purposes of this chapter, I will defer to the definition put forth by the Robert T. Stafford Act, which governs much of the use of federal historic preservation and archaeology laws and regulations in emergency management within the United States. It reads: "Disaster, Natural: any hurricane, tornado, storm, flood, high water, wind-driven water, tidal wave, tsunami, earthquake, volcanic eruption, landslide, mudslide, snowstorm, drought, fire, or other catastrophe in any part of the United States which causes, or which may cause, substantial damage or injury to civilian property or persons" (Blanchard 2008, 184). In specific, for this chapter, I will focus my attention on the natural disaster that most impacts the eastern coast of the United States—hurricanes.

While I defer to the Stafford Act definition of disaster for the majority of this chapter for its use in the laws and regulations in my discussion, I would be amiss if I did not address that the catastrophic aspect to the geological event is the impact to humans and the built environment, not the event itself. However, there is an inextricable link between the frequency and intensity of these events and the human activity, including policy and development decisions, the reality of living in the Anthropocene. While this chapter's primary focus will not be on discussing the human actions that has led to this new epoch we live in, it informs all that is discussed forthwith. As Roberto Barrios (2016, 30) has stated, "Disasters are more often than not shaped through longstanding human practices that (1) enhance the destructive and socially disruptive capacities of geophysical phenomena, and (2) inequitably distribute the effects of these phenomena along socially produced gender, ethnic, race, and class differentiations" (also see Button and Schuller 2016). This acknowledgment is key when assessing rebuilding and recovery efforts and the communities they involve. Many communities that experience the greatest impact from a disaster are also communities that are already marginalized, on the verge of displacement due to socioeconomic forces rooted in these inequities of power. In New York City, neighborhoods built on landfill like Manhattan's Lower East Side, ones that once served as industrial areas such as Red Hook, Brooklyn, and low-lying coastal waterfront spaces like Far Rockaway, Queens, are just a few of the areas impacted by Superstorm Sandy. These communities, many of which contain large public housing developments, are located on the urban periphery that was once seen as the least desirable and cheapest space in the city, but these residents now find themselves on prime urban real estate and victims to various displacement policies and projects.

Here is where the terms "gentrification" or "displacement," "sustainability," and "resiliency" arrive into the discussion. Ruth Glass coined the term "gentrification" in the 1960s to explain the increase in middle-class residents displacing lower-class ones in urban neighborhoods. Sharon Zukin added to this definition in the late 1980s by stating it was "the conversion of socially marginal and working-class areas of the central city to middle-class residential use, [which] reflects a movement, that began in the 1960s, of private-market investment capital into downtown districts of major urban centers" (Zukin 1987, 129). From the 1980s onward, the term has migrated into public discourse and comedic sketches (see *The Daily Show* and *The Unbreakable Kimmy Schmidt* for some recent pop-culture examples) and has been the focus of many grassroots community movements. The term has also been coupled with defining signifiers from various subareas such as green gentrification and resiliency gentrification, describing the various causes and effects to the wide variety of displacement processes. Kenneth Gould and Tammy Lewis (2018, 12) describe the green gentrification process as a relatively new phenomenon, coinciding with the public's rising knowledge of climate change within the last decade, that has transformed former industrial waterfronts of New York City into green spaces, such as parks, for the sustainability class. They define the sustainability class as a group that is "well-educated, holds overt sustainability-oriented values, can afford sustainability themed consumption, and touts their green urbanism (such as living on the waterfront or near green spaces) to brand their lifestyle."

With the naming of a sustainability class, one must ask, what does sustainability mean? In their introduction to *The Anthropology of Sustainability: Beyond Development and Progress*, Marc Brightman and Jerome Lewis (2017, 2) highlight that sustainability from an anthropological viewpoint is "best understood as the process of facilitating conditions for change by building and supporting diversity—ontological, biological, economic and political diversity." In essence, as Brightman and Lewis (2017, 20) advocate further:

> The challenge of sustainability demands much more than the protection or preservation of communities or nature reserves, and more than technical fixes for CO_2 production or resource limitations: it requires re-imagining and reworking communities, societies and landscapes, especially those dominated by industrial capitalism, to help us build a productive symbiosis with each other and the many nonhumans on whom we depend.

Yet, for many who use this term, including governments, agencies, and organizations, this definition is not truly comprehended. Rather sustainability is realized through the use of top-down management strategies that include little to no involvement or even input from local communities and populations and basically only offer a stopgap to the situation at hand. This disparity tends to alienate and dislocate groups of people from their land or, in urban spaces, from their social networks in the community. Many of these communities and green projects lie on waterfronts or low-lying areas, which are also vulnerable to natural events like hurricanes and tropical storms. Preparedness and mitigation projects, therefore, link to this new green development with structural mitigation projects like floodwalls, structural elevation, and other climate change resiliency measures. As Gould and Lewis (2018, 13) point out, structural mitigation raises building costs, which are then passed onto the consumer or sustainability class gentrifiers, creating what they describe as resiliency gentrification and others call environmental gentrification (see also Checker 2016). This green development is then used as a branding strategy to label and sell to the sustainable or creative class projects that are part of the rebuilding efforts in New York City post-Sandy (Checker 2016; Greenberg 2015).

The term "resiliency" has had a similar trajectory of use as "sustainability." Federal, state, and city officials use these terms to create position titles, such as "resiliency planner," or offices like the New York City's Mayor's Office of Recovery and Resiliency. These terms have entered the policy and public domains, laying foundations for private and public rebuilding and development efforts like none seen before. Barrios and others have eloquently detailed the various and contested origins and definitions of resiliency (Barrios 2016; see also Clark 2015; MacKinnon and Derickson 2013). As Barrios explains, the term adopted from ecology and physics is not necessarily conducive for studying people, communities, and networks of social engagement. Many of these definitions focus on the ideas of adaptation and change to resist the level of impact from disasters so communities can return back to a level of stability pre-disaster. As this chapter will show, the laws and regulations are written to reflect this returning concept, not taking into consideration that change is inevitable, particularly climate change and its effects on humans and their environment. Yet, as Barrios illustrates, these definitions leave out the anthropological lens and do not take into consideration that communities are never stable, that they are forever changing from internal and external factors, and therefore, returning to a pre-state condition is inefficient. Essentially, his conclusion is that "a model that assumes a stable community with unchanging membership preexists a catastrophe, experiences a shock, and then recovers is too simple to account for the political entanglements and social movements that routinely characterize disasters" (Barrios 2016, 30).

As Melissa Checker has noted in her anthropological work on Staten Island post–Superstorm Sandy, "Disasters are deeply entangled in extensive political and economic webs that stretch across time and space. Viewed in this way, disasters make visible the ways that local ecologies and communities, however far-flung or historically distant from one another they may seem, are actually connected to each other" (Checker 2016, 173). I hope to build upon Barrios's suggestion to shift the focus from "building resilience that works in conjunction with development process that creates vulnerability" (Barrios 2016, 29) and Brightman and Lewis's definition of sustainability to promote a reduction of environmental impacts by taking into consideration sociopolitical needs and vulnerabilities of communities. Additionally, I would add that while communities can rebuild in ways that reduce their physical and social vulnerability to events, they need to be an integral part of the process, not forgotten about until the end. For this reason, MacKinnon and Derickson's (2013, 250) critique on resilience policy in which they state, "Resilience is serving to reinforce and extend existing trends in urban regional development policy towards an increased responsiveness to market conditions, strategic management and the harnessing of endogenous regional assets," and their suggestion for a "politics of resourcefulness," which emphasizes "forms of learning and mobilization based upon local priorities and needs as identified and developed by community activists and residents" (McKinnon and Derickson 2013, 263–64), are an important shift in focus for how heritage management fits into the post-disaster picture. For heritage management, which plays a part in this rebuilding and building process, the current laws and regulations actually have the provision already in place for this dialogue to happen, yet are rarely utilized.

Laws, Ordinances, and Regulations

Understanding aspects of climate change terminology is only a portion of what is needed for setting the context. Having a better understanding of the laws, regulations, and ordinances that govern how communities can and do respond is the other half of the equation. Who, what, when, where, and how questions regarding the phases of disaster and where heritage management fits in are also necessary components to understanding the current nature of disasters in the United States and outlining the possible ways to evolve this process holistically. While there are state and local laws, regulations, and ordinances that may affect the disaster cycle, this chapter will focus on the federal legal attributes this sequence entails.

When most people think of archaeology, heritage management, and the US federal government, the Federal Emergency Management Agency is not the first agency that comes to mind. However, after disaster strikes and federal funds are determined, the Stafford Act, a 1988 version of the Disaster Relief Act of 1974, swings into motion. This act created a system by which a US presidential disaster declaration can provide communities with assistance by FEMA. With the federal financial support the Stafford Act brings, the required adherence to other federal environmental and historic preservation laws such as the National Historic Preservation Act (NHPA) and the National Environmental Policy Act (NEPA), as well as regulations and ordinances, becomes mandatory.

National Historic Preservation Act

While there are many federal environmental and historic preservation laws federal agencies need to work with on a daily basis, the main law that historic preservationists and archaeologists encounter while working in the public sector is the National Historic Preservation Act of 1966, which was amended in 1992 (Public Law 89-665; 16 U.S.C. 470 et seq). This act is the nation's primary historic preservation law that defines the legal responsibilities of federal agencies with respect to the preservation and stewardship of historic properties. It states that the nation's legacy should be preserved as an important living part of a community putting into law the importance of preserving a community's past for the present. The main components of the act were the creation of the National Register of Historic Places (NR or the Register), the Advisory Council on Historic Preservation (ACHP), State Historic Preservation Offices (SHPOs), and then in 1992 the Tribal Historic Preservation Offices (THPOs). Two main sections of the act are section 106, which mandates that federal agencies consider the effect of their projects on historic properties and is known as 36 CFR 800; and section 110, which ensures that historic preservation is integrated into every federal agency's mission by obligating federal agencies to adequately care for agency-owned or agency-maintained historic properties, directs federal agencies to establish historic preservation programs and a federal preservation officer (FPO), and provides protection of National Historic Landmarks (NHLs).

Essentially, if one federal dollar is spent on a project or the endeavor is being conducted on one inch of federal lands, compliance with federal environmental and historic preservation laws is *required*. Compliance, or conformity of adhering to official, in this case, federal requirements, is the backbone to heritage management in the United States. In several instances, federal agencies do not full comply with these laws (consciously or not) and regulations, or controversies emerge over the interpretation of the level of compliance, as was witnessed in the Dakota Access Pipe Line (DAPL), but essentially agencies are responsible for completing the compliance process for all projects under their purview.

The majority of the projects FEMA processes must meet these compliance regulations due to the fiscal nature of the agency's involvement in a project, with some exceptions. At FEMA, federal spending can be seen in a variety of grant programs that correspond to the various points of the disaster management cycle, from the onset of an event to the response, recovery, mitigation, and preparation phases. The response and recovery phase usually comprises the largest amount of allocated grants and dollars and therefore is where the majority of compliance work is done. There are many misconceived notions that FEMA responds to a disaster as a first responder, such as police or fire departments would to an event. However, while all staff are emergency managers and are deployed into action at the beginning of a potential disaster event, they are there to respond to state and local needs when requested. These needs usually are met by assisting the municipalities receiving the items (e.g., generators, water), helping with communication needs, and so forth. In actuality, FEMA is not a first responder but a granting agency, providing two different types of funding assistance: first, to individuals to fund rebuilding of privately owned buildings, such as housing or commercial properties; and second, to public entities such as tribal nations and states, which then direct the funds to municipalities, such as counties, cities, or towns, who applied for funding either to rebuild to pre-disaster conditions or to mitigate and prepare for future disasters. Funding for either individual or public assistance can only be applied for once a disaster declaration has been made by the president of the United States. Disaster declarations that are presented to Congress for disaster relief funds must be petitioned to the president of the United States by state governors or, until very recently, by tribal nations directly. It is only when the president formally declares a "disaster" that full federal involvement takes place.

After a disaster has been declared by the president of the United States, the Stafford Act is put into place, and federal funds are allocated for public projects, it is at this point that FEMA now has an *obligation* to adhere to these laws, which is generally completed by staff within the Environmental and Historic Preservation Cadre (EHP) of the agency. How that obligation is interpreted and carried out depends on various factors, including the current administration's position on particular issues, the department that oversees the federal agency, which in this instance is the Department of Homeland Security (DHS), the agency's missions and policies, regional or district guidelines and procedures, and finally, but most importantly, individual praxis on a day-to-day basis. It is within this praxis, language and action can be used to shape how consultation or collaboration occurs.

Part II: The Narrative

What Makes a Place? Disasters, Heritage, and Communities in Transition

Rebuilding post-disaster is a complex, lengthy, emotional, and costly endeavor. Recovery from large storms, like Superstorm Sandy, includes rebuilding infrastructure, utilities, and structures; it also consists of reconstructing homes, relationships, networks, and communities both large and small. After safety and security of life and basic property have been re-established, focus can begin on other important aspects of society that help mend the wounds of the transition from pre- to post-disaster living, and heritage and historic sites play an important key role in this psychological process (Rico 2014). As can be seen in areas of conflict, heritage and history play a crucial role in establishing or re-establishing power relations and control. New Jersey's post–Sandy slogan "Stronger Than the Storm" that ran on TV and print media was geared toward empowering residents and reassuring tourists that their sense of place was not lost, but rather being rebuilt better than before. It demonstrates points made by Barrios and others of the government's and public's notion of resiliency and rebuilding. To build back "stronger" equates to building back to pre-disaster state and, in this slogan, even better, extra-resilient to future events. But to build back "stronger" may make many more vulnerable, less connected, and further displaced.

By rejoining individuals and communities to their heritage, sites help people and communities reconnect. Yet how heritage value is created and managed varies, whether by a top-down nationalist viewpoint, from expert advice via heritage professionals, or a bottom-up grassroots movement. As Trinidad Rico (2014, 160) states, "cultural heritage is constructed in relation to its vulnerability, in specific contexts. Due to their high visibility and global translatability, disasters mobilize concerns for cultural heritage and amass large-scale support for the preservation mission." Risk value establishes a general focus on either a dominant discourse such as known damaged sites or those at risk from disaster (Rico 2014). Yet, the post-disaster road to recovery is riddled with heritage potholes of sorts, emerging in least expected spaces, yet also filled with meaning and memory.

In a term borrowed from Christopher Mathews, "an idea of a site" is at the center of much of post-disaster recovery for heritage and non-heritage sites alike. The physical creation of a heritage site serves as a place and space for mediation and social awareness within the community itself. This makes the heritage site formation or re-formation process not divorced from the disaster, but rather very much wedded in the present. This creation or re-creation within communities "represents the community to itself and to others in an accessible material medium" (Mathews 2006, 76). This materiality is seen in the making of these places and claimed by the community providing meaning to them. Moreover, for many sites that are national and international tourist destinations, it provides meaning to those visitors who venture to experience the site as well.

As Barbara Kirshenblatt-Gimblett states, "Heritage is created through a process of exhibition (as knowledge, as performance, as museum display). Exhibition endows heritage thus conceived with a second life. This process reveals the political economy of display in museums and in cultural tourism more generally" (1998, 149). Heritage adds value to existing objects, sites, and buildings that ceased to be viable or perhaps were never economically productive (Kirshenblatt-Gimblett 1998, 150). Heritage also transforms a local landscape into an exportable product, by changing a historic site into a heritage destination. The first stage is to imbue uniqueness in the site in order to give it value, and the second stage is to create a sense of "hereness" that will be accessible to and valued by tourists (Kirshenblatt-Gimblett 1998, 153).

It is important to recognize, however, that "heritage" is not always generated solely for export, nor is it always directly connected with historical events or history. Heritage sites are also important for local residents and influence how they view themselves and their surroundings (Glassberg 2001, 117), which is why they are so crucial in rebuilding efforts post-disaster. David Glassberg asks us to question "collective memory" as being the principal source of a community's sense of place. He argues that there are conflicts with political implications of the meanings attached to places and that the invention of a "collective" sense of place as the source of invention of a public history reflects the power struggle among the various groups and stakeholders (2001, 117). Heritage landscapes and places are often inscribed with meaning from a dominant individual or group and are subsequently interpreted through the lens of their ideological hegemony (Cosgrove and Domosh in Glassberg 2001, 117). This begs the question, what ideology was and still is leading the rebuilding process post-Sandy? The simple answer: neoliberal policy and politics.

The Golden Apple—Bloomberg's Luxury Urban Destination

Mayor Michael Bloomberg came into office after 9/11, and his twelve-year term (he managed to extend a two-year term limit to three) fell during Hurricane Sandy's landfall on the metropolis. While rebuilding the city after such massive disasters is beyond a daunting task, it provided the perfect impetus for Bloomberg's neoliberal policies that focused on remaking New York City into a luxury destination, particularly on the city's deindustrialized waterfront areas, devastated by the storm and desperate for rebuilding. Many authors and documentary filmmakers have focused on this time period and the social and economic effect Bloomberg's plans and policies had on the city, and I will not focus on them here (e.g., Anderson 2012; Galinsky and Hawley 2011; Brash 2011; Greenberg 2015). However, now, four years after Bloomberg left office, six years after Superstorm Sandy, the effects of the Bloomberg administration's decisions have taken root and are spreading furiously like choking weeds, dividing the city, which many local journalists and the current mayor's running platform have referred to as "a tale of two cities" (see Pilkington 2013). Despite current Mayor Bill de Blasio's stand to spread the wealth, much of the building and rebuilding are directly tied to post-Sandy efforts and Bloomberg's 2007 PlaNYC 2030, to build a "greener and greater New York," which was last updated in 2011. Many of these plans and policies are laced with problematic terminology listed above, such as climate resilience and focus on adaptation and mitigation projects, including working with FEMA to reassess the flood maps. But as also stated above, building back to a more "resilient" state requires extensive funding; New York City fought back in 2015 and appealed the new flood maps created by FEMA in order to reduce cost of insurance and the expenditure to build in accordance with flood zone regulations. In 2016 FEMA agreed to remap the city's flood zones so rates would be affordable to city residents (Chen 2018). As the maps are being redrawn, the city is using the 2007 Flood Insurance Rate Maps (FIRMs) for guidance. While the goal was to reduce costs, in essence this created a liminal space, one where those who live in coastal communities, many in public housing, are at the highest risk of being affected by another major hurricane. Either they will be able to build back more cost-effectively but at a higher risk, or they will need extraordinary amounts of funding to build back and "adapt" to the worst-case scenario projections. Needless to say, the new private-funding luxury residential spaces are being built with these higher-cost "resilient" measures, creating new communities existing in all-encompassing residential silos, while the former residents in public housing or middle-class residences will be more directly affected by future disaster events, displaced and disconnected to the heritage spaces that are tied to their built environment.

Social Networks as the Key to Survival

Many communities protect their heritage and historic resources through state or federal programs such as the State and National Registers for Historic Places, local historical commissions, and other private and public institutions. With these resources come regulations, codes, and other guidelines that individuals and organizations need to adhere to in order to qualify for funds, and many groups, particularly small nonprofits are reliant on these funds to survive and preserve heritage for the community. Money is the nonhuman tie that binds. Funding for large- or small-scale projects is needed to rebuild and recover, and as with many forms of funding, regulations and policies also play a large part in who gets what and how much. But navigating what funding opportunities individuals and organizations can qualify for and the application process can be so overwhelming. With massive disasters, individuals and even individual organizations cannot rebuild alone; therefore community-led endeavors emerged that are trying to bridge the gap between policy and implementation, between people and politics, and between disaster and resilience.

Key Players: Remaking Identities, Rebuilding Spaces

In the aftermath of Sandy, one thing became abundantly clear: there was a significant gap between entities that provide the physical and monetary resources needed to prepare for or recover from a disaster and those that need it most. The individuals, organizations, and governmental agencies form what Simon Sinek (2014, 26) calls "the circle the safety." This is a circle of trust providing the structure to survive and thrive as a unified team rather than individuals looking out for themselves. These networks, nonprofits, and grassroots organizations can provide the bridge needed between the local and federal to assist in creating this circle of safety needed for recovery and in turn help shape the ideology of rebuilding. Eric Klinenberg's (2018) recent book *Palaces for the People* takes this concept further by illustrating examples from various parts of the globe in a range of circumstances of the importance of social infrastructure for communities' civic survival, especially in times of crisis such as when disaster strikes. I feel this has become even more true in the more recent period of austerity, particularly when it comes to funding for education, social programs, and organizations. This infrastructure was key to many communities' endurance following Sandy, to obtain basic provisions and shelter and help rebuilding. Additionally, cultural and heritage organizations and networks were instrumental in assisting in the recovery of a particular segment of the city's population and changed the way cultural organizations and institutions prepared and mitigated for, responded to, and recovered from disasters. I will highlight just a few of these organizations here, starting with the federal, state, and locally supported ones down to the more grassroots or public/private programs.

Starting with the federal, the National Disaster Recovery Framework (NDRF) of FEMA enables recovery support to states, tribal nations, and territories impacted by disasters. Its goal is to facilitate more interagency problem-solving that will improve recovery and foster resilience in the communities in which they work (FEMA 2011). There were six Recovery Support Functions (RSFs) during Sandy recovery efforts, with Natural and Cultural Resources being one of them, which can link communities with federal and state partners for opportunities to rebuild the heritage spaces that are important to them. The goal is a community-focused recovery process. Hurricane Sandy was the first large-scale disaster during which the framework was activated, so as with many first runs, there were growing pains. Having served a ninety-day detail, which is a temporary assignment to a different position or a different agency, as Environmental and Historic Preservation (EHP) liaison between FEMA EHP staff and the Natural and Cultural Resources RSF, approximately six months into the recovery phase of Superstorm Sandy, I can speak from personal experience. As with any endeavor with a large staff, there are always aspects of basic personality conflicts and values. However, as the RSFs were staffed from other federal agencies, such as the National Oceanic Atmospheric Administration (NOAA), National Park Service (NPS), United States Geological Services (USGS), Housing and Urban Development (HUD), United States Army Corps of Engineers (USACE), along with others, for generally a period of ninety days, they would then rotate back to their home agency, and a new person would be sent, having to learn the ropes, meet the people, and understand the situations at hand. While policy, programs, and projects did not change, consistency was lacking in personnel, making some initiatives or potential projects harder to get off the ground than others. However, through Volunteer Organizations Active in Disaster (VOAD), organizations such as religious organizations, animal shelters, and cultural institutions could link via a liaison and provide that social infrastructure needed on a local level, with some federal support.

One of the major volunteer organizations active in New York City that was key to connect people working in the cultural and heritage sector to resources after Sandy was Alliance for Response, New York City. It was formerly part of Heritage Preservation and now part of Foundation of American Institute for Conservation of Historic and Artistic Works (FAIC). The New York City Alliance for Response chapter founded in 2004 as a local volunteer organization connecting community cultural heritage professionals with emergency responders is comprised of various sectors of society, from private institutions to individuals and public agencies. Its goal is to provide a space for partnerships to develop, which in turn strengthens mitigation and response to disasters to the art and cultural heritage of the city. It was integral to many post-Sandy, for basic conservation tips or links to professionals. Many informational meetings for the public took place in the "palaces for the people" Klinenberg (2018) discusses that are integral in civic life—museums and libraries became meeting spaces, informational gathering spots, and most importantly places of support, both physically and emotionally, for many.

Culture Active in Disasters–CultureAID NYC was founded through a collaborative working process led by the New York City Department of Cultural Affairs (DCLA) and FEMA's Sandy Recovery Office, along with a group of cultural service organizations. Its mission is to serve the entire City of New York's cultural community, which includes artists and organizations, and it works to maintain relationships with the national arts sector and emergency management agencies, providing resources and updated disaster-related information to the field. Much like Alliance for Response, it connects people with a wide variety of resources, gives out small grants and awards, and provides a network people can reach out to in times of need.

Rebuild by Design was developed by Housing and Urban Development (HUD) after Hurricane Sandy and provides a new way to design, fund, and implement rebuilding a resilient community after disasters. It is an interagency collaboration that "delivers innovative, implementable, large-scale infrastructural solutions that embody a people's unique vision of their own resilient future" (http://www.rebuildbydesign.org/). The goal is to redevelop communities in the wake of disasters that puts the community and its needs first. Over $930 million was given to six winning ideas for rebuilding efforts after Sandy. While most designs focus on rebuilding that mitigates for future disasters, the goal is to have the community at the center of the dialogue, providing information about what is most important to them. As with many large-scale projects, design and implementation can vary greatly, usually due to budget constraints and permitting, and several of the large-scale projects that won face those same challenges. Questions have arisen such as the following: Where and what gets cut—do you sacrifice communities needs versus "resiliency" measures? Is it sustainable? Who pays for the upkeep? How are communities involved or not involved in the decision-making process? Many community members are not even aware these large-scale projects are even underway and what it will mean to their neighborhood. Many local community nonprofits and advocate organizations are trying to bring the voice of the community to the project; with deadlines to use the funding and finish the project looming, this is a daunting task and does not always meet the needs of the community or the project.

These entities are just a few of the ways people have organized to recover from and prepare for disasters within the cultural sector. Many more neighborhood grassroots organizations and groups were formed that provided resources for a variety of residents needs, and I would be amiss to not acknowledge them here. These networks provide links to resources that are desperately needed post-disaster but rarely discussed. While these networks are necessary to link the circle of safety and rebuild post-disaster, there are still issues of politics and regulations that need to be navigated, which are inherent in the building-back discourse.

The Materiality of Heritage: Negotiating Politics, People, and Place

Superstorm Sandy hit coastal communities that are familiar with hurricanes and storm surges; therefore, they felt they were prepared for this storm but unfortunately were sadly mistaken. Historic structures were impacted in ways most of their communities could never have imagined. Places like Camp Osborne and Mantoloking Historic District in New Jersey and Coney Island in New York all saw a shift not only in their built environment, but in their natural environment as well. Barrier islands like Fire Island off the southern coast of Long Island traveled sixty-five to eighty-five feet (nineteen to twenty-five meters) from just one storm. The twentieth and twenty-first centuries have brought development to these areas and created a local history for the community. Many communities exist in landscapes never meant to be permanently inhabited or in marginalized areas where transportation and amenities are few and expensive. Yet, for many, moving away from an area lived in by generations is just not an option, for moving away would be to lose one's soul.

Many of these communities are comprised of people of color or lower-income residents, and many public housing facilities are located in these low-lying, heavily impacted areas. Post-disaster, some were or are still rebuilding; others have yet to return. Many public housing projects under care by the New York City Housing Authority (NYCHA) have yet to be fixed. New development in many of these communities fits into the neoliberal plan by former mayor Bloomberg, to develop the city as a luxury city, with high-rise developments that are inclusive in terms of amenities (e.g., interior dog parks, bowling alleys, schools, gyms, restaurants) but exclusive in terms of availability, where the majority of the properties are available only to the 1 percent or elite population.

The majority of physical damage during Sandy was due to coastal flooding and storm surge, creating havoc particularly for historic properties ill-equipped for their location in floodplains. At the same time Sandy struck, regulations were changing to properties located in these high-risk areas prone to flooding and damage. In addition, new rules for the National Flood Insurance Program (NFIP) and what is determined as the Advisory Base Flood Elevation also played a part in the rebuilding process. While communities can install a variance for historic properties, many communities have historic properties located in the floodplain or floodway and are some of the hardest hit structures. Furthermore, communities with buildings in flood zones that remain below the Advisory Base Flood Elevation will pay higher premiums for flood insurance.

With all these issues and constraints, what happens to a community's historic and cultural spaces? Some communities have active historical preservation commissions, but these commissions are required to balance the preservation needs of the community with rising risks of future damage from disasters. Are communities' desires for pristine historical heritage sites changing in the wake of large-scale disasters? Are new areas becoming favored over others? Is the risk value of a site taking precedence over other forms of value? In addition, how do the regulations, the law, and the enforcement change with the times and people's desires?

State Historic Preservation Offices (SHPOs) that review projects using federal funds or projects on federal land for section 106 of the National Historic Preservation Act regulate how to rebuild historic properties. These primarily are based on the Secretary of the Interior's Standards for the Treatment of Historic Properties. These standards are guidelines, not regulations, for maintaining, repairing, and replacing historic materials. These treatment guidelines, along with National and State Register of Historic Places requirements, are what SHPOs rely on to carry out their responsibility as part of section 106. However, these guidelines were written before Sandy, before the large natural disasters that have affected the United States, and long before climate change was a topic of discussion. It is here where the quandary really lies for rebuilding. In order to build back to protect properties and lives, the flood insurance standards and the Secretary of the Interior's guidelines need to complement each other but currently are at times in direct opposition and are in desperate need of updating. In addition, many communities are losing entire historic districts—either to the storms themselves or to funding programs like FEMA's Hazard Mitigation Grant Program (HMGP), which purchases and demolishes structures that have suffered from repeated damage and returns the land to open space. How does a community rebuild an entire district that has been part of the local identity for generations? While this is a question for the entire community, it is one wrought with individual thoughts and emotions—collective versus individual identity politics at play.

Part III: Resolution or Revolution?

Community Archaeology, Federal Agencies, and the Decolonialization Process

The history of anthropology and archaeology is embedded in a colonial discourse, complete with nationalistic, racist, sexist, and elite notions of looking at the past (Gosden 2002; Kohl and Fawcett 1996; Nassaney 2012; Thomas 1991, 2000; Watkins 2001). Critiques from outside the field including indigenous perspectives have led to additional assessments from practitioners within the field as well. Anthropological methodology, specifically with reference to advocacy, reciprocity, and accountability, has been evaluated, questioned, and altered. It requires anthropologists and archaeologists to "unthink" how many have been taught to think. It necessitates re-evaluating paradigms, epistemology, theory, and practice.

Community archaeology allows for this historical narrative to be critiqued and for the colonial lens in which archaeologists have viewed the past to be removed for a more inclusive practice that provides a space for archaeology to be conducted, as Atalay (2006, 283) has stated from Nicholas (1997, 85), "'with, for and by' indigenous communities."

While many archaeologists and anthropologists working in the federal government may subscribe to a community-based research agenda, history and historical interactions with communities, particularly indigenous communities, are steeped in colonialism and colonialist ideological practices. This mars the present with the past and scars contemporary interactions with policies or customs that built on these ideals or centrist procedures. So how do we use the obligation of communication that comes with these policies to get outside these historical dialogues and into a present that recognizes past inequalities, critiques them, but also moves beyond to support a decolonized practice of archaeology in the federal government?

The word "obligation" is chosen purposefully. But it is not a word that comes to mind when thinking of community engagement and working with indigenous populations. As Watkins notes when discussing legislated ethics, obligation comes from the portions of compliance archaeology that were once "left to the judgment of the individual archeologist" but are now regulated (Watkins 2001, 173). While this obligation is now regulated, it is here where an agency's staff and their commitment to a decolonized practice can make a difference, or not. If there is no commitment from staff to relook at past practices and no awareness present for change, we are basically treading water in a proverbial postcolonial sea. In required re-examination and commitment from staff, obligation can be the stepping-stone to a more dialogic community approach to federal archaeology projects. This form of collaboration can provide space for indigenous perspectives to be listened to and be incorporated into and guide projects, even if doing so is not an easy or straightforward process.

Many federal projects, particularly FEMA projects, are judged by the time it takes to complete them, with a desired termination date of yesterday. Much like developers use archaeology as a scapegoat for project delays or increased costs, so too is archaeology sometimes seen as a hindrance to the final goal with disaster recovery. Therefore, convincing a room of federal employees, community members affected by disaster, and congressional representatives that historic preservation is important can be trying at times. I have witnessed that having the law on your side has only assisted in bringing an alternative (albeit forced) view of archaeology to the table, for adhering to the law is non-negotiable.

As several scholars have noted, politics and political action can encourage archaeologists as well as the general public to consider perspective and multi-vocality in the consultation process (Nicholas 2006; Nassaney 2012). As Michael Nassaney (2012, 9) has explained, "The hermeneutical circle begins with socio-political relations grounded in experience, which in turn influences archaeological theory, thereby shaping archaeological practice," and I would add, the reverse could also be true where the *required* practice of inclusion by laws such as NHPA can influence theory and also shape practice.

The National Historic Preservation Act has evolved over its fifty-year history, finally including tribal nations into the conversation in the last amendment in 1992. And while it has progressed in some areas, it has lagged behind in others, leaving much of future progress in the hands of those who use and implement it (see Preservation Leadership Forum 2015). In previous papers, I have written about how the NHPA can be used as a vehicle toward collaboration with indigenous communities versus mere coordination for the sake of it. FEMA Region II (encompassing New York, New Jersey, Puerto Rico, and the Virgin Islands) made baby steps forward during my tenure as regional archaeologist, collaborating with tribal nations in the required consultation process for compliance with the National Historic Preservation Act. This included yearly cultural sensitivity trainings with New York's federally recognized tribal nations, conducting yearly Nation to Nation summits, listening to nations' requests for desired terminology such as "nation" versus "tribe," and folding the Tribal Historic Preservation Officers (THPOs) into the review process early on in a project. These actions, while small steps, provided a way forward to make mandated collaboration more than a check in a box and rather a more collaborative endeavor. Yet, I realize much more work is needed, such as more training for employees and bringing in state-only and non-recognized tribal nations to erode some of the long-lasting colonial legacies that the laws embody. I hope to be able to see the trajectory of this work move forward rather than back. Ideas such as incorporation of other communities into the collaboration process, such as citizens of neighborhoods whose historic districts are affected or residents of public housing developments with notable historic heritage spaces, can essentially change the current top-down approach to compliance to a more democratically centered one. Required outreach dictated by law is not the same as collaborative community engagement. While the law requires consultation, the consultation process can provide a space for redistribution of power and an opening of new interpretations based on dialogue and exchanges—in essence it's a resource for a community's voice to be heard.

Resilient Heritage, Resistant Communities, or Resourceful Opportunities? A Relational Approach

In March 2015 New York State governor Andrew Cuomo announced $4.9 million would go to assist thirteen counties in rebuilding historic properties damaged by Sandy. The grants are available to provide repair and assistance to historic and archeological resources that were damaged. In the announcement, Governor Cuomo said, "New York has a rich history, and many places important to it were damaged in Superstorm Sandy, making them more vulnerable to future severe storms. These grants will help build back these significant sites and ensure they remain important parts of New York's heritage, and tourism economy, for generations to come" (New York State 2015). Eligibility requirements are based on location of property, whether the property or historic district is listed or eligible for listing in the National Register of Historic Places and all work needs to adhere to the Secretary of the Interior's Standards for the Treatment of Historic Properties. While this provides some state support, it does not alleviate the power struggle Glassberg noted regarding collective memory: What if your property does not meet the criteria but is important to individuals and the community? Are only at-risk properties to be considered? And with the historic property regulations of rebuilding dictated by the Secretary of the Interior's Standards, created in a pre-climate-change worldview, how does one mitigate these disconnects between policy and reality?

Obviously there are still major gaps in the system, and in some instances, it is the system itself that is the gap. Many of these questions cannot be adequately answered or in some cases even addressed; however, I propose to borrow from Brightman and Lewis's (2017, 2) words on sustainability and MacKinnon and Derickson's (2013, 263) notes on a "politics of resourcefulness" to offer some possible ways forward. Change can happen, but "it requires re-imagining and reworking communities, societies and landscapes" (Brightman and Lewis 2017, 2), and these changes cannot take place without the will of the people; but how can the will of the people manifest without a seat at the table?

It is here where I have found that MacKinnon and Derickson offer specific concepts to a politics of resourcefulness that prove fruitful for discussion and a potential framework from which to build. Foremost, they see resourcefulness as a process, not as a product that is relational, or as they state, "It is the act of fostering resourcefulness, not measuring it or achieving it that should motivate policy and activism" (McKinnon and Derickson 2013, 264). The first step in this process revolves around "problematiz[ing] both the uneven distribution of material resources and the associated inability of disadvantaged groups and communities to access the levers of social change" (MacKinnon and Derickson 2013, 263). This is at the heart of Barrios's (2016) critique of the notion of resiliency and its use in post-disaster frameworks, which was illustrated throughout this chapter. This uneven distribution of resources prior to any catastrophic event means building back post-event reconstitutes those inequalities that existed pre-event both materially and socially. Yet, before change can happen, acknowledgment and discussion of these inequities needs to take place so redistribution can occur. The section 106 process can provide one space to bring communities to the table to begin to address some long-standing inequitable distribution of resources, in this instance individual and collective heritage.

Second, as McKinnon and Derickson (2013, 263–64) illustrate, the needs of a community should be defined by the community rather than removed governmental agents. They argue, "Resourcefulness is a material property and a relational term that seeks to problematize the often-profound inequalities in the distribution of resources by the state that further disadvantage low-income communities" (MacKinnon and Derickson 2013, 264). Access to community-based organizations and existing social infrastructure, as Klinenberg (2018) also notes, can provide a means for community needs to be democratically determined, shared, and disseminated, as can be seen in arts and heritage organizations that were illustrated in this chapter, such as Alliance for Response and CultureAID. These organizations provide a relational process to community or local autonomy—a processual relationship between the local and the larger communities. These organizations or community groups, organized or formed through grassroots movements, can provide skill sets or even just a place to exchange knowledge or information about procedures, technology, or ideas. Alliance for Response and CultureAID are examples of these networks of social infrastructure that assist communities and individual members in navigating the post-disaster event process, in some ways bridging the gap between the local and the larger government. Not all gaps will be linked; however, as seen in this chapter, the process of addressing those gaps can commence.

Third, MacKinnon and Derickson stress that "resilience policy tends to reify different spatial scales such as the urban and regional as discrete, self-organizing units, requiring local actors to adapt to turbulent external environment which is taken for granted and naturalized" (2013, 264). Their notion of resourcefulness provides a more scalar approach with community capacity building and that relational link of local to regional or national. I would add that time could be a relational tool as well—time as in looking at the past through history, heritage, and indigenous knowledge as modes of yoking past or indigenous ways of knowing, in particular around disasters, as potential ways of capacity building in the future. Heritage and historic properties can provide a means to new ways of thinking about catastrophes, such as how we as a community prevent, respond, and heal from these events.

The last element in MacKinnon and Derickson's framework in some ways brings us back to their first point, for they state that recognition of differences is key to mobilize social justice. I would add, without that recognition first, you can't have discussions about the unequal access to resources that need to occur and provide those relational links in community-based organizations. This chapter highlights this point clearly through the various ways that historic preservation policy can be used as a tool to recognize difference and inequalities (systemic and resource based), bring people to the table, and acknowledge, discuss, and formulate potential changes to move forward. For instance, recognition of unacceptable terms, such as "tribe," acknowledges a of different ways of seeing, and opens space to look at solutions that expand outside the regional or federal framework. MacKinnon and Derickson (2013, 265) underscore the following:

> Recognition promotes a sense of self-confidence, self-worth and self-community-affirmation that can be drawn upon to fuel the mobilization of existing resources and argue for and pursue new resources. Additionally, recognition confers group status upon the community in question on the basis of common attributes and a shared understanding that the community is itself a subject of rights and receiving body for state resources.

As stated at the beginning of this chapter, a primary goal of this work is to provide a theoretical framework for potential suggestions that can be put into practice in catastrophic contexts. I hope readers looking at the specific contexts illustrated throughout this chapter and the larger volume in which it sits, will see the benefits to shifting the conversation back into the communities that are affected, allowing them to build capacity and alter the systemic circle of inequality that has persisted in disaster frameworks. Heritage and historic preservation policies, such as section 106 of the National Historic Preservation Act, while still a top-down colonial process, do provide spaces to start that shift in discussion from one of being resilient to one of resourcefulness. To provide a more relational approach to how communities react to climate change, we all must do the following: acknowledge communities' unequal access to resources; use social infrastructure to provide space for communities to build knowledge; give space to alternative modernities, particularly those situated in indigenous lifeways; and recognize all voices at the table.

Abbreviations

ACHP—Advisory Council on Historic Preservation
DAPL—Dakota Access Pipe Line
DCLA—(New York City) Department of Cultural Affairs
DHS—Department of Homeland Security
EHP—Environmental and Historic Preservation
FAIC—Foundation of American Institute for Conservation of Historic and Artistic Works
FEMA—(United States) Federal Emergency Management Agency
FIRM—Flood Insurance Rate Map
FPO—Federal preservation officer
HMGP—Hazard Mitigation Grant Program
HUD—Housing and Urban Development
NDRF—National Disaster Recovery Framework
NEPA—National Environmental Policy Act
NFIP—National Flood Insurance Program
NHL—National Historic Landmark
NHPA—National Historic Preservation Act
NOAA—(United States) National Oceanic and Atmospheric Administration
NPS—National Park Service
NR—National Register of Historic Places
NYCHA—New York City Housing Authority
RSF—Recovery Support Function
SHPO—State Historic Preservation Office
THPO—Tribal Historic Preservation Office
USACE—United States Army Corps of Engineers
USGS—United States Geological Services
USVI—United States Virgin Islands
VOAD—Volunteer Organizations Active in Disaster

Acknowledgments

Disclaimer: While no longer a federal employee, I would like to state that opinions presented in this chapter are the personal thoughts of the author and do not represent the Federal Emergency Management Agency (FEMA), Brooklyn College, or any other agency, professional organization, or institution.

In addition, certain aspects of this chapter have evolved from papers presented and panel discussions at various conferences such as the Theoretical Archaeology Group, the Society of Historical Archaeology Annual Meetings, the Society for American Archaeology Annual Meetings, and finally the Graduate Center at the City University of New York's Colloquia Series. Some focused more on the community efforts of post-disaster recovery and how grassroots organizations supplement and at times take over governmental responsibilities, other discussions concentrated more on a decolonial process of engagement with tribal nations, and lastly another paper discussed the overlooked aspect of yoking heritage sites to the healing process of communities during recovery. This chapter tries to marry many of the individual concepts previously discussed in a more holistic manner as well as introduce the complexities urbanization makes in the post-disaster recovery. By interweaving them together, I hope to illustrate the connections, disconnections, political complexities, and at times controversial nature of heritage management and disaster recovery in the United States. I thank present and former colleagues at FEMA and Brooklyn College for ongoing discussions, thoughts, and suggestions. I also would like to personally thank Mark Schuller for inviting me into this conversation and Felix Riede and Payson Sheets and all the collaborators in the volume for the discussion and dialogue on this very important subject. All errors and mistakes are mine.

Kelly M. Britt, PhD, RPA, graduated from Columbia University with a doctorate in anthropology and is currently an assistant professor of Urban Archaeology at Brooklyn College, focusing on activist-centered, community-based historical archaeology of urban spaces. She is currently interested in two areas of research: (1) exploring the intersection of gentrification, activism, and materiality and (2) disasters and heritage management—locally and globally.

References

Anderson, Kelly, dir. 2012. *My Brooklyn*. Kanopy Streaming.

Atalay, Sonya. 2006. "Indigenous Archaeology as Decolonizing Practice." *American Indian Quarterly Special Issue: Decolonizing Archaeology* 30 (3/4): 280–310.

Barrios, Roberto. 2016. "Resilience: A Commentary from the Vantage Point of Anthropology." *Annals of Anthropological Practice* 40 (1): 28–38.

Blanchard, B. Wayne. 2008 [2007]. *Guide to Emergency Management and Related Terms, Definitions, Concepts, Acronyms, Organizations, Programs, Guidance and Legislation: A Tutorial on Emergency Management, Broadly Defined, Past, Present, and Future*. 22 October. Retrieved 16 February 2019 from https://training.fema.gov/hiedu/docs/terms%20and%20definitions/terms%20and%20definitions.pdf.

Brash, Julien. 2011. *Bloomberg's New York: Class and Governance in the Luxury City*. Athens: University of Georgia Press.

Brightman, Marc, and Jerome Lewis. 2017. "Introduction: The Anthropology of Sustainability; Beyond Development and Progress." In *The Anthropology of Sustainability: Beyond Development and Progress*, edited by Marc Brightman and Jerome Lewis, 1–34. New York: Palgrave Macmillan.

Button, Gregory V., and Mark Schuller, eds. 2016. *Contextualizing Disaster*. New York: Berghahn Books.

Checker, Melissa. 2016. "Tempests, Green Teas, and the Right to Relocate." In *Contexualizing Disaster*, edited by Gregory V. Button and Mark Schuller, 171–95. New York: Berghahn Books.

Chen, David W. 2018. "In New York, Drawing Flood Maps Is a 'Game of Inches.'" *New York Times*, 7 January 20. Retrieved 22 September 2018 from https://www.nytimes.com/2018/01/07/nyregion/new-york-city-flood-maps-fema.html.

Clark, John. 2015. "The Katrina Disaster and the Politics of Disavowal." New Clear Vision, 21 September. Retrieved 16 February 2019 from http://www.newclearvision.com/2015/09/21/against-resilence/.

Cosgrove, Denis, and Mona Domosh. 1993. "Author and Authority: Writing the New Cultural Geography." In *Place/Culture/Representations*, edited by James Duncan and David Ley, 25. New York: Verso.

FEMA (Federal Emergency Management Agency). 2011. *National Disaster Recovery Framework: Strengthening Disaster Recovery for the Nation*. Retrieved 15 May 2015 from http://www.fema.gov/pdf/recoveryframework/ndrf.pdf.

Galinsky, Michael, and Suki Hawley, dir. 2011. *Battle for Brooklyn*. RUMUR.

Glassberg, David. 2001. *Sense of History: The Place of Past in American Life*. Amherst: University of Massachusetts Press.

Gosden, Christopher. 2002. "Postcolonial Archaeology: Issues of Culture, Identity and Knowledge." In *Archaeology Theory Today*, edited by Ian Hodder, 241–61. Malden, MA: Blackwell.

Gould, Kenneth, and Tammy Lewis. 2018. "From Green Gentrification to Resilience Gentrification." *City and Community* 17 (1): 12–15.

Greenberg, Miriam. 2015. "The Sustainability Edge: Competition, Crisis and the Rise of Green Urban Planning." In *Sustainability in the Global City: Myth and Practice*, edited by Cynthia Isenhour, Gary McDonogh, and Melissa Checker, 106–30. New York: Cambridge University Press.

Kirshenblatt-Gimblett, Barbara. 1998. *Destination Culture: Tourism, Museums and Heritage*. Berkeley: University of California Press.

Klinenberg, Eric. 2018. *Palaces for the People: How Social Infrastructure Can Help Fight Inequality, Polarization, and the Decline of Civic Life*. New York: Crown.

Kohl, Philip L., and Clare Fawcett., eds. 1996. *Nationalism, Politics and the Practice of Archaeology*. Cambridge: Cambridge University Press.

MacKinnon, Danny, and Kate Driscoll Derickson. 2013. "From Resilience to Resourcefulness: A Critique of Resilience Policy and Activism." *Progress in Human Geography* 37 (2): 253–70.

Mathews, Christopher. 2006. "The Idea of the Site: History, Heritage, and Locality in Community Archaeology." In *Landscapes under Pressure: Theory and Practice of Cultural Heritage Research and Preservation*, edited by Ludomit Lozny, 75–91. New York: Springer.

Nassaney, Michael. 2012. "Decolonizing Archaeological Theory at Fort St. Joseph: An Eighteenth-Century Multi-Ethnic Community in the Western Great Lakes Region." *Midcontinental Journal of Archaeology* 37 (1): 5–24.

NOAA (National Oceanic Atmospheric Administration). 2018. "What Is a Hurricane?" Retrieved 11 September 2018 from https://oceanservice.noaa.gov/facts/hurricane.html.

New York State. 2015. "Governor Cuomo Announces $4.9 Million to Repair Historic Properties Damaged by Superstorm Sandy." Retrieved 22 September 2018 from https://www.governor.ny.gov/news/governor-cuomo-announces-49-million-repair-historic-properties-damaged-superstorm-sandy.

Nicholas, George P. 1997. "Education and Empowerment: Archaeology with, for and by the Shuswap Nation, British Colombia." In *At a Crossroads: Archaeology and First Peoples of Canada*, edited by George P. and Thomas D. Andrews, 85–104. Burnaby, BC: Archaeology Press.

——— 2006. "Decolonizing the Archaeological Landscape." *American Indian Quarterly Special Issue: Decolonizing Archaeology* 30 (3/4): 350–80.

Pilkington, Ed. 2013. "A Tale of Two Cities: Poor New Yorkers Demand a Slice of Manhattan's Action." *The Guardian*, 14 September. Retrieved 22 September 2018 from https://www.theguardian.com/world/2013/sep/14/new-york-tale-of-two-cities.

Preservation Leadership Forum. 2015. *NHPA Section 106 and Tribes: A Look Back and Paths Forward*, 13 March (Special Contributor). Retrieved 26 March 2015 from http://blog.preservationleadershipforum.org/2015/03/13/section-106-and-tribes/#.VRRrzI7wLK0.

Rico, Trinidad. 2014. "The Limits of a 'Heritage at Risk' Framework: The Construction of Post-disaster Cultural Heritage in Banda Aceh, Indonesia." In *Journal of Social Archaeology* 14 (2): 157–76.

Sinek, Simon. 2014. *Leaders Eat Last: Why Some Teams Pull Together and Others Don't*. New York: Penguin.

Thomas, David Hurst, ed. 1991. *Columbian Consequences*. Vol. 3, *The Spanish Borderlands in Pan-American Perspective*. Washington, DC: Smithsonian Institution Press.

——— 2000. *Skull Wars: Kennewick Man, Archaeology, and the Battle for Native American Identity*. New York: Basic Books.

Trenberth, Kevin E., Lijing Cheng, Peter Jacobs, Yongxin Zhang, and John Fasullo. 2018. "Hurricane Harvey Links to Ocean Heat Content and Climate Change Adaptation." *Earth's Future* 6: 730–44.

Watkins, Joe. 2001. *Indigenous Archaeology: American Indian Values and Scientific Practice*. Walnut Creek, CA: AltaMira Press.

Zukin, Sharon. 1987. "Gentrification: Culture and Capital in the Urban Core." *Annual Review of Sociology* 13: 129–47.

CHAPTER 9

Mound-Building and the Politics of Disaster Debris

SHANNON LEE DAWDY

Summary for Stakeholders

The debris pile from approximately 134,000 New Orleans buildings damaged or destroyed by Hurricane Katrina is visible from space. Although there was some effort to recycle materials through a little-known global market in demolition debris, most of the rubble amassed in place. In the future, archaeologists might reasonably consider the hurricane landfill a monumental structure. I use the example of the Katrina landfills to think about the political effects of disaster and what archaeologists call taphonomy—the formation process of landscapes and deposits. I examine the political formation of three landfills in New Orleans, one a superfund site and the other two major sites of contestation and accumulation post-Katrina. I look at everything from the percentage of plastics and "putrescibles" (foul-smelling organic matter that normally decays rapidly) in the landfills, to headline news about political bribes and kickbacks tied to the profitable disaster debris business. I also look at how local communities rose up to protest what they could see would be a longer, slower disaster they would have to live with in the form of toxic leaching. As protestors against one post-Katrina landfill chanted on the streets, "Don't dump on us." Disasters, I argue, produce "contingent publics" (Bennett 2010) that form around the resolution of a problem such as what to do with debris or how to rebuild. While a hazard may be experienced in the short term, its reverberations through the debris it creates may have social effects for generations. Many scholars today are bringing attention to processes of slow violence. When it comes to the environmental impacts of debris clearance and concealment of social failures, we should also talk about slow politics. Only when we can see the long-term consequences of today's political actions in the wake of disaster can we be empowered to redirect the slow politics of climate change.

Speculative Archaeology

I would like you to engage with me in a thought experiment—to imagine how New Orleans, Louisiana, will appear to archaeologists in the future, perhaps five hundred to a thousand years from now. The point is not fantasy or child's play, although it resembles the new genre of "cli-fi," or climate fiction, particularly in the case of the award-winning young adult novel *Ship Breaker* (Bacigalupi 2010) set on the Gulf Coast of the United States.

The fictionalized description I am about to present will help introduce the topic of this chapter—disaster debris. More specifically, I focus on the landfills created by the destruction of Hurricane Katrina and its aftermath. First, it needs to be said that in this future, if climate change and rising sea levels proceed according to even conservative estimates, most of the former city will be the domain of underwater archaeologists and recreational scuba divers. Like the prehistoric Mississippian mounds that were the only above-water features to be seen in the Great Flood of 1927, the only terrestrial exception to this future watery domain that New Orleans will become is an island in an eastern part of the city. There, manmade mounds that at one time rose eighty feet above ground surface now form islands that peak out of the murky surrounding water about fifty feet tall, although they are soft and erode with toxic leaching at a relatively quick pace from the battering of rain and waves in the now year-round tropical heat. Some hardy plants such as giant kudzu, cat's claw, and stinging nettles create a tangled, prickly barrier. Visible just below the water level is a line of multicolored large metal objects, heavily oxidized but which remote sensing has been shown to be the ruins of automobiles. These encircle the site, whether serving as some sort of ornamental or ritual purpose is unclear, although they were clearly marking off this space before the floods.

When archaeologists first arrive, they will have to cut the plants back with machetes. A flamethrower would cause an explosion due to the methane gas emitting from vents on the island. And by this time, humans will have learned the hard way that herbicides just create super weeds through fast-acting natural selection. Whether these future archaeologists will have a preserved paper archive to understand these mounds before their excavation is uncertain. Wars, continuing climate disasters, and the collapse of the United States in the twenty-first century may have created significant gaps in the record. They also know that newspaper and media accounts from this era were highly unreliable, prone to repetitive narratives, omissions, exaggeration, and what was at the time called fake news. Let's assume their record is minimal. So they rely heavily upon the archaeological record to reconstruct this time period. Their initial survey of the area indicates that these are definitely man-made features. The local geomorphology indicates that in the first half of the Anthropocene, without modification, the nonhuman landscape would have had undulations of only one to five meters.

After site clearing and testing for toxins, they don hazmat suits and commence excavation and core sampling of one of the islands that appear semi-rectangular in plan view from drone and satellite imagery. In fact, they look remarkably similar to the yet older abandoned Mississippian mounds that archaeologists of this lost culture once excavated themselves. Below the top levels of humic soil formed from generations of weeds and decay, they encounter a lens of about five centimeters thick consisting of a pulverized mix of organics and plastic, with a small amount of metal. Next comes an introduced clay cap about ten centimeters thick, although it varies across the site due to erosion and what appears to have been the rough movements of mass machinery used to bucket it and compact it into place. Below this clay cap, they encounter a significant layer of broken concrete and twisted metal, interspersed with broken glass and occasional sections of metal and plastic pipe and wet gypsum board (drywall), which emits hydrogen sulfide, making gas masks a requirement of the job. This extremely thick (over ten meters) deposit is heavy and, they realize, has caused the lower, softer layers to "hamburger" out, such that there is a ring of smaller, more diverse and toxic materials both surrounding the mound and deep within its center. This fifth stratum is incredibly diverse, with large to medium fragments of household furnishings and consumer waste. The shapes of couches, televisions, toys, and polyester clothing can be made out (some are whole and mostly intact), along with a dizzying array of ceramic types and plastic bottles and containers, which present a nightmare of a classification challenge to the archaeologists back in the lab. Due to the anaerobic conditions of the mound, some organics are relatively well preserved, from architectural wood to faunal remains. Occasionally, among the bone, lab technicians identify a lone fragment of a human tibia or mandible. This presents one of the great mysteries of the site, as well as the fact that most of the massive mound appears to have been built during a very short time frame—less than three years. Below this stratum they encounter another clay cap, and below that the water table, within which sits the seventh man-made stratum. It is much more mixed than the newer levels, with the contents more fragmented and much less plastic in evidence. Further, this stratum is distinguished from the others because it appears to be the result of a more gradual accumulation over decades. The archaeologists scratch their heads. They also try to figure out a sampling strategy. There is no way they want to curate even one-tenth of 1 percent of this material. It *is* full of information, and some of the pieces, such as small plastic human figurines with elongated legs and large breasts, are evocative, but there is simply too much of it. And it is full of toxins.

What I have just described is 90 percent real. It is based on what we already know about the contents and taphonomic processes taking place at the Katrina landfills. "Taphonomy" is a word that archaeologists and geologists use to describe the process by which the record of the ground is created—the science of deposition and decay. The primary thing I added with my imagination was the archaeologists themselves. Maybe no one five hundred to a thousand years from now will care about this past. But I already do. I want to expand on this speculative archaeology to think about disaster taphonomy and the politics of trash. I will bring together some of my thoughts through the literature on garbology—or the science of garbage, but also the post-human ontological turn. My main question is: what can disaster deposits tell us about politics?

Political Taphonomy

In an earlier piece I wrote shortly after Hurricane Katrina struck the Gulf Coast of the United States in 2005, I (Dawdy 2006, 720) made the claim that paying attention to taphonomic processes following a major disaster had revelatory possibilities.

> The active creation of a new archaeological record during recovery from disaster, I argue, is a primary medium through which individuals and communities reconstitute themselves. Thus, it pays to pay attention to the major and minor decisions people make regarding debris and dirt. Stratigraphy in this case does not merely reflect other, more socially significant, behaviors removed by one or two degrees from the record left in the earth but, rather, burial itself is a deliberate part of the recovery effort. Struggles over how to sort trash, where and how to deposit it, what to do with the dead, where to rebuild, how to memorialize the event in space, and, quite literally, the movement of dirt (for levee building, mudslide and earthquake stabilization, fire gaps, etc.) all factor into social transformation and cultural preservation.

At the time of that writing, some of the political and material processes related to debris removal, sorting, and disposal were beginning to emerge. The political activation of the Vietnamese-American community located adjacent to one of the new landfills, for example, had just begun and not yet resulted in its closure, nor the community's new electoral power, nor a documentary film that vaunted them into the national spotlight (Chiang 2009). But that is just the tip of the iceberg. Or tip of the landfill. The political history of the Katrina landfills in the years after the storm (and in the years since I wrote that first piece on disaster archaeology) is so tangled and fascinating that I am uncertain whether to characterize it as scandal, tragedy, or comedy. Perhaps some combination. In what follows, I will describe some of the contemporary events and facts related to the disaster debris and add some ethnographic observations before moving on to a more theoretical discussion of garbology and object-oriented ontology. The point of doing this is to demonstrate—with examples and details lacking in that first article—that taphonomic processes can be highly political.

As other contributions to this volume note, both "fast" and "slow" disasters produce political effects, sometimes in the all too predictable way of disproportionately affecting the poor and the vulnerable (see chapters 8 and 14 in this volume), but in other ways they can produce new forms of mobilization that shift the political landscape like a storm surge shifts a barrier island. Disasters, I argue, produce "contingent publics" (Bennett 2010, after Dewey) that form around the resolution of a problem such as what to do with debris or how to rebuild. Importantly, these publics also form around different temporal imaginaries that disasters can trigger, such as a concern with the salvage of heritage (see chapter 8 in this volume; Dawdy 2016) or a deep anxiety about the future (see chapter 2 in this volume). How we imagine the past and the future has everything to do with how we imagine political rights and responsibilities in the present. My experiment in speculative archaeology that opened this chapter is a natural impulse for someone who has lived through catastrophe. Your temporal horizons expand; your political sensibilities sharpen.

Temporal politics often get expressed through monuments and ruins. As one journalist quipped, the main landfill is "an accidental monument to Katrina" (Curtis 2006). A second landfill, located down the road, was more short-lived but fascinating as a political artifact. In fact, although few people venture out to the abject part of town where both are located, these two mounds are the only significant monuments to the storm that will likely survive long into the future. The history and ethnography of landfills in and around New Orleans, and many other metropolitan areas, could be a fascinating book-length study unto itself, as has been demonstrated by Robin Nagle's (2013) lively study of the New York City Sanitation Department. But I will try to curb my enthusiasm and give you the short story here, which involves three landfills with different trajectories over the course of 113 years.

Since 1906, when the Agriculture Street Landfill first opened, New Orleans has directed its waste to the swampy and generally low-value land along its eastern and northeastern boundaries. As the city grew, the landfills moved further northeast but were never detached from residential neighborhoods, although they were usually poor ones. The Agriculture Street landfill in the Upper Ninth Ward took in the city's refuse up through the early 1950s (of note for the future archaeologist: this means that most of the landfill dates to the period just before the widespread adoption of disposable plastics). It often smoldered and caught fire, earning the local nickname "Dante's Inferno." In 1965 Hurricane Betsy, the last major storm to make a direct hit on the city before Katrina, caused the landfill to be reopened to take in demolition debris. While household and industrial toxins were undoubtedly present in the landfill prior to Betsy, local perception is that the weight of the disaster debris exacerbated seepage. Despite its hellish reputation, the city's mayor encouraged development over the site after it was closed in the late 1970s. A public housing development, a school, and dozens of businesses were built and hundreds of new houses were made available to qualifying first-time buyers (largely African American) to become part of the Press Park neighborhood. Due to bioturbation and the movement caused by methane and other gases, within a few years, residents were finding trash literally bubbling up to the surface. They became concerned about lead and arsenic levels affecting children and a suspiciously high breast cancer rate in the area. By 1994 the former Agricultural Street Landfill had been designated a Superfund site—a federal designation meaning that the Environmental Protection Agency has ordered the site be cleaned up and remediated. It remains the only Superfund site in the city limits. Katrina put a stop to the slow cleanup and repair of the neighborhood. It is now mostly a ghost town of abandoned brick ranch houses and strip malls.

In the 1950s municipal trash disposal turned more intensively to incineration (in hindsight, a shortsighted move that essentially puts our trash into our lungs and into the overheating atmosphere). According to city records, the city's second official landfill opened around 1960 in an effort to move the nuisance business further east. The Old Gentilly Landfill was named after a colonial road of the same name, but in archaeological anticipation, one reporter after Katrina rather humorously referred to it as an "ancient dump" (Roig-Franzia 2005). This landfill operated until 1985, taking in all manner of household trash and debris. In 1985, it was closed and capped with clay, and the city's trash started to be exported to a neighboring suburb. Still squatting on over one hundred acres in a part of the city made undesirable by industrial canals, salvage yards, illegal dumping, and even an indigent cemetery that receives the remains of the city morgue's unclaimed dead (sadly also referred to as a type of "disposal"), the Old Gentilly Landfill was reopened immediately after Katrina, in September 2005. Using his emergency powers, the mayor bypassed environmental regulations to reopen it and, at the same time and in the same extrajudicial manner, approved opening a brand-new landfill down the road, at the extreme eastern end of the city near a coffee roasting plant and a shuttered factory for the US space shuttle.

This new site for a third city landfill also abutted the Bayou Sauvage Wildlife Refuge. At twenty-three thousand acres, it is the largest urban wildlife area in the United States and home to alligators, white-tailed deer, and tens of thousands of water birds and ducks. The Chef Menteur ("chief liar") Landfill opened in April 2006 amid ongoing controversy and resistance not only from the neighboring Vietnamese and African American communities (Chiang 2009), who created a new political alliance for this purpose, but from several local, state, and national environmental groups (Eaton 2006; Hau 2014). Even the US Fish and Wildlife Service became involved, going on record to state that the landfill should not be used without a liner installed to prevent seepage into the wildlife refuge and nearby waterways. Opposition was so fierce that the landfill was closed and capped in August 2006, less than five months after it opened.

The controversy over Chef Menteur at first overshadowed any objections to the re-opening of the older Old Gentilly Landfill, which had been authorized by the Federal Emergency Management Agency (FEMA) to accept a staggering one hundred thousand cubic yards of disaster waste *per day*. At first this landfill took in the vast majority of the debris from post-Katrina cleanup. But waste is big business. FEMA paid out over $130 million in "tipping fees" (an obscure term for the fee paid to accept waste—measured per ton, truckload, or large item) for the New Orleans metro area. Of that, $60 million went to the owners of the Old Gentilly Landfill. But competition was fierce and through political maneuvers that involved not only lobbying but allegedly bribes, owners of two competing landfills located well outside the city limits in Jefferson Parish successfully diverted some of this business. Meanwhile, the city of New Orleans received a 3 percent "royalty" (actual language) on these tipping fees, because it was presumed to be the owner of the land on which the main dump sits, though not its operator. Nevertheless, this was a political kickback (since the city itself made the licensing and tonnage limit decisions) that the US Congress, with the help of the FBI, later decided was "inappropriate" and possibly illegal (Hadley to Stark, Office of the Inspector General, 15 December 2006). The corrupt world of trash disposal was starting to be exposed to public view. Almost overnight, southeastern Louisiana landfill operators developed a keen interest in public policy.

After Katrina, several of them became major campaign donors to politicians at the city, state, and federal levels. The Jefferson Parish landfill operators also became concerned environmentalists, throwing their weight into the movement to close the competing Chef Menteur Landfill (*Times Picayune* 2011; Russell 2015b).

From there, the politics become even more twisted. It turns out that up to 80 percent of the land upon which the Old Gentilly Landfill sat was actually owned not by the city, but by hundreds of private landowners who had been duped in a land speculation scheme decades earlier. As with the Agricultural Street Landfill, there were once plans for a future housing development to be built on the trash-filled site that would be called "Flowerdale." These landowners had speculated and lost. Still, they held deeds to a mountain of garbage. Through a class action lawsuit, it was found that the city owed them $8 million if it wanted clear title to the land, a suit that was not settled until 2015 (Russell 2015a).

Disaster Debris

These political and economic vectors in the taphonomy of disaster debris provide a snapshot of the high-stakes interests and conflicts that contribute to a landfill and/or a mass disaster deposit. But let me now turn briefly to a description of the material process, as we know it so far. The formation processes, of course, will continue as the Old Gentilly Landfill settles and ages. The site, although reopened under emergency measures to receive disaster debris, has now once again reverted to taking construction debris. On a visit I made in August 2018, the supervisor directed me to the sector of the site where they were currently depositing new loads daily—directly over Katrina debris, which is such a massive deposit that it still lies exposed ten years after the first phase of major cleanup was completed. He said it is about 80 percent covered over at the moment and that it will take them probably another two years before they have completed the new stratum of regular trash over the hundred-acre site. I observed oversized bulldozers grinding and spreading the new deposits evenly over the new sector. This means is that it will take twelve years to cover over a much thicker deposit that, essentially, is a snapshot of one day in the life of a city—29 August 2005.

Going back to that period, within a few weeks of the storm, the enormity of the task at hand was starting to sink in, even before the floodwaters had receded. To quote one FEMA official speaking in mid-September of 2005, "The Hurricane Katrina cleanup represents the biggest waste-disposal job in U.S. history, dwarfing in volume the debris carted off after the World Trade Center's twin towers fell in 2001" (Associated Press 2005). This early coverage claimed that house debris (e.g., lumber, vinyl siding, damaged furniture and belongings) would be separated from dangerous household chemicals and AC units with coolant. Plastic and metal would be recycled, and trees would be would chipped for landscaping.

This was a very optimistic projection. In reality, very little sorting (perhaps 20 percent) was accomplished on storm debris due to the overwhelming scale of the task, labor shortages, and the fact that local salvaging and recycling facilities were themselves wiped out by the storm. Add to this the reality that waterlogged houses quickly became rusting and rotting amalgams of mixed household chemicals, personal effects, appliances, and building materials and it becomes understandable how so much debris was simply dumped as waste rather than sorted and recycled. That said, a bit later in the cleanup process (2007–11), when vehicles, industrial appliances, and larger concrete and rebar buildings were salvaged, materials were not only separated but put on barges and ships bound for places as far away as India for recycling in a little-documented international trade in demolition debris (Hazal Corak, personal communication 2018). Dealers found, however, that the Katrina debris was either so rusted or mixed that it was unsalvageable and not worth their time or the already expended transport cost. Somewhere on the other side of the planet, archaeologists of the future may become quite confused by massive piles of cars with Louisiana license plates. Although Hurricane Katrina is now tied with Harvey (August 2017) as the costliest US hurricane, in terms of storm debris it still breaks all records. Landfills in southeastern Louisiana received an estimated thirty-eight million cubic tons, while in Houston collection is estimated to come in around eight million (Niiler 2017).

A congressional report on Katrina prepared in April 2008 describes the content and challenges of disaster debris, in an effort to explain why cleanup was not yet complete two and a half years after the storm and why more funds were needed for the job:

> Hurricane Katrina is also unique because of the type of waste generated. Generally, "disaster debris" includes waste materials created as the result of a man-made or natural disaster, such as an earthquake, flood, hurricane, or terrorist attack. Debris created from flooding is often quite different from debris created from an earthquake or storm. Disaster debris from Hurricane Katrina involves two types of waste—waste generated immediately during and after the storm (e.g., from high winds and flooding related to rainfall and coastal storm surge) and extensive flooding related to the levee failure in New Orleans (resulting in deep flood waters that left some areas submerged for weeks).
>
> The primary types of disaster debris being removed in the wake of Hurricane Katrina fall into the following categories: Municipal solid waste—general household

> trash and personal belongings. Construction and demolition (C&D) debris—building materials (which may include asbestos-containing materials), drywall, lumber, carpet, furniture, mattresses, plumbing. Vegetative debris—trees, branches, shrubs, and logs. Household hazardous waste—oil, pesticides, paints, cleaning agents. White goods—refrigerators, freezers, washers, dryers, stoves, water heaters, dishwashers, air conditioners. Electronic waste—computers, televisions, printers, stereos, DVD players, telephones. (Luther 2008, 3)

In addition, the report notes that the Corps of Engineers (the federal agency responsible for overseeing debris removal) had removed thirty-six million pounds of rotting meat, besides other "putrescibles" (a waste industry term for organic matter subject to putrefaction, generally food, animal carcasses, and excrement); 350,000 damaged automobiles and trucks and 60,000 abandoned and damaged watercraft (e.g., boats, barges) had also been picked up (Luther 2008, 4). It is from this report that we learn that the Old Gentilly Landfill, once it hits approved capacity, will reach a height of eighty feet (twenty-four meters) in a landscape where the highest natural point is three meters. We also learn that "another complicating factor is the potential presence of human remains in some of the destroyed homes. As a result, canine search teams must search debris before it is removed. Also, demolition teams must use excavators to remove the homes in layers instead of 'bulldozing' them to prevent any human remains from being lost" (Luther 2008, 16).

By now it should be clear that my opening fictional account of archaeologists exploring the mound culture of twenty-first-century Louisiana is not all that fictional after all. Having moved from speculation to the facts of Katrina debris, I will now present some broader theoretical considerations for the politics of disaster debris.

Theoretical Considerations

In terms of the politics of garbage, the Katrina disaster was used at first to impose a what philosopher Giorgio Agamben (2005) calls a "state of exception," when executive or military orders override the rule of law. FEMA and the mayor bent the already weak rules for recycling and separation of consumer waste in the United States in order to open and operate the Katrina landfills. A month after the storm, Chuck Carr Brown, the Louisiana state official responsible for landfill regulation, "bristled at the notion that residents, who approved a bond measure to clean up the site, might complain once they return and find it reopened. 'What taxpayers?' he said. 'They're all displaced. I don't think anybody's worried about garbage'" (Roig-Franzia 2005). As he and the soon-embattled mayor were to find out, however, when the taxpayers returned they *did* care about "garbage"—an inadequate term for the collapsed remnants of their lives, and even their loved ones, as well as the chemical residue of the present that they anticipated would seep into the future. In a creepy echo of the too frequently expressed sentiments of the American gun lobby, members of the country's major waste professional association noted their sympathy for those affected by a tragedy from which they would profit hundreds of millions of dollars: "The thoughts and prayers of the members of the Solid Waste Association of North America are with those who have been impacted by Hurricane Katrina" (SWANA 2005, 1).

Bill Rathje's decades-long archaeological study of garbage and landfills that came to be called "garbology" started in Tucson, Arizona, and later expanded to the site of the Fresh Kills Landfill on New York's Staten Island. The project ran from the 1970s through the 1990s, focused not only on the content of US landfills (and thus was taken to be a mirror of what Americans actually consumed, as opposed to what they *said* they consumed), but on taphonomic processes (Rathje and Cullen 2001). His work was pathbreaking and is considered to be a pioneering effort in the archaeology of the contemporary world, the sub-branch of archaeology in which I have been immersed for the last few years. One of Rathje's key findings was that due to the rapid burial of artifacts in landfills, their microenvironment was relatively anaerobic, and biodegradation (or decay through microorganisms and fungi) happens at a much slower rate than previously assumed. Another major finding was that landfills produce a toxic slurry (or leachate) that seeps out at their base and borders. While Rathje was interested in the contents of landfills as middens of contemporary life, he was equally interested in what happens to the organic and inorganic material amassed in these huge man-made features. His study has had significant effects in the world of waste management and remains one of the most significant cases of archaeology applied to contemporary problems.

Rathje's general approach helps me think through the various phases of US consumer culture reflected in what we know of New Orleans's landfills—from the largely pre-plastic Agricultural Street Landfill (Rathje found that plastics account for 20–24 percent of disposables in the 1970s) to the verifiable environmental concerns about toxic sludge leaching into bordering neighborhoods and wildlife habitats. The alarms raised by the Versailles community living adjacent to the short-lived Chef Menteur Landfill were reasonable and valid. However, when considered comparatively, I can also see how the Katrina landfills stand out as exceptional. Rathje presumed that landfills are in some sense total, typical, and *normative* samples of consumer behavior. Although he and his students might have discerned small trash disposal events (akin to basketloads of soil seen in Mississippian mound profiles), he shared the widely held archaeological assumption that most trash deposits and middens are accumulations of small events that are largely inconsequential by themselves but, amassed and analyzed, can hold up a mirror to lived life. Still, the human behaviors so interpreted were thought to be largely unconscious and not intentionally political. But as the Katrina landfills demonstrate, large disposal features can be reflections of mass disruptions and exceptional events. Some trash deposits are formed through processes that are not only conscious but highly charged, both emotionally and politically. While admittedly it would be difficult to get at the political intrigues that accompanied the Katrina landfills through archaeology alone, the sudden starts and stops and the efforts to seal the site will be stratigraphically quite clear to future archaeologists, as will the short life and abandonment of the Chef Menteur Landfill. It is not so much of a stretch, I would argue, to interpret these deliberate efforts to manage a massive amount of trash in a short period of time as an archaeological signature of major political events in the wake of disaster. In short, I want to argue for putting considerations of political processes into garbology.

One of the most intriguing, but underdeveloped, implications of Rathje's work is the agency of these assemblages. Toxins, in particular, have been a locus of recent anthropological concerns in object ontology. In Jane Bennett's (2010) work, we find an opening through which to consider the politics of taphonomy, and of landfills. She asks, "How would political responses to public problems change were we to take seriously the vitality of (nonhuman) bodies?" (Bennett 2010, viii). I would argue, and hope that I have demonstrated, that in fact many New Orleans residents *already* take the politics of nonhuman bodies quite seriously. I have often thought that object ontologists have simply been catching up with how most people think about and interact with the world in the first place. Although they may not have a developed philosophy about the agentive capacity of the nonhuman or the status of the subject-object divide that Western scholarship has been fretting about since at least the Greek skeptics, they take object agency seriously enough to feel threatened by materials. And they know that objects are political—that lawsuits, bribes, lobbying, and regulation can mitigate, or exacerbate, the more dangerous agentive capacity of objects.

Within the broad swath of Bennett's version of actor-network theory (Latour 2005), she lobs a specific cultural critique that also feels quite relevant here. She says, "It hit me in a visceral way how American materialism, which requires buying ever-increasing numbers of products purchased in ever-shorter cycles, is *anti*materiality. The sheer volume of commodities, and the hyperconsumptive necessity of junking them to make room for new ones, conceals the vitality of matter" (Bennett 2010, 5). She is onto something, but this concealing function requires a concealing of waste, in which the vitality of matter is scattered, crushed, and compacted into a potent but never inert mass. It is a concentrate of vitality. This operation of concealment is itself a form of labor. To quote Robin Nagle, the ethnographer of New York City trash, "Garbage is itself the great unmarked and purposely unseen result of a lushly consumptive economy and culture. The work is further unmarked and unseen because it exists along both physical and cognitive edges" (Nagle 2013, 22). One of the many ways in which disaster debris in a modern context is exceptional is that the tremendous volume, redundancy, wealth, and waste of this consumer society could not be concealed—it lay scattered like a moldering rat's feast across the breadth of the city for not just months, but years.

As archaeologist Bjørnar Olsen observes, "Since the nineteenth century, mass production, consumerism, and thus cycles of material replacement have accelerated; increasingly larger amounts of things are, with increasing rapidity, victimized and made redundant. At the same time processes of destruction have immensely intensified" (Olsen 2010, 168–69). Olsen is among several historical archaeologists who have noted that one of the challenges of doing archaeology of the modern period is the sheer volume of material presented for analysis.

While not as visually arresting as Pompeii, the Katrina landfills do come close to representing an exact moment on 29 August 2005. It is just that they are chewed and churned up. In doing an archaeology of modernity, and especially of supermodernity (González-Ruibal 2008), we need to pull away from the artifacts as signs and instead go immediately to the levels of the assemblage and the feature. While the fact of the sheer volume, mass, and standardization of artifacts will be an important datum to archaeologists of the future, what may be more revelatory is close attention to how this predestined trash—this massive collection of material—was collected, concentrated, and managed over the long term and through short-term intensive events. And many of these events are irrefutably political. Once we recognize this, efforts to separate the human and the nonhuman and privilege object agency do not make a lot of sense. Like the very mixture of human remains with household trash that the Katrina landfills contain, I suggest that it would be better to consider the human and nonhuman as a co-formed, constantly shifting assemblage (see also Dawdy 2016b).

My effort here has been to shift attention from the acute failures of George W. Bush and his military men that resulted in thousands of preventable deaths to the formational processes of Mayor Nagin and his business pals, which were no less political but where the stakes revolved around the reconstitution of the local landscape. In her effort to bring out the political life of vital matter, Bennett adopts Dewey's notion of a public: "A public does not pre-exist its particular problem but merges in response to it. A public is a contingent and temporary formation existing alongside many other publics, protopublics, and residual or postpublics" (Bennett 2010, 100). As we saw in the brief political histories of the Katrina landfills, publics formed around the problem of disaster debris—the newly empowered Vietnamese community (whose voter registration rate has soared since the threat of the Chef Menteur Landfill), as well as a coalition of environmentalists, political lobbyists for competing waste management companies, and a residual public from the Agricultural Street Superfund lawsuit. In what ways might it be helpful to conceive of disaster management and waste disposal as a problem that activates a contingent public—in the deep past, in the present, and in the future? What sort of publics were activated in the cleanup after the earthquakes on Santorini and Crete (Driessen 2001), in the forced migrations after the 536 CE climate event in northern Europe (see chapter 4 in this volume), or after the trauma of major volcanic eruptions on New Britain Island (see chapter 5 in this volume)? What problems were people trying to solve in the aftermath of disaster? What possible publics might have been summoned into existence by these problems?

The correlation between political crisis and disaster is a thick vein in the archaeological literature. As Sheets and Cooper (2012, 8) state, "Populations can be quick to apportion blame and can quickly change their allegiance should they feel failed by a social or religious elite in the face of an environmental hazard." Indeed, many have attributed the Obama election win of 2008 to the spectacular failure of George W. Bush's administration to adequately respond to Hurricane Katrina and its aftermath. And former mayor Nagin, who was responsible for the backroom deals over disaster debris kickbacks, is currently serving out a federal sentence on twenty-one corruption charges at a Texarkana work camp, without possibility of parole until 2023. While a hazard may be experienced in the short term, its reverberations through the debris it creates may have social effects for generations. Many scholars today are bringing attention to processes of slow violence (see chapter 14 in this volume). When it comes to the environmental impacts of debris clearance and concealment of social failures, we should also talk about slow politics. It is not so much that political actors miscalculate the consequences of their actions, it is that some may deliberately attempt to defer them into a distant, hazy future, while others are motivated by a very clear vision of what waits on the horizon. My effort to imagine the long-term future of New Orleans is itself a kind of political resistance to the veil of irresponsibility. Only when we can see the long-term consequences of today's political actions can we be empowered to redirect the slow politics of climate change.

Acknowledgments

I am grateful to Felix Riede and Payson Sheets for the invitation to return to disaster studies in a time when we all need to feel that our work matters in a world at risk. This sense of mattering deepened with an invitation to polish the work and present it to a broader audience through the Center for Translating Research into Practice at Indiana University–Purdue University Indianapolis, and I am grateful to colleagues there for their hospitality. In terms of thanks with a deeper history, I want to recognize James Crouch and other colleagues at FEMA for their expertise and camaraderie back in the worst days of Katrina triage. More recently, I am indebted to my son, Asa McNaughton, for his patience in accompanying me one time too many to the landfill. This work was made possible by the Lichtstern Fund of the Department of Anthropology, University of Chicago.

Shannon Lee Dawdy's fieldwork combines archival, ethnographic, and archaeological methods with a regional focus on the coastal communities of the United States, Caribbean, and Mexico. She is the author of *Building the Devil's Empire: French Colonial New Orleans* (2008), *Patina: A Profane Archaeology* (2016), and *American After-Life* (forthcoming). Her current work focuses on climate change and futurities.

References

Agamben, Giorgio. 2005. *State of Exception*. Translated by Kevin Attell. Chicago: University of Chicago Press.

Associated Press. 2005. "Where Will Garbage from Katrina Cleanup Go? Katrina Recovery Represents Biggest Waste-Disposal Job in U.S. History." *NBC News*, 19 September. Retrieved 2 April 2018 from http://www.nbcnews.com/id/9375252/ns/us_news-katrina_the_long_road_back/t/where-will-garbage-katrina-cleanup-go/#.WsKZDsgh3jA.

Bacigalupi, Paolo. 2010. *Ship Breaker*. New York: Little, Brown.

Bennett, Jane. 2010. *Vibrant Matter: A Political Ecology of Things*. Durham, NC: Duke University Press.

Chiang, S. Leo, dir. 2009. *A Village Called Versailles*. Walking Iris Films.

Curtis, Wayne. 2006. "A Controversial New Orleans Landfill Is Set to Close, but Eco-disaster Still Looms," *Grist*, 11 August. Retrieved 2 April 2018 from https://grist.org/article/curtis/.

Dawdy, Shannon Lee. 2006. "The Taphonomy of Disaster and the (Re)Formation of New Orleans." *American Anthropologist* 108 (4): 719–30.
———. 2016a. *Patina: A Profane Archaeology*. Chicago: University of Chicago Press.
———. 2016b. "Profane Archaeology and the Existential Dialectics of the City. *Journal of Social Archaeology* 16 (1): 32–55.
Driessen, Jan. 2001. "Crisis Cults on Minoan Crete?" In *Potnia: Deities and Religion in the Aegean Bronze Age. Proceedings of the 8th International Aegean Conference, Göteborg, 12–15 April 2000*, edited by Robert Laffineur and Robin Hägg, 361–9. Liège: Université de Liège.
Eaton, Leslie. 2006. "A New Landfill in New Orleans Sets Off Battle." *New York Times*, 8 May. Retrieved 2 April 2018 from https://www.nytimes.com/2006/05/08/us/08landfill.html.
González-Ruibal, Alfredo. 2008. "Time to Destroy: An Archaeology of Supermodernity." *Current Anthropology* 49 (2): 247–79.
Gould, Richard A. 2007. *Disaster Archaeology*. Salt Lake City: University of Utah Press.
Hadley, Tonda L. 2006. "Congressional Inquiry, Landfill Cost Issues Related to Disposal of Debris in the City of New Orleans Report Number DD-0703." Homeland Security, U.S. Office of Inspector General, Hadley to Stark, memorandum of 15 December 2006.
Hau, Vanessa. 2014. "Standing Up for the Vietnamese Community of New Orleans." *Citylab*, 27 October. Retrieved 2 April 2018 from https://www.citylab.com/environment/2014/10/standing-up-for-the-vietnamese-community-of-new-orleans/381865/.
Latour, Bruno. 2005. *Reassembling the Social: An Introduction to Actor-Network-Theory*. Oxford: Oxford University Press.
Luther, Linda. 2008. "Disaster Debris Removal After Hurricane Katrina: Status and Associated Issues." CRS Report for Congress, updated 2 April.
Nagle, Robin. 2013. *Picking Up on the Streets and behind the Trucks with the Sanitation Workers of New York City*. New York: Farrar, Straus and Giroux.
Niiler, Eric. 2017. "Where Do They Put All That Toxic Hurricane Debris?" *Wired*, 17 September. Retrieved 2 April 2017 from https://www.wired.com/story/where-do-they-put-all-that-toxic-hurricane-debris/.
Olsen, Bjørnar, 2010. *In Defense of Things: Archaeology and the Ontology of Objects*. Plymouth, UK: Altamira Press.
Rathje, William, and Cullen Murphy. 2001. *Rubbish! The Archaeology of Garbage*. Tucson: University of Arizona Press.
Roig-Franzia, Manuel. 2005. "Hurricane Bands Landfill Rules." *Washington Post*, 29 October. Retrieved 2 April 2018 from http://www.washingtonpost.com/wp-dyn/content/article/2005/10/29/AR2005102900939.html.
Russell, Gordon. 2015a. "City of N.O., Landfill Operators Settle Lawsuit with Land's Real Owners." *New Orleans Advocate*, 26 January. Retrieved 2 April 2015 from http://www.theadvocate.com/new_orleans/news/article_b1693e74-6768-5c53-89bb-eaf5566820b9.html.
———. 2015b. "Hurricane Katrina Was a Bonanza for Local Landfills, and River Birth Fought to Get Every Scrap of Debris." *Nola.com*, 24 February. Retrieved 2 April 2015 from http://www.nola.com/politics/index.ssf/2012/09/hurricane_katrina_was_a_bonanz.html.
Schiffer, Michael B. 1983. "Toward the Identification of Formation Processes." *American Antiquity* 48 (4): 675–706.

Sheets, Payson, and Jago Cooper. 2012. *Learning to Live with the Dangers of Sudden Environmental Change*. Boulder: University Press of Colorado.

SWANA (Solid Waste Association of North America). 2005. "Hurricane Katrina Disaster Debris Management: Lessons Learned from State and Local Governments." Briefing report, December.

Times Picayune. 2011. "Hurricane Katrina Pushed Landfill Business into Overdrive." *Times Picayune*, 20 March. Retrieved 2 April 2018 from http://www.nola.com/katrina/index.ssf/2011/03/hurricane_katrina_pushed_landf.html.

CHAPTER 10

Catastrophe and Collapse in the Late Pre-Hispanic Andes

Responding for Half a Millennium to Political Fragmentation and Climate Stress

NICOLA SHARRATT

Summary for Stakeholders

Unlike earthquakes, hurricanes, or volcanic eruptions, which bring sudden devastation to communities, drought can last for decades, even centuries, and impact multiple generations of people in an affected region. Because archaeology is particularly suited to documenting human behavior over long time periods, archaeological case studies of drought in the past are especially relevant sources of data to policy makers in the present. Specifically, they provide an opportunity to examine not only the long-term impacts of drought but also how people responded to challenging subsistence conditions and, critically, to identify responses that have been successful in building resilient communities.

Beginning around 1000 CE, the south-central Andes, which today includes areas of Peru, Bolivia, Chile, and Argentina, experienced a drought that lasted for several hundred years and was punctuated by episodes of particularly severe conditions. Notably, the communities who lived through this drought had to adapt not only to environmental difficulties but also to radical political changes following the collapse of the Tiwanaku state, which had dominated for the previous five hundred years.

This chapter explores how communities were impacted by and reacted to both drought and political instability in the region. By drawing on archaeological evidence that spans 1000 CE to almost 1500 CE, it describes how communities initially chose to respond to subsistence stress by building local networks through which resources were exchanged and by developing relationships between villages through collective gatherings. I argue that by doing this, communities essentially maintained peace. However, circa 1250 CE, those practices of exchange and interaction were abandoned, and in their wake, hostilities developed between villages.

I propose that the findings of this archaeological case study offer three lessons relevant to policy makers concerned with the impact of climate catastrophe in the present. First, developing connections between communities can be critically effective in mitigating disruption to resource access and so alleviate subsistence difficulties. Second, participation in intercommunity networks must be equitable or mechanisms of interconnectivity risk becoming sources of inequality. Third, social practices that promote solidarity between people can enhance policies that facilitate resource exchange.

Introduction

Accelerated glacial melt constitutes a very real and urgent danger to communities in Andean South America, one with potentially catastrophic impacts on subsistence practices (Brown 2017; Casey 2016, 2017: Fraser 2009; Kozhikkodan Veettil and Florêncio de Souza 2017). While current human-driven rapid climate change risks calamity in the Andes, societies in this region, which is characterized by significant ecological variability, climatic extremes, and recurrent episodes of catastrophic weather events (see chapter 13 in this volume), have been impacted by and responding to uncertain and shifting environmental conditions for millennia (illustrations 10.1a–d). As such, diachronic archaeological data from Andean South America offer opportunity to examine successful and unsuccessful human responses to severe climatic stress.

Given the centrality of irrigation and hydraulic management technologies in the development and maintenance of agricultural systems in Andean South America, the connection between significant changes in precipitation and sociopolitical transformation is a recurrent theme in the archaeology of the region, as it is in many global contexts (Dillehay and Kolata 2004; Shimada et al. 1991; Weiss 2017a, 2017b: Weiss and Bradley 2001; Weiss et al. 1993). The relationship between environmental conditions and the political rise and decline of the Tiwanaku polity, one of the earliest expansive states in Andean South America, has been subject to particular debate (figure 10.1). Discussion focuses especially on the role that drought played in the state's political fragmentation, a process that is archaeologically visible beginning around 1000 CE (Abbott et al. 1997; Binford et al. 1997; Erickson 1993, 1999; Kolata et al. 2000, Kolata and Ortloff

a b c d

Illustrations 10.1a–d. Environmental diversity of Andean South America showing mountainous sierra (a), arid Pacific coast (b), high-altitude plains (c), and fertile river valleys (d). Author's images.

2003; Ortloff and Kolata 1993; Thompson and Kolata 2017; Thompson et al. 1985; Thompson et al. 1986; P. Williams 2002, 2006).

This chapter seeks neither to participate in these debates nor to diminish their significance. Instead, it presents a detailed, local, and diachronic perspective on the aftermath of Tiwanaku decline. It is clear that whatever the role of drought in causing radical sociopolitical change in the south-central Andes circa 1000 CE, the region was characterized by more arid, challenging subsistence conditions for the following five hundred years (Thompson and Kolata 2017). This chapter draws on extensive excavation data from the Moquegua Valley, one of the Tiwanaku state's largest and most significant provinces before collapse. Reconstructing how communities were impacted and how they responded to both changes in regional sociopolitical organization and enduring climate change, I describe two distinct phases. The first (called the Tumilaca phase) dates to the first two to three hundred years after Tiwanaku political decline. These centuries are characterized by considerable maintenance of past practices but also by evidence for the emergence of local exchange networks and intercommunity ceremonial activities, which served to integrate communities across the valley. Although there are clear indicators that in a number of ways life became more challenging for Moquegua Valley inhabitants after the collapse of the Tiwanaku state and the onset of increasingly arid subsistence conditions, there is little evidence for conflict within the valley. The second phase (the Estuquiña phase) begins in the mid-thirteenth century CE and is distinguished by complete rejection of Tiwanaku materials but also by isolated, nucleated, defensive communities. Newly generated bio-distance data (Sharratt and Sutter 2018) indicate that this alteration in the local sociopolitical landscape was not a consequence of incursion by outsiders but instead a reorientation of intercommunity relationships.

Situating these data in published paleoclimatic reconstructions (Abbott et al. 1997; Thompson and Kolata 2017) and in recent refinements to the Moquegua Valley's chronology (Sharratt 2019), I make the case that the ultimate abandonment of integrative economic and ritual practices during the Tumilaca phase made communities especially vulnerable to decades of particularly severe drought, which began around 1250 CE and exacerbated tensions within and between communities. In diachronically reconstructing responses to enduring climate and political change, this analysis of a case study from the late pre-Hispanic southern Andes has three implications for policy makers concerned with fostering effective responses for and by communities impacted by climate catastrophe in the present. First, in agreement with other contributions to this volume, the emergence of local exchange networks in the initial Tumilaca phase indicates that interconnectivity can promote resilience. Second, evidence that access to exchange networks was shared across communities suggests that equitable

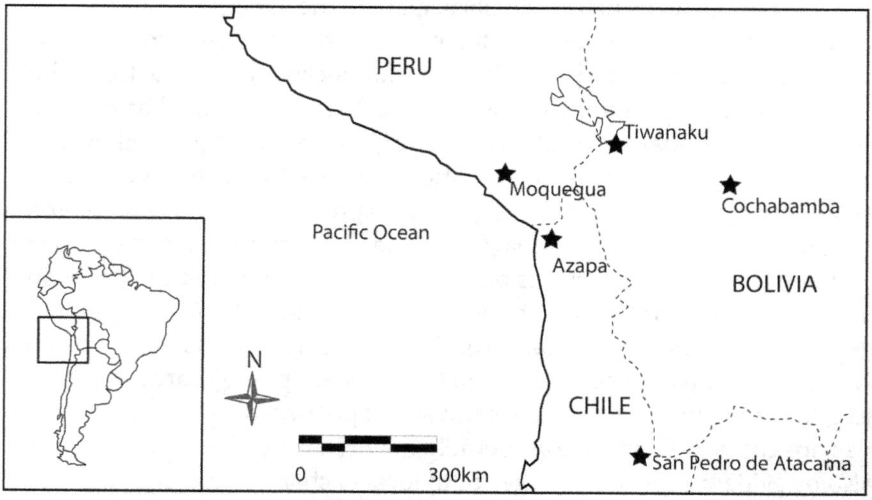

Figure 10.1. The south-central Andes showing location of the city of Tiwanaku and the state's principal provinces. Author's image.

participation in mechanisms of interconnectivity is important in avoiding the possibility that post-disaster responses become a source for tension. Finally, while developing systems of interconnectivity may primarily be motivated by the need to alleviate subsistence challenges, these systems will be strengthened by policies and institutions that also foster collective identity and solidarity between people.

The Tiwanaku

Although now recognized by many Andean archaeologists as an expansive state that exerted political, religious, and economic influence across large areas of the south-central Andes (Stanish 2013), the Tiwanaku polity confused a number of nineteenth-century European travelers who encountered the ceremonial core of the state's urban capital. The city of Tiwanaku is located at 3,800 meters above sea level, close to the shores of Lake Titicaca in the altiplano. This region of high-altitude, windswept, and arid plains, which span parts of both modern western Bolivia and southern Peru and where temperatures fall below freezing as much as twenty-five nights per month, is today one of the most impoverished areas of South America. European scholars and visitors expressed disbelief that anyone should live in the altiplano, let alone that a major expansive state could have developed there. These skeptics proposed outlandish alternative explanations for the presence of monumental architecture and elaborate carved monoliths (Janusek 2004b; Posnansky 1945; Posnansky 1912; Squier 1877; Vranich 2013).

Yet, extensive research over the past century reveals that Tiwanaku became the dominant polity in this tough physical setting around 300–400 CE (Bandy 2001, 2013; Janusek 2008; Levine et al. 2013; Stanish 2003). Between 400 and 800 CE, extensive construction in the urban core of the state's capital, also called Tiwanaku, produced a ritual landscape of monuments, many of which remain partially standing today (Isbell 2013; Janusek 2004a; Vranich 2001, 2006; Yaeger and Vranich 2013). Ceremonial spaces at Tiwanaku were vertically and horizontally expansive, incorporating pyramids and plazas, defined and connected by passageways and carved portals. These established the site as a symbolically potent center, which surrounding and distant communities referenced in the creation of their own ritual spaces (Goldstein 1993b; Goldstein and Sitek 2018).

Residential neighborhoods at Tiwanaku stretched over four to six square kilometers (Koons 2013) and were characterized by significant economic disparity. Palatial elite residences were located in the monumental core of the city and distinguished by elaborate architectural features as well as high status and imported goods (Couture and Sampeck 2003). The majority of the city's twenty thousand residents lived in neighborhoods further out from the core. These comprised large walled compounds that shared ceremonial space (Janusek 2008). In neighborhoods on the outskirts of the city, houses were small, rustic, and made of adobe, and crude wares dominate excavated ceramic assemblages. Tiwanaku's "middle class" lived closer to the urban center in houses made from field stones (Couture 2003; Janusek 1999, 2002; Rivera Casanovas 2003).

In the city's hinterland, a four-tier settlement hierarchy was arguably connected to state-sponsored agricultural production, which relied on raised field systems (Albarracin-Jordan 1996, Albarracin-Jordan and Mathews 1990; Bandy 2001; Janusek and Kolata 2003; McAndrews, Albarracin-Jordan, and Bermann 1997). These fields mitigate the effects of both aridity and cold by facilitating the movement of water through troughs and by protecting crops from nighttime temperatures, which can reach as low as -10°C in the dry winter months of June through August (Binford and Kolata 1996; Erickson 1993). Both the degree to which these fields were under state control and the impact of climate change on their use are central to ongoing debates about the role of drought in the state's political decline (Erickson 1999; Kolata et al. 2000).

From 800 CE, the Tiwanaku state extended its influence into ecologically diverse places across the south-central Andes (figure 10.1). This expansion was likely motivated at least in part by desire for access to resources, especially maize and coca leaves, that are exotic to the altiplano. In some regions, such as northern Chile, expansion was facilitated by consolidating existing connections with local elites, while in others, including Cochabamba in lowland Bolivia and the Moquegua Valley in southern Peru, by establishing colonies of altiplano people (Anderson 2013; Blom et al. 1998; Goldstein 2005, 2009, 2013; Stovel 2001; Torres-Rouff 2008; Torres-Rouff and Hubbe 2013). The Tiwanaku inhabitants of those provinces asserted their affiliation with the state heartland through the consumption and representation of resources and products derived from the altiplano, over time crafting regional variants of Tiwanaku styles, variants that in turn appear in specific neighborhoods of the city of Tiwanaku as people moved around the growing Tiwanaku realm (Janusek 2008; Kolata 1993; Rivera Casanovas 2003).

Around 1000 CE, this political, economic, and cultural network across the south-central Andes began to fragment (Augustyniak 2004; Janusek 2004a, 2005; Sharratt 2019; P. Williams 2002) in a manner illustrative of Conlee's definition of state collapse as "the process in which the political system breaks down and society becomes organized on a less complex scale" (Conlee 2006, 99). In the south-central Andes, this process of collapse was drawn out. In both the state heartland and the provinces, it included a decline in monumental construction, destruction of palatial structures, episodes of violence targeted against elite tombs and monuments, abandonment of urban cores, and radical alterations in settlement patters as populations dispersed and formed smaller communities (Albarracin-Jordan 1996; Bandy 2001; Bermann et al. 1989; Couture and Sampeck 2003; Goldstein 2005; Janusek 2004a; Owen 2005; Vranich 2006).

Alterations in sociopolitical organization were long-lasting. State authority was not reinstituted in the south-central Andes until the fourteenth to fifteenth centuries, during Inca imperial incursion into the region. The intervening four centuries were characterized by a mosaic of local polities, turbulence, and increasing violence (Arkush 2005, 2006, 2008, 2011; Covey 2008; Kurin 2016; Tung 2008). In the altiplano, a number of independent and competing kingdoms emerged and jostled for prestige and power (Frye and De la Vega 2005; Stanish 2003), while in some of Tiwanaku's previous colonies, social organization was even more locally concentrated (Conrad 1993; Stanish 1985). Tiwanaku's collapse, then, drastically impacted the south-central Andes, and the effects lasted for as long as five centuries. To date, interest in that collapse has largely focused on understanding why it happened.

Catastrophic Climate Change: The Paleoclimate Record

Extensive, detailed, and multifaceted data derived from ice cores of the Quelccaya ice cap in southern Peru as well as sediment cores collected from Lake Titicaca reveal the onset of drought, a rise in temperatures, and a significant drop in lake levels in the Andes beginning around 1100 CE (Abbott et al. 1997; Thompson and Kolata 2017; Thompson et al. 1985; Thompson et al. 1986). Those data are integrated into an explanation for political collapse in which the pan-Andean rise in temperatures coupled with decreased precipitation led to the deterioration and ultimate abandonment first of irrigation-based agricultural systems in Tiwanaku's lowland enclaves and then of the raised field systems in the altiplano, and that this agricultural failure undermined the economic basis of the political authority of Tiwanaku elites (Binford et al. 1997; Kolata et al. 2000; Kolata and Ortloff 2003; Ortloff and Kolata 1993; Thompson and Kolata 2017).

Challenges to this interpretation include the argument, based on archaeological evidence that raised field systems endured despite Tiwanaku political collapse and on ethnographic data that suggest that state organization is not necessary for raised field farming, that Tiwanaku's political power was not dependent upon control of agriculture and therefore an explanation that relies on the climate-driven decline of the economic base is problematic (Albarracin-Jordan 1996; Erickson 1993, 1999; Graffam 1992). Janusek (2005) emphasizes the role internal schisms played in collapse, proposing that increased control and competition resulted in Tiwanaku populations fragmenting into factions. In the Moquegua Valley enclave, evidence that political decline predates the onset of drought presents a particular challenge to climate stress as a stand-alone explanation for collapse (P. Williams 2002).

Interest in Tiwanaku collapse has focused on its proximate causes. Concern with its aftermath is largely concerned with identifying shifts in settlement patterns and the impact on subsistence economy (Graffam 1992; Owen 2005; Thompson and Kolata 2017). In the following, I complement existing scholarship by examining how local communities were affected by and how they responded to organizational changes over time. I draw on fine-grained excavation data spanning five hundred years of the Moquegua Valley's late pre-Hispanic archaeological record to explore the local and peripheral experience of Tiwanaku collapse. I contextualize these diachronic data with the published high-resolution paleoclimatic reconstructions for the southern Andes (Abbott et al. 1997; Thompson and Kolata 2017; Thompson et al. 1985; Thompson et al. 1986). Climate-driven explanations for the decline of the Tiwanaku state have emphasized the onset of overall drier climate after 1000 CE. However, the evidence from ice and lake cores indicates not only that communities faced an altered climate, but that the generally drier and warmer conditions were punctuated by decades of particularly severe drought (Ortloff and Kolata 1993).

I describe two sequential phases, differentiated by distinct social dynamics and response in Moquegua (table 10.1). The first (the Tumilaca phase: 1000–1250 CE) was characterized by cultural maintenance, local network building, and the emergence of integrative mechanisms that drew communities together. The second phase (the Estuquiña phase: 1250–1470s CE) contrasts starkly with the first and is characterized by isolated communities, growing tensions, and a concern with violence. I

Table 10.1. The chronology of the Moquegua Valley, 500–1470s CE.

Approximate Dates	Moquegua Nomenclature	Andean Chronology	Sociopolitical Environment
500–1000 CE	Tiwanaku	Middle Horizon	Tiwanaku state influence
1000–1250 CE	Tumilaca	Terminal Middle Horizon	Aftermath of state "collapse"
1250–1470s CE	Estuquiña	Late Intermediate period	Instability, tension

then discuss the implications of recent radiocarbon dates and preliminary bio-distance analyses for explaining this dramatic change in the post-collapse social landscape of the Moquegua Valley (Sharratt 2019; Sharratt and Sutter 2018). I contend that the alterations in social dynamics were a consequence of changes by existing populations and not a consequence of incursion by outsiders. I note that the shift in intervalley relations corresponds temporally to the onset of several decades of particularly severe drought. Finally, I suggest that despite this, climate stress alone does not explain why communities became isolated and fearful in the second phase but that choices made during the first phase, specifically the abandonment of integrative mechanisms, contributed to exacerbated tensions after 1250 CE.

The Moquegua Valley

Located approximately 350 kilometers from the Tiwanaku heartland and spanning considerably lower altitudes, the Moquegua Valley was attractive to Tiwanaku immigrants from the altiplano (as well as to later arrivals, among them Inca and then Spanish colonists) for its temperate climate and soils that, with irrigation, are highly productive and conducive to raising crops like maize, coca, and fruits that do not grow in the altiplano (D. Rice 1989; P. Rice 2012, 2013). Itinerant Tiwanaku camelid herds probably first came to Moquegua as early as the sixth century CE, evidenced by temporary shelters in the archaeological record, but it was in the late eighth century CE that a permanent colony was established and Moquegua became home to the largest Tiwanaku province (Goldstein 1993a, 2005).

Immigrants from the altiplano and generations of their descendants occupied towns of several thousand that were situated in an area of Moquegua called the middle valley (figure 10.2). The middle valley spans altitudes of one thousand to fifteen hundred meters above sea level and is characterized by wide bluffs that rise above the river (Blom 1999; Blom et al. 1998; Goldstein 2005; Knudson et al. 2004; Knudson and Price 2007; Knudson et al. 2014). Extensive agricultural fields were established around these fields (P. Williams 1997, 1998, 2013). Inhabitants of Tiwanaku provincial towns in Moquegua largely replicated altiplano traditions. Ceramic forms and decorative repertoires exhibit regional variations but are rooted in heartland styles (Goldstein 1985) (illustrations 10.2a–c). Residential and monumental architecture mimics that seen in the Tiwanaku core (Goldstein 1989a, 1989b, 1993b, 2005; Goldstein and Sitek 2018; Owen and Goldstein 2001). For approximately three centuries, the population of the Moquegua province asserted a clear Tiwanaku identity and maintained

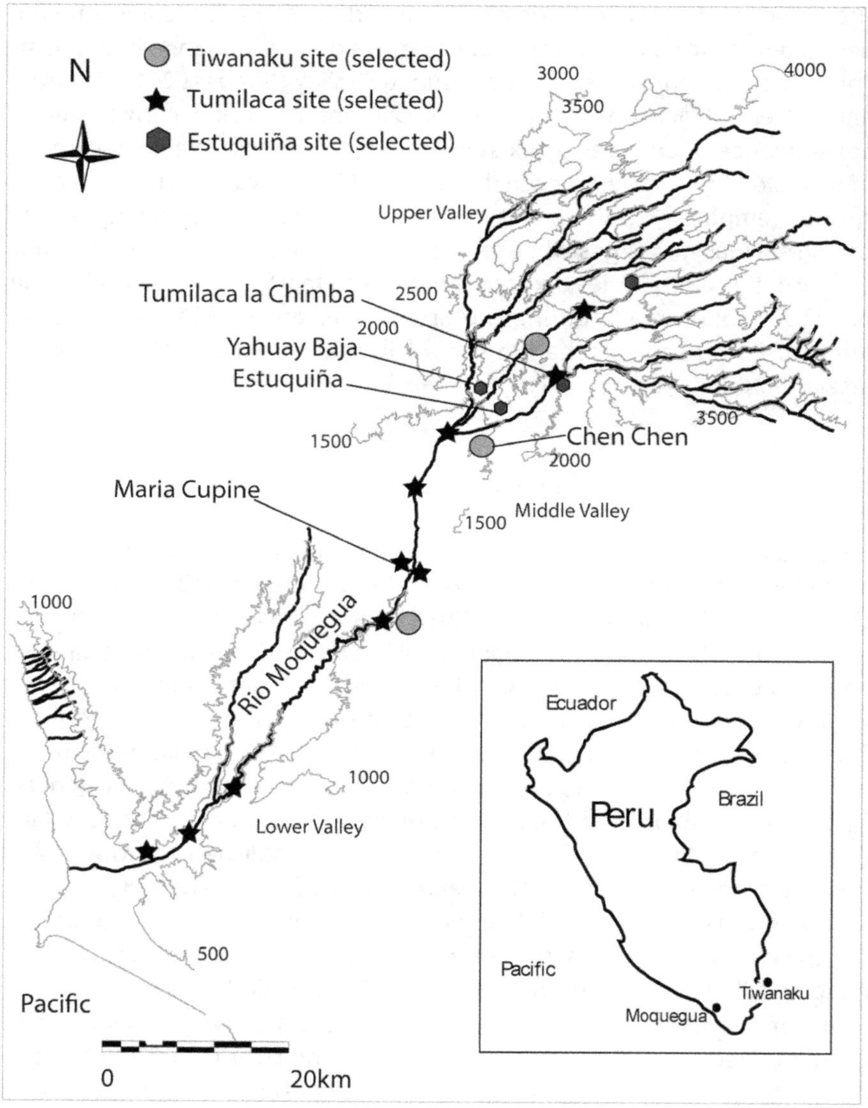

Figure 10.2. The Moquegua Valley, showing selected Tiwanaku, Tumilaca, and Estuquiña sites, including sites mentioned in the text. Author's image.

ongoing connections with the altiplano through the movement of people, animals, and goods.

As noted, the decline of Tiwanaku in Moquegua slightly predates the beginnings of the pan-Andean drought (P. Williams 2002, 2006). Stress on Tiwanaku's agricultural system there may have resulted initially from Wari (a contemporaneous expansive state that also established an outpost in

a

b

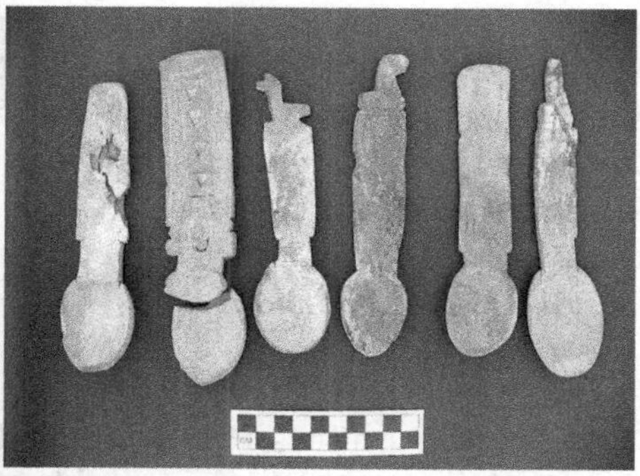

c

Illustrations 10.2a–c. Moquegua Valley Tiwanaku craft goods referencing altiplano imagery and resources. Author's images.

Moquegua) colonists' hydraulic activities upriver from the Tiwanaku fields. These activities reduced the amount of water available to Tiwanaku farmers, and the significant reduction in farmable land may have motivated rebellion among the colonial population in Moquegua (Goldstein 2005). Rebellion was manifested in violence targeted toward temples and elite burials (Goldstein 2005). It also resulted in the abandonment of the Tiwanaku immigrant towns beginning around 1000 CE. Populations dispersed into new territory and ecological zones, where they established smaller villages (Owen 2005). Although a few villages are found in the middle valley, close to the earlier towns, they are also located sixty kilometers away near the Pacific coast and in the upper valley, where steep slopes rise above a narrow river bottom and elevations span fifteen hundred to three thousand meters above sea level (Bermann et al. 1989; Owen 1993, 1999, 2005; Owen and Goldstein 2001; Stanish 1985) (figure 10.2).

Ongoing archaeological work at these villages seeks to elucidate the local, peripheral, and non-elite response to macroscale sociopolitical change and climate stress in the half millennium following the decline of the Tiwanaku state (Lowman, Sharratt, and Turner 2019; Parker and Sharratt 2017; Sharratt 2010, 2011, 2015b, 2016a, 2016b, 2017, 2019; Sharratt, Golitko, and Williams 2015; Sharratt et al. 2012; Sutter and Sharratt 2010). To date, that work has focused on one site, Tumilaca la Chimba. Located in the upper valley, fifteen kilometers from the abandoned Tiwanaku towns, at nineteen hundred meters above sea level, the site was occupied throughout the five hundred years under examination in this chapter (figure 10.2). The following discussion draws on extensive excavations conducted at Tumilaca la Chimba since 2006 but is complemented by existing published work at other post–1000 CE sites in Moquegua (Burgi et al. 1989; Conrad 1993; Goldstein 2005; Owen and Goldstein 2001; R. Williams et al. 1989).

The Tumilaca Phase (1000–1250 CE): Maintenance, Network Building, and Integrating Communities

The settlements established during abandonment of Tiwanaku towns and population dispersal throughout the Moquegua Valley, as well as the materials recovered from them, are called Tumilaca. They are dated to approximately 1000–1250 CE (Owen 2005; Sharratt 2019; Sims 2006; Stanish 1992). Bio-distance analyses derived from nonmetric dental traits confirm that these sites were founded by descendants of the earlier Tiwanaku migrants to Moquegua (Sutter and Sharratt 2010). In many ways Tumilaca sites present a picture of cultural continuity, with considerable maintenance of Tiwanaku concepts, practices, and styles visible in community organization, in residential architecture, in funerary practice, and in the forms and decorative repertoires of craft goods (Goldstein 1985, 2005; Owen 1993, 2005; Owen and Goldstein 2001; Sharratt 2011, 2016a, 2016b; Sharratt et al. 2012; Stanish 1991) (illustrations 10.3a–c).

Despite this continuity, the community at Tumilaca la Chimba (the only Tumilaca site for which detailed bioarchaeological and geochemical analyses exist) certainly felt the impacts of both increasingly challenging subsistence conditions and regional sociopolitical fragmentation. Analyses of pathologies on human skeletons excavated from the site's four Tumilaca-phase cemeteries indicate an increase in the frequency of cribra orbitalia and porotic hyperostoses compared with populations at the Tiwanaku towns (Lowman et al. 2019). Preliminary isotopic data derived from bone and teeth samples suggest that the community at Tumilaca la Chimba also experienced reduced access to maize compared with those at Tiwanaku towns (Quispe Vilcahuaman 2018).

Participation in long-distance economic networks declined. This is clear in a significantly reduced presence of nonlocal pottery in the Tumilaca ceramic assemblage at Tumilaca la Chimba compared with assemblages prior to 1000 CE (from 10 percent to 2 percent) (Sharratt 2015a, 2016b). The nearest obsidian sources to the Moquegua Valley are several hundred kilometers away (Burger 2000). Although documented in quantity at Tiwa-

a

b

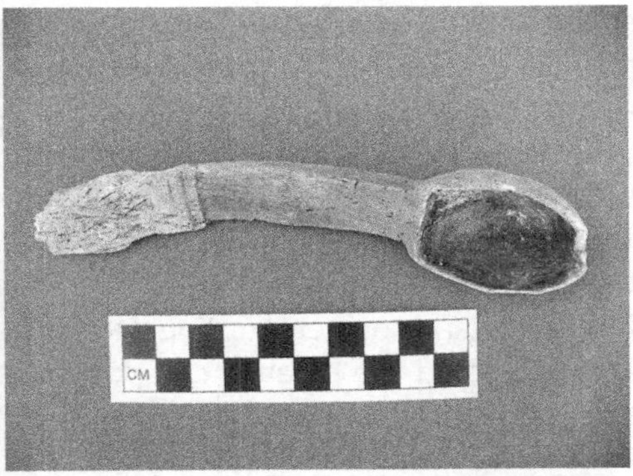

c

Illustrations 10.3a–c. Tumilaca craft goods. Author's images.

naku towns in Moquegua (Goldstein 2005), the only obsidian recovered from Tumilaca contexts at Tumilaca la Chimba is small flakes, possibly scavenged from earlier sites (Goldstein 2005). Finally, the textile assemblage at the site indicates a reduction in a material of especial value in Tiwanaku craft production—camelid fiber. Conceptually associated with the altiplano heartland (Goldstein 2005), camelid fiber was the exclusive shroud of the dead during the height of Tiwanaku authority. During these centuries, herds of alpaca and llama were herded between the altiplano, where they thrive, and Moquegua. At Tumilaca la Chimba, camelid fiber was used only to wrap adult corpses, and local cotton was used for infants, raising the possibility that access to this resource was limited as exchange networks with the heartland diminished (Sharratt 2016b). Moreover, weavers used what camelid fiber they did have more sparingly in cloth production by reducing the number of weft threads in shawls and blankets (Sharratt 2016b).

However, although long-distance exchange networks appear to have fallen apart, local networks of exchange emerged in Moquegua during the Tumilaca phase. This is most clearly illustrated through compositional data derived from LA-ICP-MS (laser ablation inductively coupled plasma mass spectrometry) analyses of Tumilaca pottery. When compared with a compositional database on local clays (Sharratt et al. 2009), these analyses reveal that although clays are available within one kilometer of Tumilaca la Chimba, the majority of analyzed ceramic from the site was still largely produced using clays from the middle valley (Sharratt et al. 2015). As such, Tumilaca-phase potters were securing raw materials likely located further than estimates derived from ethno-archaeological research in the Andes for the distance potters routinely travel for clays (Arnold 1993). The mechanisms behind the ceramic compositional data from Tumilaca la Chimba are unclear, namely whether people at Tumilaca la Chimba traveled to the middle valley to collect clays or procured them (or ceramic vessels) from communities there, but these data do suggest the emergence of an intra-valley network around pottery production.

The analyzed sherds were excavated from the four Tumilaca-style cemeteries at the site. It is thought that each cemetery was used by an intra-community (possibly extended kin) group in line with Tiwanaku concepts of social organization (Blom 1999; Sharratt 2011). Pottery produced with middle-valley clays was recovered from all four of the cemeteries, suggesting cross-community participation in local pottery exchange networks at Tumilaca la Chimba.

Preliminary data from other sites indicate the local circulation of other resources. Although marine resources are relatively scarce in Tumilaca-phase faunal assemblages from Tumilaca la Chimba, abundant marine shells on the surface of a middle-valley Tumilaca site called Maria Cupine indicate that this community engaged in networks with the coast, some sixty kilometers away (illustration 10.4).

I propose that local interactions were not only about the exchange of goods and materials but that they were also mediated and reinforced through collective ritual practice. Tumilaca la Chimba stands out among Tumilaca-phase sites in the Moquegua Valley for the presence of a rustic, ceremonial structure located in the middle of the village (illustrations 10.5a–b). Excavations in this structure revealed evidence for the kinds of practices conducted in earlier Tiwanaku ritual spaces in the altiplano and in the Moquegua Valley. These included the smashing of vessels, subfloor burial of ritually significant material goods, and possibly the installation of rus-

Illustration 10.4. Marine resources on the surface of Maria Cupine. Author's image.

a   b

Illustrations 10.5a–b. Rustic ceremonial space and zoomorphic *incensario* at Tumilaca la Chimba. Author's images.

tic monoliths. However, at Tumilaca la Chimba, the open and unassuming physical space where these practices were enacted contrasts starkly with the exclusive, restricted monuments controlled by the political elite during state authority (Sharratt 2016a). This re-situating of religious practice in the aftermath of state collapse arguably served as an integrating mechanism at Tumilaca la Chimba, one that drew people together and fostered solidarity (Sharratt 2016a). Perhaps, given the absence (to date) of similar structures identified at other Tumilaca sites, this ceremonial space and the activities conducted within it served to integrate people at an extra community level by drawing people together from multiple villages, serving both to facilitate economic exchanges and cultivating a pan-valley identity rooted in shared ancestry.

The Tumilaca phase, the approximately 250 years following the violent disintegration of Tiwanaku political authority in Moquegua, was one in which people were clearly impacted by macroscale sociopolitical and environmental change, but also one in which considerable maintenance is apparent and in which both economic and ritual practices played a role in building new local networks. However, that maintenance and the relative stability came to an end circa 1250 CE.

The Estuquiña Phase (1250–1470s CE): Rejection and Isolation

Beginning in the mid- to late thirteenth century CE, the archaeological record of the middle and upper Moquegua Valley is dominated by materials and settlements collectively called Estuquiña (Chacaltana-Cortez 2015; Conrad 1993; Stanish 1991). Some Estuquiña sites superimpose earlier Tumilaca villages, including at Tumilaca la Chimba, where Estuquiña-style domestic structures and an Estuquiña cemetery overlay the eastern part of the Tumilaca village (Parker and Sharratt 2017; Sharratt 2017). Other Estuquiña settlements, including the type site (called Estuquiña) in the middle valley, were established in previously unoccupied locations.

By almost every measure, Estuquiña is materially distinct from Tumilaca. All traces of Tiwanaku ceramic forms are absent from Estuquiña assemblages, which instead comprise crude, dark-red slipped shallow bowls and pitchers, with little decoration (Bawden 1989; Lozada Cerna 1987) (illustration 10.6). Textiles are also significantly different (Clark 1993). After 1250 CE, domestic architecture took on forms and masonry styles distinct from that documented in Tiwanaku and Tumilaca communities (Bawden 1989, 1993; Conrad 1993; Goldstein 2005; Parker and Sharratt 2017). Finally, agricultural practices were reworked with a shift from farming the valley bottom to terraced slopes (P. Williams 1997, 2006).

In addition to these material shifts, there were significant changes to social dynamics both between and within communities after 1250 CE. While the visual differences between pre- and post-1250 pottery were documented several decades ago (Stanish 1991), comparison of compositional data derived from LA-ICP-MS analyses of Tumilaca and Estuquiña ceramic assemblages sheds light on how economic networks shifted in the five hundred years after Tiwanaku political fragmentation. Significantly, they suggest that the local exchange networks identified for the Tumilaca phase and evidenced by the use of middle-valley clays for pottery consumed at the upper-valley Tumilaca la Chimba site were no longer in use after 1250 CE. Recently generated compositional data from an assemblage of Estuquiña pottery at Tumilaca la Chimba and comparison with the compositional database of locally available clays (Sharratt et al. 2009) reveals that after 1250 CE, pottery there was crafted from clays located within a few kilometers of the site. There is no evidence for the inclusion of middle-valley resources in Estuquiña pottery at Tumilaca la Chimba, in contrast with the earlier Tumilaca-style assemblage (Sharratt 2018).

Illustration 10.6. Estuquiña bowl. Author's image.

Architectural patterns provide additional evidence for increasing isolation of communities in Moquegua after 1250 CE. As other scholars have noted, in contrast to the relatively standardized Tumilaca-style domestic architecture, which exhibits strong continuity in form and layout with Tiwanaku traditions at both middle- and upper-valley Moquegua sites, Estuquiña domestic architecture is much more variable (Smit 2012). Highly localized traditions are visible, specifically between the middle valley (Conrad 1993) and the upper valley (Parker and Sharratt 2017). Architectural differences between Estuquiña sites may suggest declining interactions across the valley, but perhaps the absence of shared architectural language in turn contributed to a reduced sense of shared identity.

Architecture and site location suggest not only reduced inter-community interaction after 1250 CE, but also increasing hostilities. Estuquiña villages are considerably more fortified than their Tumilaca predecessors and included highly defensive hilltop refuges, a shift documented elsewhere in the south-central Andes (Arkush 2011; Bawden 1989, 1993) (illustrations 10.7a–b). I propose that even within communities, people became increasingly nucleated. Regardless of overall form, Estuquiña domestic architecture is characterized by agglutinated rooms and walled compounds that contrast with the accessible house patios and open plazas common at Tumilaca sites. This architectural change reveals an emphasis on protection and exclusion not only between communities but even between households (figure 10.3).

A focus on independent households is perhaps also indicated by the use of subfloor residential burials, as well as cemeteries (Burgi et al. 1989; S. Williams 1990; S. Williams et al. 1989). This represents a marked change from Tiwanaku and Tumilaca mortuary traditions in which community members were buried in remarkably standardized ways in cemeteries spatially segregated from residential neighborhoods, practices that I have previously argued served to assert and reinforce a collective identity within communities (Sharratt 2010, 2011). Moreover, large aboveground tombs that held multiple members of kin groups were first constructed in Moquegua during the Estuquiña phase (illustration 10.8). These are inter-

a

b

Illustrations 10.7a–b. Estuquiña fortifications at Tumilaca la Chimba (a) and Yahuay Baja (b). Author's images.

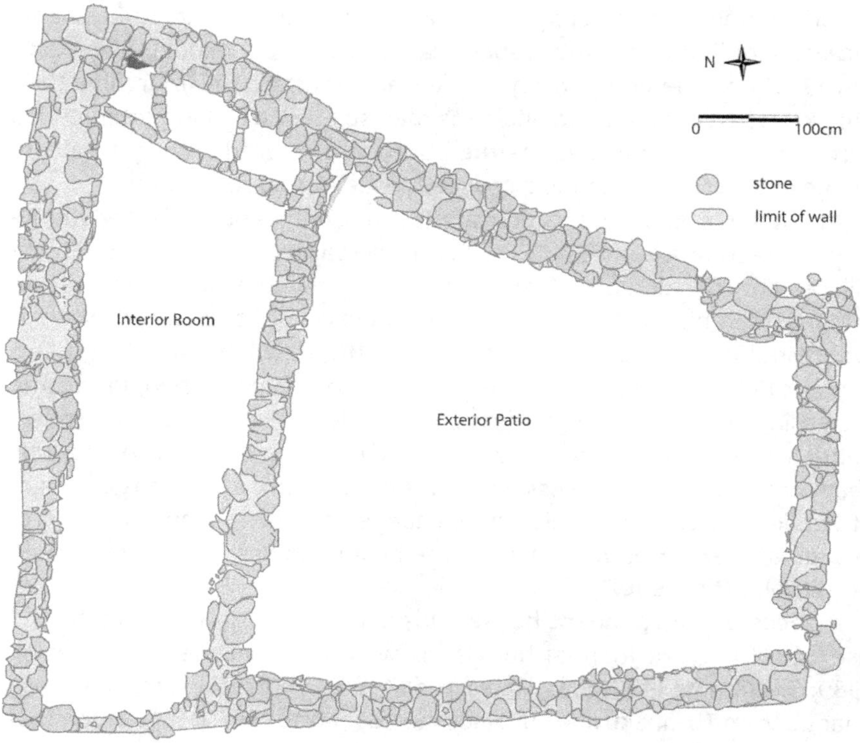

Figure 10.3. Estuquiña residential architecture at Tumilaca la Chimba. Author's image.

Illustration 10.8. Estuquiña-style aboveground tomb at Estuquiña. Author's image.

preted by scholars as territorial markers, as media for competitive display, and as venues for emphasizing kin allegiances (Arkush 2011; Stanish 2012).

The transition from Tumilaca to Estuquiña several centuries after Tiwanaku political decline is clearly visible in the archaeological record of the Moquegua Valley. Significantly, however, it constituted not only a radical material change and a rejection of Tiwanaku-derived styles, but also a fundamental reorientation of social dynamics as villages and possibly even households became more isolated and independent, rejected the local networks that had emerged during the Tumilaca phase, and constructed defenses that suggest a growth in local tension and hostility.

Discussion

Ethnohistoric data offer one explanation for the changes visible in the archaeological record beginning around 1250 CE, namely that inhabitants of Estuquiña sites represent a new wave of migration to Moquegua from the altiplano (Murra 1968). Criticisms of this explanation have to date relied on analyses of domestic architecture (Conrad 1993; Stanish 1989). However, preliminary bio-distance analyses based on scoring of highly heritable nonmetric dental traits from individuals excavated in both the Tumilaca and the Estuquiña cemeteries at Tumilaca la Chimba as well as from the type site of Estuquiña indicate that the Estuquiña population was almost certainly directly descended from previous Tumilaca populations. These findings signal that the alterations in material culture and in social dynamics are not attributable to migration but instead resulted from decisions by the post-collapse communities to discard remnants of their Tiwanaku heritage as well as cross-valley connections (Sharratt and Sutter 2018).

Recently generated radiocarbon dates from Tumilaca la Chimba also refine the chronology of the Tumilaca to Estuquiña shift. While earlier chronologies presented Tumilaca as obsolete by 1200 CE and Estuquiña as present from around 1300 CE (Conrad 1993; Moseley 2001, Owen 2005, Sims 2006), forty accelerator mass spectrometry (AMS) dates that were calibrated using the SHCal13 curve (Hogg et al. 2013; Marsh et al. 2018) and subject to Bayesian modeling reveal that Tumilaca contexts at Tumilaca la Chimba date a little later and Estuquiña contexts at the same site possibly a little earlier than previously thought. A phase analysis of these dates places the end of the Tumilaca occupation at 1301–1415 cal CE and the beginning of the Estuquiña occupation to 1253–1383 cal CE (Sharratt 2019).

These dates are significant when compared with the paleoclimatic data from the southern Andes. Although scholars who propose that the decline of the Tiwanaku state resulted from climate change emphasize the overall warming and reduced precipitation after 1000–1100 CE, those data also indicate episodes of particularly stressful conditions in subsequent centuries. In particular, data on snow layer thickness from the Quelccaya ice cap, used as a proxy for annual rainfall, reveal that even within the context of several centuries of a drier, warmer climate post–1000 CE, the period from 1245 to 1310 CE was characterized by particularly severe drought (Ortloff and Kolata 1993; Thompson and Kolata 2017; Thompson et al. 1985; Thompson et al. 1986).

Discussing the construction of fortified settlements in the altiplano, Arkush (2008, 2011) has proposed that increased violence can be understood as a response to drought and harsh subsistence conditions. Although no evidence of large-scale interpersonal violence has yet been documented in Estuquiña skeletal samples (Lowman et al. 2019; S. Williams 1990), the location and architectural features of Estuquiña sites coupled with evidence for the disintegration of local networks does suggest heightened tensions and insecurity in the Moquegua Valley. However, I also suggest that in Moquegua, choices made by communities, as well as the onset of exacerbated environmental stress, contributed to the development of a social landscape characterized by isolation and hostility.

AMS dates from Tumilaca la Chimba reveal that although Tumilaca-style household and funerary contexts at the site were in use until at least 1300 CE, the rustic ceremonial context was abandoned by 1200 CE (Sharratt 2019). When subsistence conditions became particularly difficult in the mid- to late thirteenth century, the physical space and arguably the practices that had been undertaken in it were no longer in use. As discussed above, I propose that this structure served to foster solidarity both within and beyond the community at Tumilaca la Chimba and in doing so may also have promoted the exchange of resources in local economic networks. With the abandonment of collective ceremonial space, the cohesion it had nurtured was unable to withstand the especially acute stress of the mid-thirteenth century, and a landscape of nucleated, defensive, and isolated communities emerged.

Concluding Thoughts: Policy Implications

Because of its temporal scope, archaeology provides a unique diachronic perspective on human response to episodes such as climate stress. The south central Andes post–1000 CE presents an example of what Shepherd (chapter 14 in this volume) describes as a "slow catastrophe." Unlike the sudden devastation of an earthquake or volcano, the onset and impact of warming temperatures, reduced precipitation, and drought extended across centuries (Thompson and Kolata 2017; Thompson et al. 1985; Thompson et al. 1986). During that time, human populations experienced particularly pronounced decades of subsistence stress. What archaeology offers to policy makers is the opportunity to take a long view on how slow catastrophes unfold. What the Moquegua Valley case study discussed here specifically offers is a detailed reconstruction of half a millennium of human responses to climate change. Significantly, it reveals how responses can either mitigate or exacerbate the impacts of disaster on social stability and can make the difference between climate stress and climate catastrophe.

Regardless of whether drought was the proximate cause of Tiwanaku state collapse, the communities who lived through both radical sociopolitical change and increasingly difficult subsistence conditions beginning around 1000 CE were impacted in negative ways. Populations experienced displacement and resettlement. Access to resources, especially nonlocal goods, was reduced. Health and nutrition were negatively affected. Thus, contrary to some archaeological scholarship that suggests that the breakdown of political authority has few impacts on non-elites (Graffam 1992), the data from the Moquegua Valley after 1000 CE indicate that ramifications can be felt across society.

However, despite this, the first two to three hundred years (the Tumilaca phase) after Tiwanaku political disintegration appear to have been relatively peaceful centuries in the Moquegua Valley. In this respect, they contrast significantly with the evidence for hostility, tension, and social insecurity that is apparent after 1250 CE (during the Estuquiña phase). Although this shift toward hostility (if not full-blown violence) is roughly contemporaneous with the onset of especially pronounced drought, I propose that it was also a consequence of the abandonment of integrative social practices that had served both to alleviate stress through resource distribution and to build cohesion within and between communities. The success of these practices and the dramatic worsening of social conditions when they were abandoned perhaps offer the following three lessons for policy makers in the present:

1) As other scholars note, interconnectivity can serve to promote resilience in the face of subsistence stress (see chapters 4 and 7 in this volume). When regional interconnectivity and access to long-distance networks was compromised by political fragmentation, populations in Moquegua were impacted, but the emergence of localized interconnectivity between refugee communities in different ecological zones likely both alleviated subsistence challenges and promoted cross-valley cohesion.

2) Significantly, policies of interconnection must be shared equitably. As noted in this volume (chapter 14) and elsewhere (Scanlon 1988), the impacts of disaster often fall disproportionately on the poor and other disenfranchised members of society. Moreover, catastrophe can intensify preexisting inequalities (Barrios 2017). In Moquegua, access to emerging local exchange networks appears to have been spread across communities and did not become a source for entrenching inequality.
3) Finally, policies that foster resource exchange and economic interdependence are strengthened by practices and institutions that promote solidarity and commonality. Archaeologists studying the earliest permanent villages note the importance of mechanisms for minimizing the conflict that can result from increasing population density (Bandy and Fox 2010; Pluckhahn 2010; Varien and Potter 2008). In particular, group ritual activity that routinely brought people together appears to have served to promote collective identity (Stanish and Haley 2005). I propose that in the Moquegua Valley, while tension was a product of climatic and political stress, solidarity was fostered by similar mechanisms as in early villages, namely by the periodic gatherings of people in architectural spaces that emphasized equality and downplayed hierarchy. While local economic exchange was important to alleviate resource stress, I suggest that the social interactions facilitated by integrative mechanisms that brought people together (in this case ritual practice) were important to minimizing tension. It is notable that it was after those architectural spaces had been abandoned that hostility became prevalent in Moquegua. I propose then that while the most immediate and pressing concern in the aftermath of climate disaster is of course subsistence and survival, policy makers ought also to consider the role that integrative mechanisms can play in minimizing and countering the potentially long-lasting social tensions and conflicts that can develop from those subsistence challenges.

Acknowledgments

Archaeological research in Moquegua was supported by the National Science Foundation (BSC 1347166 and DDIG 0937303), the National Geographic Society (9096-12), the Archaeological Institute of America, the Curtiss T. and Mary G. Brennan Foundation (2012 and 2016), Fulbright IIE, and Dumbarton Oaks. Additional support was provided by the Graduate College and Department of Anthropology at the University of Illinois of

Chicago, the Women's Board and the Department of Anthropology at the Field Museum, and the Center for Latin American and Latino Studies at Georgia State University, a Georgia State University Research Initiation Grant, and a GSU Arts & Sciences Dean's Early Career Award. Fieldwork was conducted with permission from the Ministerio de Cultura del Perú, Lima (RDN 1208/INC in 2006/7; RDN 1350/INC; RDN 301-2012; RDN 24-2015; RDN 412-2018). The radiocarbon dates were generated by the Arizona Accelerator Mass Spectrometry (AMS) Laboratory at the University of Arizona. Thanks to the various field crews, the Museo Contisuyo, and colleagues, especially P. Ryan Williams and Bruce Owen. Any errors or oversights are mine alone.

Dr. Nicola Sharratt is associate professor in the Department of Anthropology at Georgia State University. She directs an ongoing archaeological project in southern Peru that examines the diachronic impacts on and responses of local communities to radical sociopolitical transformation. Her research foci include state collapse, identity construction, craft production, and compositional analyses of material culture.

References

Abbott, M. B., Michael W. Binford, Mark Brenner, and K. R. Kelts. 1997. "A 3500 ^{14}C yr High-Resolution Sediment Record of Lake Level Changes in Lake Titicaca, Bolivia/Peru." *Quaternary Research* 47 (2): 169–80.

Albarracin-Jordan, Juan. 1996. "Tiwanaku Settlement System: The Integration of Nested Hierarchies in the Lower Tiwanaku Valley." *Latin American Antiquity* 7 (3): 183–210.

Albarracin-Jordan, Juan, and James Edward Mathews. 1990. *Asentamientos Prehispanicos del Valle de Tiwanaku*. Vol. 1. La Paz, Bolivia: Producciones CIMA.

Anderson, Karen. 2013. "Tiwanaku Influence of the Central Valley of Cochabamba." In *Visions of Tiwanaku*, edited by Alexei Vranich and Charles Stanish, 87–112. Los Angeles: Cotsen Institute of Archaeology.

Arkush, Elizabeth N. 2005. "Interpreting Conflict in the Ancient Andes: Implications for the Archaeology of Warfare." *Current Anthropology* 46 (1): 3–28.

———. 2006. "Collapse, Conflict, Conquest: The Transformation of Warfare in the Late Prehispanic Highlands." In *The Archaeology of Warfare*, edited by E. Arkush and M. Allen, 286–87. Gainesville: University of Florida Press.

———. 2008. "War, Causality, and Chronology in the Titicaca Basin." *Latin American Antiquity* 19 (4): 339–73.

———. 2011. *Hillforts of the Ancient Andes: Colla Warfare, Society, and Landscape*. Gainesville: University of Florida Press.

Arnold, Dean, E. 1993. *Ecology and Ceramic Production in an Andean Community*. New Studies in Archaeology. Cambridge: Cambridge University Press.

Augustyniak, Szymon. 2004. "Dating the Tiwanaku State: Analisis Cronologico del Estado Tiwanaku." *Chungara* 36 (1): 19–35.

Bandy, Matthew. 2001. "Population and History in the Ancient Titicaca Basin." PhD dissertation. University of California at Berkeley.

———. 2013. "Tiwanaku Origins and Early Development: The Political and Moral Economy of a Hospitality State." In *Visions of Tiwanaku*, edited by Alexei Vranich and Charles Stanish, 135–50. Los Angeles: Cotsen Institute of Archaeology.

Bandy, Matthew S., and Jake R. Fox. 2010. "Becoming Villagers: The Evolution of Early Village Societies." In *Becoming Villagers: Comparing Early Village Societies*, edited by Matthew S. Bandy and Jake R. Fox, 1–16. Tucson: University of Arizona Press.

Barrios, R. E. 2017. "What Does Catastrophe Reveal for Whom? The Anthropology of Crises and Disasters at the Onset of the Anthropocene." *Annual Review of Anthropology* 46: 151–66.

Bawden, Garth. 1989. "The Tumilaca Site and Post-Tiahuanaco Occupational Stratigraphy in the Moquegua Drainage." In *Ecology, Settlement and History in the Osmore Drainage, Peru*, edited by Don S. Rice, Charles Stanish, and Phillip R. Scarr, 287–302. Oxford: BAR.

———. 1993. "An Archaeological Study of Social Structure and Ethnic Replacement in Residential Architecture of the Tumilaca Valley." In *Domestic Architecture, Ethnicity, and Complementarity in the South-Central Andes*, edited by Mark S. Aldenderfer, 42–54. Iowa City: University of Iowa Press.

Bermann, Marc, Paul S. Goldstein, Charles Stanish, and Luis Watanabe. 1989. "The Collapse of the Tiwanaku State: A View from the Osmore Drainage." In *Ecology, Settlement and History in the Osmore Drainage, Peru*, edited by Don S. Rice, Charles Stanish and Phillip R. Scarr, 269–85. Oxford: BAR.

Binford, Michael W., and Alan K. Kolata. 1996. "The Natural and Human Setting." In *Tiwanaku and Its Hinterland: Archaeology and Paleoecology of an Andean Civilization*, edited by Alan K. Kolata, 23–56. Washington, DC: Smithsonian Institution Press.

Binford, Michael W., Alan L. Kolata, Mark Brenner, John W. Janusek, Matthew T. Seddon, Mark Abbott, and Jason H. Curtis. 1997. "Climate Variation and the Rise and Fall of an Andean Civilization." *Quaternary Research* 47 (2): 235–48.

Blom, Deborah E. 1999. "Tiwanaku Regional Interaction and Social Identity: A Bioarchaeological Approach." PhD dissertation, University of Chicago.

Blom, Deborah E., Benedikt Hallgrimsson, Linda Keng, Maria Cecilia Lozada Cerna, and Jane E. Buikstra. 1998. "Tiwanaku 'Colonization': Biological Implications for Migration in the Moquegua Valley, Peru." *World Archaeology* 30 (2): 238–61.

Brown, Rachel. 2017. "Photos Reveal How Climate Change Affects the High Andes." *National Geographic*, 3 March.

Burger, Richard L. 2000. "Through the Glass Darkly: Prehispanic Obsidian Procurement and Exchange in Southern Peru and Northern Bolivia." *Journal of World Prehistory* 14 (3): 267–362.

Burgi, Peter T., Sloan A. Williams, Jane E Buikstra, Niki R. Clark, Maria Cecilia Lozada Cerna, and Elva Torres Pino. 1989. "Aspects of Mortuary Differentiation at the Site of Estuquina, Southern Peru." In *Ecology, Settlement and History in the Osmore Drainage, Peru*, edited by Don S. Rice, Charles Stanish and Phillip R. Scarr, 347–69. Oxford: BAR.

Casey, Nicholas. 2016. "Climate Change Claims a Lake, and an identity." *New York Times*, 7 July.

———. 2017. "A Lifetime in Peru's Glaciers, Slowly Melting Away." *New York Times*, 26 January.

Chacaltana-Cortez, Sofia. 2015. "Regional Interfaces between Inca and Local Communities in the Colesuyo Region of Southern Peru." PhD dissertation, University of Illinois at Chicago.

Clark, Niki R. 1993. "The Estuquina Textile Tradition: Cultural Patterning in Late Prehistoric Fabrics in Moquegua." PhD dissertation, Washington University.

Conlee, Christina A. 2006. "Regeneration as Transformation: Postcollapse Society in Nasca, Peru." In *After Collaspe*, edited by Glenn M. Schwartz and John J. Nichols, 99–113. Tuscon: University of Arizona Press.

Conrad, Geoffrey W. 1993. "Domestic Architecture of the Estuquina Phase: Estuquina and San Antonio." In *Domestic Architecture, Ethnicity, and Complementarity in the South-Central Andes*, edited by Mark S. Aldenderfer, 55–65. Iowa City: University of Iowa Press.

Couture, Nicole C. 2003. "Ritual, Monumentalism, and Residence at Mollo Kontu, Tiwanaku." In *Tiwanaku and Its Hinterland: Archaeology and Paleocology of an Andean Civilization* 2, edited by Alan L. Kolata, 202–25. Washington, DC: Smithsonian Institution Press.

Couture, Nicole C., and K. Sampeck. 2003. "Putuni: A History of Palace Architecture in Tiwanaku." In *Tiwanaku and Its Hinterland: Archaeology and Paleoecology of an Andean Civilization*, edited by Alan L. Kolata, 226–63. Washington, DC: Smithsonian Institution Press.

Covey, R. Alan. 2008. "Multiregional Perspectives on the Archaeology of the Andes during the Late Intermediate Period (c. A.D. 1000–1400)." *Journal of Archaeological Research* 16 (3): 287–338.

Dillehay, Tom D., and Alan L. Kolata. 2004. "Long-Term Human Response to Uncertain Environmental Conditions in the Andes." *Proceedings of the National Academy of Sciences* 101 (12): 4325–30.

Erickson, Clark L. 1993. "The Social Organization of Prehispanic Raised Field Agriculture in the Lake Titicaca Basin." Supplement, *Research in Economic Anthropology* 7: 369–426.

———. 1999. "Neo-environmental Determinism and Agrarian 'Collapse' in Andean Prehistory." *Antiquity* 73 (281): 634–42.

Fraser, Barbara. 2009. "Climate Change Equals Culture Change in the Andes." *Scientific American*, 5 October.

Frye, Kirk Lawrence, and Edmundo De la Vega. 2005. "The Altiplano Period in the Titicaca Basin." In *Advances in Titicaca Basin Archaeology*, edited by Charles Stanish, Amanda B. Cohen, and Mark S. Aldenderfer, 173–84. Los Angeles: Cotsen Institute of Archaeology, UCLA.

Goldstein, Paul S. 1985. "Tiwanaku Ceramics of the Moquegua Valley, Peru." MA thesis, University of Chicago.

———. 1989a. "Omo: A Tiwanaku Provincial Center in Moquegua, Peru." PhD dissertation, University of Chicago.

———. 1989b. "The Tiwanaku Occupation of Moquegua." In *Ecology, Settlement and History in the Osmore Drainage, Peru*, edited by Don S. Rice, Charles Stanish and Phillip R. Scarr, 219–55. Oxford: BAR.

———. 1993a. "House, Community, and State in the Earliest Tiwanaku Colony: Domestic Patterns and State Integration at Omo M12, Moquegua." In *Domestic Architec-*

ture, Ethnicity, and Complementarity in the South-Central Andes, edited by Mark S. Aldenderfer, 25–41. Iowa City: University of Iowa Press.
———. 1993b. "Tiwanaku Temples and State Expansion: A Tiwanaku Sunken-Court Temple in Moquegua, Peru." *Latin American Antiquity* 4 (1): 22–47.
———. 2005. *Andean Diaspora: The Tiwanaku Colonies and the Origins of South American Empire*. Gainesville: University Press of Florida.
———. 2009. "Diasporas within the Ancient State: Tiwanaku as Ayllus in Motion." In *Andean Civilization: A Tribute to Michael E. Moseley*, edited by Joyce Marcus and Patrick Ryan Williams, 277–301. Los Angeles: Cotsen Institute of Archaeology.
———. 2013. "Tiwanaku and Wari State Expansion: Demographic and Outpost Colonization Compared." In *Visions of Tiwanaku*, edited by Alexei Vranich and Charles Stanish, 41–63. Los Angeles: Cotsen Institute of Archaeology Press.
Goldstein, Paul S., and Matthew J. Sitek. 2018. "Plazas and Processional Paths in Tiwanaku: Divergence, Convergence, and Encounter at Omo M10, Moquegua, Peru." *Latin American Antiquity* 29 (3): 455–74.
Graffam, Gray. 1992. "Beyond State Collapse: Rural History, Raised Fields, and Pastoralism in the South Andes." *American Anthropologist* 94 (4): 882–904.
Hogg, Alan G., Quan Hua, Paul G. Blackwell, Mu Niu, Caitlin E. Buck, Thomas P. Guilderson, Timothy J. Heaton, Jonathan G. Palmer, Paula J. Reimer, Ron W. Reimer, Chris S.M. Turney, and Susan R. H. Zimmerman. 2013. "SHCal13 Southern Hemisphere Calibration, 0–50,000 Years cal BP." *Radiocarbon* 55 (4): 1889–1903.
Isbell, William H. 2013. "Nature of an Andean City: Tiwanaku and the Production of Spectacle." In *Visions of Tiwanaku*, edited by Alexei Vranich and Charles Stanish, 167–96. Los Angeles: Cotsen Institute of Archaeology.
Janusek, John W. 1999. "Craft and Local Power: Embedded Specialization in Tiwanaku Cities." *Latin American Antiquity* 10 (2): 107–31.
———. 2002. "Out of Many, One: Style and Social Boundaries in Tiwanaku." *Latin American Antiquity* 13 (1): 35–61.
———. 2004a. *Identity and Power in the Ancient Andes*. London: Routledge.
———. 2004b. "Tiwanaku and Its Precursors: Recent Research and Emerging Perspectives." *Journal of Archaeological Research* 12 (2): 121–83.
———. 2005. "Collapse as Cultural Revolution: Power and Identity in the Tiwanaku to Pacajes Transition." In *Foundations of Power in the Prehispanic Andes*, edited by Kevin J. Vaughn, Dennis Ogburn, and Christina A. Conlee, 175–210. Arlington, VA: American Anthropological Association.
———. 2008. *Ancient Tiwanaku, Case Studies in Early Societies*. Cambridge: Cambridge University Press.
Janusek, John W., and Alan L. Kolata. 2003. "Prehispanic rural history in the Katari Valley." In *Tiwanaku and Its Hinterland; Archaeology and Paleoecology of an Andean Civilization*, edited by Alan K. Kolata, 129–72. Washington, DC: Smithsonian Institution Press.
Knudson, Kelly J., Paul S. Goldstein, Allisen Dahlstedt, Andrew Somerville, and Margaret J. Schoeninger. 2014. "Paleomobility in the Tiwanaku Diaspora: Biogeochemical Analyses at Rio Muerto, Moquegua, Peru." *American Journal of Physical Anthropology* 155 (3): 405–21.
Knudson, Kelly J., and T. D. Price. 2007. "Utility of Multiple Chemical Techniques in Archaeological Residential Mobility Studies: Case Studies from Tiwanaku and Chiribaya Affiliated Sites in the Andes." *American Journal of Physical Anthropology* 132 (1): 25–39.

Knudson, Kelly J., T. D. Price, J. E. Buikstra, and D. E. Blom. 2004. "The Use of Strontium Isotope Analysis to Investigate Tiwanaku Migration and Mortuary Ritual in Bolivia and Peru." *Archaeometry* 46 (1): 5–18.

Kolata, Alan L. 1993. *The Tiwanaku: Portrait of an Andean Civilization*. Oxford: Blackwell.

Kolata, Alan L., Michael W. Binford, Mark Brenner, John W. Janusek, and Charles Ortloff. 2000. "Environmental Thresholds and the Empirical Reality of State Collapse: A Response to Erickson (1999)." *Antiquity* 74 (284): 424–26.

Kolata, Alan L., and C. R. Ortloff. 2003. "Agroecological Perspectives on the Decline of the Tiwanaku State." In *Tiwanaku and Its Hinterland: Archaeology and Paleoecology of an Andean Civilization*, edited by Alan K. Kolata, 181–202. Washington, DC: Smithsonian Institution Press.

Koons, Michele L. 2013. "Reexamining Tiwanaku's Urban Renewal through Ground-Penetrating Radar and Excavation: The Results of Three Field Seasons." In *Advances in Titicaca Basin Archaeology* 2, edited by Alexei Vranich and Abigail Levine, 147–65. Los Angeles: Cotsen Institute of Archaeology.

Kozhikkodan Veettil, Bijeesh, and Sergio Florêncio de Souza. 2017. "Study of 40-Year Glacier Retreat in the Northern Region of the Cordillera Vilcanota, Peru, Using Satellite Images: Preliminary Results." *Remote Sensing Letters* 8 (1): 78–85.

Kurin, Danielle S. 2016. *The Bioarchaeology of Societal Collapse and Regeneration in Ancient Peru*. Switzerland: Springer International.

Levine, Abigail, Charles Stanish, Patrick Ryan Williams, Cecilia Chavez, and Mark Golitko. 2013. "Trade and Early State Formation in the Northern Titicaca Basin, Peru." *Latin American Antiquity* 24 (3): 289–308.

Lowman, Shannon A., Nicola Sharratt, and Bethany L. Turner. 2019. "Bioarchaeology of Social Transition: A Diachronic Study of Pathological Conditions at Tumilaca la Chimba, Peru." *International Journal of Osteoarchaeology* 29 (1): 62–72.

Lozada Cerna, Maria Cecilia. 1987. "La Ceramica del Componente Mortuorio de Estuquina, Moquegua." Bachiler, Facultad de Ciencias Historico—Arqueologicas, Universidad Catolica Santa Maria.

Marsh, Erik J., Maria C. Bruno, Sherilyn C. Fritz, Paul Baker, Jose M. Capriles, and Christine A. Hastorf. 2018. "IntCal, SHCal, or a Mixed Curve? Choosing a ^{14}C Calibration Curver for Archaeological and Paleoenvironmental Records from Tropical South America." *Radiocarbon* 60 (3): 1–16.

McAndrews, Timothy L., Juan Albarracin-Jordan, and Marc Bermann. 1997. "Regional Settlement Patterns in the Tiwanaku Valley of Bolivia." *Journal of Field Archaeology* 24 (1): 67–83.

Moseley, Michael E. 2001. *The Incas and Their Ancestors: The Archaeology of Peru*. 2nd ed. London: Thames and Hudson.

Murra, John V. 1968. "An Aymara Kingdom in 1567." *Ethnohistory* 15 (2): 115–51.

Ortloff, C. R., and Alan L. Kolata. 1993. "Climate and Collapse: Agro-ecological Perspectives on the Decline of the Tiwanaku State." *Journal of Archaeological Science* 20 (2): 195–221.

Owen, Bruce. 1993. "A Model of Multiethnicity: State Collapse, Competition, and Social Complexity from Tiwanaku to Chiribaya in the Osmore Valley, Peru." PhD dissertation, UCLA.

———. 1999. *Proyecto "Vecinos de Cerro Baúl" 1997: Informe de Campo e Informe Final*. Report presented to the Instituto Nacional de Cultura, Lima, Peru.

———. 2005. "Distant Colonies and Explosive Collapse: The Two Stages of the Tiwanaku Diaspora in the Osmore Drainage." *Latin American Antiquity* 16 (1): 45–80.

Owen, Bruce, and Paul S. Goldstein. 2001. "Tiwanaku en Moquegua: Interacciones Regionales y Colapso." *Boletin de Arqueologia PUCP* 5: 169–88.

Parker, Bradley J., and Nicola Sharratt. 2017. "Fragments of the Past: Applying Microarchaeological Techniques to Use Surfaces at Tumilaca La Chimba, Moquegua, Peru." *Advances in Archaeological Practice* 5 (1): 71–92.

Pluckhahn, Thomas. 2010. "The Sacred and the Secular Revisited: The Essential Tensions of Early Village Society in the Southeastern United States." In *Becoming Villagers: Comparing Early Village Societies*, edited by Matthew S. Bandy and Jake R. Fox, 100–118. Tucson: University of Arizona Press.

Posnansky, Arthur. 1945. *Tihuanacu, the Cradle of American Man*. New York: J. J. Augustin.

Posnansky, Arturo. 1912. *Guia General ilustrada para la Investigacion de los Monumentos prehistoricos de Tihuanacu e Islas del Sol y la Luna (Titicaca y Koaty)*. La Paz, Bolivia: Hugo Heitmann.

Quispe Vilcahuaman, Breidy. 2018. "Investigating Paleodiet and Mobility through Stable Isotope Analyses at the site of Tumilaca la Chimba, Moquegua, Peru." MA thesis, Georgia State University.

Rice, Don S. 1989. "Osmore Drainage, Peru: The Ecological Setting." In *Ecology, Settlement and History in the Osmore Drainage, Peru*, edited by Don S. Rice, Charles Stanish, and Phillip R. Scarr, 17–34. Oxford: BAR.

Rice, Prudence M. 2012. "Torata Alta: An Inka Administrative Center and Spanish Colonial Reduccion in Moquegua, Peru." *Latin American Antiquity* 23 (1): 3–28.

———. 2013. *Space-Time Perspectives on Early Colonial Moquegua*. Boulder: University of Colorado Press.

Rivera Casanovas, Claudia. 2003. "Ch'iji Jawira: A Case of Ceramic Specialization in the Tiwanaku Urban Periphery." In *Tiwanaku and Its Hinterland: Archaeology and Paleoecology of an Andean Civilization*, edited by Alan L. Kolata, 296–315. Washington, DC: Smithsonian Institution Press.

Scanlon, J. 1988. "Winners and Losers: Some Thoughts about the Political Economy of Disaster." *International Journal of Mass Emergencies and Disasters* 6 (1): 47–63.

Sharratt, Nicola. 2010. "Identity Negotiation During Tiwanaku State Collapse." In *Identity Crisis: Archaeological Perspectives on Social Identity*, edited by Lindsay Amundsen-Meyer, Nicole Engel, and Sean Pickering. Calgary: Chacmool Archaeological Association.

———. 2011. "Social Identities and State Collapse: A Diachronic Study of Tiwanaku Burials in the Moquegua Valley, Peru." PhD dissertation, University of Illinois at Chicago.

———. 2015a. "From Dispersal to Disappearance: AD 1000–1250 in the Upper Moquegua Valley." 80th Annual Meeting of the Society for American Archaeology, San Francisco, 15–19 April.

———. 2015b. "Viviendo y Muriendo en medio de la efervescencia política: excavaciones en una aldea Tiwanaku terminal (950–1150 D.C) del valle de Moquegua, Perú." In *El Horizonte Medio en los Andes Centro Sur: Nuevos aportes sobre la arqueología del sur de Perú, norte de Chile y altiplano de Bolivia*, edited by Antti Korpisaari and Juan Chacama, 201–23. Lima: IFEA.

———. 2016a. "Collapse and Cohesion: Building Community in the Aftermath of Tiwanaku State Breakdown." *World Archaeology* 48 (1): 144–63.

———. 2016b. "Crafting a Response to Collapse: Ceramic and Textile Production in the Wake of Tiwanaku State Breakdown." In *Beyond Collapse*, edited by Ronald K. Faulseit, 407–30. Carbondale, IL: CAI Press.

———. 2017. "Steering Clear of the Dead: Avoiding Ancestors in the Moquegua Valley, Peru." *American Anthropologist* 119 (4): 645–61.

———. 2018. "Tradition and Transformation during the Middle Horizon to LIP Transition: Visual and Compositional Analyses of Tumilaca and Estuquiña Pottery in the Moquegua Valley, Peru." 83rd Annual Meeting of the Society for American Archaeology, Washington D.C.

———. 2019. "Tiwanaku's Legacy: A Chronological Reassessment of the Terminal Middle Horizon in the Moquegua Valley, Peru." *Latin American Antiquity* 30 (3): 529–49.

Sharratt, Nicola, Mark Golitko, and Patrick Ryan Williams. 2015. "Pottery Production, Regional Exchange and State Collapse during the Middle Horizon (A.D. 500–1000): LA-ICP-MS analyses of Tiwanaku Pottery in the Moquegua Valley, Perú." *Journal of Field Archaeology* 40 (4): 397–412.

Sharratt, Nicola, Mark Golitko, Patrick Ryan Williams, and Laure Dussubieux. 2009. "Ceramic Production during the Middle Horizon; Wari and Tiwanaku Clay Procurement in the Moquegua Valley, Peru." *Geoarchaeology* 24 (6): 792–820.

Sharratt, Nicola, and Richard Sutter. 2018. "Late Intermediate Period Ethnogenesis in the Moquegua Valley, Peru: A Bioarchaeological Perspective on the Emergence of Estuquiña Communities." 46th Annual Midwest Conference on Andean and Amazonian Archaeology and Ethnohistory, Chicago.

Sharratt, Nicola, Patrick Ryan Williams, Maria Cecilia Lozada Cerna, and Jennifer Starbird. 2012. "Late Tiwanaku Mortuary Patterns in the Moquegua Drainage, Peru: Excavations at the Tumilaca la Chimba Cemetery." In *Advances in Titicaca Basin Archaeology III*, edited by Alexei Vranich, Elizabeth Klarich and Charles Stanish, 193–203. Ann Arbor: Museum of Anthropology Publications.

Shimada, Izumi, C. B. Schaaf, Lonnie G. Thompson, and E. Mosley-Thompson. 1991. "Cultural Impacts of Severe Droughts in the Andes: Application of a 1,500 Year Ice Core Precipitation Record." *World Archaeology* 22 (3): 247–70.

Sims, Kenny. 2006. "After State Collapse: How Tumilaca Communities Developed in the Upper Moquegua Valley, Peru." In *After Collapse: The Regeneration of Complex Societies*, edited by Glenn M. Schwartz and John J. Nichols, 114–36. Tucson: University of Arizona Press.

Smit, Douglas. 2012. "Examining Estuquina Architecture in the Upper Osmore Drainage during the Late Intermediate Period." 77th Annual Meeting of Society for American Archaeology, Memphis, TN, 18–22 April.

Squier, E. George. 1877. *Peru: Incidents of Travel and Exploration in the Land of the Incas*. London: Macmillan.

Stanish, Charles. 1985. "Post-Tiwanaku Regional Economics in the Otora Valley, Southern Peru." PhD dissertation, University of Chicago.

———. 1989. "Household Archaeology: Testing Models of Zonal Complementarity in the South Central Andes." *American Anthropologist* 91 (1): 7–24.

———. 1991. *A Late Pre-Hispanic Ceramic Chronology for the Upper Moquegua Valley, Peru, Fieldiana*. Chicago: Field Museum of Natural History.

———. 1992. *Ancient Andean Political Economy*. Austin: University of Texas Press.

———. 2003. *Ancient Titicaca: The Evolution of Complex Society in Southern Peru and Northern Bolivia*. Berkeley: University of California Press.

———. 2012. "Above-Ground Tombs in the Circum-Titicaca Basin." In *Advances in Titicaca Basin Archaeology III*, edited by Alexei Vranich, Elizabeth Klarich, and Charles Stanish, 203–20. Ann Arbor: Museum of Anthropology, University of Michigan.
———. 2013. "What Was Tiwanaku?" In *Visions of Tiwanaku*, edited by Alexei Vranich and Charles Stanish, 151–66. Los Angeles: Cotsen Institute of Archaeology.
Stanish, Charles, and Kevin J. Haley. 2005. "Power, Fairness, and Architecture: Modeling Early Chiefdom Development in the Central Andes." In *Foundations of Power in the Prehispanic Andes*, edited by Kevin J. Vaughn, Dennis Ogburn, and Christina A. Conlee, 53–70. Washington DC: Archeological Papers of the American Anthropological Association.
Stovel, Emily. 2001. "Patrones funerarios de San Pedro de Atacama y el problema de la presencia de los contextos Tiwanaku." *Boletin de Arqueologia PUCP* 5: 375–96.
Sutter, Richard C., and Nicola Sharratt. 2010. "Continuity and Transformation during the Terminal Middle Horizon (AD 950–1150): A Bioarchaeological Assessment of Tumilaca Origins within the Middle Moquegua Valley, Peru." *Latin American Antiquity* 21 (1): 67–86.
Thompson, Lonnie G., and Alan L. Kolata. 2017. "Twelth Century AD: Climate, Environment, and the Tiwanaku State." In *Megadrought and Collapse: From Early Agriculture to Angkor*, edited by Harvey Weiss, 231–46. Oxford: Oxford University Press.
Thompson, Lonnie G., M. E. Moseley, J. F. Bolzan, and B. R. Koci. 1985. "A 1500-Year Record of Climate Variability Recorded in Ice Cores from the Tropical Quelccaya Ice Cap, Peru." *Science* 229 (4717): 971–73.
Thompson, Lonnie G., M. E. Moseley, W. Dansgaard, and P. M. Grootes. 1986. "The Little Ice Age as Recorded in the Stratigraphy of the Tropical Quelccaya Ice Cap." *Science* 234 (4774): 361–64.
Torres-Rouff, Christina. 2008. "The Influence of Tiwanaku on Life in the Chilean Atacama: Mortuary and Bodily Perspectives." *American Anthropologist* 110 (3): 325–37.
Torres-Rouff, Christina, and Mark Hubbe. 2013. "The Sequence of Human Occupation in the Atacama Oases, Chile: A Radiocarbon Chronology Based on Human Skeletal Remains." *Latin American Antiquity* 24 (3): 330–44.
Tung, Tiffiny A. 2008. "Violence after Imperial Collapse: A Study of Cranial Trauma among Late Intermediate Period Burials from the Former Huari Capital, Ayacucho, Peru." *Nawpa Pacha* 29 (1): 101–17.
Varien, Mark D., and James M. Potter. 2008. "The Social Production of Communities: Structure, Agency, and Identity." In *The Social Construction of Communities: Agency, Structure, and Identity in the Prehispanic Southwest*, edited by Mark D. Varien and James M. Potter, 1–18. Lanham, MD: AltaMira Press.
Vranich, Alexei. 2001. "La Piramide de Akapana: Reconsiderano el Centro Monumental de Tiwanaku." *Boletin de Arqueologia PUCP* 5: 295–308.
———. 2006. "The Construction and Reconstruction of Ritual Space at Tiwanaku, Bolivia (A.D. 500–1000)." *Journal of Field Archaeology* 31 (2): 121–36.
———. 2013. "Visions of Tiwanaku." In *Visions of Tiwanaku*, edited by Alexei Vranich and Charles Stanish, 1–9. Los Angeles: Cotsen Institute of Archaeology Press.
Weiss, Harvey. 2017a. *Megadrought and Collapse: From Early Agriculture to Angkor*. Oxford: Oxford University Press.
———. 2017b. "Megadrought, Collapse, and Causality." In *Megadrought and Collapse: From Early Agriculture to Angkor*, edited by Harvey Weiss, 1–31. Oxford: Oxford University Press.

Weiss, Harvey, and Raymond S. Bradley. 2001. "What Drives Societal Collapse." *Science* 291 (5504): 609–10.

Weiss, Harvey, M. A. Courty, W. Wetterstrom, F. Guichard, L. Senior, R. Meadow, and A. Curnow. 1993. "The Genesis and Collapse of the Third Millenium North Mesopotamian Civilization." *Science* 261 (5124): 995–1004.

Williams, Patrick Ryan. 1997. "The Role of Disaster in the Development of Agriculture and the Evolution of Social Complexity in the South-Central Andes." PhD dissertation, University of Florida.

———. 1998. *Proyecto Rescate Chen Chen 1995: Levantamiento y Sectores Agricolas Informe Final*. Report presented to the Instituto Nacional de Cultura, Lima, Peru.

———. 2002. "Rethinking Disaster-Induced Collapse in the Demise of the Andean Highland States: Wari and Tiwanaku." *World Archaeology* 33 (3): 361–74.

———. 2006. "Agricultural Innovation, Intensification, and Sociopolitical Development: the Case of Highland Irrigation Agriculture on the Pacific Andean Watersheds." In *Agricultural Strategies*, edited by Joyce Marcus and Charles Stanish. Los Angeles: Cotsen Institute of Archaeology Press.

———. 2013. "Tiwanaku: A Cult of the Masses." In *Visions of Tiwanaku*, edited by Alexei Vranich and Charles Stanish, 27–40. Los Angeles: Cotsen Institute of Archaeology.

Williams, Sloan R. 1990. "The Skeletal Biology of Estuquina: A Late Intermediate Period Site in Southern Peru." PhD dissertation, Northwestern University.

Williams, Sloan R., Jane E. Buikstra, Niki R. Clark, Maria Cecilia Lozada Cerna, and Elva Torres Pino. 1989. "Mortuary Site Excavations and Skeletal Biology in the Osmore Project." In *Ecology, Settlement and History in the Osmore Drainage, Peru*, edited by Don S. Rice, Charles Stanish, and Phillip R. Scarr, 329–46. Oxford: BAR.

Yaeger, Jason, and Alexei Vranich. 2013. "A Radiocarbon Chronology of the Pumapunku Complex and a Reassessment of the Development of Tiwanaku, Bolivia." In *Advances in Titicaca Basin Archaeology* 2, edited by Alexei Vranich and Abigail Levine, 127–46. Los Angeles: Cotsen Institute of Archaeology.

CHAPTER 11

Beyond One-Shot Hypotheses

Explaining Three Increasingly Large Collapses in the Northern Pueblo Southwest

TIMOTHY A. KOHLER, LAURA J. ELLYSON, and R. KYLE BOCINSKY

Summary for Stakeholders

The pre-Hispanic history of the northern US Southwest is well known because of relatively good preservation, high-resolution dating from tree rings, and large amounts of research. In this chapter we especially capitalize on recent work by the Village Ecodynamics Project. We are able to reconstruct population levels, potential maize production, and several features of the lived experience in the central Mesa Verde area of southwestern Colorado, including levels of violence and the degree of wealth differentiation among households through time, at generational resolution or better, for the seven centuries from about 600 to 1300 CE. In this area, high levels of current potential maize production per capita tend to accompany low levels of violence and also set the stage for low levels of violence in the next generation. On the other hand, low per-capita production accompanies high levels of concurrent violence and foreshadows continuing high levels of violence in the next generation. High violence also tends to diminish wealth differentiation among households, though the effect is weak. It is perhaps not surprising to learn that production crises—especially in contexts of dense population—frequently destabilized ancient societies and led to high levels of violence and alterations to social relationships amid violence. We cannot assume that all our technology and ingenuity guarantee that similar forces today could not lead to similar outcomes. We can work on structural conditions such as reducing cleavages in identity and strengthening institutions that make violence accompanying resource shortfalls less likely.

Coincidence and Causation

Processual archaeologists were so deeply motivated by a desire to identify the causes for various aspects of the archaeological record that they sometimes even included the word "explanation" in their titles (e.g., Watson, LeBlanc, and Redman 1971). Often they focused on explaining quite small-scale patterning in the archaeological record, such as the spatial clustering of particular design elements on sherds from a southwestern pueblo (Longacre 1964). Much larger-scale patterns of change were equally within their sights, however; the origins of agriculture and increasing social complexity constitute classic examples (Binford 1983, 195–232; Wenke 1981).

Fast-forward a decade or two and discussions of causation are hard to find in an archaeology dominated by discourses on social theory, and especially on agency and identity. Neither "explanation" nor "causation" figures in the titles (or even the indexes) of such classic works of theory as Hodder (1986, 2012). In a sense, identification of agency had become the only sort of explanation needed, since "agency is an ability to act *to some effect* in a particular context" (Robb 2010, 513, emphasis added). Given the recognition that "virtually all actions occur in chains of cause, effect and context involving other people . . . [so that] social actions involve a palimpsest of purposes, some of which may be quite disparate" (Robb 2010, 503), how could it ever be possible to detail such chains adequately, and at long-enough lengths, to ever "explain" large-scale change over considerable time spans? The task must have seemed overwhelming unless agents were effectively cut out, which was not an option. Nor, apparently, was it an option to assume that agents were so constrained by their circumstances as to make the directions taken by their agency predictable from structural conditions. Better to relinquish the possibility of looking for cause and effect in the structural debris left by agents than to elide agency.

Over time, though, even some archaeologists sympathizing with the displacement of processualism by other isms emphasizing social theory have come to recognize that they "have missed the boat on long-term change" in their focus on the more comfortable (and less politically fraught) "small worlds of agency and meaning understandable at strictly local scales" (Robb and Pauketat 2013, 5).

On Not Missing the Boat

Our goal in this paper is unabashedly explanatory; we are interested in seeing whether we can identify causality at work when multiple contextual variables that theory suggests might have causal power are all changing at various rates. In our view this does not mean abandoning an interest in agency. It does though require assuming that the actions of agents averaged over the periods in which these emerge into archaeological visibility will exhibit central tendencies that are interpretable, in the main, in terms of structural imperatives and constraints. But that diagnosis does not necessarily mean that it is easy to determine which are the causes and which the effects in the changes we perceive in the archaeological record. Or maybe the variability we see in various traces is just random, and apparent conjunctures coincidental? It does seem highly plausible that not all human action is either a cause or an effect of another action or some structural contingency (Camus 1942). But unless we adopt an approach that helps us identify outcomes of agency that are heavily channeled by constraints and structural imperatives, we give up any ability to recognize agency not so structured.

We will explore these issues in the context of a particular time and area that is relatively well known. For almost two decades a small band of archaeologists and allied researchers from other disciplines loosely organized as the Village Ecodynamics Project (VEP)—plus a large number of other archaeologists and much previous work of course—has been assembling an account of what happened in eastern Pueblo history before the Spanish incursion of the early sixteenth century. We have concentrated on two regions. Our original study area, chosen to build on the successes of the Dolores Archaeological Program and on pioneering work estimating maize productivity through time for this area (Burns 1983; Van West 1994), was an 1,817-square-kilometer portion of Southwest Colorado centered on the Great Sage Plain. A few years later we expanded this rectangle considerably to encompass an area that we call VEPIIN, including most of what archaeologists traditionally refer to as the central Mesa Verde (CMV) region. We will use these terms interchangeably. At the same time, we added a second study area in the northern Rio Grande (NRG) region of New Mexico (Kohler and Varien 2012; see figure 11.1).

In this chapter we try to see how far we can go in assigning causation for a series of changes in the northern study area, which was densely occupied between 600 and 1280 CE by farmers heavily dependent on maize produced mostly through dry (rain-fed) farming, complemented by smaller amounts of squash, beans, and (after the mid-1000s) turkey raising. Within these seven centuries we can distinguish fourteen periods averaging about fifty years long, primarily using changes in ceramic assemblages that are in turn calibrated by abundant tree-ring dates from numerous well-excavated sites.[1] Although there are many interesting puzzles in these data, we are going to focus on trying to disentangle cause and effect in the extreme variability in levels of violence, wealth inequality, population size, degree of aggregation (village size), and climatically sensitive measures of farming production that characterize this seven-century record. We are sensitive to the dangers of "data-dependent analysis" or "the garden of forking paths" (Gelman and Loken 2014) that are especially hard to avoid in observational fields such as archaeology where replication (strictly defined) is impossible. Thus, we will concentrate on the behaviors of this subset of variables, while introducing other variables that put our catastrophes in context.

Building the Data Set

Population History

Extensive survey within this area in conjunction with relatively well-preserved and legible signatures for households allow us to develop paleodemographic histories with fairly high confidence, using methods developed by and explained in Ortman, Varien, and Gripp (2007) and Schwindt et al. (2016). The VEP estimates for momentary number of households through time in the VEPIIN area appear in figure 11.2. This shows a global population peak between 1225 and 1260 CE, toward the end of the

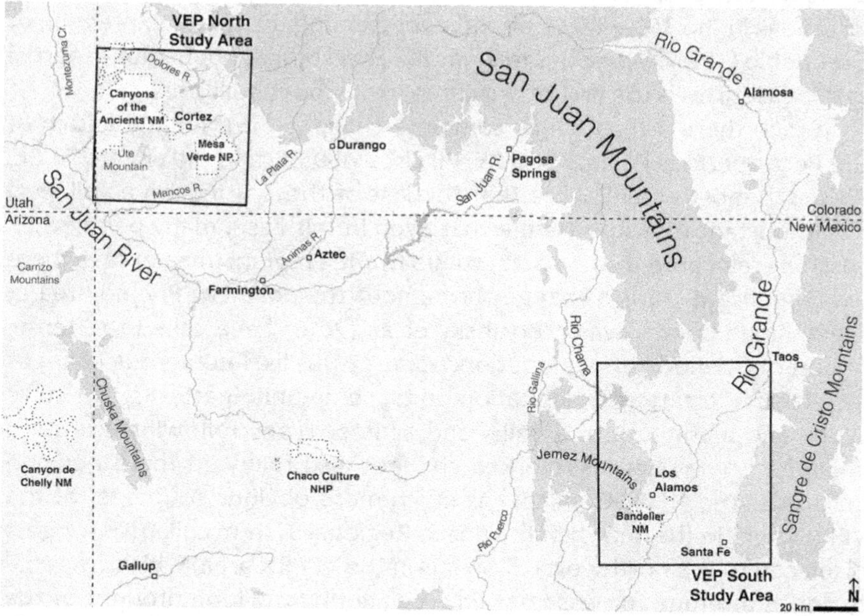

Figure 11.1. Location of the VEP study areas in the northern US Southwest. Figure created by the authors.

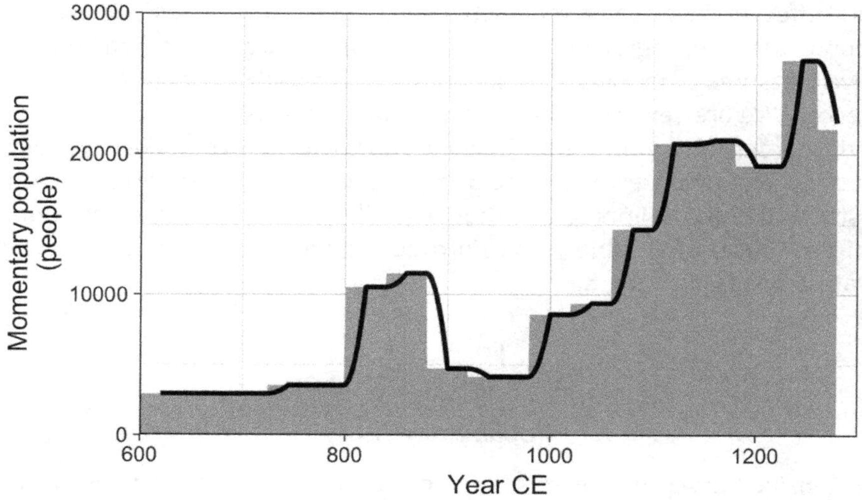

Figure 11.2. Momentary population in the central Mesa Verde region. Figure created by the authors.

Pueblo III (PIII) period, which is followed by the famous rapid and complete depopulation of the entire northern Southwest (Douglass 1929; Kohler et al. 2008), including the VEPIIN area (Schwindt et al. 2016). This is the third and largest collapse referenced in our title. There is a second local peak in the 840–880 CE period, representing the fullest expression of the Pueblo I (PI) villages; this too was followed by a depopulation—partial in this case. This is the first of our three eponymous collapses.

In fact, there are partial or complete collapses at the end of each of the Pecos periods PI circa 900 CE, PII circa 1150 CE, and PIII circa 1270 CE. Although most would agree that the last of these is indeed a collapse, it is important to acknowledge that even in this case, many people successfully relocated to the northern Rio Grande region. In each case there was significant culture change throughout the northern Pueblo area at these hinge points, which Bocinsky et al. (2016) have called the termination of "periods of exploitation." Lipe (2010) lists numerous changes in settlement patterns, habitation units, community patterns, structure types and architectural details, and artifact types following the third collapse. Somewhat less-marked changes also followed the other two collapses. The 1150 CE collapse is much more obvious southeast of the VEPIIN, where the hearth of the Chaco Regional System collapses (or gets displaced to the northwest), than it is in the VEPIIN area, which was able to act as a refuge for less-favored areas during the long drought of the mid-1100s CE.

Figure 11.2 and most of the following figures present a smoothing in addition to the raw data. The black line is the unweighted average of the current year and the previous twenty (thus, a lagging indicator). Therefore, any particular year from these series in essence contains a memory of the previous twenty years. After presenting and briefly discussing each series, we will systematically sample these linear-smoothed series to develop a causal analysis.

History of Aggregation

In this area the degree of aggregation varies markedly through time; documenting and explaining changes in typical settlement size were chief goals of VEPI. Figure 11.3 displays the estimated momentary number of households in the largest site in each period, one plausible measure of aggregation. We have previously shown a different measure of aggregation (for just the VEPI area) to be significantly positively correlated with current momentary population size and with current levels of violence (Kohler 2012a). We also know that in the VEPI area the peak population of the largest sites—often called community centers—is significantly but weakly positively related to the estimated maize production of their two-kilometer catchments, averaged across the entire 600–1280 CE period (Glowacki and Ortman 2012).

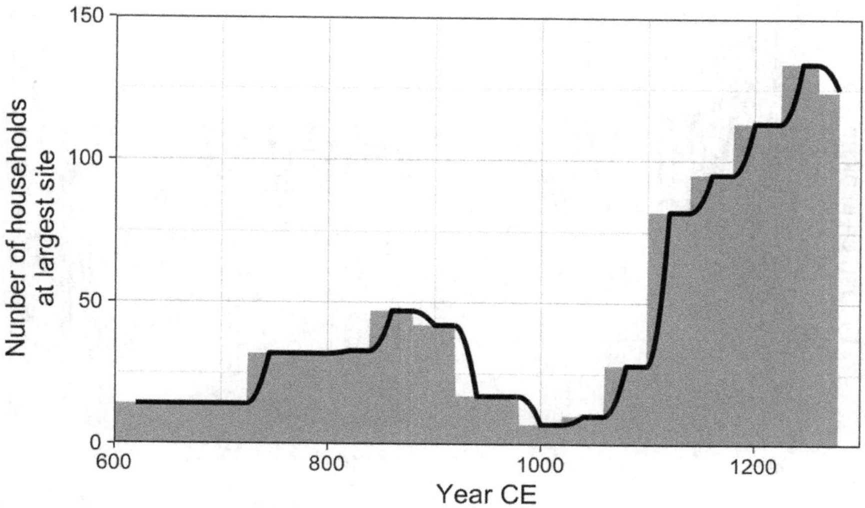

Figure 11.3. Estimated momentary number of households in the largest site in the central Mesa Verde region. Figure created by the authors.

Two Views on Maize Production History

Some aspects of this population history appear to be related to changing climates for maize production. We graph two views on maize production in figures 11.4 and 11.5. In figure 11.4 we reconstruct the spatial extent of the maize dry-farming niche using combinations of tree-ring sequences sensitive to either temperature or precipitation as explained in Bocinsky and Kohler (2014) and using the reconstruction from Bocinsky et al. (2016). Readers unfamiliar with the difficulties of dry farming in the upland Southwest should note the very high variance in this unsmoothed series. There appear to be years in which no dry farming was possible in the VEPIIN area, as well as years when one could successfully dry-farm maize anywhere.[2] Averaging across years, though, over two-thirds of the area was productive for dry farming, which is likely higher than any other area of comparable size in the northern Southwest.

Figure 11.5 is a maize productivity reconstruction ultimately based on regression relationships with historic maize production and climate in this area from 1931 to 1960, as explained in Kohler (2012b). These estimates have been evaluated by Bocinsky and Varien (2017) using contemporary experimental maize production data. They found the mean estimates to be approximately correct but the amplitude of the variability to be too low. In other words, figure 11.5 likely underestimates production in the best years, but overestimates it in the worst years. We

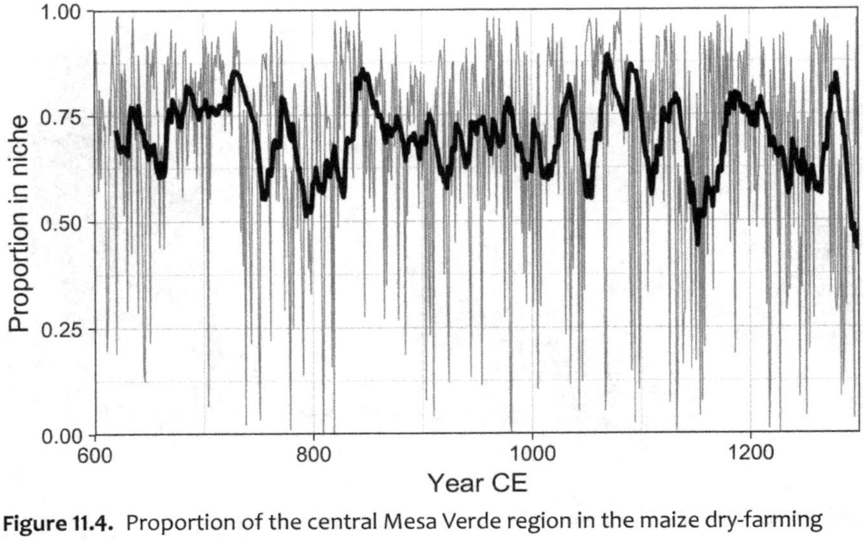

Figure 11.4. Proportion of the central Mesa Verde region in the maize dry-farming niche. Figure created by the authors.

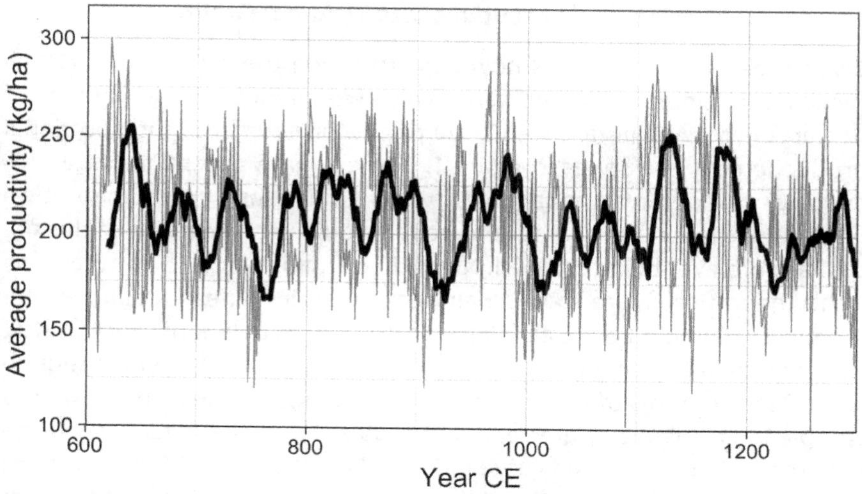

Figure 11.5. Estimated potential average maize yield (kilograms per hectare) in the central Mesa Verde region. Figure created by the authors.

remind our readers that since both of these approaches to reconstructing maize production depend on tree rings, they may also underestimate the impact of low-frequency trends, especially in temperature (Kohler 2010).

From these graphs, the demise of the PI villages circa 900 CE looks like it might be correlated with a marked downturn in production (which of course could be an underestimate of the severity of the actual conditions) accompanied by a fairly marked constriction in the maize niche. Another rather large constriction in the maize niche in the mid-1100s CE (slightly less marked in the productivity series) is reflected only in a slight decrease in the momentary population size that marks the end of the Pueblo II (PII) period. This event—the second of our three collapses—appears to be relatively minor in the VEPIIN area, at least from the perspective of the population history. It is well marked though in the local history of violence, as we will soon see. Moreover, as mentioned, further southeast in the Chaco Canyon area, the mid-1100s CE downturn was coincident with the demise of the Chaco Regional System (Lekson 2015, chapter 5), which sent ripples throughout the eastern Southwest. The 1200s CE appear to be fairly low in production throughout, with further marked declines in both niche size and production beginning in the 1270s CE, by which time the final depopulation of this area (along with the rest of the northern Southwest) was already well underway.

Estimated Potential Maize Yield per Capita

Given these sequences, it is now easy to divide the series in figure 11.5 (which is in kilograms per hectare, which we multiply by the number of hectares in the VEPIIN area, 460,400 to get the estimated total potential production) by the series in figure 11.2 to estimate potential maize productivity in kilograms per capita. Of course, this represents a theoretical figure, since labor and access constraints would prevent much of this potential from ever being realized. Nevertheless, it is useful in part because if this theoretical figure should ever decline to a level near actual per capita needs, it would be a clear signal that these populations were at risk. Roughly speaking, an adult male working six hours per day would require some 234 kilograms of maize per year,[3] assuming resources necessary to complement this diet were readily available. Thus, the minimum potential production of the study area in figure 11.6 of around 3,000 kilograms per person is over twelve times that minimum. Nevertheless, this figure makes clear that if there were maize shortfalls resulting from extreme aggregation or other impediments to access, or stemming from our likely overestimation of production in poor years, they were most likely to affect the thirteenth century. As we saw in figure 11.3, that was indeed the time of maximum aggregation. High degrees of aggregation kept people from distributing themselves to best profit from the distribution of potential production.

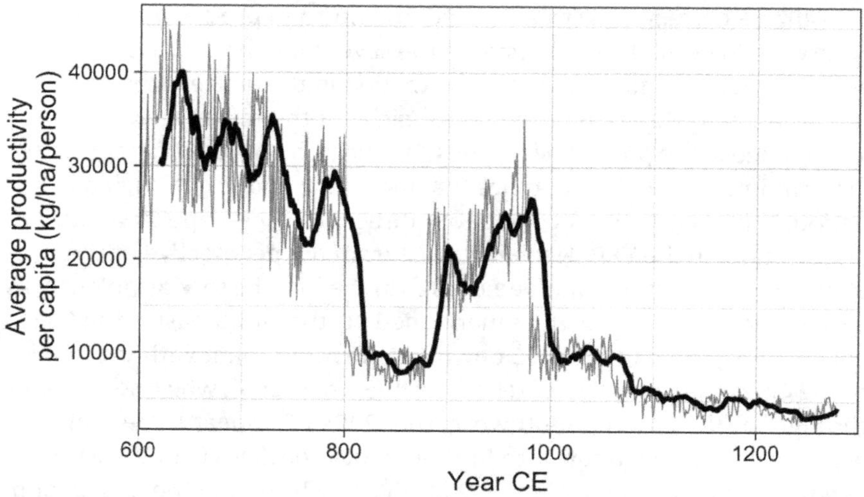

Figure 11.6. Potential per capita maize yield (kilograms) in the central Mesa Verde region. Figure created by the authors.

Construction Investment History

The counts of tree-ring dates (both cutting and near cutting) in this area are shown in figure 11.7. Nearly all of these dates come from wood used for construction, so this series can be viewed as a direct indicator for amount of construction (all of which used at least some wood). Some portions of this series are plausibly correlated with aspects of farming. For example, the peak in cutting in the mid-800s CE seems to be correlated with a peak in productivity (though not in niche size). All three series show declines in the early 900s CE. The increase in tree-ring dates in the mid-1000s CE appears to be associated with a clear expansion of the maize niche, though productivity increases only slightly. In short, relationships for this series appear to be somewhat mixed and are probably driven in part by episodes of immigration (which could well be correlated with unfavorable balances between population and maize production—or political developments—well outside the VEPIIN area). If so, we might expect these peaks in tree-ring dates to be correlated with changes in ceramic types.

Looking at the tree-ring record from the entire upland Southwest, Bocinsky et al. (2016) (see also Kohler and Bocinsky 2017) suggested that four "periods of exploration" could be identified: 500–600, 700–790, 890–1025, and 1145–1200 CE. These can be contrasted with four "periods of exploitation": 600–700, 790–890, 1035–1145, and 1200–1285 CE. Peaks in the tree-ring-cutting record are a key defining feature of the periods

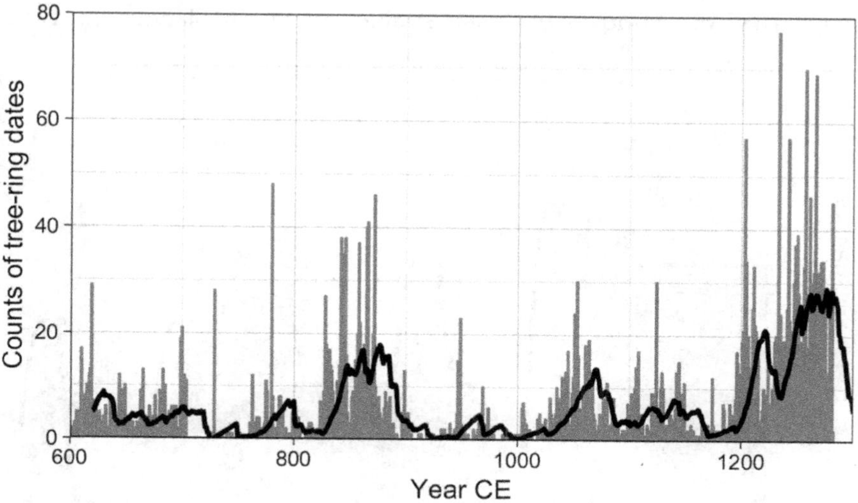

Figure 11.7. Counts of cutting and near-cutting tree-ring dates in the central Mesa Verde region. Figure created by the authors.

of exploitation. Other factors important to their identification were high frequencies of cutting dates relative to non-cutting dates, and significant spatial clustering of cells with tree-ring dates. Finally, it was suggested that periods of exploitation should be marked by establishment of relatively stable stylistic canons—visible in ceramic materials and architecture for example.

Typological Changes in Ceramic Inventories through Time

To examine this suggestion more thoroughly, we calculate the rate of change in ceramic types in this record in two different ways. The VEP ceramics database (Ortman et al. 2007; Schwindt et al. 2016) tracks the abundance of twenty-four diagnostic ceramic types and categories in the CMV region; the probability of finding any given type is modeled as a unimodal (though not necessarily Gaussian) distribution. In figure 11.8 we simply count the number of ceramic types that either appear in the record for the first time or disappear from the record (where "appear" and "disappear" are defined as rising above or falling below a 0.01 threshold of probability of finding that type). Defined in this way, changes in ceramic frequencies must be correlated with period boundaries.

We also developed another, potentially higher temporal resolution way of determining timing and rate of ceramic change. In figure 11.9, we begin with the same record of relative frequencies of ceramic types in each of the periods used above. Then we create an annual record in which all years in a given period have the same values for a particular ceramic type,

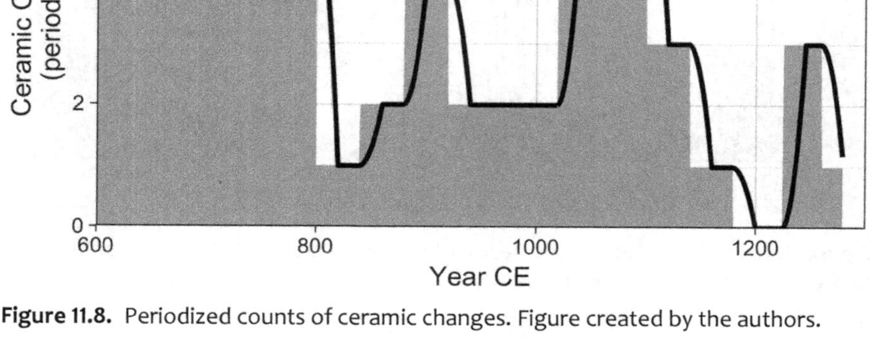

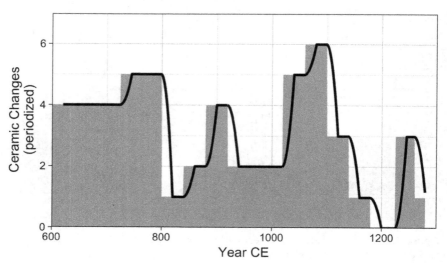

Figure 11.8. Periodized counts of ceramic changes. Figure created by the authors.

which is the relative frequency of each ceramic type. We then smoothed that record for each ceramic type using the twenty-one-year linear lagged smooth. This creates a monotonically increasing and then a monotonically decreasing annual series for each ceramic type. We mark the first year in which each type increases above a proportion of 0.01 and also the first year when each type later decreases below 0.01. This creates an annual record of mostly 0s (no change), and a few 1s and exactly one 2, in years with one or more changes, which is then also smoothed, with the results as shown in figure 11.9.

These two ways of identifying when ceramic change at the typological level is most common yield generically similar results. Both identify the early to mid-700s, the mid-800s, the mid-1000s, and the mid-1200s CE as times of rapid change. The last three of these fall squarely within the periods of exploitation identified by Bocinsky et al. (2016), though the first does not. All four represent times of population growth in our study area, possibly including immigration. The suspicion that the record of annualized ceramic change tracks episodes of immigration is strengthened by the fact that it has a positive though nonsignificant correlation with the record of tree-ring cutting ($r = 0.49$).

Changing Wealth Inequality through Time

The disappearance of elites, often amid violence, is a classic index of collapse, for which the Mayan case (e.g., Dunning, Beach, and Luzzadder-Beach 2012) is archetypal. We therefore want to add here a consideration

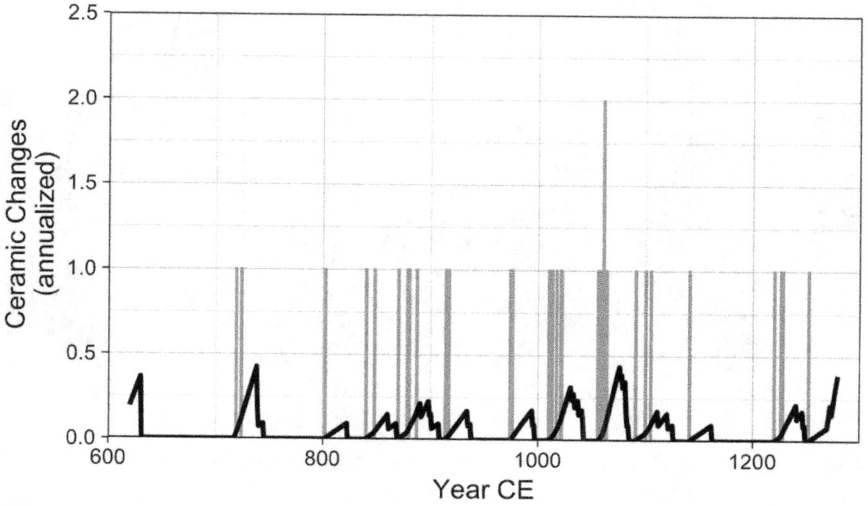

Figure 11.9. Annualized counts of ceramic changes. Figure created by the authors.

of the degree of wealth inequality proxied from distributions of house sizes, as explained by Kohler and Ellyson (2018; see also Ellyson, Kohler, and Cameron 2019). Elsewhere we argue that the concept of wealth (as developed by Borgerhoff Mulder et al. 2009) measured in this way is a much broader concept than its contemporary definition in finance would suggest (see Rakopoulos and Rio 2018 for a critique of a narrow association of wealth with capital accumulation). It includes property but also participates in reproductive and relational dimensions of well-being.

Briefly, the Gini indices we display here are bounded between zero and (almost) one. Higher values represent periods in which we infer relatively high wealth differentiation among households. Lower Ginis mark periods of greater equality in household wealth. The sequence in Kohler and Ellyson (2018) has been updated by Ellyson, and the numbers in figure 11.10 match those recently presented in Ellyson et al. (2019).

Figure 11.10 shows that the early 1100s CE, when the Chaco Regional System was best expressed in this area, presents the greatest wealth inequalities in this sequence. The significant decline in inequality after this period is our second collapse. Looking just at the central tendencies for the Gini calculations, other periods of relatively high inequality were the late 1100s/early 1200s, the early 800s, and the 600s and early 700s. Note that inequality declined markedly in each of our three collapses, circa 900, 1140, and the late 1200s. The marked decline circa 1000 does not coincide with our other indices of collapse but should perhaps be

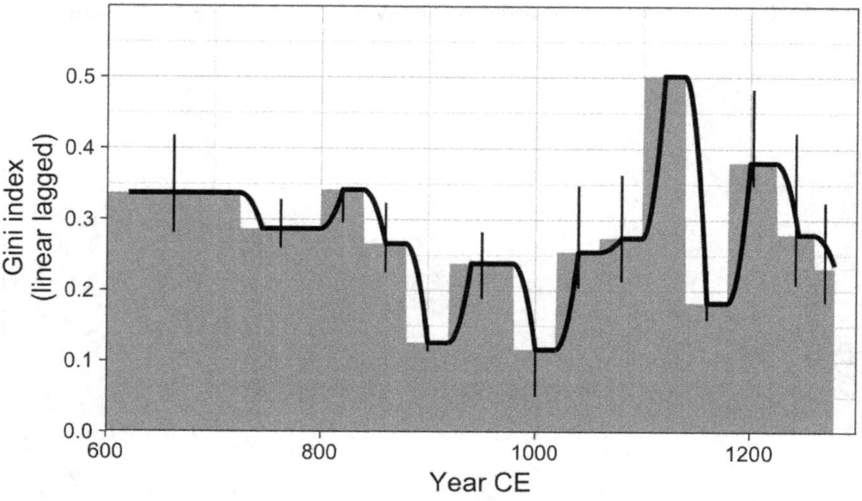

Figure 11.10. Wealth inequality (Gini indices) through time, with 80 percent Confidence Intervals (CIs). Figure created by the authors.

ignored, as based on only three households. (See Ellyson et al. 2019 for sample sizes.)

History of Violence

Walter Scheidel (2017) argues that in normally functioning societies, wealth inequalities tend to remain stable or increase, noting that rapid declines in Ginis can be expected only alongside massive disruption and violence. We can examine this suggestion here using a violence index created by Sarah Cole (2012). As part of her MA thesis research at Washington State University, using the periodization established by the VEP, Cole combed through published and gray literature to tabulate the proportions of sets of human remains bearing marks of violence-induced trauma for the central Mesa Verde region. Her results are in figure 11.11.

Comparison of figures 4, 5, 10, and 11 in this chapter, though, leads to a conundrum phrased by Kohler and Ellyson (2018, 146) as follows:

> We now raise the possibility that some of the episodic violence we see in the CMV may have been intended to challenge high levels of social inequality; each local peak in violence occurred immediately after, or during, a local peak in inequality. . . . Of course, we cannot entirely rule out a different causality: episodes of violence could have been brought on by decreasing productivity causing social chaos as existing social contracts collapsed. In fact, there is no reason to believe that both of these causal paths might not have been effective and mutually constitutive.

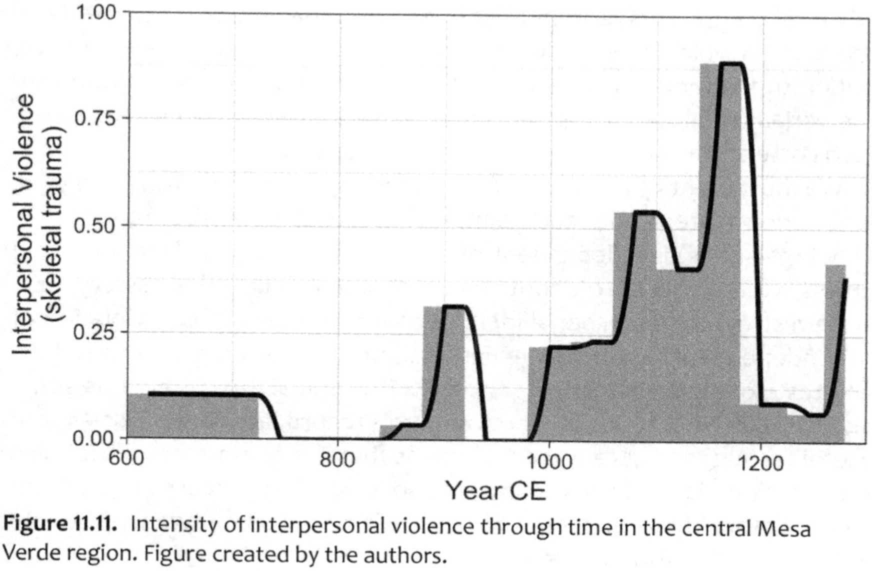

Figure 11.11. Intensity of interpersonal violence through time in the central Mesa Verde region. Figure created by the authors.

Putting It All Together

Finally, then, we arrive at our main problem. Can we unravel cause and effect in the coincidence of decreases in maize production/niche size, decreases in inequality, and increases in violence that we see at the ends of the PI, PII, and PIII periods? The quantitative resources available for this job are collected in figure 11.12, which displays the linear-lagged versions of these variables.

We will begin with a classic social science move, called cross-sectional or synchronic analysis, examining the relative importance of various potential regressors in three linear models, where "importance" is defined as relating to the amount of explained variance (Gromping 2006). These will work on a version of the data set displayed above, from which we sampled one year every twenty-five years beginning in 679 CE and ending in 1279, giving us twenty-five cases (observations). We also carried out the same analysis using thirty-one time slices of twenty years each, with similar results. Of the fourteen periods identified by the VEP, that from 600–725 CE is by far the longest. Thus, there is no change in any of the variables presented as period averages during the 600s, so we would gain nothing by including more years in that century.[4]

The first model takes violence as the dependent (variable to be explained). The method we employ follows a suggestion by Lindeman, Merenda, and Gold[5] (1980) as implemented in the R package *relaimpo* (Gromping 2006). It is designed to work well for cases, such as here, where the regressors (potential independent variables) are correlated and the order in which they are considered will influence their apparent contribution to the model R^2. However, to simplify the discussion we removed the variable "04-Average prod" from these analyses given its extremely high correlation with "05-Average prod per capita."

We must point out that one key assumption of the following analyses, which we violate, is that each sample (here, each time-slice from the VEPIIN time series) is independent of all the others. This is clearly not true unless we are willing to adopt the untenable position that history, ecosystem structure, and spatial identity count for nothing. Our violation of this independent random sampling assumption prevents us from taking any tests of significance too seriously. These analyses do give us some insight as to what tends to co-occur in this record, across periods—more useful for suggesting causal connections than for testing them. They also suggest directions of causal influence so long as both causes and effects could reasonably be expected to occur within the same twenty-five-year windows distinguished here.

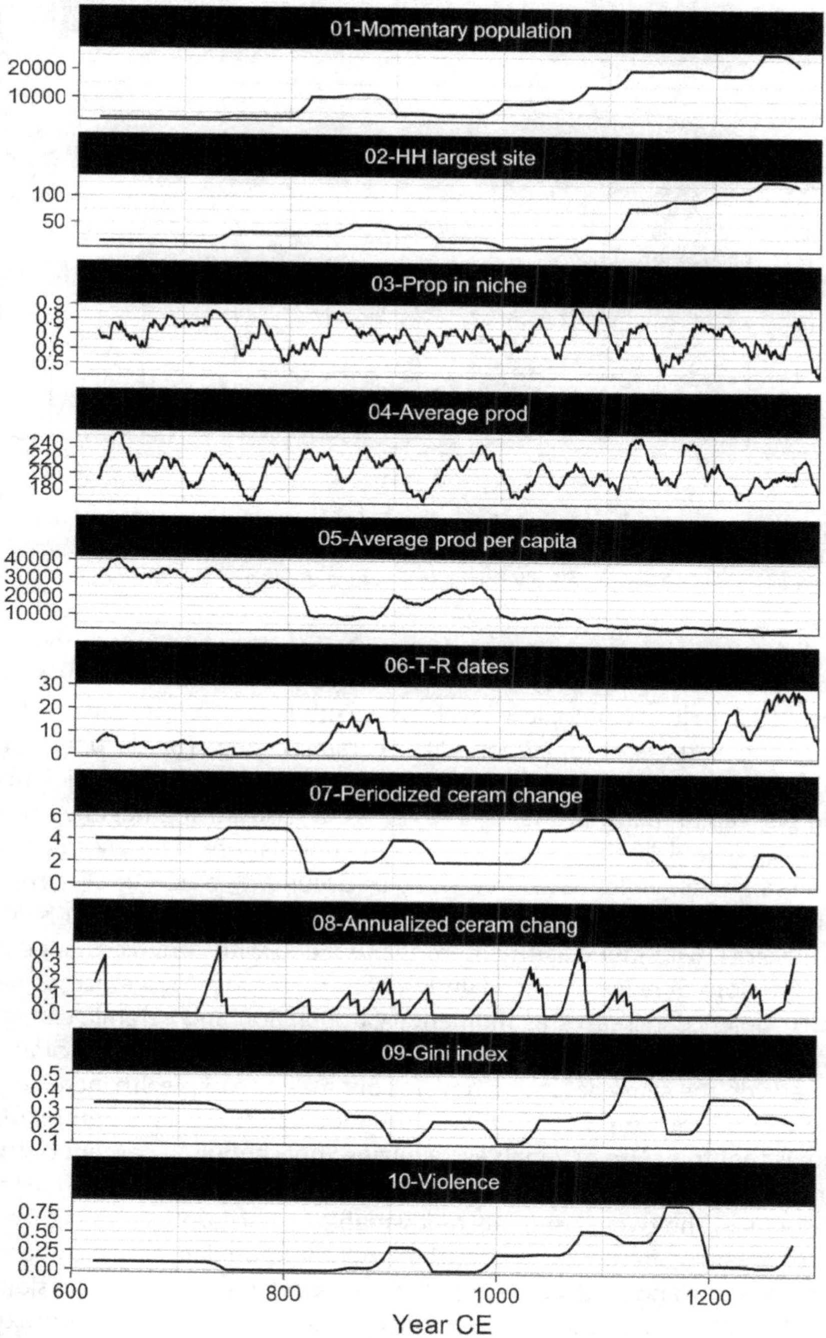

Figure 11.12. Linear-lagged variables, combined; see preceding figures for *y*-axis units and more detail. Figure created by the authors.

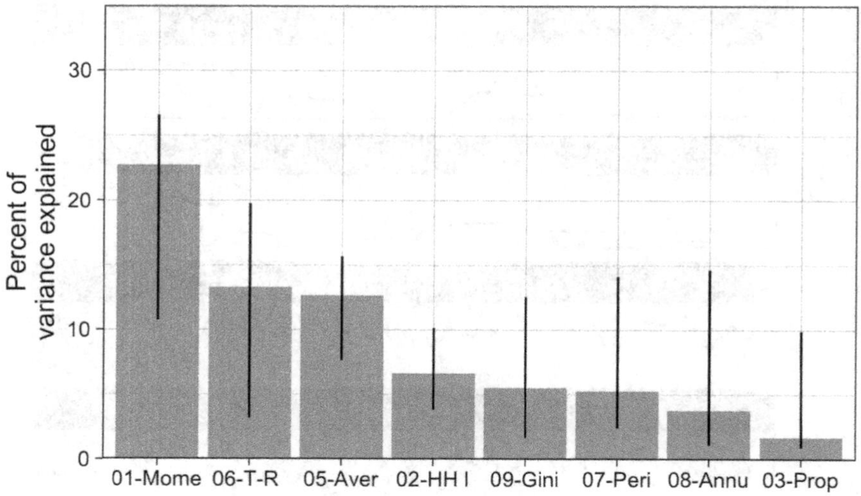

Figure 11.13. Relative importance of predictors of violence. Total $R^2 = 0.716$. Of the four variables significantly related to violence, 01 and 07 are positively correlated, whereas 06 and 09 are negatively correlated. Figure created by the authors.

High levels of violence strongly co-occur with high values for 01-momentary population ($p>|t| = 0.03$), low values for current construction (06-tree-ring dates, $p>|t| = 0.005$), low levels of wealth inequality (09-Gini, $p>|t| = 0.01$), and high values for 07-periodized ceramic change ($p>|t| = 0.09$) (figure 11.13).[6] None of the other variables has a $p>|t| < 0.36$, although violence and per capita maize production (05) have a fairly strong negative relationship. In words, then, violence and high populations strongly co-occur across periods. Violence also tends to co-occur with a dearth of current construction (and with disaggregation, although this relationship is not significant), with low wealth differentiation, and with ceramic change at the typological level. Stated slightly differently, as we move across periods, violence increases as momentary population and ceramic change increase, but as construction and levels of wealth inequality are declining.

Let's do the same operation now for our measure of wealth inequality. The co-occurrence pattern for wealth inequality is weaker; figure 11.14 shows that this suite of variables "explains" only about 46 percent of the Gini variability, whereas we explained about 72 percent of the variability in violence. The two most important variables co-occurring with high levels of wealth differentiation are 01-momentary population, which has a positive slope and $p>|t| = 0.04$ and 10-violence, which has a negative slope ($p>|t| = 0.05$). In words, high wealth inequalities tend to occur in contexts offering high populations and low violence. Although they are less important, it is interesting to note that the two next-most-important variables

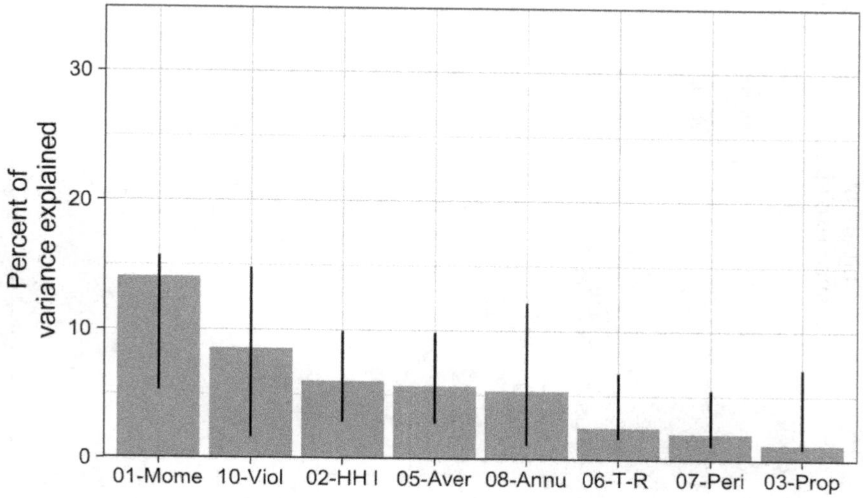

Figure 11.14. Relative importance of predictors of Gini coefficients. Total $R^2 = 0.456$. Momentary population (01) is significantly positively correlated with the Ginis; violence (10) is significantly negatively correlated. Figure created by the authors.

are 02-degree of aggregation and 05-per capita production, both of which are positively related to Gini indices.

Clearly we could continue this exercise for each of our variables, but not wanting to get disoriented in the garden of forking paths let's limit ourselves to examining the factors influencing momentary population size, since theory—and the results above—suggests its centrality to the changes of interest here. Figure 11.15 shows that momentary population strongly covaries with 05-per capita maize production, with which it has a strong mechanical, negative correlation. It positively covaries with 02-degree of aggregation ($p>|t| < 0.001$), 10-level of violence ($p>|t| = 0.03$), and 09-Gini index ($p>|t| = 0.04$). It also positively covaries with counts of tree-ring dates (06), since increasing populations require new housing but declining ones can make do with existing infrastructure, though the relationship is not significant ($p>|t| < 0.29$). The predictability of momentary population ($R^2 = 0.96$) is considerably larger than that for either wealth inequality or violence. This echoes results by Turchin et al. (2018), who found that "Polity Population" was linked to eight other "complexity characteristics" more strongly than any other variable in a global cross-cultural data set, Seshat, in development by this group. However, our inclusion of per capita maize production among the independents undoubtedly boosts this measure of multiple R^2.

While these synchronic comparisons help us understand how all these variables interact, it is important to remember that we would get these

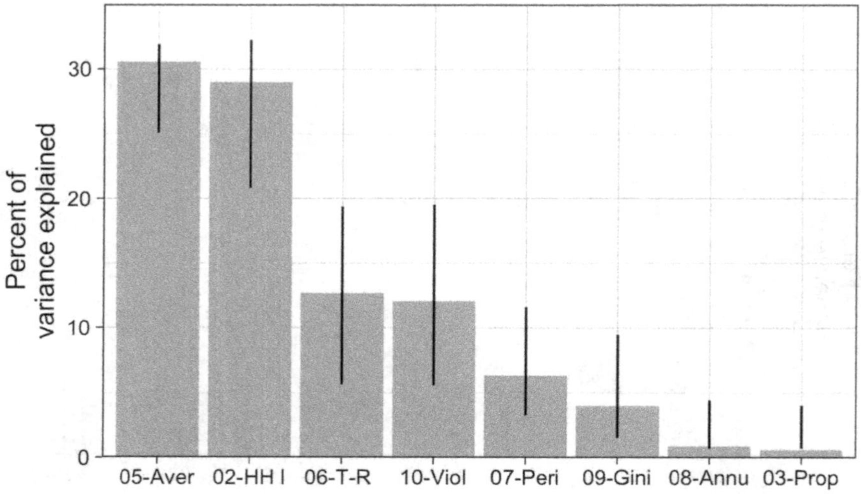

Figure 11.15. Relative importance of predictors of momentary population size. Total $R^2 = 0.962$. Of the four variables significantly related to momentary population, 05 is negatively correlated, and 02, 06, and 10 are positively correlated. Figure created by the authors.

same results no matter what order we use to sort the snapshots representing these periods. In other words, in the analyses so far, their *actual* sequence counts for nothing. This seems unreasonable—archaeologists work very hard to get the timing right after all! To make full use of the temporal structure of our data requires turning to a style of analysis that honors the historical sequence of the periods. Such an analysis might be called "longitudinal" by sociologists, though a typical longitudinal analysis in that field might follow individuals for a few years or perhaps a few decades—rarely or never a region over many centuries. Temporal precedence is an important factor in determining causation, so having a data set in which regular time steps are encoded is advantageous (to say the least) for any analysis hoping to identify causes and effects.

Saving Time Using Granger Causality

The literature on causal analysis of time series is little known or used by archaeologists outside of a few specialized subfields such as analysis of tree-ring sequences. The most similar study we have seen, by Zhang et al. (2011), draws on both textual and geoscience data to look for causal structure among variables such as population growth, temperature, famine, epidemics, and war in Europe from 1500 to 1800 CE. Benefiting greatly from the annual granularity in many of these series, they were able to demonstrate that temperature variability caused variability in bioproductivity, with cascading effects on agricultural productivity, food supply per capita, and a suite of variables including social disturbances, war, and famine. Another relevant application is by Turchin (2018), who works with one-hundred-year time slices and lags of up to two (two hundred years) in his attempt to identify the causes of the evolution of the Seshat measure of information complexity in thirty-two regions. Turchin settles on a nonlinear model to explain the growth of information complexity. In this model the most important term is the value of information complexity in the previous century, followed by a square of that term and the lag2 of information, followed in turn by a number of less-influential variables, of which complexity of governing structures and increasingly sophisticated monetary instruments are the most important.

Both of these studies utilize a concept called "Granger causality" (Granger 1969), which provides a statistical test as to whether one variable is useful in forecasting another. Specifically, do past values of *x* enable significantly better prediction of current values of *y* than do past values of *y* alone? Almost needless to say, causal systems can be much more complex than that: two or more variables acting together might influence a third; there can be transitive relationships in which *x* affects *y*, which then affects *z*; and there can be cyclic (recursive) variants of any of these. Even so, bivariate examination of Granger causality is a good place to start.

We consider the following analyses to be exploratory, for two reasons.[7] First, our sample of twenty-five observations is very modest in size for any kind of time-series analysis. Second, there is some uncertainty on how to respond to one complexity of time-series data: that serial autocorrelation within variables may lead to biased estimates of regression coefficients between variables. Although the literature dealing with these issues is not completely concordant, the general recommendation is to remove trends within variables by differencing at some temporal lag. Stated more formally, if a standard test such as the Augmented Dickey-Fuller (ADF) test cannot reject the null hypothesis of "no unit root" (Said and Dickey 1984), one creates a new series in which each observation is the difference between the present value and a previous value at some lag.

Of the variables relevant to the analyses that follow, the ADF test cannot reject H_0 ($p > 0.38$) for those prefixed 01, 02, and 05; for those prefixed 03 and 04, the H_0 can be rejected (at $p < 0.05$) (these are our maize-production variables, which display no significant serial autocorrelation at temporal lags of twenty-five years). Results were intermediate for 09-Gini index ($p = 0.18$) and 10-violence ($p = 0.14$). For 01, 02, 05, 09, and 10 we created new variables by differencing at a lag1 (twenty-five years); higher-order lags were of less importance both for theoretical and statistical reasons. These differenced variables have a "d" following their numeric prefix. Given the rather ambiguous test results for 09-Gini index and 10-violence, we explored the behavior of both the raw and detrended (differenced) versions of these variables.[8]

Given the negative synchronic relationship between violence and wealth differentiation (figures 11.13 and 11.14), we first examine whether either of these variables also Granger-causes the other at a lag of 1. This is in effect asking (for example) whether the previous values of violence *plus* the previous values of Gini predict the current values of Gini better than do just the previous values of the Gini. The answer in both cases is maybe: there is weak evidence that violence Granger-causes Ginis (p = 0.1) and roughly comparable evidence that Ginis Granger-cause violence (p = 0.13). Both effects disappear after differencing, where 09d-Gini index does not Granger-cause 10d-violence (p = 0.28), and 10d-violence does not Granger-cause 09d-Gini index (p = 0.97).

These somewhat ambiguous results may suggest that in addition to some negative correlation between current values of wealth differentiation and violence, high violence in the previous generation (generally accompanying low Ginis) may positively influence current tendencies to differentially accumulate wealth—a relationship that seems puzzling. Likewise, high wealth differentiation in the previous generation may increase current levels of violence—an effect that is easier to understand. This lagged, weak reciprocal causal relationship between these two variables records the tendencies of these two variables to flip states through time, with high wealth inequality/low violence followed by low wealth inequality/high violence (and vice versa).

The other interesting relationship pointed up in the Granger causality analyses targeted on these variables is for high momentary population in the previous period to contribute to aggregation (02-HH largest site) in the current period (p = 0.02). We might speculate that this is due to a landscape- or ecosystem-memory effect. For example, recent high population may locally deplete slowly renewing resources such as deer, making life in villages, with their greater opportunities for balanced reciprocal exchange, more attractive (Kohler and Van West 1996). On the other hand, average production per capita may play a regulatory function for aggregate size in the next period, since these two variables are linked by a weak negative relationship (p = 0.12). Neither of these relationships remains significant after lag1 differencing, however.

Average per capita production also has a strong, significant, negative effect on violence in the next period. That is, high current per capita production leads to low violence in the next generation. Part of this is surely due to a storage effect, since high production allows stores to be topped up. We also speculate that habits of peaceful relationship developed in periods of high production may somewhat outlive high production itself. Since low current per capita production leads to high violence in the next period, the converse also appears possible, unfortunately. Per capita production has no significant effect on current or subsequent Ginis.

Discussion and Conclusions

In figure 11.16 we summarize the main lessons learned here on the relationships among violence, wealth differentiation, and maize production in the central Mesa Verde region.

Beginning with the most exogenous variable, decreasing average per capita maize production (resulting in part from high momentary population) tends to accompany increasing aggregation and increasing violence. High violence tends to suppress current wealth differences (figure 11.12), though the effect is slightly too weak to be shown among the synchronic relationships in figure 11.16. Over time—as shown by the diachronic dynamics—low Ginis tend (rather weakly) to entrain low violence. On the other hand, high Ginis eventually (but weakly) also entrain high violence.

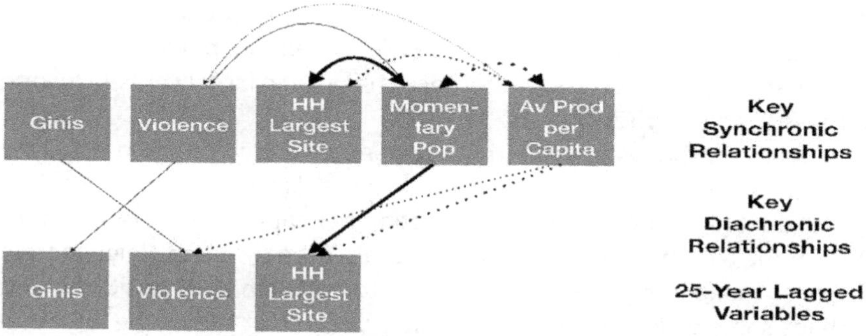

Figure 11.16. Sketch of causal relationships among focus variables. Synchronic correlation coefficients and *p* values apply the Holm adjustment for multiple comparisons (Holm 1979); only *r* values > |0.49| are shown. Thicker lines/dots denote lower *p* values (i.e., relationships less likely to be due to chance); dotted lines show negative relationships. Granger-causality probabilities in the diachronic comparisons are derived by comparing the fit of models with and without the ancillary variable and do not employ the lag1-differenced versions of the variables. Key synchronic relationships affecting the variables lagged twenty-five years are not shown but are the same as those shown for the upper row of variables. Figure created by the authors.

Figure 11.16 also shows a weak positive diachronic effect of violence on Ginis. Putting these two tendencies together (and using the operator → to indicate "leads in the next generation to") suggests that

high Ginis → high violence → high Ginis, and
low Ginis → low violence → low Ginis

across three generations, signaling two possible attractors in this dynamic. But figure 11.12 shows that this is clearly *not* what actually happens, and the reason is that the synchronic positive effect of high population on violence and the synchronic negative effect of production per capita on violence are both stronger than the diachronic reinforcing effects that Ginis and violence have on each other.

Thus, the apparent symmetry lamented by Kohler and Ellyson (2018) is broken. We can say with some confidence that agricultural production crises (led either by climatically or demographically induced shortfalls) lead to violence, which then has a (slight but immediate) negative effect on wealth differentiation. (Note that figure 11.16 shows two causal paths between average production per capita and violence, but no direct path between average production per capita and Ginis.) In this specific history, though, high violence then entrains high Ginis in the following generation: it does not take long for wealth differences to rebound. We would like to know whether the critical factor in this rebound is differences in quality of lands held by specific households or lineages, or differential labor capacities, or the structural imperatives of ceremonial systems. Whatever the case, the (inferred) prevailing system of balanced reciprocal exchange appears able to rebuild notable wealth differences among households within a generation, even after such differences have been largely erased by one of these "catastrophes."

In overview then, shortfalls in maize per capita are likely to precipitate violence, either in the current period or more likely yet in the following generation. (Shortfalls in maize production per capita are of course more likely in the context of high population levels.) The resulting violence then seems to make it more difficult for elites to maintain their positions, and perhaps some violence was preferentially directed at them. The hypothesis we form from this case is for transitive causality from decreases in production through increased violence to decreased wealth differentiation.

This scenario strengthens the supposition that the variability in maize production seen here, in combination with the surprisingly variable population levels, "means something." It is certainly relevant to the levels of violence in this society, probably to the degree of aggregation, and likely (but more indirectly) relevant to the levels of wealth inequality that can be supported. Although this finding does not address whether avoiding imbalances between population and resources has been a *general* structuring principle in human societies (a view derided by George Cowgill in 1975 as "strictly from hunger"), it demonstrates that population and resource balances are relevant to human security and well-being in some cases.

Thus we echo conclusions reached by Sharratt, in chapter 10 in this volume for the late pre-Hispanic Andes, that marked climatically induced downturns in farming production may lead to violence. Our strategy for argument has been different than is typical for discussions of "catastrophes" in prehistory though, since we compute correlations across our entire sequence rather than just connecting a particular downturn with a specific episode of social crisis through logic and ancillary evidence. This allows us to conclude with equal confidence that (for example) *high* current per capita production tends to both accompany low current violence and lead to low violence in the next generation. We consider our approach to explanation preferable, since it is more complete. However, we agree with Currie (2019) that the more common approach—which he calls "one-shot hypotheses"—can still productively highlight dependencies between variables and provide "explanatory resources" to construct more complete and complex explanations.

In chapter 12 in this volume, Detlef Gronenborn and colleagues attribute the final decline of the Württemberg LBK (of Southwest Germany) to a combination of factors related to social identity, social diversity, unfavorable climatic variability, and population increases during previous climatically favorable periods. We suggest that wealth inequality as discussed here can be viewed as a component of social identity within the framework established by Gronenborn and colleagues, in that wealth inequalities that are too high may undermine social solidarity. (Paskov and Dewilde [2012] present evidence for this effect in contemporary Europe.) And indeed, we have demonstrated that high wealth inequality has a tendency to precipitate violence in the next generation. In the long run, to make larger-scale comparisons possible, we should work to harmonize the set of variables we attempt to consider in such studies, as well as the manner in which they are considered.

Our results provide some deep-time perspective on the vexed question of whether a relationship exists between climatic variability and violence in the world today—a literature partly motivated by anxiety about possible increased violence under global warming. Recent reviews (Koubi 2019; Theisen 2017) converge on the view that although violence in current and recent societies does not necessarily have climatic causes, some conditions do contribute to the likelihood that climatic variability provoking scarcity will precipitate violence. These include high dependence on agriculture, a standard of living near the subsistence level, existence of politically salient identity cleavages, and low capacity of the state (or other institutions). The societies discussed here seem to satisfy most or all of these conditions.

In closing, we have demonstrated that systematic and rigorous approaches to explanation are within the reach of archaeology. If archaeologists choose to pursue nonexplanatory narratives, it is due to prior theoretical commitments or interests, not necessity. Archaeology plays from a stronger hand in its attempts to use prehistory to inform contemporary policy when it deals in causality and not just examples. Perhaps this chapter, and allied work, can begin to rescue archaeology from the lagged effects of rejection of the possibility of detecting large-scale causal structure in human history.

Acknowledgments

This material is based upon work supported by the National Science Foundation under grants BCS-0119981 (VEP I), DEB-0816400 (VEP II), IBSS-1620462, and SMA-1637171 (SKOPE). We thank the many contributors to the VEP and these other projects over the years. Kohler also acknowledges the TransMonDyn project, especially Laure Nuninger and Lena Sanders, the Santa Fe Institute, and Crow Canyon Archaeological Center. The participants in the delightful Aarhus symposium, and Keith Kintigh, provided many useful comments on an earlier version of this chapter. Finally, we thank Felix Riede and Payson Sheets for the invitation to Aarhus and Moesgård, and the Research Institute for Humanity and Nature, Kyoto, where Kohler completed final edits to this chapter.

Timothy A. Kohler is a regents professor of archaeology and evolutionary anthropology at Washington State University, an external faculty member at the Santa Fe Institute, a research associate with the Research Institute at Crow Canyon, and was in residence as an invited scholar at the Research Institute for Humanity and Nature, Kyoto, during final edits to his contribution here. In 2019 he received a Presidential Recognition Award from the Society for American Archaeology "in appreciation of efforts in helping SAA examine ways in which professional archaeologists can better share the value of our research with the contemporary world."

Laura J. Ellyson is a PhD candidate in the Department of Anthropology at Washington State University. Her contribution to this volume expands her dissertation research on the emergence of wealth inequalities in the pre-Hispanic American Southwest. Her research has been published by the *Journal of Anthropological Archaeology*, the *Journal of Anthropological Research*, and in the volume *Ten Thousand Years of Inequality: The Archaeology of Wealth Differences* edited by Timothy A. Kohler and Michael E. Smith.

R. Kyle Bocinsky is the William D. Lipe Chair in Research and director of the Research Institute at Crow Canyon Archaeological Center in Cortez, Colorado, and a research scientist with the Montana Climate Office at the University of Montana. He received his PhD in anthropology from Washington State University in 2014, where he was the recipient of the College of Arts and Sciences Graduate Achievement Award in the Social Sciences. His research on human responses to environmental change has appeared in the *Proceedings of the National Academy of Sciences*, *Science*, *Nature Communications*, *Science Advances*, and *Current Anthropology*.

Notes

1. Here we seek a higher temporal resolution of about a generation by truncating the long first period (600–725 CE) to its final portion. The remaining thirteen periods average about forty-three years in length. As described below, we smooth each data series using a twenty-one-year linear filter and sample them at twenty-five-year intervals.
2. In the niche reconstruction we do not remove cells with very high slopes, or composed mostly of bedrock, or having other edaphic barriers to successful farming, as we do in the productivity reconstruction.
3. Assuming that maize provides 3,610 calories/kg; other values required for this estimate are from Kohler (2012c, table 4.1).
4. Ortman et al. (2016) have recently suggested a mechanism for dividing this long period into two portions; unfortunately this cannot be applied retroactively to the VEP demographic estimates.
5. Also known as Shapley Value Regression.
6. *p* values here and in the following are taken from multiple linear regression models on the dependent variable in the saturated model (composed of all the variables graphed in each figure).
7. We use the function grangertest from the R package lmtest (Zeileis and Hothorn 2002), specifying "order = 1" (lag = 1).
8. For comparison, Zhang et al. (2011) conducted ADF tests and used detrended variables in subsequent analyses when suggested by the outcomes of the test; Turchin (2018) does neither. We prefer the non-detrended results for our case, given the small number of observations and the rather large time steps between them.

References

Binford, Lewis R. 1983. *In Pursuit of the Past: Decoding the Archaeological Record*. New York: Thames Hudson.

Bocinsky, R. Kyle, and Timothy A. Kohler. 2014. "2,000-Year Reconstruction of the Rain-Fed Maize Agricultural Niche in the US Southwest." *Nature Communications* 5 (5618).

Bocinsky, R. Kyle, Johnathan Rush, Keith W. Kintigh, and Timothy A. Kohler. 2016. "Exploration and Exploitation in the Macrohistory of the Pre-Hispanic Pueblo Southwest." *Science Advances* 2: e1501532.

Bocinsky, R. Kyle, and Mark D. Varien. 2017. "Comparing Maize Paleoproduction Models with Experimental Data." *Journal of Ethnobiology* 37 (2): 282–307.

Borgerhoff Mulder, Monique, Samuel Bowles, Tom Hertz, Adrian Bell, Jan Beise, Greg Clark, Ila Fazzio, et al. 2009. "Intergenerational Wealth Transmission and the Dynamics of Inequality in Small-Scale Societies." *Science* 326 (5953): 682–88.

Burns, Barney T. 1983. "Simulated Anasazi Storage Behavior Using Crop Yields Reconstructed from Tree-Rings: A.D. 652–1968." Unpublished PhD dissertation, University of Arizona, Tucson.

Camus, Albert. 1942. *L'Étranger*. Paris: Gallimard.

Cole, Sarah M. 2012. "Population Dynamics and Warfare in the Central Mesa Verde Region." In *Emergence and Collapse of Early Villages: Models of Central Mesa Verde Archaeology*, edited by Timothy A. Kohler and Mark D. Varien, 197–218. Berkeley: University of California Press.

Cowgill, George. 1975. "On the Causes and Consequences of Ancient and Modern Population Changes." *American Anthropologist* 77 (3): 505–25.

Currie, Adrian. 2019. "Simplicity, One-Shot Hypotheses and Paleobiological Explanation." *History and Philosophy of the Life Sciences* 41 (10).

Douglass, A. E. 1929. "The Secret of the Southwest Solved by Talkative Tree Rings." *National Geographic Magazine* 56: 736–70.

Dunning, Nicholas P., Timothy P. Beach, and Sheryl Luzzadder-Beach. 2012. "Kax and Kol: Collapse and Resilience in Lowland Maya Civilization." *Proceedings of the National Academy of Sciences* 109 (10): 3652–57.

Ellyson, Laura J., Timothy A. Kohler, and Catherine M. Cameron. 2019. "How Far from Chaco to Oraibi? Quantifying Inequality among Pueblo Households." *Journal of Anthropological Archaeology* 55: 101073.

Gelman, Andrew, and Eric Loken. 2014. "The Statistical Crisis in Science." *American Scientist* 102 (6): 460–65.

Glowacki, Donna M., and Scott G. Ortman. 2012. "Characterizing Community-Center (Village) Formation in the VEP Study Area, A.D. 600–1280." In *Emergence and Collapse of Early Villages: Models of Central Mesa Verde Archaeology*, edited by Timothy A. Kohler and Mark D. Varien, 219–46. Berkeley: University of California Press.

Granger, Clive W. 1969. "Investigating Causal Relations by Econometric Models and Cross-Spectral Methods." *Econometrica* 37 (3): 424–38.

Gromping, Ulrike. 2006. "Relative Importance for Linear Regression in r: The Package Relaimpo." *Journal of Satatistical Software* 17 (1): 1–27.

Hodder, Ian. 1986. *Reading the Past: Current Approaches to Interpretation in Archaeology*. Cambridge: Cambridge University Press.

———. 2012. *Entangled: An Archaeology of the Relationships between Humans and Things*. Chichester, UK: Wiley-Blackwell.

Holm, S. 1979. "A Simple Sequentially Rejective Multiple Test Procedure." *Scandinavian Journal of Statistics* 6 (2): 65–70.

Kohler, Timothy A. 2010. "A New Paleoproductivity Reconstruction for Southwestern Colorado, and Its Implications for Understanding Thirteenth-Century Depopulation." In *Leaving Mesa Verde: Peril and Change in the Thirteenth-Century Southwest*, edited by Timothy A. Kohler, Mark D. Varien, and Aaron M. Wright, 102–27. Tucson: University of Arizona Press.

———. 2012a. "The Rise and Collapse of Villages in the Central Mesa Verde Region." In *Emergence and Collapse of Early Villages: Models of Central Mesa Verde Archaeology*, edited by Timothy A. Kohler and Mark D. Varien, 237–62. Berkeley: University of California Press.

———. 2012b. "Modeling Agricultural Productivity and Farming Effort." In *Emergence and Collapse of Early Villages: Models of Central Mesa Verde Archaeology*, edited by Timothy A. Kohler and Mark D. Varien, 85–112. Berkeley: University of California Press.

———. 2012c. "Simulation Model Overview." In *Emergence and Collapse of Early Villages: Models of Central Mesa Verde Archaeology*, edited by Timothy A. Kohler and Mark D. Varien, 59–83. Berkeley: University of California Press.

Kohler, Timothy A., and R. Kyle Bocinsky. 2017. "Crises as Opportunities for Culture Change." In *Crisis to Collapse: The Archaeology of Social Breakdown*, edited by Tim Cunningham and Jan Driessen, 263–74. Aegis 11. Belgium: Presses Universitaires de Louvain, Louvain-la-Neuve.

Kohler, Timothy A., and Laura J. Ellyson. 2018 "In and Out of Chains? The Changing Social Contract in the Pueblo Southwest, A.D. 600–1300." In *Ten Thousand Years of Inequality: The Archaeology of Wealth Differences*, edited by Timothy A. Kohler and Michael E. Smith, 130–54. Tucson: University of Arizona Press.

Kohler, Timothy A., and Carla R. Van West. 1996. "The Calculus of Self Interest in the Development of Cooperation: Sociopolitical Development and Risk among the Northern Anasazi." In *Evolving Complexity and Environment: Risk in the Prehistoric Southwest*, edited by Joseph A. and Bonnie Bagley Tainter, 169–96. Santa Fe Institute Studies in the Sciences of Complexity, Proceedings 24. Reading, MA: Addison-Wesley.

Kohler, Timothy A., and Mark D. Varien, eds. 2012. *Emergence and Collapse of Early Villages: Models of Central Mesa Verde Archaeology*. Berkeley: University of California Press.

Kohler, Timothy A., Mark D. Varien, Aaron M. Wright, and Kristin A. Kuckelman. 2008. "Mesa Verde Migrations." *American Scientist* 96 (2): 146–53.

Koubi, Vally. 2019. "Climate Change and Conflict." *Annual Review of Political Science* 22: 343–60.

Lekson, Stephen H. 2015. *The Chaco Meridian: One Thousand Years of Political and Religious Power in the Ancient Southwest*. 2nd ed. Lanham, MD: Rowman & Littlefield.

Lindeman, R. H., P. F. Merenda, and R. Z. Gold. 1980. *Introduction to Bivariate and Multivariate Analysis*. Glenview, IL: Scott, Foresman.

Lipe, William D. 2010. "Lost in Transit: The Central Mesa Verde Archaeological Complex." In *Leaving Mesa Verde: Peril and Change in the Thirteenth-Century Southwest*, edited by Timothy A. Kohler, Mark D. Varien, and Aaron M. Wright, 262–84. Tucson: University of Arizona Press.

Longacre, William A. 1964. "Archeology as Anthropology: A Case Study." *Science* 144 (3625): 1454–55.

Ortman, Scott G., Shanna Diederichs, Kari Schleher, Jerry Fetterman, Marcus Espinosa, and Caitlin Sommer. 2016. "Demographic and Social Dimensions of the Neolithic Demographic Revolution in Southwest Colorado." *Kiva* 82 (3): 232–58.

Ortman, Scott G., Mark D. Varien, and T. Lee Gripp. 2007. "Empirical Bayesian Methods for Archaeological Survey Data: An Application from the Mesa Verde Region." *American Antiquity* 72 (2): 241–72.

Paskov, Marii, and Caroline Dewilde. 2012. "Inequality and Solidarity in Europe." GINI Discussion Paper 33. Amsterdam Institute for Social Science Research. http://www.gini-research.org/system/uploads/379/original/DP_33_-_Paskov_Dewilde.pdf?1345621096.

Rakopoulos, Theodoros, and Knut Rio. 2018. "Introduction to an Anthropology of Wealth." *History and Anthropology* 29 (3): 275–91.

Robb, John. 2010. "Beyond Agency." *World Archaeology* 42 (4): 493–520.

Robb, John, and Timothy R. Pauketat. 2013. "From Moments to Millennia: Theorizing Scale and Change in Human History." In *Big Histories, Human Lives: Tackling Problems of Scale in Archaeology*, edited by John Robb and Timothy R. Pauketat, 3–34. Santa Fe, NM: School for Advanced Research.

Said, S. E., and D. A. Dickey. 1984. "Testing for Unit Roots in Autoregressive-Moving Average Models of Unknown Order." *Biometrika* 71 (3): 599–607.

Scheidel, Walter. 2017. *The Great Leveler: Violence and the History of Inequality from the Stone Age to the Twenty-First Century*. Princeton: Princeton University Press.

Schwindt, Dylan M., R. Kyle Bocinsky, Scott G. Ortman, Donna M. Glowacki, Mark D. Varien, and Timothy A. Kohler. 2016. "The Social Consequences of Climate Change in the Central Mesa Verde Region." *American Antiquity* 81 (1): 74–96.

Theisen, Ole Magnus. 2017. "Climate Change and Violence: Insights from Political Science." *Current Climate Change Reports* 3: 210–21.

Turchin, Peter. 2018. "Fitting Dynamic Regression Models to Seshat Data." *Cliodynamics* 9 (1): 25–58.

Turchin, Peter, Thomas E. Currie, Harvey Whitehouse, Pieter François, Kevin Feeney, Daniel Mullins, Daniel Hoyer, et al. 2018. "Quantitative Historical Analysis Uncovers a Single Dimension of Complexity That Structures Global Variation in Human Social Organization." *Proceedings of the National Academy of Science* 115 (2): E144–E151.

Van West, Carla R. 1994. *Modeling Prehistoric Agricultural Productivity in Southwestern Colorado: A GIS Approach*. Reports of Investigations 67. Pullman: Department of Anthropology, Washington State University.

Watson, Patty Jo, Steven A. LeBlanc, and Charles L. Redman. 1971. *Explanation in Archaeology: An Explicitly Scientific Approach*. New York: Columbia University Press.

Wenke, Robert J. 1981. "Explaining the Evolution of Cultural Complexity: A Review." In *Advances in Archaeological Method and Theory* 4, edited by Michael B. Schiffer, 79–128. New York: Academic Press.

Zeileis, Achim, and Torsten Hothorn. 2002. "Diagnostic Checking in Regression Relationships." *R News* 2: 7–10. https://CRAN.R-project.org/doc/Rnews/.

Zhang, David D., Harry F. Lee, Cong Wang, Baosheng Li, Qing Peia, Jane Zhang, and Yulun An. 2011. "The Causality Analysis of Climate Change and Large-Scale Human Crisis." *Proceedings of the National Academy of Sciences* 108 (42): 17296–301.

CHAPTER 12

Inherent Collapse?

Social Dynamics and External Forcing in Early Neolithic and Modern Southwest Germany

DETLEF GRONENBORN, HANS-CHRISTOPH STRIEN, KAI WIRTZ, PETER TURCHIN, CHRISTOPH ZIELHOFER, and ROLF VAN DICK

Summary for Stakeholders

Doubtlessly the next decades will be among the most challenging periods in the history of humankind. In this they bear a tragic component: for the first time humanity as a whole will be challenged by problems induced by humans themselves, by the Anthropocene and its major alterations in the Earth system, one component being global warming. In the light of this challenge also archaeology, anthropology, and the historical sciences have addressed the topic of climate impacts on human history.

This has particularly been the case for one of the most important quantum leaps in the history of humankind, the emergence and the dispersal of farming. Numerous studies have been undertaken, sometimes with data sets of considerable detail. But while earlier studies had proposed almost exclusive external mechanisms in that climate might have triggered and shaped the dispersal of farming, newer studies have adopted a much more nuanced approach. When we look at case studies with high-resolution data sets, simplistic scenarios become inapplicable. Any historic process must nowadays be understood as a result of complex positive and negative feedbacks, and it appears that from early farming societies onward endogenous social dynamics had played considerable and hitherto often overlooked roles. This is of course not to say that each decline or collapse in the course of human history was induced solely by internal processes, but these factors need to be addressed. Therefore, we have focused on an important social factor, namely social cohesion.

Our two case studies, being seven thousand years apart, suggest that early farmers and modern industrial societies underwent fluctuations in social dynamics that were and are inherent. The degree of social cohesion might determine the effectiveness with which societies were and will be able to cope with external stress factors.

So, for the future, ameliorating the possibly grave challenges of global change may greatly depend on the social cohesion of human societies, on local, regional, and global scales.

The Setting: The Neolithic Expansion in Western Eurasia

The emergence and the expansion of early farming societies is one of the most consequential socioeconomic shifts in human history (Diamond and Bellwood 2003; Barker 2006; Shennan 2018). The effects of this process are evident in the current genetic makeup of populations almost anywhere on Earth and are even visible in the physical properties of the human skeleton (Ruff et al. 2015). As various studies have shown, early farming is also accompanied by enormous population booms and busts, often associated with cultural disintegration or even collapse (Bocquet-Appel 2011; Shennan and Edinborough 2007; Shennan et al. 2013). While causation for these disintegrative phases is often unclear (Zahid, Robinson, and Kelly 2016; Weitzel and Codding 2016) and certainly the term "collapse" must be taken with caution (McAnany and Yoffee 2010a), it nevertheless describes actual periods of disintegration and shifts to succeeding periods, often with changes in genetic population composition (Lipson et al. 2017; Mathieson et al. 2018).

While farming emerges at different periods during the Holocene and at different locations on the globe (Fuller 2006; Fuller and Hildebrand 2013; Larson and Fuller 2014; Gallagher, Shennan, and Thomas 2015), one of the most consequential shifts was the emergence and the spread of farming societies in western Eurasia (Shennan 2018). Given the impacts of this process on global history, it has been the focus of continuous scholarly attention. Numerous hypotheses have been proposed concerning—what may have initiated the emergence of farming in the Near East and what may have forced the expansion of farming across western Eurasia (figure 12.1). With the study of "human-environment interactions" having been classified as one of the "grand challenges for archaeology" in Kintigh et al. (2014, 15–16), it is not surprising that early to mid-Holocene climate fluctuations have been suggested as forcing factors both for the emergence and the expansion of farming as well as the internal dynamics.

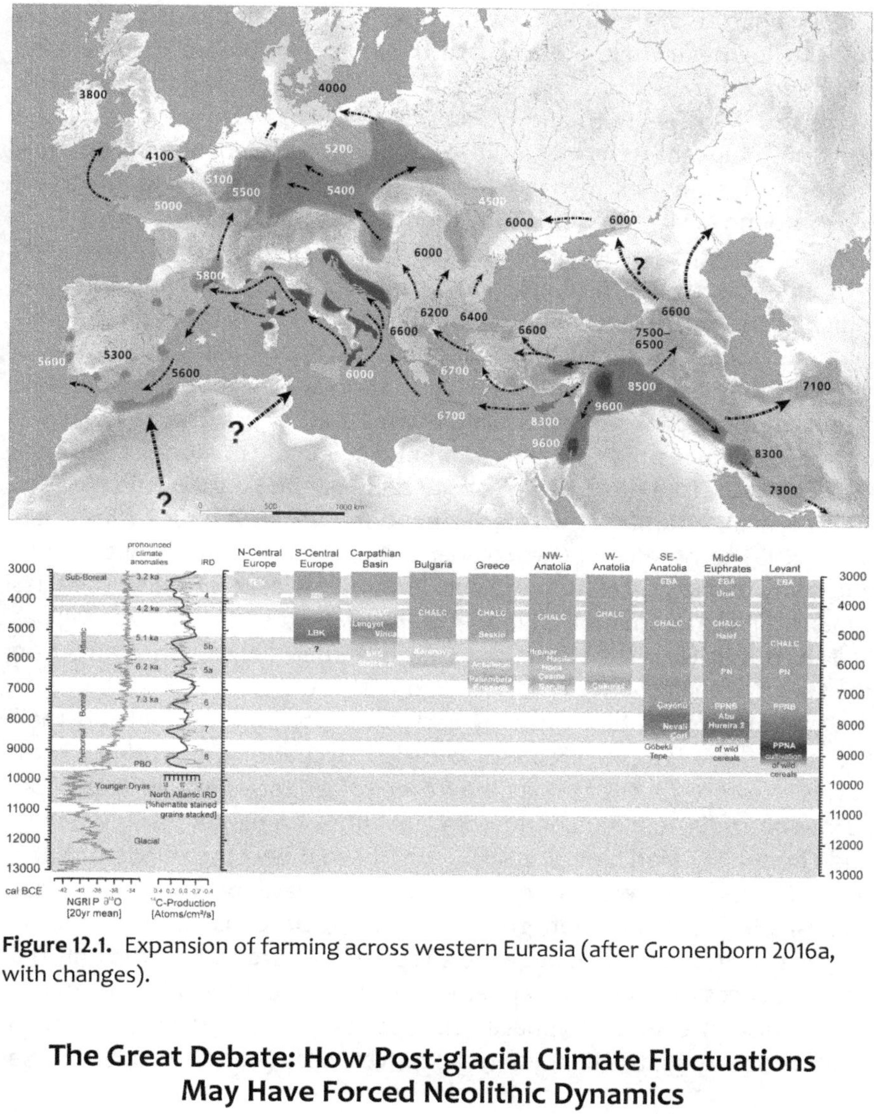

Figure 12.1. Expansion of farming across western Eurasia (after Gronenborn 2016a, with changes).

The Great Debate: How Post-glacial Climate Fluctuations May Have Forced Neolithic Dynamics

Climate excursions during the Holocene, often termed "Holocene rapid climate change (RCC) events" (Mayewski et al. 2004; Weninger et al. 2014; Rohling et al. 2019), are seen as key forcing events for Neolithic dynamics. Massive iceberg discharges into the North Atlantic, so-called ice-rafted debris (IRD) events, are considered to have been a significant component for the North Atlantic region, western Eurasia, and the Mediterranean basin (Bond et al. 2001; Wassenburg et al. 2016; Zielhofer et al. 2019). While a cycling nature of these RCC events has been challenged (Wanner et al. 2008), they nevertheless punctuate the Holocene with a certain regularity and are particularly characteristic for the earlier parts (figure 12.1), with the 7.3 ka (cal BCE) and 6.2 ka (cal BCE) cooling phases being the most pronounced (Berger et al. 2016). Less pronounced, but still possibly important for Neolithic dynamics in Europe are fluctuations at 5.1 ka (cal BCE), around 4.2 ka (cal BCE), and around 3.5 ka (cal BCE).

North Atlantic cooling can reduce the moisture content of the prevailing westerlies over western Eurasia and thus modifies regional hydroclimates, which in turn drive significant environmental changes in Mediterranean drylands (Migowski et al. 2006; Zielhofer et al. 2012; Rohling et al. 2019). A number of archeological studies have therefore focused on the possible effects of these pronounced cooling phases on the spread of farming and on the dynamics of these early farming societies. Opinions are opposing and reach from postulating considerable effects (e.g., Weninger et al. 2009; Weninger and Clare 2017; Gronenborn 2010a; Düring 2013; Horejs et al. 2015) to no effects (Reingruber 2018; Wainwright and Ayala 2019) and lastly to the postulation of considerable resilience of these societies against climate fluctuations (Flohr et al. 2016). Mathematical modeling has indicated that climate fluctuations may have had only a minor effect on the speed of the advance (Lemmen and Wirtz 2014).[1]

One common feature of many earlier climate impact studies is their focus on the negative effects of climate fluctuations on early farming societies. More recent studies, however investigate positive feedbacks (Gronenborn 2016a; Sánchez Goñi et al. 2016; Weninger 2017; Weiberg and Finné 2018; Clarke et al. 2016). From these it becomes evident that if the full historic process is to be understood, climate forcing on economic flourishing and population growth needs to be considered as well—maybe even more so than negative effects, which are quite often only the consequences of what had happened before. A theoretical framework to include history effects and phase dependency in social dynamics has been proposed through the concept of adaptive cycles (Redman 2005). These

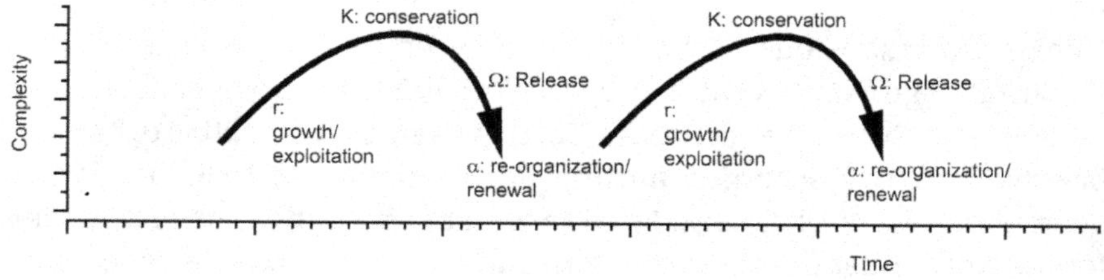

Figure 12.2. Adaptive cycles (after Gronenborn et al. 2014, with changes).

theories have been successfully applied on data from central Europe, a region on which this chapter will focus further on.

Adaptive Cycles and Resilience: A Coupled Culture-Environment Model

The concept of adaptive cycles in archaeology has been adopted from the environmental sciences (Redman and Kinzig 2003; Redman 2005; Dearing 2008). Subsequently, various groups and individual scholars within archaeology have suggested slight changes in the terminology and in concepts (Bradtmöller, Grimm, and Riel-Salvatore 2017).

For example, the original visualization has been simplified into a two-dimensional graph (figure 12.2), which would be better suited for the representation of archaeological time series (Gronenborn et al. 2014). The parameter "connectedness" of the adaptive cycles model by Holling and Gunderson (2002) had been changed into "complexity," a term archaeology may be more comfortable with (e.g., Price and Brown 1985; McIntosh 1999; Chapman [2003] 2008; Gunderson and Holling 2002). Lastly, we suggested an arrangement of nested and interrelated cycles on different regional and temporal scales (figure 12.3), a construct related to the panarchy concept of Gunderson and Holling (2002) in that coarser scales are at least partly composed out of finer-grained ones and information flows between the different scales of these cycles (Dearing 2008, 118; Bradtmöller, Grimm, and Riel-Salvatore 2017, 11). One major component of the adaptive cycles is resilience, and most of the archaeological studies have applied a definition based on Holling and Gunderson (2002), or derivatives (Bradtmöller, Grimm, and Riel-Salvatore 2017, 3). Here, as before (Gronenborn, Strien, and Lemmen 2017), we apply the definition by Walker et al. (2004), who introduced resilience as the capacity of a system to absorb disturbance and reorganize while undergoing change so as to still retain essentially the same function, structure, identity, and

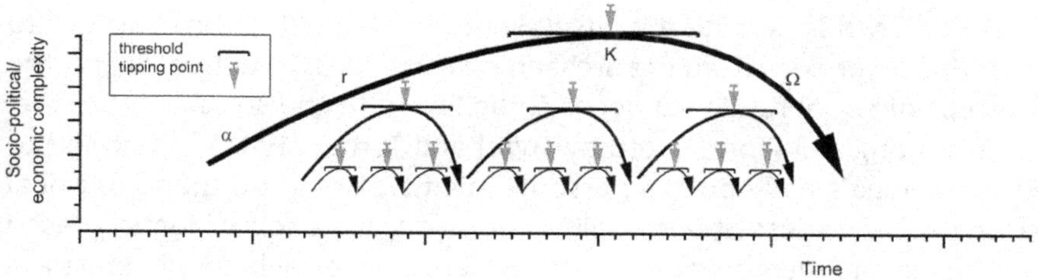

Figure 12.3. Nesting of cycles (after Gronenbern et al. 2014, with changes).

feedbacks. Obviously, this approach is but one out of many applications of the term (e.g., Barrios 2016), but it seems still applicable because of its general orientation.

The cycling structure and the entailed concept of resilience had proved quite helpful in understanding the complex interrelationships between socioeconomic developments and external influences, namely climate and environment, particularly in study areas where data is dense. It encompassed the interdependencies of human and nonhuman systems and helped in conceptualizing processes on various scales (e.g., Dearing 2008; McAnany and Yoffee 2010b; Zimmermann 2012a; Bradtmöller, Grimm, and Riel-Salvatore 2017).

Adaptive Cycles Refined: Social Identity Theory

While the concepts of adaptive cycles and resilience were a definite step forward in coming to grips with climate-culture interdependencies, one major problem remained, already addressed by Scheffer (2009, 79): Adaptive cycles work well conceptually but are also "intuitive metaphors" rather than "rigorous models." If these metaphors were to be used as an analytical tool, they would need to be tied to quantifiable proxy signals reflecting human activities. These rather ecology-based definitions, work agreeably well if proxies are analyzed that reflect human activities tied to the field of economics or population dynamics. However, when social parameters are concerned, these definitions may become problematic, and the concept of social resilience needs to be invoked (Gronenborn, Strien, and Lemmen 2017, 55). Being decoupled from the component of environment, social resilience focuses on inherently in-group organizational forms emphasizing individuality and agency (Keck and Sakdapolrak 2013; Maclean, Cuthill, and Ross 2014). The ostensibly determinant curve progression of cycles becomes subject to human forcing. Within this theoretical realm, social resilience is conceived as an active component controlled and shaped by human agency, which as a factor can prolong, abbreviate, or amplify processes.

However, this definition by itself is rather abstract and has no ties to quantifiable proxies from the archaeological record. To extract these, the concept of social resilience needs to be linked to the social identity theory (SIT) originally formulated by Tajfel and Turner (1986). According to SIT, individuals have both a personal identity, based on their individual strengths, weaknesses, personality, and so on, and a social identity, based on their group memberships. A strong sense of social belongingness is a basic motivation for any human and enhances the effective functioning of groups and societies (Baumeister and Leary 1995). Thus, group identities are formed by similarities and individuals' identification with their group, whereas differences or diversity within groups may contribute to misunderstandings and conflicts (van Knippenberg, Dreu, and Homan 2004). Therefore, groups that are more homogenous have a stronger sense of shared identities. Resilience as part of the SIT concept is thus determined by the degree with which group identity promotes effective reactions against both internal and external threats. This does not mean, though, that higher group homogeneity is generally more advantageous, as often these situations lead to the classical rigidity traps (Schultz and Searleman 2002; Carpenter and Brock 2008). In fact, higher diversity may at times be necessary to increase the number of possible solutions when individuals value diversity for completing certain tasks or overcoming challenges (van Dick et al. 2008).

Theoretically, then, any social history of a set period may be understood as a series of fluctuations between extremes of group diversity and group homogeneity. This idea is not new and can be traced back to Classical Greek historiography (Ryffel 1949), Durkheimian concepts (Gane 1992), but also to earlier theoretical studies in archaeology (Renfrew 1984; Renfrew and Cherry 1986; Blanton et al. 1996). The cyclical nature of these fluctuations and their possible effects on elite emergence have been discussed elsewhere (Gronenborn 2009; Gronenborn 2016b; Gronenborn et al. 2018; Turchin and Nefedov 2009), as have their possible effects on shifts in population densities (Zimmermann 2012a). Many of these previous studies had not yet explicitly embedded SIT, although they did encompass similar concepts (Kohler, VanBuskirk, and Ruscavage-Barz 2004; Gronenborn et al. 2014). SIT may help to further substantiate these approaches (Gronenborn et al. 2018).

Identifying Fluctuations in Group Diversity and Group Homogeneity in the Archaeological Record

The question then emerges as to how cycles between group diversity and group homogeneity as components of resilience may be identified, classified, and measured in the archaeological record. When this task is tackled, it becomes clear that components of social resilience may be reflected rather unevenly in the archaeological record and often may be reflected only very coarsely or not at all. But even if the archaeological preservation is good and the data sets are robust, different levels of resolution of social resilience may be reflected in different data sets. To come to grips with this problem of scales, we have suggested disentangling the concept of

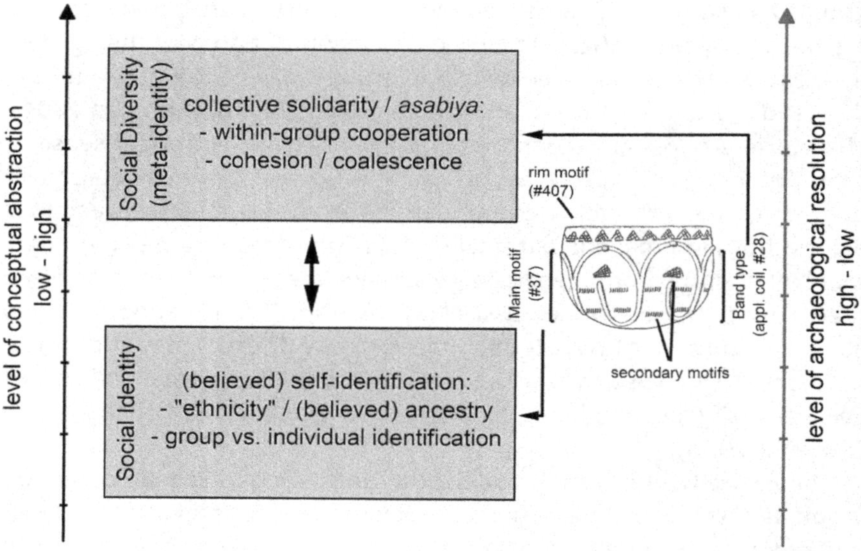

Figure 12.4. The difference between the concepts of social diversity in the sense of a meta-identity, social identity, and their respective degrees of archaeological visibility (modified after Gronenborn et al. 2018, 210, fig. 7). Manifestation of social diversity and social identity on a typical linear pottery ceramic vessel, coding after Kerig et al. (2010), accessed 23 May 2019. Reprinted here with Permission.

social resilience into two interrelated sub-concepts (figure 12.4). Within the proposed scheme, "social diversity" is a rather abstract entity reflecting within-group cooperation or group cohesion. It basically describes the rate of homogeneity in identification within groups or societies, with societies being more homogenous at the beginning and toward the end of cycles, and more diverse in phases in between (Gronenborn, Strien, and Lemmen 2017, 55; Gronenborn et al. 2018, 209).

In a way, "social diversity" (SD) may be understood as a meta-identity, although this sociological concept is ill-defined and appears to be applied to various scales, from cooperations and organizations to supranational levels (e.g., Kim 1994; Ro'i and Wainer 2009; Harris 2011). "Social identity" (SI), on the other hand, goes down to the level of the individual, reflecting self-identification (or, in the terminology of SIT, self-categorization) and the relationship between group and individual identification. Both concepts are preserved differently in the archaeological record, and both are preserved in different levels of resolution, with markers of social identity requiring rather fine-grained and high-resolution data sets (Gronenborn et al. 2018, 208). Nevertheless, both concepts do relate to each other, as social diversity is lastly composed out of individual identities and out of how individuals define themselves in relation to their own group and other groups (Tajfel and Turner 1986).

But, as both concepts operate on different scales, they may progress at nonidentical speed. Social diversity, as defined by us for this purpose, possibly operates on longer timescales and may be decoupled from population dynamics, as was previously demonstrated for central European early farming societies (Gronenborn, Strien, and Lemmen 2017; and below). Social identity, with its firm link to the individual, may progress on shorter timescales and more dynamically, as the proxy presented here shows. With this approach, social diversity and social identity then become quantifiable resilience factors. Other proxies, like those reflecting also economic components, may follow different curve progressions. Nevertheless, all these signals together compose the "metaphorical" adaptive cycles (figure 12.5).

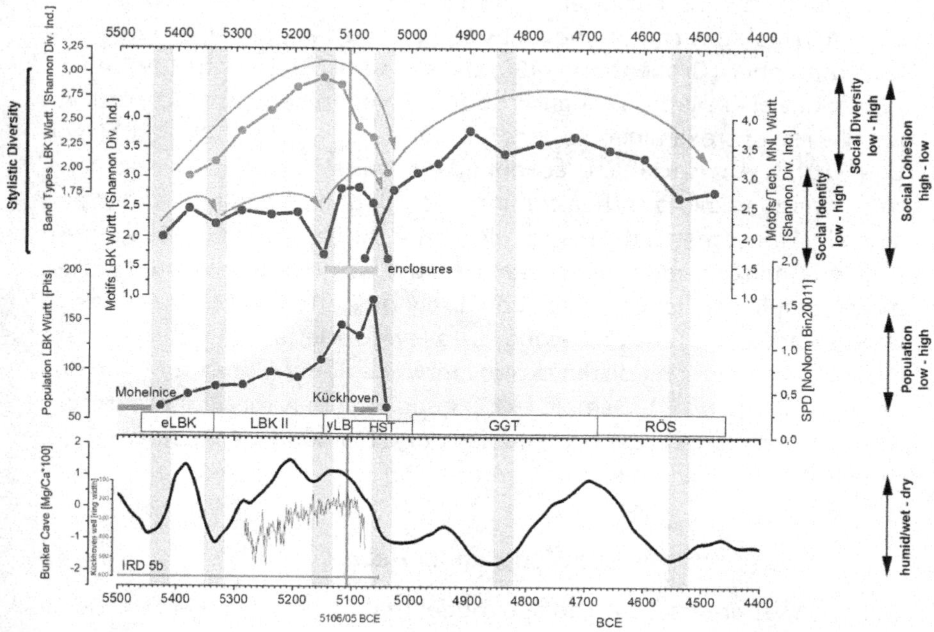

Figure 12.5. Social diversity and social identity fluctuations in the Early and Middle Neolithic of Southwest Germany. The Shannon diversity index serves as an indicator for stylistic diversity. Added are proxies for population changes, and climate proxies for western central Europe. Gray bars mark periods of higher precipitation. The drought of 5106–5105 BCE is highlighted by a dark-gray line. Population density for the Württemberg region was reconstructed using radiocarbon dates (neolithicRC). Local variability can be expected to average out at a sample size of $n = 1232$. Radiocarbon dates were binned within 200 ^{14}C years and summed probability distribution (SPD) calculated without normalization to avoid artificial peaks (Weninger et al. 2015). Palaeoclimate proxy data are from Helle and Schleser (1998), and Fohlmeister et al. (2012).

A Natural Experiment of History: Western Central Europe between 5400 and 4300 cal BCE

Previously we have considered the Neolithic expansion from a broader perspective (Gronenborn 2010a; Gronenborn 2016a) but also zoomed in and focused on simple farming societies from western central Europe (Strien 2000; Strien 2005; Gronenborn et al. 2014). Apart from our expertise in the region and the period, this was due to other reasons, one being the high density of data in the study area, the other the local to regional confinement of these simple farming societies such that in case of shortages no means for amelioration through extensive exchange or even trade were available. They seem to have been organized as segmentary societies along descent lines (Strien 2005; Bentley et al. 2012; Bogaard, Krause, R., and Strien 2011). At least for the early Neolithic Linearbandkeramik (LBK), any greater external impetus by other societies would have been minimal; this can be shown by the so-called import finds, which are few in number (Gronenborn 1990; Gronenborn 2010b; Löhr 1991; Allard 2005), but also by physical anthropology and archaeogenetics, at least for the regions examined so far (Szécsényi-Nagy et al. 2015; Mathieson et al. 2018). Any social and economic dynamics took place within territorial limits, within a rather confined population. While migrations and individual movements did play a role (Strien 2010a; Hofmann 2016), these simple farming societies operated in relative isolation, compared to later, more-complex societies, which could rely on better and more intensive long-distance transport, let alone state-level societies with an elaborate infrastructure for long-distance transport, like Rome (Jongman 2014; Wilson and Bowman 2018). Simple farming societies may therefore represent a near-perfect natural experiment of history (Diamond and Robinson 2010; Dunning 2012; Scheffer 2016).

Age Model under Debate

Our analyses are based on an age model that has emerged in the course of more than fifty years of continuous fine-grained typo-chronological studies, combined with ^{14}C-date models based on wiggle matching (Stehli 1987; Spatz 1996; Jeunesse 1998–99; Strien 2000; Bronk Ramsey, van der Plicht, and Weninger 2001; Eisenhauer 2002). This age model has been described in detail elsewhere (Gronenborn et al. 2014; Gronenborn, Strien, and Lemmen 2017) and will therefore be presented only briefly here. It is based on calculations of house generations, referring to the so-called compound model (Germ. *Hofplatzmodell*—Zimmermann 2012b), an artificial mean duration entity per longhouse of twenty-three to twenty-four years (Strien 2000; Claßen 2011). We use the dendrochronological ages of the Kückhoven and the Mohelnice wells as chronological anchor points (figure 12.5). Due to the imprecision of the Mohelnice date and the adding inaccuracies in counting back mean duration spans of house generations, our age model becomes increasingly imprecise toward the older phases (Gronenborn, Strien, and Lemmen 2017, 58).

It needs to be noted, however, that in the course of the emergence and the increasing popularity of Bayesian modeling of ^{14}C dates, new age models have been suggested that seem to contradict the earlier endeavors. This has been formulated for the beginning of the LBK (Stäuble 1995; Jakucs et al. 2016; Fröhlich and Lüning 2017), its further course and the beginning of the Middle Neolithic (Bánffy et al. 2018), and lastly the Middle Neolithic and the early Young Neolithic (Denaire et al. 2017; Riedhammer 2018). However, while we do acknowledge the need to revise the earlier age models of the central European Neolithic, we caution that methodological implications and problems be addressed (Schier 2014; Weninger et al. 2015; Strien 2019). We therefore stick, for the time being, to the scheme we had used previously and which has provided fine-grained archaeological time series. This approach has produced reasonably robust explanatory results on internal dynamics as well as climate-culture interrelations (Peters and Zimmermann 2017; Gronenborn et al. 2014; Gronenborn, Strien, and Lemmen 2017).

The Data Sets

In our previous studies we had used data sets from the LBK and the consecutive middle Neolithic (Gronenborn et al. 2018), both from Southwest Germany. Both LBK as well as Middle Neolithic pottery is richly decorated and may be arranged in fine-grained schemes chronologically as well as spatially (Spatz 1996; Strien 2010b; Kerig 2010). Given the segmentary lineage form of organization of at least the LBK societies and their scale, ceramic production would have been household-based and thus reveals fine-grained information on group and sub-subgroup affiliation (Strien 2005; Bogaard, Krause, R., and Strien 2011). It needs to be remembered, however, that signals that were transported by pottery in early farming societies likely reflect social dynamics and social networks mainly maintained by females (Hart et al. 2016). Nevertheless, these dynamics may have played a considerable role for the shaping of entire societies (Birch and Hart 2018).

For our previous studies we had used band types, as have Peters and Zimmermann (2017), as well as secondary motifs in between main motifs. For this study we have added a new set of data for the LBK, namely the main motifs, the typical angular bands and spirals (figure 12.5). We assume that these contain coded social information, which in detail is largely unknown, but which may have differed from the contents of the secondary motifs. Despite these social contents are main motifs not well suited for typo-chronological studies, as often they are preserved only as fragments and may thus not be identified in sufficient numbers. Also, the coded social information may have been important over long stretches of time and may therefore have carried only little or even no chronological information.

On the other hand, band types may not have contained as much detailed social information and may therefore have been more variable in their realization and used for a variety of main motifs. The data availability for both sets is the same, the Württemberg LBK, as is the statistical method applied, namely the Shannon diversity index (Shannon 1948).

Interestingly, the motif time series is more dynamic than the band-type series and also follows the population peak during the final phases (figure 12.5). The LBK main motif data set is also linked closer to the Middle Neolithic data set, as the latter encompasses a combination of both motifs and technique, which cannot be split due to the data coding method applied by Spatz (1996). Reassuringly, the difference in curve progression in both data sets supports our previous theoretical postulations (figure 12.3).

Various components of material culture reflect various levels of social resilience processes, from the group level down to the level of the individual (Gronenborn et al. 2014; Gronenborn et al. 2018). According to the definition laid out above, the term "social diversity" reflects group-level factors like group cohesion, and "social identity" reflects the level of self-identification and the transition zone between group and individual identification (figure 12.4).[2]

For the new sets of data, we suggest that band types reflect our concept of social diversity on the level of within-group cooperation and cohesion. Main motifs may primarily reflect our concept of social identity on the level of group versus individual identification and ancestral beliefs. According to our model of nested cycles (figure 12.3), social diversity band-type time series proceed in coarser and longer intervals, whereas social identity main motif time series proceed in shorter intervals (figure 12.6).

If our approach is anywhere near interpretational precision, we also need to sharpen our terminology and need to carefully distinguish between technical and motif diversity with much more rigor than we have done hitherto. We therefore suggest to apply the term "stylistic diversity" as a generic term encompassing both signals for social diversity—in our LBK case the technical diversity reflected in the variation of band types—

and social identity—in our case the motif diversity reflected in the variation of motives (figure 12.4).

Both curves—together with other signals (Peters and Zimmermann 2017)—then constitute components of what we have called the sociopolitical and economic-ecological cycle (SPEEC—Gronenborn 2016b). Referring to the secular cycles dealt with by Turchin and Nefedov (2009), we divided the template into an integrative and disintegrative part and ascribed patterns of societal behavior to the successive stages of this cycle (figure 12.6). Basically, these are similar to empirical predictions presented by Turchin and Nefedov (2009, 33–34) for state-level societies. One major difference, though, is that the template presented here does not include elite political maneuvering, as presumably elites, if at all existent, may not have been all that influential in these societies. We therefore take this template as a basic phase-dependent behavioral pattern for simple sedentary societies and at the same time as an underlying template for all farming-based and industrialized societies. Whether mobile and sedentary forager and hunter-gatherer or fisher societies basically followed the same pattern will have to be investigated.

Obviously, this is just a very coarse scheme, following an ideal curve progression, in a way a metaphor similar to the adaptive cycles. However, with the methodology described here and in our previous publications, the challenge of how to visualize parameters shaping the curve may gradually be met. Signals of social diversity and social identity as components of stylistic diversity that may then again be an indicator for social cohesion and resilience processes are—under fortunate circumstances—distinguishable in the archaeological record. With these signals, it becomes possible to subtly quantify and plot resilience strategies and their dynamics along a time axis and on various scales.

Discussion

The calculations and the model we have applied previously and that we have modified here are primarily geared toward understanding the dynamics operating within simple farming societies and their possible forcing and triggers. We ascribe the various curve progressions of indicators of stylistic diversity to the apparently distinguishable social factors of "diversity" and "identity," using various pottery decoration motifs and techniques.

As hitherto laid out, the entire span of the LBK in Württemberg is marked by one single curve—or cycle—with a tipping point at the shift from the earlier LBK to the younger phases, around 5150 cal BCE in our age model (figure 12.5). From then on, what we have called social diversity decreases continuously, indicating a general decrease in the diversity of collective solidarity, cooperation, and coalescence. These disintegrating mechanisms are accompanied by an increase in population, but also an increase in the construction of enclosures, signaling an increasing importance of defense and territorial marking (Gronenborn et al. 2014).

The social diversity curve is complemented by the social identity curve, representing sub-cycles: a decrease in main motifs or the diversity of social identity marks the beginning and the end of chronological entities like earliest LBK (eLBK), and earlier LBK (LBK II—Flomborn) and the later and terminal phases (yLBK) (figure 12.5). It is interesting to note that the steep decline in the diversity of social identity around 5150 cal BCE—during the shift from LBK II to yLBK—is paralleled by the appearance of enclosures, an indicator of increased territorialism and the desire to defend communities. During that time we do see an increase in humid/wet conditions, but no decrease in population. Thus we assume that this brief phase of low diversity of social identity was forced by mainly internal processes that were, however, amplified by adverse climate conditions. This correlation is also evident for the last LBK social identity cycle, the younger LBK. While social diversity is already declining, social identity undergoes another cycle, paralleled by a considerable population increase. This increase is punctuated by a brief drought period (Gronenborn et al. 2014) at 5106–5105 cal BCE, from which the Württemberg population seems to have recovered, only to decline rapidly after 5050 cal BCE, with this decline being paralleled by adverse climate conditions as well. The possibly considerable climate fluctuations between 5200 and 5000 cal BCE seem to have characterized the terminal centuries of IRD 5 (Gronenborn 2012). This causation would then suggest that the dynamics of the sub-periods within the Württemberg LBK were mainly forced by a social component, as predicted by the SPEEC (figure 12.6), and the final decline was a combination of internal social forcing and external factors, in this case the fluctuations around the end of IRD 5.

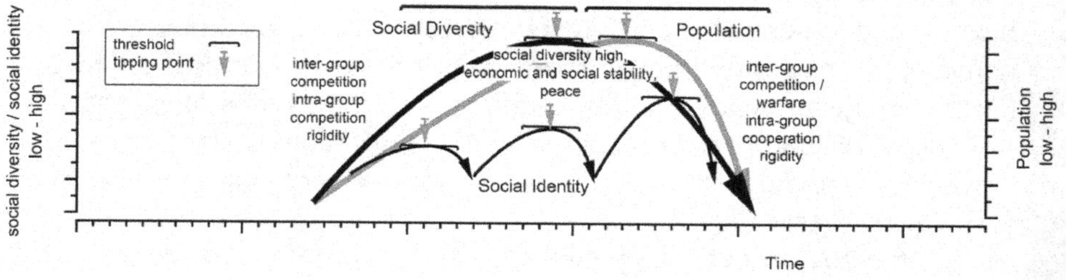

Figure 12.6. The sociopolitical and economic-ecological cycle (SPEEC) (after Gronenborn 2016b, with changes).

Cycles are never constituted by one single signal, but are rather composed out of a combination of various indicators, with the new signal from the social identity curve adding to the picture. The prediction calls for a formative stage during which groups integrate, then the stage during which they stabilize, followed by the disintegrative stage during which groups tumble into internal strife, competition, and—in extreme cases—warfare. The disintegrative stage may also be characterized by a polarization of societies, an indicator being the decrease in diversity. This polarization may be paralleled by rigidity, sometimes leading to a rigidity trap (Schultz and Searleman 2002; Carpenter and Brock 2008). As previously suggested for the later stages of the LBK, rigidity finds its expression in the outbreak of internal and external interpersonal violence, if not warfare (Gronenborn 2016b; Meller 2015; Meyer et al. 2018a). Judging from the physical anthropology evidence, violence in late LBK societies was geared to "effectively cause the identity and the individuality of the victims to be erased" (Meyer et al. 2018b, 35). This observation is particularly important, as the theory calls for an increase in polarization toward the end of cycles combined with the decrease of social diversity (figure 12.6). Apparently then, these conflicts may also be seen as conflicting social identities in a sphere of social rigidity. However, the consequences of these rigidity processes were confined to western central Europe and maybe France, as there are indications of some form of continuity in the East (Link 2014; Wollenweber 2019). Apart from the more definite evidence of violence, there are other indications for a ritual treatment of the dead in which forms of cannibalism might have been involved, reaching from southern Iberia to central Europe (Santana et al. 2019; Pechtl et al. 2018; Haack 2017). This form of treating the dead is not necessarily indicative of intergroup and intragroup violence, but may also have been some form of secondary burial tradition that had evolved toward the end of the sixth millennium cal BCE.

Internal human forcing on early farming dynamics must not be understood as a claim for an exclusive and determinant causation. What needs to be considered further is the role of disease. Tuberculosis has been detected in Early Neolithic populations and is discussed as a possible contributor to the regional decline in Alsace (Nicklisch et al. 2012; Denaire et al. 2017, 1142). The plague may have had much more devastating effects but is not yet proven for the immediate period in question (Andrades Valtueña et al. 2017; Rascovan et al. 2019). Also, while numerous studies bring disease in connection with climate change, in the past and in the present (Hoberg and Brooks 2015; Baer and Singer 2018; Harper 2017), evidence from the Neolithic suggests that epidemics did not have any substantial effects on dynamics (Fuchs et al. 2019).

Beyond Early Farming

The method applied here only works for archaeological entities that had signaled vital sociopolitical content in fine-grained and abundant material representations. Wherever such material representations are not preserved, methods of quantifying these signals must fail, and more general approaches need to be adopted, as is for instance the case for the central European Young Neolithic (Gronenborn et al. 2018, 212).

Whether the method applied here would also be applicable to state-level societies must remain unclear at this point, as due to centralization of production, signaling properties are filtered and channeled by market mechanisms. For such societies, other indicators may have to be investigated, including elite behavior and political maneuvering (Turchin et al. 2018). But it appears from the literature that many archaeological data sets reflecting identity have not yet been arranged into time series and that studies are rather situational, with earlier ones often being confined to questions of "ethnicity" (Hall 1998; Mattingly 2014; Gardner 2016; George and Kurchin 2019). Thus, to explore the possibilities for current societies, we have chosen a proxy that appears to be similar to the social identity proxy we have chosen for the early farming societies in Southwest Germany, the study area being roughly the same, the territory of the modern German state of Baden-Württemberg.

As outlined above, the social identity of the early farming societies seems to have at least partly been based on social and political lineage affiliations. As lineages have become socially and politically largely unimportant today, a comparable proxy for modern Western societies might be party identification (Greene 1999; Falter, Schoen, and Caballero 2000; Ohr and Quandt 2012). Just as Neolithic tribesmen would have identified themselves with their lineage and acted in concordance with this political group, modern citizens identify politically with the party they elect, at least to some extent. Obviously, this approach will only work in political systems with many parties, and thus the United States may not qualify. Here periods of social cohesion might be better represented by proxies for violence (Turchin 2016, 113–24). For democratic European nations, however, party diversity in parliaments may be taken as a proxy for what we have defined as social identity (figure 12.4).

We have thus calculated the diversity index of the spectrum of political parties elected into the parliament for the State of Württemberg and later the State of Baden-Württemberg, and as a reference time series the index of the party spectrum elected into the German national parliaments (Reichstag and Bundestag) (figure 12.7). Gray bars indicate the time of the German-French War of 1870–71, both world wars, and the Cold War

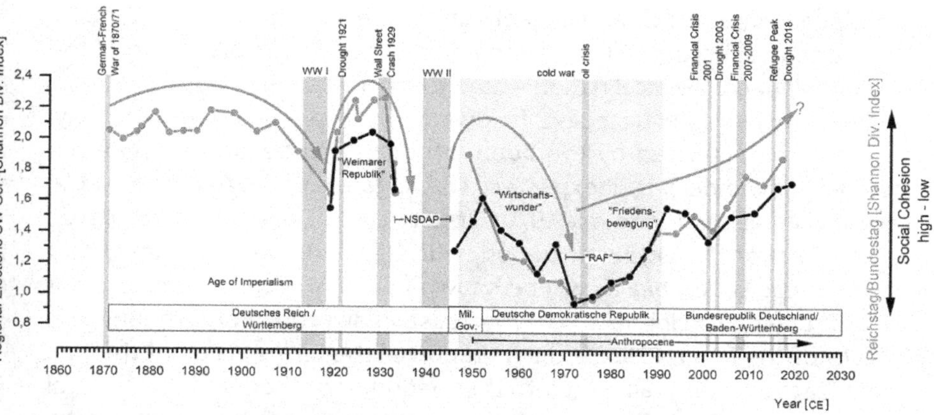

Figure 12.7. Party identification data from Württemberg and the German Reichstag and Bundestag. Plotted is the Shannon diversity index for the spectrum of political parties elected into the respective parliaments. Sources: https://www.statistik-bw.de/Wahlen/Kommunal/, accessed 22 January 2020; https://www.reichstagsprotokolle.de/en_rtbhauf.html, accessed 22 January 2020; https://www.bundestag.de/parlament/aufgaben/bundesversammlung/bundesversammlungen-seit-1949-485146, accessed 22 January 2020; http://www.bundeswahlleiter.de/de/bundestagswahlen/downloads/bundestagswahlergebnisse/btw_ab49_ergebnisse.pdf, accessed 22 January 2020.

period. Equally marked are the Wall Street crash of 1929 and the following economic crisis, the oil crisis of 1973, the global financial crises of 2001 and 2007–9, and lastly the "refugee crisis" of 2015. Intuitively, we consider these "external" factors to have had a possible implication on German and local societies within the territory of Baden-Württemberg.

It is interesting to note, but not unexpected, that the national electoral trends are reflected in the regional elections in Southwest Germany. At first sight, periods of warfare—be it open wars or the Cold War period—correlate with a decrease in party identification diversity, just as we have postulated for the Early Neolithic societies in the same region. These are clear signals for rigidity, in either type of society. It is also interesting to note that trends toward a decrease in diversification set in before the outbreaks of war for both World Wars I and II. For World War I, this might be correlated with the arms race preceding 1914 and the increasing nationalism during the age of imperialism (1890–1914). At the same time, the political opposition against these tendencies gained ground, with the rising social democratic and communist movements. Societies polarized and drifted toward rigidity. The same process is visible for the period preceding World War II, with however a more rapid decline of diversity in the course of the world economic crisis after the "Black Thursday" of 1929. Additional components of this trend toward rigidity might be the lasting effects of the reparation payments as a consequence of World War I and a national sensation of an allegedly unjust treatment by the victors. All this led to the success of the National Socialist Party (NSDAP)—an all too obvious signal of political rigidity—and to World War II.

The considerable decrease in diversity during postwar Germany, a period characterized by the boom phase of the "economic miracle" (*Wirtschaftswunder*), is unexpected. The negative tipping point of social identity is reached in the mid-1970s. Intuitively this might be interpreted as an effect of the Cold War period, with its subtle but constant threat of an atomic strike, but as will be shown below, this threat appears not to have been a forcing factor for decrease in diversity. For Germany, the attacks of the first and second generation of the terror group of the Red Army Fraction (RAF) fall right into that period. Together with the political effects of the 1968 student "revolt," this was another shift toward rigidity. The situation begins to change with the NATO Double-Track Decision of 1979, with diversity climbing considerably with the signing of the Intermediate-Range Nuclear Forces Treaty in 1987, a period in which Germany was dominated by the peace movement (*Friedensbewegung*) and the popular Easter peace marches (Schmitt 1990; Wentker, Gassert, and Geiger 2018). So despite the actual and prominent fear of an atomic strike—notably from the American side—diversity did rise during the 1980s. Apparently, fear of this external threat did not cause a decrease in diversity. Diversity rates remained stable during the 1990s, with a slight decrease around the financial crisis of 2000–2003, only to rise again, with no great effect of either the financial crisis of 2007–9 or the "refugee crisis" of 2015. In fact, diversity has continued to rise during the most recent elections, both nationally and on the state level. It needs to be noted, however, that this recent increase must be ascribed also to the rising popularity of right-wing political parties, which may well be seen as a reaction to an increasing social divergence and a stoked fear of migrants.

Apparently, climate excursions did not have any effects on the curve progression of the social identity proxy, as the drought of 1921 (Cook et al. 2015) was contemporary to a steep increase. Nor did the drought of 2018 have lasting effects, although economically implications were felt (Davydov 2019; N. N. 2019). But lasting effects of short-term climate excursions on modern industrial societies are not to be expected.

Of course many more factors may be discussed, but given the data presented, it seems justified to suggest that as from early farming onward, human societies fluctuated between group diversity and group homogeneity or between degrees of social cohesion. Sometimes, with increasing polarization, these cycles drifted toward political and social rigidity, occasionally leading to a rigidity trap. These fluctuations seem to have been an independent, inherent dynamic, regardless of the social and political complexity of societies. External factors may have provided additional forcing but were not intrinsic.

Conclusions: Looking at the Whole Range

Our previous studies and the data presented here suggest that social dynamics have played an important and hitherto somewhat underrated role in the shaping of cultural processes, both in early farming societies and today. What we have called social diversity and social identity, as components of social resilience processes, may be powerful players in the shaping of cycles and possibly also in the shaping of declines or collapses. This has already been suggested in ancient Greek historiography and has been repeated in various forms until today (Turchin 2016; Turchin et al. 2018).

What might play an overrated role in the shaping of cultural cycles are climate anomalies. This is shown here both for the prehistoric and modern case studies from Southwest Germany. While the possible roles of climate anomalies for the earlier parts of the Holocene, particularly in the Near East and across the central Eurasian landmass, are still debated (see above), more and more studies on various periods after the 6.2-ka event show that climate fluctuations might not have had any major triggering effects. We were able to demonstrate this for the final and terminal periods of the LBK in western central Europe, correcting our earlier assumptions based on the evidence of considerable fluctuations around 5000 cal BCE (Strien and Gronenborn 2005; Gronenborn 2010a; Gronenborn 2012). Recent studies on Bronze Age societies have equally shown that climate fluctuations had not triggered periods of decline or collapse (Armit et al. 2014; Weiberg and Finné 2018; Weiberg et al. 2019), despite earlier claims to the contrary (Kaniewski et al. 2013). Recent investigations on the effects of climate fluctuations in North America have also disproved earlier hypotheses or have resulted in a much more complex and interrelated net of forcing factors and triggers: Schwindt et al. (2016) show that an increase in favorable conditions, reflected in an increase in agricultural production (maize), led to an increase in population in five out of six regions, but the reverse is not the case for two regions, where population remains high in periods of drought, leading to considerable social reactions like violence and social collapse. They conclude that "it is not merely climate change, but the way in which climate change interacted with a historically constituted social landscape and a pattern of great reliance on maize agriculture" that accounted for the only partial collapse of these simple farming societies in the North American Southwest (Schwindt et al. 2016, 92). In principle, Kohler, Ellyson, and Bocinsky (chapter 11 in this volume) substantiate these earlier conclusions, suggesting a connection between climate—or rather maize production rates—and violence notably when population is high, a result supporting our conclusions for the yLBK phase.

In another recent study focusing on the same region, Kintigh and Ingram (2018, 29) did not find "a single case with statistical support for a relationship between the major transitions and episodes of climatic extremes." They also underline the fact that a construction of causality is often hindered by imprecise dating.

A more promising avenue than searching for any correlations between collapse and climate may be to switch reasoning: as suggested (Gronenborn 2016a; Weiberg and Finné 2018), periods of beneficial climate are possibly more important than periods of unfavorable climate, in that they force societies to an increasing complexity. If the present study is looked at under this perspective, the curve progression of both cycles, particularly the sub-cycles, are important. While the temporal correlation between the periods of increased precipitation, the shift from one LBK-phase to another, and the corresponding decrease in main motif diversity coupled with an increase in social cohesion indicate externally implicated stress, the period in between is the one during which societies apparently benefited from drier conditions, with populations recovering or rising. Moreover, the curve progression of the more abstract index of social diversity is largely unaffected by climate excursions; only the last phase of increasing social cohesion is punctuated by the fluctuations toward the end of IRD 5b.

It may therefore be postulated that these early farming societies were only subtly affected by climate excursions and that beneficial periods played a more substantial role in stabilizing these societies. The phase progression of the overarching social diversity cycle as well as the social identity sub-cycles was largely determined by social cohesion processes (figure 12.5). The interrelation of these processes and the climatically beneficial phases ultimately led to the population increase after 5200 cal BCE and lastly to the final decline—or collapse—which, indeed, may have been aggravated by climate anomalies.

If the above observations from central Europe and the other regions are scaled up, Holocene climate fluctuations, or RCCs, appear to have had no overall and uniform effect on internal dynamics of early farming societies nor on the spread of farming itself, as was previously considered (Weninger et al. 2009; Gronenborn 2010a). On a high-resolution level, the situation becomes quite complex. The transition to farming in western Eurasia was a millennia-long process with complex positive and negative feedbacks and shifting thresholds between factors from the social realm including political components, but also productivity, population increase, and external factors like climate and the environment. While social cohesion dynamics are only one component within a canon of factors (Cutter, Boruff, and Shirley 2003; Berkes and Ross 2013; Bradtmöller, Grimm, and Riel-Salvatore 2017), they may nevertheless have been one of considerable importance.

As our short excursion to the modern-day situation within the same study area showed, social cohesion dynamics appear to have played an equally important endogenous role in the twentieth and twenty-first centuries CE. Collapse may therefore be an inherent property of human social systems, at least since the beginning of farming.

Acknowledgments

We are indebted to Denis Scholz, Johannes-Gutenberg University, for providing and discussing the Bunker Cave data; Stefan Schreiber, Louise Rokohl, and Florian Schimmer, Römisch-Germanisches Zentralmuseum, for fruitful discussions; and last but not least Felix Riede and Payson Sheets for the invitation of one of us (DG) to the Aarhus meeting. The chapter is an outcome of the research cluster "Processes of Societal Change and Dynamics" at the Römisch-Germanisches Zentralmuseum and of the project "Resilience Factors in Diachronic and Intercultural Perspective," funded by the Leibniz Association, Leibniz Collaborative Excellence.

Detlef Gronenborn is an archaeologist at the Leibniz Research Institute for Archaeology (Römisch-Germanisches Zentralmuseum) and at Johannes Gutenberg University in Mainz, Germany. He is interested in social dynamics and their effects on processes of change in non-state and state-level societies in the past and present. Together with the other coauthors he has published a series of peer-reviewed journal articles and book chapters, but also blog contributions, on the dynamics of early farming societies in central Europe.

Hans-Christoph Strien is an archaeologist at Johannes Gutenberg University in Mainz, Germany. His research interest is focused on central European Early Neolithic and its temporal, spatial, and social differentiation, mainly based on large data sets of stone raw material and the typology of ceramic decorations.

Kai Wirtz is head of the Ecosystem Modeling Department at the Institute of Coastal Research at the Helmholtz Centre Geesthacht, Germany, and professor at the University of Kiel. As a coordinator of integrated research projects, he is a member of the advisory board of German Coastal Science. While the major branch of his research covers marine ecosystems, a second branch is focused on the dynamics of prehistoric societies. He has published six book chapters and more than seventy articles in peer-reviewed journals.

Peter Turchin is an evolutionary anthropologist at the University of Connecticut and Complexity Science Hub–Vienna. His research interests lie at the intersection of social and cultural evolution, historical macrosociology, economic history and cliometrics, mathematical modeling of long-term social processes, and the construction and analysis of historical databases (see Seshat: Global History Databank). His most recent books are *Ultrasociety: How 10,000 Years of War Made Humans the Greatest Cooperators on Earth* and *Ages of Discord* (both published in 2016).

Christoph Zielhofer is professor of physical geography and director of the Institute of Geography at Leipzig University (Germany). He has a strong research focus on geoarchaeology and paleogeography of central Europe and the Mediterranean. He serves as vice chair of the scientific advisory board of the Leibniz-Institut für Länderkunde (IfL) and published/edited more than 120 articles and monographs, including over 50 contributions in international peer-reviewed journals.

Rolf van Dick is professor of social psychology at Goethe University Frankfurt (Germany) and serves as vice president for International Affairs and Early Career Researchers. Rolf van Dick is scientific director of the interdisciplinary Center for Leadership and Behavior in Organizations (CLBO). He has published/edited almost 20 books and special issues, and he has published over 250 book chapters and papers. He was editor of the *British Journal of Management* and the *Journal of Personnel Psychology* and is a fellow of the International Association of Applied Psychology.

Notes

1. This model does not tackle the question as to whether the Neolithic as a global phenomenon was an effect of the Holocene climate amelioration (Richerson, Boyd, and Bettinger 2001).
2. The concept of social diversity applied here is more confined than the more general concept of diversity applied by Bickle and Whittle (2013). While the latter encompasses biological and economic variability, we focus solely on social processes.

References

Allard, Pierre. 2005. *L'industrie lithique des populations rubanées du Nord-Est de la France et de la Belgique*. Rahden, Westfalen: Verlag Marie Leidorf.

Andrades Valtueña, Aida, Alissa Mittnik, Felix M. Key, Wolfgang Haak, Raili Allmäe, Andrej Belinskij, Mantas Daubaras, et al. 2017. "The Stone Age Plague and Its Persistence in Eurasia." *Current Biology: CB* 27 (23): 3683–91.e8.

Armit, Ian, Graeme T. Swindles, Katharina Becker, Gill Plunkett, and Maarten Blaauw. 2014. "Rapid Climate Change Did Not Cause Population Collapse at the End of the European Bronze Age." *Proceedings of the National Academy of Sciences of the United States of America* 111 (48): 17045–49.

Baer, Hans A., and Merrill Singer. 2018. *The Anthropology of Climate Change: An Integrated Critical Perspective*. 2nd ed. Routledge Advances in Climate Change Research. London and New York: Routledge.

Bánffy, Eszter, Alex Bayliss, Anthony Denaire, Bisserka Gaydarska, Daniela Hofmann, Philippe Lefranc, János Jakucs, et al. 2018. "Seeking the Holy Grail: Robust Chronologies from Archaeology and Radiocarbon Dating Combined." *Documenta Praehistorica* (45): 120–36.

Barker, Graeme. 2006. *The Agricultural Revolution in Prehistory: Why Did Foragers Become Farmers?* Oxford: Oxford University Press.

Barrios, Roberto E. 2016. "Resilience: A Commentary from the Vantage Point of Anthropology." *Annals of Anthropological Practice* 40 (1): 28–38.

Baumeister, R., and M. R. Leary. 1995. "The Need to Belong: Desire for Interpersonal Attachments as a Fundamental Human Motivation." *Psychological Bulletin* 117 (3): 497–529.

Bentley, R. A., Penny Bickle, Linda Fibiger, Geoff M. Nowell, Christopher W. Dale, Robert E. M. Hedges, Julie Hamilton, et al. 2012. "Community Differentiation and Kinship Among Europe's First Farmers." *Proceedings of the National Academy of Sciences of the United States of America* 109 (24): 9326–30.

Berger, Jean-Francois, Laurent Lespez, Catherine Kuzucuoğlu, Arthur Glais, Fuad Hourani, Adrien Barra, and Jean Guilaine. 2016. "Interactions between Climate Change and Human Activities during the Early to Mid-Holocene in the Eastern Mediterranean Basins." *Climate of the Past* 12 (9): 1847–77.

Berkes, Fikret, and Helen Ross. 2013. "Community Resilience: Toward an Integrated Approach." *Society & Natural Resources* 26 (1): 5–20.

Bickle, Penny, and Alasdair Whittle. 2013. *The First Farmers of Central Europe: Diversity in LBK Lifeways*. Oxford and Oakville, CT: Oxbow Books and David Brown Book Co.

Birch, Jennifer, and John P. Hart. 2018. "Social Networks and Northern Iroquoian Confederacy Dynamics." *American Antiquity* 83 (1): 13–33.

Blanton, Richard E., Gary F. Feinman, Stephen A. Kowalewski, and Peter F. Peregrine. 1996. "A Dual-Processual Theory for the Evolution of Mesoamerican Civilization." *Current Anthropology* 37 (1): 1–14.

Bocquet-Appel, Jean-Pierre. 2011. "When the World's Population Took Off: The Springboard of the Neolithic Demographic Transition." *Science* 333 (6042): 560–61.

Bogaard, Amy, Rüdiger Krause, and Hans-Christoph Strien. 2011. "Towards a Social Geography of Cultivation and Plant Use in an Early Farming Community: Vaihingen an der Enz, South-West Germany." *Antiquity* 85 (328): 395–416.

Bond, Gerard C., Bernd Kromer, Juerg Beer, Raimund Muscheler, Michael N. Evans, William Showers, Sharon Hoffmann, Rusty Lotti-Bond, Irka Hajdas, and Georges Bonani. 2001. "Persistent Solar Influence on North Atlantic Climate during the Holocene." *Science* 294 (5549): 2130–36.

Bradtmöller, Marcel, Sonja Grimm, and Julien Riel-Salvatore. 2017. "Resilience Theory in Archaeological Practice: An Annotated Review." *Quaternary International* 446 (2 August): 1–14.

Bronk Ramsey, C., J. van der Plicht, and Bernhard Weninger. 2001. "'Wiggle Matching' Radiocarbon Dates." *Radiocarbon* 43 (2A): 381–89.

Carpenter, Stephen R., and William A. Brock. 2008. "Adaptive Capacity and Traps." *Ecology and Society* 13 (2): 40.

Chapman, Robert. (2003) 2008. *Archaeologies of Complexity*. Reprinted. London: Routledge.

Clarke, Joanne, Nick Brooks, Edward B. Banning, Miryam Bar-Matthews, Stuart Campbell, Lee Clare, Mauro Cremaschi, et al. 2016. "Climatic Changes and Social Transformations in the Near East and North Africa during the 'Long' 4th Millennium BC: A Comparative Study of Environmental and Archaeological Evidence." *Quaternary Science Reviews* 136 (15 March): 96–121.

Claßen, Erich. 2011. *Siedlungen Der Bandkeramik Bei Königshoven*. Rheinische Ausgrabungen 64. Mainz: Philipp von Zabern.

Cook, Edward R., Richard Seager, Yochanan Kushnir, Keith R. Briffa, Ulf Büntgen, David Frank, Paul J. Krusic, et al. 2015. "Old World Megadroughts and Pluvials during the Common Era." *Science Advances* 1 (10): e1500561.

Cutter, Susan L., Bryan J. Boruff, and W. L. Shirley. 2003. "Social Vulnerability to Environmental Hazards." *Social Science Quarterly* 84 (2): 242–61.

Davydov, Alexander. 2019. "Jeder Regentropfen zählt: Folgen der Dürre." Retrieved 16 May 2019 from https://www.faz.net/aktuell/rhein-main/folgen-der-duerre-auch-2019-zu-spueren-16091587.html.

Dearing, J. A. 2008. "Landscape Change and Resilience Theory: A Palaeoenvironmental Assessment from Yunnan, SW China." *The Holocene* 18 (1): 117–27.

Denaire, Anthony, Philippe Lefranc, Joachim Wahl, Christopher Bronk Ramsey, Elaine Dunbar, Tomasz Goslar, Alex Bayliss, Nancy Beavan, Penny Bickle, and Alasdair Whittle. 2017. "The Cultural Project: Formal Chronological Modelling of the Early and Middle Neolithic Sequence in Lower Alsace." *Journal of Archaeological Method and Theory* 24 (4): 1072–1149.

Diamond, Jared, and Peter Bellwood. 2003. "Farmers and Their Languages: The First Expansions." *Science* 300 (5619): 597–603.

Diamond, Jared M., and James A. Robinson, eds. 2010. *Natural Experiments of History*. Cambridge, MA: Belknap Press of Harvard University Press.

Dunning, Thad. 2012. *Natural Experiments in the Social Sciences: A Design-Based Approach*. Strategies for Social Inquiry. Cambridge: Cambridge University Press.

Düring, Bleda S. 2013. "Breaking the Bond: Investigating the Neolithic Expansion in Asia Minor in the Seventh Millennium BC." *Journal of World Prehistory* 26 (2): 75–100.

Eisenhauer, U. 2002. *Untersuchungen zur Siedlungs- und Kulturgeschichte des Mittelneolithikums in der Wetterau:* Universitätsforschungen zur Prähistorischen Archäologie 89. Bonn: Rudolf Habelt.

Falter, Jürgen W., Harald Schoen, and Claudio Caballero. 2000. "Dreißig Jahre danach: Zur Validierung des Konzepts 'Parteiidentifikation' in der Bundesrepublik." In *50 Jahre Empirische Wahlforschung in Deutschland: Entwicklung, Befunde, Perspekti-*

ven, Daten, edited by Markus Klein, Wolfgang Jagodzinski, Ekkehard Mochmann, and Dieter Ohr, 235–71. Wiesbaden: VS Verlag für Sozialwissenschaften.

Flohr, Pascal, Dominik Fleitmann, Roger Matthews, Wendy Matthews, and Stuart Black. 2016. "Evidence of Resilience to Past Climate Change in Southwest Asia: Early Farming Communities and the 9.2 and 8.2 Ka Events." In "Mediterranean Holocene Climate, Environment and Human Societies." Special issue, *Quaternary Science Reviews* 136 (15 March 2016): 23–39.

Fohlmeister, Jens, A. Schröder-Ritzrau, Denis Scholz, C. Spötl, D. F. C. Riechelmann, M. Mudelsee, A. K. Wackerbarth, et al. 2012. "Bunker Cave Stalagmites: An Archive for Central European Holocene Climate Variability." *Climate of the Past* 8: 1751–64.

Fröhlich, Nico, and Jens Lüning. 2017. "Neue Untersuchungen zur absoluten Datierung des Männergrabes und der Siedlung auf dem ältestbandkeramischen Fundplatz Schwanfeld, Ldkr. Schweinfurt, Unterfranken." *Germania* 95 (1–2): 43–91.

Fuchs, Katharina, Christoph Rinne, Clara Drummer, Alexander Immel, Ben Krause-Kyora, and Almut Nebel. 2019. "Infectious Diseases and Neolithic Transformations: Evaluating Biological and Archaeological Proxies in the German Loess Zone between 5500 and 2500 BCE." *Holocene* 29 (10): 1545–1557.

Fuller, Dorian Q. 2006. "Agricultural Origins and Frontiers in South Asia: A Working Synthesis." *Journal of World Prehistory* 20 (1): 1–86.

Fuller, Dorian Q., and Elisabeth Hildebrand. 2013. "Domesticating Plants in Africa." In *Oxford Handbook of African Archaeology*, edited by Peter Mitchell and Paul Lane, 507–62. Oxford Handbooks in Archaeology. Oxford: Oxford University Press.

Gallagher, Elizabeth M., Stephen Shennan, and Mark G. Thomas. 2015. "Transition to Farming More Likely for Small, Conservative Groups with Property Rights, but Increased Productivity Is Not Essential." *Proceedings of the National Academy of Sciences of the United States of America* 112 (46): 14218–23.

Gane, M. 1992. *The Radical Sociology of Durkheim and Mauss*. London and New York: Routledge.

Gardner, Andrew. 2016. *An Archaeology of Identity: Soldiers and Society in Late Roman Britain*. London: Routledge.

George, Diane F., and Bernice Kurchin, eds. 2019. *Archaeology of Identity and Dissonance: Contexts for a Brave New World*. Gainesville: University Press of Florida. https://ebookcentral.proquest.com/lib/gbv/detail.action?docID=5645968.

Greene, Steven. 1999. "Understanding Party Identification: A Social Identity Approach." *Political Psychology* 20 (2): 393–403.

Gronenborn, Detlef. 1990. "Mesolithic-Neolithic Interactions: The Lithic Industry of the Earliest Bandkeramik Culture Site at Friedberg-Bruchenbrücken (West Germany)." In *Contributions to the Mesolithic in Europe: Papers Presented at the Fourth International Symposium "The Mesolithic in Europe," Leuven 1990*, edited by P. M. Vermeersch U. P. Van Peer, 173–82. Studia Praehistorica Belgica 5. Leuven: Leuven University Press.

———. 2009. "Zur Repräsentation von Eliten im Grabbrauch—Probleme und Aussagemöglichkeiten historischer und ethnographischer Quellen aus Westafrika." In *Aufstieg und Untergang Vor- und Frühgeschichtlicher Eliten*, edited by Markus Egg and Dieter Quast, 217–45. Monographien des Römisch-Germanischen Zentralmuseums. Mainz: Verlag des Römisch-Germanischen Zentralmuseums.

———. 2010a. "Climate, Crises, and the Neolithisation of Central Europe between IRD-Events 6 and 4." In *Die Neolithisierung Mitteleuropas—The Spread of the Neolithic* to Central Europe: Internationale Tagung Mainz, 24.–26. Juni 2005*, edited by Detlef Gronenborn and Jörg Petrasch, 61–80. Mainz: Verlag des Römisch-Germanischen Zentralmuseums.

———. 2010b. "Fernkontakte aus dem nördlichen Europa während der Bandkeramischen Kultur." In *PANTA RHEI: Studies in Chronology and Cultural Development of South-Eastern and Central Europe in Earlier Prehistory Presented to Juraj Pavúk on the Occasion of His 75 Birthday*, edited by J. Suteková, P. Pavúk, P. Kalábková, and B. Kovár, 561–74. Bratislava: Comenius University.

———. 2012. "Das Ende Von IRD5b: Abrupte Klimafluktuationen um 5100 den BC und der Übergang vom Alt- zum Mittelneolithikum im westlichen Mitteleuropa." In *Siedlungsstruktur Und Kulturwandel in Der Bandkeramik: Beiträge Der Internationalen Tagung "Neue Fragen Zur Bandkeramik Oder Alles Beim Alten?!," Leipzig, 23. Bis 24. September 2010*, edited by Sabine Wolfram and Harald Stäuble, 241–50. Arbeits- und Forschungsberichte zur sächsischen Bodendenkmalpflege Beihefte 25. Dresden: Landesamt für Archäologie.

———. 2016a. "Climate Fluctuations, Human Migrations, and the Spread of Farming in Western Eurasia—Refining the Argument." In *Climate and Cultural Change in Prehistoric Europe and the Near East*, edited by Peter F. Biehl and Olivier Nieuwenhuyse, 211–36. Institute for European and Mediterranean Archaeology Distinguished Monograph Series. Albany: State University of New York Press.

———. 2016b. "Some Thoughts on Political Differentiation in Early to Young Neolithic Societies in Western Central Europe." In *Arm und Reich—Zur Ressourcenverteilung in Prähistorischen Gesellschaften: 8. Mitteldeutscher Archäologentag Vom 22. Bis 24. Oktober 2015 in Halle*, edited by Harald Meller, Hans-Peter Hahn, Reinhard Jung, and Roberto Risch, 61–76. Halle (Saale): Landesamt für Denkmalpflege und Archäologie Sachsen-Anhalt – Landesmuseum für Vorgeschichte Halle (Saale).

Gronenborn, Detlef, and Jörg Petrasch, eds. 2010. *Die Neolithisierung Mitteleuropas—The Spread of the Neolithic to Central Europe: Internationale Tagung Mainz, 24.-26. Juni 2005*. 2 vols. RGZM—Tagungen 4. Mainz: Verlag des Römisch-Germanischen Zentralmuseums.

Gronenborn, Detlef, Hans-Christoph Strien, Stephan Dietrich, and Frank Sirocko. 2014. "'Adaptive Cycles' and Climate Fluctuations: A Case Study from Linear Pottery Culture in Western Central Europe." *Journal of Archaeological Science* 51 (November):73–83.

Gronenborn, Detlef, Hans-Christoph Strien, and Carsten Lemmen. 2017. "Population Dynamics, Social Resilience Strategies, and Adaptive Cycles in Early Farming Societies of SW Central Europe." *Quaternary International* 446 (2 August): 54–65.

Gronenborn, Detlef, Hans-Christoph Strien, Rolf van Dick, and Peter Turchin. 2018. "Social Diversity, Social Identity, and the Emergence of Surplus in the Western Central European Neolithic." In *Überschuss Ohne Staat / Surplus Without the State: Politische Formen in Der Vorgeschichte / Political Forms in Prehistory*, edited by Harald Meller, Detlef Gronenborn, and Roberto Risch, 201–20. Tagungen des Landesmuseums für Vorgeschichte Halle 18. Halle: Landesamt f. Denkmalpflege u. Archäologie Sachsen-Anhalt.

Gunderson, Lance H., and C. S. Holling, eds. 2002. *Panarchy: Understanding Transformations in Human and Natural Systems*. Washington, DC: Island Press.

Haack, Fabian. 2017. "Die Grubenanlage Von Herxheim, Lkr. Südliche Weinstraße, Rheinland-Pfalz: Architektur, Verfüllungsprozesse Und Fundkonzentrationen." In *Salzmünde—Regel Oder Ausnahme?* edited by Harald Meller and Susanne Friederich, 549–60. Halle (Saale): Landesamt für Denkmalpflege und Archäologie Sachsen-Anhalt – Landesmuseum für Vorgeschichte Halle (Saale).

Hall, Jonathan M. 1998. "Ethnic Identity in Greek Antiquity." *Cambridge Archaeological Journal* 8 (2): 265.

Harper, Kyle. 2017. *The Fate of Rome: Climate, Disease, and the End of an Empire*. Princeton History of the Ancient World. Princeton, NJ: Princeton University Press.

Harris, Matthew J. 2011. "Strategic Planning in an International Nongovernmental Development Organization." *Administration & Society* 43 (2): 216–47.

Hart, John P., Termeh Shafie, Jennifer Birch, Susan Dermarkar, and Ronald F. Williamson. 2016. "Nation Building and Social Signaling in Southern Ontario: A.D. 1350–1650." *PLoS ONE* 11 (5): e0156178.

Helle, G., and G. H. Schleser. 1998. "Die Eichenbohlen des neolithischen Brunnens von Erkelenz-Kückhoven." In *Brunnen Der Jungsteinzeit. Internationales Symposium in Erkelenz 27. Bis. 29. Oktober 1997*, edited by H. Koschik (Hrsg.), 271–77. Materialien Zur Bodendenkmalpflege Im Rheinland 11. Köln: Rheinland-Verlag.

Hoberg, Eric P., and Daniel R. Brooks. 2015. "Evolution in Action: Climate Change, Biodiversity Dynamics and Emerging Infectious Disease." *Philosophical Transactions of the Royal Society of London: Series B, Biological Sciences* 370 (1665).

Hofmann, Daniela. 2016. "Keep on Walking: The Role of Migration in Linearbandkeramik Life." *Documenta Praehistorica* 43: 235–51.

Holling, C. S., and Lance H. Gunderson. 2002. "Resilience and Adaptive Cycles." In *Panarchy: Understanding Transformations in Human and Natural Systems*, edited by Lance H. Gunderson and C. S. Holling, 25–62. Washington, DC: Island Press.

Horejs, B., B. Milić, F. Ostmann, U. Thanheiser, Bernhard Weninger, and A. Galik. 2015. "The Aegean in the Early 7th Millennium BC: Maritime Networks and Colonization." *Journal of World Prehistory* 28 (4): 289–330.

Jakucs, János, Eszter Bánffy, Krisztián Oross, Vanda Voicsek, Christopher Bronk Ramsey, Elaine Dunbar, Bernd Kromer, et al. 2016. "Between the Vinča and Linearbandkeramik Worlds: The Diversity of Practices and Identities in the 54th–53rd Centuries Cal BC in Southwest Hungary and Beyond." *Journal of World Prehistory* 29: 267–336.

Jeunesse, Chr. 1998–99. "La Synchronisation Des Séquence Culturelles Des Bassins Du Rhin, De La Meuse Et De La Seine Et La Chronologie Du Bassin Parisien Au Néolithique Ancien Et Moyen (5200-4500 Av. J.-C.)." *Bulletin de la Societé Préhistorique Luxembourgeoise* 20–21: 337–92.

Jongman, Willem M. 2014. "Re-constructing the Roman Economy." In *the Cambridge History of Capitalism*. Vol. 1, *The Rise of Capitalism: From Ancient Origins to 1848*, edited by Jeffrey G. Williamson and Larry Neal, 75–100. Cambridge: Cambridge University Press.

Kaniewski, David, Elise van Campo, Joël Guiot, Sabine Le Burel, Thierry Otto, and Cecile Baeteman. 2013. "Environmental Roots of the Late Bronze Age Crisis." *PLoS ONE* 8 (8): e71004.

Keck, Markus, and Patrick Sakdapolrak. 2013. "What Is Social Resilience? Lessons Learned and Ways Forward." *Erdkunde* 67 (1): 5–19.

Kerig, Tim. 2010. "Grenzen Ziehen: Zur hronologie regionaler und sozialer Unterschiede im hessischen Altneolithikum." In *Die Neolithisierung Mitteleuropas—The Spread of the Neolithic to Central Europe: Internationale Tagung Mainz, 24.-26. Juni 2005*, vol. 2, edited by Detlef Gronenborn and Jörg 475–86. RGZM—Tagungen 4. Mainz: Verlag des Römisch-Germanischen Zentralmuseums.

Kerig, Tim, Christiane Krahn, Ulla Münch, Guido Nockemann, and Hans-Christoph Strien. 2010. "Bandkeramik Online: Merkmalskatalog Zur Aufnahme Verzierter Keramik." Retrieved 19 May 2020 from http://www.archaeologie-stiftung.de/de/wissenschaft/bandkeramik_online/bandkeramik_online_1.html.

Kim, Young Y. 1994. "Beyond Cultural Identity." *Intercultural Communication Studies* 4 (1): 1–25.

Kintigh, Keith W., Jeffrey H. Altschul, Mary C. Beaudry, Robert D. Drennan, Ann P. Kinzig, Timothy A. Kohler, W. F. Limp, et al. 2014. "Grand Challenges for Archaeology." *American Antiquity* 79 (1): 5–24.

Kintigh, Keith W., and Scott E. Ingram. 2018. "Was the Drought Really Responsible? Assessing Statistical Relationships Between Climate Extremes and Cultural Transitions." *Journal of Archaeological Science* 89 (January): 25–31.

Kohler, Timothy A., Stephanie VanBuskirk, and Samantha Ruscavage-Barz. 2004. "Vessels and Villages: Evidence for Conformist Transmission in Early Village Aggregations on the Pajarito Plateau, New Mexico." *Journal of Anthropological Archaeology* 23 (1): 100–118.

Larson, Greger, and Dorian Q. Fuller. 2014. "The Evolution of Animal Domestication." *Annual Review of Ecology, Evolution, and Systematics* 45 (1): 115–36.

Lemmen, Carsten, and Kai W. Wirtz. 2014. "On the Sensitivity of the Simulated European Neolithic Transition to Climate Extremes." *Journal of Archaeological Science* 51 (November 2014): 65–72.

Link, Thomas. 2014. "Gewaltphantasien? Kritische Bemerkungen Zur Diskussion Über Krieg Und Krise Am Ende Der Bandkeramik." In *Gewalt Und Gesellschaft. Dimensionen Der Gewalt in Ur- Und Frühgeschichtlicher Zeit / Violence and Society. Dimensions of Violence in Pre- and Protohistoric Times: Internationale Tagung Vom 14.–16. März 2013 an Der Julius-Maximilians-Universität Würzburg*, edited by T. Link, H. Peter-Röcher, Thomas Link, and Heidi Peter-Röcher, 271–86. Universitätsforschungen zur prähistorischen Archäologie 259. Bonn: Habelt.

Lipson, Mark, Anna Szécsényi-Nagy, Swapan Mallick, Annamária Pósa, Balázs Stégmár, Victoria Keerl, Nadin Rohland et al. 2017. "Parallel Palaeogenomic Transects Reveal Complex Genetic History of Early European Farmers." *Nature* 551 (7680): 368–72.

Löhr, Hartwig. 1991. "La Latéralisation Des Armatures Asymétriques À La Charnière Mésolithique-Néolithique." *Bulletin Société Préhistoire Luxembourg* 12: 53–64.

Maclean, Kirsten, Michael Cuthill, and Helen Ross. 2014. "Six Attributes of Social Resilience." *Journal of Environmental Planning and Management* 57 (1): 144–56.

Mathieson, Iain, Songül Alpaslan-Roodenberg, Cosimo Posth, Anna Szécsényi-Nagy, Nadin Rohland, Swapan Mallick, Iñigo Olalde, et al. 2018. "The Genomic History of Southeastern Europe." *Nature* 555 (7695): 197–203.

Mattingly, David J. 2014. "Identities in the Roman World: Discrepancy, Heterogeneity, Hybridity, and Plurality." In *Roman in the Provinces: Art on the Periphery of Empire*, edited by Lisa R. Brody and Gail L. Hoffman, 35–60. Chestnut Hill, MA: McMullen Museum of Art Boston College.

Mayewski, Paul A., Eelco J. Rohling, J. C. Stager, Wibjörn Karlén, Kirk A. Maasch, L. D. Meeker, Eric A. Meyerson, et al. 2004. "Holocene Climate Variability." *Quaternary Research* 62 (3): 243–55.

McAnany, Patricia, and Norman Yoffee, eds. 2010a. *Questioning Collapse: Human Resilience, Ecological Vulnerability, and the Aftermath of Empire*. New York: Cambridge University Press.

———. 2010b. "Why We Question Collapse and Study Human Resilience, Ecological Vulnerability, and the Aftermath of Empire." In *Questioning Collapse: Human Resilience, Ecological Vulnerability, and the Aftermath of Empire*, edited by Patricia McAnany and Norman Yoffee, 1–20. New York: Cambridge University Press.

McIntosh, Susan K. 1999. "Pathways to Complexity: An African Perspective." In *Beyond Chiefdoms: Pathways to Complexity in Africa*, edited by Susan K. McIntosh, 1–30. Cambridge: Cambridge University Press.

Meller, Harald. 2015. "Krieg im europäischen Neolithikum." In *Krieg—eine archäologische Spurensuche: Begleitband zur Sonderausstellung im Landesmuseum für Vorgeschichte Halle (Saale); 6. November 2015 bis 22. Mai 2016*, edited by Harald Meller and Michael Schefzik, 109–16. Halle (Saale), Darmstadt: Landesamt für Denkmalpflege und Archäologie Sachsen-Anhalt Landesmuseum für Vorgeschichte; Theiss.

Meyer, Christian, Corina Knipper, Nicole Nicklisch, Angelina Münster, Olaf Kürbis, Veit Dresely, Harald Meller, and Kurt W. Alt. 2018a. "Early Neolithic Executions Indicated by Clustered Cranial Trauma in the Mass Grave of Halberstadt." *Nature Communications* 9 (1): 2472.

Meyer, Christian, O. Kürbis, V. Dresely, and K. W. Alt. 2018b. "Patterns of Collective Violence in the Early Neolithic of Central Europe." In *Prehistoric Warfare and Violence: Quantitative and Qualitative Approaches*, edited by Andrea Dolfini, Rachel J. Crellin, Christian Horn, and Marion Uckelmann, 21–38. Quantitative Methods in the Humanities and Social Sciences. Cham: Springer International.

Migowski, Claudia, Mordechai Stein, Sushma Prasad, Jörg F.W. Negendank, and Amotz Agnon. 2006. "Holocene Climate Variability and Cultural Evolution in the Near East from the Dead Sea Sedimentary Record." *Quaternary Research* 66 (3): 421–31.

N. N. 2019. "Lebensmittelpreise bleiben trotz Dürresommer stabil: Der Schaden der Landwirte ist allerdings in Milliarden-Höhe—Und die Auswirkungen der Dürre, wie das Niedrigwasser, sind noch nicht vorüber." Retrieved 16 May 2019 from https://www.handelsblatt.com/unternehmen/handel-konsumgueter/duerrefolgen-lebensmittelpreise-bleiben-trotz-duerresommer-stabil/23757240.html?ticket=ST-3461979-ScW1C7OgfjbAf6xHTrNu-ap6.

Nicklisch, Nicole, Frank Maixner, Robert Ganslmeier, Susanne Friederich, Veit Dreseley, Harald Meller, Albert Zink, and Kurt W. Alt. 2012. "Rib Lesions in Skeletons from Early Neolithic Sites in Central Germany: On the Trail of Tuberculosis at the Onset of Agriculture." *American Journal of Physical Anthropology* 149 (3): 391–404.

Ohr, Dieter, and Markus Quandt. 2012. "Parteiidentifikation in Deutschland: Eine Empirische Fundierung Des Konzepts Auf Basis Der Theorie Sozialer Identität." In *Wählen in Deutschland*, edited by Rüdiger Schmitt-Beck, 186–209. Politische Vierteljahresschrift Sonderheft 45. Baden-Baden: Nomos-Verl.-Ges.

Pechtl, Joachim, Stefa Hanöffener, Anja Staskiewicz, and Henriette Obermeier. 2018. "Die linienbandkeramische Gräbergruppe von Niederpöring-„Leitensiedlung", Gde. Oberpöring, Lkr. Deggendorf." In *Vorträge des 36. Niederbayerischen Archäologentages*, edited by Ludwig Husty and Karl Schmotz, 29–84. Rahden/Westf.: Verlag Marie Leidorf.

Peters, Robin, and Andreas Zimmermann. 2017. "Resilience and Cyclicity: Towards a Macrohistory of the Central European Neolithic." *Quaternary International* 446 (2 August): 43–53.

Price, T. D., and James A. Brown. 1985. "Aspects of Hunter-Gatherer Complexity." In *Prehistoric Hunter-Gatherers: The Emergence of Cultural Complexity*, edited by T. D. Price and James A. Brown, 3–20. Orlando and San Diego: Academic Press.

Rascovan, Nicolás, Karl-Göran Sjögren, Kristian Kristiansen, Rasmus Nielsen, Eske Willerslev, Christelle Desnues, and Simon Rasmussen. 2019. "Emergence and Spread of Basal Lineages of Yersinia Pestis during the Neolithic Decline." *Cell* 176 (1–2): 295-305.e10.

Redman, Charles L. 2005. "Resilience Theory in Archaeology." *American Anthropologist* 107 (1): 70–77.

Redman, Charles L., and Ann Kinzig. 2003. "Resilience of Past Landscapes: Resilience Theory, Society, and the *Longue Durée*." *Conservation Ecology* 7 (1): 14. Retrieved 14 May 2019 from http://www.consecol.org/vol7/iss1/art14.

Reingruber, Agathe. 2018. "Geographical Mobility and Social Motility in the Aegean before and after 6600 BC." *Praehistorische Zeitschrift* 93 (1): 1–24.

Renfrew, Colin. 1984. "Social Archaeology, Societal Change and Generalisation." In *Approaches to Social Archaeology*, edited by Colin Renfrew, 3–21. Edinburg: Edinburgh University Press.

Renfrew, Colin, and J. F. Cherry. 1986. *Peer Polity Interaction as Socio-political Change.* Cambridge: Cambridge University Press.

Richerson, P. J., R. Boyd, and R. L. Bettinger. 2001. "Was Agriculture Impossible during the Pleistocene but Mandatory during the Holocene? A Climate Change Hypothesis." *American Antiquity* 66 (3): 387–422.

Riedhammer, Karin. 2018. "Die sbsolute Datierung des südostbayerischen Mittelneolithikums, des Mittelneolithikums westdeutscher Prägung, der Stichbandkeramik und der frühen Lengyel-Keramik Mährens und Ostösterreichs." In *Neue Materialien Des Bayerischen Neolithikums 2: Tagung Im Kloster Windberg Vom 18. Bis 20. November 2016*, edited by Ludwig Husty, Thomas Link, and Joachim Pechtl, 41–124. Würzburger Studien zur Vor- und Frühgeschichtlichen Archäologie 3. Würzburg: Würzburg University Press.

Rohling, Eelco J., Gianluca Marino, Katharine M. Grant, Paul A. Mayewski, and Bernhard Weninger. 2019. "A Model for Archaeologically Relevant Holocene Climate Impacts in the Aegean-Levantine Region (Easternmost Mediterranean)." *Quaternary Science Reviews* 208 (15 March): 38–53.

Ro'i, Yaacov, and Alon Wainer. 2009. "Muslim Identity and Islamic Practice in Post-Soviet Central Asia." *Central Asian Survey* 28 (3): 303–22.

Ruff, Christopher B., Brigitte Holt, Markku Niskanen, Vladimir Sladek, Margit Berner, Evan Garofalo, Heather M. Garvin, et al. 2015. "Gradual Decline in Mobility with the Adoption of Food Production in Europe." *Proceedings of the National Academy of Sciences of the United States of America* 112 (23): 7142–52.

Ryffel, Heinrich. 1949. *Metabole Politeion. Der Wandel der Staatsverfassungen.* Noctes Romanae, Forschungen über die Kultur der Antike 2. Bern: Paul Haupt.

Sánchez Goñi, María F., Elena Ortu, William E. Banks, Jacques Giraudeau, Chantal Leroyer, and Vincent Hanquiez. 2016. "The Expansion of Central and Northern European Neolithic Populations Was Associated with a Multi-century Warm Winter and Wetter Climate." *The Holocene* 26 (8): 1188–99.

Santana, Jonathan, Francisco J. Rodríguez-Santos, María D. Camalich-Massieu, Dimas Martín-Socas, and Rosa Fregel. 2019. "Aggressive or Funerary Cannibalism? Skull-Cup and Human Bone Manipulation in Cueva De El Toro (Early Neolithic, Southern Iberia)." *American Journal of Physical Anthropology* 169 (1): 31–54.

Scheffer, Marten. 2009. *Critical Transitions in Nature and Society*. Princeton Studies in Complexity. Princeton, NJ: Princeton University Press.

———. 2016. "Anticipating Societal Collapse: Hints from the Stone Age." *Proceedings of the National Academy of Sciences of the United States of America* 113 (39): 10733–35.

Schier, Wolfram. 2014. "Zeitbegriffe und chronologische Konzepte in der Prähistorischen Archäologie." *Praehistorische Zeitschrift* 88 (1–2).

Schmitt, Rüdiger. 1990. *Die Friedensbewegung in der Bundesrepublik Deutschland: Ursachen und Bedingungen der Mobilisierung einer neuen sozialen Bewegung*. Studien zur Sozialwissenschaft 90. Wiesbaden: VS Verlag für Sozialwissenschaften.

Schultz, P. W., and Alan Searleman. 2002. "Rigidity of Thought and Behavior: 100 Years of Research." *Genetic, Social, and General Psychology Monographs* 128 (2): 165–207.

Schwindt, Dylan M., R. K. Bocinsky, Scott G. Ortman, Donna M. Glowacki, Mark D. Varien, and Timothy A. Kohler. 2016. "The Social Consequences of Climate Change in the Central Mesa Verde Region." *American Antiquity* 81 (1): 74–96.

Shannon, C. E. 1948. "A Mathematical Theory of Communication." *Bell System Technical Journal* 27: 379–423.

Shennan, Stephen. 2018. *The First Farmers of Europe: An Evolutionary Perspective*. Cambridge World Archaeology. Cambridge: Cambridge University Press.

Shennan, Stephen, Sean S. Downey, Adrian Timpson, Kevan Edinborough, Sue Colledge, Tim Kerig, Katie Manning, and Mark G. Thomas. 2013. "Regional Population Collapse Followed Initial Agriculture Booms in Mid-Holocene Europe." *Nature Communications* 4: 2486.

Shennan, Stephen, and Kevan Edinborough. 2007. "Prehistoric Population History: From the Late Glacial to the Late Neolithic in Central and Northern Europe." *Journal of Archaeological Science* 34 (8): 1339–45.

Spatz, Helmut. 1996. *Beiträge zum Kulturkomplex Hinkelstein-Großgartach-Rössen: Der keramische Fundstoff des Mittelneolithikums aus dem Mittleren Neckarland and seine zeitliche Gliederung*. 2 vols. Stuttgart: Materialhefte zur Archäologie in Baden-Württemberg.

Stäuble, Harald. 1995. "Radiocarbon Dates of the Earliest Neolithic in Central Europe." *Radiocarbon* 37 (2): 227–37.

Stehli, P. 1987. "Zur relativen und absoluten Chronologie der Bandkeramik in Mitteleuropa." In *Bylany Seminar 1987: Collected Papers*, edited by Jan Rulf, 69–78. Praha: Archeologický ústav AV CR.

Strien, Hans-Christoph. 2000. *Untersuchungen Zur Bandkeramik in Württemberg*. Universitätsforschungen zur prähistorischen Archäologie 69. Bonn: Habelt.

———. 2005. "Familientraditionen in Der Bandkeramischen Siedlung Bei Vaihingen/Enz." In *Die Bandkeramik Im 21. Jahrhundert: Symposium in Der Abtei Brauweiler Bei Köln Vom 16.9–19.9.2002*, edited by Jens Lüning, Christiane Frirdich, and Andreas Zimmermann. Internationale Archäologie. Arbeitsgemeinschaft, Symposium, Tagung, Kongress 7. Rahden/Westf.: Marie Leidorf.

———. 2010a. "Ein Komplexes Geflecht: Bandkeramische Kommunikationsnetze." In *Vernetzungen: Aspekte Siedlungsarchäologischer Forschung; Festschrift Für Helmut Schlichtherle Zum 60. Geburtstag*, edited by Irenäus Matuschik, Christian Strahm, Beat Eberschweiler, Gerhard Fingerlin, Albert Hafner, Michael Kinsky, Martin Mainberger, and Gunter Schöbel, 76–80. Freiburg, Br. Lavori.

———. 2010b. "Mobilität in Bandkeramischer Zeit im Spiegel der Fernimporte." In *Die Neolithisierung Mitteleuropas / The Spread of the Neolithic to Central Europe*, part

2, edited by Detlef Gronenborn and Jörg Petrasch, 497–508. Mainz: Verlag Des Römisch-Germanischen Zentralmuseums.

———. 2019. "'Robust Chronologies' or 'Bayesian Illusion'? Some Critical Remarks on the Use of Chronological Modelling." *Documenta Praehistorica* 46: 204–215.

Strien, Hans-Christoph, and Detlef Gronenborn. 2005. "Klima- Und Kulturwandel Während Des Mitteleuropäischen Altneolithikums (58./57.-51./50. Jahrhundert V. Chr.)." In *Klimaveränderung Und Kulturwandel in Neolithischen Gesellschaften Mitteleuropas, 6700-2200 V. Chr. RGZM—Tagungen 1*, edited by D. Gronenborn, 131–50. Mainz: Verlag Des Römisch-Germanischen Zentralmuseums.

Szécsényi-Nagy, Anna, Guido Brandt, Wolfgang Haak, Victoria Keerl, János Jakucs, Sabine Möller-Rieker, Kitti Köhler, et al. 2015. "Tracing the Genetic Origin of Europe's First Farmers Reveals Insights into Their Social Organization." *Proceedings of the Royal Society B: Biological Sciences* 282 (1805).

Tajfel, H., and J. C. Turner. 1986. "The Social Identity Theory of Intergroup Behavior." In *Psychology of Intergroup Relations*, edited by S. Worchel and W. G. Austin, 7–24. Chicago: Nelson-Hall.

Turchin, Peter. 2016. *Ages of Discord: A Structural-Demographic Analysis of American History*. Chaplin, CT: Beresta Books.

Turchin, Peter, and Sergey A. Nefedov. 2009. *Secular Cycles*. Princeton, NJ: Princeton University Press.

Turchin, Peter, Nina Witoszek, Stefan Thurner, David Garcia, Roger Griffin, Daniel Hoyer, Atle Midttun, James Bennett, Knut Myrum Næss, and Sergey Gavrilets. 2018. "A History of Possible Futures: Multipath Forecasting of Social Breakdown, Recovery, and Resilience." *Cliodynamics* 9 (2).

Van Dick, Rolf, Daan van Knippenberg, Silvia Hägele, Yves R.F. Guillaume, and Felix C. Brodbeck. 2008. "Group Diversity and Group Identification: The Moderating Role of Diversity Beliefs." *Human Relations* 61 (10): 1463–92.

Van Knippenberg, Daan, C. K. de Dreu, and A. C. Homan. 2004. "Work Group Diversity and Group Performance: An Integrative Model and Research Agenda." *Journal of Applied Psychology* 89 (6): 1008–22.

Wainwright, John, and Gianna Ayala. 2019. "Teleconnections and Environmental Determinism: Was There Really a Climate-Driven Collapse at Late Neolithic Çatalhöyük?" *Proceedings of the National Academy of Sciences of the United States of America* 116 (9): 3343–44.

Walker, Brian, C. S. Holling, Stephen R. Carpenter, and Ann P. Kinzig. 2004. "Resilience, Adaptability and Transformability in Social-Ecological Systems." *Ecology and Society* 9 (2): 5. http://www.ecologyandsociety.org/vol9/iss2/art5/.

Wanner, Heinz, Juerg Beer, Jonathan Bütikofer, Thomas J. Crowley, Ulrich Cuibash, Jacqueline Fluckiger, Hugues Goosse, et al. 2008. "Mid- to Late Holocene Climate Change: An Overview." *Quaternary Science Reviews* 27 (19–20): 1791–1828.

Wassenburg, Jasper A., Stephan Dietrich, Jan Fietzke, Jens Fohlmeister, Klaus P. Jochum, Denis Scholz, Detlev K. Richter, et al. 2016. "Reorganization of the North Atlantic Oscillation during Early Holocene Deglaciation." *Nature Geoscience* 9 (8): 602–5.

Weiberg, Erika, Andrew Bevan, Katerina Kouli, Markos Katsianis, Jessie Woodbridge, Anton Bonnier, Max Engel, et al. 2019. "Long-Term Trends of Land Use and Demography in Greece: A Comparative Study." *The Holocene* 24 (1): 095968361982664.

Weiberg, Erika, and Martin Finné. 2018. "Resilience and Persistence of Ancient Societies in the Face of Climate Change: A Case Study from Late Bronze Age Peloponnese." *World Archaeology* 72 (1): 1–19.

Weitzel, Elic M., and Brian F. Codding. 2016. "Population Growth as a Driver of Initial Domestication in Eastern North America." *Royal Society Open Science* 3 (8): 160319.

Weninger, Bernhard. 2017. "Niche Construction and Theory of Agricultural Origins: Case Studies in Punctuated Equilibrium." *Documenta Praehistorica* 44: 6–17.

Weninger, Bernhard, and Lee Clare. 2017. "6600–6000 Cal BP Abrupt Climate Change and Neolithic Dispersal from West Asia." In *Megadrought and Collapse: From Early Agriculture to Angkor*, edited by H. Weiss, 69–92. Oxford: Oxford University Press.

Weninger, Bernhard, Lee Clare, Fokke Gerritsen, Horejs, Barbara, Krauß, Raiko, Jörg Linstädter, Rana Ozbal, and Eelco J. Rohling. 2014. "Neolithisation of the Aegean and Southeast Europe during the 6600–6000 CalBC Period of Rapid Climate Change." *Documenta Praehistorica* 41: 1–31.

Weninger, Bernhard, Lee Clare, Olaf Jöris, Reinhard Jung, and Kevan Edinborough. 2015. "Quantum Theory of Radiocarbon Calibration." *World Archaeology* 47 (4): 543–66.

Weninger, Bernhard, Lee Clare, Eelco J. Rohling, Ofer Bar-Yosef, et al. 2009. "The Impact of Rapid Climate Change on Prehistoric Societies during the Holocene in the Eastern Mediterranean." *Documenta Praehistorica* 34: 7–59.

Wentker, Hermann, Philipp Gassert, and Tim Geiger, eds. 2018. *Zweiter Kalter Krieg und Friedensbewegung: Der NATO-Doppelbeschluss in deutsch-deutscher und internationaler Perspektive*. Schriftenreihe der Vierteljahrshefte für Zeitgeschichte Sondernummer. Munich and Vienna: De Gruyter Oldenbourg.

Wilson, Andrew, and Alan K. Bowman, eds. 2018. *Trade, Commerce, and the State in the Roman World*. Oxford Studies on the Roman Economy. Oxford: Oxford University Press.

Wolfram, Sabine, and Harald Stäuble, eds. 2012. *Siedlungsstruktur Und Kulturwandel in Der Bandkeramik: Beiträge Der Internationalen Tagung "Neue Fragen Zur Bandkeramik Oder Alles Beim Alten?!", Leipzig, 23. Bis 24. September 2010*. Arbeits- und Forschungsberichte zur sächsischen Bodendenkmalpflege Beihefte 25. Dresden: Landesamt für Archäologie.

Wollenweber, René. 2019. "The Oldest Box-Shaped Wooden Well from Saxony-Anhalt and the Stichbandkeramik Culture in Central Germany." In *Contacts, Boundaries and Innovation in the Fifth Millennium: Exploring Developed Neolithic Societies in Central Europe and Beyond*, edited by Ralf Gleser and Daniela Hofmann, 159–79. Leiden: Sidestone Press.

Zahid, H. J., Erick Robinson, and Robert L. Kelly. 2016. "Agriculture, Population Growth, and Statistical Analysis of the Radiocarbon Record." *Proceedings of the National Academy of Sciences of the United States of America* 113 (4): 931–35.

Zielhofer, Christoph, Lee Clare, Gary Rollefson, Stephan Wächter, Dirk Hoffmeister, Georg Bareth, Christopher Roettig, et al. 2012. "The Decline of the Early Neolithic Population Center of 'Ain Ghazal and Corresponding Earth-Surface Processes, Jordan Rift Valley." *Late Quaternary Tropical Ecosystem Dynamics* 78 (3): 427–41.

Zielhofer, Christoph, Anne Köhler, Steffen Mischke, Abdelfattah Benkaddour, Abdeslam Mikdad, and William J. Fletcher. 2019. "Western Mediterranean Hydro-Climatic Consequences of Holocene Ice-Rafted Debris (Bond) Events." *Climate of the Past* 15 (2): 463–75.

Zimmermann, Andreas. 2012a. "Cultural Cycles in Central Europe during the Holocene." *Quaternary International* 274 (October): 251–58.

———. 2012b. "Das Hofplatzmodell: Entwicklung, Probleme, Perspektiven." In *Siedlungsstruktur Und Kulturwandel in Der Bandkeramik: Beiträge Der Internationalen Tagung "Neue Fragen Zur Bandkeramik Oder Alles Beim Alten?!," Leipzig, 23. Bis 24. September 2010*, edited by Sabine Wolfram and Harald Stäuble, 11–19. Arbeits- und Forschungsberichte zur sächsischen Bodendenkmalpflege Beihefte 25. Dresden: Landesamt für Archäologie.

CHAPTER 13

El Niño as Catastrophe on the Peruvian Coast

DANIEL H. SANDWEISS and KIRK A. MAASCH

Summary for Stakeholders

El Niño is a climatological phenomenon centered in the Pacific basin but with global reach. Although there are different kinds of El Niños, the best known is the Eastern Pacific (EP) El Niño. Some world regions benefit from these events—warmer winters in the northeastern United States, fewer hurricanes in the Caribbean. Many areas, however, are devastated. As ground zero for El Niño, the Peruvian coast is particularly hard hit, with damage to the normally rich fisheries matched by destruction of infrastructure on land, including the canal and field systems essential for productivity in this desert environment. Epidemic diseases such as malaria and dengue also run rampant during EP events. We have been studying ancient El Niños and their effects on prehistoric people and resources on the northern Peruvian coast. Our work and that of many colleagues on this topic offers a number of insights of potential importance to modern societies. These observations may be of particular use for planners on the Peruvian coast.

1. Archaeological proxies for El Niño give us unique data to help refine the climate models that are the best hope of predicting and mitigating El Niño events.
2. The archaeology of coastal Peru teaches us how earlier people faced the stresses of El Niño—there may well be appropriate technologies of the past yet to be discovered, such as rainwater capture in low-flow gullies.
3. Data from archaeology and studies of the ancient environment around the archaeological sites show medium- and long-term pro-

cesses that are not obvious in the short term. For instance, we identified a cycle of earthquakes, El Niño mudslides and floods, beach ridges, and blowing sand that can impact agricultural systems as easily today as it did in the past—if appropriate mitigation is not undertaken.

4. Not all effects of El Niño are negative. Proper planning can take advantage of the upside of El Niño.
5. The long-term correlations of El Niño frequency change and cultural change suggest that loss of faith may lead to regime change. This has consequences for political stability.

Introduction

In a recent review, Roberto Barrios (2017, 151) wrote that anthropologists define catastrophes "as the end result of historical processes by which human practices enhance the materially destructive and socially disruptive capacities of geophysical phenomena, technological malfunctions, and communicable diseases and inequitably distribute disaster risk according to lines of gender, race, class, and ethnicity." El Niño events on the Peruvian coast fit this consensus definition of disaster, catastrophe, and inequitably distributed risk. In this chapter, we consider the prehistory of El Niño on the north coast of Peru as a socio-ecological process and demonstrate how geophysical phenomena intersected with human practice and may have resulted in change in the material correlates of culture.

El Niño events on the Peruvian coast offer a useful lens for viewing past human behavior in the face of catastrophe, because (1) they are sometimes extreme events that destroy or damage infrastructure, curtail subsistence production, and bring negative health consequences including death; and (2) the frequency of large-magnitude events has changed through time. Thus, El Niño allows us to assess the human impact of catastrophic events with variable recurrence intervals. Some positive effects of El Niño offer opportunities for resilient mitigation (including accrual of power through crisis management), but on the whole events are negative, even catastrophic, for most humans in their path and following a latitudinal gradient of decreasing negative effects north to south, from Ecuador through Peru and Chile. Here, we focus on the Peruvian coast north of Lima (12° S; see figure 13.1 for location of all places and sites mentioned in the text), where El Niño is most catastrophic for humans in its path.

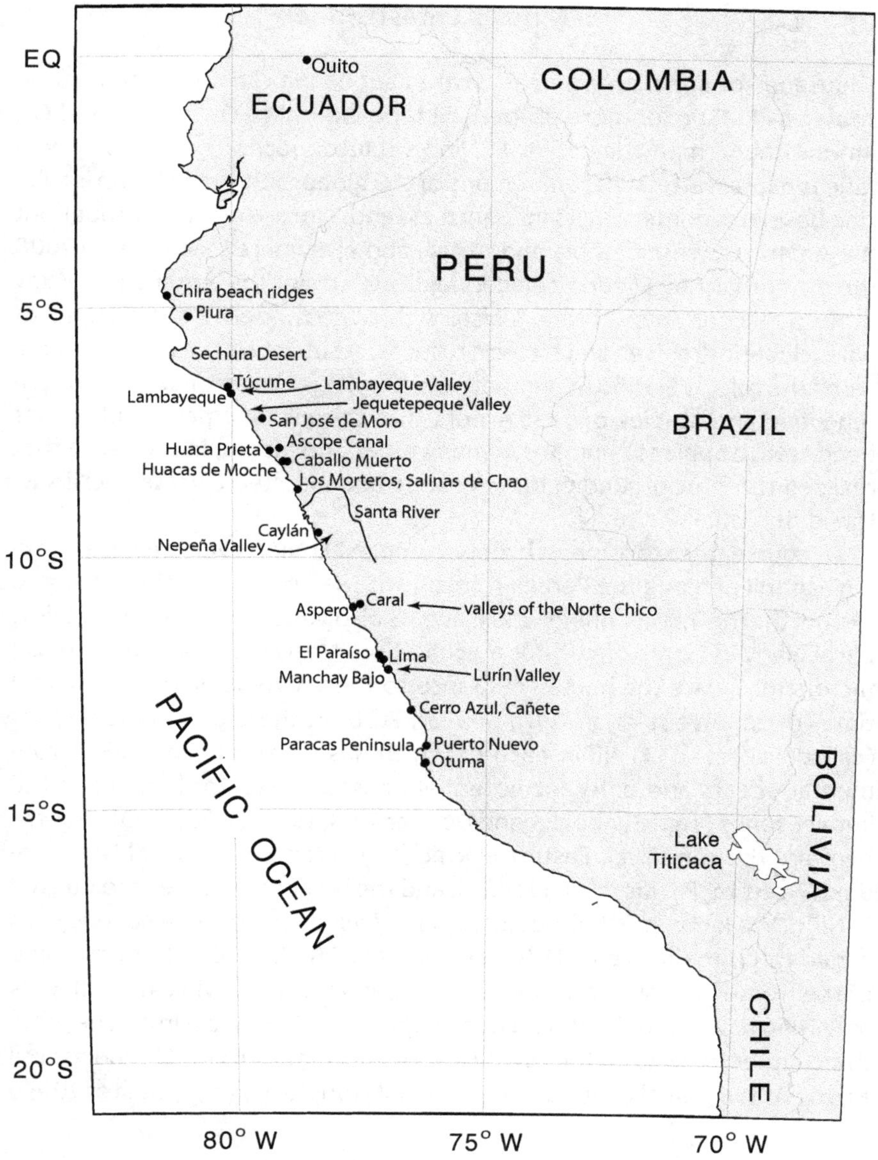

Figure 13.1. Locations of sites and places mentioned in the text. The north coast as defined here runs from Lima north to the border between Peru and Ecuador. Figure created by Kirk A. Maasch.

El Niño as Catastrophe

Thousands of papers have been written about the climatic phenomenon known as El Niño, or more properly El Niño–Southern Oscillation (ENSO). Among them, many deal with El Niño's teleconnections, that is, how El Niño is expressed in different regions of the globe; although El Niño is a Pacific basin phenomenon, its influence extends north and east throughout the Americas, west to India and Africa, and elsewhere (see Maasch 2008 for a summary of El Niño teleconnections across the Americas). Many other papers address El Niño's history through modeling and analysis of paleoclimatic archives and historic records. A subset of these papers concerns the role of El Niño in human prehistory. It is clear from both modern reporting and studies of past events that this climatic perturbation has been catastrophic for humans in many times and places, in the sense that realized risk precipitated cultural change and affected diverse social sectors differentially.

Of course, the story is much more complex. El Niño events have a latitudinal gradient along the Peruvian coast, with severity usually increasing to the north. The impact of individual events also varies from valley to valley, particularly in terms of coastal precipitation. Many cultural and historical factors modulate the human response to these events across space and time (D. Sandweiss et al. 2001, 605–6). Further, there are multiple types (called flavors) of El Niño, each of which has different climatic/environmental effects and different potential consequences for humans in the impact zones (e.g., Banholzer and Donner 2014; Hu et al. 2018). Of concern here are the canonical, Eastern Pacific (EP) El Niño, La Niña, El Niño Modoki (= central Pacific or CP El Niño), and the recently experienced Coastal El Niño. We know most about EP El Niño, including that its frequency has varied through time (e.g., D. Sandweiss et al. 2007, 2020), although some of the frequency variation may involve Coastal El Niño. While most flavors of El Niño have climatic influence throughout the Pacific basin and beyond, this chapter focuses on the coast of Peru—ground zero for El Niño as well as one of the global centers of early social complexity (e.g., Quilter 2014).

Flavors of El Niño and Consequences for Coast Dwellers in Peru

Eastern Pacific El Niño

The canonical El Niño captured global attention with the large-magnitude events of 1982–83 and particularly 1997–98, when El Niño became part of popular culture in the United States (e.g., Shropshire 2000) and elsewhere. These events are characterized by weakened trade winds and by anomalous warming in the Central Pacific that propagates eastward to the coast of the Americas. During normal (non-EP) years, the Humboldt or Peru Current flows north along the Chilean and Peruvian coasts, bringing cool, deep, nutrient-rich water to the surface through intense upwelling; under these conditions, the thermocline (the division between warm, mixed, nutrient-depleted surface water and cool, nutrient-rich deeper water) is near the surface. As the pulse of warm water reaches the coastal zone during an EP event, the thermocline deepens and upwelling weakens, with warmer sea surface temperatures (SSTs) and depleted nutrients. Marine biomass is reduced, from plankton to fish to sea birds and sea mammals (UCAR/NOAA 1994). Around the Pacific basin, normal precipitation patterns tend to reverse: the western Pacific becomes drier while the Eastern Pacific gets wetter. Under normal conditions, the coast of Peru is an arid desert, caught between the cool sea surface and the rain shadow of the Andes. During an EP El Niño, the warming of the coastal water leads to convective storms onshore that cause destructive flooding across the desert.

On the Peruvian north coast, El Niño rainfall drives massive quantities of sediment into the rivers and down to the coast, causing the shoreline to prograde (expand seaward) in the form of temporary deltas. Longshore drift subsequently transports this sediment north to form enduring beach ridges (Moseley, Wagner, and Richardson 1992; D. Sandweiss 1986; D. Sandweiss et al. 1998; Shafer Rogers et al. 2004). This new land was later used by people. For example, sequential camps show that fisher-gatherers followed the Chira beach ridges westward through time (Richardson 1983). Wells (1992) demonstrated that flooding of the Santa River in northern Peru created new land at the river mouth throughout the mid- to late Holocene, as well as building beach ridges to the north of the valley; she tracked the westward progradation of the valley by the first appearance of archaeological sites on each newly created tract of land.

For millennia, two complementary resource bases have sustained the large, increasingly complex human populations of the Peruvian coastal desert: fishing in the rich waters of the Humboldt Current and irrigation-based farming in the river valleys that run west from the adjacent Andes mountains, fed by highland precipitation and glacial melt. Both resource bases are vulnerable to EP El Niño; the decline in marine biomass is matched by destructive flooding of coastal infrastructure, including irrigation and field systems. Standing water has its own hazards, both in destroying crops and in promoting insect-borne diseases (e.g., Gagnon, Smoyer-Tomic, and Bush 2002; Kovats et al. 2003); during the 2017 Coastal El Niño, malaria, dengue, Zika, and chikungunya were all reported in Peruvian newspapers as epidemic on the north coast.

The first large magnitude EP (or Coastal) El Niño following the Spanish conquest of Peru in 1532 CE occurred in 1578 CE. In 1580, Spanish colonial authorities in Lima sent a scribe to the north coast to find out what had happened. We are fortunate to have about half of the resulting interviews of eyewitnesses to this event (see below, "Coping with El Niño on the North Coast of Peru") (Alcocer 1987 [1580]). A Spanish priest described the consequences of the event for agriculture in the Lambayeque Valley:

> After the canals were fixed, the Indians hurried to plant and there came the plagues . . . such that any seed that grew a hand's width above the ground was eaten by crickets and locusts and some green worms and yellow ones and other black ones that were bred from the putrefaction of the earth because of the said rains. . . . [After several plantings], when the fruit was ready to harvest there was such a multitude of mice that this witness didn't believe the Indians and went to some fields and saw mounds of mice like piles of sand . . . the mice were the size of medium rabbits . . . this witness counted a mound of them and there were 500 more or less.[1] (Alcocer 1987 [1580], 42 [f. 220v./221r.], translated by D. Sandweiss)

La Niña

La Niña is the reverse of EP El Niño: an exaggeration of normal (non-Niño) conditions (Glantz 2002; McPhaden 2003). Instead of anomalous warming, the Pacific basin cools. The Eastern Pacific, including Peru, gets drier (Cai et al. 2015). On the Peruvian coast, the human consequences of La Niña are much less severe than EP El Niño. Although malarial epidemics are not reported for La Niña (Gagnon et al. 2002), health consequences include respiratory problems on the north coast of Peru (Ordinola 2002). Fisheries are enhanced by the intensified cooling of La Niña, while agricultural outcomes are mixed (Ordinola 2002).

Central Pacific El Niño (Modoki)

In the early 2000s, Japanese scientists recognized a new flavor of ENSO: CP El Niño or El Niño Modoki. "'Modoki' is a classical Japanese word, which means 'a similar but different thing'" (Ashok et al. 2007). In a Modoki event, the Central Pacific warms anomalously, but the warm water does not propagate to the east. Peru, for instance, has near neutral to slightly negative SST anomalies during Modoki events. El Niño Modoki does have atmospheric teleconnections around the Pacific basin that have consequences for air temperature and precipitation, generally resulting in an opposite precipitation signal to EP El Niño (e.g., Ashok et al. 2007; Taschetto and England 2009; Weng et al. 2009; Zhang, Jin, and Turner 2014). For the north coast of Peru, Modoki is associated with a 50 percent reduction in normal stream flow (A. Sandweiss 2019; Sulca et al. 2018). Unlike EP El Niño events, during which river discharge doubles in the austral summer due to rainfall in the normally arid coastal zone, Modoki-related reduction in river discharge results from reduced precipitation and/or reduced glacial melting in the adjacent Andes mountains. Presumably, this recently recognized reduction in flow has negative consequences for irrigation-based agriculture on the Peruvian north coast.

Coastal El Niño

In February and March of 2017, the north coast of Peru was devastated by an event that looked—from the local perspective—like a large-magnitude EP El Niño. Climatologically, it was quite different. Although the Peruvian coast experienced extraordinarily high SSTs and torrential rainfall, especially from Lima north, SSTs in the Central Pacific remained normal. Subsequent reanalysis of records from 1979–2017 recognized seven Coastal El Niños, some of which followed on the heels of large-magnitude EP El Niño events and extended the negative consequences of those events for coast dwellers (Hu et al. 2018). At the end of the 2017 event (31 March 2017), the Peruvian government reported over 140,000 people homeless, close to 1,000,000 affected, 101 dead, 353 missing, and 19 disappeared as a result of the two-month Coastal El Niño (Radio Programas del Perú 2017). Later accounts put the numbers even higher: "158 flood-related deaths, 1,372,260 people displaced, and 3.124 billion dollars in damage" (Caramanica 2018)—over 1 percent of Peru's GDP. From the perspective of a Peruvian coast dweller (especially from Lima north), a Coastal El Niño is indistinguishable from an EP El Niño: fishing is diminished, coastal valley infrastructure (e.g., canals) is damaged or destroyed, insect-borne diseases are rampant, and sediment transport enables coastal progradation. However, Coastal El Niños are generally much shorter in duration than similarly intense EP El Niños. The 2017 Coastal EP lasted for 2 months, while the 1982–83 and 1997–88 EP events lasted for 13 and 14 months, respectively, including a short Coastal El Niño at the end of each event (Hu et al. 2018).

Opportunities on the Peruvian Coast during Eastern Pacific El Niño/Coastal El Niño

Few natural hazards have only negative consequences for humans. EP El Niño and Coastal El Niño (which manifest similarly along the Peruvian coast, particularly from Lima north) are no exception. Resilience requires opportunities; in this section we review the positive correlates of EP/Coastal El Niño (henceforth El Niño unless otherwise specified).

Arntz (1986; Arntz, Landa, and Tarazona 1985) catalogued many of the positive and negative effects of the 1982–83 large-magnitude El Niño on marine resources in Peru. At the start of some El Niño events in this region, warm water and reduced nutrients cause fish to flee from north to south, coming inshore on the central coast (i.e., near Lima). As Marcus et al. (2020) have noted, on the central and south central coast, during El Niño events scallops boom in response to increased dissolved oxygen in their habitat (Wolff 1985), and shrimp also become abundant (Weisburd 1984). The extensive, monospecific Otuma shell middens on the Paracas Peninsula (about two hundred kilometers south of Lima) date to about 3850 cal BP (Craig and Psuty 1971). The Otuma middens suggest that El Niño scallop booms are not new and that pre-Columbian inhabitants of the region took advantage of these temporary increases in marine resources.

Analysis of El Niño's effects on the Peruvian fishery during the late twentieth century found that, in general, "at the end of the El Niño phenomenon [there was] less productivity but more diversity in the pelagic ecosystem" (Ñiquen and Bouchon 2004, 563). This corresponds with informal interviews with artisanal fishermen on the north coast of Peru several years after the 1982–83 El Niño: fish were present, but there were less, some preferred species were gone, and new species were present but less abundant. At Cerro Azul, Cañete, a fishing village about 150 kilometers south of Lima, Marcus et al. (2020) documented the response of the fishery to the 1982–83 El Niño: as in the north, many species suffered mass mortality or migrated away or out of reach of artisanal fishermen, while new species appeared; some of these were abundant, valuable, and available until normal, cool-water species recovered in 1985–86. These different cases reflect a climatic divide at about 12° S latitude (D. Sandweiss 2003, 26; D. Sandweiss et al. 2020).

Although flooding and landslides associated with El Niño destroy canal intakes and other features of the irrigation systems that make the desert coast of Peru so productive, it is possible to mitigate some of this resource loss. One option is rainfall-fed farming on the desert during the longer and more intense events (Caramanica 2018a). Another is through the construction of dams that capture floodwater in smaller drainages (A. Sandweiss 2019). During and after the 2017 Coastal El Niño, Caramanica (2018a, 2018b) provided proof of this concept with observations of fields that had been planted successfully in gullies blocked by the aqueducts of the massive Ascope Canal in the Chicama Valley, which dates to the Late Intermediate period (1000–1400 CE) (Huckleberry, Caramanica, and Quilter 2018).

Xerophytic (fog-based) plant communities called *lomas* normally grow in the western foothills of the Andes between about two hundred and nine hundred meters above sea level (e.g., Dillon et al. 2011; Rundel et al. 1991). Some *lomas* plants are edible, while others serve as wood, fuel, or forage for animals (see Beresford-Jones et al. 2015, 206–9). During El Niño events, rainfall on the desert slopes causes extraordinary growth in the *lomas* (Dillon and Rundel 1990; Cano et al. 1999), providing another partial alternative for the agricultural produce lost to El Niño's rains, floods, insects, and rodents. For the Early and Middle Preceramic periods (before about 5000 cal BP), several investigators have pointed to the importance of *lomas* stands or "fog oases" (Engel 1973) for coastal hunter-gatherers (Lanning 1967; Beresford-Jones et al. 2015).

Algarrobo (*Prosopis* spp.) is one of the most common tree genera on the desert coast of Peru. The pods of this legume are edible, and the wood has been a primary source of building material and fuel for millennia, appearing frequently in archaeological and paleobotanical contexts across the region (e.g., Beresford-Jones 2011; Nordt et al. 2004). The ENSO cycle of El Niño rains and normal aridity play essential roles in the reproduction of *algarrobo* forests (Salazar et al. 2018). Were the Peruvian coast a desert without periodic El Niños, this important resource would not exist.

Although El Niño takes away, it also gives. El Niño–associated rainfall is erosive along both established channels and new channels that form during floods, but the same overbank flooding that encourages disease epidemics also deposits replenishing soil on the irrigated desert fields. For instance, Nordt et al. (2004, 30) found silt introduced during El Niño events in pre-Hispanic fields in the Lambayeque Valley on the north coast.

Within the channels and across the floodplains of the desert coast, sediments deposited by El Niño–related flooding build landscapes. Eventually, segments of these landscapes rise above the one-thousand-year floods and become flood-proof bases for construction. Working with our colleague Alice Kelley and our student Paul Pluta (Pluta 2015), we found that the Moche (north coast, first millennium CE) took advantage of this process, constructing at least two sites on top of landscapes that had reached safe elevations. San José de Moro (SJM) is a Moche and post-Moche site located on the north side of the Jequetepeque Valley in the Chamán River drainage. SJM is an ideal test case for El Niño erosion and deposit: the Chamán's headwaters are on the western slopes of the Andean cordillera and below seasonal highland rainfall, so the river only flows during El Niño events.

Luis Jaime Castillo has been excavating at SJM since 1990 (e.g., Castillo Butters 2011). Beginning at about 400 CE, occupants of the site began accumulating cultural strata that are now over 4 meters deep. Nowhere are these deposits disturbed by channelized erosion. Below the archaeological levels, however, it is a different story. There, a 2.75-meter deep test pit found channelized deposits overlying broad floodplain sediments (Pluta 2015). All of these water-lain deposits must have been deposited during El Niño events. Although we have not yet succeeded in dating these pre-occupation deposits, the final pre-occupation, flood-built surface seems to have been used for floodwater farming—we found regular furrows in profile, and samples from within the furrows had maize phytoliths with processing damage (L. Perry, pers. comm.). This surface must date to the Middle or Late Holocene and may immediately predate the beginning of intensive occupation at 400 CE.

Two valleys to the south, we found a similar sequence at the Huacas de Moche site (e.g., Uceda 2010). Under the northwest corner of the massive Huaca del Sol (estimated to have been built with 143 million adobe bricks [Hastings and Moseley 1975, 197]), we found another pre-occupational sequence of flood deposits (Pluta 2015). Mound construction began at about 400 CE, as at SJM (S. Uceda, pers. comm). Once the Huaca del Sol was built, it shows no evidence of erosive flooding.

Preliminary OSL (optically stimulated luminescence) dates from the flood deposits under Huaca del Sol are consistent with natural accumulation up to the start of mound building. These flood deposits are fine-grained (Pluta 2015), indicating low-energy overbank deposits, as in the lower section at SJM. Within these deposits, we found angular rocks that would have required much more energy to move than indicated by the surrounding grain size; this suggests a human presence in the area while the landscape was under construction.

There may well be other sites along the Peruvian coast that were also built on flood-safe, El Niño–constructed landscapes; this is a question for future research.

Finally, we might also ask whether multi-sectorial natural hazards associated with large-magnitude El Niño events inspired political entrepreneurs to offer solutions in exchange for power. As President Obama's chief of staff Rahm Emanuel famously put it, successful politicians "never let a good crisis go to waste."

Summary of El Niño Flavors and Effects of El Niño on Peruvian Coastal Landscapes, Ecologies, and Communities

El Niño comes in many flavors. Those with important consequences for humans are (in order of decreasing negative effects) Eastern Pacific (EP) El Niño, Coastal El Niño, El Niño Modoki, and La Niña. The downside of EP and Coastal El Niño in coastal Peru is abundantly clear: marine biomass loss, insect plagues, torrential rains leading to desert erosion and debris flows, destruction of crops, destruction of infrastructure, coastline change, disease epidemics, and population dislocation. There are also upsides, some concurrent with the event and others resulting from longer-term processes set in motion by El Niño. Concurrent mitigating factors include some marine species replacement, *lomas* blooms, floodwater capture, opportunistic rainfall farming, and perhaps crisis management. Longer-term processes are soil replenishment, *algarrobo* forest growth, and positive landscape modification. El Niño Modoki's effects are subtler, consisting of changes in precipitation and/or temperature in the Andean highlands leading to reduced water flow to the coast. This flavor was discovered recently and has not yet been addressed in terms of consequences for prehistoric Peruvian coast dwellers. La Niña mainly affects human health through decreased temperatures.

Coping with El Niño on the North Coast of Peru: Lessons from 1578

In 1578 the Peruvian coast was devastated by the first large-magnitude El Niño following the Spanish conquest of 1532 (Alcocer 1987 [1580]; Huertas Vallejos 2001). The Spaniards had not accumulated knowledge of such events—in terms of landscape learning, they lacked limitational and social knowledge about El Niño (Rockman 2009a, 2009b). Not having experienced a major El Niño since arriving on the Peruvian coast, the Spaniards could not have acquired limitational knowledge on their own, nor had they succeeded in acquiring and acting upon an adequate stock of social knowledge from the native inhabitants. That such knowledge existed is implied by the long-term, pre-contact trajectory of increasing population and social complexity evidenced in the archaeological record (e.g., Quilter 2014; D. Sandweiss and Quilter 2012; Roscoe, Sandweiss, and Robinson, forthcoming). Some indicators of this knowledge are preserved in the strategies employed by native inhabitants in 1578 and summarized below (Alcocer 1987 [1580]; Huertas Vallejos 2001). *Why* the Spaniards were seemingly caught unaware by the event is an interesting question for future research; it would have been to the natives' interest to prepare their new overlords for the recurrence of El Niño, given how much they suffered from inappropriate Spanish management, some of which was apparent prior to the event. An equally interesting question is whether, or when, Spaniards learned to plan for and react appropriately to El Niño. The colonial and republican periods on the Peruvian coast offer a potentially powerful opportunity to assess the landscape learning model (Rockman 2009a, 2009b).

Between 1532 and 1578 CE, much had changed: demography (drastic depopulation [Cook 1981]), settlement pattern (the *reducciones*, or re-settlements that concentrated the declining native population in central villages), power relations (Incas and paramount local lords replaced by Spaniards), and economics (there had been no money in most of the pre-Columbian Andean world; redistribution and reciprocity structured most exchanges of goods and services [Murra 1980]). However, the 1578 CE event occurred only forty-six years after the conquest, when native lords still held some authority and while there were still people living who had been born during Inca rule. The testimonies recorded by Alcocer (1987 [1580]) are the closest we have to eyewitness accounts of pre-Columbian responses to El Niño.

Indeed, the consequences of this first large-magnitude post-conquest El Niño were particularly dire precisely because of the recent Spanish re-settlement policy—as their populations declined, natives were concentrated in central villages for easier control and catechizing. In the valleys of the north coast, these villages were often squarely in the paths of El Niño floods; canals, fields, houses, public buildings, animals, stores—everything was washed away by El Niño's waters (Alcocer 1987 [1580]; Huertas Vallejos 2001; Copson and Sandweiss 1999).

During and in the immediate aftermath of the events, Spaniards in charge of native groups insisted that tribute continue to be paid and that native laborers rebuild the master canals before working to recover their own infrastructure and livelihoods. In response, native lords petitioned the *Real Audiencia* (royal authorities) in Lima for tribute relief until they had recovered from the event. In 1580 CE the *Real Audiencia* sent an inspector, the scribe Francisco de Alcocer, to find out what had happened. He came prepared with two versions of a fourteen-point questionnaire, one for witnesses brought forward by the local Spanish *encomenderos* (Spaniards given charge of native groups' labor in exchange for catechizing the natives) and one for witnesses speaking on behalf of native lords. About half of the responses have been found in the archives and published by Lorenzo Huertas in 1987 and 2001 (Alcocer 1987 [1580]; Huertas Vallejos 2001). These are rich and fascinating records; of interest here are coping strategies extracted from the testimonies.

Coping Strategies from Alcocer (1987 [1580])

Relocation. A number of witnesses recounted different relocation strategies. Some simply moved to higher ground in their vicinity. One witness from the village of Túcume in the Lambayeque Valley said that "because all the valley was like a sea they went up to the huacas [archaeological mounds] and the high hills." One of us [D. Sandweiss] worked at the archaeological site of Túcume for three years beginning in 1989 (Heyerdahl et al. 1995). Memories of the catastrophic 1982–83 El Niño were fresh in local memory, and more than one Tucumano spoke of the valley flooding and villagers moving to the huacas and high hills during the event—the same effects and coping strategies as in 1578, recounted using identical words (D. Sandweiss 1999).

Other natives relocated further away: north to Quito on the equator in the high Andes of present-day Ecuador, east into the adjacent mountains, south to Lima. Not all had returned by 1580 CE.

Replanting. As we have seen already in the priest's testimony, replanting in the inundated fields was not initially successful. The witnesses are silent about whether they tried any rain-fed farming in the desert margins where inundation may have been less of a problem.

Building/rebuilding. Some witnesses spoke of building platforms and shelters to keep their goods and supplies dry. A number complained of being forced to spend several months rebuilding the main canal.

Refinancing. Some natives sold textiles and animals at low prices to raise funds to pay taxes. Textiles, mostly cotton on the coast, were highly valued in the pre-Columbian Andes and in the Spanish colonial world (e.g., Murra 1962). Others exchanged maize (corn) from their diminished stock to pay tribute. Some offered service to the Spaniards in exchange for food. Two witnesses admitted to stealing.

Foraging. As often happens during famines, witnesses spoke of eating wild foods such as lizards, grasses, fruits, and seeds.

Emotional responses. Some witnesses said they cried, complained, or begged the king for mercy. It is unlikely that these strategies helped much in terms of economic recovery. They may, however, be seen as indicative of (post-traumatic) stress that is well-recorded from recent disasters, which in turn may have influenced decision-making in other areas (F. Riede, pers. comm. 2019). Again, this is an unexplored topic that could be productively pursued in the archives.

Paleo-Niños

When EP, Coastal, and CP El Niños occurred during pre-Columbian times, they must have provoked some response from Peruvian coastal people.

Geographically, we would expect the clearest responses from Lima (12° S) north, where the negative consequences for humans are most dire. Temporally, human response to El Niño would have increased rapidly after about 4800 cal BP as coast dwellers began to rely on irrigation agriculture, with its vulnerable infrastructure and related demographic growth. The largest pre-Columbian canal systems are also located north of Lima (e.g., Huckleberry et al. 2018) for reasons of deep geological history. The earliest canal known from Peru dates to about 5400 cal BP but was very small and was located in the Andean foothills about sixty kilometers east of the coast (Dillehay, Eling, and Rossen 2005). Multiple large, Late Preceramic period mound sites such as Caral (Shady, Haas, and Creamer 2001) dating between about 4800 and 3800 cal BP are found inland along the coastal valleys of the Norte Chico (centered about two hundred kilometers north of Lima) and elsewhere on the north coast. Remains of domesticated plants (mainly cotton and gourd) are major components of the midden at these sites. Together with locations twenty-plus kilometers to the east of the shoreline, the abundant agricultural produce strongly suggests the development of large-scale irrigation systems in the Late Preceramic period, after about 4800 cal BP.

In this context, understanding the timing and frequency of paleo-Niños becomes urgent. Multiple proxies from natural and anthropogenic archives provide insight, particularly concerning frequency variability. Climate modelers have also addressed paleo-Niños. Although one of the first studies to recognize that El Niño frequency has not been stationary across the Holocene was based on marine biota found in Peruvian coastal archaeological sites (Rollins, Richardson, and Sandweiss 1986; D. Sandweiss et al. 1996), there are now hundreds to thousands of paleo-Niño studies (see Lu et al. 2018 for a recent review of proxy data and model simulations).

To understand the human eco-dynamics of El Niño in pre-Columbian coastal Peru, we should use data that are directly relevant to the region. As a tropical desert coast washed by a cool eastern boundary current, the region lacks many of the standard high to mid-resolution natural archives. Corals are absent. There are no glaciers on the Peruvian coast; there are glaciers on the east side of the adjacent Andes, but records are complicated because much of the input comes across the Amazon from the Atlantic, whereas El Niño is a Pacific phenomenon. With one quasi-exception (Lake La Niña) discussed later, there are no lakes along the Peruvian coast except those created by irrigation runoff. Like the glaciers, highland lakes respond in part to Amazonian/Atlantic climate. To be clear: many glaciers, corals, and lakes are located in areas affected by ENSO and thus hold important archives relevant to understanding the global behavior of ENSO through time (e.g., Thompson et al. 2017), but they are not ideal for learning what took place on the Peruvian coast (D. Sandweiss et al. 2020).

Fortunately, there are El Niño archives embedded in or preserved near archaeological sites on the Peruvian coast. We have previously reviewed the climate archives that are most relevant for the Peruvian coast during the Terminal Pleistocene and the Holocene (D. Sandweiss 2003; D. Sandweiss et al. 2007, 2020). These include the following:

- Biogeography of marine animals (mollusks, fish, sea mammals) and plants (e.g., *lomas* plants)
- Growth increment analysis (mollusks, fish otoliths)
- $\partial^{18}O$ and $\partial^{14}C$ profiles (mollusks, fish otoliths)
- Differential preservation in archaeological sites
- Paleo-flood deposits
- Beach ridge sequences
- Ephemeral lake deposits
- Cores from the continental shelf

Our reconstruction of EP/Coastal El Niño frequency on the Peruvian north coast shows transitions approximately every three thousand years. In summary (D. Sandweiss 2003; D. Sandweiss et al. 2007, 2020; unpublished data):

- Before ca. 9000/8000 cal yr BP: El Niño present, frequency unknown
- Ca. 9000/8000–5800 cal yr BP: El Niño absent or very low frequency
- Ca. 5800–2900 cal yr BP: El Niño present, frequency lower than modern
- After ca. 2900 cal yr BP: El Niño present, frequency within modern range of variability, particularly high frequency for several centuries after 2900 cal BP

The data for this history of El Niño frequency mostly come from the north coast of Peru and directly or indirectly measure SST change. It has long been clear that climatic conditions were different south of Lima (12° S) (D. Sandweiss et al. 1996, 1997, 2007, 2020; D. Sandweiss 2003): soil development shows long-term hyperaridity south of 12° S and greater moisture to the north (Noller 1993); *lomas* plant communities north of that point are a single community (suggesting periods of frequent rainfall to allow communities to intermingle), while to the south each stand has a high degree of endemism (Rundel and Dillon 1998; Rundel et al., 1991). Carré et al. (2014) recently published a study of Holocene El Niño frequencies based on the geochemistry of growth increments in archaeological shells from sites at and south of Lima (12° S). Their results differ from ours for some periods; both reconstructions of El Niño frequency may be correct for their respective regions. For much of the period when we see an absence of El Niño, Carré et al. (2014) suggest that El Niño Modoki (CP mode) was operating; Modoki does not raise SST on the Peruvian coast and therefore would not be visible in our proxies. Carré et al. see minimum El Niño at times when we see it present but reduced in frequency. Coastal El Niños could account for this pattern, as the recent events indicate that Coastal El Niños affect the coast much more to the north of Lima than to the south: five-day average SSTs for eight stations along the coast from start of collection (variably 1970–89) to September 2017 show that Coastal El Niños are strongly attenuated south of Lima (data from IMARPE/Peruvian Institute of the Sea; D. Sandweiss et al. 2020).

Although much research remains to be done on the history of El Niño frequency, including the kinds of events predominating at different times, archaeological indicators from north coast sites strongly support our reconstruction, particularly the shift from low frequency (5800–2900 cal BP) to high frequency at about 2900 cal BP. The final section of this chapter examines human eco-dynamics on the north coast of Peru before and after this transition.

Case Studies

El Niño and the End of a Multi-millennial Mound Building Tradition at ~2900 cal BP

Fifty years ago, Edward Lanning (1967) was among the first to note the widespread, early appearance of temple mounds on the Peruvian central and north central coast. A decade later, Michael Moseley (1975) defied archaeological orthodoxy by proposing that this Late Preceramic (ca. 5800–3600 cal BP) complexity was underwritten by marine resources from Peru's rich ocean. He noted then, and continued to stress (Moseley 1992), that agriculture was also practiced but that the bulk of crops were "industrial" rather than food: cotton for nets and textiles, gourds for containers and net floats. Domesticated plants were part of the diet as well but occurred in lesser quantities than industrial plants. The modified "Maritime Foundations" hypothesis (Moseley 1992) has been supported as an economic model (D. Sandweiss 2009).

Since 1975, however, the inventory of confirmed Late Preceramic mounds has increased both latitudinally (north as far as Lambayeque at 6°48′ S) and in number. The greatest surprise—albeit suspected by Lanning and others—was the Late Preceramic age of Caral in the Supe Valley

(10°53′ S; Shady et al. 2001) and the subsequent confirmation that dozens of mound sites in the Norte Chico (Huacho, Huara, Supe, Fortaleza, and Pativilca Valleys, 11°12′ S to 10°38′ S) are also Late Preceramic (see Haas, Creamer, and Ruiz 2004; Shady et al. 2015). Although small-scale monumental structures appear first in the Middle Preceramic period (e.g., Huaca Prieta in the Chicama Valley, 7°55′ S; Dillehay et al. 2012), the earliest large mound is Los Morteros (8°40′ S) in the Salinas de Chao, which began before 5400 cal BP (Mauricio Llonto 2015).

We have suggested previously that there may be a connection between the beginning of large-scale monumental temple construction and the return of low-frequency El Niño events following the mid-Holocene hiatus (D. Sandweiss et al. 2007). Settlement pattern data for the Late Preceramic and Initial periods (about 5800 to 2900 cal BP) from Lima north to Lambayeque show temple mounds beginning by 5400 cal BP and increasing in size, number, and latitudinal spread throughout these periods. The correlation between the increase in frequency of El Niño and the start of a multi-centennial cessation of mound building is more tightly constrained in time, dating toward the end of the Initial period (~2900 cal BP). When we first identified the increase in El Niño frequency from the biogeography of mollusks in north coast archaeological sites (D. Sandweiss et al. 2001), we could only place the change between about 3200 and 2800 cal BP. Working with paleolimnologist Curt Stager and other colleagues on ephemeral lake deposits in the Sechura Desert, we have recently refined the timing of the frequency increase to circa 2900 cal BP, that is, right at the end of the Initial period and beginning of the subsequent Early Horizon.

Nesbitt's (2016) excavation and analyses at the monumental Initial period site of Caballo Muerto in the Moche Valley (8°4′ S) provide strong support for a causal role for El Niño in the abandonment of the site at the end of the Initial period. Nesbitt identified water-lain deposits from several El Niño events at the Huaca Cortada, one of the mounds at Caballo Muerto. The first dates to 3550–3400 cal BP, prior to mound construction. Three events occurred during mound use, between the pre-mound event and 3050–2950 cal BP. In our reconstruction of El Niño for the north coast between 5800 and 2900 cal BP, event frequency is low, with large-magnitude events occurring only once or twice per century (D. Sandweiss et al. 2001). This is consistent with Nesbitt's event frequency at Caballo Muerto. Between 2950 and 2850 cal BP, a final El Niño event (or possible multiple, closely spaced events) coincides exactly with site termination.

While mound sites were abandoned all along the north coast at this time, large complex sites were still being built. For instance, Caylán (9°30′ S; Early Horizon, 2750–1951 cal BP) is "a large urban settlement interpreted as the primary center of a multi-tiered polity located in the Nepeña Valley" (Chicoine and Rojas 2013, 336; see also Chicoine and Ikehara 2014). The site covers an area of about 900 by 700 meters, with hundreds of rooms. Like other complex coastal sites of the Early Horizon, Caylán has no temple mound.

As summarized above, when El Niño frequency suddenly increased from once or twice per century to as much as once or twice per decade at about 2900 cal BP, the final north coast mound sites were abandoned. However, large sites continued to be built, suggesting that population did not decline dramatically. Did the increased frequency of El Niño events constitute a catastrophe? We would argue that it was a limited catastrophe that changed social organization from one centered on temple mounds to something different. As we have cautiously suggested before (D. Sandweiss et al. 2007), it may be that nascent religious leaders used the threat of El Niño events to mobilize labor to build mounds meant to intercede with supernatural forces to prevent El Niño's return. So long as events were infrequent, the system would appear to be working. Years ago, when less was known about El Niño's prehistory, Richard Burger (1988) suggested that a single El Niño event, then thought to have occurred at about 2500 cal BP (Nials et al. 1979), led to a crisis of faith. With a more nuanced understanding of the timing and frequency of events, we proposed that it was the sudden increase of events at 2900 cal BP that led to a crisis of faith and abandonment of the multi-millennial temple system (D. Sandweiss et al. 2007, 43–45).

Some support for this interpretation comes from Burger's excavations at Manchay Bajo (Burger 2003; D. Sandweiss et al. 2001), an Initial period site in the Lurín Valley near Lima. There, he found "evidence for El Niño mitigation by temple leaders . . . a major labor investment was made to construct a wall between the temple and the mouths of two ravines that can carry mudslide debris during El Niño rainfall events" (D. Sandweiss et al. 2001, 605; Burger 2003). To our knowledge, this is the first evidence of proactive El Niño mitigation at a temple site. Manchay Bajo's abandonment came a century later than other Initial period mound sites, at about 2800 cal BP. We might consider this an example of the building strategy seen in smaller scale on the north coast in response to the early colonial event of 1578 CE. Temple leaders did not (as far as we can see) successfully employ other coping strategies, although sites like Caylán show that other sectors of the population not only survived but seem to have thrived in a time of increased El Niño–driven stress.

One final piece of evidence supports the hypothesis that the increase in El Niño was catastrophic for north coast people, at least in the short term. The site of Puerto Nuevo (13°49′ S), on the north side of the Paracas Peninsula, was founded between about 2950 and 2750 cal BP, just as El Niño frequency increased. The site was abandoned no later than 2350 cal BP (Dulanto 2013). Although most of the pottery at this site is local, Dulanto identified sherds from the north central coast (Nepeña, where Caylán is located) and the far north coast (Piura, north of Lambayeque). These finds recall the relocation strategy used in the sixteenth century, when some people from the north coast traveled south to Lima to escape the ravages of El Niño.

Late Preceramic Florescence and the Sediment Cycle in the Norte Chico

While mound building continued unabated on the Peruvian coast as a whole throughout the Late Preceramic and Initial periods, monumental construction shows temporal variation within smaller regions. The most prominent case is the Norte Chico, centered about two hundred kilometers north of Lima. The last two decades of research by Shady et al. (2001, 2015) and Haas et al. (2004) show that this region had the highest concentration of monumental structures during the Late Preceramic period, anchored at the huge, World Heritage site of Caral. Between about 3800 and 3600 cal BP, these sites were all abandoned. Although the area was never completely depopulated, it remained a relative backwater for the succeeding millennia of Andean prehistory.

In the late 2000s, several of us worked with Ruth Shady to see if any catastrophic events were involved in this abandonment (D. Sandweiss et al. 2009). They were. To understand what seems to have happened, it is necessary to explain the sediment cycle on the Peruvian coast (D. Sandweiss 1986; Moseley et al. 1992). This cycle starts with earthquakes, which produce loose debris that sits on the unvegetated desert surface of the valley sides with only slow mass wasting to move it—until a large magnitude EP or Coastal El Niño event occurs. El Niño's torrential rains wash this debris into the rivers that traverse the valleys from the Andes to the coast. The extra water increases the competence of the rivers, which carry massive debris loads to the coast and form temporary deltas (D. Sandweiss 1986; Moseley et al. 1992; Shafer Rogers et al. 2004); in following years, longshore drift reworks the deltas, moving the sediment north to form beach ridges (D. Sandweiss 1986; Shafer Rogers et al. 2004). Constant onshore winds blowing to the north-northeast or northeast pick up the sand fraction and move it inland (Moseley et al. 1992; D. Sandweiss et al. 2009). Where the resulting sand sheets cover agricultural fields and sites, the results can be catastrophic for economic systems depending in part on irrigation agriculture.

We found evidence in the Norte Chico for all the phases of the sediment cycle in the centuries leading up to site abandonment (D. Sandweiss et al. 2009). Two Supe Valley sites, Aspero on the coast and Caral about twenty-three kilometers inland, had evidence of a powerful earthquake (calculated at M ≥ 7.2) covered by a final phase of construction. Driven by pulses of El Niño–borne sediment, a long beach ridge formed in front of the entire Norte Chico. Wind blew sand in from the ridge; this sand would also have covered agricultural fields and reduced production. We found sand covering the final floor at Aspero, just inland from the shore, and over the final preceramic occupation at Caral. Sand also blanketed two smaller mound sites near Caral, Chupacigarro, and Miraya, followed by a final, low-volume construction phase. Both the post-quake construction at Aspero and Caral and the post-sand construction at Chupacigarro and Miraya are instances of the rebuilding strategy, but they were ultimately unsuccessful—in each case there was a final, post-incident construction level, and then each site was abandoned.

The radiocarbon dates for the Norte Chico temple mound sites indicate progressive abandonment from south to north between 3800 and 3600 cal BP. This, too, supports our reconstruction of the sediment cycle and its effects on Late Preceramic societies of the Norte Chico. The direction of longshore drift is dictated by the angle of incidence of waves on the shore. Winds on the Peruvian coast are constant from southwest or south-southwest to northeast or north-northeast, so drift moves along the beach from south to north. The beach ridge that supplied the sand would have built in this direction, and the sand carried inland on the wind would also have moved from south to north. It makes sense that the first sites to be abandoned were on the south side of the Norte Chico.

Two large Late Preceramic sites continued to be occupied after the fall of the Norte Chico (Quilter 1991, 453). El Paraíso (Quilter et al. 1991) is on the north side of Lima, about 100 kilometers south-southeast along the coast from the south end of the Norte Chico. Salinas de Chao (Alva 1986) is about 240 kilometers north-northeast along the shore from the north end of the Norte Chico. Neither site is fronted by the kind of massive, sand-producing beach ridge found in the Norte Chico, although the Santa beach ridges (D. Sandweiss 1986) are just south of the Salinas de Chao site and there are large dune trains passing nearby. Both El Paraíso and Salinas de Chao maintained a preceramic (or aceramic) lifeway while most sites around them had adopted pottery. Perhaps this conservative lifestyle was promoted by climate migrants from the Norte Chico, another potential echo of the sixteenth-century relocation coping strategy.

Lessons from Ancient Niños

Riede (2017, 4) writes that "in areas where natural hazards occur frequently, the maintenance of efficient ways of responding, of so-called 'cultures of coping' (Bankoff 2009, p. 265), is likely. In contrast, when hazards occur less frequently or when we are considering high-magnitude/low-frequency hazards, a 'disaster gap' (Pfister 2009, p. 239) emerges that creates the illusion of false security from natural events."

Because of frequency changes across the Holocene, the prehistory of El Niño on the north coast of Peru offers lessons on both the "culture of coping" and "disaster gaps." Drawing in particular on the "culture of coping," paleoclimatic and archaeological data reviewed here suggest a variety of lessons for the present and future:

- Archaeological proxies for El Niño give us unique data to help refine the models that are the best hope of predicting and mitigating El Niño (e.g., diminished ENSO frequency in the Middle Holocene).
- The archaeology of coastal Peru teaches us how earlier people faced the stresses of El Niño—there may well be appropriate technologies of the past yet to be discovered or employed (e.g., rainwater capture).
- Recovering the millennial record of human responses to El Niño along the Peruvian coast may serve as a source of community social capital, where general solutions or narratives of prior vulnerability and resilience play into contemporary actions (F. Riede, pers. comm. 2019). This will require that we communicate our findings outside the academy.
- Combined archaeological and paleoenvironmental data show medium- and long-term processes that are not obvious in the short term (e.g., the earthquake–sediment–beach ridge–sand cycle).
- As with most catastrophes, there are some positive features that can be incorporated into coping strategies.
- The long-term correlations of El Niño frequency change and cultural change suggest that loss of faith may lead to regime change.

Conclusions

Perhaps because it is named for the infant Jesus, El Niño makes a convenient *deus ex machina* to explain social and cultural change on the Peruvian coast. Almost twenty years ago, van Buren (2001), reflecting a large literature on climate and culture change, reviewed studies of El Niño and culture change on the Peruvian coast and warned against uncritical correlations (see also D. Sandweiss and Quilter 2008). Nothing is simple, especially when it comes to humans. We need to continue refining climatic and cultural data, correlating them spatially and temporally, and embedding them in deeper understanding of how real humans have responded to catastrophes now and in the historic past. Scale is critical. For the Peruvian coast, available paleo-demographic reconstructions (D. Sandweiss and Quilter 2012; Goldberg, Mychajliw, and Hadly 2016; Riris 2018; Roscoe, Sandweiss, and Robinson, forthcoming) all concur that despite temporary downturns, the trend in population over the second half of the Holocene was been clearly upward, at least until 2000 cal BP. Given the estimates for the population of the coast at the time of the Spanish conquest (e.g., Cook 1981), it seems likely that demographic increase continued up to that time, although the number of radiocarbon dates decreases (possibly because pottery style in late prehistory is both effective and a cheaper dating tool).

The greatest single demographic disaster since people first arrived in South America perhaps fifteen thousand years ago had nothing to do with climate or other natural disasters—it was triggered by the anthropogenic catastrophe of the Spanish conquest (e.g., Cook 1981). Lewis and Maslin (2015, 174–75) have proposed an onset date for the Anthropocene at 1610 CE as a result of the synergistic effects of the European colonization of the New World visible in a variety of geological records. Coming full circle, accelerating climatic change in the Anthropocene is projected to intensify El Niño events (e.g., Power et al. 2013). We will need more effective responses.

El Niño is a stressor that has multiple flavors operating at variable spatial and temporal scales, as reviewed in the first section of this paper. EP and Coastal El Niños caused sudden and simultaneous downturns in primary economic bases (marine and terrestrial) for the complex pre-Columbian societies that occupied the Peruvian coast for almost five thousand years. At times El Niño happened infrequently and at times very frequently. Coast dwellers cannot have ignored these events or their temporal spacing. How they responded is partly an archaeological question. In the second section of this chapter, we reviewed two case studies that we and our colleagues have investigated over the past few decades. In the first, we note that a sudden increase in the frequency of EP/Coastal events is tightly correlated with the abandonment of temple mounds and a change in site structure on the north coast of Peru. These changes suggest a new system of governance in which temple mounds do not feature—but not a wholesale abandonment of the north coast. Perhaps following a "disaster gap" associated with mound abandonment, effective coping strategies were developed to deal with the more frequent climatic onslaughts. In the second case, we note how a cycle of sedimentary erosion and deposition led to a longer-term depression of agricultural productivity in the Norte Chico, accompanied not only by local abandonment of temple mound sites and cessation of mound building, but also permanent backwatering of the region. Even with these fuzzy data, it is clear that geophysical phenomena (El Niño) correlate with cultural change and that this change is unevenly distributed in space. Relating these changes to inequitable outcomes across "gender, race, class, and ethnicity" will require further research. If current projections for increasing frequency of El Niño are correct, this work takes on even greater urgency.

Acknowledgments

We thank Felix Riede and Paul "Jim" Roscoe for their significant help in improving this chapter. Any remaining errors or omissions are our responsibility.

Daniel H. Sandweiss is professor of anthropology and climate studies at the University of Maine. An archaeologist working on the Pacific coast of South America, he focuses on climate change and maritime adaptations during the Terminal Pleistocene and the Holocene. Sandweiss received the Rip Rapp Archaeological Geology Award from the Geological Society of America for his research on ancient El Niño and three Presidential Recognition Awards from the Society of American Archaeology for efforts to strengthen intra-hemispheric relations among archaeologists and for co-founding the SAA's climate change committee.

Kirk A. Maasch is a professor in the Climate Change Institute and School of Earth and Climate Sciences at the University of Maine. He has over thirty years of experience using climate models and statistical methods to investigate the causes of climate change across a wide range of timescales. He has worked toward developing a comprehensive theory for climate change with an emphasis on ice ages and the history of scientific research on them. Current work focuses on interannual-to-decadal-scale climate variability and the relationship between climate change and human activities.

Note

1. "Los yndios se dieron gran prisa a sembrar y vino las plagas . . . de tal manera que estando cualquier semilla un palmo de la tierra la comían los grillos y langostas y unos gusanos verdes y amarillos y otros negros que se criaban de la putrefacción de la tierra a causa de las dichas lluvias . . . quando venia a dar el fruto no hallaban nada y volvian a sembrar de nuevo y lo mismo sucedió . . . aunque no fue tanto . . . quando . . . venia a estar ya el fruto para querello coger fue tanta la multitud de ratones que este testigo no creyendo a los yndios fue a algunas chacaras y vido montones de ratones como montones de arena y que en una chacara . . . vido cinco o seis montones de ratones tamaño como conejos medianos que hizo este testigo contar un monton de aquellos que uvo quinientos poco mas o menos."

References

Alcocer, Francisco de. 1987 [1580]. *Probanzas de indios y españoles referentes a las catastróficas lluvias de 1578, en los corregimientos de Trujillo y Saña*. Transcription by Lorenzo Huertas. Chiclayo, Peru: CES Solidaridad.

Alva A. W. 1986. *Las Salinas de Chao, Un Asentamiento Temprano, Observaciones y Problemática*. Munich: Materialien zur allgemeinen und vergleichenden Archäologie, Band 34.

Arntz, W. 1986. "The Two Faces of El Nino 1982–1983." *Meeresforschung* 31: 1–46.

Arntz, W., A. Landa, and A. Tarazona, eds. 1985. "El fenómeno "El Niño" y su impacto en la fauna marina." *Boletín del Instituto del Mar del Perú-Callao*, número especial.

Ashok, K., S. K. Behera, S. A. Rao, H. Weng, and T. Yamagata. 2007. "El Niño Modoki and Its Possible Teleconnection." *Journal of Geophysical Research* 112: C11007.

Banholzer, S., and S. Donner. 2014. "The Influence of Different El Niño Types on Global Average Temperature." *Geophysical Research Letters* 41: 2093–99.

Bankoff, G. 2009. "Cultures of Disaster, Cultures of Coping: Hazard as a Frequent Life Experience in the Philippines, 1600–2000." In *Natural Disasters, Cultural Responses: Case Studies toward a Global Environmental History*, edited by C. Mauch and C. Pfister, 265–84. Lanham: Lexington Books.

Barrios, R. E. 2017. "What Does Catastrophe Reveal for Whom? The Anthropology of Crises and Disasters at the Onset of the Anthropocene." *Annual Review of Anthropology* 46: 151–166.

Beresford-Jones, D. G. 2011. *Lost Woodlands of the Ancient Nasca*. Oxford: Oxford University Press.

Beresford-Jones, D., A. G. Pullen, O. Q. Whaley, J. Moat, G. Chauca, L. Cadwallader, S. Arce, A. Orellana, C. A. Alarcón, M. Gorriti, P. K. Maita, F. Sturt, A. Dupeyron, O. Huaman, K. J. Lane, and C. French. 2015. "Re-evaluating the Resource Potential of Lomas Fog Oasis Environments for Preceramic Hunter-Gatherers under Past SO Modes on the South Coast of Peru." *Quaternary Science Reviews* 129: 196–215.

Burger, R. L. 1988. "Unity and Heterogeneity within the Chavín Horizon." In *Peruvian Prehistory: An Overview of Pre-Inca and Inca Society*, edited by R. W. Keatinge, 99–144. New York: Cambridge University Press.

———. 2003. "El Niño, Early Peruvian Civilization, and Human Agency, Some Thoughts from the Lurin Valley." In *El Niño in Perú, Biology and Culture over 10,000 Years*, edited by J. Haas and M. O. Dillon, 90–107. Fieldiana Botany 43. Chicago: Field Museum of Natural History.

Cai, W., G. Wang, A. Santoso, M. J. McPhaden, L. Wu, F.-F. Jin, A. Timmermann, M. Collins, G. Vecchi, M. Lengaigne, M. H. England, D. Dommenget, K. Takahashi,, and E. Guilyardi. 2015. "Increased Frequency of Extreme La Niña Events under Greenhouse Warming." *Nature Climate Change* 5: 132–137.

Cano, A., J. Roque, M. Arakaki, C. Arana, M. La Torre, N. Llerena, and N. Refulio. 1999. "Diversidad florística de las Lomas de Lachay (Lima) durante el evento 'El Niño 1997–98.'" *Revista Peruana de Biología* 6 (3): 125–132.

Caramanica, A. 2018a. "Land, Labor, and Water of the Ancient Agricultural Pampa de Mocan, North Coast, Peru." PhD dissertation, Harvard University.

———.2018b. "Resilience and Resistance in the Peruvian Deserts." *ReVista Harvard Review of Latin America* 13 (3): 48–50.

Carré, M., J. P. Sachs, S. Purca, A. J. Schauer, P. Braconnot, R. Angeles Falcón, M. Julien, and D. Lavallée. 2014. "Holocene History of ENSO Variance and Asymmetry in the Eastern Tropical Pacific." *Science* 345: 1045–48.

Castillo Butters, L. J. 2011. *San José de Moro y la arqueología del Valle de Jequetepeque*. Lima: Fondo Editorial de la Pontificia Universidad Católica del Perú.

Chicoine, D., and H. Ikehara. 2014. "Ancient Urban Life at the Early Horizon Center of Caylán, Peru." *Journal of Field Archaeology* 39: 336–52.

Chicoine, D., and C. Rojas. 2013. "Shellfish Resources and Maritime Economy at Caylán, Coastal Ancash, Peru." *Journal of Island & Coastal Archaeology* 8: 336–60.

Cook, D. N. 1981. *Demographic Collapse, Indian Peru, 1520–1620*. Cambridge: Cambridge University Press.

Copson, W., and D. H. Sandweiss. 1999. "Native and Spanish Perspectives on the 1578 El Niño." In *The Entangled Past: Integrating History and Archaeology; Proceedings of the 1997 Chacmool Conference*, edited by M. Boyd, J. C. Erwin, and M. Hendrickson, 208–20. Calgary: University of Calgary.

Craig, A. K., and N. P. Psuty. 1971. "Paleoecology of Shellmounds at Otuma, Peru." *Geographical Review* 61: 125–32.

Dillehay, T. D., H. H. Eling, Jr., and J. Rossen. 2005. "Preceramic Irrigation Canals in the Peruvian Andes." *Proceedings of the National Academy of Sciences* 102: 17241–244.

Dillehay, T. D., D. Bonavia, S. Goodbred, M. Pino, V. Vasquez, T. Rosales Tham, W. Conklin, J. Splitstoser, D. Piperno, J. Iriarte, A. Grobman, G. Levi-Lazzaris, D. Moreira, M. Lopéz, T. Tung, A. Titelbaum, J. Verano, J. Adovasio, L. Scott Cummings, P. Bearéz, E. Dufour, O. Tombret, M. Ramirez, R. Beavins, L. DeSantis, I. Rey, P. Mink, G. Maggard, and T. Franco. 2012. "Chronology, Mound-Building and Environment at Huaca Prieta, Coastal Peru, from 13700 to 4000 Years Ago." *Antiquity* 86: 48–70.

Dillon, M. O., S. Leiva González, M. Zapata Cruz, P. Lezama Asencio, and V. Quipuscoa Silvestre. 2011. "Floristic Checklist of the Peruvian Lomas Formations—Catálogo florístico de las Lomas peruanas." *Arnaldoa* 18 (1): 7–32.

Dillon, M. O., and P. W. Rundel. 1990. "The Botanical Response of the Atacama and Peruvian Desert Floras to the 1982–83 El Niño Event." *Elsevier Oceanography Series* 52: 487–504.

Dulanto, J. 2013. "Puerto Nuevo: redes de intercambio a larga distancia durante la primera mitad del primer milenio antes de nuestra era." *Boletín de Arqueología PUCP* 17: 103–32.

Engel, F. A. 1973. "New Facts about Pre-Columbian Life in the Andean Lomas." *Current Anthropology* 14: 271–80.

Gagnon, A., K. E. Smoyer-Tomic, and A. B. G. Bush. 2002. "The El Niño Southern Oscillation and Malaria Epidemics in South America." *International Journal of Biometeorology* 46: 81–89.

Glantz, M. H., ed. 2002. *La Nina and Its Impacts: Facts and Speculation*. Toronto, New York, and Paris: United Nations University Press.

Goldberg, A., A. M. Mychajliw, and E. A. Hadly. 2016. "Post-invasion Demography of Prehistoric Humans in South America." *Nature* 532: 232–35.

Haas, J., W. Creamer, and A. Ruiz. 2004. "Dating the Late Archaic Occupation of the Norte Chico Region in Peru." *Nature* 432: 1020–23.

Hastings, C. M., and M. E. Moseley. 1975. "The Adobes of Huaca del Sol and Huaca de la Luna." *American Antiquity* 40: 196–203.

Heyerdahl, T., D. H. Sandweiss, and A. Narváez. 1995. *The Pyramids of Túcume*. London and New York: Thames & Hudson.

Hu, Z.-Z., B. Huang, J. Zhu, A. Kumar, and M. J. McPhaden. 2018. "On the Variety of Coastal El Niño Events." *Climate Dynamics* 52: 7537–7552.

Huckleberry, G., A. Caramanica, and J. Quilter. 2018. "Dating the Ascope Canal System: Competition for Water during the Late Intermediate Period in the Chicama Valley, North Coast of Peru." *Journal of Field Archaeology* 43: 17–30.

Huertas Vallejos, L. 2001. *Diluvios andinos: a través de las fuentes documentales*. Lima: Fondo Editorial de la Pontificia Universidad Católica del Perú.

Kovats, R. S., M. J. Bouma, S. Hajat, E. Worrall, and A. Haines. 2003. "El Niño and Health." *Lancet* 362: 1481–89.

Lanning, E. P. 1967. *Peru before the Incas*. Englewood Cliffs, NJ: Prentice Hall.

Lewis, S. L., and M. A. Maslin. 2015. "Defining the Anthropocene." *Nature* 519: 171–80.

Lu, Z., Z. Liu, J. Zhu, and K. M. Cobb. 2018. "A Review of Paleo El Niño–Southern Oscillation." *Atmosphere* 9 (4): 130.

Maasch, K. A. 2008. "El Niño and Interannual Variability of Climate in the Western Hemisphere." In *El Niño, Catastrophism, and Culture Change in Ancient America*, edited by D. H. Sandweiss and J. Quilter, 33–55. Washington, DC: Dumbarton Oaks Research Library and Collection.

Marcus, J., K. V. Flannery, J. Sommer, and R. G. Reynolds. 2020. "Maritime Adaptations at Cerro Azul, Peru: A Comparison of Late Intermediate and 20th Century Fishing." In *Maritime Communities of the Ancient Andes*, edited by G. Prieto and D. H. Sandweiss, 351–65. Gainesville: University of Florida Press.

Mauricio Llonto, A. C. 2015. "Los Morteros: Early Monumentality and Environmental Change in the Lower Chao Valley, Northern Peruvian Coast." PhD dissertation, University of Maine, Orono.

McPhaden, M. J. 2003. "El Niño and La Niña: Causes and Global Consequences." In *Encyclopedia of Global Environmental Change*, vol. 1, *The Earth System: Physical and Chemical Dimensions of Global Environmental Change*, edited by M. C. MacCracken and J. S. Perry, 353–70. New York: Wiley.

Moseley, M. E. 1975. *The Maritime Foundations of Andean Civilization*. Menlo Park, CA: Cummings.

———. 1992. Maritime Foundations and Multilinear Evolution: Retrospect and Prospect. *Andean Past* 3: 5–42.

Moseley, M. E., D. Wagner, and J. B. Richardson III. 1992. "Space Shuttle Imagery of Recent Catastrophic Change along the Arid Andean Coast." In *Paleoshorelines and Prehistory: An Investigation of Method*, edited by L. L. Johnson and M. Stright, 215–35. Boca Raton, FL: CRC Press.

Murra, J. V. 1962. "Cloth and Its Functions in the Inca State." *American Anthropologist* 64: 710–28.

———. 1980. *The Economic Organization of the Inca State*. Greenwich, CT: JAI Press.

Nesbitt, J. 2016. "El Niño and Second-Millennium BC Monument Building at Huaca Cortada (Moche Valley, Peru)." *Antiquity* 90: 638–53.

Nials, F. L., E. Deeds, M. E. Moseley, S. G. Pozorski, T. G. Pozorski, and R. Feldman. 1979. "E1 Nino: The Catastrophic Flooding of Coastal Peru, Pt. II." *Bulletin of the Field Museum of Natural History* 50 (8): 4–10.

Ñiquen, M., and M. Bouchon. 2004. "Impact of El Niño Events on Pelagic Fisheries in Peruvian Waters." *Deep-Sea Research II* 51: 563–74

Noller, J. S. 1993. "Late Cenozoic Stratigraphy and Soil Geomorphology of the Peruvian Desert, 3 Degrees–18 Degrees S: A Long-Term Record of Hyperaridity and El Niño." PhD dissertation, University of Colorado, Boulder.

Nordt, L. F. Hayashida, T. Hallmark, and C. Crawford. 2004. "Late Prehistoric Soil Fertility, Irrigation Management, and Agricultural Production in Northwest Coastal Peru." *Geoarchaeology* 19: 21–46.

Ordinola N. 2002. "The Consequences of Cold Events for Peru." In *La Nina and Its Impacts: Facts and Speculation*, edited by M. H. Glantz, 146–50. Toronto, New York, and Paris: United Nations University Press.

Pfister, C. 2009. "The 'Disaster Gap' of the 20th Century and the Loss of Traditional Disaster Memory." *GAIA—Ecological Perspectives for Science and Society* 18: 239–46.

Pluta, P. M. 2015. "Fluvial Deposition, El Nino and Landscape Construction in Northern Coastal Peru." MS thesis, University of Maine, Orono.

Power, S., F. Delage, C. Chungm, G. Kociuba, and K. Keay. 2013. "Robust Twenty-First-Century Projections of El Niño and Related Precipitation." *Nature* 502: 541–45.

Quilter, J. 1991. "Problems with the Late Preceramic of Peru: Comment on a Report by T. &. S. Pozorski." *American Anthropologist* 93: 450–54.

Quilter, J. 2014. *The Ancient Central Andes*. London: Routledge.

Quilter, J., B. Ojeda E., D. M. Pearsall, D. H. Sandweiss, J. G. Jones, and E. S. Wing. 1991. "The Subsistence Economy of El Paraíso, Peru." *Science* 251: 277–83.

Radio Programas del Perú. 2017. "Estos son los colegios con las pensiones más caras de Lima," 11 March. Retrieved 5 October 2017 from http://rpp.pe/peru/actualidad/mas-de-56-mil-damnificados-por-la-temporada-de-lluvias-a-nivel-nacional-noticia-1036219.

Richardson, J. B. III. 1983. "The Chira Beach Ridges, Sea Level Change, and the Origins of Maritime Economies on the Peruvian Coast." *Annals of Carnegie Museum* 52: 265–76.

Riede, F. 2017. "Past-Forwarding Ancient Calamities: Pathways for Making Archaeology Relevant in Disaster Risk Reduction Research." *Humanities* 6 (4): 79.

Riris, P. 2018. "Dates as Data Revisited: A Statistical Examination of the Peruvian Preceramic Radiocarbon Record." *Journal of Archaeological Science* 97: 67–76.

Rockman, M. 2009a. "New World with a New Sky: Climatic Variability, Environmental Expectations, and the Historical Period Colonization of Eastern North America." *Historical Archaeology* 44: 4–20.

———. 2009b. "Landscape Learning in Relation to Evolutionary Theory." In *Macroevolution in Human Prehistory*, edited by A. M. Prentiss, I. Kuijt, and J. C. Chatters, 51–71. New York: Springer.

Rollins, H. B., J. B. Richardson III, and D. H. Sandweiss. 1986. "The Birth of El Niño: Geoarchaeological Evidence and Implications." *Geoarchaeology* 1: 3–15.

Roscoe, P. B., D. H. Sandweiss, and E. Robinson. Forthcoming. "Population Density and Size Facilitate Interactive Capacity and the Rise of the State." *Philosophical Transactions of the Royal Society B.*

Rundel, P. W., and Dillon, M. O. 1998. "Ecological Patterns in the Bromeliaceae of the Lomas Formations of Coastal Chile and Peru." *Plant Systematics and Evolution* 212: 261–78.

Rundel, P. W., M. O. Dillon, B. Palma, H. A. Mooney, S. L. Gulmon, and J. R. Ehleringer. 1991. "The Phytogeography and Ecology of the Coastal Atacama and Peruvian Deserts." *Aliso: A Journal of Systematic and Evolutionary Botany* 13 (1): Article 2.

Salazar, P. C., R. M. Navarro-Cerrillo, E. Ancajima, J. Duque Lazo, R. Rodríguez, I. Ghezzi, and A. Mabres. 2018. "Effect of Climate and ENSO Events on *Prosopis pallida* Forests along a Climatic Gradient." *Forestry: An International Journal of Forest Research* 91 (5): 552–562.

Sandweiss, A. 2019. "El Niño Modoki: A Diagnostic Study for Peru and Beyond." In *Climate Change and the Future of Water*, 133–158. Abu Dhabi: Emirates Center for Strategic Studies and Research.

Sandweiss, D. H. 1986. "The Beach Ridges at Santa, Peru: El Niño, Uplift, and Prehistory." *Geoarchaeology* 1: 17–28.

———. 1999. "El Niño and the Archaeological Record in Northern Peru." *Society for American Archaeology Bulletin* 17 (1): 1, 9–11.

———. 2003. "Terminal Pleistocene through Mid-Holocene Archaeological Sites as Paleoclimatic Archives for the Peruvian Coast." *Palaeogeography, Palaeoclimatology, Palaeoecology* 194: 23–40.

———. 2009. "Early Fishing and Inland Monuments: Challenging the Maritime Foundations of Andean Civilization?" In *Andean Civilization: Papers in Honor of Michael E. Moseley*, edited by J. Marcus, C. Stanish, and R. Williams, 39–54. Los Angeles: Cotsen Institute of Archaeology.

Sandweiss, D. H., C. F. T. Andrus, A. R. Kelley, K. A. Maasch, E. J. Reitz, and P. B. Roscoe. 2020. "Archaeological Climate Proxies and the Complexities of Reconstructing Holocene El Niño in Coastal Peru." *Proceedings of the National Academy of Sciences* 117: 8271–79.

Sandweiss, D. H., K. A. Maasch, C. F. T. Andrus, E. J. Reitz, M. Riedinger-Whitmore, J. B. Richardson III, and H. B. Rollins. 2007. "Mid-Holocene Climate and Culture Change in Coastal Peru." In *Climatic Change and Cultural Dynamics: A Global Perspective on Mid-Holocene Transitions*, edited by D. G. Anderson, K. A. Maasch, and D. H. Sandweiss, 25–50. San Diego: Academic Press.

Sandweiss, D. H., K. A. Maasch, D. F. Belknap, J. B. Richardson III, and H. B. Rollins. 1998. "Discussion of 'The Santa Beach Ridge Complex,' by Lisa E. Wells, in *Journal of Coastal Research* 12(1):1–17 (1996)." *Journal of Coastal Research* 14: 367–73.

Sandweiss, D. H., K. A. Maasch, R. L. Burger, J. B. Richardson III, H. B. Rollins, and A. Clement. 2001. "Variation in Holocene El Niño Frequencies: Climate Records and Cultural Consequences in Ancient Peru." *Geology* 29: 603–6.

Sandweiss, D. H., and J. Quilter. 2008. "Climate, Catastrophe, and Culture in the Ancient Americas." In *El Niño, Catastrophism, and Culture Change in Ancient America*, edited by D. H. Sandweiss and J. Quilter, 1–11. Washington, DC: Dumbarton Oaks.

———. 2012. "Collation, Correlation, and Causation in the Prehistory of Coastal Peru." In *Surviving Sudden Environmental Change: Answers from Archaeology*, edited by P. Sheets and J. Cooper, 117–41. Boulder: University Press of Colorado.

Sandweiss, D. H., J. B. Richardson III, E. J. Reitz, H. B. Rollins, and K. A. Maasch. 1996. "Geoarchaeological Evidence from Peru for a 5000 Years B.P. Onset of El Niño." *Science* 273: 1531–33.

———. 1997. "Determining the Beginning of El Niño: Response [to comments]." *Science* 276: 966–67.

Sandweiss, D. H., R. Shady Solís, M. E. Moseley, D. K. Keefer, and C. R. Ortloff. 2009. "Environmental change and economic development in coastal Peru between 5,800 and 3,600 years ago." *Proceedings of the National Academy of Sciences* 106: 1359–1363.

Shady Solís, R., J. Haas, and W. Creamer. 2001. "Dating Caral, a Preceramic Site in the Supe Valley on the Central Coast of Peru." *Science* 292: 723–26.

Shady, Solís, R., M. Machacuay, P. Novoa, E. Quispe, and C. Leyva. 2015. *Centros urbanos de la civilización Caral: 21 años recuperando la historia sobre el sistema social.* Lima, Peru: Zona Arqueológica Caral, Unidad Ejecutora 003, Ministerio de Cultura.

Shafer Rogers, S., D. H. Sandweiss, K. A. Maasch, D. F. Belknap, and P. Agouris. 2004. "Coastal Change and Beach Ridges along the Northwest Coast of Peru: Image and GIS Analysis of the Chira, Piura, and Colán Beach-Ridge Plains." *Journal of Coastal Research* 20: 1102–25.

Shropshire, E. 2000. "Blame It on El Niño." Released on the album *Love, Death, and Taxes* by Dr. Elmo. Laughing Stock.

Sulca, J., K. Takahashi, J.-C. Espinoza, M. Vuille, and W. Lavado-Casimiro. 2018. "Impacts of Different ENSO Flavors and Tropical Pacific Convection Variability (ITCZ, SPCZ) on Austral Summer Rainfall in South America, with a Focus on Peru." *International Journal of Climatology* 38: 420–35.

Taschetto, A., and M. England. 2009. "El Niño Modoki Impacts on Australian Rainfall." *Journal of Climate* 22: 3167–74.

Thompson, L. G, E. Mosley-Thompson, M. E. Davis, and S. E. Porter. 2017. "Ice Core Records of Climate and Environmental Variability in the Tropical Andes of Peru: Past, Present and Future—Registros en Núcleos de Hielo de la Variabilidad Climática y Ambiental en los Andes Tropicales del Perú: Pasado, Presente y Futuro." *Revista de Glaciares y Ecosistemas de Montaña* 3: 25–40.

UCAR/NOAA. 1994. "El Niño and Climate Prediction." *Reports to the Nation on Our Changing Planet* 3.

Uceda, S. 2010. "Theocracy and Secularism: Relationships between the Temple and Urban Nucleus and Political Change at the Huacas de Moche." In *New Perspectives on Moche Political Organization*, edited by J. Quilter and L. J. Castillo, 132–58. Washington, DC: Dumbarton Oaks.

Van Buren, M. 2001. "The Archaeology of El Niño Events and Other "Natural" Disasters." *Journal of Archaeological Method and Theory* 8: 129–49.

Weisburd, Stefi. 1984. "El Niño Brought the Blues, But Bliss Too." *Science News* 126: 228.

Wells, L. E. 1992. "Holocene Landscape Change on the Santa Delta, Peru: Impact on Archaeological Site Distributions." *The Holocene* 2: 193–204.

Weng, H., K. Ashok, S. K. Behera, S. A. Rao, and T. Yamagata. 2009. "Anomalous Winter Climate Conditions in the Pacific Rim during Recent El Niño Modoki and El Niño Events." *Climate Dynamics* 32: 663–74.

Wolff, Matthias. 1985. "Abundancia masiva y crecimiento de pre-adultos de la concha de abanico (*Argopecten purpuratus*) en la zona de Pisco bajo condiciones de "El Niño" 1983." In *"El Niño": Su Impacto en la Fauna Marina*, edited by Wolf Arntz, Antonio Landa, and Juan Tarazona, 87–90. Callao, Peru: *Boletín del Instituto del Mar del Perú. Volumen Extraordinario.*

Zhang, W., F.-F. Jin, and A. Turner. 2014. "Increasing Autumn Drought over Southern China Associated with ENSO Regime Shift." *Geophysical Research Letters* 41: 4020–26.

CHAPTER 14

A Slow Catastrophe

Anthropocene Futures and Cape Town's "Day Zero"

NICK SHEPHERD

Summary for Stakeholders

The current and future challenges of anthropogenic environmental change are often imagined as moments of crisis that elicit a technical and policy response at the level of management. Taking Cape Town's brush with "Day Zero" as a case study, this chapter argues that such moments of crisis are likely to be socially, politically, and economically entangled and mediated, both in the manner of their representation and in the forms of response that emerge. Notions of active citizenship and changing behaviors at the level of the individual household turned out to be key to resolving Cape Town's water crisis in 2018. Events in Cape Town open a window onto the future, to the extent that they tell us something about what happens when the added stresses of climate change are mapped onto already contested social and political situations. Thinking about water as heritage and about the entanglement between nature and culture in the Anthropocene, we need to initiate radically new, transdisciplinary research configurations and conceptual languages that cut across conventional divides among the arts, sciences, and humanities.

Slow Catastrophes

Increasingly, our journey into the Anthropocene is a journey into the unknown. In March 2018 I spent time in Cape Town, South Africa, doing work on the unfolding water crisis in the city. When I told colleagues there that I was based in Denmark, their invariable response was: This kind of thing—meaning drought, water scarcity, and the threat of wild-fires—must seem pretty remote for Scandinavians. A few weeks later I returned to Denmark to face one of the hottest and driest summers on record (Hohnen 2018). Suddenly, water-talk was part of this other, new Danish part of my world. In this chapter I track the events around the unfolding water crisis in Cape Town as a way of thinking about the catastrophic effects of anthropogenic environmental change. One of my starting points is the idea that Cape Town opens a window onto the future, to the extent that it suggests what might happen when the added stresses of climate change are mapped onto already contested social, political, and economic situations. Through the course of the chapter I make a set of linked arguments. One argument is that rather than being an inert resource, clean drinking water is a complex object, constructed at the point of intersection between natural systems, cultural imaginaries, and social, political, and economic forces and interests. A second argument is that rather than being a moment of climatic crisis that elicited a technical response—as we imagine the future shocks of the Anthropocene to play out—Cape Town's brush with Day Zero was a more layered and mediated event. As such, what we might call "the politics and poetics of water" came to the fore, in addition to questions of management, infrastructure, and the like. A third argument is that the decisive factor in averting Day Zero lay not in the realm of political leadership, astute management, or a technical quick fix, but rather in the realm of changing behaviors at the level of the individual household. In effect, the key to resolving the crisis lay in changing intimately embodied relationships to water understood as a precious resource.

But first I want to do some conceptual work, in thinking about the nature of the catastrophe itself. A typical dictionary definition of catastrophe is "an event causing great and usually sudden damage or suffering; a disaster" (*Oxford Dictionaries* n.d.). The water situation in Cape Town presents itself to us as a catastrophe, but I would argue that it is a catastrophe of a particular kind. As a way of conceptualizing the nature of this catastrophe, I want to borrow and adapt an idea from Rob Nixon: his influential notion of "slow violence." While violence (or catastrophes) is usually thought of as being sudden, disruptive, dramatic, and spectacular, Nixon has in mind another kind of violence. He writes, "Violence is customarily conceived as an event or action that is immediate in time, explosive and spectacular in space, and as erupting into instant sensational visibility. We need, I believe, to engage a different kind of violence, a violence that is neither spectacular nor instantaneous, but rather incremental and accretive, its calamitous repercussions playing out across a range of temporal scales" (Nixon 2011, 2). Extrapolating from this account, slow catastrophes have moments of drama but also moments of dormancy. Their unfolding is uneven, urgently present and pressing at one moment, seemingly gone from the world's attention at another. I speculate that many of the catastrophes of our shared Anthropocene future will be of this nature (Shepherd 2019). No doubt, there will be catastrophes whose nature will be sudden and imminent, but there are also likely to be many that announce themselves as a slow burn, a slow melt—until, that is, things accelerate and suddenly nothing is slow anymore.

There are two further ideas that I wish to borrow from Nixon. The first is that slow violence (read: slow catastrophes) present us with a problem of representation. They are not inherently media-worthy, or if they are, then they are only fitfully media-worthy. They erupt on our consciousness in bursts, but then we lose the plot—things become too complicated or seem too unresolved. This is not the territory of the explosion, the tidal wave, the deluge, the unstoppable burn, but rather something else: the unfolding human tragedy, the exponential failure of governance, the slow seeping away of will, the folding inward of expectations. Telling the story of slow catastrophes requires that, in the words of Donna Haraway, we "stay with the trouble," taking the time to unfold complexity, being comfortable with ambiguity, nuance, and irony (Haraway 2016). Especially irony. I suspect that the Anthropocene will reveal itself to be the era of irony: ironic injustices, ironic returns, the irony of good intentions, the irony of the chaos that we unleash on those that we love most, our children and our children's children.

A final idea that I wish to borrow from Nixon is the idea that slow violence (slow catastrophe) disproportionately impacts the poor of the world and already vulnerable people, communities, and nations. Of course, this is not a new idea but is one that has already been eloquently presented by, for example, the postcolonial historian Dipesh Chakrabarty, whose "The Climate of History" (2009) first alerted me to the need to rethink my own scholarly practice. This is likely to be the crowning irony of the Anthropocene: that those poor nations in the global south who bear a disproportionate cost of global capitalist development through historical processes of racial slavery, colonialism, and imperialism (the losers of the first round) are also likely to bear a disproportionate burden of the cost of Anthropogenic environmental change (the losers of the second round) (Parenti 2012; Shepherd 2019). With all of this in mind, let us move on to Cape Town.

An Anthropocene Moment

In mid-January 2018 a story broke in the global media: Cape Town, a city of some four million inhabitants, was running out of water. The immediate catalyst for this media attention appears to have been a statement made by Cape Town mayor Patricia de Lille on Monday 15 January, in which she said, "Cape Town's average daily consumption is still too high. It has increased to 618 million litres per day, up from 578 million litres (the previous week). For each day that Cape Town uses more than 500 million litres, the city moves closer to Day Zero" (*TimesLive* 2018). She announced that based on current consumption, Day Zero would arrive on Sunday, 22 April. The following day, Tuesday, she announced that Day Zero had been moved forward to Saturday, 21 April. Day Zero—the day when city managers cut off water supplies and the taps run dry—is calculated based on storage capacity in the five major dams that feed the city's water supply. The final 10 percent of water in the dams is effectively unusable, so Day Zero is pegged against the point at which dam levels fall to 13.5 percent of capacity. At the date of de Lille's announcement, dam levels stood at 28.7 percent on average, with little immediate prospect of rainfall to replenish them.

As early as 7 December 2017, a report in *Bloomberg Businessweek* asked, "Will Cape Town run out of water?" The report continued, "If 'Day Zero' comes, the 4 million residents of South Africa's second-biggest city will face a catastrophe." It quoted de Lille: "We have to change our relationship to water. We have to plan for being permanently in a drought-stricken area" (Cohen 2017). On 12 January 2018, days before de Lille's announcement, the *BBC*'s Gabriella Mulligan reported, "Cape Town, home to Table Mountain, African Penguins, sunshine and sea, is a world-renowned tourist destination. But it could also become famous for being the first major city in the world to run out of water" (Mulligan 2018). However, it was de Lille's statement setting a date for Day Zero, and thereby moving it from the realm of hypothetical possibility to imminent catastrophe, that unleashed a torrent of news. On 15 January, Aryn Baker reported for *Time* magazine ("Cape Town Is 90 Days from Running Out of Water"), "After three years of unprecedented drought, the South African city of Cape Town has less than 90 days-worth of water in its reservoirs, putting it on track to be the first major city in the world to run out of water." The report continues, "What happens when the taps are turned off? Cape Town enters Mad Max territory (well, almost). Residents will have to go to one of 200 municipal water points throughout the city where they will be allowed to collect a maximum of 25 litres (6.6 gallons) a day. Armed guards will be standing by to keep the peace" (Baker 2018).

On 16 January, the story was picked up by the *Mail Online* version of the *Daily Mail* ("Seaside Metropolis Could Become the First Major City in the World to Run Dry, Mayor Warns" (*Daily Mail* 2018), *EcoWatch* ("Will Cape

Town Become the First Major City to Run Out of Water?" (Chow 2018), and *Al Jazeera* ("Cape Town Confronts Looming 'Day Zero' Water Crisis" (Child 2018). On 18 January, Trevor Nace ran the story for *Forbes* magazine under the headline "Mad Max Scenario: Cape Town Will Run Out of Water in Just 90 Days." It continues, "The severe water shortage is due to a three year, once in a millennium drought. While meteorologists believe the drought was initially due to the strong 2015 El Niño, the drought has continued despite no longer being in El Niño conditions. Most climate models predict that as global temperatures continue to warm, South Africa will continue to receive less and less precipitation" (Nace 2018). On 19 January, the *Los Angeles Times* ran the story (Dixon 2018), as did *CBS News* ("Cape Town, on Verge of Running Out of Water, Braces for 'Chaos'" (*CBS News* 2018). On 23 January, *News24*'s Jenni Evans reported that Day Zero had been brought forward to 12 April, following an announcement by City of Cape Town deputy mayor Ian Neilson (Evans 2018). On 24 January, the BBC's Mohammed Allie reported, "Cape Town Water Crisis: "My Wife Doesn't Shower Anymore" (Allie 2018). That same day, the journal *Nature* ran the story under the headline "As Cape Town Water Crisis Deepens, Scientists Prepare for 'Day Zero'" (Maxmen 2018). It quotes Jodie Miller, a water scientist at Stellenbosch University: "To be honest, I can't wrap my head around what's happening—a major metropolitan city running out of water. There are enormous ramifications to this."

On 27 January, the story ran in the *Irish Times* (Corcoran 2018). On 29 January Aislinn Laing of the *The Times* (UK) reported, "Cape Town will run out of water within weeks" (Laing 2018). On 30 January, it made the front page of the *New York Times* (Onishi and Sengupta 2018), which also ran an op-ed piece on 1 February titled "Running Dry in Cape Town" (Kane 2018). On 1 February, The *Economist* ran the story "Why Cape Town's Water Could Run Out in April" (*Economist* 2018). And so it continued. Cape Town was facing its Anthropocene moment. This is a moment that is likely to face many, perhaps most, large cities in the coming decades and will take many forms: fire, flood, drought, mudslide, or the slow breakdown of infrastructures and institutions. In the case of Cape Town, it took—and is taking—the form of a combination of factors: an aging infrastructure; rapid population growth over the last few decades as economic migrants have poured (or flowed, or flooded) into the city from the surrounding hinterland; a severe and largely unpredicted three-year drought; and chronic political infighting within the ruling Democratic Alliance and between the Democratic Alliance and the African National Congress (Robins 2019; Shepherd 2018, 2019). This combination of social, political, economic, and climatic factors delivered up a potent moment—an Anthropocene moment—when anxieties about the future and apocalyptic imaginaries meshed with conditions on the ground, falling dam levels, and the torrent of facts and figures reported in the news and delivered up on websites like the City of Cape Town's own "Water Dashboard." The rhetorical power of the notion of "Day Zero"—a powerfully compressed metaphor containing within itself the idea of a countdown, the scene of a disaster (a ground zero), and an apocalyptic end-time (the end of days)—captured public and media attention and expressed the particular nature of the unfolding catastrophe (Shepherd 2018, 2019).

Mad Max in Cape Town

One of the themes of many of these news reports—in fact, a hook for journalistic interest—was the prediction of chaos. Mad Max scenarios imagined a quick slide into anarchy as city residents battled one another for the scarce resource or as local warlords and gang leaders seized control of water points and extorted money from city residents. On 22 January 2018, Helen Zille, the premier of the Western Cape province that includes Cape Town and thus the highest-ranking local politician, wrote in the popular online news site the *Daily Maverick*, "The question that dominates my waking hours now is: When Day Zero arrives, how do we make water accessible and prevent anarchy?" She continued, "As things stand, the challenge exceeds anything a major city has had to face anywhere in the world since the Second World War or 9/11. I personally doubt whether it is possible for a city the size of Cape Town to distribute sufficient water to its residents, using its own resources, once the underground waterpipe network has been shut down" (Zille 2018a).

And, indeed, the city's contingency plans were not promising. Come Day Zero, municipal water would only be available at two hundred points of distribution (PoDs) across the city, where residents would need to queue for a daily ration of twenty-five liters of water per person. An infographic published in the *Daily Maverick* breaks down the numbers: two hundred PoDs to service a city of four million inhabitants means—assuming that some people make alternative arrangements—ten to fifteen thousand people could be expected to converge on each water point every day. It takes two to three minutes to fill a single twenty-five-liter container. The queues would be endless, beyond imagination. Some people would be filling up on behalf of their families. This creates the practical problem of shifting fifty to a hundred kilograms of water. Identity checks would need to be in place at the PoDs to prevent water fraud, entailing further delays. Vehicle traffic in and out of the PoDs would be hellish. For those reliant on public transport—the majority of the city's population—there would be a different kind of hell. Without flushing toilets and running water and with residents spending hours each day queueing at PoDs, schools and businesses would need to close. Functioning economic life as we know it in the city would cease to exist or would be severely curtailed. Without a functioning waterborne sewerage system and with limited water for washing, the risk of epidemic diseases would be vastly increased. Outside of war zones or scenes of natural disaster, this was an almost unimaginable scenario (Shepherd 2018, 2019).

In any normal city this would present city managers with prodigious logistical challenges, but this is Cape Town, and Cape Town is far from being a normal city. Stated baldly, Cape Town is one of the most divided, disjunctive, and unequal cities on the face of the planet. At this point it becomes necessary to sketch a tale of two cities, beginning with some statistics. According to *Census 2011*, the most recent census carried out in South Africa, Cape Town had 1.068 million households. Of these, 129,918 households, or just over 12 percent, lived in "informal structures," that is, shacks made of corrugated iron and salvaged materials. Nearly 36 percent of households lived below the poverty line of less than ZAR 3500 (approximately US$250) per household per month; 13.7 percent of households reported no income at all. With regard to water, 97.3 percent of households were dependent on a regional or local water scheme (i.e., municipal water). Around 10 percent of households did not have access to a flush toilet (the alternatives are listed as: chemical toilet, "bucket toilet," or "none known") (City of Cape Town 2012). According to the *State of Cape Town Report 2016*, the most recent comprehensive report on the city, the number of households had risen to 1.26 million. The number of households living in informal housing had risen to just under 20 percent (up from 12 percent in 2011). Youth unemployment in the city is estimated at between 45 and 46 percent (City of Cape Town 2016).

On 7 March 2018, *BusinessTech* reported that Cape Town is the fifteenth most violent city in the world (*BusinessTech* 2018). This is according to a study published by the Mexican Council for Public Security and Criminal Justice (most of the world's most violent cities are in Latin America). The good news is that Cape Town had improved its position from 2016–17, when it was the thirteenth most violent city on the world, and from 2015–16, when it was listed ninth. The bad news is that in terms of absolute numbers of homicides per year, as opposed to the murder rate per one hundred thousand residents, Cape Town currently stands third in the list of the fifty most violent cities globally, with just two cities reporting a higher absolute number of homicides in the year 2017–18: Caracas in Venezuela, and Fortaleza in Brazil. By these figures, Cape Town is the most violent city in all for Africa, Asia, and Europe (Shepherd 2019).

And then there is the other face of Cape Town, a city of opulent living conditions and extraordinary natural beauty, keyed in to global tourism circuits and real estate markets. The Knight Frank Prime Global Cities Index "enables investors and developers to monitor and compare the performance of prime residential prices across key global cities," measuring the top 5 percent of the housing market. According to the Knight Frank Index for the second quarter of 2017, Cape Town was the ninth most profitable city in which to invest in real estate, ahead of Melbourne, Paris, and Hong Kong and behind Berlin (Knight Frank 2017). According to a report published in the *City Press* in July 2016, Cape Town has the world's second highest seasonal fluctuation of US-dollar multimillionaire populations in the world (after the Hamptons in New York) (Brown 2016). In 2014 the *New York Times* declared Cape Town the best place in the world to visit (Khan 2014). In 2016 the *Telegraph* published "22 Reasons Why Cape Town Is the World's Best City," based on a poll of *Telegraph Travel* readers (*Telegraph* 2016). In fact, for the five years leading up to 2017, the *Telegraph* readers had consistently voted Cape Town Britain's top travel destination.

Such statistics paint a picture of a city not so much divided, as schizophrenically at odds with itself. The subjective experience of dwelling in Cape Town is of a city that remains overwhelmingly racially divided, where extraordinary wealth exists side by side with abject poverty and scenes of bare life. The spatial layout of the city remains that of the urban plan of apartheid residential segregation, with an overlay of loosely regulated development and runaway property speculation post-1994. I can think of no other city with such starkly contrasted scenarios, vistas, and living conditions: the stately homes of Constantia and Bishopscourt, the seaside villas of Clifton and Camps Bay, the windswept shacklands of Khayelitsha, and the dystopian ganglands of the cynically named "Lavender Hill" and "Ocean View" (Shepherd 2015, 2019). Certainly, Cape Town's spectacular natural worlds, its unparalleled beaches and the stately magnificence of Table Mountain, serve to compound this sense of disjuncture when held up against the social misery that is the ineluctable other face of the city. In Cape Town, perhaps more visibly and viscerally than in other parts of South Africa, race and class coincide, so that the constant, daily reminders of white wealth and black poverty underscore this sense of disjuncture. Additionally, in Cape Town, perhaps more so than in other parts of South Africa, contemporary social injustices are often rooted in deep historical injustices. From the moment of the rounding of the Cape in the late fifteenth century and the establishment of a settlement by the Dutch East India Company in the mid-seventeenth century, the litany of Cape history has included the genocide of the Cape San (the indigenous people of the

Cape); the establishment of a brutal slave economy under the Dutch; both Dutch and British colonial orders; and—in the mid-twentieth century—the establishment of institutionalized apartheid (Shepherd 2015, 2019). In the 1960s and 1970s, urban forced removals displaced in excess of one hundred thousand black and POC residents of Cape Town, ripping apart functioning working-class communities like District Six and turning the city into a patchwork of racially segregated residential areas (Field 2002). As in other parts of South Africa, white Capetonians emerged as the beneficiaries of such policies.

My theme here is not that of South Africa's—or Cape Town's—exceptionalism, but rather the opposite: the sense that in Cape Town, a set of dynamics, forces, and social and economic trends that are present in many cities in the world are presented with an unusual directness and intensity. Jacques Derrida first makes the case for this notion of "intensification" in relation to South Africa, in an essay called "Racism's Last Word" published in the mid-1980s, at the height of apartheid repression (Derrida 1985). Derrida argues that apartheid in South Africa is the recognizable outcome of a set of social and political forces present in Europe's own history: authoritarianism, fascism, and racism. "What is South Africa?" asks Derrida. His answer is that it is a "concentration of world history." He writes, "We might be tempted to look at this region of the world as a giant tableau or painting, the screen for some geopolitical computer. Europe, in the enigmatic process of its globalization and its paradoxical disappearance, seems to project onto this screen, point by point, the silhouette of its internal war, the bottom line of its profits and losses, the double-bind logic of its national and multi-national interests" (Derrida 1985, 36–37). My argument is that this sense of intensification makes Cape Town a useful prognosticator of future trends and developments, a kind of crucible of the past and future. Living in Cape Town, as I did on and off from 1985 to 2017, I often had the sense of living in the midst of a vast social experiment, one whose outcome is uncertain. This makes for stoicism and fatalism, but it also makes for something else: black humor, irony, and a peculiar intensity to the pitch and sensation of everyday life that it is difficult to replicate elsewhere. More immediately, it makes for a city characterized by simmering social, political, and economic tensions and a deep sense of historical grievance (Shepherd 2015, 2019). Nixon (2011) and Chakrabarty (2009) both make the point that the added pressures of Anthropogenic environmental change are likely to deepen and entrench already existing social, economic, and political fault lines in impacted cities and communities. No wonder so many commentators were predicting anarchy come Day Zero.

Water as Social Leveler

In fact, from the beginning there was another, different scenario present in the reports on Cape Town's water crisis. This second scenario was present not so much in the words of the reports as in the images that accompanied these words. Many of these images were of people standing in line, patiently waiting to fill plastic containers with water from the natural springs that occur in many places in the city. Table Mountain acts as a giant sponge, and many of these springs—located on the side of the road or down a suburban street—are the result of upwelling. The springs

a

b

Illustrations 14.1a–e. Water as social leveler? Cape Town residents collect water from the Spring Street site, during the height of the Day Zero restrictions. Photos by Dirk-Jan Visser.

c

d

e

have been known about for centuries and are part of the fabric of the city (Shepherd 2019). They are tapped by industries, like the large South African Breweries site in Newlands, and by city residents who either do not have a water source of their own or are eager to access a more natural alternative to municipal water (although the quality of municipal water in Cape Town is generally excellent). In the years in which I lived in Cape Town, I would routinely collect water from these springs, using twenty-five-liter plastic containers in the back of my truck (or "bakkie") for the purpose. Now, from being an alternative lifestyle supplement, these springs had become a necessity to many residents, eking out their daily fifty-liter ration or stockpiling water for the hard times ahead.

The photographs accompanying many of the news reports were mainly taken at three sites: the South African Breweries spring off Main Road in Newlands, the spring on the side of Main Road in St. James, and the spring at the end of "Spring Street" off Kildare Road. The image of Cape Town residents queueing at the springs became a visual trope for the crisis as a whole. Part of the fascination of these images is the inter-race, inter-class nature of the queueing multitudes: white middle-class matrons from Constantia; black and POC workers from a nearby construction site; a black domestic worker on her lunch break; businessmen in suits and ties; a township entrepreneur filling a bakkie with containers of water to sell. As images, they reference and recall another New South African visual trope, the image of patient queues of people waiting to vote in the country's first democratic elections in 1994. For South Africans, such images resonate strongly. As with other highly segregated societies, there tend to be very few occasions where people meet casually in the public sphere across race and class lines. These images suggest a different meaning of water and another possible scenario, not water as scarce commodity that precipitates a Mad Max–style resource war, but water as social leveler (Robins 2019; Shepherd 2018, 2019).

For many residents of Cape Town's townships and informal settlements, the experience of queueing for water is nothing new. On 29 January 2018, the national Water and Sanitation Department announced that more than five million South African do not have reliable access to drinking water (out of a total population of around fifty-six million people), according to a report published by *EyeWitness News* (Smith 2018). The same report notes that an estimated 14.1 million people do not have access to safe sanitation. According to Statistics South Africa's "General Household Survey 2016," fewer than half of South African households (46.4 percent) have water piped in their homes, 26.8 percent of households have water on their property (usually an outdoor tap), while 13.3 percent need to share a communal tap (STATS SA 2016). Over the decades, Cape Town's city managers and wealthier residents have shown little political will to address the plight of the city's poorest and most vulnerable residents. Perhaps the water crisis would achieve what South Africa's Mandela-inspired "rainbow nation" rhetoric has so signally failed to achieve in the quarter-century following the end of statutory apartheid: bonds of empathy and solidarity that cross race and class lines and that draw South Africans together to find a common future. Perhaps this is what it takes: an embodied sense of being together in a shared crisis, having to rely on the person behind you in the queue to help you with your unwieldy container of water, or reaching out to help the person in front of you.

The idea of water as social leveler raises intriguing possibilities that strike at the heart of some core South African dilemmas. In an interesting twist, city managers announced that come Day Zero, piped water to communal taps in the city's townships and informal settlements would continue to flow, even as water supplies to the suburbs would be turned off. Would this send Cape Town's wealthier residents into the city's informal settlements, places they would normally shun? Would access to water invert accustomed relationships between the city's "haves" and "have-nots"? Informal accounts reported widespread water hoarding in early 2018, especially among the city's wealthier households. Sales of bottled water surged, and some retailers introduced twenty-liter containers of bottled water, something not before found in stores. Interesting existential questions arise off the back of such scenarios. In times of crisis, such as Cape Town's water crisis in early 2018, should you put your faith in high walls, electrified fences, and private stockpiles of water, such as many of Cape Town's wealthier residents were doing? Could you rely on your relative wealth to see you through the crisis, as it had through the social and political upheavals of the past decades? Or would you be better off pursuing a different strategy, putting your faith in a developed social network, offering favors and expecting favors in return, relying on friends and neighbors to tell you about where the queues are shortest or which shops still stock water? There is something foundational about such questions. They speak to the very basis of our understanding of society, and they are sure to become more pointed and more relevant as we face the rocky road ahead (Shepherd 2018, 2019).

Day Zero Deferred

Up to this point the story of Cape Town's water crisis is not so much a slow catastrophe as a rapidly accelerating one, with a recognizable plot: a city held hostage by a critical shortage of potable water, predictions of anarchy, and the scramble by citizens to make do. Then, suddenly, the message changed. On 7 March 2018, Mmusi Maimane, national leader of the Democratic Alliance (DA), the governing party in the Western Cape and official opposition to the African National Congress, called a press briefing at the DA's Cape Town office. Calling the city's residents "Day Zero heroes" and surrounded by six flat screens reading "Act Now. We Must #DefeatDayZero," Maimane said that he had "some encouraging news for the drought-stricken city." He announced that "Day Zero will not occur in 2018" (Dougan 2018; Brandt 2018; Pather 2018). Underlining the surprising nature of this announcement, "the party admitted that it had not yet informed the national water department about its prediction that Day Zero will not occur in 2018" (Pather 2018). At this point we need to pause in the narrative to review some of the statistics. In early January, when Mayor de Lille made her dramatic Day Zero announcement, dam levels stood at 28.7 percent of capacity. On 6 March, the day before Maimane's announcement, dam levels had dropped to 23.6 percent. No rain had fallen in the intervening months. In fact, following Maimane's announcement, it would be nearly two months before any appreciable rain fell in Cape Town (in late April), and it would be fully three months before the long-anticipated winter rains finally arrived. In the meantime, dam levels continued to fall.

Thus it is that we need to detour away from a story that up to this point has been told via the technical detail of rainfall statistics and dam-level reports, to consider the role of other factors in social responses to catastrophic events. Clues appear in the language used in this and other reports originating from the DA around this time. In his briefing of 7 March, Maimane is reported as saying that he was not satisfied with the way the city has responded to the crisis: "Many residents blamed the DA, and as Cape Town is a DA government, it was important that I intervene to ensure that residents received the level of service and honest government that they expect from the DA" (Brandt 2018). Writing on 12 March in a column published on *News24*, an online news site, Helen Zille said, "The idea of 'Day Zero' hovering on the horizon has had a major effect on the big pillar of our economy, tourism. Visitors stay away from a city at risk of running out of water. Many also cancel their bookings. And this has a knock-on effect through the entire pipeline of tourism offerings. We simply cannot afford to lose jobs" (Zille 2018b). Here is Maimane again, as reported by the *Mail & Guardian*: "Cape Town and the Western Cape are open for business" (Pather 2018). In a column written on 19 March, journalist Melanie Gosling wrote, "The decision to scrap Day Zero has left many residents confused. One day it was hovering on the horizon, the next it was gone. Yet the dam levels are still dropping, there has been almost no rain. . . . Trawling through statements, opinions and conversations with people from different sectors, it appears that the decision was political, designed to limit the negative impact on tourism and investment in the city" (Gosling 2018).

Maimane's political gamble paid off when winter rains topped up dam levels and forestalled the collapse of the city's water infrastructure. By late June, dam levels had risen to 42.7 percent. However, there was a second crucial factor in the events around Day Zero and its deferment—a widespread change in behavior. In a widely quoted set of figures, average daily water consumption in the city dropped from around 1.2 billion liters per day in February 2015 to between 510 and 520 million liters per day in early 2018 around the time of Maimane's announcement, a drop of almost 60 percent (Brandt 2018; Robins 2019; Shepherd 2019). Robins (2019) notes that this drop in consumption is especially significant when we consider that 70 percent of the water usage in the city is residential. In other words, the saving in water consumption was achieved at the level of the individual household, as the result of a widely shared set of behaviors. By early October, dam levels stood at 76.2 percent of capacity, and average daily water usage in the city was around 546 million liters per day. Day Zero had been averted, at least for the time being.

The Politics and Poetics of Water in the Anthropocene

So much of the discussion on anthropogenic environmental change focuses on water: too much water, too little water, melting ice, rising sea levels. In fact, we might say that water—along with fire—is one of the elemental languages through which anthropogenic environmental change expresses itself. It was always going to be about the water. Water-focused research is a burgeoning area of study. Some of the most engaging work in this expanding field understands fresh drinking water not simply as an inert resource, but rather as a complex object constructed at the intersection between natural systems, cultural imaginaries, and social, political, and economic forces and considerations (Shepherd 2019). Jamie Linton writes of the development of "modern water" as a way of knowing water based on its "abstract, metric identity" (Linton 2010, 13). He writes, "One virtue of modern water is that it is not complicated by ecological, cultural, or social factors. This has made it relatively easy to manage. Another virtue of modern water is its universality—all waters, in whatever circumstances they may occur, are reducible to this abstraction" (Linton 2010, 8). He continues, "The business of fixing water, in other words, is hardly just an intellectual performance; in each instance, it allows for certain hydrosocial realities while making it difficult or impossible for others to spring to life" (Linton 2010, 13). Graeme Wynn writes, "Developing a quantitative view of water was part of the process that enabled science, in the words of German philosopher Martin Heidegger, 'to pursue and entrap nature as a calculable coherence'" (Heidegger [1977], quoted in Wynn 2010, xiii). Nikhil Anand's study of water supply in Mumbai considers the many social, political, and infrastructural factors needed to keep water flowing in the city. He develops a notion of "hydraulic citizenship," which he defines as "a form of belonging to the city enabled by social and material claims made to the city's water infrastructure" (Anand 2011, 545). Kirsten Hastrup and colleagues write about the agentive power of water to impact on social worlds, constructing what she calls "waterworlds" (Hastrup and Hastrup 2015). Astrida Neimanis develops a post-human feminist phenomenology of water, understood as a transcorporeal agent in colonial and decolonial worlds. She writes, "Colonialism is carried by currents in a weather-and-water world of planetary circulation, where we cannot calculate a politics of location according to stable cartographies or geometries. . . . These waters gather and distribute the liquid runoff of a global political economy and techno-industrial capitalism that produces vastly divergent body burdens, but which nevertheless gathers us all" (Neimanis 2017, 36, 40).

In early 2018, working with a group of junior colleagues, I started a research project at Aarhus University called "The Politics and Poetics of Water in the Anthropocene," focused on the unfolding events in Cape Town. In part, this draws from my own research biography. I have written extensively about the city, usually from the perspective of questions of history, memory, representation, and social justice (Shepherd 2003, 2007, 2008, 2012, 2015, 2017). The events of Day Zero gather up many of these themes but reframe them in interesting ways by situating them in relation to natural systems and climatic events. Like Chakrabarty (2009), my sense is that available social theory is only just beginning to grapple with the implications of these new, emergent conjunctions. I come from an intellectual background—Marxism, feminism, postcolonial theory, decolonial thinking—which is intensely skeptical of what it terms "environmental determinism." The social constructedness of the past, present, and future is almost an article of faith for such approaches, opposed as they are to attempts to naturalize racism, sexism, and unequal social arrangements. And yet, my strong sense is that we stand at a novel historical conjunction, which challenges such articles of faith and asks us fundamentally to rethink the relationship between nature and culture. Following Latour (2014), questions of agency become more complexly entangled in the Anthropocene, as we are asked to consider the agentive power of water, weather, and infrastructure. Following Chakrabarty, one of the challenges for scholars of a certain generation is the challenge of "learning to unlearn," as the decolonial thinkers put it. In his 2009 "climate change" essay, Chakrabarty makes an extraordinary admission. He writes, "As the crisis gathered momentum in the last few years, I realized that all of my readings in theories of globalization, Marxist analysis of capital, subaltern studies, and postcolonial criticism over the last twenty-five years, while enormously useful in studying globalization, had not prepared me for the making sense of this planetary conjunction within which humanity finds itself today" (Chakrabarty 2009, 199). He goes on to wonder what it will mean to think and practice, as he puts it "under the cloud of the Anthropocene" (Chakrabarty 2009, 212).

One of the starting points for our project is an interest in Anthropocene futures and an idea, shared by many commentators, that events in Cape Town open a window onto the future to the extent that they begin to suggest what happens when the stresses of anthropogenic environmental change are mapped onto complex social and political situations (for example, see Newkirk 2018). Do new forms of empathy and solidarity emerge out of moments of crisis like Cape Town's brush with Day Zero? Or can we expect the opposite: the collapse of civil society and the breakdown of social systems? And what tips the balance between the two? Allied to this interest is an attempt to forge a new kind of conceptual language through which to attempt to grasp the full meaning of the events around Day Zero and the changing social meanings of water as a once taken-for-granted resource becomes something else: a cherished necessity for life itself. What follows are a set of field notes based on the events around Cape Town's Day Zero and the new hydro-social realities that they reveal.

Field Notes from the Future

Objective and Subjective Relationships to Water

Our relationship to water needs to be understood in both its objective and subjective aspects. There is a substantial literature focused on questions of water policy, management, and infrastructure and on the macro-politics of water in southern Africa (for example, see Fallon 2018). The events in Cape Town reveal a second, more intimate, embodied, and subjective aspect of our relationship to water. They also speak of the micro-politics of water in everyday life (Shepherd 2019). A host of questions come to the fore. What are the social meanings of water, and how do these change in times of shortage? What new forms of value emerge? What imaginaries of water come to the fore? Making do on fifty liters of water a day requires careful management when this needs to cover all of one's needs: drinking, cooking, cleaning, and flushing. Common middle-class household practice during Cape Town's water crisis involved taking a quick shower standing in a plastic tub to catch the run-off, then using this water to wash clothes or flush the toilet (usually limited to a single flush per day). An *NBC News* report that appeared at the height of the Day Zero crisis quotes 26-year-old Sitara Stodel: "I'm constantly thinking about running out of water and worrying about 'Day Zero.' I'm even having nightmares about wasting water. The other day I had a dream that I took a long shower by mistake" (Monteiro 2018).

Anthropocene Vernaculars

The debate around the Anthropocene has tended to be conducted as a matter of high theory, by researchers based for the most part in the global north. In the events around Cape Town's Day Zero, it was fascinating to see how core Anthropocene concepts and concerns were translated into everyday terms and became the stuff and substance of casual encounters and dinner-table conversations (Shepherd 2018, 2019). Anthropologist Steven Robins calls this "water-talk" and notes that it became an integral part of the events around Day Zero (Robins 2019). Such water-talk often involved surprisingly detailed technical knowledge of water policy and management. People followed information on dam levels and daily water consumption closely and could quote statistics back at you. For its part, the City of Cape Town published a weekly, online "Water Dashboard," which broke down the statistics via a series of graphs. In January 2018 the city published an online, interactive "City Water Map," which showed average water consumption at a household level via a series of colored dots. This informal means of surveillance meant that householders could monitor the behavior of their neighbors and single out the water wasters from the "Day Zero heroes."

The Entanglement of "Nature" and "Culture"

A core argument of the debate around the Anthropocene in the work of Latour (2014), Chakrabarty (2009), and others concerns the entanglement of "nature" and "culture." Even at this early stage of analysis I think it is clear that both the crisis and the post-crisis moments in Cape Town's Day Zero were produced at a complex point of intersection between climatic, social, political, and economic factors. Rather than being a climatic event that elicited a technical response—as we tend to imagine such shocks and crises to play out—Cape Town's Anthropocene moment was, and continues to be, a more layered event. I would argue that future Anthropocene crises are likely to be socially, economically, politically, and culturally entangled and mediated in similar ways (Shepherd 2018, 2019). In the Anthropocene, perhaps more than ever before, empirically based scientific knowledge will be entangled with forms of discourse and systems of meaning and value as natural-world facts and events strike deep into the domain of "culture." On the one hand, this points to potentially exciting new knowledge conjunctions and collaborations. On the other hand, it points to the outmoded nature of current disciplinary configurations and the urgent need to "catch up."

The Unthinkability of Climate Change

Slavoj Zizek has an interesting line on anthropogenic climate change. He writes (in paraphrase), "We know it . . . but we don't believe it" (2011). One of the most important and perceptive interventions on the unthinkability of climate change is Amitav Ghosh's *The Great Derangement* (2016), in which he tracks the rise of the modern novel, with its depiction of stable, bourgeois worlds and the "calm passion" of daily life. This prompts Ghosh to describe the crisis of the Anthropocene as being, in part, a cultural crisis, or a crisis of forms: nothing in our cultural apparatus equips us to think about abrupt discontinuities, ruptures, and the derangement of nature. Such events belong in the realm of discredited forms: science fiction or gothic horror.

Since we have been confronted with a barrage of statistics and reports on anthropogenic environmental change, it has become common to encounter the sentiment: But where do I begin? How do I make a difference when the scale of the challenge is so vast? One of the interesting aspects of Cape Town's Day Zero was that it translated such large-scale and intractable challenges down to the level of the individual household. Not only was anthropogenic environmental change immediately perceptible, but doing something about it was as immediate as the decision not to flush, to re-wear a shirt, or to let your hair go another day between washes. There is something empowering about such a realization. After so much uncertainty and helplessness, it comes as a relief to know where to begin.

Survivalist States

What does it mean to live in a survivalist state? While for many people daily life is a matter of survival, for most middle-class households this is a new and uncomfortable state of being. Extrapolating from Ghosh (2016), we might say that to a very great extent, middle-class life has been constituted around ensuring against risk and managing future outcomes. Such horizons and expectations begin to break down in the face of the shocks and crises of the Anthropocene. In Cape Town it was interesting to see how, at an early stage, the realization set in that the state was unlikely to intervene in a decisive way to rescue the situation and that the responsibility devolved to individual households (Shepherd 2018, 2019). Social media sources were full of suggestions for everyday technologies and "hacks" to recycle gray water or to transport heavy twenty-five-liter containers of water (Shepherd 2018; Robins 2019). Innovation and improvisation were the order of the day, as was the idea of living with uncertainty. Survivalism—promoted by real or imagined threats—would seem to be an ambiguous and double-edged state of being, never far from paranoia, and beloved of right-wing fundamentalists. And yet, it may be useful and even inescapable as we journey deeper into the Anthropocene.

Changing Behaviors

One of the most important takeaways from the events around Cape Town's Day Zero was the widespread change in behavior evidenced in people's reduced consumption of water. Described as "unprecedented," the collective drop in consumption was remarkable. By comparison, at the height of its drought in 2015, California residents achieved a 27 percent reduction in water consumption, and in response to their "Millennium Drought," Melbourne residents took twelve years to reach a similar percentage reduction to that achieved by Cape Town residents in 2018 (Robins 2019; Shepherd 2019). It was this, rather than any action on the part of the DA or the City of Cape Town that averted the collapse of the city's water infrastructure, Maimane's statements notwithstanding. In part, the reduced consumption is likely to have been the result of increased tariffs and surveillance. However, the decisive factor appears to have been the manner in which householders internalized the risk and acted decisively to reduce consumption. This social mobilization is all the more remarkable for having taken place across lines of race and class in a historically divided city. There is some attention to changing behaviors in the debate around the Anthropocene (for example, see Jones, Pykett, and Whitehead 2013); however, I would anticipate that this important topic will become more central in years to come. Indeed, in an entirely personal way, each of us will be confronted soon—or has already been confronted—by the urgent need to change our patterns of consumption as an ethical and political concern "under the cloud of the Anthropocene" (Chakrabarty 2009, 212).

Defense of the Commons

Michael Hardt and Antonio Negri write, "By the 'common' we mean, first of all, the common wealth of the material world—the air, the water, the fruits of the soil, and all nature's bounty—which in classical European political texts is often claimed to be the inheritance of humanity as a whole, to be shared together. . . . Neoliberal government policies throughout the world have sought in recent decades to privatize the common" (Hardt and Negri 2009, vii). In March 2018, Cape Town was alive with rumors: the City of Cape Town was using the water crisis as an excuse to raise tariffs and to force the privatization of water, which in South Africa remains largely in municipal hands. There were signs that this was indeed the case (Robins 2019). Certainly, the crisis was being seen by some as a moment of opportunity. Retailers were quick to exploit the market demand for bottled water and developed new forms of packaging that allowed consumers to buy water in large volumes. One of the most remarkable Day Zero stories concerns Riyaz Rawoot, the "Water Master," who informally adopted and managed the freshwater spring on Spring Street. When we visited Spring Street in March 2018, a whole careful ecology was in operation, via an intricate system of PVC pipes, special queues for the elderly, and trolley operators who would transport your water for a small fee. As told by Steven Robins, a few weeks after our visit, the City of Cape Town closed down Riyaz's operation and poured concrete over the source of the spring (Robins 2018). It appears that such uncaptured and unmonetized sources of water were perceived by city managers as a threat, even as Cape Town faced an unprecedented shortage of potable water.

The Role of Social Movements

With much at stake and with a strong tradition of social activism in South Africa, it is perhaps inevitable that water-focused social movements would organize around Day Zero. Groups like the Water Crisis Coalition mobilized to pressure the city to lower tariffs, to oppose the use of controversial and inefficient water management devices, and to demand transparent and accountable governance. In the context of a low-trust environment with a comparatively weak state, social movements play an important role in producing a notion of active citizenship. This form of active citizenship was arguably a key factor in the events around Cape Town's Day Zero as citizens absorbed the message and took matters into their own hands (Shepherd 2018, 2019). Like the notion of survivalist states, a notion of active citizenship becomes useful in thinking about how populations adapt to the stresses of anthropogenic environmental change. It becomes interesting to speculate that these forms of social resilience may be more accessible to populations in the global south, accustomed by long experience to shocks, crises, and taking matters into their own hands, than to their counterparts in the more settled environments of the global north, who tend to look to the state to solve infrastructural and other challenges.

Water as Heritage

How will we tell the story of water in future years? Perhaps we will say that for a brief moment in human history, for a privileged few, it was a taken-for-granted fact of everyday life that you turned on a tap and the water would flow. Or we could describe how piped, potable water became one of the indexes of modernization, just as in previous eras the control of water had been the foundation of civilizations. And then we would need to tell the rest of the story—how this brief flourishing was truncated by the harsh new regimes of the Anthropocene. According to the United Nations World Water Development Report of 2018, water shortages could affect five billion people by 2050, with likely "conflict and civilizational threats" (Watts 2018). It seems clear that we have to value water differently. Rather than thinking about water as a right, as a resource, or as a commodity, we should perhaps be thinking about clean drinking water as a precious heritage, to be held in stewardship and handed down to our children and to their children. The story of the earth's water is remarkable and uncanny. Delivered to a dry earth by asteroids, individual water molecules have been cycled through the earth's natural systems and through every form of life, only now to be filtered through our carbon civilization and through our own bodies. If there was ever a case for the entanglement of "natural heritage" and "cultural heritage," then water most eloquently presents it (Shepherd 2019).

Empathy and Anthropocene Futures

Taking a leaf from Mike Davis's (1990) brilliant excavation of the future in dystopian 1980s Los Angeles, I think it is possible to view events in Cape Town as opening a window onto the future of the Anthropocene. The question might be framed as follows: What happens when the added stresses of anthropogenic environmental change are mapped onto already contested social, political, and economic situations? In the case of Cape Town, this remains an open question. Day Zero has been deferred for now, but the specter of drought haunts the city. By some reports, southern Africa is a climate change "hot spot," with an expected average temperature rise roughly twice the global average (Bloom 2018). It is common in the literature to see anthropogenic environmental stress referred to as a "magnifier," exacerbating already existing tensions, but the events in Cape Town suggest other possible outcomes: the emergence of new forms of solidarity, improvised solutions, and modes of active citizenship.

To a significant extent, Cape Town's Day Zero was a middle-class crisis. At the height of the Day Zero events, township dwellers were heard to say that they would count themselves fortunate to have access to fifty liters of clean water each day. As I write, the idea of fifty liters of water per day remains an aspiration for many of Cape Town's poorest residents, as does access to a flushing toilet. However, rather than detracting from the seriousness of events in Cape Town, if anything, this underlines them. Globally, the future shocks of the Anthropocene will strike nations, classes, and bodies differently, depending on their levels of wealth and forms of governance, as well as on accidents of geography. Very little of this will be fair, as the already underdeveloped territories of the global south and vulnerable populations everywhere find themselves most at risk (Parenti 2012). Entanglement is not the same as empathy and connectedness. We are all in this together, but some are more *in* it than others, in the sense that some will pay a disproportionately higher cost as the world warms. A central question is whether we are able to find—or evolve—the forms of empathy that allow us to imagine a common human future. The alternative, as Christian Parenti points out, is the "politics of the armed lifeboat" in a dog-eat-dog world in which those with means scramble for survival at any cost (Parenti 2012; Shepherd 2019).

In March 2019, exactly one year after the high point of the events around Day Zero, I again visited Cape Town. For the moment, the dams supplying the city are comfortably full, and talk of Day Zero has receded. Indeed, the focus of attention in early 2019 has shifted to another infrastructure—electricity supply—and the failings of ESCOM, the state power utility. At the same time, everyone I spoke to—friends, family, colleagues, city officials, activists—understands that the water crisis is not over. In part, the geographical focus of attention has shifted, with some small towns in the interior experiencing severe droughts over the summer, and rivers running dry for the first time in living memory. The narrative of the slow catastrophe shifts, complicates, draws in other factors, even as the general drift and direction of the narrative is not in doubt. Water flows, seeps, and pools. It travels upward against the force of gravity. Full of surprises, it is at the same time utterly commonplace. It seems clear that we are entering an ambiguous new phase in human history, in which many of the old certainties fall by the wayside. We need new metaphors, new metrics, new disciplines, new forms of analysis, a whole new language, to describe these new realities. For scholars, there are many ways of reaching for this new language. For me, for now, I am going to follow the water.

Nick Shepherd is an associate professor of sustainable heritage management at Aarhus University and extraordinary professor at the University of Pretoria. In 2017–18 he was artist-in-residence at the Amsterdam University of the Arts. He has been a visiting professor at Harvard University, Brown University, the University of Basel, and Colgate University. His current project, "Heritage and the Anthropocene (HATA)," is a joint project between Aarhus University and the University of Cape Town's Future Water Institute.

References

Allie, M. 2018. "Cape Town Water Crisis: 'My Wife Doesn't Shower Anymore.'" *BBC News*, 24 January. Retrieved 17 May 2020 from https://www.bbc.com/news/world-africa-42787773.

Anand, N. 2011. "Pressure: The PoliTechnics of Water Supply in Mumbai." In *Cultural Anthropology* 26 (4): 542–64.

Baker, A. 2018. "Cape Town Is 90 Days from Running Out of Water." *Time*, 15 January 15. Retrieved 17 May 2020 from http://time.com/5103259/cape-town-water-crisis/.

Bloom, K. 2018. "Interview: South Africa Climate Change 'Hot Spot.'" *Daily Maverick*, 7 November. Retrieved 17 May 2020 from https://www.dailymaverick.co.za/article/2018-11-07-interview-south-africa-climate-change-hot-spot/.

Brandt, K. 2018. "Maimane: Day Zero May Not Happen in 2018." *EyeWitness News*, 7 March. Retrieved 17 May 2020 from https://ewn.co.za/2018/03/07/maimane-day-zero-may-not-happen-in-2018.

Brown, J. 2016. "Wealthy Flock to Cape Town." *City Press*, 11 July. Retrieved 17 May 2020 from https://city-press.news24.com/Business/wealthy-flock-to-cape-town-20160711.

BusinessTech. 2018. "Cape Town Is One of the Most Violent Cities in the World." *BusinessTech*, 7 March. Retrieved 17 May 2020 from https://businesstech.co.za/news/lifestyle/230123/cape-town-is-one-of-the-most-violent-cities-in-the-world/

CBS News. 2018. "Cape Town, on Verge of Running Out of Water, Braces for 'Chaos.'" *CBS News*, 19 January. Retrieved 17 May 2020 from https://www.cbsnews.com/news/cape-town-drought-water-shortage-south-africa/.

Chakrabarty, D. 2009. "The Climate of History." *Critical Inquiry*, 35 (2): 197–222. https://www.jstor.org/stable/10.1086/596640.

Child, D. 2018. "Cape Town Confronts Looming 'Day Zero' Water Crisis." *Al Jazeera—English*, 16 January. Retrieved 17 May 2020 from https://www.aljazeera.com/news/2018/01/cape-town-confronts-looming-day-water-crisis-180114121145902.html.

Chow, L. 2018. "Will Cape Town Become the First Major City to Run Out of Water?" *EcoWatch*, 16 January. Retrieved 17 May 2020 from https://www.ecowatch.com/cape-town-water-crisis-2525997846.html.

City of Cape Town. 2012. *City of Cape Town—2011 Census—Cape Town*. Strategic Development Information and GIS Department. Retrieved 17 May 2020 from http://resource.capetown.gov.za/documentcentre/Documents/Maps percent20and percent20statistics/2011_Census_Cape_Town_Profile.pdf.

City of Cape Town. 2016. *State of Cape Town Report 2016—Overview with Infographics*. Development Information and Geographic Information Systems Department. Retrieved 17 May 2020 from http://maitcid.co.za/wp-content/uploads/2017/01/State-of-Cape-Town-Report-2016.pdf.

Cohen, M. 2017. "Will Cape Town Run Out of Water?" *Bloomberg Businessweek*, 8 December. Retrieved 17 May 2020 from https://www.bloomberg.com/news/features/2017-12-08/will-cape-town-run-out-of-water.

Corcoran, B. 2018. "Time Trickling Away for Cape Town's Water Supply." *Irish Times*, 27 January. Retrieved 17 May 2020 from https://www.irishtimes.com/news/world/africa/time-trickling-away-for-cape-town-s-water-supply-1.3369700.

Daily Mail. 2018. "Cape Town Is 90 DAYS Away from Running Out of Water: Seaside Metropolis Could Become the First Major City in the World to Run Dry, Mayor Warns." *Mail Online / Daily Mail*, 16 January. Retrieved 17 May 2020 from https://www.dailymail.co.uk/news/article-5275997/Cape-Town-90-DAYS-away-running-water.html.

Davis, M. 1990. *Cities of Quartz: Excavating the Future in Los Angeles*. London and New York: Verso.

Derrida, J. 1985. "Racism's Last Word." *Critical Inquiry* 12 (1): 290–99.

Dixon, R. 2018. "In Cape Town, 'Day Zero' Is Coming Very Soon—the Day the Water Runs Out." *Los Angeles Times*, 19 January. Retrieved 17 May 2020 from https://www.latimes.com/world/africa/la-fg-south-africa-water-crisis-20180119-story.html.

Dougan, L. 2018. "Cape Town: 'Day Zero' Will Not Occur in 2018, Announces Mmusi Maimane." *Daily Maverick*, 7 March. Retrieved 17 May 2020 from https://www.dailymaverick.co.za/article/2018-03-07-cape-town-day-zero-will-not-occur-in-2018-announces-mmusi-maimane/.

Economist. 2018. "Why Cape Town's Water Could Run Out in April." *Economist*, 1 February. Retrieved 17 May 2020 from https://www.economist.com/the-economist-explains/2018/02/01/why-cape-towns-water-could-run-out-in-april.

Evans, J. 2018. "Day Zero Now on April 12 for Cape Town." *News24*, 23 January. Retrieved 17 May 2020 from https://www.news24.com/SouthAfrica/News/day-zero-now-on-april-12-for-cape-town-20180123.

Fallon, A. 2018. "A Perfect Storm: The Hydropolitics of Cape Town's Water Crisis." Global Water Forum, 17 April. Retrieved 17 May 2020 from http://www.globalwaterforum.org/2018/04/17/the-hydropolitics-of-cape-towns-water-crisis-a-perfect-storm/.

Field, S. 2002. *Lost Communities, Living Memories: Remembering Forced Removals in Cape Town*. Cape Town: New African Books/University of Cape Town.

Ghosh, A. 2016. *The Great Derangement. Climate Change and the Unthinkable*. Chicago: University of Chicago Press.

Gosling, M. 2018. "Analysis: Why Day Zero Was Scrapped." *News24*, 19 March. Retrieved 17 May 2020 from https://www.news24.com/SouthAfrica/News/analysis-why-day-zero-was-scrapped-20180319.

Haraway, D. 2016. *Staying with the Trouble: Making Kin in the Chthulucene*. Durham: Duke University Press.

Hardt, M., and A. Negri. 2009. *Commonwealth*. Cambridge, MA: Belknap Press/Harvard University Press.

Hastrup, K., and F. Hastrup, eds. 2015. *Waterworlds: Anthropology in Fluid Environment*. New York: Berghahn Books.

Hohnen, M. 2018. "Nu er det slået fast: Vi har aldrig haft en varmere sommer end i år." *Jyllands-Posten*, 1 September. Retrieved 17 May 2020 from https://jyllands-posten.dk/indland/trafik/ECE10842123/nu-er-det-slaaet-fast-vi-har-aldrig-haft-en-varmere-sommer-end-i-aar/.

Jones, R., J. Pykett, and M. Whitehead. 2013. *Changing Behaviours: On the Rise of Psychological State*. Cheltenham: Edward Elgar.

Kane, D. 2018. "Running Dry in Cape Town." *New York Times*, 1 February. Retrieved 17 May 2020 from https://www.nytimes.com/2018/02/01/opinion/cape-town-drought-day-zero.html.

Khan, S. 2014. "52 Places to Go in 2014." *New York Times*, 12 January. Retrieved 17 May 2020 from https://www.nytimes.com/interactive/2014/01/10/travel/2014-places-to-go.html.

Knight Frank. 2017. "Residential Research: Prime Global Cities Index; Second Quarter 2017." Knight Frank. Retrieved 17 May 2020 from https://content.knightfrank.com/research/323/documents/en/prime-global-cities-index-q2-2017-4862.pdf.

Laing, A. 2018. "Cape Town Will Run Out of Water within Weeks." *The Times* (UK), 29 January 29. Retrieved 17 May 2020 from https://www.thetimes.co.uk/article/cape-town-weeks-away-from-running-out-of-water-stgfdx0g6.

Latour, B. 2014. "Agency at the Time of the Anthropocene." *New Literary History* 45: 1–18. http://www.bruno-latour.fr/sites/default/files/128-FELSKI-HOLBERG-NLH-FINAL.pdf.

Linton, J. 2010. *What Is Water? The History of a Modern Abstraction*. Vancouver: UBC Press.

Maxmen, A. 2018. "As Cape Town Water Crisis Deepens, Scientists Prepare for 'Day Zero.'" *Nature: International Journal of Science*, 24 January 24. https://www.nature.com/articles/d41586-018-01134-x.

Monteiro, C. 2018. "Water Crisis Grips Cape Town after South African Drought Stretching Years." *NBC News*, 29 January. Retrieved 17 May 2020 from https://www.nbcnews.com/news/world/water-crisis-hits-cape-town-south-africa-day-zero-looms-n841881.

Mulligan, G. 2018. "Will Cape Town Be the First City to Run Out of Water?" *BBC News*, 12 January. Retrieved 17 May 2020 from https://www.bbc.com/news/business-42626790.

Nace, T. 2018. "Mad Max Scenario: Cape Town Will Run Out of Water in Just 90 Days." *Forbes*, 18 January. Retrieved 17 May 2020 from https://www.forbes.com/sites/trevornace/2018/01/18/mad-max-scenario-cape-town-run-out-water-90-days/#4859f9675414.

Neimanis, A. 2017. *Bodies of Water: Posthuman Feminist Phenomenology*. London and New York: Bloomsbury.

Newkirk, V. R. 2018. "Cape Town Is an Omen." *The Atlantic*, 11 September. Retrieved 17 May 2020 from https://www.theatlantic.com/science/archive/2018/09/cape-south-south-africa-water-crisis/569317/.

Nixon, R. 2011. *Slow Violence and the Environmentalism of the Poor*. Cambridge, MA: Harvard University Press.

Onishi, N., and Somini Sengupta. 2018. "Dangerously Low on Water, Cape Town Now Faces 'Day Zero.'" *New York Times*, 30 January. Retrieved 17 May 2020 from https://www.nytimes.com/2018/01/30/world/africa/cape-town-day-zero.html.

Oxford Dictionaries. N.d. "Catastrophe." Accessed 2 April 2019. https://en.oxforddictionaries.com/definition/catastrophe.

Parenti, C. 2012. *Tropic of Chaos: Climate Change and the New Geography of Violence*. New York: Bold Type Books.

Pather, R. 2018. "Maimane: #DayZero Will Not Occur in 2018." *Mail & Guardian*, 7 March. Retrieved 17 May 2020 from https://mg.co.za/article/2018-03-07-maimane-dayzero-will-not-occur-in-2018.

Robins, S. 2018. "The Kildare Road Spring: A Place Buried under Concrete." *Daily Maverick*, 4 June. Retrieved 17 May 2020 from https://www.dailymaverick.co.za/article/2018-06-04-the-kildare-road-spring-a-place-buried-under-concrete/.

———. 2019. "'Day Zero,' Hydraulic Citizenship and the Defence of the Commons in Cape Town: A Case Study of the Politics of Water and Its Infrastructures (2017–2018)." *Journal of Southern African Studies* 45 (1): 5–29.

Shepherd, N. 2003. "When the Hand That Holds the Trowel Is Black . . .": Disciplinary Practices of Self-Representation and the Issue of "Native" Labour in Archaeology. *Journal of Social Archaeology* 3 (3): 334–52.

———. 2007. "Archaeology Dreaming: Postapartheid Urban Imaginaries and the Bones of the Prestwich Street Dead." *Journal of Social Archaeology* 7 (1): 3–28.

———. 2008. "Heritage." In *New South African Keywords*, edited by N. Shepherd and S. Robins, 116–28. Cape Town and Athens, OH: Jacana Media and Ohio University Press.

———. 2012. "Ruin Memory: A Hauntology of Cape Town." In *Reclaiming Archaeology: Beyond the Tropes of Modernity*, edited by A. Gonzalez-Ruibal, 233–43. Oxford: Routledge.

———. 2015. "Digging Deep: A Hauntology of Cape Town." In *Archaeology for the People: Joukowsky Institute Perspectives*, edited by J. Cherry and F. Rojas, 96–107. Oxford: Oxbow Books.

———. 2017. "La Mano del Arqueologo: Ensayos 2001–2015. [The Hand of the Archaeologist: Essays 2001–2015]." Jointly published by Universidad del Cauca (Colombia), JAS Arqueología (Spain), and Noches Blancas (Argentina).

———. 2018. "Cape Town Water: Anthropocene Futures." In *The Walking Seminar: Embodied Research in Emergent Anthropocene Landscapes*, edited by N. Shepherd, C. Ernsten, and D.-J. Visser, 40–50. Amsterdam: Reinwardt Academy Press.

———. 2019. "Making Sense of "Day Zero": Slow Catastrophes, Anthropocene Futures, and the Story of Cape Town's Water Crisis." *Water* 11 (9): 1744.

Smith, G.-L. 2018. "Over 5 Million South Africans Don't Have Access to Reliable Drinking Water." *EyeWitness News*. Retrieved 17 May 2020 from https://ewn.co.za/2018/01/26/over-5-million-south-africans-don-t-have-access-to-reliable-drinking-water.

STATS SA. 2016. "General Household Survey 2016: Statistical Release." Statistics South Africa. Retrieved 3 April 2019 from http://www.statssa.gov.za/publications/P0318/P03182016.pdf.

Telegraph. 2016. "22 reasons Why Cape Town Is the World's Best City." *Telegraph*, 16 July. Retrieved 17 May 2020 from https://www.telegraph.co.uk/travel/destinations/africa/south-africa/galleries/reasons-why-cape-town-is-the-best-city-in-the-world/.

TimesLive. 2018. "April 21 Is Cape Town's New 'Day Zero.'" *TimesLive*, 16 January. Retrieved 17 May 2020 from https://www.timeslive.co.za/news/south-africa/2018-01-16-april-21-is-cape-towns-new-day-zero/.

Watts, J. 2018. "Water Shortages Could Affect 5bn People by 2050, UN Report Warns." *Guardian*, 19 March. Retrieved 17 May 2020 from https://www.theguardian.com/environment/2018/mar/19/water-shortages-could-affect-5bn-people-by-2050-un-report-warns.

Wynn, G. 2010. "Foreword: Making Waves." In *What Is Water? The History of a Modern Abstraction*, by Jamie Linton, ix–xvi. Vancouver: UBC Press.

Zille, H. 2018a. "From the Inside: The Countdown to Day Zero." *Daily Maverick*, 22 January. Retrieved 17 May 2020 from https://www.dailymaverick.co.za/opinionista/2018-01-22-from-the-inside-the-countdown-to-day-zero/.

———. 2018b. "4 Things That Helped Us Dramatically Push Back Day Zero." *News24*, 12 March. Retrieved 17 May 2020 from https://www.news24.com/Columnists/GuestColumn/4-things-that-helped-us-dramatically-push-back-day-zero-20180312.

Zizek, S. 2011. *Living in the End Times*. London and New York: Verso.

Conclusion

Rewriting the Disaster Narrative, an Archaeological Imagination

MARK SCHULLER

As we just read, our new geological epoch heralds greater uncertainty. Will human beings survive the coming climate catastrophe of our own making? Cape Town's water crisis and countdown to Day Zero inspired apocalyptic doomsday predictions of another "Mad Max." This disaster narrative draws on racialized legacies of postcolonial fearmongering, not unlike Haiti after the earthquake (Schuller 2016; Ulysse 2015); the reality, as Shepherd documented, is more complex, replete with contradictions but ultimately solidarity. Shepherd's chapter offers important lessons for humanity as a species to survive our own shortsightedness, arguing that Cape Town is far from being exceptional, rather a canary in a coal mine: a warning for the pent-up inequalities in racial capitalism and colonization. Crises like these are what the Anthropocene foretells. Those of us concerned with the survival of our species would do well to learn the lessons of how humanity has survived catastrophes in our deep past. As Holmberg aptly reminds us, we are *all* stakeholders.

Confronting contemporary climate change through an archaeological imagination offers us an ability to assess just how significant, how out of step, or how severe the current anthropogenic climate change actually is. Archaeological research is ignored at our own peril. This is what Riede and Sheets outline as the "mandate of the Anthropocene." If there's anything we can be sure of, we are heading toward the unknown, the "black swan." This volume assembles an exhaustively researched and diverse set of case studies that offer timely analysis of contemporary and future crises. The last volume in this series (Hoffman and Barrios 2019) highlighted gaps between knowledge, policy, and practice regarding disasters, arguing that ethnographical engagement, deep connection with local populations and tapping into their understandings, is a necessary step to "close the gap." It is fitting that this next volume takes this a step further, to include lessons that span millennia of human history and experience. As the editors and several contributors note, an archaeological approach expands our time horizon, being able to see well past the triggering events and their immediate aftermath. Additionally, an archaeological imagination allows us to see the material remains of their ways of life offering context fleshing out or challenging the written records of well-connected urban, literate elite populations whose perspectives define "history."

It is no exaggeration to say that human beings face increasingly unpredictable large-scale catastrophes as a result of anthropogenic climate change. While the term "Anthropocene" is on its way to formal adoption, increasingly scholars are pushing back against the erasures implied by lumping all humans in the same category. Davis and Todd (2017) argue for the necessity of decolonizing the Anthropocene, to center Indigenous perspectives. In effect, Indigenous peoples have already faced the apocalypse and total destruction of their environments as European settlers took their land (Whyte 2017, 2019). Scholars of the African Diaspora, particularly the plantations of the Caribbean and North America, discuss the central roles that plantation slavery played in those "anthropogenic" factors (Davis et al. 2019). As Dipesh Chakrabarty (2009) demonstrated, black and brown colonized peoples were systematically exploited (if not outright killed) during capitalist development's initial accumulation and now disproportionately pay for the effects of global climate change, what Melissa Checker (2008) calls "eco-apartheid."

Two concepts predominate within disaster scholarship, policy, and practice: vulnerability and resilience. While definitions abound, vulnerability is the human-produced amplification of hazards' destructiveness (Bankoff, Frerks, and Hilhorst 2004; Wisner et al. 2004), and resilience is human groups' capacity to "rebound" after a disaster (Barrios 2016; Gaillard 2007; Guest Editorial 2011). While ethnographic scholarship has steadily chipped away at the edges of these concepts, their utility within government agencies and nonprofits assures their long shelf life. In contemporary disasters like Haiti's 2010 earthquake, "resilience" has been used in racialized, postcolonial contexts either to justify sending less aid because Haitian people need less, because of their extraordinary "resilience" (Ulysse 2011), or as cover for disaster capitalism, embodied by Bill Clinton's slogan of "building back better." From her years of experience in FEMA, Britt details the ways in which discourses of resilience can be used to exacerbate inequality. She challenges us to move from resilience to resourcefulness.

As some scholars are beginning to note, vulnerability and resilience—both products of human action, shaped by society, quickly glossed as "social constructs"—are not so distinct as they first appear (Barrios 2017; Barrios 2016; Schuller, Gebrian, and Lewis 2019; Alexander 2013). They are like the yin and the yang within Taoist cosmology: not oppositional but interrelated. An archaeological imagination—looking at material cultures within a vast timescape—reveals that they are co-productions of human society. As chapters in this volume like Dugmore et al.'s demonstrate, a *longue durée* approach helps us identify the ways in which the very same human activity can increase resilience in the short and medium term while deepening vulnerability in the long term.

What lessons does this book offer to planners, responders, communities, and scholars regarding present and future disasters? Facilitating the distillation process, particularly useful considering a specialist social science like archaeology, each chapter includes an executive summary outlining lessons for today's policy makers and disaster managers.

A typical disaster narrative typically focuses media (Adams 1986; Benthall 1993)—and therefore philanthropic and agency (Olsen, Carstensen, and Hoyen 2003; Eisensee and Strömberg 2007)—attention on the event: the photo op. However, a generation of political ecology-oriented disaster social science since sociologist Enrico Quarantelli (1998), geographer Ben Wisner (2004; Wisner et al. 2004), and anthropologist Tony Oliver-Smith (1999, 2002) has argued for moving away from events and toward process to understand disasters. As this volume demonstrates, archaeological research is particularly well suited to contribute to understanding disasters within a larger time horizon. Several contributors in this volume build on Rob Nixon's "slow violence" (2011). Several chapters discuss recurrent or repeating disasters. Citing contributor Shannon Dawdy, Karen Holmberg reminds readers that "methodological materialism of archaeology permits us to show that catastrophes are rarely, if ever, terminal and that they are recurrent and multi-scalar." Holmberg argues that like layers of tephra, hazards sit atop one another—in Masco's terms, "multiple overlapping crises," such as Fukushima's nuclear crisis triggered by the 2011 earthquake and tsunami. The Indonesian government's promotion of nuclear power in the volcanically active "Ring of Fire" increases risk exponentially; it is a "disaster upon disaster" (Hoffman and Barrios 2019). While the case of Iceland discussed in chapter 6 is a particularly salient example, authors of other chapters, such as Torrence, Gjesfjeld and Brown, and Sandweiss and Maasch, all discuss repeated disasters in the same place over a long time period. Each of these chapters offers a different set of analyses regarding human societies' preparation and response, what Gregory Button (2010) called a "disaster culture." Sharratt's chapter reminds us that some hazards, like drought, are themselves experienced as long-term phenomena, lasting years and even generations.

A related point made by disaster scholars is that there is no such thing as a "natural" disaster (Alexander 1997; Barrios 2017; Oliver-Smith 2002; Reed 2006; Wijkman and Timberlake 1984). Hazards may be natural—although with anthropogenic climate change several of even these taken-for-granted hazards are increasing in either number or intensity—but disasters are produced by human activity, both conscious policy and long-term processes of extraction and inequality built up over time. Vulnerability is not only a key ingredient in a disaster's destructiveness; it is the one over which humans have the most control. As such, reducing vulnerability should be a primary focus of scholarship, policy, and practice. As this volume underscores, an archaeological imagination offers a unique vantage point to support disaster social science. As Riede and Sheets argue in their introduction, "social inequality is at the root of most if not all disasters." Nearly all chapters make this point in some way. For example, Sharratt argues that rituals that reinforced egalitarian relationships increased communities' resilience to disaster. In a frighteningly detailed parable of an archaeology of the present, Dawdy demonstrates that elite groups made strategic decisions that put hazardous waste, including "putrescibles" (rotting meat and dead bodies), in communities predominated by low-income people and/or people of color. Contemporary examples such as Hurricane Katrina, Haiti's 2010 earthquake, and Hurricane Maria highlight how disasters increase inequality. However, in a provocative argument, Sheets concludes from archaeological data in Costa Rica and Pueblo that disasters do not necessarily lead to increased inequality

Directly addressing vulnerability, disaster risk reduction (DRR) arose out of focused attention and conscious policy from hazard-endemic societies. DRR isn't owned by any ideology or political economy; earthquake-prone Japan and Cuba, where hurricanes are a regular reality, both have made significant contributions to DRR. Internationally, given its centrality to the world economy and its ties to other capitalist societies such as the United States, Japan has hosted several DRR conferences, leading to frameworks for action, such as 2005 in Hyogo (Prevention Web n.d.) and 2015 in Sendai (United Nations Office for Disaster Risk Reduction 2016). Much less resourced, Cuba centers DRR in their regional networks such as the Organization for Caribbean States (United Nations Development Programme 2015). As this book demonstrates, archaeological research has much to contribute to DRR. Chapters in this volume have argued that local, bottom-up initiatives are more successful, tapping into local knowledge is key, activating social networks is essential, and solidarity is central to resilience.

Several chapters have argued that local initiative leads to successful outcomes. As Shepherd argues, far from Mad Max, individuals set up user-friendly ways to access collective resources, and central to averting the water crisis was the fact that local households (yes, middle class) decided to drastically cut their water consumption. Sheets concludes that local people taking initiative, like the Latinx community during the 1995 Chicago heat wave, is key to saving lives, a point he makes to help interpret the archaeological data from Mesoamerica. Discussing the successful repopulation of the Willaumez Peninsula in Papua New Guinea, Torrence comes to the same conclusion: people with ancestral ties to the land did not wait for government evacuation orders. In prehistory, communities visited areas impacted by the volcano and sped up intervals to repopulate the affected areas. In his cross-cultural analysis, Peregrine concludes that space for participation in decision-making was the most significant factor in successful post-disaster recovery.

On the other end of the spectrum, several chapters discuss elites' attempt to use disasters for their own gain. Britt recounts how New York City mayor Michael Bloomberg weaponized the Historic Preservation Act to promote a neoliberal rebuilding agenda, what in other contexts has been critiqued as "disaster capitalism" (Gunewardena and Schuller 2008; Klein 2007). Whose losses count and whose histories matter are inherently political questions. Sandweiss and Maasch ague that elite groups tend to attempt to instrumentalize disasters in their governance or at the very least legitimation strategies. As they quote Obama's chief of staff Rahm Emanuel, later to become mayor of Chicago, "Never let a good crisis go to waste." As they argue, disasters such as increasing frequency of the El Niño events can trigger a "crisis of faith" and a challenge to their power. A couple of authors note that the same occurred in Teotihuacan and China's Wei dynasty, as the mid-sixth century drought indicated that the Chinese rulers had lost their "Mandate of Heaven." Readers from the United States are familiar with the role that President George W. Bush's botched response to Katrina played in voters' disenchantment with his ruling Republican Party, which subsequently lost the majority in Congress the following year.

The archaeological cases conclude that local embodied knowledge is key to communities' survival. Given the interval between volcanic eruptions, in Papua New Guinea or Mesoamerica, with an average periodicity of 250 years, it is not usual that living elders can offer warnings. Instead, as both Sheets and Torrence document, this knowledge is passed down through what is often dismissed as "folklore"—oral history or even mythology. Yet, this knowledge can be quite detailed and effective.

This book has also argued that social networks and regional cooperation are keys to survival. In addition to Sheets and Torrence, who discuss the cultivation of networks that tied differing villages together, several other chapters detail diverse sets of geographically dispersed social ties. Using a social network analysis, Gjesfjeld and Brown outline the strength of "weak ties" (Granovetter 1973). Discussing how communities use geographical space to facilitate network interaction, they conclude that the more diverse and richly connected a community is, the greater resilience it has. Sharratt's chapter argues against an environmental or climatic determinism in the collapse and aftermath of the Tiwanaku in the Andes. Accessing data that span five hundred years, from 1000 to 1500 CE, Sharratt notes that the region faced severe droughts. Before 1250, communities engaged in group ritual activities that built on egalitarian tendency and suppressed hierarchies. These activities built local networks between villages, fostering collaboration and ensuring survival despite protracted drought.

As disaster researchers have documented, catastrophic events can inspire solidarity (Benadusi 2015; Dynes 1970; Kroll-Smith 2018; Quarantelli 1984; Schuller, Gebrian, and Lewis 2019; Solnit 2009; Vélez-Vélez and Villarrubia-Mendoza 2018; Zhang 2016). This present volume pushes this conversation a step further. Dawdy discusses "emergent publics"—solidarity between two marginalized groups within New Orleans traditionally set in opposition to one another, Vietnamese and African Americans—to oppose the Chef Menteur ("chief liar") landfill in the Upper Ninth Ward. In one of the most unequal cities on the planet, with a legacy of colonial contact and apartheid, new forms of solidarity began to develop in Cape Town during the acute water crisis. Solidarity is more difficult to "see" within the material remains, but Sharratt discusses religious observances and shared cultural materials, which facilitated trade connections and possibly a shared regional identity.

With these solidarity ties actively maintained—through means such as ritual or trade—*the* biggest predictor of community survival and resilient communities in several cases in this book was migration. Fleeing a volcano, a hurricane, earthquake and tsunami, El Niño event, or drought was literally the difference between life and death. For all but the very last bit of human history, we have been on the move; national borders are a recent phenomenon. An anthropological imagination reminds us—all of us—about our shared interest in defending immigration: for our species to survive, humans need to keep being human, being allowed to move (Schuller 2021). This lesson may be the hardest to swallow given the rise of anti-immigrant xenophobia engulfing the United States, the United Kingdom, India, and elsewhere.

Taken as a whole, the book offers policy makers, as well as ourselves, answers to urgent questions about our future on this earth. Not only going forward by looking back, an archaeological imagination is useful—if a harsh—look at ourselves in the present, as Dawdy concludes, "Only when we can see the long-term consequences of today's political actions can we be empowered to redirect the slow politics of climate change."

Mark Schuller is associate professor—and from late 2020 full professor—of anthropology and nonprofit and NGO studies at Northern Illinois University and affiliate at the State University of Haiti. Supported by the National Science Foundation Senior and CAREER Grant, Bellagio Center, and others, Schuller's research is published in over forty scholarly articles or book chapters. He has authored or coedited eight books and co-directed/co-produced the documentary *Poto Mitan*. Recipient of the Margaret Mead Award and Anthropology in Media Award, he is president of the Haitian Studies Association and active as a solidarity activist.

References

Adams, W. C. 1986. "Whose Lives Count? TV Coverage of Natural Disasters." *Journal of Communication* 36 (2): 113–22.

Alexander, David E. 1997. "The Study of Natural Disasters, 1977–97: Some Reflections on a Changing Field of Knowledge." *Disasters* 21 (4): 284–304.

———. 2013. "Resilience and Disaster Risk Reduction: An Etymological Journey." *Natural Hazards and Earth System Sciences* 13 (11): 2707–16.

Bankoff, Greg, Georg Frerks, and Dorothea Hilhorst. 2004. *Mapping Vulnerability: Disasters, Development, and People*. London: Earthscan.

Barrios, Roberto. 2017. "What Does Catastrophe Reveal for Whom? The Anthropology of Crises and Disasters at the Onset of the Anthropocene." *Annual Review of Anthropology* 46: 151–66.

Barrios, Roberto E. 2016. "Resilience: A Commentary from the Vantage Point of Anthropology." *Annals of Anthropological Practice* 40 (1): 28–38.

Benadusi, Mara. 2015. "Cultivating Communities after Disaster: A Whirlwind of Generosity on the Coasts of Sri Lanka." In *Governing Disasters: Beyond Risk Culture*, edited by Sandrine Revet, Julien Langumier and Ethan Rundell, 87–125. New York: Palgrave Macmillan.

Benthall, Jonathan. 1993. *Disasters, Relief, and the Media*. London: I. B. Tauris.

Button, Gregory V. 2010. *Disaster Culture: Knowledge and Uncertainty in the Wake of Human and Environmental Catastrophe*. Walnut Creek: Left Coast Press.

Chakrabarty, Dipesh. 2009. "The Climate of History: Four Theses." *Critical Inquiry* 35 (Winter): 197–221.

Checker, Melissa. 2008. "Eco-Apartheid and Global Greenwaves: African Diasporic Environmental Justice Movements." *Souls: A Critical Journal of Black Politics, Culture, and Society* 10 (4): 390–408.

Davis, Heather, and Zoe Todd. 2017. "On the Importance of a Date, or, Decolonizing the Anthropocene." *ACME: An International Journal for Critical Geographies* 16 (4): 761–80.

Davis, Janae, Alex A. Moulton, Levi Van Sant, and Brian Williams. 2019. "Anthropocene, capitalocene, . . . Plantationocene? A Manifesto for Ecological Justice in an Age of Global Crises." *Geography Compass* 13 (5): e12438.
Dynes, Russell. 1970. *Organized Behavior in Disasters*. Lexington, MA: Heath.
Eisensee, Thomas, and David Strömberg. 2007. "News Droughts, News Floods, and U.S. Disaster Relief." *Quarterly Journal of Economics* 122 (2): 693–728.
Gaillard, Jean-Christophe. 2007. "Resilience of Traditional Societies in Facing Natural Hazards." *Disaster Prevention and Management: An International Journal* 16 (4): 522–44.
Granovetter, Mark S. 1973. "The Strength of Weak Ties." *American Journal of Sociology* 78 (6): 1360–1380.
Guest Editorial. 2011. "Disaster Resilience: A Bounce Back or Bounce Forward Ability?" *Local Environment: The International Journal of Justice and Sustainability* 16 (5): 417–24.
Gunewardena, Nandini, and Mark Schuller. 2008. *Capitalizing on Catastrophe: Neoliberal Strategies in Disaster Reconstruction*. Lanham, MD: Alta Mira Press.
Hoffman, Suanna, and Roberto Barrios. 2019. *Disaster upon Disaster: Exploring the Gap between Knowledge, Policy and Practice*. New York: Berghahn Books.
Klein, Naomi. 2007. *The Shock Doctrine: The Rise of Disaster Capitalism*. New York: Metropolitan Books.
Kroll-Smith, Stephen. 2018. *Recovering Inequality: Hurricane Katrina, the San Francisco Earthquake of 1806, and the Aftermath of Disaster*. Austin: University of Texas Press.
Nixon, Rob. 2011. *Slow Violence and the Environmentalism of the Poor*. Cambridge, MA: Harvard University Press.
Oliver-Smith, Anthony. 1999. "What Is a Disaster?" In *The Angry Earth: Disaster in Anthropological Perspective*, edited by Anthony Oliver-Smith and Susanna M. Hoffman, 18–34. New York: Routledge.
———. 2002. "Theorizing Disasters: Nature, Power, and Culture." In *Catastrophe & Culture: The Anthropology of Disasters*, edited by Susanna M. Hoffman and Anthony Oliver-Smith, 23–47. Santa Fe: School of American Research Press.
Olsen, Gorm Rye, Nils Carstensen, and Kristian Hoyen. 2003. "Humanitarian Crises: What Determines the Level of Emergency Assistance? Media Coverage, Donor Interests and the Aid Business." *Disasters* 27 (2): 109–26.
Prevention Web. N.d. "About the Hyogo Framework for Action." Retrieved 6 July 2020 from https://www.preventionweb.net/english/hyogo/framework/.
Quarantelli, E. L. 1984. *Emergent Behavior and the Emergency Time Period of Disasters: Final Report*. Newark: Disaster Research Center, University of Delaware.
Quarantelli, Enrico. 1998. *What Is a Disaster? Perspectives on the Question*. New York: Routledge.
Reed, Betsy. 2006. *Unnatural Disaster: The Nation on Hurricane Katrina*. New York: Nation Books.
Schuller, Mark. 2016. "The Tremors Felt Round the World: Haiti's Earthquake as Global Imagined Community." In *Contextualizing Disaster*, edited by Gregory V. Button and Mark Schuller, 66–88. New York: Berghahn Books.
———. 2021. *Humanity's Last Stand: Confronting Global Catastrophe*. New Brunswick, NJ: Rutgers University Press.
Schuller, Mark, Bette Gebrian, and Judy Lewis. 2019. "'Yon Lòt Ayiti Posib': Glimmers of Another Haiti Following the 2010 Earthquake and 2016 Hurricane Matthew." *Human Organization* 78 (4): 267–77.

Solnit, Rebecca. 2009. *The Paradise Built in Hell: The Extraordinary Communities That Arise in Disaster*. New York: Penguin Books.

Ulysse, Gina Athena. 2011. *Fascinating! Her Resilience*. Middletown, CT: Wesleyan University Center for the Arts.

———. 2015. *Why Haiti Needs New Narratives: A Post-quake Chronicle*. Middletown, CT: Wesleyan University Press.

United Nations Development Programme. 2015. "A Cuban Model for a Resilient Caribbean," 25 February. Retrieved 6 July 2020 from https://www.undp.org/content/undp/en/home/presscenter/articles/2015/02/25/a-cuban-model-for-a-resilient-caribbean.html.

United Nations Office for Disaster Risk Reduction. 2016. *Sendai Framework for Disaster Risk Reduction, 2015–2030*. Retrieved 6 July 2020 from https://www.preventionweb.net/files/43291_sendaiframeworkfordrren.pdf.

Vélez-Vélez, Roberto, and Jaqueline Villarrubia-Mendoza. 2018. "Cambio desde abajo y desde adentro: Notes on Centros de Apoyo Mutuo in post-María Puerto Rico." *Latino Studies* 16 (4): 542–47.

Whyte, Kyle Powys. 2017. "Indigenous Climate Change Studies: Indigenizing Futures, Decolonizing the Anthropocene." *English Language Notes* 55 (1–2): 153–62.

———. 2019. "Way Beyond the Lifeboat: An Indigenous Allegory of Climate Justice." In *Climate Futures: Reimagining Global Climate Justice*, edited by Kum-Kum Bhavnani, John Foran, Priya Kurian, and Debashish Munshi. London: Zed Books.

Wijkman, Anders, and Lloyd Timberlake. 1984. *Natural Disasters: Acts of God or Acts of Man?* London: Earthscan.

Wisner, Ben. 2004. "Assessment of Capability and Vulnerability." In *Mapping Vulnerability: Disasters, Development, and People*, edited by Greg Bankoff, Georg Frerks, and Dorothea Hilhorst, 183–93. London: Earthscan.

Wisner, Ben, Piers Blaikie, Terry Cannon, and Ian Davis. 2004. *At Risk: Natural Hazards, People's Vulnerability and Disasters*. 2nd ed. New York: Routledge.

Zhang, Qiaoyun. 2016. "Disaster Response and Recovery: Aid and Social Change." *Annals of Anthropological Practice* 40 (1): 86–97.

Index

W

Y

Z

CPSIA information can be obtained
at www.ICGtesting.com
Printed in the USA
JSHW012020050323
38444JS00003B/10

9 781800 739284